EU Banking Union

EU Banking Union

Law, Institutions, and Co-operation

Edited by

JONATHAN BAUERSCHMIDT

Member of the Legal Service, Visiting Professor, Université catholique de Louvain, Council of the European Union, Brussels, Belgium

RAFFAELE D'AMBROSIO

Deputy Head of the Legal Services Directorate, Banca d'Italia, Italy

DIANE FROMAGE

Professor of European Law, Law Faculty & SCEUS, University of Salzburg, Austria

DANIELA JAROS

Team Lead of International Affairs and EU Integration, Austrian Financial Market Authority, Austria

PAUL WEISMANN

Associate Professor of European Union Law, Law Faculty and Salzburg Centre of European Union Studies, Salzburg Centre of European Union Studies at the University of Salzburg, Austria

OXFORD
UNIVERSITY PRESS

OXFORD
UNIVERSITY PRESS

Great Clarendon Street, Oxford, OX2 6DP,
United Kingdom

Oxford University Press is a department of the University of Oxford.
It furthers the University's objective of excellence in research, scholarship,
and education by publishing worldwide. Oxford is a registered trade mark of
Oxford University Press in the UK and in certain other countries.

Published in the United States of America by Oxford University Press
546 Fifth Avenue, New York, NY 10036, United States of America.

British Library Cataloguing in Publication Data
Data available

Library of Congress Control Number: 2026936553

ISBN 9780198949749

DOI: 10.1093/9780198949756.001.0001

Printed and bound by
CPI Group (UK) Ltd., Croydon, CR0 4YY

The manufacturer's authorised representative in the EU for product safety is
Oxford University Press España S.A. of El Parque Empresarial San Fernando de Henares,
Avenida de Castilla, 2 – 28830 Madrid (www.oup.es/en or
product.safety@oup.com). OUP España S.A. also acts as importer into Spain
of products made by the manufacturer.

MIX
Paper | Supporting
responsible forestry
FSC® C013604
FSC
www.fsc.org

In memory of our dear colleague and friend Luís Silva Morais.

Contents

Detailed Contents

Table of Cases

CASES OF THE COURT OF JUSTICE OF THE EUROPEAN UNION

Court of Justice of the European Union

General Court

European Court of Human Rights

Court of the European Free Trade Association (EFTA)

NATIONAL CASES

Austria

Germany

Norway

Table of Legislation

TREATIES AND CONVENTIONS

DIRECTIVES

REGULATIONS

RECOMMENDATIONS

RESOLUTIONS

NATIONAL LEGISLATION

Austria

United Kingdom

Abbreviations

ABoR	Administrative Board of Review
ACER	Agency for the Cooperation of Energy Regulators
AG	Advocate General
AI Act	Artificial Intelligence Act
ALE	Greens/European Free Alliance
AML	anti-money laundering
AMLA	Authority for Anti-Money Laundering and Countering the Financing of Terrorism (Anti-Money Laundering Authority)
AMLAR	Authority for Anti-Money Laundering and Countering the Financing of Terrorism and amending Regulations
AP	Appeal Panel
APA	Approved publication arrangement
ARM	Approved reporting mechanism
AT1	Additional Tier 1
BA	Banking Act (Switzerland)
BBM	borrower-based measure
BCBS	Basel Committee on Banking Supervision
BIS	Bank of International Settlement
BLCI	Bulgarian Law on Credit Institutions
BMA	Business Model Analysis
BNB	Bulgarian National Bank
BRRD	Bank Recovery and Resolution Directive
BU	Banking Union
BWG	Bankwesengesetz
C&E	climate-related and environmental
CBR	combined buffer requirement
CCIA	Croatian Credit Institution Act
CCP	central counterparty
CCyB	countercyclical capital buffer
CEO	chief executive officer
CET1	Common Equity Tier 1
CFR	Charter of Fundamental Rights of the European Union
CFT	combating the financing of terrorism
CHF	Swiss franc
CJ	Court of Justice
CJEU	Court of Justice of the European Union

CMDI	Crisis Management and Deposit Insurance
COM	European Commission
CP	Core Principle
CRA	credit ratings agency
CRD	Capital Requirements Directive
CRR	Capital Requirements Regulation
CTP	Consolidated tape provider
DCC	Decision on close cooperation
DG	Directorate-General
DG IPOL	Directorate-General for Internal Policies of the Union
DGS	deposit guarantee scheme
DGSD	Deposit Guarantee Schemes Directive
DIF	Deposit Insurance Fund
DORA	Digital Operational Resilience Act
DSSR	Directorate Supervisory Strategy and Risk
EBA	European Banking Authority
EBA ITS	EBA Implementing Technical Standards
EBU	European Banking Union
ECA	European Court of Auditors
ECB	European Central Bank
ECB ABoR	European Central Bank's Administrative Board of Review
ECHR	European Convention on Human Rights
ECtHR	European Court of Human Rights
ECJ	European Court of Justice
ECON	Committee on Economic and Monetary Affairs
ECSC	European Coal and Steel Community
EDIS	European Deposit Insurance Scheme
EEA	European Economic Area
EEC	European Economic Community
EFSF	European Financial Stability Facility
EFTA	European Free Trade Association
EFTA SA	EFTA Surveillance Authority
EGOV	Economic Governance and EMU Scrutiny Unit
EIOPA	European Insurance and Occupational Pensions Authority
EMIR	European Market Infrastructure Regulation
EMU	Economic and Monetary Union
ENISA	European Network and Information Security Agency
EP	European Parliament
ERM-II	Exchange Rate Mechanism
ESA	European Supervisory Authority
ESCB	European System of Central Banks
ESFS	European System of Financial Supervision
ESG	environmental, social, and governance

ESM	European Stability Mechanism
ESMA	European Securities and Markets Authority
ESRB	European Systemic Risk Board
ESRC	European Systemic Risk Council
EU	European Union
FCA	Financial Conduct Authority
FINMA	Swiss Financial Market Supervisory Authority
FINMASA	Federal Act on the Swiss Financial Market Supervisory Authority
FIU	Financial Intelligence Unit
FMA	Financial Market Authority
FM-GwG	Austrian Financial Markets Anti-Money Laundering Act
FOLTF	failing or likely to fail
FSB	Financial Stability Board
FSC	Financial Stability Committee
FSR	Financial Stability Review
GC	General Court
GFC	Great Financial Crisis
GDP	gross domestic product
GovC	Governing Council of the ECB
G-SIB	global systemically important bank
G-SII	global systemically important institution
G-SIIB	buffers for identified global systemically important institutions
G10	Group of Ten
HERA	Health Emergency Preparedness and Response
HNB	Croatian National Bank
IADI	International Association of Deposit Insurers
IAIS	International Association of Insurance Supervisors
IGA	intergovernmental agreement
IIA	Interinstitutional Agreement
INTOSAI	International Organization of Supreme Audit Institutions
IOSCO	International Organization of Securities Commissions
IRB	internal ratings-based
IRT	internal resolution team
IT	information technology
ITS	implementing technical standards
JBoA	Joint Board of Appeal
JET	Joint Examination Team
JST	Joint Supervisory Team
LAA	loss-absorbing amount
LCR	Liquidity Coverage Ratio
LGD	loss given default
LSI	Less Significant Institution
MDA	maximum distributable amount

MEP	Member of the European Parliament
MFF	Multi-Annual Financial Framework
MFSA	Malta Financial Services Authority
MiCA	Market in Crypto Assets Act
MiFID	Markets in Financial Instruments Directive
MiFIR	Markets in Financial Instruments Regulation
ML	money laundering
M-MDA	Maximum Distributable Amount related to MREL
MNB	[queried with author]
MoU	memorandum of understanding
MREL	minimum requirement for own funds and eligible liabilities
MS	Member State
NCA	National Competent Authority
NCWO	no-creditor-worse-off
NDA	national designated authority
NGEU	Next Generation EU
NMA	national macroprudential authorities
NOK	Norwegian krone
NPE	non-performing exposure
NPL	non-performing loan
NRA	national resolution authority
NSFR	Net Stable Funding Ratio
OCR	Overall Capital Requirement
OJ	Official Journal of the European Union
OMT	outright monetary transactions
O-SII	other systemically important institution
O-SIIB	buffer for other systemically important institutions
OTC	Over-the-counter
P1	Pillar 1
P2G	Pillar 2 guidance
P2R	Pillar 2 requirements
PEP	Politically Exposed Persons
PONV	point of non-viability
PPE	European People's Party
RCA	recapitalization amount
RTS	regulatory technical standards
RWA	risk-weighted asset
SA	Standardised Approach
SAI	supreme audit institution
S&D	Socialists and Democrats
SEC	Securities and Exchange Commission
SI	significant institution
SIF	State Secretariat for International Finance (Switzerland)

SIU	Savings and Investments Union
SNB	Swiss National Bank
SOEs	selected obliged entities
SRB	Single Resolution Board
SRB AP	Single Resolution Board's Appeal Panel
SREP	Supervisory Review and Evaluation Process
SRF	Single Resolution Fund
SRM	Single Resolution Mechanism
SRMR	Single Resolution Mechanism Regulation
SSM	Single Supervisory Mechanism
SSMFR	SSM Framework Regulation
SSMR	Single Supervisory Mechanism Regulation
SSR	Short Selling Regulation
SyRB	systemic risk buffer
TCR	total capital requirement
TEU	Treaty on European Union
TF	terrorism financing
TFEU	Treaty on the Functioning of the European Union
TLAC	Total Loss-absorbing Capacity
TREA	total risk exposure amount
TSCR	Total SREP Capital Requirement
UK	United Kingdom
US	United States
VCLT	Vienna Convention on the Law of Treaties

Contributors

Vanessa Aichstill, University of Salzburg, Salzburg, Austria

Mads Andenas is Professor, Faculty of Law, University of Oslo, Oslo, Norway

Filipe Brito Bastos is Associate Professor and Vice-President of the Pedagogical Council, NOVA School of Law, Lisbon, Portugal

Jonathan Bauerschmidt is Member of the Legal Service, Council of the European Union, Brussels, Belgium, and Visiting Professor, Université catholique de Louvain, Belgium. https://orcid.org/0000-0003-2691-3150

Concetta Brescia Morra is Full Professor of EU Financial Law. Law Department, Roma Tre University, Rome, Italy

David M Brinkman is Principal Legal Counsel, DG Legal Services, European Central Bank, Frankfurt am Main, Germany. https://orcid.org/0009-0007-1262-8128

Gaia Chiarini, University of Salzburg, Salzburg, Austria

Raffaele D'Ambrosio is Deputy Head of the Legal Services Directorate, Banca d'Italia, Italy

Matthias Deissenberger is Legal Officer, Legal and Enforcement Department, European Securities and Markets Authority (ESMA), France

Eugénie d'Ursel is Legal Adviser, European Commission, Brussels, Belgium

Mariolina Eliantonio is Professor of European and Comparative Administrative Law and Procedure, Maastricht University, Netherlands

Diane Fromage is Professor of European Law, Law Faculty & SCEUS, University of Salzburg, Austria. https://orcid.org/0000-0001-6911-0468

Alberto de Gregorio Merino is Director-General of the Legal Service, European Commission, Brussels, Belgium

Ursula Hauser-Rethaller is Senior Expert, Banking Supervision, Austrian Financial Market Authority, Austria

Pavlína Hubková is a Researcher, University of Exeter, Exeter, United Kingdom

Ieva Hūna is Doctoral Researcher, European University Institute, Florence, Italy. https://orcid.org/0000-0001-9109-5874

Daniela Jaros is Team Lead of International Affairs and EU Integration, Austrian Financial Market Authority, Austria

Jakub Kerlin is Case Handler at Directorate-General for Competition, European Commission, Brussels, Belgium. https://orcid.org/0000-0001-5146-2369

Asen Lefterov is Principal Legal Counsel, Legal Services, European Central Bank, Frankfurt am Main, Germany

Carlo Lombardini is Professor of Banking Law/Attorney-at-law, University of Lausanne/Geneva Bar, Switzerland

Menelaos Markakis is Associate Professor of International and European Union Law, Erasmus School of Law, Erasmus University Rotterdam, Netherlands and Scientific Coordinator, Erasmus Center for Economic and Financial Governance. https://orcid.org/0000-0002-4243-3715

Christy Ann Petit is Assistant Professor, Dublin City University, School of Law and Government, Dublin, Ireland

Federico Pistelli is Researcher of Private Law, University of Trento, Faculty of Law, Trento, Italy. https://orcid.org/0000-0003-3050-7550

Agnese Pizzolla is Lead Legal Counsel, Supervisory Law Division, European Central Bank, Frankfurt am Main, Germany

Edoardo Rulli is Policy Officer, European Commission, Belgium. https://orcid.org/0000-0003-4115-6864

Carlos Soler Ruiz is Policy Officer, European Anti-Fraud Office (OLAF), European Commission, Luxembourg, Luxembourg, formerly Senior Auditor at the European Court of Auditors, Luxembourg, Luxembourg

Audronė Steiblytė is a Member of the European Commission Legal Service, Brussels, Belgium.

Paul Weismann is Associate Professor of European Union Law, Law Faculty and Salzburg Centre of European Union Studies, Salzburg Centre of European Union Studies at the University of Salzburg, Austria. https://orcid.org/0000-0002-4414-3586

Andrea Westerhof Löfflerová is Senior Legal Adviser in the Legal Service, Council of the EU, Brussels, Belgium

Carsten Zatschler is a member of the Bar of Ireland and Adjunct Full Professor, Sutherland School of Law, University College Dublin, Ireland

Introduction

EU Banking Union: Law, Institutions, and Co-operation

Jonathan Bauerschmidt, Raffaele D'Ambrosio, Diane Fromage, Daniela Jaros, and Paul Weismann

I Introduction: Why study the Banking Union? Remaining open questions after a decade of practice

The Banking Union created in 2012[1] has been one of the European Union (EU)'s most ambitious policy projects of the past 10 years.[2] It has revolutionized the EU's grip on the banking sector by installing the European Central Bank (ECB) as the dominant banking supervisor within the EU;[3] by introducing a banking resolution regime headed by an EU agency, the Single Resolution Board (SRB);[4] and by pooling financial resources to make the banking sector more resilient.[5] While the EU actors in charge play an important role in setting up and implementing this regime, they do not act in isolation. Instead, they build a network with the National Competent Authorities (NCAs) and

[1] Commission, 'A Roadmap towards a Banking Union' COM (2012) 510 final, 12 September 2012.

[2] On the project and its inception, see Stefan Grundmann and Hans-W Micklitz (eds), *The European Banking Union and Constitution: Beacon for Advanced Integration or Death-Knell for Democracy?* (Bloomsbury Publishing 2019), esp ch 1; Pedro Gustavo Teixeira, *The Legal History of the European Banking Union: How European Law Led to the Supranational Integration of the Single Financial Market* (Bloomsbury Publishing 2020).

[3] This was achieved by means of the institution of the Single Supervisory Mechanism: Council Regulation (EU) 1024/2013 of 15 October 2013 conferring specific tasks on the European Central Bank concerning policies relating to the prudential supervision of credit institutions [2013] OJ L287, pp 63–89.

[4] This is the result of the adoption of the Single Resolution Mechanism: Regulation (EU) 806/2014 of the European Parliament and of the Council of 15 July 2014 establishing uniform rules and a uniform procedure for the resolution of credit institutions and certain investment firms in the framework of a Single Resolution Mechanism and a Single Resolution Fund and amending Regulation (EU) 1093/2010 [2014] OJ L225, pp 1–90.

[5] This notably happened thanks to the establishment of the Single Resolution Fund, on which see Christos Hadjiemmanuil, 'Bank Resolution Financing in the Banking Union' in Jens-Hinrich Binder and Dalvinder Singh (eds), *Bank Resolution: The European Regime* (OUP 2016) and Eugénie d'Ursel's chapter, in this volume.

Jonathan Bauerschmidt, Raffaele D'Ambrosio, Diane Fromage, Daniela Jaros, and Paul Weismann, *Introduction* In: *EU Banking Union*. Edited by: Jonathan Bauerschmidt, Raffaele D'Ambrosio, Diane Fromage, Daniela Jaros, and Paul Weismann, Oxford University Press.
DOI: 10.1093/9780198949756.003.0001

the national resolution authorities (NRAs). These originally only stemmed from euro area Member States. Since 2020, the authorities of Bulgaria, which joined the Banking Union, have also been involved.[6] EU authorities (the ECB and SRB) rely on NCAs' and NRAs' knowledge and experience, and cooperate with them in the context of the so-called Joint Supervisory Teams and Internal Resolution Teams.[7]

Despite more than 10 years of progress, the Banking Union remains a dynamically evolving project. This is due to the ongoing development of complementary rules, the unfolding case law of the Court of Justice of the EU (CJEU),[8] and the participation of Member States outside the euro area. The cooperation of these multiple actors is framed by an intricate system of constitutional, legislative, and executive rules, administrative instructions, and exchanges of information anchored in sources of hard and soft law.[9]

Against this background, we present a book which addresses current legal questions relating to the Banking Union and regimes closely connected to, but not part of, the Banking Union, such as the European System of Financial Supervision or the Authority for Anti-Money Laundering and Countering the Financing of Terrorism (AMLA). The Banking Union still remains incomplete, which is why further reforms are under way. Indeed, the Banking Union was originally conceived of as a three-pillar structure, with a Supervisory, a Resolution, and a Deposit Guarantee pillar. However, while the first and the second pillars have been set in place and are now properly functioning, the third one—the European Deposit Insurance Scheme (EDIS), as proposed by the Commission—has not been introduced yet.[10] Therefore, the legal

[6] It is indeed possible for Member States outside the euro area to join the Banking Union only (so-called Member States in close cooperation). This was Bulgaria's and Croatia's choice, although Croatia has since joined the euro area as well. On close cooperation, see Agnese Pizzola, in this volume, and María J Nieto and Dalvinder Singh, 'Incentive-Compatible Relationship between ERM II and Close Co-operation in the Banking Union: The Cases of Bulgaria and Croatia' (2022) 47(2) European Law Review 200–21.

[7] Laura Wissink, 'Challenges to an Efficient European Centralised Banking Supervision (SSM): Single Rulebook, Joint Supervisory Teams and Split Supervisory Tasks' (2017) 18(3) European Business Organization Law Review 431–56; Christy Ann Petit, 'Differentiated Governance in the Banking Union: Single Mechanisms, Joint Teams, and Opting-ins' (2022) European Papers – A Journal on Law and Integration 889–907; and Marta Božina Beroš, 'Developing banking union's common supervisory culture: a look into the 'black box' of joint supervisory teams' (2023) 45(1) Journal of European Integration 103–20.

[8] Federico della Negra and René Smit regularly update a list of cases: EU Cases or Jurisprudence—EBI Europe. Also: Chiara Zilioli and Karl-Philipp Wojcik (eds), *Judicial Review in the European Banking Union* (Edward Elgar Publishing 2021); Chs 6 and 7 in Marco Lamandini and David Ramos Muñoz, *Finance, Law, and the Courts* (OUP 2024); and Menelaos Markakis, 'Judicial Review of Actions by EU Financial Agencies: European Supervisory Authorities, Single Resolution Board' in Annalisa Volpato and others (eds), *EU Agencies before the Court of Justice* (Edward Elgar, forthcoming).

[9] On the latter, see Mariolina Eliantonio and *Pavlína* Hubková, in this volume.

[10] On which, see Gaia Chiarini and Diane Fromage, in this volume.

questions addressed in this book are both topical and cutting-edge, while also being informed by the existing knowledge of the Banking Union's development, pertinent court cases, and the discussions already present in relevant literature. Similarly, while maintaining high academic quality and offering original perspectives, the individual contributions are designed to have practical value and to inform ongoing debates, notably on the reform of the bank crisis management and deposit insurance framework (CMDI Framework).[11]

II The originality of this edited volume

(Legal) scholarship has given ample attention to the creation, conception, and future completion of the Banking Union. A focus on the Banking Union's development over the first decade since its formation, however, does not exist. While there are significant earlier works,[12] the Banking Union has progressed considerably, necessitating a fresh perspective that is both broad and deep in scope. Some of the legal issues addressed in this book have come up or developed further in recent times, and so far have hardly resulted in academic output (eg EU-Member States outside Banking Union or the Court of Auditor's role in the Banking Union), or have been dealt with only *en passant*, but not as a topic of their own.

There have been works considering various aspects of banking regulation (Single Rulebook), supervision (pillar 1—SSM), resolution (pillar 2—SRM), and developments regarding deposit guarantee schemes (pillar 3). Some works have focused on Economic and Monetary Union in more general terms, without dedicating an in-depth analysis to the Banking Union. Various other monographs and edited volumes offer a constitutional law analysis of the Banking Union, but also a broader analysis of its components. These works were written not only by lawyers, but also by authors with a different academic background, such as political scientists. It appears, however, that the academic discourse has focused on the possible completion of the Banking Union, but has not so much engaged in reflections on the performance of the past years,

[11] Commission, 'Reform of the bank crisis management and deposit insurance framework', 18 April 2023 https://finance.ec.europa.eu/publications/reform-bank-crisis-management-and-deposit-insurance-framework_en, accessed 9 June 2026.

[12] The literature on the Banking Union is very rich, and cannot possibly be cited here in its entirety. Some of the main sources were already mentioned in nn 2 and 8, while additional useful references include Gianni Lo Schiavo (ed), *The European Banking Union and the Role of Law* (Edward Elgar Publishing 2019); Nicolas Véron, *Europe's Banking Union at Ten: Unfinished Yet Transformative* (Bruegel 2023); Danny Busch and Guido Ferrarini (eds), *European Banking Union* (2nd edn, OUP 2020); Gianni Lo Schiavo (ed), *EU Banking Law and Regulation* (OUP 2024).

let alone engaged in the multidimensional analysis proposed here. In particular, beyond the still-evolving regulatory landscape, the quickly evolving case law related to the Banking Union has not been sufficiently reflected in a comprehensive volume. It also seems that existing broader approaches towards the Banking Union appeared in the early days of this policy field, which means that they are, at least in part, outdated by now. This edited volume makes a significant contribution to filling this gap by providing an account of *horizontal*, *substantive*, *institutional*, *cooperative*, *review* and *external* aspects of the Banking Union as it has developed over the past 10 years.

III The multidimensional approach of this edited volume

This book takes a comprehensive approach by examining the Banking Union through its various dimensions. Instead of focusing on its constituent pillars, we take a *multidimensional approach*, traversing the various pillars. 'Dimension' derives from the Latin word *dimensio*, meaning 'measurement'. In classical physics, dimensions are used to measure fundamental units such as length, allowing for the location of a point in three-dimensional space; time is used to make temporal measurements; and mass is used to determine the mass of an object.[13] Social sciences use dimensions to structure complex concepts that allow both the making of theoretical propositions and the measurement of empirical evidence. Thus, dimensions transcend the theory–fact divide and allow a given object to be observed and evaluated. Moreover, rather than treating a given object as an isolated and separate entity, dimensions show the relations to other objects and can help uncover the underlying structure of the whole.[14]

Applying this multidimensional approach to the Banking Union enables us to take its individual pillars seriously while acknowledging that its components form part of a whole. This is not only important for understanding the economic and political challenges the Banking Union strives to overcome; even more so, it facilitates a focus on the various legal problems the three pillars of the Banking Union have in common and the mechanisms developed to solve these problems. Taken together, this multidimensional approach allows us to present an original survey of the Banking Union a decade after it started to function. It promises to shed new light on seemingly known topics,

[13] James Clerk Maxwell, *A Treatise on Electricity and Magnetism* (Clarendon Press 1873) 1–4.
[14] Gary Goertz, *Social Science Concepts and Measurement* (Princeton University Press 2020) 1–5.

but also to uncover how the various dimensions analysed contribute to the overall functioning of the Banking Union. This edited volume distinguishes between a *horizontal*, a *substantive*, an *institutional*, a *cooperative*, a *review*, and an *external* dimension. To each of these dimensions, one part of the book is dedicated.

First, the *horizontal dimension* covers a number of cross-cutting themes that traverse the whole of the Banking Union. Since the Banking Union was conceived in the wake of, and as a reaction to, the Great Financial Crisis, *Alberto de Gregorio Merino* explores how the EU Treaties respond to crises threatening the constitutional fabric of the Union. His finding is that the Treaties have not only proven to be a living constitution which contributes to an ever-closer union, but that they have also given birth to a new law of crisis in the EU, of which the Banking Union is a prominent example. Subsequently, *Mariolina Eliantonio* and *Pavlína Hubková* identify soft law as a transversal method for regulating actors in the Banking Union. In contrast to hard legal obligations that are binding and directly enforceable, soft law allows for novel ways of affecting the multiple actors and governing their complex relationships, thereby also producing significant legal effects. Whereas soft law broadens the reach of regulators, fundamental rights are supposed to restrict the exercise of public power. *Paul Weismann* thus examines the fundamental rights protection in banking supervision and resolution. He puts particular emphasis on the proportionality test and how financial stability and the considerate use of taxpayers' money are balanced against individual interests of banks and their respective shareholders and creditors. Finally, *Concetta Brescia Morra* and *Federico Pistelli* zoom in on the relations between the various bodies in the Banking Union. A plethora of Union institutions and agencies are tasked to pursue financial stability as a common objective. This raises a fundamental problem of coordination between entities that do not share the same scope of action and possess different powers. By highlighting the obstacles that can endanger the proper coordination between the various bodies in the Banking Union, and their different decision-making procedures, they aim to formulate proposals for the creation of a more integrated system of European authorities within the Banking Union.

Second, the *substantive dimension* surveys how the Banking Union is constituted in material terms. *Daniela Jaros* investigates the application of national law by the ECB and other EU bodies. Under EU legislation, these Union authorities are called upon to apply national law transposing directives and other EU acts that are not directly applicable to banks. When applying such substantive banking law, EU authorities have to strike a balance between the interpretation of EU law and established interpretations under national law, which has already led to important case law by the CJEU. Subsequently, *Diane Fromage* and *Gaia Chiarini* seek to answer the question whether, in light of the political stalemate for an EDIS, a revamped deposit guarantee scheme (DGS) would be sufficient to overcome possible crises. To this end, they explore the features and rationales of the ongoing legislative discussions on DGS and whether these proposals could compensate for the absence of an EDIS. A core component of banking supervision which is largely neglected in legal scholarship is the Supervisory Review and Evaluation Process (SREP). *Christy Ann Petit* sets out to close this lacuna. Not only does she explain how SREP is constituted and applied in practice, but she also traces the evolution of this process over time, in light of international standards, the Single Rulebook, EBA guidance, and relevant soft law, in order to evaluate whether SREP is an effective tool for crisis prevention. Finally, *David M Brinkman* and *Asen Lefterov* zoom in on a variety of substantive requirements for financial institutions under EU law. By charting the map of own funds requirements, buffers, and leverage ratios, Total Loss-absorbing Capacity (TLAC), and Minimum Requirement for Own Funds and Eligible Liabilities (MREL), they allow practitioners and scholars alike to navigate these treacherous waters. In spite of some overlap, the individual components form a whole which can be enforced by different means.

Third, the *institutional dimension* focuses on newly established structures and their organisation and powers. *Jonathan Bauerschmidt* gives an overview of how the *Meroni* doctrine has shaped the delegation of powers to EU agencies. The Banking Union exhibits three different types of dealing with the *Meroni* doctrine, whether it concerns internal delegation in the SSM, delegation of autonomous powers for ESMA, or delegation of preparatory powers for the SRB for the resolution of banks. Subsequently, *Andrea Westerhof Löfflerová* explores the reform of the European Stability Mechanism (ESM) as a backstop for the Single Resolution Fund (SRF), which again is part of the SRM. A politically highly contested measure, which for some constitutes a step towards a 'transfer Union', required to find a delicate balance between the constitutional requirements of Member States and the limits imposed by EU law. This contribution shows that the reform of the ESM, although formally outside the Treaties, continues to be loyal to the EU legal order and fully respects its primacy and autonomy. Closely related are the contributions to the SRF. *Eugénie d'Ursel* explores the legal framework governing the so-called *ex ante* contributions which are levied from banks, based on Article 114 TFEU, in an annual exercise. This has led to a plethora of legal challenges before the Union courts, where issues of equal treatment between smaller and bigger banks, as well as proportionality and legal certainty, have been raised. Despite the complexity of the calculations, it is shown that the legal framework for levying these contributions is sufficiently clear and foreseeable. Finally, *Matthias Deissenberger* gives an overview of the newest addition to the supervisory framework: the Anti-Money Laundering Authority, AMLA. This chapter puts into historical perspective the reasons for creating the EU supervisory authorities, and how, building on the examples of the ESAs and the SRB, the EU legislator again pushed the limits imposed by primary law and conferred far-reaching yet specifically circumscribed powers on AMLA to tackle challenges posed by money laundering.

Fourth, the *cooperative dimension* examines the cooperation between EU and national authorities in the Banking Union, considering the intricate distribution of tasks between the EU and the Member State level, which is strongly determined not only by legal rules, but also by administrative practice. *Filipe Brito Bastos* and *Ieva Hūna* investigate composite administrative procedures, which are an important expression of the vertical cooperation between the EU and its Member States. Drawing on the experience in other areas of EU law, they show that the legal framework for supervision and resolution allows for a fruitful pooling of resources to come up with fully informed and legitimate decisions. Moreover, general principles of EU law and the Charter of Fundamental Rights are crucial to fill gaps and overcome obstacles. Closely related, *Edoardo Rulli* explores the cooperation between European and national authorities in banking resolution and the various mechanisms which were devised in the core decision-making phases regarding resolution planning, MREL, and the adoption and implementation of resolution schemes. It is argued that the SRB's leading role is likely to increase in the future because of legislative reforms and the development of a European 'resolution-administrative practice'. Subsequently, *Audronė Steiblytė* uncovers the complementary nature of State aid for banks and how the Commission's regulatory framework for this aid interacts with the bank resolution regime. The resolution framework leaves a specific window open for State aid intervention, provided that the struggling bank is solvent and the State aid is of a precautionary and temporary nature and is not used to offset any losses of the bank. This not only closes a largely neglected research gap; it also serves to address whether national deposit guarantee schemes could be used to support measures preventing bank resolution. Moving away from resolution, *Ursula Hauser-Rethaller* gives an overview of the legal and institutional framework for cooperation in macroprudential policy for banks. While the current macroprudential framework defines a strong role for the National Competent Authorities, this contribution takes a closer look at the legal and practical challenges for the necessary cooperation with the ECB. It establishes how the current framework strikes the balance between subsidiarity and country-specific differentiation, on the one hand, and the objective of financial stability, on the other. Finally, *Agnese Pizzolla* calls, in close cooperation, for a test as to how non-euro-area Member States can join the Banking Union. This specifically designed 'opt-in' mechanism has been used over the past decade, first by Croatia, and then by Bulgaria, although both have since adopted the common currency. Denmark and Sweden have also undertaken studies and released reports exploring their potential participation in the Banking Union. This chapter explores the effectiveness of the existing legal framework and how it has fared in practice.

Fifth, the *review dimension* addresses questions of accountability and judicial review in the Banking Union. To begin with, *Jakub Kerlin* makes a comparative study of the SRB's Appeal Panel and the ECB's Administrative Board of Review, asking whether these quasi-appeal bodies exhibit more commonalities or differences. Despite their similar legal frameworks providing for independent and impartial review, in terms of scope and outcome of control, the Banking Union seems to have created two very different bodies. This will be important to keep in mind also in light of recent reforms of the Statute of the Court of Justice and the Rules of Procedure of the General Court. *Menelaos Markakis* examines the accountability and transparency arrangements in the SSM and the SRM, focusing on the accountability of the ECB and the SRB to the European Parliament. The public hearings with the chair of the ECB's Supervisory Board and the chair of the SRB, at the European Parliament in the 2019–24 legislative term, take a most prominent position in this contribution on the democratic accountability of the Banking Union. *Carlos Soler Ruiz* then focuses on the role of the European Court of Auditors (ECA) in the Banking Union. Taking a deep dive into administrative accountability and the auditing powers of the ECA, this chapter shows how financial and compliance audits, special reports, and the like have contributed to ensuring that the Banking Union could deliver its main objectives. At the same time, there remain gaps in the administrative accountability framework, and the chapter makes suggestions to close them.

Sixth, the *external dimension* takes a hitherto largely neglected look at the Banking Union and its relation to states on its outside. *Jonathan Bauerschmidt*, *Diane Fromage*, and *Vanessa Aichstill* look at the cooperation and information exchange inside and outside the Banking Union, and how Memoranda of Understanding (MoUs) structure this cooperation by way of soft law. Numerous and quite diverse MoUs have been concluded in recent years by the ECB and the SRB, with their respective counterparts from non-Banking Union Member States and third states, which reflects that financial institutions operate on a global scale and that authorities need flexible instruments to keep up with them. *Mads Andenæs* and *Carsten Zatschler* then look at the effects of Banking Union on EEA/EFTA states. By virtue of the EEA Agreement, these states are part of the EU's internal market, and the four freedoms apply to the financial services sector. Moreover, through the EFTA Surveillance Authority, they are within the ambit of the ESAs' regulatory and supervisory powers. While many aspects of this cooperation run smoothly, the slow pace of incorporation of EU law within the EEA Agreement and, eventually, within national law poses problems which the chapter exemplifies through some of the contentious cases of the past decade. Finally, *Carlo Lombardini* zooms in on Switzerland. Banks in Switzerland are not supervised by the Swiss National Bank, but by FINMA, an independent supervisory authority. This chapter sets out the supervisory, resolution, and anti-money laundering frameworks and traces how the crisis of *Credit Swiss* has led to a critical review, at least for systemically important banks in Switzerland.

1
The EU Treaties as Living Constitution of the Union in Times of Crisis

Alberto de Gregorio Merino

I Introduction

Since 2009, the Union has undergone a succession of crises. It is even said to be in a sort of permacrisis: the financial crisis and banking crisis from 2009 to 2015; the debt and euro crisis from 2010 to 2015; the migration crisis, especially felt in 2015; the rule-of-law crisis afflicting some of its Member States since 2016; the process of withdrawal of the UK from the Union, since 2017; the pandemic crisis of 2020 and 2021, with its manyfold ramifications—medical, social, and economic; the war in Ukraine.

These crises have tested the constitutional fabric of the Union, since the Union responded to each of them with unprecedented measures, while hardly amending the Treaties. The latter have proven to be a living document, whose interpretation through well-settled methods allows the challenges of the times to be addressed.

The Treaties are not a rigid text but lend themselves to an evolutive reading that contributes to the process of an 'ever-closer union' to which the preamble of the TEU refers. An evolutive interpretation of the Treaties allows legislation and societal choices to be factored in, as well as articulating the different societal interests at stake. This evolutive interpretation, however, does not amount to a blank cheque for the legislator to break free of the Treaties, nor is it a recipe to twist them to accommodate the legislator's political preferences in an arbitrary manner.

The importance of this evolutive capacity of the Treaties becomes even greater due to their apparent 'freezing': if, since the 1980s, there has been a proliferation of Treaty amendments—Single European Act in 1987, Treaty of Maastricht in 1993, Treaty of Amsterdam in 1999, Treaty of Nice in 2003, Treaty

Alberto de Gregorio Merino, *The EU Treaties as Living Constitution of the Union in Times of Crisis*
In: *EU Banking Union*. Edited by: Jonathan Bauerschmidt, Raffaele D'Ambrosio, Diane Fromage, Daniela Jaros, and Paul Weismann, Oxford University Press.
DOI: 10.1093/9780198949756.003.0002

of Lisbon in 2009, which makes an average of a new Treaty every five and a half years—no such amendment has taken place in the last 15 years.[1] And despite calls by some—including the European Parliament[2]—to address the reform of the Treaties, it will probably not happen in the short or medium term, bearing in mind the uncertainties such a process would raise at the current EU political juncture. If we were to embark on a revision of the Treaties, one cannot exclude difficult national referenda that could make a negotiation process collapse, or even a result that leads to shrinking the current competences of the Union and favouring a devolution of powers upon Member States.

The living constitution of the Union manifests itself through the emergence of a law of crisis. If, as predicted by Jean Monnet, EU integration would take place through crisis—if, accordingly, in the last 15 years, integration has been forged through crisis—the law of EU integration and the theory of EU evolution can also be regarded as a law of crisis.

First, the law of crisis has entailed the broad and finalistic interpretation of legal bases provided in the Treaties, to enhance the competences of the Union when central mechanisms of decision are required.[3]

Second, the EU budget has operated as a fundamental instrument of integration through crisis.

Third, the Union has activated Treaty emergency legal bases (most notably, Article 122 of the Treaty on the Functioning of the European Union (TFEU)) which it had rarely used since the Treaty of Rome, and never with such an impact.

Fourth, where the Treaties were not sufficient, recourse has been had to intergovernmental constructions—founded on international public law—which come to the rescue of EU law by supplementing it.

Fifth, there has been a marked change of paradigm in the institutional set-up, where the Union and its institutions have been transformed from being preponderantly regulatory entities to become, also, crisis managers.

The role of the Court of Justice has also been key in the evolutive reading of the Treaties, with case law that has responded to almost each of the major

[1] With the exception of a relatively limited amendment of Art 136 of the Treaty on the Functioning of the European Union that took place in 2011, through a simplified amendment procedure, so as to make clear that mechanisms for budgetary assistance, subject to strict conditionality and indispensable to safeguard the stability of the euro area as a whole, were compatible with the Treaties.

[2] Proposals of the European Parliament for the amendment of the Treaties of 22 November 2023, P9_TA(2023)0427.

[3] On this phenomenon in general, see Diane Fromage, Adrienne Héritier, and Paul Weismann (eds), *EU Regulatory Responses to Crises: Adaptation or Transformation?* (OUP 2025).

crisis/integration EU decisions in the last years. It has led, eventually, to the development of the notion of EU constitutional identity.

This chapter will briefly explore, in turn, each of the dimensions evoked above, to offer a general cartography of the law of crisis.

II A broad interpretation of EU Treaties: The case of Article 114 TFEU

The Union has relied on 'classical' legal bases provided in the Treaties, used in normal times for common regulatory purposes, to establish mechanisms leading to enhanced integration.

This is especially the case of Article 114 TFEU, a core internal market provision. It empowers the EU legislator to adopt measures for the approximation of national laws of the Member States, which measures have as their object the establishment and functioning of the internal market. The use of Article 114 TFEU has extended to address crisis actions which do not directly consist of approximating or harmonizing national law, but which are instrumental to achieving ongoing harmonisation processes.

Recourse to Article 114 TFEU has been had during the banking crisis, where the EU established the Banking Union that aims at supervising banks located in the euro area (mostly), as well as resolving those which are non-viable and insolvent. Article 114 TFEU was relied upon to establish centralized crisis decision-making bodies such as the Single Resolution Board, on which the capacity to resolve a bank and to make use of a Fund (the Single Resolution Fund) to finance resolution operations was conferred.[4] Article 114 TFEU was also relied upon to establish the European Supervisory Authorities, EU agencies to which the legislator has granted tasks of regulation, and of intervention in exceptional circumstances where financial stability is affected, such as the temporary prohibition or restriction of short-selling operations.[5]

Article 114 also witnesses a very interesting recent development of the internal market: the legislative alignment between the internal market and social

[4] Regulation (EU) 806/2014 of the European Parliament and of the Council of 15 July 2014 establishing uniform rules and a uniform procedure for the resolution of credit institutions and certain investment firms in the framework of a Single Resolution Mechanism and a Single Resolution Fund, [2014] OJ L225, p 1.

[5] See Art 28 of Regulation (EU) 236/2012 of the European Parliament and of the Council of 14 March 2012 on short selling and certain aspects of credit default swaps, [2012] OJ L86, p 1; also Case C–270/12 *United Kingdom v Parliament and Council*, ECLI:EU:C:2014:18.

values that go beyond the pure integration of economic or production factors, including, of course, the values of Article 2 TEU.

In the important judgments of the Court of Justice concerning rule-of-law conditionality (which ruled on appeals brought by Poland and Hungary against the Conditionality rule-of-law Regulation, in Cases C-156/21 and C-157/21),[6] the Court of Justice held that the values of Article 2 TEU are at the heart of the European constitutional identity. The Court also states in those judgments that respect for the values of Article 2 TEU is bound to penetrate legislative action. The Court, in some way, calls on the legislature to incorporate respect for values into the various policies and acts of the Union, and in so far as such incorporation is necessary for the attainment of the objectives of the act in question.[7]

There is, accordingly, a recent trend in which internal market acts are subject to a 'valuative' dimension, where the establishment of fundamental freedoms (free movement of goods, free provision of services, freedom of persons, and free movement of capital) goes hand in hand with the achievement of broader social objectives and respect for fundamental values:

- The Media Freedom Act, which aims at establishing common rules for the proper functioning of the internal market for media services, and which assumes that the internal market for media services can only be established if pluralism is ensured.[8]
- The Regulation on the transparency of political advertising, aimed at protecting electoral integrity and fostering a democratic and open debate, through rules governing the provision of advertising services in electoral and political matters.[9]
- The Digital Services Act (DSA), which aims at ensuring the proper functioning of the internal market for intermediary digital services through rules for content moderation, user data handling, and liability of digital service providers, in a way that effectively protects fundamental rights

[6] Case C–156/21 *Hungary v European Parliament and Council*, ECLI:EU:C:2022:97; Case C–157/21 *Poland v European Parliament and Council*, ECLI:EU:C:2022:98.

[7] See para 268 of the judgment in *Poland v Parliament and Council* (n 6).

[8] Regulation (EU) 2024/1083 of the European Parliament and of the Council of 11 April 2024 establishing a common framework for media services in the internal market and amending Directive 2010/13/EU, [2024] OJ L2024/1083.

[9] Regulation (EU) 2024/900 of the European Parliament and of the Council of 13 March 2024 on the transparency and targeting of political advertising, [2024] OJ L2024/900.

under the Charter, including freedom of expression and information, and media freedom and pluralism.[10]

- The new Defence of Democracy proposal, which will regulate certain commercial services, such as offices of political interests, in order to promote free and fair elections, step up the fight against disinformation, and support freedom and pluralism by confronting external interests.[11]

III The EU budget as fundamental instrument of integration through crisis

On a different note, Next Generation EU (NGEU) consisted of the financial response to the dramatic economic consequences of the pandemic in the continent.[12] It is endowed with 750 billion euros. For the first time, the Union went to the markets to borrow for spending—338 billion out of the 750 billion euros was granted as subsidies—a moment that some (too) enthusiastically qualified as the Hamiltonian moment of the Union, namely the creation of an EU Treasury.

This unprecedented step had to be compatible with fundamental rules at the core of the economic constitution of the Union, most notably the principle of budgetary balance laid down in Article 310 TFEU, under which the EU budget cannot run a deficit and must be in balance at the end of each year, and the principle of integrity of the own resources system laid down in Article 311 TFEU, whereby the EU budget shall be financed wholly from own resources (which are, in turn, transferred by Member States, with proceeds from borrowing in the markets not being considered as own resources).

A broad and evolutive interpretation of these provisions was followed by the Union institutions when setting up NGEU: the latter is accompanied by a definitive, irrevocable, earmarked, and enforceable commitment of payment by Member States, which ensures the budget neutrality of the operation,

[10] Regulation (EU) 2022/2065 of the European Parliament and of the Council of 19 October 2022 on a Single Market for Digital Services and amending Directive 2000/31/EC, [2022] OJ L277, p 1.

[11] Proposal for a Directive of the European Parliament and of the Council establishing harmonised requirements in the internal market on transparency of interest representation carried out on behalf of third countries and amending Directive (EU) 2019/1937 COM (2023) 637 final.

[12] See, for an overview, Federico Fabbrini, 'The Legal Architecture of the Economic Responses to COVID-19: EMU beyond the Pandemic' (2022) 60 Journal of Common Market Studies 186–203; Paul Dermine, 'The EU's Response to the COVID-19 Crisis and the Trajectory of Fiscal Integration in Europe: Between Continuity and Rupture' (2020) 47 Legal Issues of Economic Integration 337–57; Ruth Weber, 'Introduction' in Ruth Weber (ed), *The Financial Constitution of European Integration* (Hart 2023) 1–18.

and hence guarantees that a deficit will not arise; it is a temporary facility—available up to the end of 2026—of an exceptional nature, and as such does not constitute a new budgetary paradigm of the Union which is to be consolidated and continued indefinitely, and cannot be seen as deconstructing the integrity of the own resources system.

Borrowing for spending under NGEU comes with many guarantees which make it compatible with the Treaties, be it the principle of budgetary balance or the integrity of the own resources system. It is designed to be budgetarily neutral and not to engender deficits. Bearing in mind its special characteristics and the very particular needs it intends to address, it can be regarded as complementary to the own resources system of the Union, and respectful of its integrity. NGEU does not constitute a new budgetary paradigm of the Union that is called to be consolidated throughout time. Borrowing for spending cannot become a permanent feature of the EU budget to finance regular EU policies, unless the Treaties were to be changed. It is from this perspective that it must be concluded that we are not in a Hamiltonian moment of the Union, which can be understood as the leap towards a common Treasury of the Member States. NGEU is far away from constituting a genuine European Treasury.[13]

Another fundamental dimension of integration through budget can be found in the rule-of-law conditionality mechanism—tangentially referred to in the previous section, and enshrined in Regulation 2020/2092 ('the conditionality rule-of-law Regulation').[14]

As is the case regarding the NGEU, the interest of this Regulation is not exhausted in its budgetary dimension: the conditionality rule-of-law Regulation is essentially an instrument of great constitutional and institutional value. It expresses fundamental principles of the EU legal order, such as solidarity and mutual trust, and gives legislative translation to the values set out in Article 2 of the TEU, which include respect for the rule of law.

The Commission presented its proposal on the conditionality rule-of-law Regulation in May 2018.[15] The proposal was framed in a double context. On the one hand, it was part of the Commission's overall strategy to address the challenges to the rule of law that existed in some Member States at the time of this proposal; on the other hand, the proposal is an integral part of the

[13] Alberto de Gregorio Merino, 'Follow the Money, Follow the Values' in Weber (ed), *The Financial Constitution of European Integration* (n 12) 113–30.

[14] Regulation (EU, Euratom) 2020/2092 of the European Parliament and of the Council of 16 December 2020 on a general regime of conditionality for the protection of the Union budget, [2020] OJ L433I, p 1.

[15] COM/2018/324 final - 2018/0136 (COD).

Commission's Multi-Annual Financial Framework (MFF) legislative package for the period 2021–27.

The negotiations for the current MFF revolved around three pillars: the MFF proposal; the NGEU programme, explored previously; and, finally, the conditionality rule-of-law proposal. The latter is, therefore, imbricated into the overall MFF and the NGEU negotiations and cannot be politically understood outside that context.

The general conditionality mechanism aims at protecting the EU budget in case of breaches of the principles of the rule of law in the Member States. It is based on the idea that Member States can ensure the sound financial management of EU money only if their public authorities act in accordance with the law.[16] Its legal basis is Article 322(1)(a) TFEU, which allows for the adoption of financial rules on the procedure for establishing and implementing the budget.

It has relied on a budget legal basis of the Treaties, Article 322(1)(a) TFEU, which allows for the adoption of financial rules on the procedure for establishing and implementing the budget.

There is no doubt that the conditionality rule-of-law Regulation is an example of 'marriage' between the principles of solidarity and responsibility. Integration processes brought about by recent crises are founded on a trade-off between the two principles: the public debt crisis led to instruments such as the European Stability Mechanism (ESM), which may mobilize huge amounts of money to assist Member States suffering liquidity or insolvency problems, in exchange for these states adopting measures of budgetary responsibility; and in the face of the financial crisis, the Banking Union was created, in which the risks of banks are mutualized through a single resolution fund in exchange for a mutualization of the control of those risks (through the Single Supervisory System, which has been in the hands of the European Central Bank (ECB) since 2014). The convergence of solidarity and responsibility arises in other EU policies where Member States share a common good such as asylum and immigration, and thus Article 80 TFEU reflects both principles on an equal footing.

The conditionality rule-of-law Regulation and the particular context in which it appears (the massive mobilization of funding under the MFF and NGEU) is another example of this interaction between solidarity and responsibility. As stated by Advocate General Campos Sánchez Bordona, NGEU is possibly 'the largest solidarity effort launched by the Union in its history'.[17]

[16] Recital 8 of the preamble to the conditionality rule of law Regulation (n 14).
[17] See conclusions of Advocate General Campos Sánchez Bordona in *Germany v Poland* C–848/19, ECLI:EU:C:2021:218, in footnote 43.

In its two conditionality judgments, the Court dwells on the relationship between the principles of solidarity and responsibility. It establishes a sort of 'super-conditionality', recalling that respect by the Member States of the values set out in Article 2 TEU is a necessary condition for them to enjoy their rights under the Treaties.[18] It recalls that the Union budget is one of the main instruments that gives concrete form to the principle of solidarity. The principle of solidarity, in turn, presupposes the principle of mutual trust between the Member States. There can be no solidarity, nor the mutual confidence that it presupposes, without respect by Member States of the values of Article 2 TEU.[19] The Court concludes by recalling that respect for the rule of law, which presupposes judicial independence, is essential for the sound financial management and protection of the Union's financial interests.[20]

Conditionality is the link between solidarity and responsibility. Conditionality, especially budgetary conditionality, has become an important vector of integration. And, one should not forget, the negotiation of the last MFF, as well as of the NGEU programme, has been very much marked by the establishment of different budgetary conditionalities, aimed at ensuring a responsible execution of the huge solidarity effort at stake. Suffice it to mention some of those conditionalities, such as environmental and climate conditionality; the one based on respect for 'horizontal principles' relating to the protection of fundamental rights and compliance with the Charter of Fundamental Rights; or macroeconomic conditionality linking the provision and effectiveness of funds to the respect for budgetary obligations and sound economic governance.[21]

The mechanism demonstrates the *structuring* function of the values referred to in Article 2 TEU. That article does not constitute a legal basis conferring competences on the Union. However, the values it mentions do not have a mere aspirational function. They are not a constitutional dead letter; Article 2 is not just constitutional iconography, in the words of Joseph Weiler.[22] Article 2 TEU has full normative value, intended to irrigate EU legislation.

[18] See para 144 of the judgment in *Poland v Parliament and Council* (n 6).
[19] See ibid, para 147.
[20] See ibid, paras 148–51.
[21] These conditionality rules are laid down in Regulation (EU) 2021/1060 laying down common provisions on the European Regional Development Fund, the European Social Fund Plus, the Cohesion Fund, the Just Transition Fund and the European Maritime, Fisheries and Aquaculture Fund and financial rules for those and for the Asylum, Migration and Integration Fund, the Internal Security Fund and the Instrument for Financial Support for Border Management and Visa Policy, [2021] OJ L231, p 159. Environmental conditionality is laid down in arts 6 and 9(4) thereof; respect for horizontal principles (as fundamental rights) in art 9; and macroeconomic conditionality in art 19.
[22] Joseph HH Weiler, 'On the power of the word: Europe's constitutional iconography' (2005) 3(3) International Journal of Constitutional Law 173 ff.

The two conditionality judgments of the Court confirm this. The Court repeatedly states that Article 2 TEU is legally binding for the Member States. In particular, respect for the values of Article 2 TEU constitutes an obligation of result, in the sense that, while the Member States have a margin of discretion for their internal organization to ensure respect for the principles of the rule of law, each of them must ensure an equivalent and effective level of respect for these values.[23] Moreover, the obligation to respect the values of Article 2 TEU is subject to a principle of non-regression: such an obligation is not only a condition of accession to the EU within the meaning of Article 49 TEU, but a requirement which must be complied with on a continuous basis once accession has taken place.[24]

And because Article 2 TEU has full normative value, its interpretation belongs to the EU and, ultimately, to the Court. These values are not an intangible part of the national constitutional identity but are at the core of what the Court calls the *European constitutional identity*. National constitutional identity cannot make the defence of the values under Article 2 TEU a task left to the sole discretion of each Member State. The Union cannot outsource in full the definition, content, and scope of these values to the Member States. It is for the Union to define and defend them on the basis of the autonomy enjoyed by its legal order vis-à-vis the law of the Member States.[25] And outside Article 7 TEU, which establishes a procedure subject to primarily political considerations, the monitoring of compliance by the EU institutions with the values of Article 2 TEU must be subject to legal criteria.[26]

Finally, as mentioned earlier when examining the intertwinement between Article 114 TFEU and values, respect for the values of Article 2 TEU is, according to the Court, bound to penetrate legislative action. Moreover, the Court refers to a kind of duty on the part of the EU legislator to proactively defend the values of Article 2.[27] It seems to be a message to Brussels: the Court should not bear the burden to enforce respect for the values, notably of the rule of law, alone. The political institutions should also assume their responsibility.[28]

[23] See paras 142–45, 168, 169, 179, and 263–65 of the judgment in *Poland v Parliament and Council* (n 6).
[24] See ibid, paras 143, 144, and 223.
[25] See ibid, para 143.
[26] See ibid, paras 200 and 203.
[27] See ibid, para 268.
[28] See, in this sense, Jean-Paul Jacqué, 'Le juge de l'Union saisi par la politique' (2021) 57(4) Revue Trimestriel de Droit Européen 799–802.

IV The use of the emergency clause of the Treaties, Article 122 TFEU

The Union has recently started having recourse to Article 122 TFEU more frequently. This provision, which corresponds to the TFEU title on economic and monetary policy, is certainly the most important crisis clause of the EU Treaties.

Article 122 TFEU corresponds to Chapter 1 (economic policy) of Title VIII (economic and monetary policy) TFEU. It reads as follows:

1. Without prejudice to any other procedures provided for in the Treaties, the Council, on a proposal from the Commission, may decide, in a spirit of solidarity between Member States, upon the measures appropriate to the economic situation, in particular if severe difficulties arise in the supply of certain products, notably in the area of energy.
2. Where a Member State is in difficulties or is seriously threatened with severe difficulties caused by natural disasters or exceptional occurrences beyond its control, the Council, on a proposal from the Commission, may grant, under certain conditions, Union financial assistance to the Member State concerned. The President of the Council shall inform the European Parliament of the decision taken.

Article 122 TFEU has been a kind of 'sleeping beauty' provision, hardly used before the succession of crises that have afflicted the Union since 2010—the financial crisis, the public debt crisis, the migration crisis, the Covid-19 crisis, and the war in Ukraine. Since then, the Union has relied on this provision as a legal basis on six occasions: the adoption of the European Financial Stability Mechanism,[29] which aims at providing financial assistance to Member States undergoing problems of budgetary liquidity or solvency; the adoption of the Emergency Support Instrument,[30] which initially aimed at providing financial support to Member States that suffered most the consequences of the 2016 migration and refugee crisis, and which eventually evolved towards supporting the sanitary consequences of the Covid-19 crisis; the establishment of a European instrument for temporary support to mitigate unemployment

[29] Council Regulation (EU) 407/2010 of 11 May 2010 establishing a European financial stabilisation mechanism [2010] OJ L118, p 1.

[30] Council Regulation (EU) 2016/369 of 15 March 2016 on the provision of emergency support within the Union [2016] OJ L70, p 1.

risks (SURE)[31] following the Covid-19 outbreak; the establishment of the Health Emergency Preparedness and Response (HERA),[32] a new Commission department that brings together experts from the Commission and Member States' representatives, and whose objective is to prevent, detect, and rapidly respond to health emergencies; the adoption of the EU Recovery Instrument,[33] on which we are focusing here; and, finally, at the date of publication of this contribution, the adoption of the Regulation on an emergency intervention to address high energy prices.[34]

Crisis clauses exist in most constitutions. Typically, they allow for prompt action of the executive, which can rely on wide powers with limited parliamentary control. Moreover, their activation normally involves simplified, less burdensome procedures adapted to the gravity of the situation.

Yet, although recourse to crisis clauses is legitimate, their use must rely on principles of prudence and exceptionality. Otherwise, they risk becoming a vehicle that may erode a constitutional order for reasons of political convenience and opportunity. History is enlightening in this respect. One of the most telling examples relates to Article 48 of the Weimar Constitution, the emergency provision of that constitution. It empowered the president of the republic to enforce the constitution against 'disobedient' Länder or to adopt the necessary measures, decrees, or orders, in cases of serious disturbances or risks to public order and security. The president of the republic undertook a widespread use of this article as from 1920, and most notably in the years 1930 and 1931, both in quantitative and qualitative terms. That use went beyond security and public order issues and comprised decrees and orders in the financial and economic field.[35] The relentless use of Article 48 of the Weimar Constitution ultimately led to its mutation, to the creation of a parallel legal order detrimental to parliamentarism, and to the progressive transformation of the Weimar Republic into an authoritarian regime.

[31] Council Regulation (EU) 2020/672 of 19 May 2020 on the establishment of a European instrument for temporary support to mitigate unemployment risks in an emergency (SURE) following the COVID-19 outbreak [2020] OJ L159, p 1.

[32] Council Regulation (EU) 2022/2372 of 24 October 2022 on a framework of measures for ensuring the supply of crisis-relevant medical countermeasures in the event of a public health emergency at Union level, [2022] OJ L314, p 64.

[33] Council Regulation (EU) 2020/2094 of 14 December 2020 establishing a European Union Recovery Instrument to support the recovery in the aftermath of the COVID-19 crisis [2020] OJ L433I, p 23.

[34] Council Regulation (EU) 2022/1854 on an emergency intervention to address high energy prices [2022] OJ L261I, p 1.

[35] Between 1920 and 1924, more than 100 presidential decrees were adopted on the basis of art 48 of the Weimar Constitution. In 1932, 60 presidential decrees were adopted. See Josu de Miguel Bárcena and Javier Tajadura Tejada, *Kelsen versus Schmitt, política y derecho en la crisis del Constitutionalismo* (Guillermo Escolar Editor 2019) at pp 249 ff.

Of course, one should not dramatize the evolution of the law of the Union when it comes to Article 122 TFEU. The ghost of the Weimar Constitution does not risk haunting the Union legal order. Nevertheless, the evocation of the Weimar experience of exceptionality may be useful to warn against the dangers that an excessive use of exceptionality clauses, such as Article 122 TFEU, entails.

Arguably, the wording of Article 122(1) TFEU confers upon the Council a wide margin of discretion for its use. It empowers the Council to adopt the 'measures appropriate to the economic situation' in a 'spirit of solidarity', without specifying the situations which qualify for recourse to that provision or the particular form, nature, and content of the measures that may be adopted on its basis. Article 122(1) TFEU simply refers 'in particular' to severe difficulties in the supply of certain products, notably in the area of energy, but does not specify exhaustively either the kind of situations which may give rise to the use of that provision or the specific measures that the Council is empowered to adopt. Despite this wide margin of discretion, and bearing in mind its expansive scope and strength, the use of Article 122 TFEU must be subject to strict limits—to an overall rule of prudence and of self-restraint—so that the legal fabric of the Union, founded on the principle of attribution of competences, is not affected. What are those limits?

First, Article 122 TFEU must be exclusively used in situations of exceptionality leading to severe difficulties in the economic situation of the Member States which cannot be addressed by means of the ordinary Union measures.[36] Not every exceptional situation should qualify for the use of that provision. The bar is very high: the gravity of the situation must be especially qualified. Situations where particular individual or specific sectors of the economy are affected would not be sufficient for its activation. It is necessary that the situation in question presents a systemic nature affecting, or threatening to affect, the fundamentals of the economy of the Union or of its Member States in a generalized manner, in terms of, for instance, evolution of GDP and growth, unemployment rates, productivity and competitiveness indicators, or financial stability and the solvability of liquidity of the Member States.

Second, recourse to Article 122 TFEU must be temporary. It cannot be used for the purpose of regulating a matter on a permanent basis or to replace the ordinary financing of EU policies, since this would encroach on the relevant

[36] The wording of art 122(1) TFEU does not expressly mention the condition of urgency, as is the case for art 122(2). However, the two paragraphs need to be read jointly and on the basis of the specific purpose of art 122 TFEU in the system of the Treaties: both contextual and systemic methods of interpretation point, therefore, at an 'emergency rationale' that applies to the whole provision.

substantive legal bases provided for in the Treaties. The introductory words, 'without prejudice to any other procedures provided for in the Treaties', underscore the exceptional and temporary nature of measures under Article 122(1) TFEU, as recourse to that provision may not undermine or circumvent the use of other legal bases laid down in the Treaties for use in 'normal times'.

Third, Article 122 TFEU belongs to Chapter 1 of Title VIII TFEU, which deals with economic policy. The objective and the content of measures adopted under Article 122(1) TFEU must, therefore, be economic in nature.

Fourth, Article 122 TFEU must be used for providing support to Member States of the Union, and not as an instrument of external policy to the benefit of third countries. The competence set out in Article 122 TFEU is based on the particular *spirit of solidarity* between Member States, which justifies taking exceptional action when Member States experience situations of severe economic difficulties. The position of third countries in that regard is, in principle, fundamentally different. Article 122 TFEU cannot be used as an instrument of external policy.[37]

V The intergovernmental method

In those instances where the Treaties were not able to cater for solutions to crises, namely when they did not provide a suitable legal basis and/or where the budgetary availabilities of the Union were not sufficient, recourse has been had to the intergovernmental method, where the Member States of the Union conclude *inter se* agreements of international public law. Intergovernmentalism has allowed the EU to overcome the rigidity of the EU Treaties amendment process during particularly challenging economic and financial conditions when time was a scarce resource, to address issues with a major constitutional and institutional dimension. It has also allowed the desire for integration of a majority of Member States, despite the persistent reticence of a few.[38]

[37] The General Court has clarified that 'the spirit of solidarity between Member States that must inform the adoption by the Council of measures appropriate to the economic situation, within the meaning of Article 122(1) TFEU, indicates that such measures must be founded on assistance between the Member States' (judgment of 30 September 2015, T-450/12 *Anagnostakis v Commission*, ECLI:EU:T:2015:739, para 42). This finding has been confirmed by the Court of Justice on appeal: judgment of 12 September 2017, C-589/15 P, EU:C:2017:663, para 71.

[38] See, in general, Jean-Claude Piris, *The Future of Europe: Towards a Two-speed EU?* (CUP 2012).

This is the case of the Treaty establishing the European Stability Mechanism (the ESM), an international financial organization located in Luxembourg which can mobilize up to 500 billion euros in assistance through loans subject to strict conditionality, in order to safeguard the stability of the euro area and of its Member States; this is also the case of the Treaty on Stability, Convergence and Growth (also called the Fiscal Compact), a Treaty of international public law concluded in 2012 by all Member States, which aims at reinforcing the Stability and Growth Pact under the EU Treaties—whose governance and functioning proved flawed during the economic crisis—through the establishment of enhanced budgetary obligations; and of intergovernmental mechanisms supplementing the budget of the Union, such as the Facility on the Refugees in Turkey during the migration crisis (where Member States pooled 6 billion euros outside the EU budget).

However, the fact that crisis instruments have been created outside the EU Treaties does not mean that they are completely unrelated to the law of the Union. Contrary to the fears of many, intergovernmentalism has not proven to be a threat to, or actual deconstruction of, the EU method, but a loyal supplement to it. It has allowed the achievement of the EU's objectives and the furthering of its policies though a legal architecture which ensures the anchoring of the intergovernmental instruments into the law of the Union.

These *inter se* treaties have incorporated clauses of consistency, by virtue of which measures laid down on their basis must be compatible with and subordinated to EU law. Consistency provisions are the corollary of the principles of sincere cooperation laid down by Article 4(3) TFEU,[39] and of primacy of EU law. Moreover, those instruments make extensive use of institutions of the Union—the Commission and the Court of Justice—on which they confer, respectively, powers for the execution of some of some of these tasks under these treaties, and of jurisdictional control, thus contributing to preserving the loyalty of the intergovernmental instruments to the EU.[40]

[39] Under the principle of sincere cooperation, Member States shall take any appropriate measure, general or particular, to ensure fulfilment of the obligations arising out of the Treaties or resulting from the acts of the institutions of the Union, and they shall facilitate the achievement of the Union's tasks and refrain from any measure which could jeopardize the attainment of Union objectives.

[40] The attribution of jurisdiction to the Court of Justice in the different intergovernmental constructions has been operated by means of art 273 TFEU. According to this provision, the Court shall have jurisdiction in any dispute between Member States which relates to the subject matter of the Treaties if the dispute is submitted to it under a special agreement between the parties. See also Case C-370/12 *Pringle*, ECLI:EU:C:2012:756, paras 173–77 and, more generally, Bruno de Witte and Thibault Martinelli, 'Treaties between EU Member States as Quasi-Instruments of EU Law' in Marise Cremona and Claire Kilpatrick (eds), *EU Legal Acts: Challenges and Transformations* (OUP 2018) 157–88.

VI Crisis and EU institutional shifts

As stated earlier, crises have brought about important steps of integration. Decisive actions have, in turn, entailed important consequences for the inter-institutional balance of the Union.

On the one hand, crises have made the European Council emerge, together with the Council, as the main decision-making body in the EU. Integration during the crisis has followed growing coordination in the European Council. The European Council, which gathers the heads of state and government of the 27 Member States, was established as an institution by the Treaty of Lisbon. It isn't but logical that the different existential decisions taken at the occasion of the different crises, those which have made the Treaties evolved, have been agreed by the institution that reunites the national Leaders.

This preponderant role of the European Council, which directly decides on initiatives and actions, enters into competition with the power of initiative of the Commission. An interesting question is how to reconcile the European Council's power to define the general political directions and priorities of the Union (as laid down in Article 15(1) TEU) and the Commission's power to 'promote the general interest of the Union and take appropriate initiatives to that end' (Article 17 TEU).

In any event, the role of the Commission as vector of integration and Treaty evolution has been remarkable, and has even been reinforced during the various crises. This is especially true in relation to the latest two completed Commission mandates, under presidents Juncker and von der Leyen. The Commission has had a protagonist role in putting forward crisis initiatives and in implementing them in a coordinated manner. Crises require joint responses—not national ones—and the Commission is best placed for actions that presuppose centralization. The evolution of the Treaties during the crises has entailed a federalization effect that has, in turn, made the role of the Commission grow, as the institution which best safeguards the common interest of the Union and its Member States: it is the institution that coordinated the major responses to the pandemic crisis; it has pushed through and executed restrictive measures against Russia; it has coordinated the European Peace Facility for the supply of munitions to Ukraine; it has managed the Next Generation EU—both borrowing in the markets and the spending in the Member States. Even when acting in an intergovernmental manner, Member States have, as stated earlier, decided to entrust it with tasks of coordination and management. In the landscape of EU institutions, the Commission has thus become the key crisis manager. This has entailed consequences in the functioning of the Commission itself, which has become subject to a more presidential and centrally managed model than a (traditional) collegial one where all Commissioners decide collectively and on an equal footing.

The European Council has also 'funnelled' the powers of the European Parliament and the Council as co-legislators, marking their tempos and, in some ways, guiding their legislative choices. Again here, a very interesting issue arises, namely how to reconcile the European Council's influence on legislative processes with the Treaty rule that this institution 'shall not exercise legislative functions' (Article 15(1) TEU). It is not by surprise that the European Parliament has been especially sensitive and vigilant on the possible intrusions of the European Council on legislative functions.

And this leads to another interesting institutional remark that concerns the European Parliament. The successive Treaty reforms have considerably increased the powers of this institution, which has now become co-legislator together with the Council in the vast majority of EU policies. Yet, if this guarantees the participation of the Parliament as a legislative and regulatory body, the same cannot be said in relation to many of the crisis decisions, where the involvement of that institution has been limited, by comparison to its legislative role. It has no role in relation to the emergency measures adopted under Article 122 TFEU; it has not been involved in the intergovernmental mechanisms referred to above; it had a limited participation in the measures to face the migratory crisis of 2015—the activation of quotas mechanisms among Member States. To put it otherwise, while the European Parliament is a powerful regulatory institution, it cannot yet be regarded as a crisis manager. This means that it has had a limited say in the evolution of the Treaties as living documents.

For some, this limited role of the European Parliament poses questions on the democratic legitimacy of the crisis decisions adopted by the Union. For others, to the extent that those decisions are of a rather constitutional nature, the involvement of Member States through the means of the European Council, or through intergovernmental methods, is the highest democratic guarantee, because legitimacy is ultimately provided by national legislatures.[41]

[41] See only Commission, 'Q&A: Next Generation EU – Legal Construction' (9 June 2020) https://ec.europa.eu/commission/presscorner/detail/en/QANDA_20_1024/, accessed 9 June 2026: 'The authorisation of the borrowing will need the approval of all Member States, and, depending on national procedures, of their national parliaments. This provides for the necessary democratic legitimacy of that innovative proposal necessary to fulfil the Union's objectives.' See, in addition, for an overview of the debate, Karolina Borońska-Hryniewiecka and Diane Fromage, 'Parliaments in Times of Crises: Democratic Accountability in the EU Economic Governance from the Euro to the COVID Crisis' (2022) 28 Journal of Legislative Studies 299–312.

The final institutional point refers to non-political institutions of the Union, specifically the Court of Justice and the ECB. Both of these have a mandate rooted in independence and insulation from political considerations. Yet, the two of them have been drawn in by the frenzy of crises, and have been instrumental in addressing them.

In order to guarantee the singleness of the euro, the ECB has had recourse to unconventional monetary policy instruments, such as outright monetary transactions (OMT) and operations of quantitative easing, taking that institution to the very limits of its monetary mandate under the Treaties.

The Court of Justice has had to deal with almost every one of the crisis responses, through judgments such as *Pringle* (which concerned the ESM),[42] or *Gauweiler*[43] and *Weiss*,[44] which concerned the legality of ECB unconventional monetary operations, or its rule-of-law case law, including the rule-of-law conditionality decisions already referred to.[45] The Court was also actively solicited during Brexit talks, for example in the *Wightman* case.[46] In short, there will be case law on the conditions for having recourse to Article 122 (with cases *sub iudice* where Poland has contested 122 TFEU measures adopted during the energy crisis). The Court's intervention during crises has given rise to seminal jurisprudence that has underscored and developed the constitutional audacity of the EU political institutions.

Some criticize EU political institutions as being too reliant on non-political institutions to solve the problems raised by crises: in accordance with these views, political institutions would adopt a sort of contemplative attitude where they are, for instance, comfortable seeing Draghi's ECB recourse to the OMT programme as a measure to alleviate the tensions in the euro area, instead of discussing effective budgetary discipline or fiscal capacity; where they are, for instance, comfortable seeing the ECJ dealing with the crisis of the rule of law in some Member States, instead of themselves applying decisively the political mechanisms laid down in the Treaties (Article 7 TEU).

Yet, one cannot expect non-political institutions to carry the main responsibility of addressing crises which are preponderantly political in nature. This may entail a big reputational cost for those institutions, take their mandates to the limits, and cause constitutional tensions between the Union and Member

[42] Judgment of the Court of 27 November 2012, *Pringle* (n 40).

[43] Judgment of the Court of 16 June 2015, C-62/14 *Gauweiler*, ECLI:EU:C:2015:400.

[44] Judgment of the Court of 11 December 2018, C-493/17 *Weiss*, ECLI:EU:C:2018:1000.

[45] Judgment of the Court of 27 February 2018, C-64/16 *Associação Sindical dos Juízes Portugueses*, ECLI:EU:C:2018:117.

[46] Judgment of the Court of 10 December 2018, C-621/18 *Wightman*, ECLI:EU:C:2018:999.

States (including with their constitutional courts, as the *Weiss* saga—where the mandates of the ECB and of the ECJ were contested—shows).

VII Looking into the future by means of conclusion

This contribution aspires to make a grammar of the living constitution of the Union, namely an account of the many ways in which it has evolved in the last years, in view of crises. Whether the trend of almost permanent crisis will continue in the coming years is unknown.

The coming years seem, however, to call for an evolution rooted in the idea of strategic autonomy or European sovereignty. Strategic autonomy is a concept especially dear to EU leaders in the face of the changing geostrategic situation, where the EU has to navigate among the tensions of a not-so-friendly US administration, the nationalistic pulsion of China, the belligerent threat of Russia, and a Global South that seems progressively misaligned with EU's priorities. EU law is called on to evolve as the law of European sovereignty, and this may be the next challenge for its living constitution. It suffices to have a look at the political guidelines of President von der Leyen for her second mandate, where the ritornello is security and autonomy on many different fronts.

There are several questions in this context whose response will require recourse to constitutional identity, and where the Treaties as the living constitution of the Union will be proven again. These questions include the development of the common defence policy of the Union, including its financing dimension; the development of a Defence of Democracy Shield, to face hybrid threats such as disinformation or manipulation of civic discourse; the adequacy of the Treaties and their decision-making processes—where unanimity is still required for a number of paramount decisions—for an enlarged EU with 30+ Member States; the development of industrial models able to reconcile the Union's competitiveness needs with the Green Deal, as required by international engagements, as well as with the internal market and competition requirements; the establishment of common goods which ensure a sufficient level of autonomy, such as capital or energy unions; the safeguarding of economic security while remaining loyal to the EU's approach to open trade and international trade obligations; and last—but definitely not least—the consolidation of the Union of values as part of the constitutional identity of the Union, which is a necessary condition of its constitutional autonomy.

2

EBA Guidelines and Recommendations as Part of the European Single Rulebook in Banking

Soft Law Acts with Hard Effects

Mariolina Eliantonio and Pavlína Hubková

I Introduction

One of the key actors in the Banking Union is the European Banking Authority ('EBA'), which plays a crucial role in ensuring the stability and effectiveness of the Union's financial system. It is specifically tasked with promoting effective and consistent regulation and supervision, facilitating international supervisory coordination, safeguarding customer and consumer protection, and preventing money laundering and terrorist financing.[1]

The EBA, one of three so-called European Supervisory Authorities,[2] is an independent EU agency to which all competences were delegated by secondary legislation with the aim to engage technical expertise that is not subject to short-term political agendas or political interventions.[3] It follows that it does not have any legislative power, and—as the doctrine of non-delegation requires—it cannot adopt legislative or quasi-legislative acts.[4] Nevertheless,

[1] See art 1(5) of Regulation (EU) No 1093/2010 of the European Parliament and of the Council of 24 November 2010 establishing a European Supervisory Authority (European Banking Authority), amending Decision No 716/2009/EC and repealing Commission Decision 2009/78/EC [2010] OJ L331, pp 12–47. Henceforth referred to as the 'EBA's founding Regulation' or the 'founding Regulation'.

[2] The other two being the European Securities and Markets Authority (ESMA) and the European Insurance and Occupational Pensions Authority (EIOPA).

[3] cf Deirdre Curtin, 'Delegation to EU Non-Majoritarian Agencies and Emerging Practices of Public Accountability' in Damien Geradin, Rodolphe Muñoz, and Nicolas Petit (eds), *Regulation Through Agencies in the EU: A New Paradigm of European Governance* (Edward Elgar 2005).

[4] Merijn Chamon and Nathan de Arriba-Sellier, 'FBF: On the Justiciability of Soft Law and Broadening the Discretion of EU Agencies: ECJ (Grand Chamber) 15 July 2021, Case C-911/19, Fédération Bancaire Française (FBF) v Autorité de Contrôle Prudentiel et de Résolution, ECLI:EU:C:2021:599' (2022) 18 European Constitutional Law Review 1; and 'The Law of Banking

Mariolina Eliantonio and Pavlína Hubková, *EBA Guidelines and Recommendations as Part of the European Single Rulebook in Banking* In: *EU Banking Union*. Edited by: Jonathan Bauerschmidt, Raffaele D'Ambrosio, Diane Fromage, Daniela Jaros, and Paul Weismann, Oxford University Press.
 DOI: 10.1093/9780198949756.003.0003

the EBA participates in EU rule-making and contributes to the creation of the Single Rulebook in banking.[5]

First, it drafts regulatory technical standards to ensure consistent harmonization as well as implementing technical standards for the implementation of the banking legislation, which are subsequently adopted by the Commission as delegated acts or implementing acts, respectively.[6] At that point, they gain binding legal force and become directly applicable in the Member States. Second, in the framework of supervisory coordination and convergence, the EBA issues various forms of soft law, ie legally non-binding acts having normative ambitions and producing legal and practical effects.[7]

This chapter focuses on one type of such soft law, namely guidelines and recommendations under Article 16 of the founding Regulation. In order to explore the phenomenon of soft law within the Banking Union, this chapter starts, in section II, by framing soft law (and guidelines and recommendations under Article 16 in particular) as a tool of regulatory governance in the Banking Union. In section III, the peculiar legal effects produced by guidelines through the so-called 'comply-or-explain' mechanism will be discussed. Section IV will present the available control mechanisms against these soft law measures, before section V offers some concluding remarks. Overall, this chapter will show that, while formally not binding, EBA soft law is capable of producing significant legal effects within the Banking Union. Notwithstanding the clear regulatory capacity of these measures, however, the control mechanisms available vis-à-vis EBA soft law are currently subject to several limitations.

II EBA and its soft law

1 Soft law within the regulation of banking and finance

Soft law encompasses a wide variety of legally non-binding acts. In the form of opinions, recommendations, suggestions, standards, best practices, guidance, or guidelines, soft law acts are considered a natural part of not only EU law

Union: *Meroni* Doctrine and the Delegation of Powers to EU agencies' (Jonathan Bauerschmidt) in this volume.

[5] cf Stefano Cappiello, 'The EBA and the Banking Union' (2015) 16 European Business Organization Law Review 421.

[6] Arts 10–14 and 15 of the founding Regulation, respectively.

[7] cf Francis Snyder, 'The Effectiveness of European Community Law: Institutions, Processes, Tools and Techniques' (1993) 56 The Modern Law Review 19.

but also of global regulation. Adopted by public or private actors or through the cooperation of both, they are meant to be alternatives or complements to standard legislation or other legally binding rules.[8]

The primary advantage of soft law is its ease of adoption and modification. Soft law is also flexible in its application and adaptable to regulatory needs, practical circumstances, and rapid developments.[9] The less stringent requirements for adopting soft law make the process more cost-effective, simpler, and faster compared with the adoption of hard law norms.[10] Moreover, it is believed that compliance with soft law rules in the technical or economic domains can be more effectively ensured through market pressure, peer pressure, naming-and-shaming, collaborative networking, or other alternative enforcement mechanisms.[11] Last but not least, the expertise of those who draft and approve soft law is a key factor in its legitimacy.[12] All of these are possible reasons for the widespread use of soft law techniques in the global regulation of finance and banking.[13] The soft law production of the EBA is hence a part of the global trend.[14]

The EBA's founding Regulation empowers the EBA to adopt a variety of soft law instruments: warnings (Article 9); no-action letters (Article 9c); guidelines and recommendations (Article 16); opinions and technical advice (Article 16a); questions and answers (Article 16b); and various recommendations, which are issued in the event of a breach of Union law (Article 17), in the identification of an emergency situation (Article 18), in order to correct issues

[8] The literature on soft law is large. For an overview of various aspects linked to soft law as a tool of regulation, see Mariolina Eliantonio, Emilia Korkea-aho, and Ulrika Mörth (eds), *Research Handbook on Soft Law* (Edward Elgar 2023). Specifically with a focus on *EU* soft law, see the chapter therein by Francis Snyder (Francis Snyder, 'Bamboo, or Governance through Soft Law: Hybridity, Legitimacy, and Sustainability') 10, with the literature contained therein.

[9] Emilia Korkea-aho, 'EU Soft Law in Domestic Legal Systems: Flexibility and Diversity Guaranteed?' (2015) Scandinavian Studies in Law 155.

[10] Kenneth W Abbott and Duncan Snidal, 'Hard and Soft Law in International Governance' (2000) 54 International Organization 421–56, 423.

[11] cf David M Trubek, Patrick Cottrell, and Mark Nance, '"Soft Law", "Hard Law", and European Integration: Toward a Theory of Hybridity' in Gráinne De Búrca and Joanne Scott (eds), *Law and New Governance in the EU and the US* (Hart 2006) 78–80.

[12] cf Jakob Schemmel, 'The ESA Guidelines: Soft Law and Subjectivity in the European Financial Market - Capturing the Administrative Influence' (2016) 23 Indiana Journal of Global Legal Studies 455–504, 461; Niamh Moloney, 'The European Supervisory Authorities and Discretion. Can the Functional and Constitutional Circles Be Squared?' in Joana Mendes (ed), *EU Executive Discretion and the Limits of Law* (OUP 2019) 85–86. See also Marloes van Rijsbergen, *Legitimacy and Effectiveness of ESMA's Soft Law* (Edward Elgar 2021).

[13] Chris Brummer, 'Why Soft Law Dominates International Finance—and Not Trade' (2010) 13 Journal of International Economic Law 623; Chris Brummer, *Soft Law and the Global Financial System: Rule Making in the 21st Century* (2nd edn, CUP 2015); Abraham Newman and Elliot Posner, *Voluntary Disruptions: International Soft Law, Finance, and Power* (OUP 2018).

[14] Schemmel (n 12).

identified in stress tests (Article 21), in cases of systemic risk (Article 22), or in peer reviews (Article 30); and opinions to national authorities (Article 29).

What these have in common is that they are, in themselves, legally non-binding, but otherwise they differ in their content, in the context in which they are adopted, in the type of addressees, or in the type of consequences they have. For instance, recommendations issued in cases of a breach of Union law (Article 17) serve as individual alerts, advising national authorities on how to comply with Union law; failure to adhere to such a recommendation may lead to infringement proceedings. Opinions (Article 16a), on the other hand, are addressed to the European Parliament (EP), the Council, or the Commission upon their own request. Meanwhile, answers published under Article 16b allow the EBA to respond to questions from any natural or legal person, including national and EU authorities, concerning the interpretation and application of legally binding provisions or other soft law acts.

2 Focus on recommendations and guidelines under Article 16

Guidelines and recommendations adopted in accordance with Article 16 present a considerable and—from the legal point of view—very interesting part of the EBA's soft law production. As of November 2024, the EBA has adopted five recommendations, almost 150 guidelines, and seven additional joint guidelines issued together with the ESMA and the EIOPA.[15] While intended merely as non-binding suggestions for complying with the mandatory rules in EU directives or regulations, the sheer volume, length (often comprising hundreds of provisions), and level of detail of these regulatory instruments indicate that they form a significant and influential component of the EBA's 'shadow rulemaking'.[16]

According to Article 16 of the founding Regulation, the purpose of guidelines and recommendations, which are addressed to competent authorities or to financial institutions under their supervision,[17] is to help with establishing consistent, efficient, and effective supervisory practices within the European

[15] The summary compliance table is available at https://www.eba.europa.eu/about-us/legal-and-policy-framework/compliance-eba-regulatory-products, accessed 30 November 2024. We are referring to the version last updated on 14 November 2024.

[16] Heikki Marjosola, 'Shadow Rulemaking: Governing Regulatory Innovation in the EU Financial Markets' (2022) 23 German Law Journal 186.

[17] According to art 16, as amended in 2020, the guidelines are addressed to all competent authorities or all financial institutions, while recommendations are addressed to one or more competent authorities or to one or more financial institutions.

Financial Stability Facility (ESFS), and to ensure the common, uniform, and consistent application of Union law. Since recommendations are used rather rarely, the remainder of this chapter will focus only on guidelines.

The wording of Article 16 indicates that EBA guidelines are not meant to offer alternative rules to legislation, but that their goal is to offer guidance on how to correctly interpret and apply already existing rules contained in EU regulations or directives, and therefore they fulfil what soft law literature has referred to as a function of post-legislative guidance.[18] However, in practice, they include more than a mere suggestion how to interpret those rules. The detail and depth of their provisions demonstrate their ability to propose specific new rules which are only derived from or based on binding EU acts.

An example can be seen in the EBA guidelines on internal governance under Directive 2013/36/EU.[19] Several provisions of that Directive serve as the legal basis for the given guidelines.[20] These provisions establish simple yet often broad and open-ended rules, such as the duty of financial institutions 'to have robust governance arrangements, including a clear organisational structure with well-defined, transparent and consistent lines of responsibility' (Article 74), and the duty of competent authorities to require financial institutions 'to have in place adequate risk management processes and internal control mechanisms' (Article 123). These vague rules are expanded into more than 200 detailed provisions within the guidelines, which direct financial institutions on exactly what actions to take and which practices to adopt in order to comply with the requirements of the Directive. For example:

> 69. The structure of the institution should not impede the ability of the management body to oversee and manage effectively the risks the institution or the group faces or the ability of the competent authority to effectively supervise the institution.
> 76. Institutions should avoid setting up complex and potentially non-transparent structures.
> 91. The management body should approve and regularly review and update the outsourcing policy of an institution, ensuring that appropriate changes are implemented in a timely manner.

[18] cf Linda Senden, 'Soft Post-Legislative Rulemaking: A Time for More Stringent Control' (2013) 19 European Law Journal 57. The other two main functional categories of soft law are preparatory or testing soft law (pre-law) and alternative, free-standing, or steering instruments (para-law). For a detailed explanation of these categories, see mainly Linda Senden, *Soft Law in European Community Law* (Hart 2004) 123–231.

[19] EBA/GL/2021/05, 2 July 2021.

[20] Namely art 47, art 74(1), art 76, art 88, art 109, and art 123(2).

It is evident that, rather than being purely interpretative aids, the EBA guidelines serve as de facto implementing acts because they suggest specific rules to be followed or steps to be taken by the financial institutions. Albeit written in non-mandatory language (using 'should' instead of 'shall'),[21] the guidelines look like standard binding legal acts of general application. However, the overall appearance of the guidelines and the sole choice of language cannot determine what (legal) effects these regulatory instruments produce or are capable of producing.[22] As the following section will show, the decisive factors lie outside the acts themselves.

3 The effects of EBA guidelines

According to the CJEU, by being authorized to adopt guidelines, the EBA was conferred 'a power to exhort and to persuade, distinct from the power to adopt acts having binding force'.[23] Under this logic, guidelines—unlike legally binding acts—produce effects solely through their persuasiveness:[24] they are followed or complied with when they persuade their addressees that their content is good and worth respecting. However, the EBA guidelines appear to have more than a content-dependent persuasive power, because they are accompanied by additional duties and alternative enforcement mechanisms.

First of all, the EBA's founding Regulation states a clear duty for the addressees to 'make every effort to comply' with the respective guidelines.[25] Conceptually, this duty should be distinguished from the duty to comply which accompanies legally binding acts, but it indicates that the guidelines are not meant to be complied with only if the addressee finds them suitable or to be

[21] The use of the modal verb 'should' and other non-binding linguistic constructions (such as 'are invited to' or 'are recommended to') can be regarded as verbal indicators of the non-binding nature of an act. cf Petra Lea Láncos and Eljalill Tauschinsky, 'Verbal Markers of "Softness" in EU Law? A Computer-Based Analysis to Delimit Soft Law and Hard Law Focusing on Directive-like Recommendations' in Petra Lea Láncos, Napoleon Xanthoulis, and Luis Arroyo Jiménez (eds), *The Legal Effects of EU Soft Law: Theory, Language and Sectoral Insights* (Edward Elgar 2023) 111.

[22] For an overview of the possible legal effects produced by EU soft law in general, see Luis Arroyo Jiménez, 'Beyond Bindingness: A Typology of EU Soft Law Legal Effects' in Láncos, Xanthoulis, and Arroyo Jiménez (eds) (n 21) 9.

[23] Case C–911/19 *Fédération bancaire française*, ECLI:EU:C:2021:599, para 48.

[24] cf Corina Andone and Florin Coman-Kund, 'Persuasive Rather than "Binding" EU Soft Law? An Argumentative Perspective on the European Commission's Soft Law Instruments in Times of Crisis' (2022) 10 The Theory and Practice of Legislation 22. Concerning the concept of persuasive authority, see, eg Ingo Venzke, 'Between Power and Persuasion: On International Institutions' Authority in Making Law' (2013) 4 Transnational Legal Theory 354.

[25] Art 16(3) of the founding Regulation.

easily ignored. In other words, there is no clear duty to follow the content of the guidelines, but the regulation still imposes a certain legal obligation of effort.

National Competent Authorities (NCAs)[26] are still left with a discretion to make a final decision whether to comply with the guidelines or not. However, if they find that, despite their best efforts, they cannot comply, they must inform the EBA of their decision within two months following the adoption of the guidelines and provide an explanation for their choice.[27]

This mechanism is commonly known as 'comply or explain'. Having its roots in the corporate governance of private companies,[28] the comply-or-explain mechanism provides the addressees with certain rules and leaves a possibility to either choose compliance or explain why they do not intend to comply. Under the founding Regulation, NCAs must notify the EBA of whether they comply or intend to comply with the given guidelines, or they must provide justification for non-compliance.[29] Arroyo Jiménez argues that EU soft law acts, when accompanied by such a mechanism, have indirect invalidating effects, as non-compliance without justification would constitute a breach of the hard law provision—in this case, Article 16 of the founding Regulation.[30]

The explanatory aspect of the comply-or-explain mechanism is further reinforced by the publication of the reasons for non-compliance.[31] The fact that the notified reasons are published in the compliance tables which are available on the EBA's website can be taken as a lighter version of the 'naming-and-shaming' mechanism.[32] The NCAs are not explicitly 'shamed' for their decision not to comply, but given that the reasons for non-compliance will be disclosed to the public, authorities are aware that they must have strong and valid justification.[33]

[26] According to art 4(2)(i) of the founding Regulation, the European Central Bank is also included among competent authorities 'with regard to matters relating to the tasks conferred on it by Regulation (EU) No 1024/2013'. However, this contribution focuses only on NCAs.

[27] ibid.

[28] See, eg John Roberts and others, 'The UK Corporate Governance Code Principle of "Comply or Explain": Understanding Code Compliance as "Subjection"' (2020) 56 Abacus 602; Bjorn Fasterling and Jean-Christophe Duhamel, 'Le Comply or explain: la transparence conformiste en droit des sociétés' (2009) t XXIII, 2 Revue internationale de droit économique 129; Andrew Keay, 'Comply or Explain in Corporate Governance Codes: In Need of Greater Regulatory Oversight?' (2014) 34 Legal Studies 279. See also Commission Recommendation of 9 April 2014 on the quality of corporate governance reporting ('comply or explain') (2014/208/EU) [2014] OJ L109, pp 43–47.

[29] Art 16(3) of the founding Regulation.

[30] Arroyo Jiménez (n 22) 21–22.

[31] Art 16(3) of the founding Regulation.

[32] Judith van Erp, 'Naming and Shaming in Regulatory Enforcement' in Christine Parker and Vibeke Nielsen (eds), *Explaining Compliance* (Edward Elgar 2011) 322.

[33] For details, see Pavlína Hubková, 'Limiting or Empowering? Soft Rulemaking of the European Supervisory Authorities and Its Impact on National Administrative Authorities' (2023) Revue de la Faculté de droit de l'Université de Liège 247.

In practice, the notified reasons are usually of a practical nature: the NCA does not have competence under national law to enforce the content of the guidelines, there is no proper national legal basis for a specific rule, the authority has a different policy approach, or the content of the guidelines lacks usefulness.[34] Moreover, it is not unusual that an NCA notifies non-compliance only with regard to an individual provision of the given guidelines.[35] It follows that the national authorities consider the content of the guidelines with due care and choose non-compliance only as the ultimate option.

In addition to the powerful comply-or-explain mechanism, there is a clear tendency towards compliance also because officials from the NCAs participate in the drafting process of the guidelines within the respective EBA working groups.[36] Furthermore, NCA representatives are members of the Board of Supervisors, which approves the final text by a qualified majority.[37] During the discussions, NCAs already begin to form an opinion on whether they intend to comply with the guidelines, and they may influence the text to align with their policy preferences. This further helps to rebut the idea that the EBA guidelines are impactful only due to their persuasiveness, because their direct addressees—as co-creators—are mostly persuaded already at the time when the guidelines are adopted.

As a result, there are only a few notifications of non-compliance.[38] In the vast majority of cases, the NCAs notify compliance or at least an intention to comply. On average, there are only 1.34 notifications of non-compliance per soft law document.[39] Each Member State, out of almost 150 soft law documents, notifies an average of only three cases of non-compliance. There are also instances where multiple competent authorities exist within a Member State but only one of them submits a notification of non-compliance, usually

[34] Vojtěch Belling, 'Obecné pokyny evropských orgánů finančního dohledu a úskalí jejich vnitrostátní aplikace' in Michal Bobek, Petr Bříza, and Pavlína Hubková (eds), *Dvacet let vnitrostátní aplikace práva EU* (CH Beck 2024) 372–76. The compliance tables with reasons for non-compliance are available on eba.europa.eu, usually next to the text of the respective guidelines.

[35] cf Pavlína Hubková, 'Soft law Evropských orgánů dohledu před českými orgány: vnitrostátní možnosti kontroly a soudního přezkumu' [2024] Právní rozhledy 537, 538–39.

[36] For details, see Pavlína Hubková, 'Soft Rulemaking through Multi-Level Administrative Practice: Replicating the Aesthetics of Law' (2023) 14 Transnational Legal Theory 499, 513.

[37] Art 4(8) of the EBA Rules of Procedure (Decision of the European Banking Authority of 22 January 2020 concerning the Rules of Procedure of the Board of Supervisors, EBA/DC/2020/307).

[38] The following calculations are based on the data from the summary of compliance notifications table, last updated on 14 November 2024, available at https://www.eba.europa.eu/about-us/legal-and-policy-framework/compliance-eba-regulatory-products, accessed 30 November 2024.

[39] This calculation includes data with regard to recommendations, guidelines, and joint guidelines (147 documents in total) adopted from 2011–23. The data regarding soft law acts adopted in 2024 are not complete in the summary table yet.

because of the lack of competences according to national law. Therefore, the average rate of non-compliance per Member State as a whole is even lower.

As a consequence, financial institutions under the supervision of the NCAs have a very limited space to assess whether they want to 'be persuaded' by the EBA guidelines and to comply with them.[40] Formally, they are only obliged to 'make every effort to comply'. The comply-or-explain mechanism applies to them only if the concrete guidelines say so, and this situation is very rare, or rather non-existent.[41] However, if the NCA decides to comply, it makes a promise that it intends to implement the guidelines into its enforcement activities and eventually to enforce them on financial institutions. In this way, guidelines become indirectly binding on financial institutions.

EU law does not prescribe how exactly Member States should integrate the content of the EBA guidelines into their national systems. Beyond the obligation to make every effort to comply and the duty to notify in cases of non-compliance, no specific requirements are imposed on them. Member States are free to convert the content of the guidelines into binding national rules through legislation. Depending on national rules, the NCAs can transpose the guidelines into binding administrative acts of general application (such as decrees) or into national soft law. The NCAs may also adopt their own acts that specifically refer to the EBA guidelines and outline how they should be complied with by financial institutions. Alternatively, they can issue a statement expressing their intent to comply with the guidelines and expecting financial institutions to do the same.

Unless the EBA guidelines are transposed into national legislation, the actual impact of the guidelines will ultimately depend on the policy choices and enforcement strategies of the respective NCA. Depending on national law, it can incorporate the content of guidelines into its own legally binding acts, thereby transforming the originally soft rules into binding ones *de iure*. But even if there is no such formal hardening and the guidelines remain formally non-binding and hence non-enforceable, NCAs can find indirect ways to enforce their content on financial institutions under their supervision.

[40] This applies to guidelines addressed both to NCAs and financial institutions under their supervision. There are also guidelines which address only NCAs and affect their internal activities or co-operation with other authorities (eg Joint Guidelines on the oversight cooperation and information exchange between the ESAs and the competent authorities under Regulation (EU) 2022/2554 of 17 July 2024) and, therefore, the following analysis is not applicable to such acts.

[41] This rule has been applicable only since 2020, when the amendment of the regulation came into effect (Regulation (EU) 2019/2175 of the European Parliament and of the Council of 18 December 2019 [2019] OJ L334, pp 1–145).

An example can be found in the French practice: as explained in the opinion of the rapporteur public of the Conseil d'État, a financial institution cannot be directly sanctioned for not complying with the EBA guidelines. However, the competent French authority views these guidelines as 'best practices' that must be followed as a legal obligation. If a financial institution fails to comply, it is considered bad practice, which can result in an individual warning and potentially lead to disciplinary proceedings under the Code monétaire et financier (Monetary and Financial Code).[42] Comparable practices are observed in other Member States where the competent authorities do not sanction non-compliance on its own, but failure to adhere to the guidelines is regarded as indicative of a breach of binding legal provisions.[43]

It can, therefore, be argued that, although the EBA guidelines are adopted as a legally non-binding EU act, the enforcement strategies of the NCAs make it likely that the guidelines will create binding legal effects for the financial institutions as the final targets. Depending on how national authorities choose to enforce them, what starts as a suggestion, recommendation, or invitation is often turned into a (de facto) legal obligation through the regulatory practice of these authorities.

The quasi-binding effect of the EBA guidelines is not accidental. The ultimate (de facto) bindingness of the guidelines appears to be a deliberate aspect of the system, which aims to promote effective supervision in the sector of banking, to ensure proper and consistent implementation of EU law across Member States, and to prevent consumer harm, bankruptcy of banks and, eventually, financial crises.[44] The system foresees that the guidelines are followed in as many cases as possible, not just when the financial institutions decide that the content of guidelines is good enough or persuasive enough to direct or change their behaviour.

Although the EBA guidelines may be perceived as an additional regulatory burden for financial institutions, their existence and functioning can also be assessed positively. The guidelines clearly outline concrete steps to be taken

[42] Conseil d'État, Opinion of Ms Emilie Bokdam, rapporteur public, of 4 December 2019 in case No 415550—Fédération bancaire française, 6, available at https://www.conseil-etat.fr, accessed 30 November 2024.

[43] See, eg Jacopo Alberti, 'The Unbearable Lightness of European Security and Markets Authority's Soft Law: An Italian Perspective' in Martina Buscemi and others (eds), *Legal Sources in Business and Human Rights* (Brill/Nijhoff 2020) 309; Niels Rogge, 'The Role of EBA Guidelines in Private Law Disputes: Assessing Civil Fault in the Legal Framework of Belgium' (2023) Financial Law Institute Working Paper Series, Universiteit Gent 21; Pavlína Hubková, 'The National Life of ESA Guidelines: Effective Enforcement of EU Soft Law in the Czech Republic and the Issue of Control and Remedies', forthcoming in Journal of Banking Regulation.

[44] See art 1(5) of the founding Regulation.

by financial institutions in order to comply with the requirements of 'root' binding legal provisions and are, therefore, capable of enhancing legal certainty and preserving legitimate expectations. The EBA guidelines also offer practical benefits to NCAs by clarifying the ambiguities found in binding legal provisions. When enforcing these provisions, the national authority can rely on the EBA guidelines to define the standards expected of financial institutions, saving time and effort in interpreting and justifying the specific requirements of the law.[45]

However, despite the potential benefits for both NCAs and financial institutions, it remains the case that the EBA guidelines hold a significant regulatory power. While the direction of banking regulation comes from legislation, the EBA, in cooperation with the NCAs, has an important role in determining how exactly the legal rules are implemented in practice. Like any public actor, the EBA cannot escape accountability. Moreover, its exercise of public authority must be subject to effective control, in accordance with the rule of law. It is to this discussion that the chapter now turns.

III Control and remedies

In the EU legal order, European agencies are subject to multiple controls, each with a different purpose and operating through different mechanisms.[46]

The EBA's founding Regulation provides, first of all, a mechanism of political accountability before the EP and Council (Article 3), which requires the preparation of an Annual Report, adopted in accordance with Article 43(5), to be transmitted to the EP, to the Council, to the Commission, to the Court of Auditors, and to the European Economic and Social Committee.[47] As Article 16(4) specifically requires, the Annual Report must include information upon the issuance of the guidelines and recommendations. However, it is doubtful whether this mechanism, which merely provides for information on the

[45] For details, see Hubková, 'Limiting or Empowering? (n 33). With regard to the usefulness of EU soft law in general, see eg Emilia Korkea-aho, 'Legal Interpretation of EU Framework Directives: A Soft Law Approach' (2015) 40 European Law Review 70.

[46] For an overview, see Miroslava Scholten and Alex Brenninkmeijer (eds), *Controlling EU Agencies: The Rule of Law in a Multi-Jurisdictional Legal Order* (Edward Elgar 2020).

[47] Originally, art 3 was very brief, stating only that 'The Authorities referred to in Article 2(2)(a) to (d) shall be accountable to the European Parliament and the Council.' The mechanism of accountability was significantly broadened by Regulation (EU) 2019/2175 of the European Parliament and of the Council of 18 December 2019 [2019] OJ L334, pp 1–145.

adopted instruments, entails a meaningful control of the Authority's soft law measures by the EU political institutions.[48]

Furthermore, the legislative framework provides for forms of administrative review. These are, however, either inapplicable or toothless when it comes to EBA soft law. Firstly, the founding Regulation foresees, in Article 60, a Board of Appeal, with the aim of providing an internal review mechanism for the EBA's actions.[49] However, this mechanism can only be brought against 'decisions' of the Authority, thereby excluding guidelines and recommendations under Article 16. While, as reported by Chamon and Fromage, the EP had suggested to allow review, by the Board of Appeal, of guidelines and recommendations, this proposal was not followed up.[50]

A second mechanism of administrative review specifically geared towards guidelines is provided by Article 60a of the founding Regulation, which foresees the possibility for natural and legal persons to send reasoned advice to the Commission if they are of the opinion that a guideline has been adopted in breach of the principle of proportionality. However, it is doubtful whether this mechanism is anything more than the dog that barks but does not (because it actually cannot) bite.[51] Indeed, the provision limits the possibility to send reasoned advice, granting it only to those natural or legal persons who are directly and individually concerned by a guideline. While there is no case law which could shed light on the interpretation to be given to the notion of 'individual and direct concern' contained in Article 60a, it would be hard to overlook the interpretation of this very same notion by the CJEU under Article 263(4) TFEU.[52] Looking specifically at the notion of 'direct concern', and its interpretation by the CJEU as the capacity to directly affect the legal position of

[48] cf Madalina Busuioc, *European Agencies: Law and Practices of Accountability* (OUP 2013) 48.

[49] In general on boards of appeal, see Merijn Chamon, Annalisa Volpato, and Mariolina Eliantonio (eds), *Boards of Appeal of EU Agencies: Towards Judicialization of Administrative Review?* (OUP 2022). Specifically on the ESA's boards of appeal, see Merijn Chamon, 'The Joint Board of Appeal as an Accountability Mechanism for the ESAs' in Carl Fredrik Bergström and Magnus Strand (eds), *Legal Accountability in EU Markets for Financial Instruments: the Dual Role of Investment Firms* (OUP 2021) 55.

[50] Merijn Chamon and Diane Fromage, 'Between Added Value and Untapped Potential: The Boards of Appeal in the Field of EU Financial Regulation' in Chamon, Volpato, and Eliantonio (eds) (n 49) 20–21.

[51] cf Opinion of AG Bobek in Case C-911/19 *Fédération bancaire française*, ECLI:EU:C:2021:294, points 92–93.

[52] Apart from the textual equivalence, an argument supporting the likelihood that these notions will be interpreted in line with those contained in the TFEU in respect of the action for annulment comes from the experience of the Joint Board of Appeal of the European Supervisory Authorities, which has argued that the notion of 'direct and individual interest' (ie the standing test to bring an action before the Joint Board of Appeal) reflects the similar wording of art 263 TFEU. See Decision 2014 C1 02, *SV Capital OÜ v EBA*, para 27.

the applicant,[53] one might actually wonder whether this threshold could ever be fulfilled by a soft law measure, given that the EU soft law measures will need invariably to be concretized through measures (soft or otherwise) adopted at the national level. Furthermore, as has been correctly pointed out, 'the provision offers no clue as to what would happen next' in terms of possible responses of the Commission.[54]

Finally, (soft) acts of EU agencies could, in principle, be subject to the judicial control of the CJEU. That the soft law measures adopted by EU agencies in general need to be judicially controlled has been stated in no unclear terms by the Court, not least to comply with the requirements of the *Short Selling* ruling.[55] In the *Fédération bancaire française* ruling,[56] which concerned precisely EBA guidelines, the CJEU considered that, 'since it is apparent from [the EBA's founding Regulation] that the EU legislature has precisely delineated the EBA's power to issue guidelines, on the basis of objective criteria, the exercise of that power must be amenable to stringent judicial review in the light of those objective criteria'.[57]

The judicial control of EBA guidelines is theoretically possible through two avenues: directly, through an action for annulment under Article 263 TFEU, and indirectly, through a preliminary question of validity sent by a national court under Article 267 TFEU.

In respect of this last possibility, the CJEU has stated that a preliminary question is open on the validity of all acts of EU institutions 'without exception'.[58] The direct avenues of judicial control are, however, very limited for soft law acts, since the CJEU has interpreted the requirement to produce 'legal effects' (which is a precondition for the reviewability of an act under Article 263 TFEU)[59] as the capacity of an act to produce 'binding legal effects'.[60] While no EBA soft law act has ever been brought to the attention of the CJEU through

[53] See, eg Case 21–24/72 *International Fruit Company*, ECLI:EU:C:1972:115, paras 23–29; and Case C-404/96 P *Glencore*, ECLI:EU:C:1998:196, para 41.

[54] Marloes van Rijsbergen, Heikki Marjosola, and Miroslava Scholten, 'How to Exhort and to Persuade with(out Legal) Force: Challenging Soft Law after FBF' (2022) 59 Common Market Law Review 1523, 1539–40.

[55] Case C-27/12 *United Kingdom v Parliament and Council (Short Selling)*, ECLI:EU:C:2014:18.

[56] *Fédération bancaire française* (n 23).

[57] ibid, para 67.

[58] Case C-322/88 *Grimaldi*, ECLI:EU:C:1989:646, para 8.

[59] The requirement was first enunciated by the CJEU in the *ERTA* ruling (Case C-22/70 *Commission v Council*, ECLI:EU:C:1971:32). See further, on the genesis of the 'legal effects' formula, Pavlína Hubková, 'Getting Rid of Historic Relics – A Proposal to Modify Article 263 TFEU' in Darren Harvey and others (eds), *Reforming the EU Treaties Proposals for Amendments to the TEU, TFEU and the Charter by Young Scholars of European Law* (Nomos/Hart 2023) 101.

[60] See, eg Joined Cases C-463/10 P and C-475/10 P *Deutsche Post and Germany v Commission*, ECLI:EU:C:2011:656, para 36.

an action for annulment, the literature is virtually unanimous in considering that, on the basis of the current case law, such an action would be declared inadmissible.[61]

The Court's interpretation of 'legal effects', which has been criticized in literature as excessively formalistic,[62] and even in contradiction with the rule of law tenets under the EU Treaties,[63] has recently been reiterated in the *BT v Balgarska Narodna Banka*[64] and above-mentioned *Fédération bancaire française* rulings, both concerning the EBA soft law acts. These rulings gave the CJEU the opportunity to sketch its understanding of the supposedly 'complete system of remedies'[65] available against acts of EU soft law.

The cases were both sent through preliminary questions of validity by national courts, and they in fact constitute the first examples of preliminary questions being sent in respect of soft law measures (a recommendation and a set of guidelines by the EBA, respectively), with the *BT v Balgarska Narodna Banka* case leading to the annulment of a provision of the contested recommendation.[66]

As the case law now stands, therefore, judicial control of EBA recommendations and guidelines is ensured through the preliminary question of validity.[67]

[61] See, in general, on the test and its consequences for soft law, Mariolina Eliantonio and Francesco Liguori, 'EU Soft Law Measures before the CJEU – An Empirical Investigation into Bindingness and Legal Effects in Annulment Actions' (2026) European Law Review (forthcoming); Mariolina Eliantonio, 'Judicial Review of Soft Law before the European and the National Courts. A Wind of Change Blowing from the Member States?' in Mariolina Eliantonio, Emilia Korkea-aho, and Oana Ştefan (eds), *EU Soft Law in the Member States: Theoretical Findings and Empirical Evidence* (Hart 2021) 283; Napoleon Xanthoulis, 'Legal Effects and Reviewability of EU Acts: Between Institutional Intentions and Perceptions of Concerned Parties' in Mariolina Eliantonio, Emilia Korkea-aho, and Oana Ştefan (eds), *EU Soft Law in the Member States: Theoretical Findings and Empirical Evidence* (Hart 2021) 303; Joanne Scott, 'In Legal Limbo: Post-Legislative Guidance as a Challenge for European Administrative Law' (2011) 48 Common Market Law Review 329. With respect to EU agencies' soft law, see eg Oana Stefan and Marina Petri, 'Too Weak to Be Controlled: Judicial Review of ACER Soft Law' (2018) 37 Yearbook of European Law 525.

[62] Giulia Gentile, 'Ensuring Effective Judicial Review of EU Soft Law via the Action for Annulment before the EU Courts: A Plea for a Liberal-Constitutional Approach' (2020) 16 European Constitutional Law Review 466.

[63] Pavlína Hubková, 'Judicial Review of EU Soft Law Acts as a Matter of the Rule of Law' (2023) 29(2) European Public Law 181.

[64] Case C–501/18 *BT v Balgarska Narodna Banka*, ECLI:EU:C:2021:249. Further on this case and its implications, see Pavlína Hubková, 'Judicial Review of EU Soft Law: A Revolutionary Step Which Has Not Fully Happened (Case Note on BT v Balgarska Narodna Banka, C-501/18)' (2021) Revista General de Derecho Europeo 174; Giulia Gentile, 'To Be or Not to Be (Legally Binding)? Judicial Review of EU Soft Law after BT and Fédération Bancaire Française' (2021) Revista de Derecho Comunitario Europeo 981.

[65] The formula comes from the *Les Verts* ruling and has been repeated invariably ever since in respect of the relationship between the action for annulment and the preliminary question of validity. Case 294/83 *Les Verts v Parliament* ECLI:EU:C:1986:166.

[66] An annulment which is not uncontested. See further Hubková, 'Judicial Review of EU Soft Law' (n 64) 191–95.

[67] It could be argued that even the preliminary reference of interpretation could be considered an indirect means of judicial control of soft law: if the Court provides for interpretation of soft law, it

The question which arises in this context is whether the 'indirect' route to judicial review provides a mechanism which is sufficient to comply with the rule of law and effective judicial protection tenets of the EU legal order.[68]

Indeed, regardless of the legitimate question (raised by AG Bobek in the *Fédération bancaire française* case) of how soft law can be 'dead' (ie incapable of producing legal effects for the purposes of the action for annulment) and 'alive' (ie endowed with regulatory power which renders its control necessary) at the same time,[69] there are strong arguments to argue that the preliminary question of validity does not offer a comparable avenue of judicial protection to a direct action.[70]

First of all, and regardless of an action being directed against an EU soft law measure, preliminary questions of validity take longer than direct actions, they may be brought only after infringements to individuals' legal spheres have occurred, and they strongly depend on the willingness of national courts to refer such questions to the CJEU.[71] In respect of the latter point, it is specifically not entirely clear whether the duty for national courts to send preliminary questions to the CJEU when they have doubts on the validity of an EU law measure, as established by the *Foto-Frost* ruling,[72] applies also to soft law.[73] Furthermore, the preliminary question of validity entails a number of procedural disadvantages for private applicants, in particular linked to its nature as a 'dialogue' between courts.[74]

Second, looking specifically at the soft law nature of an act, the current case law has the paradoxical consequence of placing Member States and EU institutions at a 'procedural disadvantage' compared with private parties. While the latter, being non-privileged applicants in direct actions, have access to national courts to challenge EU soft law indirectly, privileged applicants do not have

implicitly confirms its validity. See, eg Case C–526/14 *Kotnik*, EU:C:2016:570, where the Court was asked to review the validity of a soft law act but provided, rather, an interpretation thereof. cf Hubková, 'Getting Rid of Historic Relics' (n 59) 109.

68 Arts 2 and 19 TEU; art 47 of the Charter of Fundamental Rights.

69 Opinion of AG Bobek in *Fédération bancaire française* (n 51), point 132.

70 See, for a different opinion, Chamon and de Arriba-Sellier (n 4) 306.

71 These well-known points have been enunciated already by AG Jacobs in Case C-50/00 P *Unión de Pequeños Agricultores*, ECLI:EU:C:2002:197.

72 Case 314/85 *Foto-Frost*, ECLI:EU:C:1987:452.

73 In favour of this duty, see Francesco Liguori, 'Taking Soft Law Into Account . . . of Course! But What Does That Concretely Mean?' (2023) 16 Review of European Administrative Law 37, 58–60; Jacopo Alberti, 'Un Atto Non Vincolante Può Essere Dichiarato Invalido? Le Guidelines Di EBA Dinanzi Alla Corte Di Giustizia' (2022) Il diritto dell'Unione Europea 425, 452–54. For a contrary opinion, see Giulia Gentile, 'To Be or Not to Be (Legally Binding)? Judicial Review of EU Soft Law after BT and Fédération Bancaire Française' (2021) 70 Revista de Derecho Comunitario Europeo 981, 1000–01; and Opinion of AG Bobek in *Fédération bancaire française* (n 51), points 121–33.

74 Alberti, 'Un Atto Non Vincolante Può Essere Dichiarato Invalido?' (n 73) 462.

this option, a situation which is clearly misaligned with the set-up foreseen by the Treaties.[75]

Third, focusing particularly on EBA soft law, much of the chance of success of indirectly getting the CJEU to review its validity depends on the national procedural ecosystem and whether actions against national (soft) law measures implementing the EBA guidelines are deemed admissible, a matter which is uncertain.[76] A related matter is whether there is a national act to be challenged in the first place, which may not always be the case for all of EBA soft law (such as in the case of opinions and Q&As).[77] Equally uncertain is whether the competent instances ruling on claims where such guidelines are at stake would qualify as courts or tribunals for the purposes of sending preliminary questions under Article 267 TFEU.[78]

Be that as it may, it is by now clear that, with all its limitations, the CJEU will hear claims concerning the validity of EBA soft law in preliminary questions. The final point to be discussed concerns the 'intensity' of this review. In the *Fédération bancaire française* case, the CJEU insisted that that review should be 'stringent',[79] which the Court justified on the basis of the potential effects of the guidelines as well as the duty of national courts to take soft law measures into account, as established by the *Grimaldi* ruling.[80] This consideration might be regarded as serving to strengthen the effectiveness of the judicial control over soft law measures. However, the *Fédération bancaire française* case reveals a 'daunting gap between the stated intent and the actual outcome'.[81] If one considers that soft law is increasingly used by EU agencies, arguably (also) as a way to circumvent the limitations imposed by the *Meroni* and *Short Selling* rulings,[82] 'mellowing' the *Short Selling* threshold, which is in itself already a

[75] Opinion of AG Bobek in *Fédération bancaire française* (n 51), point 137.

[76] See Eliantonio (n 61) and case law cited concerning the French legal system, which provided the suitable conditions for the case to eventually be brought to the attention of the CJEU. For an examination of the follow-up of the ruling at the national level, see Daniela Quelhas, 'The EBA Guidelines on Retail Banking Products' Saga. Lessons from an Attempted Judicial Review of European Supervisory Authority-Guidelines' (*EU Law Live, Weekend Edition*, 19 September 2022) www.eulawlive.com.

[77] Chamon and de Arriba-Sellier (n 4) 308; Merijn Chamon, 'Soft Law and Challenges to Access to Justice' in Melanie Fink (ed), *Redressing Fundamental Rights Violations by the EU: The Promise of the 'Complete System of Remedies'* (CUP 2024) 383–84.

[78] As pointed out by Alberti, this would, for example, not be the case for the Italian Arbitro per le Controversie Finanziarie and Arbitro Bancario e Finanziario, the main dispute resolution bodies where EBA guidelines would come to the fore in the Italian legal system. Alberti, 'Un Atto Non Vincolante Può Essere Dichiarato Invalido?' (n 73) 459–60.

[79] *Fédération bancaire française* (n 23), para 67.

[80] ibid, paras 70–72.

[81] Chamon and de Arriba-Sellier (n 4) 308–09.

[82] Merijn Chamon, 'Le recours à la soft law comme moyen d'éluder les obstacles constitutionnels au développement des agences de l'UE' (2014) Revue de l'Union européenne 152–60.

'mellowing' of its predecessor *Meroni*, is a concerning development in terms of respect of institutional balance.

IV Conclusion

This chapter sought to examine the role of soft law, particularly guidelines and recommendations issued by the European Banking Authority (EBA), in the regulation of the Banking Union. While these instruments are formally non-binding, they create significant regulatory effects at the national level, often resembling hard law in practice. These effects are generated, first of all, by the 'comply-or-explain' principle, which requires NCAs to either comply with the guidelines or justify non-compliance, thereby promoting adherence through peer pressure and public accountability. Furthermore, NCAs participate in the drafting process of the guidelines, fostering a high compliance rate and limiting room for non-compliance. Additionally, the EBA guidelines often become de facto mandatory because NCAs may enforce them indirectly on financial institutions, integrating them into national regulatory frameworks.

Despite these strong regulatory effects, EBA soft law is subject to limited political, administrative, and judicial oversight. Judicial control in particular is mostly indirect, with national courts referring validity questions to the CJEU, with a number of hurdles to full accountability ensuing. As a consequence, the limitations of administrative review possibility through, for example, the control exercised by the Board of Appeal can be regarded as a missed opportunity to ensure the control of these increasingly important tools in the Banking Union.

3

Fundamental Rights Protection in the Banking Union

Paul Weismann

I Introduction

With the gradual creation of the Banking Union, banking law has emerged as a new field involving, on a large scale, the implementation of EU law by EU actors directly vis-à-vis natural and legal persons. This means that EU fundamental rights may be invoked, in particular, against the European Central Bank (ECB) and the Single Resolution Board (SRB) in supervisory and resolution proceedings. While the implementation of EU law by the Member States is still the rule,[1] over the years the EU has gained experience in the direct implementation of EU law vis-à-vis individual actors, notably with regard to the role of the Commission in competition law, and of (selected) European agencies.[2] This experience is also relevant in the context of banking law. This field displays some peculiarities, though, which also raise unprecedented fundamental rights questions. In order to exemplify this variety, three fundamental rights issues located in the Banking Union will be presented in this chapter.

To begin with, however, we should take a look at the role the prominent goal of banking law—to achieve financial stability—plays in the context of fundamental rights.[3] According to Article 52(1) Charter of Fundamental

[1] See art 291(1) TFEU.

[2] For this development see, eg Edoardo Chiti and Joana Mendes, 'The Evolution of EU Administrative Law' in Paul Craig and Gráinne de Búrca (eds), *The Evolution of EU Law* (3rd edn, OUP 2021) 339; Merijn Chamon, *EU Agencies: Legal and Political Limits to the Transformation of the EU Administration* (OUP 2016).

[3] See Case C-83/20 *BPC Lux 2*, ECLI:EU:C:2022:346, para 54, with further references; see also Joined Cases C-498/22 to C-550/22 *Novo Banco and Others*, ECLI:EU:C:2024:686, para 120; Case T-360/21 *Portigon AG*, ECLI:EU:T:2024:332, para 63. Financial stability is also pursued outside the Banking Union, eg by the ESFS, and by the ESCB as part of its monetary policy, or even by the Commission in its role as a competition authority: see https://ec.europa.eu/commission/presscorner/detail/es/ip_23_2889, accessed 11 September 2025. For different functions of this concept, see Jonathan Bauerschmidt, 'Financial Stability as the Objective of the Banking Union' (2020) 17 European Company and Financial Law Review 155, 179–82.

Paul Weismann, *Fundamental Rights Protection in the Banking Union* In: *EU Banking Union*.
Edited by: Jonathan Bauerschmidt, Raffaele D'Ambrosio, Diane Fromage, Daniela Jaros, and Paul Weismann, Oxford University Press. DOI: 10.1093/9780198949756.003.0004

Rights of the European Union (CFR), any 'objective[] of general interest recognised by the Union', or the 'need to protect the rights and freedoms of others', may justify a limitation of fundamental rights. Defined by the ECB as 'a condition in which the financial system—which comprises financial intermediaries, markets and market infrastructures—is capable of withstanding shocks and the unravelling of financial imbalances',[4] financial stability is, in all pillars of the Banking Union, one of the goals—if not *the* ultimate goal—to be achieved.[5] Additional, more concrete objectives are reflected upon as well, but often they just seem to be specifications—certain aspects of financial stability which partially need to be balanced against each other (eg to maintain a bank's critical functions in resolution procedures, or to protect depositors).[6]

Financial stability is relevant not only for banks and other actors on the financial market, but, due to the interrelation specifically of banks with the real economy, also for the economy as a whole.[7] Due to the complexity of the subject and the strong economics component of relevant decision-making, courts, when deciding on alleged fundamental rights violations, grant the EU and its Member States a particularly broad discretion in their efforts to ensure financial stability.[8]

[4] ECB, 'Introduction to financial stability', as provided on its website; https://www.ecb.europa.eu/paym/financial-stability/html/index.en.html, accessed 11 September 2025.

[5] For references in pertinent legislation, see, by way of example, recitals 2 and 55 SSMR; art 14(2)(b) SRMR; art 124(2)(b) Regulation 575/2013 (as part of the Single Rulebook).

[6] See Case T–481/17 *Fundación Tatiana Pérez*, ECLI:EU:T:2022:311, para 216; Case C–551/22P *Commission v SRB*, ECLI:EU:C:2024:520, para 81; see also Case C–526/14 *Kotnik*, ECLI:EU:C:2016:570, para 91 on potential conflicts between these specifications; for the importance of savers' trust in the banking system, see Concetta Brescia Morra, 'The New European Union Framework for Banking Crisis Management: Rules versus Discretion' (2019) 16 European Company and Financial Law Review 349, 352.

[7] This is succinctly put in Case C–501/18 *Balgarska Narodna Banka*, EU:C:2021:249, para 108, with further references.

[8] See Niamh Moloney, 'Banking Union and the Charter of Fundamental Rights' in Chiara Zilioli and Karl-Philipp Wojcik (eds), *Judicial Review in the European Banking Union* (Edward Elgar 2021) 209, 218, with references to the CJEU's case law; for the ECtHR see, eg case *Camberrow MM5 AD v Bulgaria* (dec.), no 5035799, 1 April 2004. With regard to the risk that the complexity of financial stability may overstrain courts when assessing the legality of pertinent measures, see Marco Lamandini, David Ramos, and Javier Solana, 'The European Central Bank (ECB) Powers as a Catalyst for Change in EU Law. Part 2: SSM, SRM, and Fundamental Rights' (2017) 23 Columbia Journal of European Law 199, 214.

II Specific questions related to fundamental rights

1 Fundamental right to property

A common feature of crisis management during the Great Financial Crisis (GFC) was the bail-out of banks by Member States' governments. This practice of resorting to taxpayer's money in order to rescue troubled banks further strained public households. It was one of the causes for the ensuing euro crisis. In an attempt to cut off this inauspicious link between banks and sovereigns, the EU legislator adopted the bank resolution regime. One of the instruments this regime provides for is the bail-in instrument, ie the write-down and conversion of relevant capital instruments.[9] Thereby, shareholders and eligible creditors, first and foremost, should bear the losses of a bank which is in trouble ('failing or likely to fail'). In view of the many bail-outs performed during the GFC, the introduction of this instrument was meant to be a paradigm change. At the same time, by law, shareholders and eligible creditors should not be put in a worse situation than under national insolvency law (which would have applied if no resolution procedure had been initiated). This guarantee is referred to as the no-creditor-worse-off (NCWO) principle, to which we will come back again. In spite of its name, it also protects shareholders.

In a fundamental rights perspective, a bail-in above all affects the fundamental right to property of the shareholders and creditors concerned. Not only shares, but also bonds and other claims qualify as property within the meaning of the fundamental right to property,[10] even if their actual value is reduced significantly, for example because the debtor is in financial troubles.[11] Thus, an interference with the right to property, as laid down in Article 17 CFR or in Article 1, 1st Protocol of the European Convention on Human Rights (ECHR),[12] must be examined. These provisions distinguish two specific forms of interference with the right to property: the deprivation (ie the

[9] The 'write-down and conversion powers' according to art 21 SRMR must be distinguished from the bail-in instrument. The former do not qualify as resolution tool. They can be applied before the conditions for resolution have been met, but also in the course of a resolution procedure (in combination with a resolution tool): see Karl-Philipp Wojcik, 'Bail-in in the Banking Union' (2016) 53 Common Market Law Review 91, 111 f.

[10] See *BPC Lux 2* (n 3), paras 39 f.

[11] See ECtHR case *Pintar and others v Slovenia*, no 49969/14 and others, 14 September 2021, paras 90 f. While shares with no economic value qualify as 'possessions' pursuant to art 1, 1st Protocol ECHR, the ECtHR avoids answering the question whether bonds (which do not, like shares, allow the undertaking's conduct to be influenced) with no economic value also qualify as property (para 92).

[12] It follows from art 52(3) CFR that art 17 CFR shall have the same meaning and scope as art 1, 1st Protocol ECHR; see also explanation on art 17 in the Explanations relating to the CFR (2007/C 303/02), [2007] OJ C303, pp 17–35.

expropriation) of property, and the regulation of the use of property.[13] The European Court of Human Rights (ECtHR), and recently also the Court of Justice of the European Union (CJEU), have also acknowledged the concept of a de facto expropriation, for example where the state makes intense use of somebody's real estate without formally expropriating the owner.[14]

In a resolution procedure involving the instruments of bridge institution and asset separation, the CJEU held that the application of these instruments constitutes a regulation of the use of property within the meaning of Article 17 CFR.[15] The ECtHR, too, saw the regulation of the use of property in the foreground in this resolution procedure.[16] The courts did not consider these measures to be a form of expropriation, or at least of a de facto expropriation. This assessment is based on the assumption that the loss in value of the relevant capital instruments—which the applicants claimed to be a result of the resolution measures in question—would also have occurred without their adoption. This loss, the CJEU concluded, is due to the fact that the bank stopped or was about to stop its payments, and not due to the resolution measures at issue.[17] AG Pitruzzella expressed this in the following words: 'From an economic point of view, the position of the investors, on the whole, remains unchanged in principle.'[18] From a legal perspective, the situation does change, though. Against this background, arguably also the conversion of debt instruments into equity qualifies as regulation of the use of property. But what about a mere write-down? Unlike with the instruments just addressed, here it could be argued that the legal situation also does not change. However, even a mere write-down is not as 'natural' as it may seem at first sight. It involves a different treatment of different categories of creditors, depending on their respective rank. This distinction according to a certain hierarchy of creditors follows only from the law,[19] not from the situation on the market. Thus, a mere write-down

[13] These interferences are to be understood against the general rule contained in the first sentence of both provisions, which, in the ECHR, is described as 'peaceful enjoyment' of one's possessions.

[14] See Case C-535/22 P *Aeris*, ECLI:EU:C:2024:819, para 215, with references to the case law of the CJEU and of the ECtHR.

[15] See *BPC Lux 2* (n 3), para 50.

[16] ECtHR case *Freire Lopez v Portugal* (dec.), no 58598/21, 31 January 2023, para 87: *'réglementation de l'usage de biens'*.

[17] See *BPC Lux 2* (n 3), paras 45–48.

[18] Opinion of AG Pitruzzella in Case C-83/20 *BPC Lux 2*, ECLI:EU:C:2021:853, para 116.

[19] Shareholders with a critical amount of shares, in addition to the loss in value, also lose their grip on the bank's management. However, this latter loss is not specifically due to the write-down, but due to the initiation of the resolution procedure more generally: see, eg art 63(1)(b) BRRD; for the different treatment of different categories of creditors in the context of art 21 CFR, see Juliane Kokott, 'Bank Resolution and Fundamental Rights' (2024) Zeitschrift für Bankrecht und Bankwirtschaft/Journal of Banking Law and Banking 33, 36 f; for the reconsideration of this hierarchy, see Council, 'Bank resolution: Council and Parliament strike deal to strengthen the EU crisis management framework' (press release of 25 June 2025); https://www.consilium.europa.eu/en/press/press-releases/2025/06/

prescribed by the resolution authority also constitutes a regulation of the use of property.

What does a regulation of the use of property now require to be lawful? It must be 'necessary for the general interest'. Unlike the deprivation, regulation of the use of property, pursuant to Article 17 CFR, does not explicitly require 'fair compensation being paid in good time' for the loss. Thus, fair compensation, in principle, is not necessary for such regulation to be justified.[20] If compensation is granted, nevertheless, this is to be taken into account when assessing the overall proportionality of the regulation at issue.[21] The CJEU has confirmed this also in the specific context of bank resolution.[22] Under EU secondary law, following a bail-in, compensation may very well be paid. This brings us back to the NCWO principle. This principle provides for the outcome of a (hypothetical) insolvency procedure applicable in the Member State at issue as a baseline.[23] This insolvency procedure is perceived as the alternative to the resolution of the bank, because if no resolution measure had been taken it would probably have been wound up in the course of an insolvency procedure. The decision as to which of the two procedures is applied in a concrete case cannot be determined by the shareholders or creditors of the bank concerned. Against this background, the NCWO principle also has an equal-treatment thrust.[24]

The NCWO principle underlies the question of causation of the interference with the right to property: is the resolution procedure a *conditio sine qua non* for the loss of shareholders and creditors? The mental exercise does not stop at removing the presumably harmful action, ie the resolution procedure, though. Rather, it is replaced by an alternative form of interference, namely the normal insolvency procedure. Even though the loss of assets is caused by the bank's insolvency as such, and not by the insolvency procedure,[25] this procedure also leads to an interference with the right to property.[26] The interference under

25/bank-resolution-council-and-parliament-strike-deal-to-strengthen-the-eu-crisis-management-framework/, accessed 11 September 2025.

[20] Only exceptionally is compensation required: see ECtHR case *Immobiliare Staffi v Italy*, no 22774/93, 28 July 1999, paras 57 and 59.

[21] See ECtHR case *Depalle v France* (GC), no 34044/02, 29 March 2010, para 91.

[22] See *BPC Lux 2* (n 3), paras 61 f.

[23] cf the 'least-cost principle', applicable in the context of deposit guarantee schemes, which is inspired by a similar economic logic; see ch 6.

[24] See art 21 CFR.

[25] See also ECtHR case *Kotov v Russia* (GC), no 54522/00, 3 April 2012, para 116.

[26] The conclusions the General Court made in this context are ambiguous. It held that the burden sharing (prescribed by the Banking Communication) 'cannot cause any detriment to the right to property of subordinated creditors that those creditors would not have suffered within insolvency proceedings'. From this, it deduces that 'it cannot reasonably be maintained that the burden-sharing

resolution may not go beyond this baseline. Whether or not the national insolvency procedure complies with the fundamental right to property is not assessed; it is assumed.[27] Otherwise, the Court could not agree with the conclusion that compliance with the NCWO principle means that the resolution measures at issue do not 'disproportionately restrict the right to property'.[28]

Pursuant to the NCWO principle, compensation is paid only to the extent that shareholders/creditors bear greater losses under the resolution procedure than they would have borne under the insolvency procedure applicable in the relevant Member State. Whether or not there is a difference in the losses to be borne can only be found out by applying both procedures.[29] As they are alternative procedures—and as, when the NCWO principle applies, the resolution procedure was already chosen as the way to go—the actual application of the insolvency procedure is counterfactual.[30] The outcome of this hypothetical application is calculated in the course of a validation (see section II.2 below). If and to the extent that the outcome for shareholders/creditors would be better under the mock insolvency procedure than under the resolution procedure, the shareholders/creditors will be compensated. The General Court qualifies this compensation as 'fair compensation in accordance with the requirements of Article 17(1) of the Charter'.[31] As explained above, this provision explicitly requires 'fair compensation' only in the case of a deprivation. The bail-in instrument, however, results in a regulation of the use of property. To call it 'fair compensation', thereby referring to Article 17(1) CFR, is, at best, misleading.

measures . . . constitute interference in the right to property of the shareholders and the subordinated creditors'. While conceding that insolvency proceedings cause a 'detriment' to the right of property, it seems to argue that a burden sharing which does not go beyond the outcome of insolvency proceedings does not result in an interference: Case T–510/17 *Del Valle Ruíz*, ECLI:EU:T:2022:312, para 520; see already *Kotnik* (n 6), paras 74 and 79.

[27] Since the insolvency law (hypothetically) applied here belongs to national law, the trust which is put in this national law also seems to reflect the different facets of art 4 TEU; for an example of amendments to (German) insolvency law due to the unconstitutional discrimination it entailed, see Robert F Adam, 'Insolvenzrecht und Grundgesetz' (2009) 19 Deutsche Zeitschrift für Wirtschafts- und Insolvenzrecht 441.

[28] This wording is taken from the Commission's impact assessment, which the General Court quotes in support of its argumentation: *Del Valle Ruíz* (n 26), para 514; see also recital 62 SRMR.

[29] A fundamental-rights-related argument in favour of applying the NCWO principle can be based not only on the right to equal treatment (as mentioned before), but also on the quest for legal certainty and the protection of legitimate expectations (which weigh heavily, in particular, in matters related to property). After all, the resolution procedure replaces the insolvency procedure only if the public interest is confirmed in a concrete case. As it cannot be anticipated by the shareholders/creditors whether this threshold will be met, their reliance on the insolvency procedure may be protected.

[30] See also Paolo Stancanelli and Alejandro Menéndez Fernández, 'The respect of Fundamental Rights in the EU bank resolution legal framework' (2024) Zeitschrift für Bankrecht und Bankwirtschaft/Journal of Banking Law and Banking 52, 54: 'counterfactual analysis'.

[31] *Del Valle Ruíz* (n 26), para 522; Case T–628/17 *Aeris Invest*, ECLI:EU:T:2022:315, para 208; Joined Cases T–302/20, T–303/20 and T–307/20 *Del Valle Ruíz*, ECLI:EU:T:2023:735, para 200.

On appeal, the Court of Justice did not repeat this argument. Rather, it held that, in this case, the granted compensation is not required under Article 17(1) CFR, but that it contributes to the proportionality of the resolution measure.[32]

Leaving aside the issue of compensation, in the context of justification it is worth recalling the public interests pursued by a resolution procedure, on the one hand, and by an insolvency procedure, on the other. For the latter, the main public interest is the satisfaction, as far as possible, of creditors in an equitable manner,[33] thereby preventing the arbitrary treatment of creditors' claims by the insolvent debtor. In the case of resolution, the public interests pursued are to ensure the continuity of the bank's critical functions; to protect financial stability; to minimize reliance on taxpayers' money; and to protect depositors. These public interests are not only more numerous than in the case of insolvency proceedings; they also have a heavier weight.[34] Given the high pertinence of the public interests at issue here, in the case of resolution, the threshold for rendering proportionate interferences with the right to property may be lower than in the case of an insolvency procedure. Against this background, and given the broad discretion public authorities have when adopting 'economic decisions',[35] from a fundamental rights perspective a treatment of shareholders and creditors which is *worse* than under insolvency law may very well be lawful, too.[36]

2 Procedural fundamental rights

The NCWO principle leads us to a procedural issue, namely the question of how to assess compliance with this principle, and the review of this assessment,

[32] *Aeris* (n 14), paras 237 f.

[33] See IMF, *Orderly & Effective Insolvency Procedures. Key Issues* (1999) https://www.imf.org/external/pubs/ft/orderly/, accessed 11 September 2025. 'Equitable treatment' does not mean 'equal treatment'.

[34] For the interest of protecting financial stability in this context, see Joined Cases C-775/22, C-779/22 and C-794/22 *Banco Santander (Résolution bancaire Banco Popular II)*, ECLI:EU:C:2024:679, para 56; see also *Aeris Invest* (n 31), para 163; ECtHR case *Albert and others v Hungary* (GC), no 5294/14, 7 July 2020, para 167.

[35] *BPC Lux 2* (n 3), para 55, with a further reference; see also ECtHR case *Grainger and others v United Kingdom* (dec.), no 34940/10, 10 July 2012, para 36.

[36] The CJEU does not explicitly confirm this finding (as it bases its arguments on the assumption that, under national law, compensation would be possible, even though it is not explicitly provided for in the concrete case), but stresses the leeway art 17(1) CFR grants; see *BPC Lux 2* (n 3), paras 54–56 and 61 f; see also Opinion of AG de la Tour of 21 March 2024 in Joined Cases C-498/22 to C-500/22 *Novo Banco*, ECLI:EU:C:2024:269, para 119; for an even broader reading of the Court, see Kokott (n 19) 35 f: 'judgment . . . seems prima facie contradictory'; for the case law of the ECtHR, see *Micallef v Malta*, no 23264/18, 28 October 2021, para 41; *Azzopardi v Malta*, no 22008/20, 9 June 2022, para 55, both with further references to case law.

respectively. Both the Bank Recovery and Resolution Directive (BRRD) and the Single Resolution Mechanism Regulation (SRMR) require, as soon as possible after the resolution action, a valuation by an 'independent person',[37] for example a consulting firm. In the course of this valuation—'valuation 3'—a mock application of the national insolvency procedure is performed at the point in time when resolution action was taken,[38] and the (hypothetical) outcome of this procedure is compared with the (actual) outcome of the resolution procedure. On this basis, the resolution authority in charge takes its decision as to whether the NCWO principle was complied with. The valuation report is 'expected to clearly explain and justify the assumptions and the methodologies adopted in [it]'.[39] It is worth emphasizing that valuation 3 involves both an economic and a legal assessment of how national insolvency proceedings would presumably be applied, and with what result. That in matters of law—for example, taking into account 'applicable insolvency law and practice in the relevant jurisdiction, which may influence factors such as the expected disposal period or recovery rates'[40]—actors other than national or EU authorities or courts shall give the main guidance is a remarkable trait of this regime.

Obviously, the scrutiny of this valuation is highly relevant for the protection of shareholders' and creditors' rights. This scrutiny may be performed by the national or EU resolution authority when taking the decision on compliance with the NCWO principle, on the one hand, and the national or EU court reviewing this decision, on the other. Where the SRB is the decision-making authority in charge,[41] and thus the CJEU may be called to review its decision, the SRB, to the extent that it actually scrutinizes the valuation, engages in the (hypothetical) application of national law. The application of national law by an EU actor has received much attention in the context of banking supervision by the ECB under the SSM.[42] Notwithstanding the significant differences between the two constellations, it is worth bearing their coexistence in mind.

With its decision to require a valuation by an independent actor, the legislator intended to facilitate objective decision-making.[43] After all, resolution authorities may be (perceived as) biased in this respect. Nevertheless, it is the

[37] See art 74(1) BRRD; art 20(16)–(18) SRMR.

[38] For the diversity of national insolvency laws, see Kokott (n 19) 37.

[39] SRB, *Framework for Valuation – Q & A*, https://www.srb.europa.eu/system/files/media/document/2019-02-01%20Framework%20for%20Valuation%20-%20%20Q%26A.pfd_.pdf, accessed 11 September 2025.

[40] Art 4(3)(a) Delegated Regulation 2018/344.

[41] Art 76(1)(e) SRMR. For the relevance of the Commission's involvement in adopting the *resolution scheme*, see *Commission v SRB* (n 6).

[42] See Daniela Jaros, in this volume, and section II.3.

[43] See, in more detail, arts 37–41 of Delegated Regulation 2016/107.

resolution authority which takes the final decision. Given this delicate balance between the independent expertise of the valuer and the democratic legitimacy of the resolution authority, it is worth considering to what extent the resolution authority—here, we shall focus on the SRB—scrutinizes the valuation report when taking its decision. If the scrutiny is too intense, the advantage of providing an independent perspective may be thwarted. If it is too mild, the valuer may be seen as a de facto decision-maker whose assessment is rubber-stamped by the SRB. The relationship between private expert bodies and EU decision-making authorities has been discussed in various contexts, for example with regard to the incorporation of technical standards in EU law. Already, the *Meroni* judgments of 1958 relate to this constellation—the relationship between the private 'Brussels agencies' and the ECSC's High Authority, in the context of discretionary decision-making.[44]

It is not the purpose of this section to analyse the legislator's decision-making set-up relating to the question whether a resolution measure complied with the NCWO principle. Instead, emphasis will be put on the practical application of this regime by the SRB and the CJEU, taking the *Banco Popular* case—the only case of bank resolution managed at EU level so far—as an example. In this case, Deloitte were appointed as valuer. On the basis of their valuation report, which denied any interference with the NCWO principle, the SRB drafted a preliminary decision. Subsequently, it sent out both documents to Banco Popular's shareholders and creditors for comments.[45] It received a total of 2,855 submissions,[46] which were then divided into comments relating to the preliminary decision but not to the valuation report, comments relating to the valuation report, and irrelevant comments. The SRB forwarded the comments related to the report to Deloitte, asking whether the report 'remained valid in light of these comments'.[47] This was confirmed by Deloitte in their 'Clarification Document', reacting to the relevant comments. In its (final) decision, the SRB took account of the valuation more generally, confirming that it was 'sufficiently reasoned and comprehensive' to form the basis of the SRB decision, and rarely even criticizing it.[48] Not only the economic assumptions made in the report, but also its legal part, were scrutinized only superficially. According to the

[44] Cases 9 and 19/56 *Meroni*, ECLI:EU:C:1958:7 and ECLI:EU:C:1958:8; the CJEU has addressed the *Meroni* case law (for procedural reasons, with some limitations) in the given context: Case T-330/20 *ACMO*, ECLI:EU:T:2023:733, paras 354–73; see also ch 9.

[45] Note recital 51 BRRD: 'As opposed to the valuation prior to the resolution action, it should be possible to challenge that comparison [ie valuation 3] separately from the resolution decision'; art 41(2)(a) CFR; for the procedure in more detail, see *ACMO* (n 44), paras 17–20.

[46] SRB, Decision SRB/EES/2020/52, recital 26.

[47] ibid, recital 28.

[48] See ibid, recital 66; for the criticism, see, eg recital 53.

SRB, the valuation 'took into account the applicable insolvency law, including the creditor hierarchy provided therein, in the relevant jurisdictions . . . and, where relevant, past insolvency cases'.[49] The largest part of its decision relates to the concerns regarding the preliminary decision, as uttered by shareholders and creditors.[50] The decision, which confirmed compliance with the NCWO principle, was challenged before the CJEU.

In matters of bank resolution more generally, the CJEU engages in a limited form of judicial review. According to its settled case law, 'complex economic assessments' undertaken by EU authorities limit the intensity of judicial review of the resulting acts.[51] This applies also in the specific context of the SRB decision on compliance with the NCWO principle, even though these assessments are essentially made by a private body.[52] Nevertheless, the General Court underlines that it is called upon to 'establish whether the evidence relied on is factually accurate, reliable and consistent but also [to] ascertain whether that evidence contains all the information which must be taken into account in order to assess a complex situation and whether it is capable of supporting the conclusions drawn from it'.[53] In order to examine whether the SRB made a 'manifest error of assessment', the Court has to examine whether the valuer made such an error in valuation 3.[54]

What the Court does not appear to consider as a separate issue is the fact that valuation 3 also involves the (hypothetical) application of (national) law. In reaction to the applicants' objections to the SRB decision which relate to Spanish insolvency law, overall the Court strongly relies on the valuer's and the SRB's assessment and also quotes the Kingdom of Spain (which joined the proceedings in support of the SRB). Partially, it also invokes concrete provisions of Spanish law, and even Spanish case law.[55] In one paragraph, it explicitly refers to 'the wording' of the relevant law, suggesting that it engages in legal interpretation.[56] Eventually, the Court concludes that the applicants could not 'validly

[49] ibid, recital 70.

[50] By asking shareholders and creditors to fill in a comment form, the SRB may actively invite objections on a broad area of issues, thereby incentivizing a comprehensive scrutiny by shareholders and creditors. This seems to be a strong contribution to provide a reasoning 'in the light of the interest which the addressees of the act may have in obtaining explanations': Joined Cases C-584/20P and C-621/20P *Landesbank Baden-Württemberg*, ECLI:EU:C:2021:601, para 104.

[51] *Del Valle Ruíz* (n 26), paras 107 f, with many further references.

[52] See *ACMO* (n 44), paras 39–41 and 61; Joined Cases T-302/20, T-303/20, and T-307/20 *Del Valle Ruíz*, ECLI:EU:T:2023:735, paras 33–40.

[53] *ACMO* (n 44), para 42.

[54] See ibid, para 61.

[55] See ibid, eg paras 84 f and 87 f.

[56] See ibid, para 101; see also Joined Cases T-302/20, T-303/20, and T-307/20 *Del Valle Ruíz*, ECLI:EU:T:2023:735, paras 81–84.

maintain that the assumptions made by the SRB or the Valuer . . . were based on a misunderstanding [of the relevant Spanish law]'.[57]

With regard to the allegedly wrongful (re)classification of loans, the Court again heavily relies on the valuation report.[58] In reaction to a complaint regarding the assessment of 'legal contingencies', the Court countered that '*it is sufficient* to note that that argument made by the applicants is based on mere statements made by their witness, A, who does not expressly refer to any provision of Spanish legislation' (emphasis added).[59] This wording reflects well the Court's unwillingness to dig deeper in matters of Spanish law.[60] The justification of the valuer's assessment by the mere facts that 'it had consulted Banco Popular's legal team', and that 'it is apparent from Valuation 3 that the Valuer relied on the applicable Spanish legislation', further underpins this impression.[61] The Court's approach is no different when economic questions are at issue (eg the valuer's assumption on prepaid performing loans or the valuation of non-performing loans).

All in all, the General Court assesses legal and economic questions—a distinction which, in the given context, is sometimes difficult to draw—relating to compliance with the NCWO principle in a similar manner: rather superficially, displaying strong deference to the SRB and the valuer. Apparently, the *mock* application of law is more similar to assumptions relating to, say, market dynamics impacting on the value of assets than to the *actual* application of national law.[62]

In a fundamental rights perspective, the SRB's limited scrutiny regarding the correct (hypothetical) application of national insolvency law may affect its duty to provide the reasons for its decisions, as laid down, inter alia, in Article 41 CFR. As long as the reasons given in the valuation report itself are sufficient, the SRB's duty to provide reasons is met. The SRB's strong dependence on, and limited scrutiny of, the independent valuation report, however, bears the risk that a flaw or incompletion in the reasoning escapes the attention of the SRB. Of key significance in this context is the legally guaranteed possibility for shareholders and creditors to react directly to the valuation report, so that questions can be answered by the valuer itself. It would be very difficult for the SRB and, eventually, the Court to adequately respond to these questions. After

[57] *ACMO* (n 44), para 105.
[58] See ibid, paras 128–38.
[59] ibid, para 233.
[60] That the Court subsequently adds further arguments, thereby again relying on the SRB's submissions, which are based on concrete provisions of Spanish law, does not challenge this assessment.
[61] *ACMO* (n 44), paras 237 f.
[62] Note the words of the valuer, as paraphrased by the Court: ibid, para 229.

all, the requirement that compliance with the NCWO principle be assessed by an independent expert (body) does not only serve the purpose of unbiased decision-making but also ought to complement the expertise of the SRB (and, eventually, the Court) in a field where they may lack in-depth expertise (ie legal and economic aspects of national insolvency proceedings). Thus, it is all the more important that compliance with the shareholders' and creditors' right to be heard be closely examined by the SRB.

As regards the judicial review exercised by the CJEU, Article 47 CFR is to be considered. While the right to an effective remedy is by no means absolute,[63] it may still be impinged on if the Court neglects the examination of matters of (national) law. Its light-touch material scrutiny applied in the given context may allow for the detection of obvious mistakes of the valuer. This must be compensated for by a more rigorous scrutiny of procedural aspects, notably of the right to be heard. Thereby, a high level of protection against potential errors in the valuer's assessment can be ensured.

Overall, the SRB's and the Court's practice seems to respect the valuer's expertise and independence while ensuring an adequate protection of procedural rights. The strong procedural guarantees seem to be intended as compensation for the limited substantive review. The (hypothetical) application of national (insolvency) law is different from the application of national law by the ECB pursuant to Article 4(3) SSM-Regulation. In our context, the EU bodies in charge treat national law as a matter of fact rather than as a matter of law.[64] Valuation 3 is qualified as an independent expert's opinion. Neither the SRB nor the Court have the competence to scrutinize the valuation in detail. Materially, they fall short of this competence for lack of in-depth knowledge, and the legal competence is restricted by the prescribed independence of the valuer, and thus of the valuation itself. The principle *iura novit curia* does not seem to apply in this context. Nevertheless, as exemplified above, obvious flaws can be detected—or their existence denied—by the SRB and the Court, which may even result in a basic form of interpretation, ie a verbal interpretation of national insolvency law.

[63] See, in the context of shareholders'/creditors' rights in bank resolution, *Banco Santander* (n 34), paras 80 f.

[64] This does not mean, however, that national law is to be treated like any other fact. After all, the meaning of law cannot be understood other than by interpreting it. For this debate, see Miro Prek and Silvère Lefèvre, 'The EU Courts as "National" Courts: National Law in the EU Judicial Process' (2017) 54 Common Market Law Review 369.

3 National fundamental rights

Under the SSM, the ECB is empowered to apply relevant national law—not as a matter of fact, but as a matter of law.[65] The case law on Article 4(3) SSMR is growing, but still some aspects of the application of national law by the ECB remain unsettled. These concern, inter alia, the role of national law other than the national legislation transposing the relevant directives or exercising options granted by regulations—for example, provisions of constitutional law informing the interpretation of the latter—and the role of national case law. While, in *Crédit Agricole* and *Crédit Mutuel Arkéa*, the Court has stressed the importance of national case law, but also of this other national law,[66] in *Berlusconi* the Court emphasized that a 'concept of Union law' was at issue, thereby diminishing the importance of national rules in the concrete case.[67] In the cases *BAWAG PSK* and *Sber*, the Court deviated from national case law by implying a margin of discretion to the relevant national law—based on the argument that the provision at issue 'does not expressly rule out th[is] possibility'—in order to achieve compliance with relevant Union law.[68] In *Corneli*, the General Court again underlined the relevance of national law transposing a directive (as opposed to the directive itself). But whereas the General Court deemed an interpretation of national law in conformity with the directive impossible (ie *contra legem*), on appeal the Court of Justice set aside the judgment of the General Court, holding that the pertinent national law can indeed be interpreted in accordance with the directive.[69]

[65] See Opinion of AG Ćapeta in Case C-579/22 P *Anglo Austrian AAB*, ECLI:EU:C:2024:296, paras 38 ff, with many further references; differently, Opinion of AG Kokott in Joined Cases C-777/22 P and C-789/22 P *Corneli*, ECLI:EU:C:2024:973, paras 128–30, again with many further references.

[66] See Joined Cases T-133/16 to T-136/16 *Alpes Provence*, ECLI:EU:T:2018:219, para 92. Here, the Court deemed the pertinent judgment of the Conseil d'État 'sufficient to establish the scope of the rules of national law that the ECB was required to apply', which was why it rejected the applicants' questioning of the interpretation provided by the Conseil d'État, including references 'to other rules of national law'. Otherwise, it is for the ECB and, eventually, the Court to take into account these other rules of national law, thereby engaging in a systematic interpretation of the provision(s) at issue: see Case T-712/15 *Crédit mutuel Arkéa*, ECLI:EU:T:2017:900, paras 132–36; confirmed on appeal, by which time the Conseil d'État had rendered a new decision: Joined Cases C-152/18P and C-153/18P *Crédit mutuel Arkéa*, ECLI:EU:C:2019:810, paras 99–107; see also Opinion of AG Ćapeta in *Anglo Austrian AAB* (n 65), paras 45 and 90. For the review, by the Court of Justice on appeal of the interpretation of national law provided by the General Court, see Case C-579/22P *Anglo Austrian AAB*, ECLI:EU:C:2024:731, paras 85–88.

[67] See Case T-913/16 *Berlusconi*, ECLI:EU:T:2022:279, paras 46–49; confirmed (with regard to this specific question) on appeal in Joined Cases C-512/22P and C-513/22P *Berlusconi*, ECLI:EU:C:2024:774, paras 48 f.

[68] Case T-667/21 *BAWAG PSK*, ECLI:EU:T:2024:131, para 76; Joined Cases T-647/21 and T-99/22 *Sber*, ECLI:EU:T:2024:127, para 77.

[69] Joined Cases C-777/22P and C-789/22 P *Corneli*, ECLI:EU:C:2025:580, paras 153–58.

It is not the purpose of this section to discuss the application of national law by the ECB more generally,[70] but to dwell on one specific question related to fundamental rights, namely on the relevance of national fundamental rights.[71] So far, there has been no case law on this question, but a potential practical example could be the following: as a banking supervisor, the ECB also assesses the personal integrity of the members of a significant bank's management body. This is provided for in the Capital Requirements Directive,[72] but the criteria to be considered are concretized by national law.[73] Let us assume that, in a given Member State, this national law requires 'past prosecutions' of the designated manager to be taken into account in the assessment of their personal integrity ('good repute'). Let us further assume that the constitutional law of this Member State, as a matter of the free choice of profession in conjunction with the presumption of innocence, forbids past *administrative* proceedings (including sanctions, eg for tax evasion below a certain threshold) from being taken into account, and that this also applies in the context of the assessment of (designated) top bank managers' 'good repute'.

This fundamental rights protection goes beyond the protection standard of the CFR. That EU fundamental rights, notably the CFR, are applicable in the context of the SSM is clear from the wording of Article 51(1) CFR, and even more so from its wide interpretation by the Court.[74] According to Article 53 CFR, '[n]othing in th[e] Charter shall be interpreted as restricting or adversely affecting human rights and fundamental freedoms as recognised . . . by the Member States' constitutions'. The Court, in its case law, has applied a restrictive interpretation of this delimitation clause. Accordingly, it allows for a higher level of protection only if 'the primacy, unity and effectiveness of EU law are not thereby compromised'.[75] Primacy means that EU law prevails over conflicting national law (including constitutional law), unity conveys the coherence (of the interpretation/application) of EU law,[76] and effectiveness

[70] For this, see Daniela Jaros, in this volume.

[71] For the potential irrelevance of national fundamental rights in this context, see Chryssa Papathanassiou, 'Fundamental Rights and Banking Supervision' (2023) 24 Journal of Banking Regulation 420, 423.

[72] Directive 2013/36/EU.

[73] For the fragmentation at national level, see Danny Busch and Annick Teubner, 'Fit and Proper Assessments Within the Single Supervisory Mechanism' in Danny Busch and Guido Ferrarini (eds), *European Banking Union* (2nd edn, OUP 2020) paras 7.88–7.95.

[74] Case C-617/10 *Åkerberg Fransson*, ECLI:EU:C:2013:105; for a differentiated analysis of this and related issues, see Lamandini, Ramos, and Solana (n 8) 204–09.

[75] Case C-399/11 *Melloni*, EU:C:2013:107, para 60. The fourth criterion, ie that 'the level of protection provided for by the Charter' is not compromised, is inherent in a 'higher level of protection' (than that of the Charter), which is why it does not require further elaboration here.

[76] See, eg Opinion of AG Mischo in Case C-133/99 *Netherlands v Commission*, ECLI:EU:C:2002:13, paras 40 and 46.

normally relates to application and enforcement of EU law in the Member States.[77] Article 4(3) SSMR distinguishes two categories of national law: that which transposes relevant directives, and that by which options explicitly granted in relevant regulations are exercised.

It could be argued that the primacy, unity, and effectiveness of EU law are not at risk, and not even at issue, to the extent Member States make use of leeway allowed for in EU law. By granting this leeway, EU law itself allows for *national* legal *choices*. Directives are conceived to grant room for manoeuvre to the Member States when transposing them, and options allow Member States to choose one out of a number of alternative measures. Thus, the above argument is valid. However, it needs to be decided on a case-by-case basis whether and to what extent there is room for manoeuvre on the part of the Member States, and thus also for increased fundamental rights protection under national law.

In the concrete case, the requirement of a 'sufficiently good repute' laid down in Article 91(1) Directive 2013/36/EU is concretized by means of EBA/ESMA and ECB soft law. These guidelines prescribe that, '[w]ithout prejudice to any fundamental rights, any relevant criminal or administrative records should be taken into account for the assessment of good repute',[78] and that 'the fact that an appointee has been convicted or sanctioned' and even 'the very fact that an individual is being prosecuted is relevant to propriety'.[79] While these guidelines are legally non-binding, they illuminate the semantics of the term 'good repute'. Good repute is not the same as having no (relevant) criminal convictions.[80] Relevant administrative records have to be considered,

[77] Case C–409/06 *Winner Wetten*, ECLI:EU:C:2010:503, paras 56 f and 61, with further references.

[78] Joint ESMA and EBA Guidelines on the assessment of the suitability of members of the management body and key function holders under Directive 2013/36/EU and Directive 2014/65/EU (2021), para 73; ECB, 'Guide to fit and proper assessments' (2021) 3.2. The reference to 'any fundamental rights' may be literally interpreted as including national fundamental rights. It does not specifically refer to national fundamental rights going beyond the CFR, though; see Summary of responses to the consultation and the EBA's analysis in the Joint ESMA and EBA Guidelines (with regard to para 75) https://www.eba.europa.eu/sites/default/files/document_library/ Publications/Guidelines/2021/EBA-GL-2021-06%20Joint%20GLs%20on%20the%20assessment%20of% 20suitability%20%28fit%26propoer%29/1022127/Final%20report%20on%20joint%20EBA%20and%20ESMA%20GL%20on%20the%20assessment%20of%20suitability.pdf, accessed 11 September 2025, at pp 89 f. In our example, giving full effect to national fundamental rights would reduce the broad range of relevant (negative) indicators for 'fit and proper assessments' referred to by the guidelines, including mere indictments, to criminal records only. Taking a teleological perspective, it is doubtful that the restriction of the list of relevant factors in this way was intended.

[79] ECB, 'Guide to fit and proper assessments' (2021) 3.2; similar content in Joint ESMA and EBA Guidelines (n 78), para 74.

[80] See, eg case T–913/16 *Berlusconi* (n 67), para 121. The fragmented legal situation across Member States apparently contrasts with the ECB's approach, according to which 'a person has either a good or a bad reputation', and according to which the underlying assessment 'should be conducted for all institutions in an equal manner': ECB, 'Guide to fit and proper assessments' (2021) 3.2. The consideration of 'good repute' as a concept of EU law could reduce Member States' leeway: see Joined Cases C–512/

as well. If the term 'sufficiently good repute' in Article 91(1) Directive 2013/36/EU is interpreted in this way, the primacy of Union law would require national law to be interpreted accordingly, if this is not *contra legem*,[81] and the deviating interpretation suggested by national fundamental rights law to be disapplied.[82] This way, the prima facie leeway of Member States is limited by a more restrictive (but equally viable) interpretation of the directive, in order to reduce legal fragmentation across Member States.[83] As a consequence, in the practical example outlined above, EU fundamental rights prevail over (a potentially further-reaching protection based on) national fundamental rights, for the sake of a uniform implementation of Union law.

The applicability of a higher fundamental rights standard under national law has, so far, been a theoretical problem in banking law, but it may very well become practical. It needs to be decided case-by-case whether the concrete issue falls within a leeway EU law grants to the Member States.[84] Only where this can be confirmed can a given higher fundamental rights standard under national law apply.

III Conclusions

As a field of law directly affecting banks as well as their respective shareholders and creditors, fundamental rights considerations—in particular, regarding the right to property and procedural rights—play a significant role in EU banking law, with a number of new justifications for interferences revolving around the primary aim of financial stability. This was showcased by three rather different examples.

22P and C-513/22P *Berlusconi*, ECLI:EU:C:2024:774, paras 48 f; see also Opinion of AG Campos Sánchez-Bordona in Joined Cases C-512/22 P and C-513/22 P *Berlusconi*, ECLI:EU:C:2024:414, para 55.

[81] Case C-212/04 *Adeneler*, ECLI:EU:C:2006:443, para 110.

[82] See Case C-573/17 *Popławski*, EU:C:2019:530, paras 55–61; with regard to an interpretation of national law implementing a directive to the detriment of individuals, see case C-106/89 *Marleasing*, ECLI:EU:C:1990:395, paras 6–8.

[83] The Court seems to favour an interpretation of 'good repute' which allows for the consideration of various factors: see Case T-323/22 *PH*, ECLI:EU:T:2024:460, para 363, with reference to the 'usual meaning' of this term.

[84] Where not the national legislator but National Competent Authorities are accorded some room for manoeuvre, the ECB aims at a convergent approach across the participating Member States: see, eg ECB Regulation 2016/445.

The particularities of the Banking Union pose fundamental-rights-related questions which cannot all be answered simply by referring to established practice (eg by the Commission, in the field of competition law)[85] and case law.

The NCWO principle is unique, and the manner in which it serves the right to property is complicated and, in part, mysterious. Rather than being 'fair compensation' pursuant to Article 17 CFR, it grants equal treatment of shareholders/creditors of failing banks, as for them, in financial terms, the outcome is the same, irrespective of whether these institutions are resolved (due to public interest) or are undergoing insolvency proceedings.

The scrutiny of compliance with the NCWO principle concerns procedural rights. On the one hand, this scrutiny is essentially performed by an independent actor (eg a consulting firm), which is intended to serve an objective outcome. On the other hand, the main decision-maker—at the EU level—that is the SRB—and the Court—exercising judicial review, must not be deprived of their genuine functions.[86] It is a delicate balance which the legislator has provided for, but which eventually needs to be struck by the SRB and the Court.

The question of to what extent national fundamental rights may come into play when the ECB applies national law under the SSM adds a new dimension to the curiosity of Article 4(3) SSMR, even though it has not had practical relevance so far.

What these cases show is that the novel tools of EU law and administration introduced by the Banking Union also raise new questions with regard to fundamental rights. Taking a step back from the intricacies of each example, however, it turns out that they just add new facets to old issues, such as the proportionality test, the adequacy of 'legitimation by procedure', and the limits of the primacy of Union law. This is not to downplay the relevance of the examples addressed here, but to underline the everlasting topicality of the 'old issues'.

[85] Some of them, however, can; for the proposal of an ECB Hearing Officer in charge of safeguarding the effective exercise of procedural rights, taking inspiration from a long-standing practice in the Commission's competition law policy, see Paola Chirulli and Luca de Lucia, 'Fundamental Procedural Rights and ECB Banking Supervision: An ECB Hearing Officer?' (2024) 61 Common Market Law Review 1191.

[86] Whereas a resolution scheme requires the approval of the Commission or the Council, the SRB, materially speaking, can still be described as the main decision-maker.

4

Relations between EU Bodies in the Banking Union

*Concetta Brescia Morra and Federico Pistelli**

I Close cooperation and financial stability in the Banking Union

The Banking Union (BU), with the establishment of a Single Supervisory Mechanism (SSM) for the supervision of banks, and a Single Resolution Mechanism (SRM) for resolving banking crises, has been a cornerstone in the European Union (EU) integration process.[1] The distinguishing feature of this new architecture is the coexistence of a wide institutional network, in which competences in regulating and supervising financial institutions are shared. Multiple bodies at EU and national level are called on to coordinate and harmonize their actions and to ensure the effectiveness and the consistency of the policies. The increasing complexity, interconnectedness, and globalization of financial markets makes the coordination and cooperation between authorities a key factor for a proper functioning of the BU. The consequence is that the interactions between EU bodies within the BU represent a major field of research.

Notwithstanding the multipolar architecture of BU governance, the European Central Bank (ECB) plays a strong role in ensuring the cooperation among the different authorities.[2] In exercising its mandate, the ECB is called

* Although this chapter is the result of a joint effort of the authors, the following sections are specifically attributable as follows: section II, Concetta Brescia Morra; section III, Federico Pistelli; sections I and IV, both authors.

[1] On the Banking Union, see, among many others, Danny Busch and Guido Ferrarini (eds), *European Banking Union* (2nd edn, OUP 2020); Stefan Grundmann and Hans-Wolfgang Micklitz (eds), *The European Banking Union and Constitution: Beacon for Advanced Integration or Death-knell for Democracy?* (Hart 2019); Angelo Baglioni (ed), *The European Banking Union* (Palgrave Macmillan UK 2016).

[2] Eddy Wymeersch, 'The Single Supervisory Mechanism or "SSM": Part One of the Banking Union' (2014) 240 ECGI Law Working Paper 26 ff.

Concetta Brescia Morra and Federico Pistelli, *Relations between EU Bodies in the Banking Union*
In: *EU Banking Union*. Edited by: Jonathan Bauerschmidt, Raffaele D'Ambrosio, Diane Fromage, Daniela Jaros, and Paul Weismann, Oxford University Press. © Oxford University Press 2026.
DOI: 10.1093/9780198949756.003.0005

on to strike a delicate balance between monetary policies and financial stability objectives. To achieve this equilibrium, the ECB must liaise with a wide range of EU and national authorities entrusted with supervisory and regulatory tasks.

To avoid excessively tightening the horizontal relationships between these authorities, the SSM Regulation (SSMR)[3] relies on a series of petitions of principle. According to Article 3 SSMR, 'the ECB shall cooperate closely with EBA, ESMA, EIOPA and the European Systemic Risk Board (ESRB), and the other authorities which form part of the ESFS, which ensure an adequate level of regulation and supervision in the Union' (para 1), 'shall carry out its tasks in accordance with this Regulation and without prejudice to the competence and the tasks of EBA, ESMA, EIOPA and the ESRB' (para 3), and 'shall cooperate closely with the authorities empowered to resolve credit institution s' (para 4). Within the SSM, both the ECB and National Competent Authorities are subject to a duty of cooperation in good faith and an obligation to exchange information (Article 6(2) SSMR). A wider look at the SSM Regulation reveals that the functioning of the SSM is essentially structured as a cooperation scheme.

Such provisions have a clear conceptual function[4] that nonetheless had a direct legal influence in guiding the cooperation between the EU bodies within the BU.

This contribution aims at investigating some cases of concrete applications of horizontal cooperation, in the context of supervision and regulation, between EU bodies in the BU, focusing on the relationships within the European System of Financial Supervision (ESFS), which comprises the three European Supervisory Authorities (ESAs), the European Systemic Risk Board (ESRB), and the national supervisors.[5] The analysis will highlight good institutional practices and question some overlap and misalignments between competences that might hinder the achievement of the objectives set out in the Treaties. Section II examines the distinction between supervisory and regulatory tasks in the banking field, revealing the existence of some weaknesses in the design of the legal framework. In particular, the cases of actions against non-performing loans (NPLs) (section II.2) and the EBA's guidelines on the acquisition of qualifying holdings (section II.3) suggest the need to rethink

[3] Council Regulation (EU) 1024/2013 of 15 October 2013 conferring specific tasks on the European Central Bank concerning policies relating to the prudential supervision of credit institutions [2013] OJ L287, 29.

[4] Eddy Wymeersch, 'The Single Supervisory Mechanism or "SSM". Part One of the Banking Union' (2014) 240 ECGI Law Working Paper 26.

[5] The cooperation among resolution authorities is examined in by Edoardo Rulli, in ch 14 of this volume.

the Lamfalussy architecture of the BU. Section III explores the distribution of competences for the macroprudential supervision. After having examined the intricate allocation of tasks and macroprudential toolkits (section III.1), the analysis shows that cooperation mechanisms rest on fragile foundations, such as soft law measures, governance structures, and peer pressure, that proved to be effective during the pandemic but raise the question of ensuring a higher degree of centralization in the long term (section III.2).

II Splitting microprudential supervision as regulation and control on sound and prudent management of banking activity

The SSMR proceeds from an apparently clear distinction between 'regulation' and 'supervision'. These functions are, theoretically, intended as different tasks that must be carried out by different subjects.[6] However, the actual discharge of regulatory and supervisory tasks is not straightforward and, despite the petition of principle in recital 31 and Article 3 SSMR, the relationships between ECB and EBA have frequently been problematic, especially before the pandemic.[7]

This model is unique, since it has not been experienced by the legislation of any country so far. In some cases, as in the UK, the word 'regulation' is even used as a synonym for 'supervision'.

As pointed out in several provisions of the SSMR, the regulation of banks remains essentially a national competence, implementing EU rules. At EU level, regulatory powers are typically exercised by the Union legislator, with the ECB enjoying a residual competence, for example where there are still options and discretions. According to Article 4(3) SSMR, the ECB shall apply all relevant Union law, and where this Union Law is composed of directives, the national legislation transposing those directives. Where the relevant Union law is composed of regulations, and where those regulations explicitly grant a certain margin of discretion for Member States (MSs), the ECB shall also apply the national legislation exercising these options. To that effect, the ECB shall adopt guidelines and recommendations, and take decisions subject to and in compliance with the relevant Union law. Moreover, the ECB shall be

[6] Eddy Wymeersch, 'The European Banking Union, a First Analysis' (2012) Financial Law Institute Working Paper Series WP 2012-07.

[7] Alexander Kern, 'European Banking Union: Effectiveness, Impact and Future Challenges' in Busch and Ferrarini (n 1) 44.

subject to binding EBA regulatory and implementing standards adopted by the Commission.

From a strict interpretation of Article 4(3) SSMR, one may conclude that the ECB has no regulatory powers over banking activities, but a systemic overview of the current legal framework contradicts this conclusion. In carrying out its supervisory tasks, the ECB shall apply EU laws and national provisions implementing EU rules. The ECB may adopt regulations 'only to the extent necessary to organise or specify the modalities for the carrying out of those tasks' (Article 4(3) SSMR). It is, therefore, a regulatory power limited to 'self-organization' for the exercise of ECB powers. The most important example of 'self-organization' rules is the SSM Framework Regulation.[8] The SSM Framework Regulation has been adopted in consultation with national authorities, 'to organise the practical arrangements' relating to the cooperation within the SSM (Article 6(7)).

The picture is less clear if we continue reading the same Article 4(3) SSMR, where it is stated that, 'before adopting a regulation, the ECB shall conduct open public consultations and analyse the potential related costs and benefits'. The need for a public consultation, normally required for the adoption of rules in the proper sense, ie provisions binding on third parties, suggests that, in the remit of the ECB, there are also regulatory powers. Typically, the Union legislator would, in most cases, enjoy regulatory powers under Articles 53, 62, and 114 of the Treaty on the Functioning of the European Union (TFEU). The residual regulatory competence of the ECB seems, thus, to be left to exercising options and discretion, which, however, depending on the circumstances, can be particularly broad. Since the first part of Article 4(3) SSMR does not seem to explicitly assign such powers to the ECB, except to the extent necessary to self-organize the supervisory function, it is unclear what the source of these powers is. Furthermore, Article 4(3) SSMR allows the ECB to exercise regulatory powers in two ways.

First, regarding prudential requirements for credit institutions, Union law provides for options and discretions that competent authorities may exercise. Considering that the ECB is the competent authority for the purpose of carrying out microprudential supervision on significant credit institutions, we should conclude that, in performing this task, the ECB enjoys all the powers and obligations that National Competent Authorities have under relevant

[8] Regulation (EU) 468/2014 of the European Central Bank of 16 April 2014 establishing the framework for cooperation within the Single Supervisory Mechanism between the European Central Bank and National Competent Authorities and with national designated authorities (SSM Framework Regulation) [2014] OJ L141.

Union law. In particular, the ECB has the power to exercise the options and discretions available according to the Union law. Following this interpretation, the ECB issued a regulation on 14 March 2016 on the exercise of options and discretions available in Union law;[9] this was significantly amended in 2022.[10] The goal of this legal act is to ensure the consistent application of prudential requirements for credit institutions within the MSs participating in the SSM.

Second, notwithstanding the non-binding nature of the regulatory acts that the ECB can adopt, their aptitude to shape the regulatory environment for banks should not be underestimated. Over the past 10 years, the ECB has issued a significant number of non-binding regulatory acts, for different purposes and under different labels: guidelines, supervisory expectations, and 'letters to managers'. The most relevant examples are the *Guide to Fit and Proper Assessment* (2021),[11] the NPL supervisory expectations (2018),[12] and the recommendation inviting banks to avoid dividend distributions during the pandemic (2020).[13] These examples show that soft law measures can have a significant capacity to influence or even direct the banks' management. As the Court of Justice of the European Union (CJEU) pointed out with regard to EBA guidelines,[14] a non-binding legal act can, nonetheless, produce legal effects. Leaving aside the specific question addressed in the decision on the reviewability of non-binding acts under Article 263 TFEU, it is relevant to point out that the CJEU affirmed its jurisdiction to assess their legality on a preliminary reference. The CJEU clarified that the ability to affect the rights of third parties depends on the content of the act, the wording used, the context, and the perception by the addressees. We can add to the ECJ reasoning that the capacity of those acts to affect the rights of third parties in the banking context also depends on the position of 'moral authority' that the supervisory authority

[9] Regulation (EU) 2016/445 of the European Central Bank of 14 March 2016 on the exercise of options and discretions available in Union law [2016] OJ L78.

[10] The recitals of the regulation specify the legal source. Indeed, the ECB is empowered to adopt regulations in accordance with art 132 of the Treaty on the Functioning of the European Union. In addition, art 132 of the Treaty and art 34 of the Statute of the European System of Central Banks and of the European Central Bank (hereinafter the 'Statute of the ESCB'), by referring to art 25.2 of the Statute of the ESCB, entrust the ECB with regulatory powers to the extent necessary to implement specific tasks concerning policies relating to the prudential supervision of credit institutions.

[11] Available at https://www.bankingsupervision.europa.eu/ecb/pub/pdf/ssm.fit_and_proper_guide_update202112~d66f230eca.en.pdf, accessed 14 May 2026.

[12] Available at https://www.bankingsupervision.europa.eu/ecb/pub/pdf/ssm.npl_addendum_201803.en.pdf, accessed 14 May 2026.

[13] Available at https://www.bankingsupervision.europa.eu/press/publications/letterstobanks/shared/pdf/2020/ssm.2020_recommendation_on_dividend_distribution_policies.en.pdf, accessed 14 May 2026.

[14] Case 911/19 *Fédération bancaire française (FBF) v Autorité de contrôle prudentiel et de résolution (ACPR)* [2021], ECLI:EU:C:2021:599.

has vis-à-vis a supervised entity. Peer pressure and the desire to maintain regulatory cohesion within the EU can reinforce the authority of European supervisors, as deviations from EU-wide standards can lead to reputational risks for national regulators.

Given the above, we can conclude that, while not benefitting from the formal conferral of regulatory powers, the ECB can shape the regulatory framework for banks by other means.

1 Weaknesses in the current legal framework having regard to the distribution of competences in regulating banks

A rigid separation between regulation and supervision can endanger the proper functioning of the SSM. Despite the progress in the harmonization process, the differences between rules and supervisory approaches between MSs remain quite significant. Up to now, such differences have mainly been due to the margin of discretion that MSs enjoyed in transposing EU directives. On this issue, the European legislation on capital requirements made substantial progress. Back in 2013, the CRD-CRR IV package replaced the Capital Requirements Directive with two different legislative instruments: a directive governing access to deposit-taking activities (CRD)[15] and a regulation establishing the prudential requirements (CRR).[16] The direct applicability of the CRR contributes to reducing the divergences between European legal systems, although it still leaves some options to MSs in its implementation. However, as demonstrated by some studies and research reports, different authorities in different EU jurisdictions can still follow different approaches to performing their supervisory duties.[17]

The harmonization of national approaches to supervision finds a further obstacle in the potential use of such margin of discretion to protect the primacy of national interests. There are various reasons for such resistance to change. In some cases, governments want to protect the competitiveness of their national intermediaries and internal market; in some other cases, the

[15] Directive 2013/36/EU of the European Parliament and of the Council of 26 June 2013 on access to the activity of credit institutions and the prudential supervision of credit institutions and investment firms, amending Directive 2002/87/EC and repealing Directives 2006/48/EC and 2006/49/EC [2013] OJ L176.

[16] Regulation (EU) 575/2013 of the European Parliament and of the Council of 26 June 2013 on prudential requirements for credit institutions and investment firms and amending Regulation (EU) No 648/2012 [2013] OJ L176.

[17] Pierre Schammo, 'Institutional Change in the Banking Union: The Case of the Single Supervisory Mechanism' (2021) 40 Yearbook of European Law 265–309.

conservative approach refers to the national regulatory framework, also given the constitutional limits, and traditional administrative culture. The different approaches to supervision led to regulatory arbitrage, giving a competitive advantage to intermediaries established in countries with a 'light-touch approach' to banking supervision.[18]

The regulatory discrepancies can impact on the correct functioning of the SSM. The ECB may find difficulties in adopting common supervisory standards due to the legislative constraint to implement the 'national rules'. This could, in turn, undermine the ECB's capacity to carry out its task and comply with one of the key principles stated in the first provisions of the SSMR.[19] Moreover, different supervisory approaches could hinder the ECB's oversight of cross-border groups.[20]

Can the EBA be the panacea for the harmonization of regulatory and supervisory approaches? Certainly, the EBA contribution to the Single Rulebook plays an important role in creating common standards, but also at a price of two counter-effects. Firstly, the proliferation of legal sources and rules cause regulated entities an increasing difficulty in the actual knowledge of the legal framework they must comply with. Secondly, the level of details reduces the discretion of supervisory authorities (even of the ECB) to adapt to individual cases. The following sections describe two cases highlighting the weaknesses embedded in the current legal framework.

2 Between flexibility and democratic legitimacy: The case of ECB Supervisory expectation for NPLs

The outbreak of the global financial crisis rose awareness in international and European authorities of the need to develop a common strategy to deal with the massive, sprawling deterioration of financial institutions' principal assets and the unprecedented increase in NPLs in banks' balance sheets. The strategy to tackle the NPLs issue showed a clear example of the consequences of multiple bodies exercising regulatory powers, thus giving rise to a complex and inflexible system of rules.

[18] Financial Services Authority, *A Regulatory Response to the Global Financial Crisis* (FSA 2009).

[19] The ECB tasks were built upon the idea that it has a 'duty of care for the unity and integrity of the internal market based on equal treatment of credit institutions with a view to preventing regulatory arbitrage' (art 1(1) SSMR).

[20] Luigi Chiarella and Guido Ferrarini, 'Common Banking Supervision in the Eurozone: Strengths and Weaknesses' (2013) 223 ECGI Law Working Paper.

In 2013, the EBA, as part of its role to foster convergence within the EU on a common system of supervisory reporting on loan quality, established uniform criteria to define non-performing exposures (NPEs), in its 'Implementing Technical Standards (ITS) on Forbearance and Non-Performing Exposures'.[21] NPEs are broadly defined and include NPLs. This framework was then implemented by the ECB in its role within the SSM. In 2017, the ECB introduced a uniform European framework of provisioning rules for NPLs, with a guidance addendum concerning the minimum coverage of NPLs,[22] followed by the publication of the final text on 15 March 2018.[23] In 2019, the European Parliament and the Council approved an amendment of the CRR containing rules on minimum loss coverage of NPLs, aligning with the ECB expectations to establish a detailed calendar provisioning.[24]

With such an approach, the European Parliament seems to reverse the four-level system established by the Lamfalussy regulatory hierarchy. Rather than setting out framework principles, level 1 regulation prescribes technical, detailed rules, which should be better placed at level 2.

What lesson we can draw from this case?

Establishing detailed rules on supervisory provisions in the level 1 regulation (amending the CRR in April 2019) can hinder a prompt and flexible reaction from supervisory authorities to an unexpected event. The rules outlined in the ECB addendum only imply an 'act or explain' mechanism, meaning that, during the supervisory dialogue in the context of the Supervisory Review and Evaluation Process (SREP), significant institutions are requested to justify any divergence from the prudential provisioning expectations outlined in the addendum. Given the specific circumstances, the Joint Supervisory Team (JST) in charge may evaluate that the coverage provided by the individual credit institution is not sufficient to cover the expected credit risk, and thus impose the adoption of 'Pillar 2' measures. This approach allows authorities to tailor

[21] EBA Final Draft Implementing Technical Standards on Supervisory reporting on forbearance and non-performing exposures under Article 99(4) of Regulation (EU) No 575/2013, EBA/ITS/2013/03/rev1, 24/07/2014.

[22] European Central Bank, 'Addendum to the ECB Guidance to Banks on Nonperforming Loans: Prudential Provisioning Backstop for Non-performing Exposures', October 2017.

[23] European Central Bank, 'Addendum to the ECB Guidance to Banks on Nonperforming Loans: Supervisory Expectations for Prudential Provisioning of Non-performing Exposures', March 2018. The Addendum only applies to significant euro-area banks and specifies quantitative supervisory expectations concerning the minimum level of prudential provisions for new NPLs (from 2018 onwards).

[24] Regulation (EU) 2019/876 of the European Parliament and of the Council of 20 May 2019 amending Regulation (EU) No 575/2013 as regards the leverage ratio, the net stable funding ratio, requirements for own funds and eligible liabilities, counterparty credit risk, market risk, exposures to central counterparties, exposures to collective investment undertakings, large exposures, reporting and disclosure requirements, and Regulation (EU) No 648/2012 [2019] OJ L150.

supervisory measures to the specific conditions of each bank. On the contrary, minimum legal coverage levels for loans, established in 2019 with the amendments to CRR, lack any flexibility in responding to bank-specific conditions.[25]

The NPLs' prudential regulation shows that the legislative instrument is not suitable to supervise banking activity in times of uncertainty.

This case shows the difficulties in reconciling two opposing needs: on the one hand, the need to have flexible rules that allow supervisors to adapt to the evolution of the macroeconomic scenario, as well as possible changes in the financial situation of individual intermediaries; on the other hand, the need for supervisory rules, given their policy implications, to be the result of a democratic debate.

3 EBA's guidelines and national laws: A complicated puzzle

The EBA's guidelines are not legally binding for national authorities, nor for the ECB. It is a case of a 'comply or explain' mechanism applied to interinstitutional relationships.

The soft law nature of this legal source raises the question on possible divergences between the EBA's guidelines and national law. This is the case of a national law which, in virtue of the transposition of the CRD, already provided a detailed discipline on the same area covered by the EBA's guidelines, such as, for instance, the Italian law implementing the European discipline on acquisition of qualifying holdings. In this matter, the CRD establishes framework principles and the Joint ESAs' Guidelines 2016 provide implementing rules to favour the convergence of supervisory practices.[26] The Italian law transposing the CRD delegates some aspects of the discipline, including those covered by the EBA's guidelines, to Banca d'Italia (Italy's National Competent Authority). The ECB issued its guidelines to disclose to supervised entities the criteria that it will follow in granting the authorization to acquire a qualifying holding.[27]

In the event that national law deviated from the EBA guidelines, the ECB, as the competent authority to grant the authorization, would find itself in an

[25] Ignazio Angeloni, 'Non-Performing Loans: An Old Problem in a New Situation' (2021) European Economy—Banks, Regulation, and the Real Sector 107 ff.

[26] Joint Guidelines on the prudential assessment of acquisitions and increases of qualifying holdings in the financial sector, 20 December 2016, JC/GL/2016/01. Available at https://www.esma.europa.eu/sites/default/files/library/jc_gl_2016_01_joint_guidelines_on_prudential_assessment_of_acquisitions_and_increases_of_qualifying_holdings_-_final.pdf, accessed 14 May 2026.

[27] ECB, 'Guide on Qualifying Holding Procedures', September 2022. Available at https://www.bankingsupervision.europa.eu/legalframework/publiccons/pdf/qh_guide/ssm.pubcon202209_qualifying_holding_guide.en.pdf, accessed14 May 2026.

awkward situation. According to Article 4 SSMR, the ECB must apply national law, including provisions, approved by national authorities, implementing national law. In the event that national law establishes rules that deviate from the provisions contained in the EBA guidelines, the ECB must apply the former.

Thus, an intricate system of interlinks between European and national standards that requires a European institution, such as the ECB, to adopt non-uniform actions within the Single Market poses some significant challenges to two cornerstones of the EU and of the BU: the principle of the level playing field/uniform application, and the principle of equal treatment.

4 The need to rethink the Lamfalussy regulatory architecture of the Banking Union

These examples highlight three weaknesses in the current regulatory framework: (i) the lack of flexibility, which limits the capacity of supervisory authorities to adapt their approach to any substantial change in the economic environment, and to specific situations of certain supervised entities; (ii) the legal uncertainty, due to possible overlap between regulatory acts coming from different public bodies; and (iii) the increasing costs of compliance for regulated entities, given the proliferation of rules and legal sources.

Could the expansion of the 'formal' regulatory powers of the ECB, within the SSM framework, be a viable solution to having a 'single' system of rules, at least at the euro-area level? Two clear benefits would arise from this expansion of regulatory powers: it would increase the flexibility of the rules, while also preserving the uniformity of the legal framework within the euro area. This solution would also align the European regulatory architecture with that of the Anglo-Saxon system. Indeed, the Bank of England, being the supervisory authority (although through a separate department, the Prudential Regulatory Authority), enjoys large discretionary regulatory powers. In the US, the Federal Reserve Board carries out both supervisory and regulatory responsibilities over a variety of financial institutions.

However, there are some critical outcomes. The distribution of regulatory tasks between the ECB and the EBA should be clearly defined, to avoid the risk of the latter becoming a redundant authority. As the competent authority for significant institutions, the ECB should enjoy at least the same 'formal' regulatory powers as those assigned to national authorities, namely the exercise of options and discretions provided by the first-level legislation. At the same time, it should not be ignored that the expansion of the regulatory capacity of the

ECB could potentially unbalance the position of strength between the EBA and the ECB. To this end, the conferral to the ECB of additional regulatory powers would have to be rebalanced by increasing the scrutiny over its decisions. For this reason, this reshuffling of competence must be accompanied by a rigorous system of checks and balances, which would comprise an increasing role for the ECB's accountability towards the Parliament, and for the judicial review of the exercise of administrative discretionary power. In any case, this proposal should be accompanied by a reform of the European regulatory architecture, aiming at simplifying the current system of prudential regulation, thus reducing the burden costs on regulated entities.

III The multilayered institutional architecture of macroprudential supervision

The area of macroprudential supervision in the BU offers another sound example of how horizontal relationships between EU bodies can be hindered by an intricate overlapping of competences.

Differently from other risks that affect financial institutions, systemic risk is particularly hard to measure and address, given its peculiar characteristics, namely the pro-cyclicality, the spillover effect, and the correlation between same exposures for different institutions.[28] The typical dimension of policies that aim at preventing and managing systemic risk would, theoretically, suggest a concentration of powers on cross-border authorities, to overcome potential lack of uniformity in national responses.[29]

Contrary to the expectations, the institutional framework of macroprudential supervision in the EU is largely fragmented, given the number of authorities involved in this complex architecture and the different mandate that each authority is entrusted with. Over time, this allocation of tasks has been at the core of tensions between the ECB and MSs regarding the exercise of primary competences on the use of macroprudential tools. A quick look over the legal framework suggests that, if not supported by a well-grounded institutional

[28] Ignazio Visco, 'Key Issues for the Success of Macroprudential Policies' (Speech, Bank of Korea–Bank for International Settlements (BOK–BIS) Conference on Macroprudential Regulation and Policy, Seoul, 18 January 2011).

[29] Alexander H Türk, 'European Banking Union and Its Relations with European Union Institutions' in Mario P Chiti and Vittorio Santoro (eds), *The Palgrave Handbook of European Banking Union Law* (Palgrave Macmillan, 2019) 46. For support of a stronger role for the ECB in macroprudential supervision, see André Sapir, 'Europe's Macroprudential Policy Framework in Light of the Banking Union' in Dirk Schoenmaker (ed), *Macroprudentialism, VoxEU eBook* (CEPR 2014) 161–70.

coordination, this fragmentation might result in material divergences of policies, thus jeopardizing the effectiveness of macroprudential measures and, in turn, endangering financial stability.[30] It is, then, worth investigating what the coordination mechanisms are between the different authorities involved in macroprudential supervision, and at which layer such interactions take place.

The coexistence of multiple bodies that share responsibilities for the oversight of systemic risk was among the initial proposals suggested by the *de Larosière Report* (2009),[31] which called, on the one hand, for the establishment of a European System of Financial Supervision (ESFS) and, on the other hand, for the creation of a new entity, the European Systemic Risk Council (ESRC). While maintaining the responsibility for implementing macroprudential policies at the level of MSs, the Report suggested that this new entity should be entrusted with the responsibility of impulse and coordination of national macroprudential policies, and should remain independent from the ECB. The architecture of macroprudential supervision suggested by *de Larosière Report* has been adopted by Regulation (EU) 1092/2010.[32]

The *de Larosière Report* reflects a widespread change of sensibility in the last two decades towards the role played by macroprudential policies in banking and financial institutions supervision. Since Basel III, capital and liquidity requirements have almost exclusively been intended to have a microprudential nature;[33] building on the experience of the global economic crises (2007–08), the new legislative framework intended to operationalize macroprudential tools at the international level.[34]

The institutional design for the oversight of the systemic risk follows a tripartite architecture which involves an active role for the ECB, the ESFS, and the national authorities. The major responsibilities are assigned to the latter,[35]

[30] Piergiorgio Alessandri and Fabio Panetta, 'The Coordination of Micro and Macro-Prudential Supervision in Europe' (2015) 3 European Economy 113 ff. Further, on the tension between financial stability and integration, see Pedro Gustavo Teixeira, *The Legal History of the European Banking Union* (Bloomsbury Publishing PLC 2020) 170 ff.

[31] Commission, 'Report of the High-level Expert Group on financial supervision in the EU, Chaired by Jaques de Larosière', 25 February 2009, 11 ff.

[32] Regulation (EU) 1092/2010 of the European Parliament and of the Council of 24 November 2010 on European Union macro-prudential oversight of the financial system and establishing a European Systemic Risk Board [2010] OJ L331.

[33] Rosa M Lastra, 'Multilevel Governance in Banking Regulation' in Chiti and Santoro (n 29) 11: 'Basel 2 was about micro-prudential supervision and did not address macro-prudential risks, the unexpressed assumption being that if financial institutions are individually sound, then the financial system as a whole will be sound.'

[34] Andrew Backer, 'The New Political Economy of the Macroprudential Ideational Shift' (2012) 18(1) New Political Economy 112–139; Luca Amorello, *Macroprudential Banking Supervision & Monetary Policy: Legal Interaction in the European Union* (Palgrave Macmillan 2018) 48 ff.

[35] The sole competence of NCAs/MSs for macroprudential supervisory tasks has been reiterated by the ECB in an advisory letter concerning 'Additional clarification regarding the ECB's competence to exercise supervisory powers granted under national law' (SSM/2017/0140 - 31 March 2017).

following the creation of national macroprudential authorities (NMAs), as recommended by the newly created European body.[36] According to the ESRB, specialized authorities at the national level should be entrusted with the tasks of identifying, monitoring, and assessing systemic risks, together with additional competences of implementing policies for their prevention and mitigation. MSs can either create an ad hoc authority or assign the role of NMA to an already existing National Competent Authority (NCA) or a national designated authority (NDA), which were established for the implementation of macroprudential policies according to the CRR/CRD IV package. The possibility to confer such competences on a plethora of authorities makes clear that the national macroprudential layer can be particularly heterogeneous.[37] According to Article 5(1) SSMR, NCAs and NDAs can apply capital buffers requirements and other measures to address systemic or macroprudential risk 'whenever appropriate or deemed required'.[38]

1 Decentralization and coordination mechanisms in the legal framework

These few remarks make it quite clear that the decentralization of the macroprudential supervision requires a strong coordination role by EU institutions, to ensure the effectiveness of systemic risk's prevision strategies. However, macroprudential policies largely fall outside the scope of the SSM framework, thus tightening the margin of intervention of the ECB in this area.[39]

The main coordination mechanisms rely on streams of information between EU bodies, which are based on a legal obligation for national authorities to notify the application of a macroprudential measure to the ECB and the

[36] ESRB recommendation of 22 December 2011 on the macro-prudential mandate of national authorities, ESRB/2011/3, sub Rec B.3. (2012/C41/01).

[37] The choice for a separated or integrated model mainly depends on the degree of interaction that each MS wants to promote between macroprudential tasks and monetary policies: see Amorello (n 34) 280–81. For a distinction between different models, see International Monetary Fund, 'Macroprudential Policy: An Organizing Framework', IMF Policy Paper, 2011.

[38] Thierry Tressel and Jianping Zhou, 'Macroprudential Oversight and the Role of the European Systemic Risk Board' in Charles Enoch and others (eds), *From Fragmentation to Financial Integration in Europe* (International Monetary Fund 2014) 380 ff.

[39] The principles for such coordination are outlined in recital 24 and art 5 SSMR. According to Raffaele D'Ambrosio (ed), 'Law and Practice of the Banking Union and of its Governing Institutions (Cases and Materials)' in *Quaderni di Ricerca Giuridica della Consulenza Legale* (Banca d'Italia 2020) 90–91, 'The Recital seems to refer to the ESRB Regulation and to the multilateral coordination procedures therein for the adoption of macro-prudential tools, whilst coordination procedures under Article 5 SSMR are on a bilateral basis between the national authorities and the ECB.'

ESRB.[40] According to Article 5(1) SSMR, this notification should take place at least ten days before taking such decision, to allow the ECB to raise any concern or to ask for additional justification, for instance, given possible conflicts with financial or price stability goals.[41] National authorities are not bound by the ECB's request, except for a general obligation to give it 'duly consideration'. The notification to the ESRB also has the aim of allowing a certain degree of consistency between national macroprudential policies, especially by recommending the reciprocation of the same or an equivalent measure to one taken by an activating MS.[42] Given the nature of this body, the reciprocity recommendations are not binding for the addressees, which are only subject to a 'comply-or-explain' mechanism.[43]

Besides the right to object, the ECB retains additional parallel and sequential competences for a smooth conduct of macroprudential policies.[44] Differently from the microprudential supervision, which presents a clear vertical structure,[45] the macroprudential supervision tends to follow a more horizontal and bottom-up approach,[46] with a few limited exceptions. The ECB's responsibilities to adjust policy stances adopted by individual national authorities, such as applying 'higher requirements for capital buffers' or 'more stringent measures aimed at addressing systemic or macroprudential risks' (Article 5(2) SSMR), or to intervene in the event of inaction, can frame the relationships with MSs in a more vertical way. The ECB exercises this margin for its supplementary role *ex officio* or following a request from a national authority (Article 5(3) SSMR).

[40] For instance, arts 129, 130, and 134 CRD V. See also Rec C of the ESRB Recommendation of 4 April 2013 on intermediate objectives and instruments of macroprudential policy, ESRB/2013/1.

[41] Johann C Bauerschmidt, 'Financial Stability as the Objective of the Banking Union' (2020) European Company and Financial Law Review 155–83.

[42] Recommendation of the European Systemic Risk Board of 15 December 2015 on the assessment of cross-border effects of and voluntary reciprocity for macroprudential policy measures (ESRB/2015/2).

[43] On the mandate of the ESRB, see Trude Myklebust, 'Form and Function of the ESRB: a Critical Analysis' in Mads Adnenas and Gudula Deipenbrock (eds), *Regulating and Supervising European Financial Markets: More Risks than Achievements* (Palgrave Macmillan 2016) 43 ff.

[44] Guido Ferrarini and Fabio Recine, 'The Single Rulebook and the SSM: Should the ECB Have More Say in Prudential Rule-Making?' in Danny Busch and Guido Ferrarini (eds), *European Banking Union* (OUP 2015) 149 ff. The exercise of such competences should be in line with the general clause of 'good faith' cooperation provided by art 3 SSMR: see Giuseppe Napoletano, 'Legal Aspects of Macroprudential Policy in the United States and in the European Union' in *Quaderni di Ricerca Giuridica della Consulenza Legale* (Banca d'Italia 2016) 185–97.

[45] Case T-122/15 *Landeskreditbank Baden-Württemberg—Förderbank v European Central Bank* [2017], ECLI:EU:T:2017:337.

[46] Though the micro- and macro-prudential competences should not be seen as fully separated competences, since these supervisory functions coordinate and complement each other through a constant exchange of data and information. The impact of systemic risk and macroprudential factors is taken into account in supervisory priorities, operational planning, and the SREP process. In turn, the results of microprudential analyses provide an important basis for understanding the various risk factors on the financial system: Raffaella Dagostino, *Vigilanza bancaria europea e stabilità sistemica* (Edizioni Scientifiche Italiane 2023) 151 ff.

In such cases, the MS affected by the macroprudential measure has a right to object analogous to the one foreseen by Article 5(1) SSMR, which is again not binding for the activating authority.

Finally, the ESAs also hold some competences in overseeing macroprudential risk within the area of their supervisory remit, both indirectly—by being part of the ESRB General Board—and directly. The ESFS is, firstly, playing a fundamental role as the main channel of communication between the bodies in the BU and other relevant authorities at international level, and supervisory fora, including the International Organization of Securities Commissions (IOSCO), the Financial Stability Board (FSB), and the International Association of Insurance Supervisors (IAIS). The ESAs have the capacity to issue level 3 soft law instruments, recommendations, and warnings, but they can also exercise some more intrusive powers, such as temporarily prohibiting or restricting certain financial activities, imposing certain behaviour on financial institutions, or adopting binding decisions to supplement any omission from an NCA. With regard to the banking sector, the EBA is also called on to provide several opinions on macroprudential topics, the most relevant of which are those on the 'national flexibility measures' related to Article 458 CRR.[47]

2 Governance structure and peer pressure in horizontal relationships: The case of actions to mitigate the impact of Covid-19 in the BU

The overview on interactions between EU bodies in the context of macroprudential supervision highlights that, in this field, the legislative framework mainly relies on 'weak' coordination mechanisms, which consist of flows of information through notification obligations, non-binding opinions, and other soft law measures.[48] As shown, there are only limited cases in which national authorities suffer some constraints in taking unilateral measures to address systemic risk; in other words, the EU authorities involved in the macroprudential oversight can rarely exercise intrusive powers vis-à-vis MS to ensure financial integration purposes.

[47] When identifying changes of intensity of systemic or macroprudential risks in the financial system, NDAs can draft national legislative proposals to address this issue. The draft proposals must be submitted to the Parliament, the Council, the Commission, and the ESRB, and are subject to a right to reject from the Council, when required by the Commission.

[48] Eilis Ferran and Alexander Kern, 'Can Soft Law Bodies be Effective? Soft Systemic Risk Oversight Bodies and the Special Case of the European Systemic Risk Board' (2010) 6 European Law Review 751.

The fragmentation of tasks, alongside a decentralized conduct of these policies, might appear paradoxical, considering the cross-border nature of systemic risk's prevention and mitigation strategies. However, there is an additional channel that supports the convergence of supervisory measures taken by authorities that liaise horizontally, namely the governance dimension and the structure of the decision-making process within the EU bodies.

At national level, NCAs and NDAs are usually strongly coordinated with central banks, especially in cases in which the latter are also entrusted with macroprudential competence or assume joint responsibility together with a supervisory authority. By participating in the boards of the EU authorities entrusted with supervisory tasks, central banks are directly involved in most of the decision-making regarding the application of macro- and microprudential measures at European level. This holds true for the composition of the ECB Governing Council, the Supervisory Board in the SSM, and the ESRB General Board. In particular, members of the ESRB are representative of national macroprudential institutions and EU institutions related to financial stability. As has been observed, such close relationships with the European System of Central Banks represent the backbone of these new institutions, such as the ESRB.[49]

The European Commission is aware of the role that horizontal dialogue plays in ensuring consistency among supervisory measures. To this end, the founding regulations of the ESRB and the ESAs have recently been amended to reflect major changes that have occurred in the BU, and to adapt the existing governance accordingly. The amendments to the ESRB Regulation reinforce the effectiveness of the ECB's role as macroprudential supervisor by changing the composition of the Board and making the president of the ECB automatically chair of the ESRB,[50] thus strengthening the interdependency between these two bodies.[51]

The wide composition of the governing structure of macroprudential authorities, alongside the existence of multiple fora for a confrontation, not only favour the horizontal dialogue for the development of supervisory policies but also enhance the dynamic of peer pressure for a consistent implementation of measures to preserve financial stability.

[49] Visco (n 28).
[50] Regulation (EU) 2019/2176 of the European Parliament and the Council of 18 December 2019 amending Regulation (EU) No 1092/2010 on European Union macro-prudential oversight of the financial system and establishing a European Systemic Risk Board [2019] OJ L334.
[51] Amorello (n 34) 282.

A clear example of horizontal cooperation based on peer pressure has been provided by the issuing and implementation of recommendations on system-wide restraints on dividend payments, share buybacks, and other payouts. At the outbreak of the pandemic emergency, the EU developed a comprehensive strategy to preserve the confidence in financial markets by preventing spillover effects and ensuring the stability of the supply of credit to the real economy. The strategy consisted of a wide range of initiatives, from monetary policies to fiscal measures, and to other measures of a macro- and microprudential nature.[52] Among these, in the first quarter of 2020, the ECB,[53] the ESRB,[54] EIOPA,[55] and EBA[56] urged financial institutions under their supervisory remit to refrain from dividend distribution and other actions which have the effect of reducing the quantity and quality of their own funds.[57] The recommendations were further reiterated in December 2020, before being progressively withdrawn with the advancement of the vaccination campaign and the improvement of the macroprudential outlook. Despite the lack of binding effects, the level of national implementation of these precautionary measures proved to be significantly high. Evidence from the assessment of compliance with the ESRB's recommendations, which were those with the broadest scope of application, show a vast majority of full compliance during the first and the second periods of application of the recommendations.[58] The alignment of policies for the preservation of financial stability and the consistency in the implementation of

[52] Christos Gortsos and Georg Ringe (eds), *Pandemic Crisis and Financial Stability* (European Banking Institute 2020).

[53] Recommendation of the European Central Bank of 27 March 2020 on dividend distributions during the COVID-19 pandemic and repealing Recommendation ECB/2020/1 (ECB/2020/19), in OJ C102I.

[54] Recommendation of the European Systemic Risk Board of 27 May 2020 on restriction of distributions during the COVID-19 pandemic (ESRB/2020/7), in OJ C212/1.

[55] EIOPA statement on dividends distribution and variable remuneration policies in the context of COVID-19, 2 April 2020. Available at https://www.eiopa.europa.eu/publications/eiopa-statement-dividends-distribution-and-variable-remuneration-policies-context-covid-19_en, accessed 14 May 2026.

[56] EBA Statement on dividends distribution, share buybacks and variable remuneration, 31 March 2020, available at https://www.eba.europa.eu/sites/default/files/document_library/News%20and%20Press/Press%20Room/Press%20Releases/2020/EBA%20provides%20additional%20clarity%20on%20measures%20to%20mitigate%20the%20impact%20of%20COVID-19%20on%20the%20EU%20banking%20sector/Statement%20on%20dividends%20distribution%2C%20share%20buybacks%20and%20variable%20remuneration.pdf, accessed 14 May 2026.

[57] Antonella Sciarrone Alibrandi and Claudio Frigeni, 'Restrictions on Shareholder's Distribution in the COVID-19 Crisis: Insights on Corporate Purposes' in Gortsos and Ringe (n 52) 429 ff.

[58] See Summary Compliance Report, September 2022, Recommendation of the European Systemic Risk Board of 27 May 2020 on restriction of distributions during the COVID-19 pandemic (ESRB/2020/7), as amended by Recommendation of the European Systemic Risk Board of 15 December 2020 amending Recommendation ESRB/2020/7 on restriction of distributions during the COVID-19 pandemic (ESRB/2020/15), available online at https://www.esrb.europa.eu/pub/pdf/recommendations/esrb, accessed 14 May 2026.

those measures were, in this case, the result of peer pressure and moral suasion drivers, which disincentivized national authorities from regulatory arbitrage and opportunistic behaviour to favour their own national champions.

Still, it is worth asking whether the success of this coordination depended only on a contingent situation or on a more profound change in the interpretation of the inter-institutional horizontal dynamics between EU bodies.

IV Conclusion

In 2014, the former Member of the Executive Board of the ECB Yves Mersch compared the governance of the Euro area to

> a set of interlocking cogs wheels: they do not all need to be of similar size—that is, we do not necessarily need the same degree of centralisation in each area—but they need to all move in the same direction. If one cog moves in the other direction, the whole machine grinds to a halt.[59]

The well-functioning of the institutional architecture of the BU and its capacity to achieve the goals set out in the Treaties strongly depends on the interlinks and cooperation among all the authorities involved in this network. Horizontal relationships imply an unavoidable room for manoeuvre for each of these bodies, to orientate their actions according to their respective mandates. To avoid fragmentation without at same time giving up on flexibility, it is therefore essential to strike a delicate balance between centralization of competences to ensure the level playing field, on the one hand, and the margin to adapt strategies and actions to concrete situations, on the other.

Significant steps were taken during the first decade of the BU, whose process was strongly influenced by the occurrence of unprecedented crises, such as the sovereign debt, the rise in NPLs, the pandemic, and the increasing inflation due to geopolitical instability. Nevertheless, the overall picture of the European regulatory framework remains incomplete. The transfer of powers to the EU institutions is still limited to a few areas. Substantive integration has involved a significant number of MSs, but not all. This results in a multilayered system of integration, with European institutions and agencies having different scopes.

[59] Yves Mersch, 'Law, Money and Market: The Legal Dimension of Monetary Policy' (Speech at the Information Club Meeting, Luxembourg, 31 May 2014) https://www.ecb.europa.eu/press, accessed14 May 2026.

A significant number of disadvantages result from the incomplete puzzle described above. Firstly, overlapping competences can lead to legal uncertainty as to where the legal powers of the EU institutions and agencies lie. Furthermore, the multilayered system can lead to an overburdening of the addressees of legal acts.

Is good-faith and close cooperation between the different actors, as currently provided for in the legal framework, the optimal solution? This chapter showed that the answer to this question is not straightforward. A clearer allocation of tasks and a reduction of overlapping competences in line with what was suggested above would solve some structural weaknesses in the system, and would also reduce opportunistic behaviour of EU and national institutions in extending their competences.

5

The Application of National Law by the ECB

Daniela Jaros[*]

I Introduction

The Regulation on the Single Supervisory Mechanism (SSMR)[1] introduced a novelty in EU law, enabling an EU institution to directly apply national law (when such national law transposed EU directives or exercised options granted in regulations) in order to fulfil its tasks.[2] Many open questions have existed and continue to exist about this provision. However, 10 years after its introduction, the Court of Justice of the European Union (CJEU) has developed some principles on its meaning and use. With the Regulation establishing the Authority for Anti-Money Laundering and Countering the Financing of Terrorism[3] introducing a similar provision[4] enabling AMLA to make use of national law where it transposes directives, it is worth looking at the challenges Article 4 (3) SSMR entails, what answers have been provided by courts and policymakers so far, and which issues remain open.

The Single Supervisory Mechanism (SSM) was set up to guarantee the uniform application of material prudential requirements with regard to credit institutions across the euro area. It was meant to strengthen the single currency and the internal market.[5] These material requirements are set in European directives and regulations as well as in soft law, constituting together the

* The views expressed by the author are strictly personal and do not engage the institution for which she works.

[1] Regulation (EU) 1024/2013 of the Council of 15 October 2013 conferring specific tasks on the European Central Bank concerning policies relating to the prudential supervision of credit institutions [2013] OJ L287, p 63.

[2] Art 4(3), SSMR.

[3] Regulation (EU) 2024/1620 of the European Parliament and of the Council of 31 May 2024 establishing the Authority for Anti-Money Laundering and Countering the Financing of Terrorism [2024] OJ L1620 (AMLAR).

[4] Art 5(6), AMLAR.

[5] Recital 2, SSMR.

Daniela Jaros, *The Application of National Law by the ECB* In: *EU Banking Union*. Edited by: Jonathan Bauerschmidt, Raffaele D'Ambrosio, Diane Fromage, Daniela Jaros, and Paul Weismann, Oxford University Press. © Oxford University Press 2026. DOI: 10.1093/9780198949756.003.0006

so-called 'Single Rulebook'. A central part of the applicable framework, containing all market-access and governance provisions, as well as all suitability requirements for credit institutions' management, is governed by the Capital Requirements Directive (CRD),[6] which has to be transposed into national law before it can be applied. In the course of the legislative process leading up to the SSM Regulation, it therefore became clear that, in order to be effective, the European Central Bank (ECB) needed the possibility to apply national law transposing Union law directly. The original legislative proposals of the European Commission (COM) only contained a rather general possibility for the ECB to instruct National Competent Authorities[7] (NCAs) under its transitional provisions in Article 27(5).[8] However, the Council agreed to amend the original proposal of the COM by adding what are now recitals 34 and 35 and amending what are now Article 4(3) and Article 9(1), subparagraphs 2 and 3 SSMR.[9] The legal framework for the ECB to apply transposed Union law directly in order to fulfil its tasks was set.

Through the SSMR, which is based on Article 127(6) TFEU, the ECB was conferred specific tasks listed in Article 4(1) and (2) as well as Article 5(2) of the SSMR. These tasks can be summarized as tasks concerning microprudential supervision, meaning that credit institutions should be supervised in sticking to rules that ensure they have a solid capital and liquidity base, robust governance arrangements, and an adequate handling of risks. In addition to that, the ECB, in its role as banking supervisor, has limited macroprudential powers.[10]

The question of which areas fall under Article 4 SSMR and which do not has been discussed in case law,[11] policy guidance,[12] and literature.[13] The main

[6] Directive 2013/36/EU of the European Parliament and of the Council of 26 June 2013 on access to the activity of credit institutions and the prudential supervision of credit institutions [2013] OJ L176, p 338; most recently amended by Directive (EU) 2024/1619, OJ L1619, of the European Parliament and of the Council of 31 May 2024 amending Directive 2013/36/EU as regards supervisory powers, sanctions, third-country branches, and environmental, social and governance risks [2014] OJ L (CRD6).

[7] Defined in Art 2(2), SSMR.

[8] Proposal for a Council Regulation conferring specific tasks on the European Central Bank concerning policies relating to the prudential supervision of credit institutions, COM (2012) 0511 final.

[9] In the amendment proposal of the Council, the new recitals were numbered 26a and 26b, and what is now art 9 was art 8; see Council of the European Union (2012) 17812. At this stage, it should also be noted that recital 36 was not changed in the amended proposal, which means that, for sanctioning powers under art 18 SSMR, a different division of tasks between the ECB and NCAs applies.

[10] This chapter will only focus on the microprudential powers of the SSM. For the macroprudential ones, see the chapter by Ursula Hauser-Rethaller in this book.

[11] See below under section II in this chapter.

[12] European Central Bank, 'National powers exercised by the ECB' https://www.bankingsupervision.europa.eu/banking, accessed 1 September 2024.

[13] Klaus Lackhoff and Andreas Witte, 'Art. 4 SSMR Tasks conferred on the ECB' in Jens-Hindric Binder and others (eds), *Brussels Commentary: European Banking Union* (Beck Hart Nomos 2022); Giovanni Bassani, *The Legal Framework Applicable to the Single Supervisory Mechanism: Tapestry or Patchwork?* (Wolters Kluwer 2019); Filippo Annunziata and Thomaz de Arruda, 'The Corneli Case (T-502/19)' (2023) Weekend Edition 131 EU Law Live; Florin Coman-Funk and Fabian Amtenbrink,

question is whether Article 4(1) SSMR allows for a static or dynamic reading; in other words, how supervisory powers linked to prudential supervision but not listed explicitly in Article 4 and supervisory powers closely intertwined with non-harmonized areas of law (company law, insolvency law) should be treated. Several aspects have been clarified by the legislator: recital 28 of the SSMR makes clear that NCAs remain competent to supervise bodies which are not covered by the definition of credit institutions under Union law[14] but which are supervised as credit institutions under national law; to supervise credit institutions from third countries establishing a branch or providing cross-border services; to supervise credit institutions in relation to markets in financial instruments; and generally, with regard to the prevention of money laundering (AML) and terrorism financing and consumer protection. However, the legislator was not clear on whether Article 4(1) SSMR can include areas that are closely linked to the tasks conferred on the ECB. It also remained unclear whether Article 4(1) SSMR can include new tasks that were not there at the time of adoption of the SSMR.

Therefore, prior to asking the question of what law the ECB will apply in the fulfilment of its tasks, one first has to determine whether the law to be applied serves the fulfilment of a task conferred upon the ECB through Article 4 SSMR.[15] Once it has been established that the ECB is competent for a task, the ECB can act directly or indirectly, depending on the nature of the applicable law. Finally, this also determines which legal remedy can be used in front of which court.

II How dynamic is Article 4 SSMR?

In the early days of the SSM, it soon became clear that certain supervisory tasks are closely linked to prudential supervision but are not explicitly mentioned in EU law (neither in the list of tasks conferred on the ECB nor in the material

'On the Scope and Limits of the Application of National Law by the European Central Bank within the Single Supervisory Mechanism' (2018) 33(2) Banking & Finance Law Review 133–72; Concetta Brescia Morra and Filippo Annunziata, 'The Banking Union and the Decisions of the CJEU Towards a Complete Legal Order?' (*Economic Governance and EMU Scrutiny Unit*, 2024) https://www.europarl.europa.eu/RegData/etudes/IDAN/2024/760253/IPOL_IDA(2024)760253_EN.pdf, accessed 19 September 2024.

[14] Art 4(1)(1) Regulation (EU) 575/2013 of the European Parliament and of the Council of 26 June 2013 on prudential requirements for credit institutions and investment [2013] OJ L176, p 1 ('CRR').

[15] Due to the specificity of the division of tasks under art 5 SSMR, this chapter refers to the contribution of Ursula Hauser-Rethaller on these aspects.

requirements for credit institutions) and, therefore, are also not harmonized across Member States. The Supervisory Board of the SSM established, in 2016 and 2017, that the ECB was competent for tasks that are connected to its other prudential tasks, such as the approval of mergers and demergers, the approval of asset transfers and divestments, the approval of a significant institution's statutes, the approval of the appointment of key function holders, certain supervisory powers with regard to external auditors, and the approvals of outsourcing of activities or supervisory powers vis-à-vis a credit institution's shareholders.[16] This clarification of competence, and its public communication, enhanced legal certainty in the SSM. In this way, the ECB demonstrated that it considered itself competent for all matters of prudential supervision, or at least that it did not have a narrow understanding of its competences under Article 4 SSMR. On the contrary, its communication of the list of national powers could be seen as proving a rather dynamic understanding of Article 4 SSMR, which is also deemed to have been the intent of the legislator.[17]

In *VTB v Finanzmarktaufsicht*,[18] the Court had to deal with the question of what constituted a prudential power for the first time. In that case, it was discussed whether a supervisory power only available under national law was sufficiently linked to a prudential task of the ECB. The national provision scrutinized was the power to impose 'absorption interest' under Article 97(1)(4) of the Austrian Banking Law (Bankwesengesetz, or BWG) allowing the competent supervisory authority to absorb interest for a breach of large exposure limits stipulated in Article 395 of the Capital Requirements Regulation (CRR). The Austrian Financial Market Authority (Finanzmarktaufsicht, or FMA) claimed, based on national case law from the highest Austrian administrative court,[19] that absorption interest constituted a national, non-punitive economic control measure unconnected to the harmonized set of supervisory penalties and measures under Articles 64 and 65 CRD, and only aimed at recovering an economic advantage wrongly obtained as a result of the breach of a rule governing prudential supervision.[20] The FMA's claim was that absorption interest was no such supervisory measure, as it did not have a prudential

[16] For a complete list, see European Central Bank, 'National Powers Exercised by the ECB' https://www.bankingsupervision.europa.eu/banking/tasks/national_powers/html/index.en.html, accessed 1 September 2024.

[17] Recital 12, SSMR; Lackhoff and Witte (n 13) 46, para 15.

[18] Case C–52/17 *VTB Bank (Austria) AG v Finanzmarktaufsichtsbehörde*, ECLI:EU:C:2018:648.

[19] Case VwGH 96/17/0006, AT:VWGH:1999:1996170006.X02; Case VwGH 96/17/0359 AT:VWGH:2000:1996170359.X03; Case VwGH Ra 2017/02/0208, AT:VWGH:2018:RA2017020208.L01.

[20] *VTB Bank* (n 18), para 37.

purpose. Therefore, it deemed itself competent for issuing a decision absorbing interest for a large exposure breach vis-à-vis VTB, which was then a significant institution within the meaning of Article 6(4) SSMR, and therefore under the direct supervision of the ECB. That decision was appealed in front of a national court that referred the question of whether the classification of absorption interest as a purely national measure was correct to the CJEU. The CJEU held that 'absorption' interest provided for in Article 97(1)(4) of the BWG must be classified as an administrative measure within the meaning of Article 65(1) CRD,[21] and therefore as a measure of prudential banking supervision.

In the recent case *Anglo Austrian AAB AG, in liquidation v ECB*,[22] the Court again dealt with the question of what exactly prudential supervision entails, notably where prudential supervision closely interrelates with areas outside the scope of the SSM, such as AML. In this case, the ECB withdrew a banking licence and based its decision to a large extent on the violation of AML provisions. The General Court had dismissed the action, where the argument that the ECB had allegedly misapplied national law transposing the directive had already been made.[23] The applicants repeated the claim in front of the Court, where it was dismissed because of lack of substantiation. On substance, the Court confirmed, however, that:

> [i]t has been held that, although the Member States remain competent to implement the anti-money laundering and counter-terrorist financing provisions, as expressly provided for in recital 28 [SSMR], the ECB has exclusive competence to withdraw authorisation, for all credit institutions, irrespective of their size, even where such withdrawal is based, as in the present case, on the grounds set out in Article 67(1)(d) and (o) of the CRD IV Directive [including violations of AML legislation].[24]

Based on this, one can argue that prudential supervision—including the control of market entry and market exit of credit institutions within the SSM through licensing and withdrawal procedures—must always take into account all kinds of risk as soon as these risks do have a proven impact on the fulfilment of prudential requirements.

[21] ibid, para 42.
[22] Case T-797/19 *Anglo Austrian AAB AG, formerly Anglo Austrian AAB Bank AG and Belegging-Maatschappij 'Far-East' BV v European Central Bank*, ECLI:EU:T:2022:389.
[23] ibid, paras 29–38.
[24] Case T-712/15 *Crédit Mutuel Arkéa v European Central Bank*, ECLI:EU:T:2017:900, para 64.

Yet another dimension of the meaning and extent of 'prudential supervision' under the SSMR was discussed in the *Crédit Mutuel Arkéa v ECB* cases.[25] In a nutshell, the applicants argued in one of their claims that the ECB, within the SSM, did not have powers vis-à-vis a group whose central body was not a credit institution, referring to the definition of 'supervised group' under the SSM Framework Regulation, which defined 'supervised group' as consisting of supervised entities.[26] The General Court, confirmed by the Court, rejected this claim essentially based on the argument that the scope of the SSMR, namely prudential supervision of credit institutions, would be jeopardized if the ECB's powers were limited in this way. The relevant provisions on the definition of supervised group 'must be interpreted in the light of the legislature's intention to enable the ECB to have an overall picture of the risks likely to affect a credit institution and to avoid the fragmentation of prudential supervision between the ECB and national authorities'.[27]

Some of the areas the ECB considered itself competent for because of their close link with its prudential tasks, back in 2016 and 2017, have in the meantime been harmonized through the CRR3/CRD6 package published in June 2024,[28] notably the approval of mergers and demergers as well as asset transfers[29] and powers related to key function holders (including heads of internal control functions)[30] and outsourcing.[31] The fact that the legislator has now explicitly included these powers in the core prudential regulatory framework of CRR/CRD proves the ECB's original assessment and the direction taken by the CJEU in interpreting the scope of prudential supervision broadly right. It also gives the SSMR a forward-looking dimension, concluding that if existing powers that are harmonized at a later stage can be subsumed under Article 4 SSMR prior to their harmonization, this can also be valid for new powers that

[25] Case T-712/15 *Crédit Mutuel Arkéa v European Central Bank*, ECLI:EU:T:2017:900; Case T-52/16 *Crédit Mutuel Arkéa v European Central Bank*, ECLI:EU:T:2017:902; both appealed in Cases C-152/18 and C-153/18 *Crédit Mutuel Arkéa v European Central Bank*, ECLI:EU:C:2019:810.

[26] Art 2(21)(c), Regulation of the European Central Bank of 16 April 2014 establishing the framework for cooperation within the Single Supervisory Mechanism between the European Central Bank and National Competent Authorities and with national designated authorities (SSM Framework Regulation) [2014] OJ L141, p 1.

[27] Case T-712/15 *Crédit Mutuel Arkéa v European Central Bank*, ECLI:EU:T:2017:900, para 64.

[28] Directive (EU) 2024/1619 of the European Parliament and of the Council of 31 May 2024 amending Directive 2013/36/EU as regards supervisory powers, sanctions, third-country branches, and environmental, social and governance risks [2024] OJ L1619 (CRD6); Regulation (EU) 2024/1623 of the European Parliament and of the Council of 31 May 2024 amending Regulation (EU) No 575/2013 as regards requirements for credit risk, credit valuation adjustment risk, operational risk, market risk and the output floor [2024] OJ L1623 (CRR3).

[29] Art 27h–27l, CRD6; see also recital 9, which clearly establishes a prudential reason for these new powers.

[30] Art 91a, CRD6.

[31] Art 85, CRD6.

are linked to the prudential tasks of the SSM. In fact, the European legislator has attributed new tasks to the ECB in its role as prudential supervisor through new regulation, such as the Digital Operational Resilience Act (DORA),[32] while refraining from doing so in two other major legislative pieces with a potential impact on the prudential requirements for banks, notably the Market in Crypto Assets Act (MiCA)[33] and the Artificial Intelligence Act (AI Act).[34]

III What is the precise content of transposed EU law?

The application of transposed EU law, and thus national law, by a European institution was a novelty in EU law, introduced through Article 4(3) SSMR. Because it was without precedent, several aspects of it had to be defined and specified.[35] Does 'national law' refer to pure 'black-letter law' or does 'transposed EU law' come with a history of national interpretation, case law, and context? When does transposition end and national law start?[36] If directly applicable EU law and national law (transposing EU law) foresee similar provisions, can the ECB choose which to use? Some of these questions have been answered by now, while some are still awaiting further clarification.

As it has been—and, to some extent, still is—disputed whether and to what extent the ECB is bound by national case law that gives national law (transposing a directive) a specific meaning, the General Court ruled, in *Caisse régionale de crédit agricole mutuel Alpes Provence v ECB*, on different aspects of this question: it made clear that 'Article 4(3) [SSMR] necessarily requires the Court to assesses the legality of the contested decisions in the light of both Article 13(1) [CRD] and the second paragraph of Article L. 511-13 of the CMF [transposing the directive].'[37] The issue at stake was whether 'effective directors', according to French law, were correctly considered as 'executive directors' within the meaning of the CRD, given the fact that the ECB, in its

[32] Regulation (EU) 2022/2554 of the European Parliament and the Council of 14 December 2022 on digital operational resilience for the financial sector [2022] OJ L333, p 1; recitals 51 and 97.
[33] Regulation (EU) 2023/1114 of the European Parliament and of the Council of 31 May 2023 on markets in crypto-assets [2023] OJ L150, p 40.
[34] Regulation (EU) 2024/1689 the European Parliament and the Council of 13 June 2024 laying down harmonised rules on artificial intelligence [2024] OJ L1689.
[35] Andreas Witte, 'When Does National Law Transpose a Directive?' (ESCB Legal Conference, 2016), 247.
[36] Giovanni Bassani, 'The Centralisation of Prudential Supervision in the Euro Area: The Emergence of a New "Conventional Wisdom" and the Establishment of the SSM' (2020) 31(6) European Business Law Review 1001–22, 1014.
[37] Joined Cases T-133/16 to T-136/16 *Caisse régionale de crédit agricole mutuel Alpes Provence and Others v European Central Bank*, ECLI:EU:T:2018:219, para 49.

original decision, did not approve that the members of the management board in its supervisory functions should simultaneously be 'effective directors'. The French Conseil d'État confirmed that the ECB was correct, and the General Court stated that the national judgment was sufficient to establish the scope of the rules of national law the ECB was required to apply according to Article 4(3) SSMR. Furthermore, it made clear that, '[w]here the interpretation of a national law provision is at issue, it should be borne in mind that, according to settled case law, the scope of national laws, regulations or administrative provisions must be assessed in the light of the interpretation given to them by national courts.'[38]

A slightly different stance was taken by the General Court in the *Berlusconi II* cases[39] (*Berlusoni I*,[40] being on composite procedures, will be discussed in the section on remedies below). In these cases, the General Court set limits on the application of national law, in so far as it held that that the concept of acquisition of qualifying holdings, as defined by EU law (notably through the SSMR itself, and through the CRD), could not be given another meaning by national law, as claimed by the applicants.[41] In its view, 'a restrictive interpretation [according to national law] would have the effect of allowing the assessment procedure to be circumvented, thus removing certain methods of acquiring qualifying holdings from the supervision of the ECB and thus undermining those objectives'.[42] This is where the General Court started to draw limits on the application of national law under Article 4(3) SSMR. Upon appeal, the Court set aside the General Court's judgment on various grounds, but did not rule on this specific issue.[43] Advocate General Campos Sánchez-Bordona supported the General Court's take on this issue.[44]

In the meantime, the much-discussed[45] case *Corneli v ECB*[46] went in the opposite direction. There was, again, no interpretation of a national court to be followed, which is why the Court analysed in depth whether, in its view, the ECB had made incorrect use of national law by misinterpreting it, as claimed by the applicant. In a nutshell, the Court first recalled the settled case law on

[38] ibid, para 84.

[39] Case T–913/16 *Finanziaria d'investimento Fininvest SpA (Fininvest) and Silvio Berlusconi v European Central Bank*, ECLI:EU:T:2022:279, appealed in C–512/22 P and C-513/22 P *Fininvest v EZB u. a.*, ECLI:EU:C:2024:774.

[40] Case C–219/17 *Silvio Berlusconi and Finanziaria d'investimento Fininvest SpA (Fininvest) v Banca d'Italia and Istituto per la Vigilanza Sulle Assicurazioni (IVASS)*, ECLI:EU:C:2018:1023.

[41] *Finanziaria d'investimento Fininvest SpA (Fininvest) and Silvio Berlusconi* (n 39), paras 47 and 48.

[42] *Finanziaria d'investimento Fininvest SpA (Fininvest) and Silvio Berlusconi* (n 39), para 56.

[43] *Fininvest v ECB* (n 39), para 113.

[44] Opinion of the Advocate General Campos Sánchez-Bordona, ECLI:EU:C:2024:414, para 57.

[45] Annunziata and de Arruda (n 13).

[46] Case T–502/19 *Corneli v ECB*, ECLI:EU:T:2022:627.

the obligation to interpret national law in conformity with EU law,[47] before concluding that this obligation cannot serve as a basis for an interpretation which runs counter to the wording used in the national measure transposing the directive. It further stated that a national provision transposing EU law cannot have

> two distinct sources of obligations, namely EU law in its entirety, including directives, to which the national law transposing them should be added. . . . Furthermore, according to settled case law, a directive cannot of itself impose obligations on an individual and cannot therefore be relied on as such against an individual.[48]

The decision was appealed, and the CJEU did not uphold this argument.[49] The CJEU argued that the General Court had erred in law when concluding that the ECB had misapplied national law by allegedly interpreting it *contra legem*.[50] On Article 4(3) SSMR, the CJEU said, rather generally, that the ECB's 'application of national law is intended to respect the choices made by the national legislature within the framework established by the relevant provisions of EU law, regardless of whether they appear in regulations or directives'.[51]

A new dimension was opened up by the General Court, on the interpretation of national law by the ECB, in *BAWAG v ECB*[52] and *Sberbank v ECB*.[53] In these cases, the ECB had relied on national case law when applying the national provision on absorption interest (the same provision that had already been discussed in *VTB v Finanzmarktaufsicht*), and the General Court set limits on the 'principle of conforming interpretation' originally stipulated in *Caisse Régionale de crédit agricole mutuel Alpes Provence v ECB*. As written above, the Court classified what was thought to be a national measure without any link to EU law as a 'transposition' of EU law under Article 4(3) SSMR, in *VTB v Finanzmarktaufsicht*. This has not only proven correct the Court's rather broad understanding of the prudential tasks of the ECB, but also its broad interpretation of 'transposed EU law' under Article 4 (3) SSMR, even more so as the ECB would have the possibility to make use of national powers. In

47 ibid, paras 102–03.
48 ibid, paras 112–13.
49 Joined Cases C-777/22 P and C-789/22 P *ECB and European Commission v Corneli*, ECLI:EU:C:2025:580, paras 116–59.
50 ibid, paras 154–58.
51 ibid, para 133.
52 Case T-667/21 *BAWAG PSK v ECB*, ECLI:EU:T:2024:13.
53 Cases T-647/21 and T-99/22 *Sber Vermögensverwaltungs AG, vormals Sberbank Europe AG v ECB*, ECLI:EU:T:2024:127.

fact, Article 9(1), paragraph 3 SSMR foresees the possibility that, for the fulfilment of its tasks under Article 4 SSMR, the ECB instructs NCAs to make use of their national powers on behalf of the ECB, where those powers are not directly available to the ECB. Consequently, if the reading of 'transposition' under Article 4(3) SSMR is broad, the scope of application of Article 9(1), paragraph 3 SSMR becomes narrow. This is relevant in the context of available legal remedies, which will be discussed in the following section.

Given the precedent of *VTB v Finanzmarktaufsicht*, the question of competence in *BAWAG v ECB* and *Sberbank v ECB* when applying Article 97(1)(2) BWG,[54] now defined as a supervisory measure, appeared to be straightforward. However, it was again discussed whether it should be applied directly (Article 9(1), paragraph 2 SSMR) or indirectly (Article 9(1), paragraph 3 SSMR). The General Court stated that the expression 'under Union law' in Article 9(1), paragraph 2 SSMR has been interpreted as:

> including all the powers resulting from the legal framework established by a directive, whether they result from an obligation or power for the Member State to legislate, as opposed to the recognition by that directive of the power which the Member States enjoy under national law to provide for stricter provisions outside the framework of the regime established by that directive.[55]

Thus, it confirmed in both cases that the power to impose absorption interest was indeed such a power under Union law, and therefore the ECB was competent to apply that measure directly.[56]

However, as in *VTB v Finanzmarkaufsicht*, where the Court somewhat overruled national case law classifying the absorption interest measure as non-prudential, the General Court overruled further elements of the absorption interest measure established by national courts. In a nutshell, the wording of the absorption interest measure foresees that, save for two exceptions stipulated by law, the competent authority *has to* impose absorption interest, calculated according to a formula stipulated by law, once the limits have been breached, and it has been confirmed by the highest Austrian administrative court that the imposition of the measure is automatic.[57] The General Court

[54] Art 97 BWG was amended through Austrian Federal Act (BGBl) I No 98/2021, in order to comply with the CJEU ruling in *VTB v Finanzmarktaufsicht*; therefore, the numbering of the subparagraphs changed. In substance, art 97(1), no 2 BWG now covers what was previously covered in art 97(1), no 4 BWG.

[55] *BAWAG* (n 52), para 41.

[56] ibid, paras 45–46.

[57] ibid, paras 49–50; *Sberbank* (n 53), para 55 and the Austrian case law cited there, notably Case VwGH 97/17/0413, AT:VWGH:1999:1997170413.X01.

ruled that, if imposing absorption interest was a supervisory measure under Article 65(1) CRD, the circumstances of the case as stipulated in Article 70 CRD had to be considered, and that the ECB had incorrectly not done so when applying this measure automatically.

In *Sberbank v ECB*, the Court comes to the same conclusion, and makes explicit reference to *Caisse Régionale de crédit agricole mutuel Alpes Provence v ECB*: while the Court acknowledges that national courts' interpretation 'is sufficient to establish the scope of that national provision where it results in a finding that is compatible with the directive which it transposes',[58] it states that the 'situation is different, however, where the interpretation of the national courts does not make it possible to ensure the compatibility of national law with a directive',[59] and adds that, in such a situation:

> compliance with the principle of the primacy of EU law means that the national law has to be interpreted as far as possible in the light of the wording and the purpose of the directive transposed. While the obligation to refer to EU law when interpreting and applying the relevant rules of domestic law is limited by general principles of law and cannot serve as the basis for an interpretation of national law contra legem, the requirement to interpret national law in conformity with EU law entails the obligation for national courts to change established case law,[60] where necessary, if it is based on an interpretation of national law which is incompatible with the objectives of a directive.[61]

In *Sberbank v ECB*, it goes one step further, quoting from *Poplawski*[62] that a national provision may be disapplied by the General Court (and the national court) if it is contrary to EU law with direct effect. It does not elaborate further on the distinction between direct effect of regulations and directives, as it does not choose to base its judgment on an eventual direct effect of the relevant CRD provisions, and therefore does not explicitly enter into a broader reasoning on the direct effect of directives[63] in the context of the SSM; instead,

[58] *Sberbank* (n 53), para 58.
[59] ibid, para 59.
[60] The Austrian case law overruled by the General Court predates the *VTB*, *BAWAG*, and *Sberbank* decisions, and therefore refers to a situation where absorption interest was not yet classified as supervisory measure within the meaning of CRD VI.
[61] *Sberbank* (n 53), paras 60 and 61.
[62] Case C-573/17 *Poplawski*, ECLI:EU:C:2019:530.
[63] Bruno De Witte, 'Direct Effect, Primacy, and the Nature of the Legal Order' in Paul Craig and Gráinne de Burca (eds), *Evolution of EU Law* (OUP 2011).

it makes clear that, by overruling national case law, the provision can be interpreted in conformity with EU law as it stands.[64]

It is, of course, interesting to hypothesize what would have happened if the Court had recognized direct effect to the CRD provisions in these cases, as this would bring a new dimension to the discussion of direct effect of directives, especially as more recent case law seems to be a bit more open towards the much-discussed horizontal direct effect of directives.[65] As argued elsewhere, the cases where direct effect has been granted to directives at all are limited; however, the Court has, so far, never precluded an EU institution from relying on direct effect explicitly, as this issue has never been raised.[66] Ideas about further harmonizing the regulatory framework as directly applicable EU law in order to limit the application of transposed Union law through Article 4(3) SSMR, and therefore avoid getting into a situation where direct effect of the directive has to be argued, have so far not been realized; no content of the CRD was transferred to the CRR in the recent banking package of CRD6 and CRR3.

Finally, AG Ćapeta delivered an interesting Opinion in *Anglo Austrian AAB AG, in liquidation v ECB*, where the issue of national law was again at stake. The Court dismissed this claim because the applicant had not sufficiently specified it. However, AG Ćapeta elaborated more on this topic, having a reading of Article 4(3) SSM that is closer to *Caisse Regionale de crédit agricole mutuel Alpes Provence v ECB* than to the above-quoted cases of *Berlusoni II*, *VTB v Finanzmarktaufsicht*, *BAWAG*, and *Sberbank*. She stated that:

> In determining and applying national law within the SSM, EU Courts must therefore use their standard methodology of legal interpretation, while placing national law within its proper national context, which may differ from one Member State to another. It is only in that way that EU Courts can give effect to the regulatory diversity across the Member States endorsed by the SSM system, a consideration that guides the ECB in exercising its supervisory powers.[67]

[64] *Sberbank* (n 53), paras 62–83.

[65] De Witte (n 63) 335; *Poplawski* (n 62); Case C-261/20 *Thelen Technopark Berlin GmbH v MN*, ECLI:EU:C:2022:33.

[66] Paul Craig and Grainne De Burca, *EU Law* (6th edn, OUP, 2015) 200; Lena Boucon and Daniela Jaros, 'The Application of National Law by the European Central Bank within the EU Banking Union's Single Supervisory Mechanism: A New Mode of European Integration?' (2018) Special Issue, European Journal of Legal Studies 155, 172.

[67] Case C-579/22 P *Anglo Austrian AAB/EZB and Far East v ECB*, Opinion of AG Ćapeta, ECLI:EU:C:2024:296.

Given this opinion, it is noteworthy that the Court continuously referred to the applicable CRD provisions as the legal basis for the withdrawal, only marginally evoking the Austrian transposition of the CRD. This may be because the Austrian transposition of Article 18(f) CRD, with its reference to Article 67(1) CRD, is tricky.[68] Without elaborating on the necessity to interpret national law in line with EU law, and without invoking the possible direct effect of the directive explicitly, the ECB, the General Court, and also the CJEU relied heavily on the CRD (which clearly allows for withdrawals on grounds of violation of AML provisions under Article 67(1) CRD).

IV The application of national law and legal remedies

Some lessons on the availability of remedies in cases where the ECB issues decisions based on national law can be drawn from the above-mentioned case law.

The question of legal remedies is what makes a significant difference between the direct application of national powers through the ECB and an indirect application by way of instruction to NCAs. In *Berlusconi I*, the Court made clear that, where the ECB has exclusive decision-making power—as is the case for all its decisions in direct supervision:

> it falls to the EU Courts, by virtue of their exclusive jurisdiction to review the legality of EU acts on the basis of Article 263 TFEU . . . to rule on the legality of the final decision adopted by the EU institution at issue and to examine, in order to ensure effective judicial protection of the persons concerned, any defects vitiating the preparatory acts or the proposals of the national authorities that would be such as to affect the validity of that final decision.[69]

From what can be seen in the case law and administrative practice so far, the use of the ECB's indirect power to issue supervisory decisions (instruction) within the remit of its direct supervision under Article 9(1), paragraph 3 SSMR has been limited in the following ways: the ECB's interpretation of prudential tasks has been broad; the Court has confirmed such a broad understanding; national powers have been read as falling within the harmonized supervisory

[68] Art 67(1) o CRD cannot be bound in art 70(4) BWG, but in the Austrian Financial Markets Anti-Money Laundering Act (Finanzmarkt Geldwäschegesetz, or FM-GwG). However, the withdrawal was also based on Art 67(1)(d) CRD, which was clearly transposed in art 70(4) BWG.

[69] *Silvio Berlusconi and Finanziaria d'investimento Fininvest SpA (Fininvest)* (n 40), para 44.

framework of the CRD and, therefore, as being directly applicable for the ECB; and finally, the EU legislator has harmonized some of the remaining national powers with CRD6. Since national decisions based on ECB instructions would be appealed in national courts, it is not easy to assess, however, whether any decisions based on instructions have ever been discussed in national courts. They have never been discussed at the CJEU, though, as national courts would, in such cases, probably make a preliminary reference to the CJEU to refer the review of the legality of the instruction.[70] In addition, the question is whether, in addition to an appeal against the NCA decision in front of the national court, the ECB's instruction to the NCA as an ECB legal instrument (decision) could be challenged separately in front of the CJEU. It has been argued that the instruction could be subject to an action for annulment under Article 263 TFEU if the addressee of the decision is directly and individually concerned by it.[71] However, this question has, so far, never been raised in front of the CJEU in the context of the SSM.

As for appeals against ECB decisions based on national law, it was at first unclear whether the Court could review the ECB's application of national law, as it has never done so. In *Caisse régionale de crédit agricole mutuel Alpes Provence v ECB*, the General Court states clearly that Union courts may review a decision in the light of national law.[72] This is also underlined by AG Ćapeta in *Anglo Austrian AAB/EZB und Far East v ECB*, when she explains that national law can be treated by EU courts as law or as fact.[73] She points out that while, generally, national law is treated as a question of fact, it should, in her view, be treated as a question of law in the SSM, because that way the CJEU can review on appeal how the General Court applied the national law.[74]

[70] In the context of the SRM, the Court has dealt with a similar question in C–414/18 *Iccrea Banca*, ECLI:EU:C:2020:49. Relying on the principles established in *Berlusoni I* quoted above, it made clear that a preliminary ruling could not be used to make national courts rule on an issue outside their jurisdiction (para 33). However, the context is different, as an 'instruction' under art 9(1)(3) SSMR differs from the process foreseen for the adoption of decisions on *ex ante* contributions to the SRM, as such decisions are taken by the SRB and are merely notified by the NRA to the entity (paras 56–59).

[71] Georg Gruber, 'Art. 9 SSMR Supervisory and Investigatory Powers' in Jens-Hindric Binder and others (n 13).

[72] *Caisse régionale de crédit agricole mutuel Alpes Provence and Others* (n 37), para 49.

[73] *Anglo Austrian AAB/EZB*, Opinion of the AG (n 67), para 38, refererring to Miro Prek and Silvère Lefèvre, 'The EU Courts as "National" Courts: National Law in the EU Judicial Process' (2017) 54(2) Common Market Law Review 369.

[74] *Anglo Austrian AAB/EZB and Far East v ECB* (n 67), Opinion of the AG, para 46.

V Conclusion

What kind of conclusion can be drawn from this multifaceted case law on the application of national law by the ECB within the context of the SSM?

The Court has made clear that, while the ECB should strive to interpret national law in line with national case law, it must disapply such case law once that case law constitutes an obstacle to an EU-law-conforming interpretation of the national provisions. National provisions should be interpreted, as far as possible, in conformity with EU law, the only limit being a *contra legem* interpretation of the national provisions, ie where an interpretation would run counter to the wording of the transposed provision. In cases where national law cannot not be applied in conformity with EU law without going *contra legem*, such national law would have to be disapplied. Instead, the underlying directive could be applied directly, provided that its provisions are sufficiently clear and precise.[75]

However, the CRD has never been explicitly granted direct effect; nevertheless, the SSM case law on Article 4(3) CRD certainly adds another dimension to the broader debate on direct effect of directives. The ECB and the Court read the provisions transposing the directive in conjunction with provisions of the directive. This may be also due to the high level of detail provided in CRD provisions. The tension inherent in the ECB's mandate to create a level playing field while respecting the diversity of the national legal frameworks it is bound to apply is reflected in this tendency to stick to the wording of the directives as far as possible.

The questions that remain open for the Court to answer are, therefore, whether direct effect of the CRD in the context of the SSM is indeed possible, and whether instructions based on Article 9(1), paragraph 3 SSMR can be separately appealed in front of the Court. Other areas yet to be explored in detail by the Court are questions of administrative procedural law, such as who grants the right to be heard, or access to files, in the context of composite procedures, or in the context of indirect application of national law. Therefore, it remains interesting what cases come up next, and what clarifications the Court can make in the future.

[75] Case 41/74 *Yvonne van Duyn v Home Office*, ECLI:EU:C:1974:133; Case 148/78 *Ratti*, ECLI:EU:C:1979:110.

6

No EDIS but Revamped DGSs

Is It Sufficient?

Diane Fromage and Gaia Chiarini

I Introduction

When the European Banking Union (EBU) was first launched in 2012,[1] its structure was conceived as relying on three pillars for supranational supervision, resolution, and deposit insurance. These were to take the form of, respectively, a Single Supervisory Mechanism (SSM), a Single Resolution Mechanism (SRM), and a European Deposit Insurance Scheme (EDIS). However, even though the European Commission made a proposal for an EDIS in 2015,[2] and even though the European Parliament (EP) adopted its report on EDIS at the end of the past legislature,[3] there appears to be no appetite to proceed on the side of Council. Member States do not want to share risks, they believe that the differences that exist across banking systems are still too large, and they disagree with the choice of legal basis for EDIS.[4] It remains nonetheless the case that more harmonization in the way in which deposits are guaranteed is necessary because, as emphasized by the Chair of the Supervisory Board, Claudia Buch:

[1] Commission, 'Communication from the Commission to the European Parliament and the Council—A roadmap towards a Banking Union' (2012) https://eur-lex.europa.eu/legal-content/EN/TXT/PDF/?uri=CELEX:52012DC0510&from=EN.
[2] Commission, 'Proposal for a Regulation of the European Parliament and of the Council amending Regulation (EU) 806/2014 in order to establish a European Deposit Insurance Scheme' (2015) https://eur-lex.europa.eu/legal-content/EN/TXT/?uri=CELEX:52015PC0586.
[3] European Parliament, 'European Parliament legislative resolution of 24 April 2024 on the proposal for a directive of the European Parliament and of the Council amending Directive 2014/49/EU as regards the scope of deposit protection, use of deposit guarantee schemes funds, cross-border cooperation, and transparency', 24 April 2024 https://www.europarl.europa.eu/doceo/document/TA-9-2024-0328_EN.html.
[4] Concetta Brescia Morra, 'The Third Pillar of the Banking Union and Its Troubled Implementation' in Mario P Chiti and Vittorio Santoro (eds), *The Palgrave Handbook of European Banking Union Law* (Palgrave Macmillan 2019) 393–407.

Diane Fromage and Gaia Chiarini, *No EDIS but Revamped DGSs* In: *EU Banking Union*. Edited by: Jonathan Bauerschmidt, Raffaele D'Ambrosio, Diane Fromage, Daniela Jaros, and Paul Weismann, Oxford University Press. © Oxford University Press 2026. DOI: 10.1093/9780198949756.003.0007

> reaching a political agreement on the banking union's third pillar, a European Deposit Insurance Scheme (EDIS), is important. European deposit insurance would ensure a more comparable level of protection of depositors, thus potentially stimulating cross-border demand for deposits. Host jurisdictions' concerns on the national costs of bank distress would be alleviated, thus reducing incentives to keep capital and liquidity resources locally. For banks, the cross-border management of capital and liquidity would become easier, thus potentially increasing incentives to go abroad. Not least, a more integrated deposit insurance framework would increase ex-ante confidence in the European crisis management framework. Progress with EDIS may also unlock political will to change the Single Rulebook by providing more room for cross-border liquidity waivers and allowing for cross-border capital waivers.[5]

This is also why the European Commission made a proposal for further harmonization in the Deposit Guarantee Schemes Directive (DGSD), as part of its Crisis Management and Deposit Insurance (CMDI) package, launched in 2022.[6]

This chapter sets forth to analyse whether the (reformed) national DGSs could in some way compensate for the absence of an EDIS. Indeed, DGSs are funds established at the national level to 'protect depositors against the consequences of the insolvency of a credit institution'.[7] To answer this question, this chapter first examines DGSs' legal regime within the EU (section II). It then turns to EDIS and considers what EDIS would have entailed (section III), before the ongoing reform to the DGS Directive is analysed (section IV) and compared with EDIS (section V), focusing on specific key elements: (a) coverage level; (b) scope; (c) temporary high imbalances; (d) payout period; (e) funding; and (f) cooperation within the system. A final section concludes (section VI).

[5] Claudia Buch, 'Financial integration in Europe: where do we stand after the banking union's first decade?' (Speech at the 'Globalisation: What's Next?' conference co-organized by the Banque de France, the Centre for Economic Policy Research, the World Bank, and the University of Surrey, April 2024) https://www.bankingsupervision.europa.eu/press/speeches/date/2024/html/ssm.sp240430~68c9861180.en.html.

[6] European Parliament, 'MEPs agreed on a toolset against bank failures to protect taxpayers and deposits', 20 March 2024 https://www.europarl.europa.eu/news/en/press-room/20240311IPR19201/meps-agreed-on-a-toolset-against-bank-failures-to-protect-taxpayers-deposits; Council of the European Union, 'Bank crisis management and deposit insurance framework: Council agrees on its position', 19 June 2024 https://www.consilium.europa.eu/en/press/press-releases/2024/06/19/bank-crisis-management-and-deposit-insurance-framework-council-agrees-on-its-position/.

[7] Recital 14, DGSD.

II Regulating DGSs at EU and international level

1 The origin

DGSs have been the subject of discussions at the supranational level since 1987, when the European Commission made a recommendation on this issue.[8] At the time, only six of the then 12 Member States had some kind of DGS. The recommendation's main aim was that all Member States would have a DGS, meeting certain basic conditions, by 1 January 1990. However, the provisions of the recommendation did not undertake to define specific issues, such as coverage level, repayment period, or level of funding,[9] and it was merely a (non-binding) recommendation. Since the recommendation did not produce the intended outcome, when the development of the EU internal market required harmonization, in 1992, the European Commission proposed a directive. Furthermore, at the time, it was necessary to achieve the protection of competition, and the unification of the legal situation of depositors from various Member States, and to grant broader operational authority to guarantee schemes.[10] In 1994, the first directive[11] introduced a first set of rules on the basis of minimum harmonization criteria and the principle of mutual recognition, after some Member States had already introduced DGSs at the national level.[12] Most notably, it made membership of a DGS mandatory for every bank. In fact, the participation in a DGS was, and still is, a prerequisite for obtaining a banking licence ('A credit institution authorised in a Member State pursuant to Article 8 of Directive 2013/36/EU shall not take deposits unless it is a member of a scheme officially recognised in its home Member State pursuant to paragraph 1 of this Article' (Art 4(3), Directive 2014/49/EC)). The rationale for the introduction of specific binding rules on DGS membership notably was, and still is, closely connected to the important function that such schemes are meant to accomplish, along with the other safety-net players, in ensuring confidence in the banking system. This approach resulted

[8] Commission Recommendation 87/63/EEC of 22 December 1986 concerning the introduction of deposit-guarantee schemes in the Community, [1987] OJ L 033/16.

[9] Veerle Colaert, 'Deposit Guarantee Scheme in Europe: Is the Banking Union in Need of a Third Pillar?' (2015) European Company and Financial Law Review 376.

[10] Jakub Kerlin, *The Role of Deposit Guarantee Schemes as a Financial Safety Net in the European Union* (Palgrave MacMillan 2017) 57–61.

[11] Directive 94/19/EC of the European Parliament and of the Council of 30 May 1994 on deposit-guarantee schemes OJ L135.

[12] This was, for instance, the case of France, where a non-binding and optional depositor compensation procedure by other credit institutions was introduced in 1984 (French Law no 84-46 of 24 January 1984).

in significant differences between national DGSs as to the level of coverage, the scope of covered depositors, and the payout delay.

Even though the directive was adopted, Germany—the only Member State that voted against the directive's adoption in the Council—brought an action for annulment under Article 173 TEC, seeking the annulment of the whole directive, or, alternatively, of some of its provisions.[13]

The principal claim of the German government was for the annulment of the directive in its entirety, based on two pleas: (i) the directive was adopted on the wrong legal basis—Article 57(2) TEC on free movement of capital, instead of Article 235 TEC (internal market harmonization clause, now Art 114 TFEU); (ii) Article 190 TEC, which contains the obligation to state reasons, had been infringed as concerns the principle of subsidiarity. Regarding the first plea, the argument was that the primary objective of the directive was to increase protection for depositors. As Article 129A TEC, which specifically concerned the protection of consumers, referred only to Article 100A TEC, and not to Article 57(2) TEC, as a legal basis for harmonization, the directive should have been based on Article 235 TEC, requiring unanimity. The Court rejected this plea, mainly because the major object of the directive was, and still is, to contribute to the abolition of obstacles to the freedom of establishment and the free provision of services that may result from diverging provisions of the Member States. Therefore, Article 57(2) TEC is to be considered the correct legal basis. The second plea of the German government related to the principle of *subsidiarity*. The German government merely claimed that the directive did not fulfil the *obligation to state reasons* (Article 190) because it did not explain how it was compatible with the principle of subsidiarity. The Court carefully delimited the scope of the German government's argument, pointing out that the German government was not claiming that the Directive itself infringed the principle of subsidiarity, but only that the Community legislature had failed to set out the ground substantiating the compatibility of its action with the principle of subsidiarity, hence whether the reasoning was adequate with Article 190 TEC. Therefore, the Court focused only on Article 190 TEC, however, thereby implicitly rejecting the exclusive competence view. With regard to the obligation to state reasons, the Court agreed on a reference to the substance of the principle whereby the EP and the Council give the reasons as to why the action could be best achieved at the Community level. No express reference to the principle shall be required. In this case, it was enough to argue

[13] Case C-233/94 *Federal Republic of Germany v European Parliament and Council of the European Union*, Judgment of 13 May 1997, [1997] ECR I-2405, ECLI:EU:C:1997:231.

that a Community-wide minimum deposit protection could be regarded as indispensable, and that the insolvency of a branch of an out-of-state credit institution could have repercussions in other Member States. Although the Court dismissed all the pleas of the German government, the judgment is noteworthy for several legal issues it deals with: the question of legal basis; the infringement of the obligation to state reasons concerning the principle of subsidiarity; the application of the principle of proportionality to Community legislation; and the relevance of the principle of home country control.[14]

The numerous banking bankruptcies and some bank runs during the global financial crisis of 2007–09 impelled a lively debate on the need to strengthen and review the structure, financial resources, and function of DGSs. In particular, the case of Northern Rock in the UK in September 2007 demonstrated how significant the impact of a panicky run may be,[15] and in 2008, the European Commission formulated a proposal to promote convergence among Members States' DGSs, which, in 2009, led to the adoption of Directive 2009/14/EC. This directive represented the first step towards a structural reform of the deposit insurance system. This reform provided a remedy to some shortcomings of the previous directive, with a view to achieving greater consistency between national DGSs.

The international debate on further strengthening DGSs, and on the possibility of establishing a centralized DGS at a European level, increased with the deepening of the crisis.[16] In 2009, the International Association of Deposit Insurers (IADI) released the Core Principles for Effective Deposit Insurance Systems. The Core Principles (CPs) can be applied by the states represented in the Association,[17] to establish or enhance their deposit guarantee schemes. In 2014, the IADI issued the Revised Core Principles for Effective Deposit Insurance Systems. The revised CPs strengthened deposit insurance standards, including reimbursement speed, coverage, funding, and governance, and added guidance on the deposit insurer's role in crisis preparedness and management.[18] Moreover, the CPs were embraced in the FSB's Key Standards

[14] Wulf-Henning Roth, 'Case C-233/94, Federal Republic of Germany v. European Parliament and Council of the European Union, Judgment of 13 May 1997, [1997] ECR I-2405' (1998) 35(2) Common Market Law Review 459–79.

[15] Giuseppe Boccuzzi, *The European Banking Union: Supervision and Resolution* (Palgrave Macmillan Studies in Banking and Financial Institutions 2016) 133.

[16] ibid.

[17] At the time of writing (2024), 99 members: IADI (International Association of Deposit Insurers), 'Who we are'. https://www.iadi.org.

[18] BIS, 'Core Principles for Effective Deposit Insurance Systems—Executive Summary' (2022) 1 https://www.bis.org/fsi/fsisummaries/iadi_core_principles.pdf.

for Sound Financial Systems.[19] To assess the compliance with the CPs, an assessment methodology which submits a set of essential criteria for each CP was issued. Although the assessment is made by the jurisdictions themselves, the IADI, from 2013, established the Self-Assessment Technical Assistance Program to enable jurisdictions to request an independent on-site review and validation of their self-assessment results by a team of IADI experts.[20]

International common standards are key because they embody a common understanding and analysis.[21] However, common standards alone are not sufficient, especially because they do not have a legally binding power; it would seem that the wide discretion within jurisdictions makes it difficult to embrace them effectively and uniformly. In addition, the recent banking turmoil in Switzerland and the US may lead to consideration of a review of the IADI Core Principles.[22]

2 DGS reform of 2014

Going back to the EU's framework concerning DGSs, it was reformed in 2014, as the one established in 2009 had been adopted hastily and remained insufficient.[23] This reform entailed keeping the 100,000 euro coverage level already provided for by the directive of 2009, but to reduce the paying-out period to seven working days. However, the most important requirements were on new financing methods for deposit insurance agencies; since then, banks must pay contributions to the guarantee schemes in the EU.[24]

At the time of writing, the DGSD has not been formally adopted. The analysis provided bases itself on the positions taken by the EP and the Council in 2024,[25] while also taking account of the provisional agreement published in

[19] The Financial Stability Board (FSB) designed these standards as key for the stability of financial systems, and they are worth of priority implementation, depending on country circumstances.

[20] BIS (n 18) 4.

[21] Robert Ophèle, 'Diversity and harmonisation of deposit insurance' (Closing speech at the IADI International ERC Conference, Paris, 2016) https://www.bis.org/review/r160621g.pdf.

[22] Alessandra Perrazzelli, 'Deposit insurance and crisis management: the current landscape and the way forward' (79th EXCO Week of IADI, Rome, 13 June 2024) https://www.bis.org/review/r240614g.pdf.

[23] François Barrière, 'Deposit-guarantee Schemes in French Law and in European Law' (2018) 1 Osservatorio del diritto civile e commerciale 268; and Directive 2014/49/EU of the European Parliament and of the Council of 16 April 2014 on deposit guarantee schemes (recast) Text with EEA relevance.

[24] Marco Bordellini, 'The Optional Measures of Deposit Guarantee Schemes: Towards a New Bank Crisis Management Paradigm?' (2021) 13 European Journal of Legal Studies 341.

[25] Council of the European Union, 'Proposal for a Directive of the European Parliament and of the Council amending Directive 2014/49/EU as regards the scope of deposit protection, use of deposit

December 2025, the role of the deposit guarantee function, and the need for a European DGS.

DGSs have played a fundamental role in the safety net established for financial stability by the EU so far.[26] Depositor protection reinforces confidence in the banking system, especially in the case of a banking crisis which could cause a bank run or contagion spread to other financial intermediaries. A DGS has been demonstrated to be able to rule out bank runs.[27]

DGSs are only one piece of a complex architecture to pursue financial stability, next to rule-making, supervision, lender of last resort, special insolvency procedures, deposit insurance schemes, and the fiscal backstop. The function they are called upon to play varies across Member States, although the DGSD[28] prescribes that they have to exercise two functions, while they may play two additional, non-mandatory ones. The two mandatory functions are: (i) pay-box function (Article 11(1) DGSD); and (ii) resolution financing (Article 11(2) DGSD). The pay-box function is considered the core function of DGSs and is exercised in the context of a winding up, and aims to protect the covered depositors of a failing bank. The resolution financing function is exercised to finance the resolution of a bank that is failing or likely to fail (FOLTF). However, this function is to be carried out according to the conditions laid out in Article 109 of the Banking Recovery and Resolution Directive (BRRD) and makes DGSs act as loss absorbers to the benefit of covered depositors. The DGS will contribute to resolution financing by an amount equal to the loss it would have incurred if it had reimbursed covered depositors in the event of the bank undergoing regular insolvency proceedings.[29] Alongside these two mandatory functions, the non-mandatory ones are: (i) the implementation of alternative measures aimed at preventing a bank's failure (Article 11(3) DGSD); and (ii) the provision of financial means, in the context of liquidation, aimed at preserving access of depositors to covered deposits (Article 11(6) DGSD). Both functions need to comply with the least-cost principle, meaning that they cannot become more costly for DGSs than the amount they would have had to pay to reimburse covered depositors should the bank have undergone a liquidation instead of resolution.[30]

guarantee schemes funds cross-border cooperation, and transparency' https://data.consilium.europa.eu/doc/document/ST-11141-2024-INIT/en/pdf/.

[26] Boccuzzi (n 15) 130–39.
[27] Brescia Morra (n 4) 393–407.
[28] Directive 2014/49/EU of the European Parliament and of the Council of 16 April 2014 on deposit guarantee schemes (recast) Text with EEA relevance.
[29] Bordellini (n 24).
[30] ibid.

The harmonization of national DGSs is, however, still insufficient and is characterized by, among others, market fragmentation and lack of identical risk calculations, as well as of equivalent governance. To remedy these issues, the European Commission published a proposal for an EDIS in 2015—on which, see more in the following section. The new reform proposed in 2023 is examined further in section IV below.

III EDIS and what it would have entailed

The constitution of the Banking Union began with the creation of a first, supervisory pillar, the SSM, followed by the establishment of a second pillar, responsible for the resolution and orderly liquidation of banks, the SRM. The next step, the third pillar, is the creation of the EDIS, which would, hence, have not been an EU-wide initiative, but a Banking Union one. According to this framework, the Banking Union, built upon three pillars, is expected to allow the creation of unified competences of institutions functioning in the financial safety net.[31]

The first proposal for establishing EDIS was presented in the *Five Presidents' Report*,[32] in which EDIS was conceived as a common, supranational deposit guarantee scheme for credit institutions in a participating Member State. The participating Member States are those belonging to the Banking Union and the other Member States that have established close cooperation with the European Central Bank to participate in the SSM.[33] EDIS should be supported by a Deposit Insurance Fund (DIF). This fund should be managed by the Single Resolution Board (SRB), considering also the role the SRB already has in managing the resolution and winding-up procedures and the Single Resolution Fund (SRF), as accredited by Regulation 806/2014. Furthermore, the SRB is supposed to become the executive organ of EDIS, in cooperation with participating DGSs and designated authorities, as an organization managing the resolution and orderly liquidation procedures of financial institutions in the Banking Union. The tasks of EDIS would be the same as those appointed to national deposit insurance agencies in Directive 2014/49/EU. The legal basis for the establishment of EDIS is provided in Article 114 of the Treaty on the Functioning of the European Union (TFEU), which provides

[31] Kerlin (n 10) 75–84.

[32] Commission, 'The Five Presidents' Report: Completing Europe's Economic and Monetary Union (2015) 11 https://commission.europa.eu/document/download/261ad02b-070a-47a1-b52b.

[33] Kerlin (n 10) 75–84.

for the harmonization of internal market rules. It is interesting to note that this stands in contrast to the legal basis used for the first DGSD, in 1994, for which Article 57(2) TEC on the freedom to provide services was used. In this case, the Commission considered that EDIS aims to preserve the integrity and enhance the functioning of the internal market, promoting the application of a single set of rules for deposit protection. Article 114 TFEU is, therefore, considered to be the appropriate legal basis.[34] Also, in the opinion of the Council Legal Service,[35] Article 114 TFEU is a suitable legal basis for the establishment of the EDIS. Indeed, EDIS is intended to avoid disparities between national rules that may obstruct the establishment of the internal market in the field of financial services. This, however, gave rise to some criticism, as EDIS would leave the internal market fragmented because it would be applied only to euro-area banks.[36]

The EDIS proposal[37] assumes the creation of the institution in three phases, by gradually increasing the scope of its responsibility and the mutualization of country deposit guarantee funds through a progressive combining of funds aggregated by country insurance agencies into one common fund for banking union countries.[38] First, a reinsurance phase would take place, followed by co-insurance, leading to full insurance, similarly to the phasing-in of the SRF. In the reinsurance phase, a national DGS could access EDIS funds only when it had first exhausted all its own resources; the EDIS addresses the initial liquidity needs of a DGS to compensate depositors within the payout deadline, but also to satisfy the request for contribution to a resolution procedure over time.[39] The funding would have to be reimbursed by the participating DGS. EDIS funds would provide extra funds to a national scheme, but only up to a certain level, and would cover a limited share of the losses of a participating DGS. In the co-insurance phase, EDIS would take over limited responsibility. A national scheme would not be required to exhaust its own funds before accessing EDIS funds. EDIS would be available to contribute a share of the costs from the moment that bank depositors need to be reimbursed. This introduces

[34] Commission, 'Proposal for a Regulation of the European Parliament and of the Council amending Regulation (EU) 806/2014 in order to establish a European Deposit Insurance Scheme' (2015) 4 https://eur-lex.europa.eu/legal-content/EN/TXT/?uri=CELEX:52015PC0586.

[35] Council of the European Union, Proposal for a Regulation of the European Parliament and of the Council amending Regulation (EU) 806/2014 in order to establish a European Deposit Insurance Scheme - Examination of the proposed legal basis (2016) https://data.consilium.europa.eu/doc/document/ST-7862-2016-INIT/en/pdf.

[36] Brescia Morra (n 4) 393–407.

[37] Commission, 'Proposal for a Regulation' (n 34).

[38] Kerlin (n 10) 75–84.

[39] Commission, 'Proposal for a Regulation' (n 34), art 41(a), (b), and (c).

a higher degree of risk sharing between national schemes, through EDIS, than is currently the case, since DGSs operate independently from each other at present. In the full insurance phase, EDIS would provide full funding of the liquidity needs and cover all losses arising from a payout event or a request to contribute to resolution.[40] Furthermore, one of the most important tasks of EDIS, enabling to perform its operational activities, would be the collection of financial resources required to face potential interventions. According to the Commission's proposal,[41] national guarantee schemes would annually pay fixed amounts to EDIS directly from their own financial resources. These contributions would not be an additional weight on banks, because banks already fulfil the requirements that should be achieved by national DGSs.[42] As a result and effect of establishing EDIS, part of the national contributions would be transferred to a higher, cross-union fund, the Deposit Insurance Fund (DIF).

A pan-European DGS (or an EDIS) has been deemed to have substantial advantages compared with the current state of affairs characterized by the existence of a network of DGSs with the (optional and unattractive) possibility for DGSs to lend funds to each other.[43] These advantages would include the decrease of administrative costs; a larger capacity compared with those of individual DGSs;[44] increased experience compared with those of national DGSs, which are rarely ever activated; better capacity to deal with cross-border institutions, and the home state would no longer have to reimburse foreign depositors; and a sounder, more symmetric structure at the EU level, as the two pillars of the Banking Union have already been supranationalized. Furthermore, as explained in the Explanatory Memorandum of the Commission proposal,[45] the creation of an EDIS would contribute to creating a true level playing field and solving the inequality that results from the uniform coverage of deposits up to 100,000 euros despite the difference in the levels of income. It would also solve the issue that derives from the fact that, in the event that *ex post* funding is required, it is called in the Member State in which the credit institution is established, even if depositors are in other Member States. The possibility to

[40] Brescia Morra (n 4) 393–407.

[41] Commission, 'Proposal for a Regulation' (n 34).

[42] According to Directive 2014/49/EU of the European Parliament and of the Council of 16 April 2014 on deposit guarantee schemes (recast) Text with EEA relevance.

[43] This analysis is largely based on Colaert's analysis: Colaert (n 9) 418 f. This option is unattractive to DGSs, as they may not know when they may need those funds themselves. Hence, they may not want to take the risk of seeing their funds (partially) depleted by lending them to other DGSs.

[44] As noted by Colaert, this could also be reached by making lending among DGSs mandatory. However, the capacity of a single EDIS may still be larger than that of a network of national DGSs.

[45] Commission, 'Proposal for a Regulation of the European Parliament and of the Council amending Regulation (EU) 806/2014 in order to establish a European Deposit Insurance Scheme—Explanatory Memorandum' https://eur-lex.europa.eu/legal-content/EN/TXT/PDF/?uri=CELEX:52015PC0586.

have reduced *ex ante* funding rates (0.5% as opposed to a minimum 0.8% of covered deposits) in Member States in which the market is highly concentrated also provides those credit institutions with a competitive advantage, since this reduction is not compensated by an increase of their contributions to the resolution fund. Amid the lack of harmonization, a supranational DGS would contribute to removing existing differences, for instance as regards target levels.[46] However, an EDIS is not necessarily needed to reach that objective. On the other hand, some have argued[47] that an argument in favour of maintaining national DGSs could be their closeness to their markets. If one considers the original institutional design of the SSM, the SRM, and other models of multilevel cooperation since established, it would not be impossible to imagine a mechanism that could guarantee that the expertise present at the national level flows into the European system. Further to this, an EDIS would reduce the burden placed on states which may be called to provide alternative funding (credit lines); it would provide more confidence in the host state, where the banks provide cross-border services or establish a branch; and it would have a larger absorption capacity.

Despite those potential advantages, criticism towards EDIS has already been voiced. This primarily relates to the differences that still exist between the banking systems of Member States. One concern is that the establishment of a single DGS at the euro-area level could increase the risk that weak banking sectors could be subsidized by other, stronger banking sectors in the euro area.[48] In particular, only the minimum level of 0.8% of covered deposits' value has been harmonized. However, a national calibration of the indicator, depending on the concentration of the banking sector in a given country and the size of its banks, is missing. Some countries—for example, Germany, France, and Italy—must accumulate much more than the required 0.8% of covered funds. Indeed, the required amount in the countries above will not allow for the payouts of even medium-sized banks. Other countries—for instance, Sweden, Finland, and Ireland—may accept the 0.8% level as sufficient for the execution of proper, effective interventions towards most of their entities.[49] These differences between Member States, stemming from different banking sectors and the specific set-ups of national DGSs, underline how Member States' preferences on the institutional design of EDIS cannot be based solely on moral

[46] ibid.
[47] Colaert (n 9) 420.
[48] Brescia Morra (n 4) 393–407.
[49] Kerlin (n 10) 81–84.

hazard concerns for uneven risk reduction in the eurozone. In a study[50] of 2020, a certain degree of alignment was shown between Germany, France, and Italy, although strong divergences remain with regard to preventive risk reduction: in Germany, savings banks and cooperative banks continue to oppose a fully fledged EDIS, in order to preserve their institutional protection schemes; in France, the banking sector has lobbied for a reinsurance system that maintains national DGS, in order to keep the target level lower and the associated costs lower for French banks; in Italy, the negative experience with the transfer of decision-making powers in bank resolution, and disagreements with the Commission on the use of deposit insurance funds for alternative measures, dampened enthusiasm for the transfer of further decision-making powers to the supranational level.[51] Another criticism lies in the change in evaluating the risk profile for banks that are obliged to pay contributions. At the moment, the level of risk of a given bank is evaluated from the perspective of a given country's entities. If the proposals enter into force, this will change: the contributions for various entities will be assigned jointly, based on comparison of all entities of the Banking Union.[52]

As mentioned before, the legal basis—namely Article 114 TFEU—for both EDIS and DIF would be the same as the one underpinning the SRM, and to a limited extent the SRF: the obligation to transfer the contributions raised at national level to the Single Fund, as well as the gradual mutualization of the Fund, were established by an intergovernmental agreement (IGA). The proposal for an EDIS does not envisage the need for an intergovernmental agreement, as was necessary in the case of the SRF. The Commission, answering a specific question on this point, in a document published on the same date as the proposal (Frequently Asked Questions), clarifies that the proposed EDIS has a very different set-up from the SRM: 'It consists of a system of insurance starting with a re-insurance of national DGS, financed by direct contributions from banks to the European Deposit insurance Fund.'[53] Therefore, the Commission deems that the EU Treaties provide a sufficient legal basis for this proposal. Indeed, in the case of EDIS, banks contribute directly to the European Fund. Therefore, there is no need for an IGA, as there is no transfer of funds already collected by national DGSs to the European level, according

[50] Mario Tummler and Matthias Thiemann, 'Beyond Moral Hazard Arguments: The Role of National Deposit Insurance Schemes for Member States' Preferences on EDIS' (2020) SAFE White Paper No 72.
[51] ibid 11–12.
[52] Kerlin (n 10) 81–84.
[53] European Commission, 'A European Deposit Insurance Scheme (EDIS) - Frequently Asked Questions' Question 21, 24 November 2015, https://ec.europa.eu/commission/presscorner/detail/en/memo_15_6153.

to some evaluations.[54] Given that these statements by the Commission have not been debated by the Member States in the numerous working documents following the one containing the first EDIS proposal, it can be considered that the need for an IA to regulate the financing of the EDIS is outdated. However, according to the Council Legal Service's opinion, Member States 'under certain conditions and with adequate safeguards, may have recourse to the intergovernmental method in respect of parts of the proposal that the EU legislature decides not to regulate',[55] and this notwithstanding considering Article 114 TFEU a suitable legal basis for the establishment of the EDIS and the DIF.

After discussions had been stalled for some time, rapporteur Othmar Karas presented a draft report[56] on EDIS on 4 March 2024, and the report was adopted by the EP's ECON Committee on 18 April 2024. However, the vote for entering inter-institutional negotiations was left to the Members of the European Parliament of the next legislature (2024–29). The report suggests the establishment of the EDIS in three phases, and provides for the first phase only, named 'EDIS I'. The report reiterates that the aim remains the completion of the Banking Union with a fully fledged EDIS mechanism providing a full insurance scheme with loss coverage. However, these later stages will be adopted through subsequent proposals by the Commission. EDIS I would establish a liquidity scheme only that provides loans to the DGSs in need of liquidity. It would be supported by a DIF funded by other DGSs and, when needed, by additional (mandatory) loans from the latter. The first phase would thus ensure liquidity provisions to DGSs in need, but not risk sharing. The institutional protection schemes (Art 113(7) of the Capital Requirements Regulation (CRR))[57] would be excluded from the scope of EDIS I. It is interesting that Karas presented his report only a few weeks prior to Parliament ending its legislative period. However, discussions had been ongoing for a year and a half prior to this, and this report contributed to triggering new discussions on a potential EDIS. This happened, though, in parallel to Parliament and Council adopting their position on the Commission's proposal for a revamped DGSD.

[54] Brescia Morra (n 4) 402.

[55] Council of the European Union, 'Proposal for a Regulation of the European Parliament and of the Council amending Regulation (EU) 806/2014 in order to establish a European Deposit Insurance Scheme - Examination of the proposed legal basis' (2016) 21 https://data.consilium.europa.eu/doc/document/ST-7862-2016-INIT/en/pdf.

[56] Othmar Karas, 'Report on the proposal for a regulation of the European Parliament and of the Council amending Regulation (EU) 806/2014 in order to establish a European Deposit Insurance Scheme', 23 April 2024 https://www.europarl.europa.eu/doceo/document/A-9-2024-0182_EN.html.

[57] Regulation (EU) No 575/2013 of the European Parliament and of the Council of 26 June 2013 on prudential requirements for credit institutions and investment firms and amending Regulation (EU) No 648/2012 Text with EEA relevance.

IV The DGS Directive (reform)

In light of the political impasse on EDIS and the continuing need to ensure financial stability also as regards deposit insurance, in April 2023, the Commission proposed to reform the EU's bank Crisis Management and Deposit Insurance (CMDI). The legislative package consists of the Bank Recovery and Resolution Directive, the Single Resolution Mechanism Regulation, and the Deposit Guarantee Scheme Directive (DGSD 2).[58] The objective of the reform is to enhance the existing arrangements for managing failing banks in the EU. In particular, arrangements for managing the failure of smaller and medium-sized banks should be made more effective in terms of their design and implementation. The main elements of the proposed reform are: (i) a clarification of the public interest assessment in managing bank crises, to ensure that a full range of crisis management tools can also be applied to failing smaller and medium-sized banks; (ii) facilitating the use of deposit guarantee scheme (DGS) funds in the financing of crisis management tools, as an alternative to the basic payout function; (iii) ensuring that the use of deposit guarantee scheme funds, when applied to smaller and medium-sized banks in resolution, including to access the SRF, should be possible only under specific conditions.[59]

The Council (on 19 June 2024) and the EP (on 24 April 2024) adopted their positions on the legislative proposals to reform the CMDI framework proposed by the Commission in 2022.[60] On 5 November 2025, the provisional agreement resulting from inter-institutional negotiations was adopted.

The adopted amendments in the DGSD 2 develop and explicate the mandate of DGSs to better protect deposits in the context of reimbursement of depositors. They also enhance the role of the DGS outside of cases in which depositors are repaid by the DGS following the failure of a bank, for the purpose

[58] Directive amending the Bank Recovery and Resolution Directive (2014/59/EU) (BRRD 3), Regulation amending the Single Resolution Mechanism (SRM) Regulation ((EU) 806/2014) (SRMR 3), Directive amending the Deposit Guarantee Schemes Directive (2014/49/EU) (DGSD 2).

[59] Communication from the Commission to the European Parliament, the Council, the European Central Bank, the European Economic and Social Committee and the Committee of Regions, on the review of the crisis management and deposit insurance framework contributing to completing the Banking Union https://eur-lex.europa.eu/legal-content/EN/TXT/?uri=CELEX:52023DC0225.

[60] European Parliament, 'MEPs agreed on a toolset against bank failures to protect taxpayers and deposits', 20 March 2024 https://www.europarl.europa.eu/news/en/press-room/20240311IPR19201/meps-agreed-on-a-toolset-against-bank-failures-to-protect-taxpayers-deposits; Council of the European Union, 'Bank crisis management and deposit insurance framework: Council agrees on its position', 19 June 2024 https://www.consilium.europa.eu/en/press/press-releases/2024/06/19/bank-crisis-management-and-deposit-insurance-framework-council-agrees-on-its-position/.

of bank crisis management, with the view to maintaining depositor confidence and financial stability.

With regard to the increased possibilities to use DGSs for the financing of preventive measures, transfer strategies in resolution, and alternative measures in insolvency, it is clarified that the mandate of DGSs encompasses not only the coverage and repayment of deposits but also the use of DGS funds to ensure that depositors maintain access to their deposits.[61]

Also, it is specified that preventive measures are DGS interventions of financial support of a bank in distress before the bank meets the conditions for FOLTF. This is to preserve the bank financial soundness. Alternative measures, however, are DGS interventions supporting the transfer of deposits and assets of the failing bank to another bank, in the context of insolvency, to preserve the access of depositors to their money.[62]

Furthermore, the protection afforded by DGSs also covers depositors located in Member States where member credit institutions exercise the freedom to provide services. The proposed directive sets the conditions to give a DGS in a host Member State the possibility to reimburse directly depositors of a branch belonging to a credit institution from another Member State, or to operate as a point of contact for depositors at credit institutions that exercise the freedom to provide services.[63]

Regarding third-country branches' DGS membership requirement, branches of credit institutions established in third countries have to join a DGS within a Member State if they want to provide banking services and take eligible deposits in the EU. In particular, the membership requirement is safeguarded and equal protection for depositors in the EU branches of third-country banks, and in EU banks and their branches in different Member States, is awarded.[64]

Besides, it is important to remark that the modifications to pave the way for DGS interventions in support of resolution tools were needed to prevent depositors from bearing losses. DGSs can be used to support transfer transactions which include covered deposits, and, under certain conditions, also eligible deposits beyond the coverage level and deposits excluded from the DGS guarantee.[65] Furthermore, any loss which the DGS comes to bear because of an intervention in resolution cannot exceed the loss, net of recoveries, that the

[61] Art 1, DGSD 2.
[62] ibid, art 11.
[63] ibid, art 14.
[64] ibid, art 15.
[65] Art 109(1) BRRD 3.

DGS would bear in insolvency if it paid out covered depositors and subrogated to their claims.[66] Moreover, in order to ensure that the contribution of the DGS is strictly used for the purposes of depositor protection, where appropriate, and not for the protection of creditors that rank below deposits in insolvency, the amount of the DGS contribution cannot exceed any shortfall in the value of the assets of the institution under resolution transferred to the buyer, or the bridge institution, in comparison with the value of the transferred deposits and liabilities with the same or a higher priority ranking in insolvency.[67]

V DGSD reform compared with EDIS

In this section, we analyse the aspects that we highlighted as being key for an EDIS and compare the Commission's proposal with the EP's and the Council's positions, with a view to determining if and to what extent DGSD 2 could in some way remedy the absence of an EDIS. The analysis also covers the provisional agreement from inter-institutional negotiations[68] (hereinafter 'provisional agreement'), to assess the compromise adopted, even though it is still subject to the EP's Committee on Economic and Monetary Affairs for decision. The identified key elements are: (a) coverage level; (b) scope; (c) temporary high balances; (d) repayment period; (e) funding; and (f) cooperation within the system.

(a) The coverage level—100,000 euros—and the possibility for the Commission to revise it every five years have not been amended. On this last element, there is agreement between all the three institutions in not amending it. Indeed, in the provisional agreement, the coverage level is not the object of amendments.
(b) Public authorities, as well as investment firms, should also be protected next to ordinary depositors (Commission), although the EP is in favour of adding public authorities only, while the Council wants investment firms to be covered instead. Also, exclusions would now apply to deposits related to terrorist financing and MSs may decide to include some

[66] ibid.
[67] ibid.
[68] European Parliament, 'Provisional agreement resulting from interinstitutional negotiations - Proposal for a directive of the European Parliament and of the Council amending Directive 2014/49/EU as regards the scope of deposit protection, use of deposit guarantee schemes funds, cross-border cooperation, and transparency' https://www.europarl.europa.eu/RegData/commissions/econ/inag/2025/11-05/ECON_AG(2025)779333_EN.pdf.

pension schemes (Commission proposal). By contrast, the EP wants to exclude deposits from terrorist financing, persons or legal entities subject to financial sanctions, and deposits by investment firms, while the Council wants to exclude public authorities and deposits related to terrorist financing. In the provisional agreement, it is stated that most public authorities cannot be considered to be professional investors, so deposits of non-professional investors, such as local authorities, small public entities, and non-profit institutions controlled by central government or state government would be able to benefit from the protection offered by a DGS.

(c) In the current DGSD, temporary high balances are covered for at least three months, and up to twelve months, but it is up to the MS to decide the exact conditions of this exception and to set the temporary maximum level of such deposits. In the Commission proposal, a maximum of 500,000 euros is protected for six months. The EP increased this minimum to a range of 500,000 to 2,500,000 euros for six months, and the Council reintroduced room for manoeuvre for Member States in defining that 500,000 euros is a minimum, which could lead to gold-plating, and is thus likely to lead to differences across the internal market, which would be avoided were an EDIS to be adopted. In the provisional agreement, the protection is aligned to a minimum amount of at least 500,000 euros for all temporary high balances, and for deposits related to real estate transactions, to a maximum of 2,500,000 euros, for a harmonized duration of six months, in addition to the coverage level of 100,000 euros.[69] These amounts should, however, be revised periodically, and at least once every five years, and the Commission should submit to the EP and to the Council a proposal for a directive, if appropriate. In particular, the periodic revision is thought to adjust amounts taking into account the evolutions of real estate prices in different Member States, ensuring proportionality and a level playing field across Member States.

(d) The repayment period should be within seven days, according to Commission and Council, whereas the EP propose, in vaguer terms,

[69] Point 6 PROVISIONAL AGREEMENT RESULTING FROM INTERINSTITUTIONAL NEGOTIATIONS—Proposal for a directive of the European Parliament and of the Coucnil amending Directive 2014/49/EU as regards the scope of deposit protection, use of deposit guarantee schemes funds, cross-border cooperation, and transparency, 5 November 2025, https://www.europarl.europa.eu/RegData/commissions/econ/inag/2025/11-05/ECON_AG(2025)779333_EN.pdf.

that the deposits be made available as soon as possible, and at the latest within seven days. In all cases, that is unless exceptions apply. In the provisional agreement, the repayment should be made available as soon as possible, and in any case within seven working days, unless exceptions apply.

(e) Rules regarding *ex ante* funding and how to replenish a DGS that has come below the target level of a minimum 0.8% are to be clarified (Commission). Neither the EP nor the Council propose an amendment of the target level, such that differences across Member States would continue to be possible, and would continue to constitute an obstacle to the creation of EDIS. *Ex post* funding is still to be possible for up to a maximum of 0.5% of covered deposits. This, again, poses an obstacle to the establishment of EDIS. It is still possible for DGSs to lend to one another on a voluntary basis only; hence, this preliminary step towards EDIS remains. But, as noted above, perhaps it cannot be otherwise. Further convergence could nonetheless still be reached because of the fact that the EBA's role could be further strengthened. The EP wants EBA to draft RTSs to specify methods for calculating contributions to DGSs; the Commission, the EP, and the Council suggest that it develops draft RTSs to specify the methodology for the calculation of available financial means qualifying for the target level, the details of the process to reach said level, and guidelines to assist DGSs with the diversification of their available financial means. In the provisional agreement, to harmonize DGSs' conditions for the fulfilment of their target level, and to ensure that DGSs' available financial means are financed by contributions from the industry, it is clarified that funds that qualify to reach the target level should be distinguished from funds that are considered as complementary sources of financing, such as borrowed funds resulting in debt liabilities due by the DGS. Indeed, certain sources of DGS financing, such as expected recoveries against DGS claims deriving from its interventions, are too contingent to be accounted as available financial means that qualify for the target level of the DGS. In addition, the replenishment period in the event of substantial (above one-third of the target level) and of smaller (below one-third of the target level) reduction of available financial means is further specified. In order to grant consistent application, the EBA should develop RTSs specifying the methodology for the calculation of the available financial means qualifying for the DGS target level and the details of the process to reach the DGS target level following reduction. Moreover, the EBA should issue guidelines to provide guidance to DGSs in making adequately diversified investment of DGSs funds, ensuring convergent practices.

(f) Finally, as regards cooperation within the European Union specifically, according to the Commission, it should be possible for a DGS in a host Member State to reimburse directly depositors of a branch of a credit institution from another Member State or to act as a point of contact for depositors of credit institutions that exercise the freedom to provide services. By contrast, the EP's proposal foresees that the DGS of the home MS provides information on the number of depositors, the amount of covered deposits, and possible relevant charges to the DGS of the host Member State, and that the EBA should draft RTSs to define the methodology for the calculation of the amount to be transferred, to ensure a neutral impact of said transfer on the financial situation of both DGSs relative to the risk they cover. The Council's position foresees that Member States shall 'ensure that DGSs cover the depositors at branches set up by their member credit institutions in other Member States and depositors at their member credit institutions exercising the freedom to provide services. The EBA shall issue guidelines on how the EBA sees the respective roles of the DGS of the home and host Member States, and containing a list of circumstances and conditions under which a DGS of the home Member State should be able to decide to reimburse depositors at branches located in another Member State.' Hence, the Council's proposal is in favour of less coordination (non-binding guidelines, as opposed to binding RTSs, and a larger role for the Member States, while the principle of neutrality is not specifically mentioned). In the provisional agreement, it is considered that, in light of the technological advancements, the DGS of the home Member State should be allowed to make repayment directly to depositors at branches located in another Member State if the administrative burden and costs are lower than if the repayment were to be carried out by the DGS of the host Member State. This allows greater flexibility, considering the quantity of cross-border banking services offered. In this framework, the EBA should issue guidelines to support DGSs in cooperation, including a list of circumstances and conditions under which a DGS of the home Member State could decide to reimburse depositors at branches located in the host Member State.

VI Conclusion: The DGSD reform as a compensation for the absence of EDIS and possible steps forward

In conclusion, the recent progress on the reform of the DGSD (and CMDI in general) represents a significant step towards the strengthening of crisis management and deposit insurance within the EU.

Despite achieving a partial harmonization of solutions, the reform of the DGSD makes further tentative steps to fill the empty space due to the absence of EDIS. Recognizing an increasingly interconnected banking system, the reform of the DGSD further develops provisions for cross-border institutions and third-country branches.

Undoubtedly, some weak points remain: a 100,000 euro threshold leaves a proportion of deposits without protection in some Member States, impacting on the credibility of the deposit guarantee system in those states, whereas it represents a full guarantee for other Member States.[70] Furthermore, only a fully mutualized EDIS would ensure depositor protection without producing cross-subsidization effects[71] (although one may consider that precisely the opposite is true). Moreover, on the one hand, the DGSD reform should allow the better evaluation of the conditions applicable across the internal market, but on the other hand, it persists in dehomogenizing and creates unfair competition between Member States.

Perhaps this negative conclusion is not as dramatic as it could seem at first sight, as the existence of a resolution regime within the EU since 2014 alleviates the role of DGSs. The question could, however, be asked whether DGSs should not be hosted by the same institutions that already play the role of NRAs, to facilitate their coordination, as is the case in the UK, even if it is also true that conflicts of interest may emerge in such a configuration.

While waiting for potential steps forward in the constitution of EDIS, the DGSD reform could reach the goal to further harmonize the regulatory framework, but according to the Commission's proposal and the Council's and the EP's positions, as well as according to the provisional agreement, only to a limited extent. A final evaluation of this reform will only be possible once the negotiations have been concluded. However, it is unlikely that giant steps will be taken in the direction of increased solidarity and risk mutualization, as important measures that would be required to prepare for the introduction

[70] Colaert (n 9) 389–92.
[71] Perrazzelli (n 22).

of an EDIS have not been included—so far—in the list of amendments proposed, and as the political appetite to go in such a direction is lacking, even if the Commission was mentioning it again towards the end of 2025. Perhaps the only real hope that something will change in this regard is if larger mergers, such as the one envisaged recently by UniCredit and Commerz Bank, did materialize.

7

Supervisory Review and Evaluation Process (SREP)

A Strengthened Common Supervisory Action for Effective Crisis Prevention?

*Christy Ann Petit**

I Introduction

With the tenth anniversary of the Single Supervisory Mechanism (SSM) in 2024, policymakers have been praising the effectiveness of European Banking Supervision.[1] The European Central Bank (ECB) started a review of its implementation of the Supervisory Review and Evaluation Process (SREP)—a central supervisory process in the first pillar of the Banking Union—following a report by a group of experts (hereinafter 'Expert Group'), published the same year.[2] This chapter focuses on the question whether, and to what extent, this common supervisory process has been strengthened in law and in action in ECB Banking Supervision with the primary goal to preserve the banks' safety and soundness. The analysis is based on European Union (EU) law,[3]

* The author wishes to warmly thank the co-editors for their careful feedback and guidance. All errors or omissions remain the author's sole responsibility. The SREP cycles covered are from 2015 until 2023, as available at the time of writing.

[1] Claudia Buch, 'European Banking Supervision at Ten: Building a Strong Institution for a Resilient Future' (speech at event celebrating the tenth anniversary of the Single Supervisory Mechanism, Frankfurt am Main, 6 November 2024), https://www.bankingsupervision.europa.eu/press/speeches, accessed 8 November 2024; Frank Elderson, 'The First Decade of European Supervision: Taking Stock and Looking Ahead' (speech at '10 Years of SSM – Looking back and looking forward' conference, Frankfurt am Main, 4 November 2024), https://www.bankingsupervision.europa.eu/press/speeches/date, accessed 8 November 2024; Frank Elderson, 'Powers, Ability and Willingness to Act – the Mainstay of Effective Banking Supervision' (speech at House of the Euro, Brussels, 7 December 2023), https://www.bankingsupervision.europa.eu/press, accessed 18 October 2024.

[2] Sarah Dahlgren and others, 'Assessment of the European Central Bank's Supervisory Review and Evaluation Process' (ECB 2023), Report by the Expert Group to the Chair of the Supervisory Board of the ECB, https://www.bankingsupervision.europa.eu/ecb, accessed 18 April 2023.

[3] Litigation on SREP has rather been limited. See Case T-712/15 *Crédit Mutuel Arkéa v ECB*, ECLI:EU:T:2017:900; and, upon appeal, Joined Cases C-152/18 P and C-153/18 P *Crédit Mutuel*

Christy Ann Petit, *Supervisory Review and Evaluation Process (SREP)* In: *EU Banking Union*. Edited by: Jonathan Bauerschmidt, Raffaele D'Ambrosio, Diane Fromage, Daniela Jaros, and Paul Weismann, Oxford University Press. © Oxford University Press 2026. DOI: 10.1093/9780198949756.003.0008

in particular the relevant provisions of the Capital Requirements Directive, the SREP Guidelines from the European Banking Authority (EBA), and the ECB's methodology,[4] and the evaluations produced in EU policy documents, together with limited recent research publications.[5] It relies, in particular, on the findings of external reviews by the European Court of Auditors (ECA) and the European Commission, published in 2023.[6]

The SREP is a supervisory process in banking supervision that aims at ensuring that supervised entities have adequate arrangements, strategies, processes, and mechanisms to comply with prudential regulation, and, in particular, that they hold enough capital (own funds) and liquidity to ensure a sound management and coverage of their risks.[7] In the EU's prudential framework, banks' capital requirements are determined on the basis of Pillar 1 and Pillar 2. Pillar 1 is a general minimum requirement applicable for all banks in accordance with EU prudential regulation and based on their risk-weighted assets. Pillar 2 is tailored to the supervised entity's risk profile and is based on the supervisors' assessment of the banks' internal capital to cover all types of risks, which can lead to Pillar 2 requirements (P2R) and capital add-ons, which may be higher than Pillar 1 minimum requirements (P1). Moreover, Pillar 2 can include a Pillar 2 guidance (P2G) that gives supervisory 'advice' on capital adequacy beyond P1 and P2R. As a supervisory guidance for additional

Arkéa v ECB, ECLI:EU:C:2019:810 (dismissed). A case on SREP and early intervention—Case T-11/19 *Mutualidad de la Abogacia and Others v ECB*—was withdrawn by the applicant (April 2025).

[4] See arts 97, 98, 104, 105 and 110 of the CRD, and, more specifically, level 2 and level 3 acts within the Single Rulebook, for which the EBA is responsible, as well as the Guidelines: see EBA, 'Final Report on Guidelines on Common Procedures and Methodologies for SREP and Supervisory Stress Testing under Directive 2013/36/EU' (European Banking Authority 2022) EBA/GL/2022/03, https://www.eba.europa.eu/sites/, accessed 8 July 2024; see section 3 of this chapter, and, among others, ECB, 'Supervisory Methodology 2023', https://www.bankingsupervision.europa.eu/banking/srep, accessed 9 July 2024.

[5] Scholarship is primarily from economics, apart from Michael Meissner, 'The Supervisory Review and Evaluation Process (SREP): Ultimate Test for the Banking Union?' (2016) 31 Journal of International Banking Law and Regulation 331; Luca Amorello, 'Europe Goes "Countercyclical": A Legal Assessment of the New Countercyclical Dimension of the CRR/CRD IV Package' (2016) 17 European Business Organization Law Review 137; in economics, see, for instance, Carlos Francisco Alves, Alberto Citterio, and Bernardo P Marques, 'Bank-Specific Capital Requirements: Short and Long-Run Determinants' (2023) 52 Finance Research Letters 103558; Niklas Witte, 'Capital Requirements in Pillar 1 or Pillar 2: Does It Matter for Market Discipline?' (2024) ECB Working Paper Series No 2988, https://www.ecb.europa.eu/pub/pdf.

[6] ECA, 'Special Report 12/2023: EU Supervision of Banks' Credit Risk—The ECB Stepped up Its Efforts but More Is Needed to Increase Assurance That Credit Risk Is Properly Managed and Covered' (2023) ECA Special Report 12/2023; European Commission, 'Report from the Commission to the European Parliament and the Council on the Single Supervisory Mechanism Established Pursuant to Regulation 1024/2013' (2023) COM (2023) 212 final, https://finance.ec.europa.eu/system, accessed 28 April 2023.

[7] See art 97(1) and (3) CRD.

capital above regulatory requirements, P2G is not legally binding. Pillar 1 and Pillar 2 form, together, the supervised entity's total capital requirement (TCR).

Therefore, the outcomes of the SREP are critical for the banks, which may receive higher capital and liquidity requirements,[8] but also an indication to hold higher capital considering the P2G,[9] and other qualitative measures. However, the SREP focus, so far, seems to have been primarily centred on (quantitative) capital measures.[10] Overall, the importance of the SREP exercise is threefold, in terms of application of EU prudential regulation, actual enforcement and administrative operations of prudential supervision, and maintaining the internationally agreed approach to risk-based supervision stemming from the Basel Committee on Banking Supervision (BCBS).

The Expert Group considered that SREP has fostered the resilience of the banking sector and contributed to a level playing field for significant institutions (SIs),[11] which are under the direct supervision of the ECB. Yet, a recalibration[12] and rescoping of the SREP is currently ongoing. Indeed, the Group considered that both the efficiency and effectiveness of supervisory processes could be improved by ensuring a more integrated and risk-based approach.[13] The reorganization of processes and practices in the SREP is further justified by the robustness and maturity of the Single Supervisory Mechanism (SSM).[14]

The supervisors need to balance the flexibility represented by some elements within the SREP with the principle of equal treatment across banks. This equal treatment is notably ensured by common approaches and methodologies, which have been developed and solidified over the first decade of the SSM and constitute the 'second line of defence'[15] which became more entrenched institutionally after the reorganization of ECB Banking Supervision in 2020.[16] This reorganization modified the scope of the ECB/SSM Directorates-General

[8] Bart PM Joosen, Marco Lamandini, and Tobias H Tröger (eds), *Capital and Liquidity Requirements for European Banks* (OUP 2022).

[9] Alessandra Melis and Katrin Weissenberg, 'EU Banks' Journey Towards an Enhanced Capital Framework' (2019) EBA Staff Paper.

[10] Recommendation 3.1, Dahlgren and others (n 2) 42.

[11] This chapter will engage primarily with SIs' direct supervision in the context of SREP. Indeed, for LSIs, the latest methodology published by the ECB dates back to 2020, while the website gives elements on the application of proportionality in SREP and for LSIs' supervision: 'SSM LSI SREP Methodology 2020 Edition' (2020), https://www.bankingsupervision.europa.eu/ecb, accessed 8 July 2024.

[12] Dahlgren and others (n 2).

[13] ibid 12.

[14] ibid 6.

[15] ECB, 'SSM Supervisory Manual' (2024) 47.

[16] ECB, 'ECB Announces Organisational Changes to Strengthen Banking Supervision' (ECB Banking Supervision, 29 July 2020), https://www.bankingsupervision.europa.eu/press, accessed 14 September 2020.

(DGs), with bank-specific supervision in three DGs, horizontal supervision in one DG, and the creation of one separate directorate to perform the second line of defence, ie 'Directorate Supervisory Strategy and Risk' (DSSR).[17]

Besides the reach for effective and efficient processes, reforming the approach to the SREP is justified primarily by the evolutions of the risks the banks are facing, namely macroeconomic, technological disruption, money laundering and terrorism financing, and geopolitical and environmental risks, which were part of legislative amendments to EU prudential regulation. Proportionality has also been strengthened in both prudential regulation and supervision after the last two legislative banking packages of 2019 and 2021. In any event, the competent authorities establish the SREP frequency and intensity, considering the supervised entities' size, systemic importance, nature, scale, and complexity, as well as the principle of proportionality.[18]

This chapter considers both the Banking Union scope (with 21 participating Member States, to date) and the EU-wide application of prudential rules through the EU Single Rulebook. While the chapter aims to discuss the first decade of SREP in ECB direct supervision, it does not fully account for the exceptional and relief measures that were adopted by the ECB during the Covid-19 pandemic,[19] when the SREP was applied in a 'pragmatic' way in 2020, following the guidance from the EBA that issued temporary adjustments.[20] In essence, in 2020, the recommendations focused on how supervised entities can face the pandemic-related challenges, keeping the P2R and P2G unchanged from 2019.[21] Nevertheless, this period created a precedent, and food for thought to simplify the 'regular' SREP in normal times.[22]

The remainder of the chapter is structured as follows: section II presents the institutional context and the legal framework for SREP. Section III focuses on the SREP methodology and its main elements, and discusses what it represents in the ongoing supervision by Joint Supervisory Teams (JSTs), in particular in

[17] There are also two other DGs dedicated, respectively, to SSM Governance & Operations, and On-site & Internal Model Inspections: see ECB, 'ECB Organigramme' (European Central Bank, 2024), https://www.ecb.europa.eu/ecb/pdf/orga/ECB_organisational_chart.pdf.

[18] As per art 97(4) CRD.

[19] Christy Ann Petit, 'Financial Union and Covid-19' in Federico Fabbrini and Christy Ann Petit (eds), *Research Handbook on Post-Pandemic EU Economic Governance and NGEU Law* (Edward Elgar 2024).

[20] ECB, 'Taking a Pragmatic Approach to SREP' (*Banking Supervision Newsletter*, 13 May 2020), https://www.bankingsupervision.europa.eu/press, accessed 17 October 2024; EBA, 'EBA Publishes Guidelines on a Pragmatic and Flexible Approach to the 2020 Supervisory Review and Evaluation Process in Light of the COVID-19 Pandemic' (European Banking Authority, 23 July 2020), https://www.eba.europa.eu/publications-and-media/press-releases, accessed 18 October 2024.

[21] ECB, 'Aggregated Results of SREP 2021' (ECB Banking Supervision, 10 February 2022), https://www.bankingsupervision.europa.eu/banking, accessed 18 October 2024.

[22] European Commission, 'Report on the SSM' (n 6) 14.

terms of scoring and constrained supervisory judgement. Section IV analyses how the SREP is recalibrated and rescoped following its reviews. The reach for efficiency and effectiveness following the SREP reform seems sound and justified, but this warrants caution given a potentially fragmented process for some of the significant institutions, as will be discussed.

II Institutional context and legal framework

The SREP takes place in a particular asymmetric institutional context in EU Banking Supervision, which reflects differentiated integration between EU-wide and Banking Union (BU)-wide constructions. Furthermore, the SREP evolved along with regulatory developments in EU prudential regulation which recentred it on microprudential supervision from 2019 and considered new types of risks. These institutional and regulatory dimensions are first discussed before examining the evolution of other important elements in EU prudential regulation.

First, the institutional context reflects the asymmetry that still exists within the EU, with 21 BU-participating Member States, and six non-participating EU Member States which are still outside the BU.[23] EU secondary law—both the Capital Requirements Regulation (CRR) and the Capital Requirements Directive (CRD)—is applicable to the whole EU, and gives several mandates to the EBA. The EBA, as a European Supervisory Agency competent for banking in the European System of Financial Supervision (ESFS),[24] is mandated to issue guidelines in the interactive EU Single Rulebook at level 3, and to adopt draft regulatory standards at level 2, which are formally adopted by the European Commission. Furthermore, more specific guidance and common methodologies are published by the ECB, as the competent authority in the BU.

Second, the relevant legal framework for SREP is constituted of EU secondary law provisions found primarily in the CRD (Articles 97, 98, 104, 105,

[23] Takis Tridimas, 'The Constitutional Dimension of the Banking Union' in Stefan Grundmann and Hans-W Micklitz (eds), *The European Banking Union and Constitution: Beacon for Advanced Integration or Death-Knell for Democracy* (Hart Publishing 2019); Alberto de Gregorio Merino, 'The Banking Union in EU Law: An EU Institutional Law Perspective' in Gianni Lo Schiavo (ed), *The European Banking Union and the Role of Law* (Edward Elgar 2019), https://www.elgaronline.com/view, accessed 20 April 2024; Christy Ann Petit, 'Differentiated Governance in the Banking Union: Single Mechanisms, Joint Teams, and Opting-Ins' (2022) 7 European Papers—A Journal on Law and Integration 889.

[24] Niamh Moloney, 'International Financial Governance, the EU, and Brexit: The "Agencification" of EU Financial Governance and the Implications' (2016) 17 European Business Organization Law Review 451.

and 110), and, more specifically, level 2 and level 3 acts within the Single Rulebook, for which the EBA is responsible. In the level 3 acts of the Single Rulebook, the EBA first issued guidelines on SREP in 2014, and these were reviewed in 2021, following the adoption of the CRD V and CRR III[25] (see section III below). The EBA elaborates and issues Guidelines with a view to 'establishing consistent, efficient and effective supervisory practices within the ESFS, and to ensuring the common, uniform and consistent application of Union law' (Art 16(1), Regulation (EU) No 1093/2010 as amended (hereinafter 'EBA Regulation')). EBA Guidelines are not legally binding, as they are precisely not among the binding technical standards, but the comply-or-explain mechanism and the effort for harmonization and convergence may nuance their legal nature and degree of bindingness.[26] As this chapter focuses on the SREP in ECB direct supervision, it is important to note the combination of Article 4(1)(f) and Article 16(2) of the SSM Regulation to empower the ECB with supervisory powers, and which provide a legal basis for the adoption of supervisory measures.[27]

The SREP-related provisions from the CRD have been amended several times in EU law, in order to focus on microprudential risks, cover new types of risks, and make the SREP methodology more proportionate. First, the 2019 legislative review led to the CRD V and confined the SREP to a microprudential approach. This change is briefly discussed in relation to the exclusion of systemic risks and hence of macrolevel direct considerations. Under the former CRD IV provision, the risks an institution posed to the financial system incorporated the identification and measurement of systemic risk.[28] However, this systemic risk was removed from the list of risks to be evaluated in the SREP in the CRD V. The rationale of this change was to confine the SREP and related Pillar 2 requirements to 'micro-prudential purposes'.[29] In its proposal, the

[25] EBA, 'Guidelines on Common Procedures and Methodologies for the Supervisory Review and Evaluation Process (SREP)' (European Banking Authority 2014) EBA/GL/2014/13, https://www.eba.europa.eu/sites/default/files/documents, accessed 18 October 2024; EBA, 'EBA Guidelines, EBA/GL/2014/13 as amended by EBA/GL/2018/03 (Consolidated version)' (European Banking Authority 2018); EBA, 'Final Report on Guidelines' (n 4).

[26] Diane Fromage, Mariolina Eliantonio, and Kathryn Wright, 'Soft Law and Multilevel Cooperation as Sources of (New) Constitutional Challenges in EU Economic and Monetary Integration: Introduction to the Special Issue' (2022) 23 Journal of Banking Regulation 1; Merijn Chamon and Nathan de Arriba-Sellier, 'FBF: On the Justiciability of Soft Law and Broadening the Discretion of EU Agencies: ECJ (Grand Chamber) 15 July 2021, Case C-911/19, Fédération Bancaire Française (FBF) v Autorité de Contrôle Prudentiel et de Résolution, ECLI:EU:C:2021:599' (2022) 18 European Constitutional Law Review 2.

[27] See section III on the SREP methodology.

[28] Former art 97(1)(b), CRD IV, deleted in CRD V.

[29] European Commission, 'Proposal for a directive of the European Parliament and the Council amending Directive 2013/36/EU as regards exempted entities, financial holding companies, mixed

Commission emphasized the need for a clearer delineation of responsibilities, to avoid a situation in which the Pillar 2 measures (competence of the ECB in the SSM) undermine the effectiveness and efficiency of macroprudential instruments (whose scope is more diffuse between the ECB's macroprudential tasks, in accordance with Article 5 of the SSM Regulation, the role of the European Systemic Risk Board (ESRB), and the National Competent Authorities (NCAs) in their notification of macroprudential requirements).[30]

Therefore, the SREP has followed a purely microprudential perspective as a result of the 2019 CRD review.[31] While, in substantive law, this change matters, in prudential supervision it was not so radical a change, considering the obligation on the ECB as competent authority to inform the EBA in the event that the supervised entity poses systemic risk (Article 97(5) CRD V, upheld from previous CRD IV, and still in force in the CRD VI). We can expect the ESRB to be kept informed too, considering its function to assess and monitor systemic risks in the ESFS, and the close cooperation of competent authorities with the ESRB.[32]

Moreover, over the course of the latest legislative reviews and alongside broader EU policy developments, the SREP elements have put particular focus on certain risk areas, such as money laundering (ML) and terrorism financing risks; environmental, social, and governance (ESG) risks; and crypto-assets-related risks.[33]

For anti-money laundering (AML), Articles 91 and 97 CRD both clarified the integration of money-laundering concerns and suspicions into prudential supervision assessment, and their reporting to competent authorities (as amended by CRD V). Prudential supervisors are required to consider AML/CFT findings within the SREP and notify the EBA or competent AML authority (as per Article 97(6) CRD V).[34] With the AML Single Rulebook and

financial holding companies, remuneration, supervisory measures and powers and capital conservation measures' COM (2016) 854 final, 11.

[30] Franklin Allen and Elena Carletti, 'Systemic Risk and Macroprudential Regulation' in Hans-W Micklitz and Takis Tridimas (eds), *Risk and EU Law* (Edward Elgar 2015); Tobias H Tröger, 'Regulatory Influence on Market Conditions in the Banking Union: The Cases of Macro-Prudential Instruments and the Bail-in Tool' (2015) 16 European Business Organization Law Review 575, 580; Alexander Kern, 'The European Central Bank and Banking Supervision: The Regulatory Limits of the Single Supervisory Mechanism' (2016) 24 European Company and Financial Law Review 467.

[31] However, it meant a reinforced flexibility being granted to macroprudential tools implemented at the national level: see Carla Stamegna, 'Amending Capital Requirements – The "CRD V Package"' (2019) European Parliamentary Research Service 11.

[32] See art 6(d) CRD.

[33] There are also IT, security, and cyber risks, as well as geopolitical risks, as mentioned in the introduction.

[34] Those ML suspicions can be part of the fit and proper assessment, another supervisory process (art 91(1) CRD V).

AML Authority in 2025, policymakers have strengthened the regulatory and supervisory framework for AML, but it remains to be seen how the interplay between prudential supervision and AML supervision will operate,[35] including in the context of the SREP. What is critical is the access to data and information of the supervised entities,[36] building upon the existing multilateral agreement between the ECB and national AML/CFT authorities in the European Economic Area (EEA), adopted in 2019.[37] The AML agreement should have already allowed some more structured exchanges of information among these authorities on a case-by-case and 'relevant and necessary'[38] to know basis, to justify information sharing. It is reported that more than 500 such exchanges took place in 2020, and 1,000 exchanges in 2022.[39] This two-way information exchange may concern the SREP, ie for supervisors to transmit targeted prudential findings to AML/CFT authorities, including from the SREP exercise, and, vice versa, AML/CFT risk assessment transmitted from AML authorities to the ECB as prudential authority,[40] which can feed into the SREP assessment of internal governance and risk management, but also the assessment of the business model (see section III.2 below).

Furthermore, the integration of ESG risks in the prudential regulatory framework also reshaped prudential supervision and the conduct of the SREP. In particular, the ECB adopted a guide to set supervisory expectations on climate-related and environmental risks (C&E risks), in 2020, followed by several items of policy guidance, which constitutes an area of increased focus of the SREP.[41] It must be noted that the CRD VI also reinforced the duty of

[35] Gianni Lo Schiavo, 'The Single Supervisory Mechanism (SSM) and the EU Anti-Money Laundering Framework Compared: Governance, Rules, Challenges and Opportunities' (2022) 23 Journal of Banking Regulation 91; Christy Ann Petit, 'Anti-Money Laundering' in Miroslava Scholten (ed), *Research Handbook on the Enforcement of EU Law* (Edward Elgar 2023), https://www.elgaronline.com, accessed 20 April 2024.

[36] Édouard Fernandez-Bollo, 'Preventing Money Laundering through European Banks' (*The Supervision Blog*, 28 February 2023), https://www.bankingsupervision.europa.eu/press/blog, accessed 4 November 2024.

[37] On the basis of art 57a(2) of Directive (EU) 2015/849, art 117(5) of the CRD, and EBA Guidelines on cooperation and information exchange between prudential supervisors, AML/CFT supervisors and financial intelligence units under Directive 2013/36/EU (EBA/GL/2021/15): see ECB and Competent Authorities, 'Multilateral Agreement on the Practical Modalities for Exchange of Information Pursuant to Article 57a(2) of Directive (EU) 2015/849', https://eba.europa.eu/documents/10180/2545547, accessed 5 November 2024.

[38] Elizabeth McCaul, 'Trends in the Prudential Supervision of Money Laundering and Terrorism Financing (ML/TF) Risks' (Compliance talks, 24 May 2021), https://www.bankingsupervision.europa.eu/press, slide 5.

[39] As of September 2020, Édouard Fernandez-Bollo, 'ECB Banking Supervision's Role in Anti-Money Laundering/Combating the Financing of Terrorism (AML/CFT)' (30 September 2020); as of June 2022, Elizabeth McCaul, 'ECB Banking Supervision's Role in AML/CFT' (22 June 2022), https://www.bankingsupervision.europa.eu/press.

[40] McCaul, 'Trends in the Prudential Supervision' (n 38), slide 5.

[41] ECB, 'ECB Banking Supervision: SSM Supervisory Priorities for 2024–2026' 12–14.

competent authorities to include ESG risks and related exposures as part of the SREP governance and risk management processes' assessment (Article 98(9) CRD VI),[42] and this effort is part of specific plans adopted by the banks' management bodies, supported with quantifiable targets and processes to address ESG risks (as per Article 76(2) CRD VI). In terms of enforcement and supervisory powers, the CRD VI includes additional supervisory powers to request the reduction of ESG risks, and specific adjustments and actions in the banks' transition plans (Article 104(m) CRD VI).

Moreover, supervisors can require banks to undertake stress testing or scenario analysis in the context of crypto-asset exposures and provision of crypto-asset services (Article 104(n) CRD VI). With the latest legislative amendments, the treatment of crypto-assets-related risks is subject to an enhanced focus, and will also be grasped in the SREP supervisory findings.[43]

The CRD V also aimed at ensuring more proportionality in the SREP, with tailored methodologies to take into account similar risk profiles, business models, and geographical location of exposures (as per Article 97(4a) CRD V), and reflects the co-legislators' intent to treat differently the 'small and non-complex institutions' (a category formally introduced by the CRR II).[44] This objective was further pursued in the context of the last CRD VI/CRR III amendments. The changes give a set of conditions for the application of a proportionate SREP, which, in a nutshell, seems primarily applicable to Less Significant Institutions (LSIs, in the SSM typology)[45] of a specific nature, as there is an express reference to 'mutuals, cooperative societies or savings institutions' (as per Article 97(4)(d)(i) CRD VI). It must be noted that the ECB, as a competent authority, must publish the criteria for applying proportionality in SREP, which is broadly explained on the ECB Banking Supervision website.[46]

The CRD VI and CRR III—both adopted in 2024—led to another review of the EBA Guidelines on SREP,[47] considering this emphasis on proportionality. The ECB's supervisory methodology for SREP is now examined below.

[42] On ESG specifically, see art 87a, CRD VI. The CRR was also amended regarding ESG risks, ie arts 430 and 501c for ESG risks exposures in reporting.

[43] See arts 79, 81, 83, and 85 CRD VI.

[44] Any tailored methodologies must be notified to the EBA, which can also issue dedicated guidelines to similar risk profiles: see art 97(4a) CRD V. As for small and non-complex institutions, see art 4(1), point 145 of Regulation (EU) 2019/876 (CRR 2).

[45] Due to a reference to a limit of total assets up to 30 billion euros, as well as the exclusion of G-SII, non-EU G-SII, O-SII: see art 97(4) CRD VI.

[46] The exact contours of the common SREP methodology for LSIs are not available publicly: see ECB, 'Supervisory Approach and Methodologies' (ECB Banking Supervision, 15 July 2024), https://www.bankingsupervision.europa.eu/banking, accessed 5 November 2024.

[47] And, in any event, of additional guidelines, for instance for the output floor: see art 104a(7) CRD VI. See the EBA's consultation opened in October 2025, available at https://www.eba.europa.eu/publi

III SREP methodology

This section reviews the detailed methodology about SREP, including its components, the four SREP elements, and the scores. Finally, it discusses the notion of supervisory engagement with constrained judgement, and to what extent horizontal inputs and benchmarking may preserve equal treatment across banks.

1 SREP Guidelines and components

Within the prudential framework set by the EU legislators, the EBA was mandated to draft Guidelines on SREP which specify the common procedures and methodologies in accordance with Article 107(3) of the CRD, together with other legal provisions applicable for the assessment of the organization and treatment of risks.[48] These Guidelines are addressed to 'competent authorities', ie to national supervisory authorities in the EU, the NCAs, and the ECB as competent authority in the BU. These Guidelines, level 3 of the Single Rulebook, are legally based on the CRD—level 1—as mentioned above.

However, EBA Guidelines are not supposed to 'merely refer to, or reproduce, elements of legislative acts': therefore, the EBA must endeavour 'to avoid any duplication' (as per Article 16(2a) of the EBA Regulation).[49] Concretely, it entails that the EBA elaborated the SREP Guidelines based on, and at the same time beyond, the level 1 provisions, and considered not only level 2 acts of the Single Rulebook (technical standards) but also level 3 acts. Indeed, the EBA expressly intends to ensure that SREP Guidelines are consistent with other EBA Guidelines,[50] assesses the information provided by the competent authorities,

cations-and-media/press-releases/eba-consults-revised-guidelines-supervisory-review-and-evaluation-process-and-supervisory-stress, accessed 26 October 2025.

[48] As per arts 76–87 CRD.

[49] Regulation (EU) 2019/2175 of the European Parliament and of the Council of 18 December 2019 amending Regulation (EU) No 1093/2010 establishing a European Supervisory Authority (European Banking Authority), Regulation (EU) No 1094/2010 establishing a European Supervisory Authority (European Insurance and Occupational Pensions Authority), Regulation (EU) No 1095/2010 establishing a European Supervisory Authority (European Securities and Markets Authority), Regulation (EU) No 600/2014 on markets in financial instruments, Regulation (EU) 2016/1011 on indices used as benchmarks in financial instruments and financial contracts or to measure the performance of investment funds, and Regulation (EU) 2015/847 on information accompanying transfers of funds [2019] OJ L334, pp 1–145.

[50] Reference is made to 'other EU regulatory products', including the Guidelines: see EBA, 'Final Report on Guidelines' (n 4) 8.

to develop consistency in the SREP, and conducts peer reviews (as per Article 107(1), second paragraph, and 107(2), second paragraph, CRD). In the 2022 review of its SREP Guidelines, the EBA outlined its objective to align 'the text with other relevant guidelines, technical standards, as well as enhancing the guidance by incorporating identified best practices'.[51]

Against this background, the EBA SREP Guidelines are not only based on, and inspired by, prudential regulation, but are also based on institutional and administrative developments, ie from national supervisory practices, and, for the BU competent authority for SIs, from the ECB's supervisory practices. In this regard, European Banking Supervision has developed specific methodologies and guidelines for SREP in the SSM (see section III.2 below) and a Supervisory Manual.[52] This manual aims at ensuring consistency for supervisors at the ECB and across the SSM, as well as transparency of supervisory expectations for supervised entities. Such iterative and co-creative administrative and regulatory process gives interesting insights into the supervisory regime in the EU and in the BU.

The SREP components aim at framing the supervisory work in terms of the *substantive* assessment (in terms of which risks or business aspects are under review—see letters (b) to (h) below), and in terms of *methods* in the process, ie categorizing the institutions (a), combining the scores for the overall SREP assessment (i), and setting the adequate supervisory measures (j). According to the EBA Guidelines, the supervisors must examine the following components:

a. categorisation of the institution and periodic review of this categorisation;
b. monitoring of key indicators;
c. business model analysis (BMA);
d. assessment of internal governance and institution-wide controls;
e. assessment of risks to capital;
f. assessment of risks to liquidity;
g. assessment of the adequacy of the institution's own funds;
h. assessment of the adequacy of the institution's liquidity resources;
i. overall SREP assessment; and
j. supervisory measures (and early intervention measures, where necessary).[53]

[51] ibid 6.

[52] It was, first, a short guide, followed by more detailed supervisory processes and defined common approaches in the Supervisory Manual, updated in 2024: see ECB, 'Guide to Banking Supervision' (2014); ECB, 'SSM Supervisory Manual' (2018); ECB, 'SSM Supervisory Manual' (n 15).

[53] EBA, 'Final Report on Guidelines' (n 4) 25.

In combining all of these components, the supervisors base their assessments on past data and developments and assess the bank's future viability, with a forward-looking approach in the risk assessment, which is supposed to be holistic. This combines both short-term and medium- or long-term approaches, which in the latter case corresponds to the sustainability[54] of the entity.

In terms of outcomes after the whole supervisory process, the supervisors will have identified the vulnerabilities, deficiencies, and risks to which the bank is exposed, and will adopt supervisory measures—quantitative and/or qualitative, as discussed in section III.2 below—to mitigate them, in a SREP decision. The measures all rely on 'supervisory findings'[55] and are based on EU banking regulation, in particular the EU Single Rulebook. SREP decisions are legally binding on the banks (administrative decisions) and applicable for the following year, for example the findings and requirements from the SREP 2024 cycle will be applicable to 2025, unless a SREP decision is adopted for a longer cycle with a multi-year assessment (see the process-oriented reforms under section IV.1 below).

2 SREP elements and phases

In the SREP cycle, four elements are assessed by the supervisors. The EBA Guidelines list them as follows: business model and strategy, internal governance and institution-wide controls, capital adequacy, and liquidity adequacy.[56] Taken together, they help to pursue a holistic approach to the risk profile of the supervised entities (holistic approach that can be, to some extent, contested in the reform of SREP (see section IV below)). The ECB's supervisory methodology also relies on these four elements. However, they are phrased slightly differently, with minor adjustments in their wording: Element 1 (business model), Element 2 (internal governance and risk management), Element 3 (risks to capital), and Element 4 (risks to liquidity and funding).[57]

The way in which the ECB conveys its approach to SREP has evolved. Beyond the Supervisory Manual mentioned above, there used to be SREP Methodology Booklets (with editions from 2015 until 2018).[58] Since 2019, a web page has been dedicated to supervisory methodology,[59] and since 2023,

[54] ECB, 'SSM Supervisory Manual' (n 15) 86.
[55] ibid 82.
[56] EBA, 'Final Report on Guidelines' (n 4) 30.
[57] ECB, 'SSM Supervisory Manual' (n 15) 84.
[58] 'SSM SREP Methodology Booklet – 2018 Edition'.
[59] ECB, 'Supervisory Methodology 2023' (n 4).

some SREP 'documents', published along that methodology, have focused on each element separately, ie internal governance and risk management, business model assessment, credit risk, and market risk.[60] There is also a SREP manual with instructions and detailed operational guidance for JSTs,[61] though it is not publicly available.

Figure 7.1 below represents the elements of the ECB Banking Supervision SREP methodology.

The approach to the four elements distinguishes risk level and risk control, which matters to determine also the supervisory engagement (see section III, hereinafter). As per the EBA Guidelines, supervisors focus on quantitative

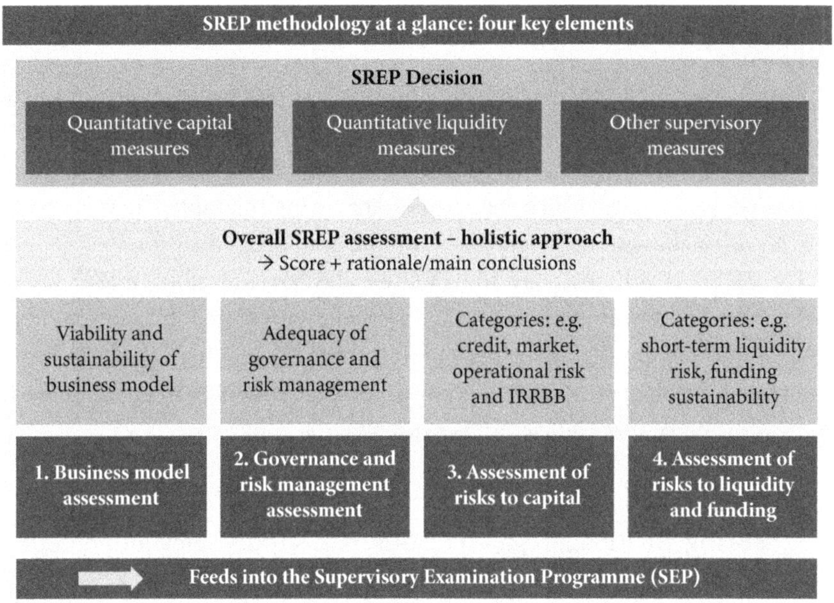

Figure 7.1 SREP methodology at a glance

Source: ECB Banking Supervision, 'Supervisory Methodology' (2023)[62] © European Central Bank, Frankfurt am Main, Germany. The information related to this figure may be obtained free of charge through the ECB Banking Supervision website, available at https://www.bankingsupervision.europa.eu/banking/srep.

[60] ECB, 'Internal Governance and Risk Management (IGRM) SREP Methodology', https://www.bankingsupervision.europa.eu/banking/srep/2023, accessed 14 October 2024; ECB, 'Business Model Assessment SREP Methodology', https://data.europa.eu/doi/10.2866/622308, accessed 14 October 2024; ECB, 'Credit Risk SREP Methodology', https://data.europa.eu/doi/10.2866/446527, accessed 14 October 2024; ECB, 'Market Risk SREP Methodology', https://data.europa.eu/doi/10.2866/648758, accessed 14 October 2024.

[61] ECA, 'Special Report 12/2023' (n 6) 18.

[62] ECB, 'Supervisory Methodology 2023' (n 4).

(risk level) and/or qualitative (risk control) approaches to the four SREP elements. Business models, capital risks, and liquidity and funding risks are assessed from a risk-level perspective, and internal governance and risk management, capital risks, and liquidity and funding risks from a risk-control perspective.

According to the ECB's supervisory methodology, the SREP cycle follows three phases. It starts with the gathering of data from the supervised entity and consideration of the materiality of each type of risk. It continues with a preliminary anchoring score for the entity's risk level (which is automated), and, for risk control, the JSTs ensure formal compliance checks.[63] Finally, the supervisors exert supervisory judgement with a 'more thorough risk assessment' in the third phase that accounts for the entity's situation. When combining the risk-level and risk-control assessment, the JSTs obtain the combined SREP score.

It must be noted that, before the approval process (with approval of the draft SREP decision by the Supervisory Board, and its adoption by the ECB Governing Council), the JSTs consult with the banks, which is part of the supervisory dialogue. Moreover, banks are formally granted a right to be heard, which allows them to comment on the draft SREP decision.[64]

The SREP is presented by the ECB as 'flexible and adjustable',[65] which means that the supervisors assess each element with varied 'frequency, scope and depth',[66] depending on the bank's circumstances. In other words, from one bank to another, supervisors have various levels of supervisory engagement to address the bank's deficiencies and ensure that the bank stays viable.

3 Scoring, SREP aggregated results, and supervisory judgement

From the assessment of the four SREP elements, each supervised entity will receive an individual SREP 'grade', which stems from a scoring exercise. The following focuses on explaining and illustrating the overall scoring made in the SREP, and how supervisory judgement is developed.

Regarding the scoring, the SREP ultimately leads supervisors to assign 'grades' to viable institutions (1 to 4) and a negative grade (F) to an entity that is failing or likely to fail (FOLTF). The supervisors, examining each of the four SREP elements, will decide on a combined score, which can range from a

[63] ibid.
[64] See art 22, SSM Regulation.
[65] ECB, 'SSM Supervisory Manual' (n 15) 82.
[66] ibid.

low-risk score (1) to a high-risk score (4); in between, (2) is medium-low, and (3) is medium-high.[67]

In order to get an overview of the supervisory practice in scoring in the ECB SREP exercise, let us compare the SREP aggregated results from 2015 until 2023.[68] The worst score (4) decreased over time (from 11% in 2015 to 3% in 2023), as a proportion of the banks receiving a SREP decision from the ECB, and no F score was attributed (or at least not disclosed publicly). Furthermore, the lowest-risk score (1) was attributed only in 2015 and 2016, and to a small proportion of banks (2%). The second-lowest-risk score (2) increased between 2015 and 2018 (from 44% to 52%), but decreased between 2019 and 2023 (from 49% to 45%).

Since the SREP 2022 results, the publications have also documented new 'buckets' or qualifiers with +/- added to the 2 and 3 scores (ie 2+, 2, 2- and 3+, 3, 3-). The main objective is to ensure 'more granular and accurate scoring' of the supervisory assessment,[69] with a 'more precise reflection of the year-to-year evolution'.[70] Over the few years for which data is available, the main findings relate to a decrease of score 4 (from 7% to 3%), which may be (partly) explained by the increase of the closest bucket, 3- (from 8% to 12%). Qualitatively, this categorization may have an influence on the perception of the banks' performances, as some of them are getting closer to lower scores (when it is in the + bucket, it shows a probability to go 'down' to the lower score, eg from 3 + to 2-). Indeed, even before this review of the scoring system, research had started to document how the disclosure of SREP scores, as taken into account by investors, can lead to market price corrections on the day of the results' publication.[71] By ensuring more dispersion across scores, there is an expectation to

[67] ECB, 'SSM Supervisory Manual' (n 15) 86.

[68] There is no aggregated score available for 2014, as the 2014 SREP cycle was based on national approaches: see ECA, 'Special Report 12/2023' (n 6) 8; and 'SSM SREP Methodology Booklet – 2015 Edition'; 'SSM SREP Methodology Booklet – 2016 Edition'; 'SSM SREP Methodology Booklet – 2017 Edition'; 'SSM SREP Methodology Booklet – 2018 Edition' (n 58); and see the aggregated results at ECB, 'Supervisory Review (SREP)' (28 May 2024), https://www.bankingsupervision.europa.eu/banking/srep/html/index.en.html, accessed 16 October 2024. The population of banks receiving this score has changed over time, in terms of both numbers and entities considered, with some exits and entries on the market or relocation in the BU area post-Brexit. Moreover, and in relation to the change of the scope of direct banking supervision, the number of SREP decisions changed over time.

[69] ECB, 'Aggregated results of SREP 2022', https://www.bankingsupervision.europa.eu/banking/srep/2023, accessed 15 October 2024.

[70] It was based on a project conducted during the 2021 SREP cycle to introduce 'more granular and accurate scoring' for the assessment of internal governance, and of the overall SREP score: see ECB, 'Supervisory Methodology 2023' (n 4).

[71] Only 43 SIs in 14 Member States were in the sample, between 2015 and 2020: see Riccardo Ferretti, Valeria Venturelli, and Alessandro Azzaretto, 'Does Individual SREP Results Reveal Real News?' (2023) 57 Finance Research Letters 104184.

decrease reputational risks, as the change across scores can be more gradual.[72] Moreover, research has shown that increased transparency reduced the pessimistic expectations from investors.[73]

In any event, regardless of the gradual and granular SREP scores, the supervisory process gives significant discretion to the supervisors. In the jargon, we refer to the fact that supervisors resort to their supervisory judgment.[74] The scoring gives a numerical representation of the viability of the institution, with primarily a holistic approach. JST members resort to their judgement, in particular in the last, third phase (as introduced in section III.2), which is flanked by some horizontal adjustments (see subsection 4 hereinafter). The supervisors resort to what is called 'constrained judgement', where the JSTs consider the risk profile of the entity; its position among other peers, through benchmarking; the macroeconomic context; the capital and liquidity planning; and the SSM risk tolerance framework.

The ECA had actually considered that there were not 'objective criteria for the exercise of constrained judgement by JSTs', in its Special Report published in May 2023.[75] This criticism reflects the significant discretion the JSTs hold in the SREP, but does not fully account for the different adjustments and safeguards in the process. Besides this criticism, the ECA adopted a nuanced perspective by acknowledging the JSTs' access to operational guidance and assessment instructions in the SREP Manual (mentioned above), and the potential factors JSTs may take into account, but it did not comprehend how consistency across JSTs is achieved in practice.[76] This point somehow overlooks the multiple institutional layers that are designed into the process, from benchmarking and horizontal inputs to legal and due process checks to indeed ensure consistency, and alignments across SIs. Moreover, the SSM risk tolerance framework, already adopted for the 2023 SREP cycle, represents a strategic steering by the Supervisory Board over the JSTs' assessment, in so far as the SSM priorities must also be considered in the SREP outcome.[77]

The framework also illustrates the objective to have a more tailor-made approach to a supervised entity in the SSM risk-based supervisory culture.[78] As

[72] The Expert Group suggested basing scores on the actual performance in addressing deficiencies: see Dahlgren and others (n 2) 36.
[73] Ferretti, Venturelli, and Azzaretto (n 71).
[74] EBA, 'Final Report on Guidelines' (n 4) 12.
[75] ECA, 'Special Report 12/2023' (n 6) 18.
[76] ibid.
[77] Elderson, 'The First Decade of European Supervision' (n 1) and Elderson, 'Powers, Ability and Willingness to Act' (n 1).
[78] ECB, 'Supervisors' Risk Tolerance: Focusing on What Matters Most' [2023] Banking Supervision Newsletter, https://www.bankingsupervision.europa.eu/press/publications/newsletter, accessed 17 October 2024.

regards SREP, this tailor-made approach implies moving away from a box-ticking exercise and an all-encompassing review, instead adopting a targeted risk focus and risk prioritization.[79] Finally, further flexibility is supposed to allow supervisors to exert additional discretion, which is, nevertheless, subject to consistency checks by other units, to ensure an equal treatment over the directly supervised banks receiving SREP decisions (see the role of benchmarking and horizontal approaches discussed hereinafter). The importance of the principle of equal treatment across banks calls for consistency across the supervisory measures, and, in concrete terms, for comparisons across the SREP results in a given cycle. The SREP scores allow this to be done in a numerical way, while new units give a 'second line of defence'.

4 Horizontal inputs, benchmarking, and governance restructuring

Supervisory judgement and discretion in the JSTs necessarily need to have checks and balances in the organization of the whole SREP process; otherwise, the process would lead to risks of unfair treatment of some entities, and disparities in supervisory approaches. Different layers are supposed to ensure the entities' equal treatment, as well as consistency in the application of EU prudential rules, and high supervisory standards in the SSM.[80]

Such layers are institutionally and materially entrenched in the SREP as a supervisory process, through guidance provision and benchmarking the JSTs' risk assessment, scores, and supervisory findings, before the SREP decisions are finalized. This is done on the basis of peer groups,[81] thanks to horizontal and specialized units for common methodology and approaches, as well as through horizontal thematic reviews. These have all been reinforced by a second line of defence, created after the 2020 reorganization of ECB Banking Supervision governance mentioned in the introduction.[82]

In particular, since 2022, a Directorate Supervisory Strategy and Risk (DSSR) has been designed to operate as an 'independent supervisory risk function'[83] whose independence is reflected at both institutional and governance levels. It is the only *Directorate*, next to the other six *Directorates-General*,[84]

[79] See Recommendations 1.1 and 1.2, Dahlgren and others (n 2).
[80] These objectives are part of the SSM Regulation itself: see arts 1 and 6, SSM Regulation.
[81] ECB, 'SSM Supervisory Manual' (n 15) 88.
[82] ECB, 'ECB Announces Organisational Changes' (n 16).
[83] ECB, 'ECB's Comments to Special Report "EU Supervision of Banks' Credit Risk: The ECB Stepped up Its Efforts, but More Is Needed to Increase Assurance That Credit Risk Is Properly Managed and Covered"' (2023) 2, 9 (hereinafter 'ECB Replies to ECA Special Report 12/2023').
[84] ECB, 'ECB Organigramme' (n 17).

and in operational processes its function is to provide inputs to other DGs, and analyses which primarily aim at ensuring consistency and common supervisory standards in direct supervision. DSSR is in charge of the benchmarking of SREP, including the scores, qualitative and quantitative measures, and horizontal analysis (which used to be undertaken by DG Microprudential Supervision IV).[85]

The second SSM Review reported that NCAs are more involved in the SREP process at the horizontal level, which may trigger some adjustments to SREP outcomes.[86] Interestingly, there is a framework 'for dealing with any dissenting views',[87] though it is not clear at which levels dissent may play out during the SREP cycle. Materially, this may lead to the adoption of other/additional supervisory measures for those peer groups of banks with similar risks and vulnerabilities. Overall, this possibility for expressing dissent may arise outside the formal decision-making process (in which NCAs' representatives are involved in the Supervisory Board for the approval of draft SREP decisions), and therefore reflects another layer for horizontal adjustments in ongoing supervision in the context of SREP.

IV Assessment of SREP effectiveness and ongoing reform

Against this background, the Expert Group mandated in 2022 to assess the SREP, and recommended some changes to ensure its effectiveness and efficiency in ECB Banking Supervision. The insights from the Expert Group assessment are extensive, as they comprehensively approached the SREP, together with other supervisory activities (ie on-site inspections, internal model investigations, fit and proper assessments, thematic horizontal reviews, deep dives, and sanctions).[88]

Stemming from the JSTs' assessment, the SREP decision may include both quantitative (for example, own funds, liquidity requirements) and qualitative measures. The qualitative measures can include changes in arrangements, processes, and strategies in the banks. For quantitative measures, as underlined in the introduction above, beyond the regulatory capital requirements (under Pillar 1), the supervisors may impose additional capital requirements—part of Pillar 2 requirements—[89] to which a leverage ratio and P2G may be added.

[85] ECB, 'SSM Supervisory Manual' (n 52) 11.
[86] Commission, 'Report on the SSM' (n 6) 7.
[87] ECB, 'ECB Replies to ECA Special Report 12/2023' (n 83) 9.
[88] Dahlgren and others (n 2) 47.
[89] Joosen, Lamandini, and Tröger (n 8).

P2G is not per se binding, but the supervisors can still implement additional measures if the bank does not comply with it.[90] Importantly, some economic research gave evidence that the imposition of capital requirements made under Pillar 1 or under Pillar 2 may not have the same effect on markets' reactions, and, as a result, on the bank.[91]

Moreover, the Expert Group considered that the supervisory approach in SREP is too centred on capital and observed that most qualitative measures are taken outside SREP; therefore, they recommended to strengthen the link between qualitative measures as appropriate with the SREP scores.[92] In particular, the risk control assessment of SREP elements (see section III.2 above) requires qualitative approaches, which may lead to supervisory measures of a qualitative nature in accordance with the CRD and EBA SREP Guidelines.[93] Therefore, supervisors may rely on these within the SREP, as well as within other supervisory procedures.

The point on underused qualitative supervisory measures is, nevertheless, partly in tension with SREP consolidated data. Indeed, while qualitative recommendations were addressed to all SIs during the 2020 SREP cycle, more recent years have seen a roughly stable number of banks receiving qualitative measures: between 96 SIs (in 2022, out of 101 SREP decisions) and 103 SIs (in 2021, out of 108 SREP decisions; and in 2023, out of 106 SREP decisions).[94] It is difficult to elaborate on this aggregated data, as we cannot associate the qualitative measures with corresponding SREP elements. In any event, this nuances to some extent the criticism from the Expert Group.

The remainder of this section focuses on effectiveness, through the changes from the viewpoint of the allocation of supervisory resources and means to reach the SREP outcomes, with methodological changes. Those changes are informed by the goals adopted by the ECB Supervisory Board to reform the SREP,[95] published after the Expert Group's report, and put in relation to the 2023 ECA recommendations and European Commission's second SSM Review. In particular, both the Expert Group and the ECA considered that the process is not efficient and not timely,[96] with too long a period allocated for the supervisory dialogue and adoption of the SREP decisions.[97]

90 ECB, 'SSM Supervisory Manual' (n 15) 90.
91 Witte (n 5).
92 Recommendation 3.1, Dahlgren and others (n 2) 42.
93 EBA, 'Final Report on Guidelines' (n 4) 12.
94 See the SREP aggregated results pages, s 4.1 for 2021, 2022, and 2023, available at: https://www.bankingsupervision.europa.eu/press/publications, accessed 10 October 2024.
95 Claudia Buch, 'Reforming the SREP: An Important Milestone towards More Efficient and Effective Supervision in a New Risk Environment' (*The Supervision Blog*, 2024), https://www.bankingsupervision.europa.eu/press/blog/2024, accessed 8 July 2024.
96 Recommendation 1.4, Dahlgren and others (n 2).
97 ECA, 'Special Report 12/2023' (n 6) 24–25, 44.

I categorize these changes as either process-oriented, methodology-driven, or enforcement-related.

1 Process and rescoping the SREP

The rescoping of the SREP is visible, with a multi-year assessment already in place in 2023, and the wish to better integrate the planning of supervisory activities also within the SREP.

First, the multi-year assessment involves choosing areas of priorities, with 'specific modules each year',[98] in line with the SSM risk tolerance framework (see section III.3 above)—which were initiatives already launched at the time of the SREP assessment by the Expert Group. Supervisors intend to widen the number of banks which would receive a SREP decision on a biannual, instead of yearly, basis. Moreover, the second SSM Review by the European Commission referred to a base SREP, complemented by a 'comprehensive SREP at least every 3 years'.[99] This illustrates well the rescoping of the SREP cycles in time and in substance, in order to use supervisory resources in relation to targeted and most pressing risks.

However, this may lead to compartmentalization of the supervisory approach to some of the supervised entities' risks, which can lead to different timelines and make horizontal analysis and consistency checks more challenging over years and peer groups. Moreover, the focus on specific risks inherently increases the likelihood that other risk areas may be overlooked or insufficiently scrutinized by the supervisors.

Second, the new approach to SREP will integrate better the planning of several other supervisory activities, 'to maximise synergies'.[100] This integrated planning might be a reaction to observations made by the ECA Special Report, on unplanned work.[101] Beyond planning, this should also implement the Expert Group recommendation at a substantive level, namely to 'better integrate the outcomes of other supervisory activities into the SREP assessments and measures'.[102] In other words, this calls the JSTs to tie other supervisory

[98] ECB, 'FAQ on the SREP of Tomorrow' (ECB Banking Supervision, 28 May 2024), https://www.bankingsupervision.europa.eu/press/publications, accessed 8 July 2024.
[99] Commission, 'Report on the SSM' (n 6) 5.
[100] Buch, 'Reforming the SREP' (n 95).
[101] ECA, 'Special Report 12/2023' (n 6) 20.
[102] Recommendation 1.3, Dahlgren and others (n 2) 24.

findings and prudential outcomes to the SREP—both the base SREP and triennial comprehensive SREP (as distinguished above).

2 Supervisory methodologies

The methodology-driven changes showcase a simplification of, as well as a qualitative leap in, the supervisory dialogue with the banks.

The objective to have consistent methodologies and approaches may be harmed by the multiplication and complexification of manifold guides, guidance, and frameworks over a decade of existence of ECB Banking Supervision. In the effort of simplification in the ECB's overall governance, the SREP is no exception. The objective is to have more stable methodologies, but also 'simpler and more transparent' ones.[103] For instance, the SREP review triggered a review of the P2R methodology, expected to be implemented in 2026.[104] This review also stems from the 2023 ECA Special Report, although the ECB considered that its P2R methodology was in line with EBA Guidelines.[105]

The supervisors wish to have more concise communication with the banks as part of their supervisory dialogue, in particular by reducing the length of SREP decisions, with better-focused decisions and clearly outlined supervisory expectations.[106] Since 2021, SREP decisions have been sent together with an 'executive letter', to draw the key priorities and also set out the key drivers for P2R.[107] The ECB, in its answer to the ECA Special Report, acknowledged that there is 'potential to further enhance transparency towards banks when communicating the main drivers of P2Rs'.[108] Moreover, the Expert Group recommended explaining more clearly the rationale behind the SREP scores; including narrative sections in the SREP decisions or executive letter to better frame supervisory findings and measures; and adding an annex providing a full overview of pending supervisory processes beyond the SREP.[109] However, it remains to be seen how these will be operationalized in the future SREP cycles.

[103] Buch, 'Reforming the SREP' (n 95).
[104] ECB, 'FAQ on the SREP of Tomorrow' (n 98).
[105] Recommendation 3, ECA, 'Special Report 12/2023' (n 6); ECB, 'ECB Replies to ECA Special Report 12/2023' (n 83) 1, 6.
[106] Buch, 'Reforming the SREP' (n 95).
[107] ECA, 'Special Report 12/2023' (n 6) 32.
[108] ECB, 'ECB Replies to ECA Special Report 12/2023' (n 83) 6.
[109] Recommendations 1.6 and 2.2, Dahlgren and others (n 2) 27, 36.

Overall, the primary concern for concise communication shows a qualitative leap forward, as, at the start of the SSM, concern was largely expressed towards higher transparency on SREP Pillar 2-related measures and their justifications.[110]

3 Enforcement-related changes and more stringent supervision

Beyond the amendments in the regulatory framework (see section II above), the supervisors are invited by SSM high-level decision-makers to use all available supervisory tools[111] and the 'escalation ladder',[112] climbing over several supervisory measures to remediate material risks and deficiencies. In other words, this means that the reform of SREP also aims at strengthening the enforcement of EU prudential regulation through more stringent supervision. For instance, the Expert Group highlighted a way forward in prioritizing qualitative measures through the existing four-point severity scale (in the escalation process) to select the 'most severe findings that warrant binding qualitative measures in the SREP decision'.[113] Any delay would be followed by enforcement actions. They also recommend a fully-fledged test to assess the effectiveness of qualitative measures, based on the following attributes: specific, measurable, achievable, relevant, and time-bound measures.[114]

4 Towards a more effective SREP?

The Expert Group considered that three to four months could be saved in the SREP cycle thanks to process-related measures and substantive changes in the assessment of risks and P2R determination.[115] How exactly the SREP may be shorter in its processes, ie with a shorter time frame for SREP and better allocation of supervisory resources for 'real-time supervision',[116] is still to be

[110] ECA, 'Single Supervisory Mechanism - Good Start but Further Improvements Needed' (2016) ECA Special Report No 29/2016 49–50; yet, see Commission, 'Report on the SSM' (n 6) 5.

[111] Buch, 'Reforming the SREP' (n 95).

[112] See an example with climate-related and environmental risks in a speech by Elderson, 'The First Decade of European Supervision' (n 1) and Elderson, 'Powers, Ability and Willingness to Act' (n 1); and the escalation framework in ECB, 'Supervisory Measures', https://www.bankingsupervision.europa.eu/banking, accessed 17 October 2024.

[113] Recommendation 3.2, Dahlgren and others (n 2) 43.

[114] Recommendation 3.4, ibid 44.

[115] ibid 25.

[116] Buch, 'Reforming the SREP' (n 95).

determined in the future SREP cycles, building on multi-year assessment and other potential changes as discussed above. Among the changes outlined by the group, I would challenge the parallel runs of multiple processes, in particular the idea to conduct the supervisory dialogue and the right to be heard at the same time.[117] The restructuring of the decision-making process for SREP decisions should be very carefully thought through to ensure full compliance with due process requirements and mitigate litigation risks.

In addition, the SREP's effectiveness could have been assessed in FOLTF cases,[118] in particular by examining the link between FOLTF assessments and prior SREP scores for banks in the years preceding their FOLTF assessment (when these did not stem from reputational issues but deficiencies and breaches of capital requirements).[119] It is not possible to do so with publicly available data from the FOLT assessments published for the nine banks assessed as FOLTF by the ECB since 2017,[120] and it remains uncertain whether this data was considered in the scope of the brainstorming and interview sessions carried out by the experts.[121]

V Conclusion

In the first decade of SREP in ECB direct Banking Supervision, we observed both regulatory changes in EU prudential regulation (from CRD IV/CRR to CRD VI/CRR III) and evolutions in prudential supervision regarding common methodologies and processes. The latter were supported by EBA SREP Guidelines and subsequent revisions, together with a significant number of guidelines and guidance from the ECB, as the competent authority in the BU.[122] The main concern in regulation and supervision has been to cater for

[117] Dahlgren and others (n 2) 25.

[118] Indeed, the EBA Guidelines on SREP closely interact with two other sets of EBA Guidelines: on the triggers to use early intervention measures (EBA/GL/2015/03), and on the interpretation of the different circumstances when an institution shall be considered as failing or likely to fail (EBA/GL/2015/07) under the Bank Recovery and Resolution Directive.

[119] ECB, '"Failing or Likely to Fail" Assessment of Veneto Banca Società per Azioni', https://www.bankingsupervision.europa.eu/ecb/pub/pdf, accessed 18 April 2022; ECB, '"Failing or Likely to Fail" Assessment of Banca Popolare Di Vicenza Società per Azioni', https://www.bankingsupervision.europa.eu/ecb/pub/pdf/ssm.2017_FOLTF_ITPVI.en.pdf, accessed 18 April 2022; ECB, '"Failing or Likely to Fail" Assessment of AS PNB Banka', https://www.bankingsupervision.europa.eu/ecb/pub/pdf/ssm.FOLTF_assessment_for_AS_PNB_Banka~48c61bec79.en.pdf, accessed 18 April 2022.

[120] Christy Ann Petit, 'Failing or Likely to Fail: Banking Union Cooperation Tested since 2017' (2023) 45 Journal of European Integration 157.

[121] See Annex 4, Dahlgren and others (n 2).

[122] Also to ensure common approaches for the SREP for LSIs.

new and emerging risks in the SREP so that the safety and soundness of banks is preserved—in line with the objectives set out at the outset of the BU for microprudential supervision. Considering the regulatory framework changes and increased supervisory powers, we can consider that the SREP has been strengthened over time.

The SSM risk tolerance framework in place in 2023 allows the prioritization of some risks, which are also considered in a more tailored approach to supervised entities in the SREP cycles. In fact, looking at the latest available SREP aggregated results, the main SREP elements that remain problematic relate to internal governance and risk management, as well as the sustainability of business models of banks.[123] The most contentious area is the non-compliance of banks with risk data aggregation and risk reporting following the BCBS principles.[124] These risks, and the regulatory developments for ESG, AML/CFT, and crypto-assets-related risks, must be adequately assessed and addressed by supervisors, which will lead to supervisory tasks being prioritized differently within the SREP, with a strategic steering by the ECB's Supervisory Board.[125] Furthermore, some of the external reviewers' recommendations (from the Expert Group, the ECA, and the European Commission) are being implemented in the second half of the 2024 SREP cycle, and in the 2025 and 2026 cycles, and therefore some elements are yet to be uncovered in the concrete SREP operations.

However, overall, the reach for more efficiency in processes might be in tension with longer-term objectives which remain embedded in the reformed SREP. Longer-term objectives include ensuring stability in methodologies, predictability of processes, and consistency. The new approach may risk giving rise to a fragmented SREP for some of the significant institutions, if some SREP elements are looked at and examined biannually, each according to a different time frame, and combining a 'base SREP' with a comprehensive SREP every three years. In this context, it may be more challenging to ensure consistency and benchmarking with different timelines across the supervised entities. While this may seem like an organizational and institutional issue at first sight,

[123] ECB Banking Supervision, 'Aggregated Results of SREP 2023', https://www.bankingsupervision.europa.eu/banking/srep, accessed 29 January 2024.

[124] ECB, 'ECB Banking Supervision: SSM Supervisory Priorities for 2024–2026' (n 41) 11; see also Elderson, 'The First Decade of European Supervision' (n 1) and Elderson, 'Powers, Ability and Willingness to Act' (n 1).

[125] Buch, 'Reforming the SREP' (n 95).

this may well have substantive implications and a detrimental effect which would risk jeopardizing what was initially intended. The articulation of the key risks assessments, the different time periods, and how they relate to the overall SREP score, to maintain a holistic approach, could be further determined in the upcoming SREP cycles.

8

Navigating Capital, Leverage, TLAC, and MREL Requirements

David M Brinkman and Asen Lefterov[*]

I Introduction

This chapter will consider the genesis of capital, leverage, TLAC, and MREL requirements in international standards and the rationale behind introducing these requirements. Second, the chapter will consider the framework for their calibration and calculation, including the related powers of public authorities in this regard. This section will, in particular, zoom in on each of the requirements, as established in Union law, and will break them down into their composite parts. Third, the chapter will seek to clarify the overlaps between some of the components of the requirements. Finally, the chapter will look at compliance issues and enforcement mechanisms applicable for the various requirements.

II Genesis of capital, leverage, TLAC, and MREL requirements

The international financial system has been periodically shaken by crises, prompting regulatory responses aimed at maintaining stability and confidence. A seminal moment in this regulatory evolution was the establishment, in 1988, of the Basel Capital Accord, commonly referred to as Basel I.[1] Central to Basel I was the introduction of a minimum capital requirement, set at 8%, which financial institutions were required to maintain relative to their risk-weighted assets.

[*] The views expressed in this chapter are those of the authors and do not necessarily reflect the views of the ECB.

[1] Basel Committee on Banking Supervision, 'The International Convergence of Capital Measurement and Capital Standards', July 1988.

David M Brinkman and Asen Lefterov, *Navigating Capital, Leverage, TLAC, and MREL Requirements*
In: *EU Banking Union*. Edited by: Jonathan Bauerschmidt, Raffaele D'Ambrosio, Diane Fromage, Daniela Jaros, and Paul Weismann, Oxford University Press. © Oxford University Press 2026.
DOI: 10.1093/9780198949756.003.0009

The 8% capital requirement emerged from a confluence of factors, including the increase in international banking activities, a series of banking crises, and competitive inequalities among international banks.[2] The early 1980s witnessed a significant rise in cross-border banking activities, accompanied by a growing concern about the adequacy of capital among banks operating internationally. This concern was exacerbated by the Latin American debt crisis and the failure of several large banks, which highlighted the systemic risks posed by undercapitalized banks to the international financial system.

In response to these challenges, the Basel Committee on Banking Supervision (BCBS), formed in 1974 by the central bank governors of the Group of Ten (G10) countries, began to work on an international framework to address the capital adequacy of banks. The 8% figure was not arrived at through empirical analysis but was, rather, a pragmatic compromise that balanced the diverse interests of participating countries while aiming to enhance the soundness and stability of the international banking system. The risk-weighted assets framework, which formed the basis for calculating the capital requirement, sought to align capital requirements with the risk profile of banks' assets.

The 1988 Accord prescribed two tiers of capital—Tier 1 (core capital) and Tier 2 (supplementary capital)—and it required banks to hold capital equivalent to at least 8% of their risk-weighted assets.[3] The general difference between Tier 1 and Tier 2 capital is the quality of the capital, and the moment the capital is meant to be absorbed.

Tier 1 capital is of the highest quality and consists of Common Equity Tier 1 capital (generally abbreviated to CET1 capital) and Additional Tier 1 capital (AT1 capital). CET1 capital instruments represent a perpetual equity stake in a credit institution that can absorb losses without any limits. AT1 instruments,[4] on the other hand, are also perpetual, but often come with call options that allow the issuer to redeem them after a certain period, typically five or ten years, subject to regulatory approval. The loss absorption of these instruments can be achieved through mechanisms such as conversion into equity or write-down of the instrument's principal value.

CET1 and AT1 capital instruments are meant to absorb losses as they occur ('going-concern basis'). In contrast, Tier 2 capital is gone-concern capital; that is, when a bank fails, Tier 2 instruments must absorb losses before depositors

[2] ibid, pp 1 and 14. See also https://www.bis.org/bcbs/history.htm, accessed 13 July 2024.
[3] See pp 3 and 4, as well as p 17 (Annex 1) of the Basel I Accord.
[4] See arts 53 and 54 of the CRR.

and general creditors do. The criteria for Tier 2 inclusion are less strict than for AT1, allowing instruments with a maturity date to be eligible for Tier 2, while only perpetual instruments are eligible for AT1. Jointly, Tier 1 and Tier 2 capital are referred to as the total available regulatory capital.[5]

The 1988 Accord was initially applied to internationally active banks in G10 countries, but it was soon adopted by a larger number of countries, reflecting its acceptance as a global standard for banking regulation. By 1999, nearly all countries, including China, Russia, and India, had—at least on paper—implemented the Basel Accord.[6] Furthermore, in 2018, the Bank of International Settlement (BIS) conducted a survey of 100 jurisdictions and concluded that all had, to some extent, implemented some iteration of the Basel framework.[7]

The implementation of the 8% capital requirement led to a significant strengthening of the capital base of many banks, as institutions that were previously undercapitalized had to increase their capital levels. However, it also had unintended consequences, such as encouraging regulatory arbitrage, and the emergence of complex financial instruments designed to optimize risk-weighted assets.

An example of such unintended side effects was the incentive for banks to securitize their corporate loans and sell off the least risky securitized assets. By 'splicing' the least risky bank loans from its loan book, a bank makes its assets riskier in de facto terms, but in the *de jure* terms of Basel I, the risk weight given to the bank's corporate loans does not change. Even more, the gains from this securitization can be added to a bank's asset reserves, allowing it to give out even more risky loans. This method—called 'cherry-picking'—creates banks that, on paper, are properly protecting themselves against credit risk, but in reality are taking on quantities of risk far greater than what Basel I intended.[8]

In view of these and other elements, the static and somewhat blunt nature of the 8% requirement came under criticism for its inability to capture the complexity and dynamism of banks' risk profiles. It was argued that the

[5] See Bank of International Settlements, 'Definition of capital in Basel III—Executive Summary', available on their website at https://www.bis.org/fsi/fsisummaries/defcap_b3.pdf, accessed 10 November 2024.

[6] Bryan J Balin, 'Basel I, Basel II, and Emerging Markets: A Nontechnical Analysis' 4 (10 May 2008), available at SSRN: https://ssrn.com/abstract = 1477712 or http://dx.doi.org/10.2139/ssrn.1477712, accessed 15 May 2026.

[7] BIS, 'The Basel framework in 100 jurisdictions: implementation status and proportionality practices', available at https://www.bis.org/fsi/publ/insights11.pdf, accessed 10 November 2024.

[8] See Balin (n 6) 5.

one-size-fits-all approach did not adequately address the varying risks across different asset classes and did not account for off-balance-sheet activities.[9]

In response to these limitations, the BCBS introduced a series of amendments and revisions, leading to the development of the more risk-sensitive Basel II framework, which was published in 2004, and amended in 2006.[10] Basel II aimed to refine the risk-weighting approach and introduced the internal ratings-based (IRB) approach, allowing banks to use their own risk assessment models as input for their capital calculation, subject to regulatory approval.[11] Despite these efforts, the Great Financial Crisis of 2007–08 revealed further deficiencies in the regulatory framework, prompting the development of Basel III, which introduced additional capital buffers and enhanced the quality of capital.[12]

Basel II was a firm-specific regulatory regime. It operated under the presumption that the whole financial system could be protected and regulated by effectively monitoring each individual firm, whereas 'Basel III is BOTH a firm-specific, risk-based framework and a system-wide, systemic risk-based framework', according to the BIS.[13]

The transition from Basel II to Basel III did not change the fundamental concept of risk-weighted assets (RWAs) as a risk-based foundation for establishing the capital levels of a bank, but it did refine and enhance the way RWAs are calculated and the amount of capital banks must hold against them. Under Basel II, the focus was on more accurately measuring the risk of a bank's assets and then assigning capital accordingly. Banks could use standardized approaches provided by regulators or more advanced internal models (if approved by regulators) to determine the risk levels of their assets. These risk levels would then be used to calculate RWAs, which in turn determined how much capital the bank needed to hold.

Basel III maintained the RWA framework but introduced several key changes to strengthen the banking sector:

[9] See recital M of European Parliament resolution of 7 October 2010 on Basel II and revision of the Capital Requirements Directives (CRD 4) (2010/2074).

[10] International Convergence of Capital Measurement and Capital Standards, A Revised Framework, June 2006, https://www.bis.org/publ/bcbs128.pdf, accessed 15 May 2026.

[11] See, for an overview of the main changes, the ECB Stability Overview December 2004, accessible at www.ecb.europa.eu/pub/pdf/fsr/art/ecb.fsrart200412_04.en.pdf, accessed 13 July 2024.

[12] Basel III: A global regulatory framework for more resilient banks and banking systems, published December 2010, revised in June 2011, accessible at https://www.bis.org/publ/bcbs189.pdf, accessed 15 May 2026.

[13] Hervé Hannoun, 'The Basel III Capital Framework: A Decisive Breakthrough' (Speech, 22 November 2010), available at http://www.bis.org/speeches/sp101125a.pdf, accessed 13 July 2024.

1. **Higher Capital Requirements**: Basel III increased the minimum capital requirements. Banks now need to hold more capital for the same level of RWAs, making them more resilient to losses.
2. **Capital Quality**: Basel III placed a greater emphasis on the quality of capital. It required a higher proportion of a bank's capital to be in the form of common equity (the highest quality of capital), which is better able to absorb losses.
3. **Capital Buffers**: Basel III introduced additional capital buffers, such as the capital conservation buffer and the countercyclical buffer, which are designed to ensure that banks build up extra capital, during good times, which they can draw down during periods of stress. The combination of both buffers adds up to 5%, which is, not coincidentally, the median of capital loss in a crisis.[14]
4. **Leverage Ratio**: A non-risk-based leverage ratio was introduced as a supplementary measure to the RWA-based requirements, to serve as a backstop and prevent banks from accumulating excessive leverage. The leverage ratio will put a cap on how much leverage a bank can have in relation to the size of its balance sheets.
5. **Liquidity Requirements**: Basel III implemented new liquidity requirements, including the Liquidity Coverage Ratio (LCR) and the Net Stable Funding Ratio (NSFR), to ensure that banks have sufficient short-term and long-term liquid assets to withstand periods of financial stress.
6. **Reducing Reliance on Internal Models**: Basel III and subsequent updates (sometimes referred to as 'Basel IV') sought to reduce the reliance on banks' internal models for calculating RWAs, as these models were sometimes criticized for being overly complex and not always reflective of the true risk. It introduced floors and standardized approaches to ensure that RWAs calculated using internal models would not fall below certain levels.

In essence, while the concept of RWAs remained intact from Basel II to Basel III, the latter introduced stricter definitions, higher capital requirements, and additional safeguards to ensure that banks are better capitalized and more liquid, thus enhancing the overall stability of the financial system.

Apart from the importance of proper capitalization, the Great Financial Crisis also underscored the need for an effective resolution regime, ie a credible

[14] Emily Lee, 'Basel III and Its New Capital Requirements, as Distinguished from Basel II' (2014) 46 University of Hong Kong Faculty of Law Research Paper 49, 50.

procedure that ensures the restructuring of failing banks while preserving their critical functions for the economy and avoiding taxpayer-funded bail-outs. The Financial Stability Board (FSB), an international body—established in 2009 by the heads of state of the G20—that monitors and makes recommendations about the global financial system, created, in 2011, the Key Attributes of Effective Resolution Regimes for Financial Institutions (the 'Key Attributes'). The Key Attributes provide a universal standard for the resolution of financial institutions, with a particular focus on systemically important financial institutions.[15] The Key Attributes outline the core elements necessary for the resolution of financial institutions in a manner that minimizes systemic disruption and avoids taxpayer exposure to loss. For example, the Key Attributes determine that there should be a recovery and resolution plan in place for firms that could be systemically significant or critical if they fail, and establish the bail-in tool, in order to absorb losses and to recapitalize the entity.

The Key Attributes, and in particular the building up of loss-absorption capacity to make resolution work, were further operationalized in 2015 with the introduction of the FSB Principles on Loss-absorbing and Recapitalisation Capacity and Total Loss-absorbing Capacity (TLAC) term sheet.[16] The principles and term sheet form an international standard for global systemically important banks (G-SIBs). A central point in the term sheet is the need for a minimum TLAC. These financial instruments, which can be common equity, subordinated debt, and some senior debt, provide the necessary loss absorption to ensure realization of losses in resolution, and for the institution to meet the minimum capital requirements after resolution. To ensure that TLAC-eligible instruments remain available when they are needed, the term sheet sets certain conditions for TLAC instruments, for example that they should be legally enforceable, and that their usage in resolution should not give rise to systemic risk or disruption to the provision of critical functions.

III Framework for calibration and calculation in the Union

The general requirements for credit institutions, stemming from the aforementioned international (non-binding) standards, have been implemented

[15] Key Attributes of Effective Resolution Regimes for Financial Institutions, October 2011, accessible at https://www.fsb.org/uploads/r_111104cc.pdf, accessed 15 May 2026.

[16] FSB, 'Principles on Loss-absorbing and Recapitalisation Capacity of G-SIBs in Resolution, Total Loss-absorbing Capacity (TLAC) Term Sheet', 9 November 2015, available at the FSB's website www.fsb.org, accessed 15 May 2026.

in the European Union (EU) via the so-called Single Rulebook.[17] Building on the European directives for credit institutions,[18] this Single Rulebook, in so far as capital requirements for credit institutions are concerned (including the leverage ratio requirements), currently comprises, notably, the Capital Requirements Directive (CRD),[19] the Capital Requirements Regulation (CRR),[20] and level 2 and level 3 acts adopted by the Commission, the European Banking Authority (EBA), and other relevant authorities.

The Single Rulebook also branches into minimum requirements for eligible liabilities (MREL requirements, which also encompass provisions implementing TLAC requirements for the relevant institutions), with the rules of the Single Resolution Mechanism Regulation (SRMR)[21] and the Bank Recovery and Resolution Directive (BRRD),[22] which are further spelled out by level 2 and level 3 rules.

It should be added that, while the objective of the Single Rulebook is to establish a uniform set of rules, certain aspects of the acts described above are provided in Union directives, which are transposed into national law.

1 Uniform requirements

The Single Rulebook governs the aspects of the calibration and the calculation of the capital, leverage, TLAC, and MREL requirements. All of these requirements involve broadly two parts: (i) a fixed component, which generally applies to all relevant entities; and (ii) a flexible additional component, which is

[17] For the Single Rulebook, see Asen Lefterov, 'The Single Rulebook: Legal Issues and Relevance in the SSM context' (2015) 15 ECB Legal Working Paper Series.

[18] See, eg Council Directive 89/647/EEC of 18 December 1989 on a solvency ratio for credit institutions [1989] OJ L386, p 14.

[19] Directive 2013/36/EU of the European Parliament and of the Council of 26 June 2013 on access to the activity of credit institutions and the prudential supervision of credit institutions and investment firms, amending Directive 2002/87/EC and repealing Directives 2006/48/EC and 2006/49/EC [2013] OJ L176, p 338.

[20] Regulation (EU) 575/2013 of the European Parliament and of the Council of 26 June 2013 on prudential requirements for credit institutions and investment firms and amending Regulation (EU) No 648/2012 [2013] OJ L176, p 1.

[21] Regulation (EU) 806/2014 of the European Parliament and of the Council of 15 July 2014 establishing uniform rules and a uniform procedure for the resolution of credit institutions and certain investment firms in the framework of a Single Resolution Mechanism and a Single Resolution Fund and amending Regulation (EU) No 1093/2010 [2014] OJ L225, p 1.

[22] Directive 2014/59/EU of the European Parliament and of the Council of 15 May 2014 establishing a framework for the recovery and resolution of credit institutions and investment firms and amending Council Directive 82/891/EEC, and Directives 2001/24/EC, 2002/47/EC, 2004/25/EC, 2005/56/EC, 2007/36/EC, 2011/35/EU, 2012/30/EU and 2013/36/EU, and Regulations (EU) No 1093/2010 and (EU) No 648/2012, of the European Parliament and of the Council [2014] OJ L173, p 190.

determined by the relevant authority, subject to its case-by-case assessment. Therefore, with a certain level of generalization, it can be posited that the risk-based capital requirements include a uniform requirement of 8% capital of risk-weighted assets, and that the leverage ratio includes a uniform requirement of 3% of a total asset measure, which is not risk-sensitive. The flexible components in this regard are the additional capital requirements that can be imposed by the supervisor,[23] as well as, for example, macroprudential buffers and a higher leverage ratio. This approach is somewhat reproduced in the area of gone-concern loss-absorption capacity. In the Union, TLAC is prescribed as the fixed component for specific credit institutions, but may be supplemented with additional MREL requirements, at the discretion of the resolution authorities. Still, for other credit institutions, a fully discretionary MREL requirement is the norm, as will be explained below.

It is appropriate to first focus on the fixed component of the relevant requirements. In other words, what are the uniform rules that apply to all relevant credit institutions in the Union, which can be determined with some degree of certainty?

a) Uniform risk-based capital requirements, leverage requirements, and TLAC requirements

The first component in the field of capital requirements, including leverage requirements, is the fixed, uniform amount of those requirements, which applies to all entities in the Union.[24] Sometimes this uniform requirement is referred to as the 'Pillar 1' requirement, following the Basel II terminology. This uniform level is set by Article 92 of the CRR, which expresses the minimum requirements in two respects: a risk-based requirement referring to the *total risk exposure amount* (TREA) of a credit institution,[25] and a non-risk-based requirement referring to all assets and, in particular, the *total exposure measure*.[26]

[23] For readability, this chapter refers to the banking supervisor as either the 'supervisor', the 'competent supervisory authority', or the 'supervisory authority'. However, within the Single Rulebook, the banking supervisor is defined in Article 4(1)(40) of the CRR simply as the 'competent authority'.

[24] There are, however, exceptions to this rule, since some entities may benefit from a specific waiver that would allow them not to comply with the uniform requirements. For example, a subsidiary entity in a banking group can benefit from a capital waiver in accordance with art 7 of the CRR, while an affiliated entity in a cooperative group can benefit from the waiver in accordance with art 10 of the CRR, to the extent that the relevant banking supervisor considers that the conditions for such waivers have been met.

[25] TREA is calculated by each credit institution in accordance with art 92(3) of the CRR and closely resembles the RWAs mentioned in section II, although it adopts a specific approach to assessing the risks from some banking activities.

[26] The total exposure measure is calculated by each credit institution in accordance with Part 7 of the CRR.

Article 92(1)(a), (b), and (c) establishes the well-known 8% of TREA figure, which is then broken down into three subcomponents, namely Common Equity Tier 1 (CET1) ratio, Tier 1 ratio, which can be met with both CET1 instruments and Additional Tier 1 (AT1) instruments, and Tier 2 (T2) ratio, setting out minimum amounts for each of these subcomponents. Likewise, Article 92(1)(d) of the CRR establishes the (non-risk-based) fixed leverage ratio of 3% of total exposure measure for the purposes of leverage. Both of these requirements—that under letters (a), (b), and (c), and that under letter (d)—are referred to, in general, as capital requirements imposed as a going concern, but are distinguished in the denominator against which they are measured, in one case accounting for risks, as measured in accordance with the framework, and in the other case with a measure that is not modified by risks.

Both the risk-based capital requirements and the leverage ratio are requirements expressed relative to a bank's balance sheet (see Table 8.1 below),[27] which are imposed in addition to the minimum requirement, expressed in absolute terms, that credit institutions in the Union must have at least 5 million[28] euros as initial capital.[29]

As noted in relation to the risk-based capital requirements, the uniform rule permits credit institutions to meet requirements with instruments of different quality. Quality, in this broad sense, refers to the loss-absorption property of the various instruments. As set out in section II above, CET1 instruments are the highest quality of capital, followed by AT1 instruments. Tier 2 capital is gone-concern capital, meaning that it must absorb losses before depositors, general creditors, and other subordinated creditors do.

Table 8.1 Simplified balance sheet of a solvent bank

Simplified balance sheet of a solvent bank (assets = liabilities)	
Assets	**Liabilities**
Loans, securities, cash, physical assets, deposits with central bank (including reserves)	Equity (shares (CET1 instruments), share premium, retained earnings, reserves, other comprehensive income, some AT1 instruments) Bonds (subordinated (T2 instruments and some AT1 instruments) and non-subordinated) Deposits

[27] As well as some off-balance-sheet items.
[28] Art 12(1) of the CRD.
[29] However, see the possible legacy exceptions in art 12(3) of the CRD and art 93(2) of the CRR.

A similar solution, with a fixed component, which does not depend on the entity's circumstances, has been established for TLAC, which is also a uniform requirement. The uniform TLAC requirement is set by Article 92a of the CRR, and with some level of generalization,[30] the TLAC requirement can be summarized as being either 18% of TREA or 6.75% of the total exposure measure. Still, as noted, the TLAC requirement only applies to certain entities,[31] and does not apply to most credit institutions in the EU, whose overall level of own funds and eligible liabilities (then termed 'MREL') is determined by the resolution authorities, in accordance with the SRMR and the BRRD. Those provisions governing the setting of MREL do not mean that other credit institutions are allowed not to have gone-concern loss-absorption capacity for a resolution. Instead the provisions empower the authorities to set the MREL requirements on a case-by-case basis, based on a number of considerations. The constituent elements of such case-by-case setting are considered in section 2(c) below. Similarly to capital requirements, under certain circumstances the SRB and other resolution authorities are empowered to waive the MREL requirement.[32]

The eligibility of TLAC and MREL instruments is similar to that of capital instruments, yet slightly broader, which permits various bonds to also qualify as TLAC and MREL, when they would not qualify as either of the three types of eligible capital instruments discussed above. The loss-absorption capacity of these instruments (which, with some level of generalization, can be described as 'bonds') is arguably lower than that of the capital instruments described above. MREL-eligible instruments, in any event, require a decision of the resolution authority in order to fully absorb losses.

b) Capital buffers

The various macroprudential capital buffers applicable to Union credit institutions are requirements of a somewhat hybrid nature, to the extent that they are partially uniformly fixed and partially discretionary. These buffers were introduced in 2013, following Basel III, and comprise, notably, the capital conservation buffer,[33] the countercyclical capital buffer,[34] the systemic risk buffer,[35]

[30] The detailed rules on TLAC, which are specified in the CRR, include a phasing-in of the requirement, as well as specific modifications depending on whether an entity in a group is a resolution entity or not.

[31] See arts 92a and 92b of the CRR.

[32] See, eg arts 12h and 12i of the SRMR. On some occasions, the MREL waivers have led to disputes between the SRB and credit institutions. See SRB Appeal Panel cases 2/2021, 3/2021, and 2/2022, and judgment of 10 July 2024, Case T-540/22 *France v SRB*, ECLI:EU:T:2024:459.

[33] See art 129 of the CRD.

[34] See arts 130 and 135–40 of the CRD.

[35] See art 133 of the CRD.

and a G-SII and an O-SII buffer.[36] The calibration of each buffer follows a different approach: some are uniformly fixed;[37] for others, their value depends on the score of the specific credit institution in a comparative overview;[38] for yet others, the value is determined as a weighted average of a number of individual buffer rates;[39] while some buffers are set partially or fully discretionarily.[40] The individual applicable capital buffers add up for each credit institution and compose a combined buffer requirement, which, in accordance with Article 128(6) of the CRD, must be met with instruments of the highest quality, namely CET1 instruments. A specificity of the capital buffers, compared with the other capital requirements which are covered in this chapter, is their enforcement, which is covered in more detail in section V below. This difference is by design, permitting capital buffers to be built up in good times, following a requirement by the relevant authority, and 'drawn down' in difficult times, following a relaxation of the requirement by the relevant authority.

2 Calibration of discretionary additional requirements

The second (flexible) component of the various requirements is the add-on determined by the supervisory authority for each credit institution and banking group. Such add-ons serve different objectives, which are described in detail below, and which guide their calibration.[41]

a) Additional risk-based capital requirements

Additional risk-based capital requirements have been in place in the EU for a significant time, notably following their introduction as 'Pillar 2' of the Basel II framework.[42] These requirements are risk-based, since, like their uniform

[36] See art 131 of the CRD.

[37] As is the case for the capital conservation buffer, which, in accordance with art 129(1) of the CRD, comprises 2.5% of total risk-exposure amount.

[38] As is the case for the G-SII buffer, which is determined primarily on the basis of the score of the entity and the buckets determined in relation to that. See art 131 of the CRD.

[39] As is the case for the countercyclical capital buffer, where the buffer rates set by the authorities where the exposures are found would determine the institution-specific buffer rate.

[40] In this category, the systemic risk buffer is rather discretionarily set in accordance with art 133 of the CRD, although, for the imposition of buffer requirements of above 3% and above 5%, specific procedures apply. Also, the O-SII buffer is set within certain ranges. See art 131 of the CRD.

[41] It should be highlighted that the presentation below does not cover guidance recommendations, be they risk-based capital guidance, leverage ratio guidance, or MREL guidance, since those are not binding requirements.

[42] CRD formally refers to these requirements as 'own funds requirements': see art 104a of the CRD. However, 'Pillar 2 capital requirements' is an often-used synonym. See, eg EBA Guidelines on common

counterpart, they are expressed as a percentage of the risk-weighted balance sheet expressed as TREA.[43] The authors consider that additional capital requirements have been the template for introducing similar case-by-case flexibility in the other areas of loss-absorption requirements for Union credit institutions.

Currently, additional capital requirements for credit institutions in the Union are regulated in a comprehensive legal framework, notably Articles 104 and 104a of the CRD,[44] and, for the ECB, in Article 16 of the SSM Regulation.[45] These additional capital requirements are meant, among others, to address risks which are not already addressed by the harmonized capital requirements.[46] An indispensable prerequisite to calibrating the additional capital requirements is the conduct of the so-called Supervisory Review and Evaluation Process (SREP), which is an analytical process conducted by the banking supervisor, generally each year,[47] and guided by granular guidance in the EBA's SREP guidelines.[48] In the context of the SREP assessment, the banking supervisor will examine three main building blocks, namely: (i) business model; (ii) internal governance and controls; and (iii) risk to capital,[49] and, based on such assessment, will exercise supervisory judgement to determine whether additional capital is needed.

b) Additional leverage requirements

While formally part of capital requirements, additional leverage ratio requirements are calibrated separately,[50] which justifies mentioning them separately. In particular, for G-SIIs, a leverage buffer applies,[51] whereas for all supervised

procedures and methodologies for the supervisory review and evaluation process (SREP) and supervisory stress testing under Directive 2013/36/EU (EBA/GL/2022/03).

[43] See art 104a(4) of the CRD.

[44] These provisions, empowering the supervisory authority to impose additional capital requirements, have been supplemented by the possibility to impose additional guidance, which is an expectation by the supervisor in order for the institution to deal with a forward-looking stress scenario. See recital 16 of Directive 2019/878.

[45] Council Regulation (EU) 1024/2013 of 15 October 2013 conferring specific tasks on the European Central Bank concerning policies relating to the prudential supervision of credit institutions [2013] OJ L287, p 63.

[46] See art 104a(1) and (2) of the CRD for the various objectives of the additional capital requirements.

[47] See also Claudia Buch, 'Reforming the SREP: an important milestone towards more efficient and effective supervision in a new risk environment', 28 May 2024, available on the ECB's website www.bankingsupervision.europa.eu, accessed 15 May 2026.

[48] EBA/GL/2022/03. See also ECB website, 'Supervisory review (SREP)', at www.bankingsupervision.europa.eu, accessed 15 May 2026.

[49] A fourth building block of SREP is assessment of liquidity, where findings are, however, more relevant for possible liquidity requirements.

[50] See arts 98(6) and 104a(3) and (4) of the CRD.

[51] See art 92(1a) of the CRR.

entities a leverage ratio add-on may be imposed,[52] which is once again expressed in terms of Tier 1 capital (CET1 and AT1 instruments).[53]

c) MREL requirements

The calibration of MREL requirements is governed by a complex framework—notably by the SRMR,[54] the BRRD,[55] and implementing national law—as well as a number of technical standards.[56] The SRB, as the main MREL setter in the Union, has also developed a number of guidance documents, explaining how it intends to exercise its discretion in setting MREL targets.[57] Procedurally, the MREL-setting process is part of the overall resolution planning process, given the significance of the chosen resolution strategy for the calibration of MREL.[58]

The two main building blocks of MREL calibration are those already established by the FSB in the TLAC term sheet,[59] namely the loss-absorbing amount (LAA) and the recapitalization amount (RCA).[60] Broadly, the main purpose of the former is to allow the realization of accrued losses, and the main purpose of the latter is to recapitalize the entity so that it can return to business as a viable going concern. The two components—LAA and RCA—but also MREL requirements in general, are determined by the resolution authority, building upon the supervisor's calibration of capital requirements, but without automaticity and subject to adjustments. To this end, the resolution authority receives, from the banking supervisor, the additional capital requirements imposed on an entity.[61]

It should be added that, for Union banking groups, MREL requirements could be imposed to be met by instruments that are externally issued to

[52] See art 104a(3) of the CRD.
[53] See ibid, art 104a(4).
[54] See, in particular, arts 12–12k of the SRMR.
[55] See, in particular, arts 45–45m of the BRRD.
[56] See, eg Commission Delegated Regulation (EU) 2016/1450 of 23 May 2016 supplementing Directive 2014/59/EU of the European Parliament and of the Council with regard to regulatory technical standards specifying the criteria relating to the methodology for setting the minimum requirement for own funds and eligible liabilities [2016] OJ L237, p 1; and Commission Delegated Regulation (EU) 2021/1118 of 26 March 2021 supplementing Directive 2014/59/EU of the European Parliament and of the Council with regard to regulatory technical standards specifying the methodology to be used by resolution authorities to estimate the requirement referred to in Article 104a of Directive 2013/36/EU of the European Parliament and of the Council and the combined buffer requirement for resolution entities at the resolution group consolidated level where the resolution group is not subject to those requirements under that Directive [2021] OJ L241, p 1.
[57] See, eg SRB, 'Minimum Requirement for Own Funds and Eligible Liabilities (MREL)', May 2024, available at the SRB's website https://www.srb.europa.eu/en, accessed 15 May 2026.
[58] With regard to resolution planning, see 'The Single Resolution Mechanism, Introduction to Resolution Planning' (2016), available at the SRB's website https://www.srb.europa.eu/en, accessed 15 May 2026.
[59] FSB, 'Term Sheet' (n 16).
[60] See art 45c(2) of the BRRD and art 12d(2) of the SRMR.
[61] art 104c of the CRD.

investors, but may also be imposed to be met by instruments[62] to be internally issued within the banking group and to be subscribed by entities which are not themselves resolution entities. Such a structure of the MREL liabilities could be permitted, given that, in single-point-of-entry resolution strategies, the losses of several of the group entities could be upstreamed to one or several resolution entities via such internal MREL instruments. Without entering into the intricate details of internal MREL, it should be mentioned that the eligibility criteria for such instruments may be slightly lighter in some respects.[63]

The precise MREL requirements are determined by the resolution authority on the basis of numerous detailed considerations, specific to each entity and, in particular, the resolution strategy to be followed by the resolution authority. It is beyond the remit of this chapter to discuss these detailed considerations.[64]

d) Additional requirements in practice

To get a sense of the significance of additional requirements, it may be useful to refer to some statistics on the requirements imposed by the ECB and the SRB. The ECB imposed, for 2025, additional risk-based capital requirements ranging between 1% and 3.7%,[65] with an average of 2.1%. To translate this to absolute numbers, for the biggest banks in the EU the combined Pillar 1 and Pillar 2 requirements may add up to more than 100 billion euros. With regard to the combined buffer requirements applicable to Union banks, Union credit institutions have between 2.5% and 8.5% in 2025.[66] The average external MREL targets set by the SRB and national resolution authorities as in 2025 were 27.9% of TREA.[67]

3 Competences and decision-making arrangements for calibrating requirements

The calibration of the capital, leverage, and MREL requirements involves numerous authorities cooperating in well-defined procedures. The involvement

[62] This can also include a guarantee. See also art 12g(3) of the SRMR, and *France v SRB* (n 32).

[63] See, eg art 12d(2) of the SRMR.

[64] In this regard, see SRB, 'Minimum Requirement for Own Funds and Eligible Liabilities (MREL)', May 2024 (n 57). See also, more generally, Marco Lamandini and David Ramos Muñoz, 'Minimum Requirement for Own Capital and Eligible Liabilities' in Mario P Chiti and Vittorio Santoro (eds), *The Palgrave Handbook of European Banking Union Law* (Palgrave Macmillan 2019) ch 14, 321–48.

[65] See Pillar 2 requirement, available at the ECB's website https://www.ecb.europa.eu/home/html, accessed 15 May 2026.

[66] ESRB, 'Combined buffer requirements as of 30 June 2025', https://www.esrb.europa.eu/home/html, accessed 15 May 2026.

[67] See SRB MREL Dashboard H1.2025, available at the SRB's website https://www.srb.europa.eu/en, accessed 15 May 2026.

of multiple authorities is necessitated notably by the fact that the requirements are often imposed on Union banking groups comprising multiple entities, established in several different Member States, and by the fact that there is an intrinsic link between going-concern and gone-concern requirements. This section pinpoints some important elements of the institutional landscape for calibrating the requirements.

a) Cooperation for decisions for cross-border banking groups

While Union law has harmonized the substantive rules for calibration of the relevant requirements to a certain extent, and the creation of the Banking Union has concentrated some decision-making on a single authority, for a banking group active in several jurisdictions there may still be multiple competent banking supervisors and resolution authorities (for example, because the group is not only active in the Banking Union, or because it is not a significant supervised group). To this end, Union law establishes rules and procedures which govern the cooperation between such authorities, in order to reach a common view on the appropriate requirements within the banking group. Such a common view is preferable in order to ensure a well-functioning Internal Market, and to avoid regulatory arbitrage and propagation of risk.[68] Union law regulates the various cooperation processes in different ways, which necessitates that one examines each and every requirement separately.

With regard to additional capital requirements, Article 113 of the CRD establishes the rules of the joint decision process to calibrate such requirements. In that process, the consolidating supervisor within the banking group and the competent authorities for the subsidiaries[69] engage in a dialogue with a view to imposing institution-specific prudential requirements.[70] While the relevant provisions seek to ensure that the relevant authorities in the supervisory college[71] reach a common solution in the form of a joint decision, which

[68] See, eg recital 13 of the CRD.

[69] Note that, in accordance with art 17(2) of the SSM Regulation, the provisions set out in the relevant Union law in relation to the cooperation between competent authorities from different Member States for conducting supervision on a consolidated basis shall not apply to the extent that the ECB is the only competent authority involved.

[70] The provision of art 113 of the CRD is supplemented by the Commission Implementing Regulation (EU) 710/2014 of 23 June 2014 laying down implementing technical standards with regard to conditions of application of the joint decision process for institution-specific prudential requirements according to Directive 2013/36/EU of the European Parliament and of the Council [2014] OJ L188, p 19.

[71] It should be emphasized that, in accordance with art 113 CRD, the joint decision is only taken by the relevant competent authorities responsible for the supervision of the entities in the banking group. Depending on the specific circumstances, a supervisory college may have a broader membership and also include authorities which do not sign the joint decision.

is thereafter implemented by each of the authorities,[72] the legal framework provides also for the possibility that the authorities do not reach a common understanding, even with the EBA's assistance. In such a case, it is possible that several different decisions will be taken within the banking group, with the consolidating supervisor notably retaining the competence to impose, on the relevant entity, capital requirements on a consolidated basis of the whole group.

The scheme of a collegial, joint decision process for setting requirements is also implemented in relation to banking groups in the resolution planning context.[73] In particular, Article 45h of the BRRD and Article 32 of the SRMR set out the rules for reaching such joint decisions,[74] providing once more the possibility to not reach a common position. It should be remarked that Article 45h of the BRRD does not apply to the SRB; hence, the SRB has a different path to concluding on MREL requirements for banking groups. While it is not the forum that decides on the specific MREL requirements within the banking group,[75] the resolution college is also a relevant forum of exchange which may influence the decision on those requirements.[76]

b) Cooperation between the competent supervisory authority and the resolution authority

The cooperation between supervisory and resolution authorities is an indispensable pillar in the calibration of the relevant requirements.[77] The additional capital requirements imposed by the supervisory authority are an important input into the decision for the setting of MREL, and Union law requires that the supervisory authorities notify such requirements to the resolution authorities.[78] In addition, the supervisory authorities have to provide resolution

[72] See art 113(4) of the CRD.

[73] Similarly to the ECB's role under art 17(2) of the SSM Regulation, the SRB is the sole decision-maker for MREL, in respect of banking groups only active in the Banking Union. See art 31(2) in conjunction with art 32 of the SRMR.

[74] On joint decisions, see Order of 11 June 2025, Case T-477/23 *DZ Bank v SRB* ECLI:EU:T:2025:602, as well as SRB Appeal Panel case 1/2022.

[75] The resolution college includes, by definition, not only resolution authorities but also competent supervisory authorities, as well as possibly other authorities. However, on the role of the resolution college in the calibration of MREL, see Order of 11 June 2025, *DZ Bank v SRB* (n 74).

[76] See, in this regard, the Commission Delegated Regulation (EU) 2016/1075 of 23 March 2016 supplementing Directive 2014/59/EU of the European Parliament and of the Council with regard to regulatory technical standards specifying the content of recovery plans, resolution plans and group resolution plans, the minimum criteria that the supervisory authority is to assess as regards recovery plans and group recovery plans, the conditions for group financial support, the requirements for independent valuers, the contractual recognition of write-down and conversion powers, the procedures and contents of notification requirements and of notice of suspension and the operational functioning of the resolution colleges [2016] OJ L184, p 1.

[77] See also the chapter by Concetta Brescia Morra and Federico Pistelli, in this volume.

[78] See art 104c of the CRD.

authorities with all relevant information needed for the calibration of MREL requirements.[79] As mentioned, resolution colleges, while not being formally competent for the adoption of MREL requirements, could also be a relevant discussion forum. The contemplated MREL requirements are also consulted on by the resolution authorities, with the supervisory authorities, pursuant to Article 45c(1) of the BRRD and Article 12(1) of the SRMR. Cooperation between supervisory and resolution authorities is also strong in the enforcement of the MREL requirements, which is discussed in more detail in section V below.

These detailed cooperation rules necessitate detailed implementation, which has been effected between the ECB and the SRB in a dedicated memorandum of understanding.[80]

IV Overlaps between the requirements

The capital, leverage, TLAC, and MREL requirements are distinct requirements, with distinct objectives, set by different authorities, in accordance with separate procedures. Yet all of these requirements apply at the same time and interact with one another, given that all of them necessitate that the relevant credit institution has a stock of capital instruments and/or other liabilities to meet those requirements. This set-up creates some overlaps, which are justified given the complementary objectives that the requirements aim to achieve, namely that the going-concern requirements assist in avoiding bank failures, while the gone-concern requirements help to restore the viability of an institution and ensure its future compliance with going-concern requirements, should the institution fail, nevertheless. Still, such overlaps create some complexity, not least on credit institutions' liability management.

1 Instruments eligible to meet requirements

As alluded to earlier, the various requirements can be met with various instruments. These instruments must meet different eligibility criteria, with many of these criteria overlapping, with a general rule that higher-quality instruments

[79] See art 11(2) of the BRRD.
[80] Memorandum of Understanding between the Single Resolution Board and the European Central Bank in Respect of Cooperation and Information Exchange, 16 December 2022, available at the ECB's website https://www.bankingsupervision.europa.eu/home, accessed 15 May 2026.

can be used to meet the requirements instead of lower-quality instruments. Therefore, at one end of the spectrum, CET1 instruments can be used to meet all of the relevant requirements, while at the other end, junior bonds that are MREL-eligible could not be used to meet the various capital requirements. In particular, bonds issued under the law of a third country may be considered eligible to meet MREL requirements, provided that they meet the additional conditions to the satisfaction of the resolution authority,[81] but they would not be eligible to meet many of the other requirements. These differences could create certain incentives for credit institutions to hold a safety buffer of high-quality instruments, which, being in surplus of what is required as additional capital requirements, could instead be used towards compliance with MREL requirements. In practice, issuance of some types of instruments is more costly for the issuer than others, with CET1 being, as a generalized rule, the most expensive, and bonds generally being the least costly. At the same time, the relatively high level of MREL-eligible instruments which are needed to meet MREL targets have meant that Union banks have needed to issue a significant number of new instruments in a relatively short period of time, therefore raising questions about the demand for such instruments.[82]

2 Stack of requirements

Conceptually, the various requirements overlap in some respects, while they add up on top of each other in other respects. Their interaction is summarized in Figure 8.1.

This refers to what are sometimes called the capital stack[83] and the MREL stack. Given the formulation of the various requirements, a priority between them can be established, with the result that a shortage in the capital and eligible instruments would result in the credit institution breaching some requirements first, and others only later. In very generalized terms, the first requirements to be breached in the case of a shortfall are likely to be the buffer requirements. They will be breached in those cases where all capital instruments are insufficient to meet: (i) the requirement of harmonized capital pursuant to Article 92(1)(a) to (c) of the CRR, combined with (ii) any additional

[81] See art 55 of the BRRD.
[82] See SRB's MREL Dashboard (n 67).
[83] Note, in this regard, that there are additional configurations, relevant in the context of supervision, such as Total SREP Capital Requirement or TSCR, which includes Pillar I and Pillar II; and Overall Capital Requirement or OCR, which includes Pillar I, Pillar II, and CBR.

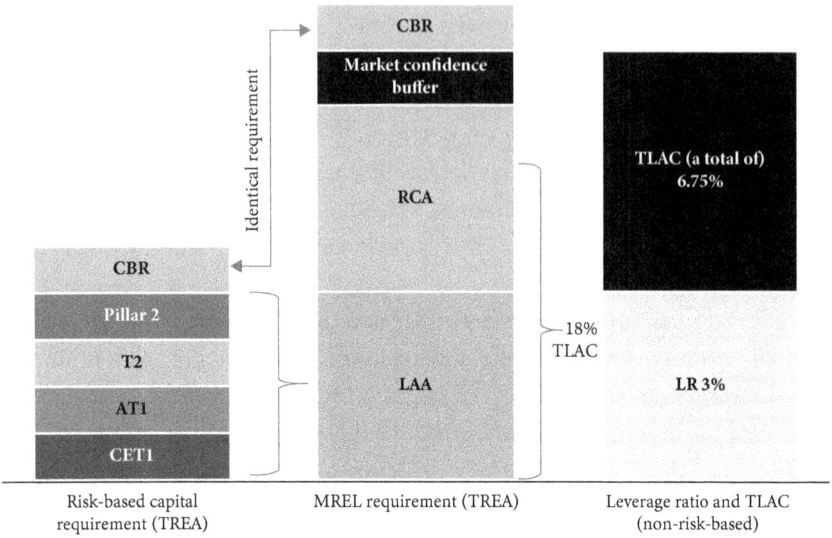

Figure 8.1 Overview of requirements

own funds requirements, and (iii) the combined buffer requirement.[84] Such a breach would result in the obligation to submit a capital conservation plan and a maximum distributable amount (MDA) calculation, as described in more detail in the next section. Once the capital buffer is fully depleted and all capital instruments are insufficient to meet the requirement of harmonized capital pursuant to Article 92(1)(a) to (c) of the CRR, combined with any additional own funds requirements, then an institution would also be in breach of additional own funds requirements imposed by the competent supervisory authority. Finally, if all capital instruments are insufficient to meet the requirement of harmonized capital pursuant to Article 92(1)(a) to (c) of the CRR, an institution will breach the harmonized risk-based capital requirement. Each of these (potentially consecutive) breaches could bring about different consequences, which are described in the next section.

A simpler stacking order applies to the leverage ratio, which must be met with Tier 1 instruments, which further shortens the stack of eligible instruments (including any additional leverage ratio imposed by the supervisory authority).

A stacking of requirements also exists for TLAC and MREL. In those cases, the capital requirements as per CRR and CRD are not formally taken into account in the compilation of the stack. Instead, the components of the stack to

[84] See art 141a of the CRD.

be considered are the MREL requirement, any subordination component, a market confidence buffer, and, once again, the combined buffer requirement. The combined buffer requirement is once again relevant, since, in accordance with the BRRD, it sits on top of the MREL requirements and is, in general, the first one to be breached.[85]

In addition, both TLAC and MREL are expressed not only by reference to TREA, but also to total risk exposure.[86] From this perspective, while TLAC and MREL do not stack on top of prudential leverage ratio, there is a certain overlap between the requirements, which may also affect the ability to release buffers.[87]

Given the different eligibility criteria for capital instruments and other eligible liabilities, depending on the specific capital and MREL requirements imposed on a specific institution, and depending on the evolution of its liability structure, shortages in certain instruments may result in different outcomes. A shortage can either result in simultaneous breach of capital, leverage, and MREL requirements, or only in a capital breach or an MREL breach. Finally, a shortage may result in a breach of the combined buffer requirement when considered in addition to either capital or MREL, or simultaneously in relation to both.

3 Analysis of overlaps in calibration

The procedures for the calibration of capital, leverage, and MREL requirements are distinct. The supervisory authority decides on the additional capital and/or leverage requirements and the resolution authority decides on the MREL requirements. At the same time, the objectives of the two sets of requirements are intrinsically linked, which suggests that a certain cohesiveness in their levels is necessary. In particular, capital requirements aim to capture and address going-concern risks, while MREL requirements aim to allow the resolution authority to clean up and stabilize a failing entity (under the assumption that all going-concern risks materialize), and to reopen that entity for business, capitalized as a going concern, to be supervised by the supervisor

[85] See art 10a of the SRMR and art 16a of the BRRD.

[86] See art 92a of the CRR, art 12a(2) of the SRMR, and art 45(2) of the BRRD.

[87] See, eg Sebastiano Laviola, 'Overlap between banks' capital buffers and minimum requirements', 17 October 2023, available at the SRB's website https://www.srb.europa.eu/en, accessed 15 May 2026; and ESRB Report of the Analytical Task Force on the overlap between capital buffers and minimum requirements, December 2021, available at the ESRB's website https://www.esrb.europa.eu/home/html/index.en.html, accessed 15 May 2026.

as a viable entity. From this perspective, the estimates of capital requirements determined by the supervisor are a useful starting point for the determination of both the loss absorption (LAA) and the recapitalization (RCA) component of the MREL requirement. With this in mind, Union legislation has embedded, in various provisions, the input from the supervisor in the calibration of the MREL.[88] Still, this is not a mechanistic process, but further analyses are carried out by the resolution authorities, with the result that the MREL can be adjusted downward or upward from simply twice the amount of the risk-based capital requirement. One important component of the upward adjustment is the additional so-called market confidence buffer,[89] which is meant to enable the institution or entity to continue to meet the conditions for authorization for an appropriate period, including by allowing the institution or entity to cover the costs related to the restructuring of its activities following resolution, and to sustain sufficient market confidence.[90]

V Compliance and enforcement

The complexity of capital and MREL requirements and the complex stacking order explained above translate into some complexity in establishing compliance and enforcement with these requirements. When a shortage in capital and eligible instruments manifests, such shortage may, depending on the circumstances, result in a breach of one or several of the concurrent requirements—risk-based capital requirements, leverage ratio, capital buffers, TLAC, or MREL. This raises the issues of monitoring such breaches, and the reaction by the authorities to such breaches.

1 Monitoring of compliance

The monitoring of compliance with the various requirements is conducted primarily on the basis of the reporting by the concerned credit institutions.

[88] See art 45c of the BRRD and art 12d of the SRMR.
[89] See art 45c(3) of the BRRD and art 12d(3) of the SRMR.
[90] See recital 13 of Regulation (EU) 2019/877 of the European Parliament and of the Council of 20 May 2019 amending Regulation (EU) No 806/2014 as regards the loss-absorbing and recapitalisation capacity of credit institutions and investment firms [2019] OJ L150, p 226.

In particular, pursuant to Commission Implementing Regulation 2024/3117 (often referred to as 'ITS on supervisory reporting'),[91] credit institutions submit, to their supervisory authority, information on their levels of capital. In addition, the supervisory authority may request additional information from credit institutions and conduct on-site inspections, which may be of relevance for the calculation of capital. The supervisory authority also verifies the eligibility of some capital instruments[92] and will monitor whether the institution is performing the necessary deductions mandated by the CRR.

Likewise, with respect to MREL compliance, in accordance with Article 45i of the BRRD, credit institutions shall report the amounts of eligible liabilities, to meet MREL. Moreover, Commission Implementing Regulation (EU) 2021/763 on MREL reporting and disclosure[93] sets out detailed rules for MREL reporting. The resolution authorities may also obtain additional information and conduct on-site inspections.

2 Redemption and reduction of capital instruments and eligible liabilities

As part of the monitoring and with a view to ensuring continued compliance, the supervisory authorities and the resolution authorities are entrusted with approving the redemption and reduction of the relevant instruments used to meet the various requirements. In this regard, Articles 78 and 78a of the CRR set out detailed rules for the approval procedures, including the criteria which the supervisory and resolution authorities apply in their assessment. Given the overlap between capital requirements and MREL requirements, the relevant provisions set out specific cooperation obligations between the authorities in the assessment.

[91] Commission Implementing Regulation (EU) 2024/3117 of 29 November 2024 laying down implementing technical standards for the application of Regulation (EU) No 575/2013 of the European Parliament and of the Council with regard to supervisory reporting of institutions and repealing Commission Implementing Regulation (EU) 2021/451 [2024] OJ L.

[92] See, eg art 26(3) of the CRR.

[93] Commission Implementing Regulation (EU) 2021/763 of 23 April 2021 laying down implementing technical standards for the application of Regulation (EU) No 575/2013 of the European Parliament and of the Council and Directive 2014/59/EU of the European Parliament and of the Council with regard to the supervisory reporting and public disclosure of the minimum requirement for own funds and eligible liabilities [2021] OJ L168, p 1.

3 Supervisory measures and sanctions to address lack of compliance with capital requirements

If a credit institution is breaching either of the capital requirements, the supervisory authority has at its disposal a broad spectrum of supervisory measures to induce a return to compliance. These measures also depend on the type of requirement breached, and may depend on the severity and duration of the breach as well as other possibly relevant considerations. While it is beyond the remit of this chapter to describe all possible supervisory measures in all possible situations of breaches of capital requirements, it should be noted that a breach of either additional own funds requirements or harmonized capital requirements could be a basis for supervisory measures under Article 104 of the CRD,[94] early intervention measures under BRRD and SRMR,[95] a pecuniary penalty,[96] and, ultimately, a withdrawal of the banking licence.[97] If the credit institution is breaching capital requirements in a way that would justify the withdrawal of its authorization, it may be declared failing or likely to fail (FOTLF), with a potential entry into resolution.[98]

4 Measures to address impediments to resolvability and other measures to address MREL breaches

Where an institution is breaching TLAC requirements, it will be breaching the directly applicable requirement of the CRR, with the relevant consequences that a breach of a CRR requirement may entail. At the same time, it should be remarked that, in accordance with the CRD, a TLAC breach has been carved out of the harmonized grounds for withdrawal of authorization.[99]

Where a credit institution is breaching MREL requirements, the resolution authority and the supervisory authority have a number of corrective measures

[94] In this regard, see art 104(1) in conjunction with art 102 of the CRD, which provide that supervisory measures can be imposed in case the credit institution does not meet the requirements of CRD or CRR or is likely to breach those requirements within the following 12 months.

[95] In this regard, see art 27(1) of the BRRD, which provides that early intervention measures can be imposed in case the credit institution infringes or is likely in the near future to infringe the requirements of CRR and CRD, among others. See also Article 13 of the SRMR as amended by Regulation (EU) 2026/808 of the European Parliament and of the Council of 30 March 2026 amending Regulation (EU) No 806/2014 as regards early intervention measures, conditions for resolution and funding of resolution action [2026], OJ L.

[96] See art 18 of the SSRM.

[97] Art 18 of the CRD.

[98] See art 32(4)(a) of the BRRD and art 18(4)(a) of the SRMR.

[99] See art 18(d) of the CRD.

they can implement. While these corrective measures are systematized and repeated in Article 12j of the SRMR and Article 45k of the BRRD, the legal bases and the conditions for the impositions of such measures are included in dedicated provisions.[100] Notably, upon finding a breach of MREL, the resolution authority may engage in a process to address impediments to resolvability, a shortage of MREL being considered such an impediment.[101] The resolution authorities may impose administrative penalties.[102]

5 Measures to address a breach of buffers

The enforcement of compliance with buffer requirements follows a separate procedure from that of capital requirements. Both supervisory authorities and resolution authorities have the power to address breaches of the combined buffer requirement (CBR), when that requirement is considered in addition to capital requirements or MREL. In the former case, Articles 141 to 142 of the CRD set out various capital conservation measures, including restrictions on distributions, in case credit institutions are in breach of buffer requirements. Some of the negative consequences from the buffer breach operate by virtue of the law, without the need for a decision by the supervisory authority.[103] Conversely, in the case where the CBR would not be breached when considered in addition to capital requirements, but would be breached when considered in addition to MREL requirements, the resolution authority may decide to limit distributions.[104] What is common between the measures to address breaches of capital buffers is the relative leeway which the credit institution can receive in how promptly it returns to compliance.

VI Conclusion

As pinpointed in this chapter, the Union has established a very comprehensive and detailed framework setting broadly three strands of requirements on credit

[100] For example, a determination that an entity is FOTLF can only be made if one of the conditions in art 32(4) of the BRRD or in art 18(4) of the SRMR has been met.
[101] Arts 17 and 18 of the BRRD and art 10 of the SRMR.
[102] See arts 110 and 111 of the BRRD.
[103] See art 141(2) of the CRD, which requires the institution to calculate a maximum distributable amount (MDA).
[104] Art 16a of the BRRD and art 10a of the SRMR.

institutions—capital requirements (both risk-based and non-risk-based), loss-absorption requirements (both risk-based and non-risk-based), and capital buffers. The advent of so many detailed and overlapping requirements in the relatively short period since the Basel Capital Accord in 1988 is remarkable. It is remarkable because it shows how quickly regulators can react to adverse events and seek to make credit institutions safer. But is also remarkable because it creates a complex regulatory landscape which both credit institutions and regulators need to master. These various requirements fundamentally make sense, to the extent that they aim to address the relevant risks from the operation and possibly the failure of credit institutions, by limiting the latitude the institutions have in their liability management, and by setting aside sufficient loss-absorption capacity to realize losses and continue the credit institutions' critical functions without taxpayer support. Yet, the requirements have various detailed subcomponents, and their calibration, as well as ensuring compliance with them, could be a challenging task. A move to take stock of how the legal framework has performed, and to seek ways to simplify it without sacrificing its effectiveness, could be on the cards.[105]

[105] See in this regard, Targeted consultation on the competitiveness of the EU banking sector, 11 February 2026, available at the European Commission's website at: https://commission.europa.eu/index_en, accessed 15 May 2026.

9

Meroni Doctrine and the Delegation of Powers to EU Agencies

Jonathan Bauerschmidt[*]

I Introduction

The Banking Union led to a proliferation of European Union (EU) agencies to effectively supervise and regulate financial markets. Agencies allow the pooling of expert knowledge, the outsourcing of certain tasks, and the depoliticization of complex decision-making procedures. At the same time, this delegation of powers creates tension with the long-standing case law of the Court of Justice of the EU, on EU agencies. In contrast to some national constitutions,[1] the Treaties do not explicitly address the possibilities and limitations for delegating powers to agencies. The relevant rules, rather, result from a series of judgments that go back to the beginning of European integration. Since the eponymous *Meroni* judgment of 1958, the ensuing case law has collectively been called the *Meroni* doctrine. It deals with the interrelated questions of what powers can be delegated, how autonomously an agency may act, and how much oversight from Union institutions is necessary.

To understand the legal constraints, an overview of the most important judgments is necessary (section II). During the Great Financial Crisis, the Banking Union pushed the boundaries of the *Meroni* doctrine and developed new legal and institutional arrangements. These can be grouped around three themes: the internal delegation within Union institutions in the Single Supervisory Mechanism (SSM) (section III); the delegation of autonomous powers for market intervention by the European Securities and Markets Authority (ESMA) (section IV); and the creation of complex administrative procedures in the Single Resolution Mechanism (SRM) (section V). These

* The views expressed by the author are strictly personal and do not engage the institution for which he works.

[1] See, eg art 37 of the French Constitution; art 86 of the German Basic Law.

Jonathan Bauerschmidt, Meroni *Doctrine and the Delegation of Powers to EU Agencies* In: *EU Banking Union.* Edited by: Jonathan Bauerschmidt, Raffaele D'Ambrosio, Diane Fromage, Daniela Jaros, and Paul Weismann, Oxford University Press. © Oxford University Press 2026. DOI: 10.1093/9780198949756.003.0010

three examples will show the significant institutional engineering undertaken, and how agencies offer more flexibilities than Union institutions within the European constitutional framework. It will reveal the many faces of the *Meroni* doctrine, which continues to guide EU lawmakers and judges to solve intricate questions surrounding the delegation of powers to agencies (section VI).

II Evolution of the *Meroni* case law

The location of the executive is difficult to pin down exactly in the EU. Not only the Commission and Member States but also the Council and other Union institutions, such as the European Central Bank (ECB), are required to implement EU law. This multiplicity of the executive is aggravated by the possibility to establish decentralized and independent new bodies, collectively called agencies.[2] To understand their legal status, it is necessary to trace the evolution of the most important case law, from the *Meroni* (1) and *Romano* (2) judgments to the more recent *Alliance for Natural Health* and *ENISA* judgments (3).

1 *Meroni* judgment of 1958

The case law on agencies started with the eponymous *Meroni* judgment of 1958. Within the framework of the European Coal and Steel Community (ECSC), the High Authority (later the Commission) set up a joint office for scrap consumers and a compensation fund for scrap, as legal entities under private law. Powers were delegated to this office and the Equalization Fund to maintain a complex regime to equalize the scrap-metal price within the ECSC. The Italian scrap-metal dealer Meroni challenged a request for payment, with the argument that a transfer of decision-making powers to the office was illegal.

In its judgment of 1958, the ECJ states that the delegation of 'clearly defined executive powers' is permissible only if the exercise of these powers can 'be subject to strict review in the light of objective criteria determined by the

[2] See, eg Edoardo Chiti, 'European Agencies' Rulemaking: Powers, Procedures and Assessment' (2013) 19 European Law Journal 93; Deirdre Curtin, *Executive Power of the European Union* (OUP 2009) 135–74; Paul Craig, *EU Administrative Law* (3rd edn, OUP 2018) 168–72; Christoph Möllers, *The Three Branches* (OUP 2013) 121–26; Stefan Griller and Andreas Orator, 'Everything under Control? The "Way Forward" for European Agencies in the Footsteps of the Meroni Doctrine' (2010) 35 European Law Review 3.

delegating authority'. Conversely, the delegation of powers which involve 'a discretionary power, implying a wide margin of discretion which may, according to the use which is made of it, make possible the execution of actual economic policy' is not permissible. While, in the first case, the delegation is not capable of significantly influencing the exercise of the delegated powers, in the second case there is an actual transfer of responsibility in which the discretion of the transferring authority is replaced by the discretion of the body to which power has been delegated. Such a wide discretion arises where different objectives have to be reconciled, and in the event of a contradiction between these objectives, priority must be given to one of these objectives. Comprehensive considerations of a political nature are reserved to the institutions established by the Treaties and may not be delegated to independent bodies.[3]

The Court combines this prohibition of delegating broad discretionary powers with a fundamental institutional principle, which was, not accidentally, established in the *Meroni* judgment: from Article 3 ECSC Treaty, 'there can be seen [a] balance of powers which is characteristic of the institutional structure of the Community a fundamental guarantee granted by the Treaty'.[4] The Court subsequently developed this idea under the term of institutional balance[5] and defined this concept in the 1990 *Chernobyl* judgment:

> The Treaties set up a system for distributing powers among the different Community institutions, assigning to each institution its own role in the institutional structure of the Community and the accomplishment of the tasks entrusted to the Community. Observance of the institutional balance means that each of the institutions must exercise its powers with due regard for the powers of the other institutions.[6]

Today, the principle of institutional balance is enshrined in Article 13(2), 1st sentence, TEU, according to which each institution shall act in accordance with the powers conferred on it by the Treaties.

Like Montesquieu's famous separation of powers at national level,[7] the principle of institutional balance entails three different

[3] Case 9/56 *Meroni v High Authority*, ECLI:EU:C:1958:7, pp 151 f.

[4] ibid, p 152.

[5] Case 25/70 *Einfuhr- und Vorratsstelle für Getreide und Futtermittel v Köster*, ECLI:EU:C:1970:115, para 9; Case 138/79 *Roquette Frères v Council*, ECLI:EU:C:1980:249, para 33; Case 149/85 *Wybot v Faure*, ECLI:EU:C:1986:310, para 23.

[6] Case C-70/88 *Parliament v Council*, ECLI:EU:C:1990:217, paras 21 f.

[7] Charles Louis de Secondat de Montesquieu, *De l'Esprit des lois* (Gallimard 1748 (1995)), XI.6, 327 ff. See also art 16 of the Declaration of the Rights of Man and of the Citizens of 1789: '*Toute société dans laquelle la garantie des droits n'est pas assurée, ni la séparation des pouvoirs déterminée, n'a pas de*

aspects:[8] first, powers must be separated, allowing each institution to enjoy a sufficient independence in order to exercise its powers;[9] second, the ban on usurpation prohibits the exercise of a particular power by an institution to which this power has not been allocated under the Treaties;[10] and third, the aspect of *balance* is already semantically underlined by the term 'institutional balance'. According to this, the powers of an institution are not to be considered in isolation, but must be understood within the institutional framework of the Treaties. In the *Meroni* judgment, the aspect of balance reinforces the allocation of powers under the Treaties and prevents arbitrary reallocation of these powers. The Court addresses the concerns precisely when it refers to the 'balance of powers' and uses this aspect to prevent the delegation of large discretionary powers to a body not governed by the Treaties.[11] For the Court, the principle of institutional balance forms the background for understanding the powers and procedures established in and under the Treaties in relation to the EU as a whole.[12]

2 *Romano* judgment of 1980

The Court revisited the delegation of powers in the *Romano* judgment of 1980. It concerns the Administrative Commission set up under Council Regulation (EEC) No 1408/71 on the application of social security systems to migrant workers.[13] Composed of government representatives from each of the Member States and a representative from the Commission, the Administrative Commission may make non-binding interpretation of EU law in the complex area of social security (and continues to do so in accordance with Article 72 of

Constitution.'; Michel Troper, *La séparation des pouvoirs et l'histoire constitutionnelle française* (LGDJ 1973 (2014)) 157 ff.

[8] Möllers (n 2), pp. 43 ff; similarly, Koen Lenaerts and Amaryllis Verhoeven, 'Institutional Balance as a Guarantee for Democracy in EU Governance' in Christian Joerges and Renaud Dehousse (eds), *Good Governance in Europe's Integrated Market* (OUP 2002) 35–88, 44 f.

[9] Case 5/85 *AKZO Chemie*, ECLI:EU:C:1986:328, paras 37–40 (internal organization of the Commission); Case C-345/95 *France v Parliament*, ECLI:EU:C:1997:450, para 32 (internal organization of the Parliament).

[10] *Einfuhr- und Vorratsstelle für Getreide und Futtermittel v Köster* (n 5), paras 8 f (interference of the Council with the implementing powers of the Commission); *Wybot v Faure* (n 5), para 23 (power of the Council and the Commission to request an extraordinary session of the Parliament).

[11] *Meroni* (n 3), p 152.

[12] See, in detail, Jonathan Bauerschmidt, *Die Rechtsperson der Europäischen Union im Wandel* (Mohr Siebeck 2019) 185 ff.

[13] Regulation (EEC) 1408/71 of the Council of 14 June 1971 on the application of social security schemes to employed persons and their families moving within the Community [1971] OJ L149, p 2.

Regulation (EC) No 883/2004).[14] Upon a Belgian request for a preliminary ruling, the Court of Justice addressed the questions of how the Administrative Commission fits into the Treaties and what the legal nature of its decisions is.

The Court of Justice inferred from the Treaties that the Administrative Commission cannot be an independent body with powers of binding legislation. From the Treaty provisions on the transfer of implementing powers (Article 155 of the EEC Treaty, today Article 291(2) TFEU) and the system of legal protection (today Articles 263 and 267 TFEU) it follows that the Administrative Commission may not be empowered by the Council to adopt acts having the force of law. While a decision of the Administrative Commission may provide an aid to social security institutions responsible for applying supranational law in this field, it is not of such a nature as to require those institutions to use certain methods or adopt certain interpretations when they come to apply the European rules.[15]

Without mentioning the *Meroni* judgment, the Court further developed the prohibition on delegating powers and the notion of institutional balance: the delegation of powers to adopt binding law would have been a usurpation of the executive powers primarily foreseen for the Commission. Only a restrictive interpretation of the powers conferred on the Administrative Commission renders this delegation compatible with the Treaty.[16] Turned positively, the *Romano* judgment shows that non-binding auxiliary activities may be transferred to bodies such as the Administrative Commission without violating the institutional balance established by the Treaties.

3 *Alliance for Natural Health* and *ENISA* judgments of 2005 and 2006

It took many years until the Court had to address the question of delegation by the European legislator, in two judgments. In 2005, the Alliance for Natural Health questioned the validity of Directive 2002/46/EC of the Parliament and the Council on food supplements.[17] The legislator had foreseen that such food

[14] Regulation (EC) 883/2004 of the European Parliament and of the Council of 29 April 2004 on the coordination of social security systems [2004] OJ L166, p 1.

[15] Case 98/80 *Romano*, ECLI:EU:C:1981:104, para 20. Similarly already, Case 19/67 *Van Der Vecht*, ECLI:EU:C:1967:49.

[16] Merijn Chamon, *EU Agencies: Legal and Political Limits to the Transformation of the EU Administration* (OUP 2016), 254 f; Lenaerts and Verhoeven (n 8) 35–88, 44 f.

[17] Directive 2002/46/EC of the European Parliament and of the Council of 10 June 2002 on the approximation of the laws of the Member States relating to food supplements [2002] OJ L183, p 51.

supplements could only be marketed if listed in annexes to the Directive, and the Commission had been authorized to amend these annexes. In response, the Court confirmed that the legislator could delegate powers to amend the annexes, provided 'that power is clearly defined and that the exercise of the power is subject to strict review in the light of objective criteria'.[18] With an explicit reference, the Court confirmed that the *Meroni* case law is also applicable to the delegation of powers by the European legislator.

Only one year later, the Court had to rule, in the *ENISA* judgment of 2006, on the legality of the establishment of the European Network and Information Security Agency (ENISA) on the basis of today's Article 114 TFEU. The United Kingdom (UK) argued that this competence for the harmonization of the internal market was not suitable for creating and empowering bodies such as ENISA.

While Advocate General Kokott expressed some doubts,[19] the Court found that there is a competence to establish an agency. On the one hand, the legislature has a margin of appreciation to assess whether a body like ENISA contributes to the realization of the harmonization process, even if this body is only allowed to adopt non-binding supporting and framework measures.[20] On the other hand, the Court stressed that the tasks entrusted to such bodies must be closely linked to the laws, regulations, and administrative provisions of the Member States, aimed to be harmonized. This is particularly the case when supranational bodies provide the national authorities and economic operators with services that can affect the homogenous implementation of the harmonization measures and facilitate their application.[21]

With the *ENISA* judgment, the Court clarified that the Union competence to regulate a certain policy field also included the competence to establish an agency.[22] As a consequence, the *ENISA* judgment contains the central requirements for establishing an agency on the basis of Article 114 TFEU: first, the legislature must, within the scope of its discretion, consider the creation of the agency to be necessary; second, the agency must contribute to the implementation of the harmonization process; third, the tasks assigned must be closely related to substantive secondary law.

[18] Joined Cases C-154/04 and C-155/04 *Alliance for Natural Health and Others*, ECLI:EU:C:2005:449, para 90.

[19] Case C-217/04 *United Kingdom v Parliament and Council (ENISA)*, ECLI EU:C:2005:574, Opinion of AG Kokott, paras 26 f.

[20] Case C-217/04, *United Kingdom v Parliament and Council (ENISA)*, ECLI:EU:C:2006:279, para 44.

[21] ibid, para 45.

[22] See also Wolfgang Weiß, *Der Europäische Verwaltungsverbund* (Duncker & Humblot 2010) 39.

These judgments form the background for setting up new bodies in the Banking Union and delegating different powers. It can be distinguished between the internal delegation within Union institutions, the delegation of autonomous powers on agencies, and the delegation within a complex administrative procedure, each of which will be examined in turn.

III Internal delegation in the Single Supervisory Mechanism

The internal delegation within the ECB, as a Union institution, is one example of how to address the *Meroni* case law. The SSM contributes to the stability of the financial system by conferring supervisory powers on the ECB for systemically important banks. To this end, the Union legislator adopted the SSM Regulation (EU) 1024/2013,[23] which seeks to contribute to the safety and soundness of credit institutions and the stability of the financial system in the Union, in accordance with Article 1 of the SSM Regulation. Although initially there were some doubts whether such supervisory powers could be conferred on the basis of Article 127(6) TFEU,[24] neither the Court of Justice[25] nor the German Constitutional Court[26] came to the conclusion that the Union legislator had exceeded its competence.[27]

The SSM addresses the *Meroni* case law by establishing the Supervisory Board as an internal body of the ECB (1). This allows compliance with the Treaty obligations to separate between monetary and supervisory functions (2) and confirms the ECB's responsibility for the execution of the Union's supervisory policy (3).

[23] Regulation (EU) 1024/2013 conferring specific tasks on the European Central Bank concerning policies relating to the prudential supervision of credit institutions [2013] OJ L287, p 63.

[24] See, in particular, German-language contributions: Matthias Herdegen, 'Europäische Bankenunion' (2012) Wertpapiermitteilungen 1889, 1891 f; Ann-Katrin Kaufhold, *Systemaufsicht* (Mohr Siebeck 2016) 285 ff; Benedikt Wolfers and Thomas Voland, 'Europäische Zentralbank und Bankenaufsicht – Rechtsgrundlage und demokratische Kontrolle des Single Supervisory Mechanism' (2014) Zeitschrift für Bank- und Kapitalmarktrecht 177, 178 f.

[25] See, indirectly, Case T–122/15 *Landeskreditbank Baden-Württemberg v ECB*, ECLI:EU:T:2017:337, paras 50–64 on the competence of the ECB, which was confirmed on appeal in Case C–450/17 P, ECLI:EU:C:2019:372, paras 36 ff.

[26] Bundesverfassungsgericht (German Constitutional Court), 30 July 2019 – 2 BvR 1685/14 and 2 BvR 2631/14, ECLI:DE:BVerfG:2019:rs20190730.2bvr168514, paras 171–96.

[27] See, for a concise summary of the arguments, Jonathan Bauerschmidt, 'Financial Stability as the Objective of the Banking Union' (2020) 17(2) European Company and Financial Law Review 155, 167 ff.

1 The Supervisory Board as internal body of the ECB

The execution of supervisory policy is not a mere apolitical task. Rather, it requires a considerable margin of discretion making it possible to execute actual economic policy in the meaning of the *Meroni* case law.[28] Therefore, the relevant competences cannot be delegated to a body without appropriate supervision by a Union institution. Moreover, in accordance with Article 129(1) TFEU, in the ECB only the Governing Council and the Executive Board are decision-making bodies. From this it follows that the Union legislator could not establish a new body based on Article 127(6) TFEU which would implement supervisory policy autonomously.

The SSM Regulation does not even attempt to completely outsource supervisory tasks. Rather, Article 26 SSM Regulation establishes the Supervisory Board as an internal body of the ECB, which plans and executes supervisory tasks as a preparatory body.[29] The Supervisory Board has the exclusive right to initiate supervisory measures by preparing complete decisions which are then adopted by the Governing Council unless the latter objects within a period of not more than 10 working days. This non-objection procedure ensures that the Supervisory Board gives its input on supervisory matters, and that the Governing Council assumes full legal and political responsibility, on behalf of the ECB, for the final acts.

The Supervisory Board is composed of a chair and a vice-chair, four other representatives of the ECB, and the representatives of national supervisory authorities from all participating Member States.[30] In principle, decisions of the Supervisory Board are taken by a simple majority of its members, and in the event of a draw, the chair has a casting vote. However, when the Supervisory Board prepares regulations with general application, it acts by qualified majority as defined in Article 16(4) TEU.

2 Separation between monetary and supervisory functions

The internal delegation of supervisory functions to the Supervisory Board ensures the Treaty obligation to separate strictly between monetary and

[28] *Meroni* (n 3), pp 151 f.

[29] Klaus Lackhoff, *Single Supervisory Mechanism* (CH Beck 2017) 60 ff; Christy Ann Petit, 'The SSM and the ECB Decision-making Governance' in Gianni Lo Schiavo (ed), *The European Banking Union and the Role of Law* (Edward Elgar 2019) 108–29, 111 ff.

[30] See, for the current composition, European Central Bank, 'Supervisory Board', https://www.ecb.europa.eu/ecb/orga/decisions/ssm/html/index.en.html, accessed 9 June 2026.

supervisory functions within the ECB. The separation between monetary and supervisory functions is of fundamental importance and not a purely theoretical problem. Rather, the ECB may be tempted to lower its interest rates or loosen the conditions for its purchases in order to facilitate access to liquidity for banks, thereby undermining banking supervision through monetary policy. Conversely, the central bank relies on a functioning banking system that serves as a transfer mechanism for its monetary policy. Banking supervision may thus spill over into monetary policy.[31]

An adequate separation of monetary and supervisory functions is based on the distinction between price and financial stability. Under Articles 127(1) and 282(2) TFEU, the primary objective of monetary policy is to ensure price stability. By contrast, the SSM Regulation, based on Article 127(6) TFEU, pursues the objective of financial stability. This is accompanied by an important distinction in the separation of competences: while monetary policy in the euro area is an exclusive competence, the SSM Regulation[32] and the rules to be applied by the ECB in the Capital Requirements Regulation[33] and the Capital Requirements Directive[34] fall into the area of shared competence.[35] The different objectives of stability have a direct impact on the separation of functions. Thus, the SSM Regulation requires a strict separation of supervisory and monetary functions: according to Article 25(1), when exercising supervisory tasks, the ECB may only pursue the objective of the SSM Regulation and, in particular, the objective of financial stability. In addition, supervisory tasks must be exercised separately from monetary policy, according to Article 25(2).

[31] On the tension between monetary policy and supervisory policy, see Cornelia Manger-Nestler and Robert Böttner, 'Ménage à trois? – Zur gewandelten Rolle der EZB im Spannungsfeld zwischen Geldpolitik, Finanzaufsicht und Fiskalpolitik' (2014) 49(6) Europarecht 621–38, 630 ff; and Kern Alexander, 'The European Central Bank and Banking Supervision' (2016) 13(3) European Company and Financial Law Review 467, 488 f.

[32] This is not called into question by the findings in *Landeskreditbank Baden-Württemberg v ECB* (n 25), paras 54, 63, and 72 (confirmed on appeal in Case C-450/17 P, ECLI:EU:C:2019:372, para 49), that art 4(1) of the SSM Regulation confers an 'exclusive competence' on the ECB, as the exclusivity relates to the tasks enumerated in this provision and applies to the banks under direct ECB supervision but not to the entire field of prudential supervision.

[33] Regulation (EU) 575/2013 of the European Parliament and of the Council of 26 June 2013 on prudential requirements for credit institutions and investment firms [2013] OJ L176, p 1.

[34] Directive 2013/36/EU of the European Parliament and of the Council of 26 June 2013 on access to the activity of credit institutions and the prudential supervision of credit institutions and investment firms [2013] OJ L176, p 338.

[35] See art 4(2)(a)TFEU regarding the Internal Market; and Martin Nettesheim, 'Artikel 4 AEUV' in Eberhard Grabitz, Meinard Hilf, and Martin Nettesheim (eds), *Das Recht der EU* (CH Beck 2023), para 6 on shared competence as a 'catch-all' category for those instances where the category of competence is not laid down in the Treaties.

In order to categorize a specific measure in an individual case, regard must be had to the objective and the effect of that measure. First, it must be determined whether the measure pursues the objective of financial stability or price stability.[36] For this, the content and justification of the measure must be evaluated. Second, a supervisory measure must be assessed as to whether it interferes with, or is determined by, monetary policy. Whether there is an interference with monetary policy can be assessed by means of the case law of the Court of Justice. In *Pringle*, the Court held that an indirect effect on price stability was not sufficient to classify a measure as monetary policy.[37] However, this also means that direct effects on price stability affect monetary policy and that such supervisory measures are prohibited.

Whether or not a supervisory measure is determined by monetary policy can be examined by having recourse to the *Gauweiler* and *Weiss* cases. According to the Court, indirect effects on the stability of the euro area are not sufficient to treat a monetary policy measure as equivalent to an economic policy measure.[38] However, it can also be deduced that monetary policy measures with a direct effect on financial stability go beyond the monetary mandate and improperly determine supervisory measures.

This normative separation of functions is accompanied by further institutional arrangements. In order to settle disagreements regarding the separation of functions between the Governing Council and the Supervisory Board, Article 25(5) of the SSM Regulation creates a mediation panel. This should not only avoid conflicts of interest but also ensure that each function is exercised in accordance with the applicable objectives, as recital (65) of the SSM Regulation explains. The ECB has also adopted further internal measures[39] to ensure the separation of functions, including IT systems and information exchange.[40] These normative and institutional safeguards seem to work well in practice, which is shown not least by the fact that the mediation panel has, so far, never been called upon to settle disagreements.

[36] See, on the scope of review, Case C-370/12 *Pringle*, ECLI:EU:C:2012:756, paras 53 and 55; Case C-62/14 *Gauweiler*, ECLI:EU:C:2015:400, para 46; Case C-493/17 *Weiss*, ECLI:EU:C:2018:1000, para 53.

[37] *Pringle* (n 36), para 56.

[38] *Gauweiler* (n 36), para 52; *Weiss* (n 36), para 61.

[39] Decision of the ECB of 17 September 2014 on the implementation of separation between the monetary policy and supervision functions (ECB/2014/39) [2014] OJ L300, p 57.

[40] Lackhoff (n 29) 79 ff.

3 The ECB as executor of the Union's supervisory policy

While the internal delegation to the Supervisory Board helps to separate functions, it leaves intact the overall responsibility of the ECB. This also means that the ECB assumes a new executive role in supervision: in contrast to monetary policy, which the ECB (together with national central banks) conceives and implements on its own to achieve price stability, the rules for supervisory policy with the objective of financial stability are set by the Union legislature (with some options and discretions),[41] and the ECB has to implement this supervisory policy.

The ECB's new executive role is also shown by the quickly growing number of direct actions against this Union institution and preliminary references regarding banking supervisions. Beyond some fundamental questions, such as the nature of the ECB's supervisory competences, these cases deal with details of administrative law. Thus, the Union courts have had to examine the principle of good administration, which also entails the duty of the competent institution to examine carefully and impartially all the relevant aspects of the individual case.[42] Moreover, they pronounced themselves on questions related to the calculation of administrative penalties,[43] the alleged misuse of powers by the ECB,[44] and the intricacies of standing of shareholders against ECB decisions.[45]

A particular challenge arises from composite administrative procedures involving the assessment of national supervisory authorities which are subsequently used by the ECB in its final decision.[46] In such cases, the Union courts alone have jurisdiction to determine, as an incidental matter, whether the legality of the ECB's decisions is affected by any defects rendering unlawful the preparatory acts. As a consequence, the legal remedies to review the acts of the ECB under Article 263 TFEU preclude national courts from hearing actions against national preparatory acts.[47] The underlying rationale is to treat

[41] See, on the ECB, Regulation (EU) 2016/445 of 14 March 2016 on the exercise of options and discretions available in Union law (ECB/2016/4) [2016] OJ L78, p 60, as well as the accompanying Guideline (EU) 2017/697 of 4 April 2017 (ECB/2017/9) [2017] OJ L101, p 156.

[42] See only *Landeskreditbank Baden-Württemberg v ECB* (n 25), paras 146–50; Case T-733/16 *Banque postale v ECB*, ECLI:EU:T:2018:477, para 70.

[43] Case T-203/18 *VQ v ECB*, ECLI:EU:T:2020:313.

[44] Case T-52/16 *Crédit mutuel Arkéa v ECB*, ECLI:EU:T:2017:902, paras 210–13.

[45] Joined Cases C-663/17 P, C-665/17 P, and C-669/17 P *ECB v Trasta Komercbanka and Others*, ECLI:EU:C:2019:923, paras 102–15.

[46] See also the chapters by Christy Ann Petit on supervisory review, and by Filipe Brito Bastos and Huna on complex administrative procedures, in this book.

[47] Case C-219/17 *Berlusconi and Fininvest*, ECLI:EU:C:2018:1023, paras 57–59. See, for an assessment, Filipe Brito Bastos, 'Judicial Review of Composite Administrative Procedures in the Single Supervisory Mechanism: Berlusconi' (2019) 56 Common Market Law Review 1355–78.

composite administrative procedures as a unified process leading to one final act rather than emphasizing fragmentation into multiple parts.[48] From the point of view of good administration, enshrined in Article 41 of the Charter, and the right to effective judicial protection, under Article 47 of the Charter, this is a welcome development. And the ECB is at the forefront of this development, as the main executor of the Union's supervisory policy.

IV Autonomous market intervention by the European Securities and Markets Authority

The *Meroni* doctrine was again tested during the Great Financial Crisis, when the Union legislator established the European Supervisory Authorities (ESAs). Based on Article 114 TFEU, the European Banking Authority (EBA), the ESMA, and the European Insurance and Occupational Pensions Authority (EIOPA) are to safeguard financial stability.[49] The ESAs, together with national authorities, conduct microprudential supervision of individual financial actors and their conduct on the market. While many of the powers conferred on the ESAs remained within the advisory logic and soft law instruments envisaged by the *Romano* judgment,[50] some also contained delegated autonomous powers. In particular, ESMA may, in exceptional cases, prohibit short selling on European financial markets (1), an empowerment challenged before the Court of Justice (2). Following this judgment, ESMA used its powers for the first time during the Covid pandemic (3).

1 ESMA intervention powers in exceptional circumstances

The Short Selling Regulation 236/2012[51] (SSR) was adopted in spring 2012 to create a harmonized framework to deal with those financial transactions. During financial instability, short selling can aggravate a downward spiral in the prices of shares in a way that could ultimately threaten financial institutions

[48] Yves Mersch, 'Mehrteilige Verwaltungsverfahren in der Aufsichtspraxis der EZB' (2020) Europäische Zeitschrift für Wirtschaftsrecht 781–86, at 786.
[49] Established, respectively, by the EBA Regulation (EU) 1093/2010, EIOPA Regulation (EU) 1094/2010, and ESMA Regulation (EU) 1095/2010.
[50] See section II.2 above.
[51] Regulation (EU) 236/2012 of the European Parliament and of the Council of 14 March 2012 on short selling and certain aspects of credit default swaps [2012] OJ L86, p 1.

and create systemic risks. In accordance with the principle of indirect implementation enshrined in Article 291(1) TFEU, a broad set of intervention powers are foreseen for National Competent Authorities, in Articles 18–23 SSR. To ensure transparency, these measures must be notified to other competent authorities and ESMA, in accordance with Article 26 SSR. These provisions are an expression of the principle of loyal cooperation, enshrined in Article 4(3) TEU, in both its horizontal and vertical dimensions.[52]

ESMA is also empowered to intervene on financial markets if there are serious threats to the integrity of financial markets or to financial stability. Pursuant to Article 28 SSR, ESMA may order all persons to disclose their short-selling positions (letter a) or prohibit them from entering into short-sale or similar transactions (letter b).[53] For such interventions, substantive and procedural conditions must be met.[54]

In substance, ESMA may only intervene to address the orderly functioning and integrity of financial markets or the stability of the financial system in the Union (Article 28(2)(a) SSR). In order to further guide ESMA in the exercise of its powers, the Commission has adopted a delegated regulation setting the criteria to be taken into account when determining when adverse events or developments have arisen.[55] Moreover, as an expression of the principle of subsidiarity enshrined in Article 5(3) TEU, ESMA may only act if no national authority has taken measures, or if such measures do not adequately address the threat. Finally, the measures must be proportionate, without too far-reaching detrimental effects on the efficiency of financial markets.

As regards procedure, ESMA must consult the European Systemic Risk Board (ESRB) before imposing any measure (Article 28(4) SSR), and needs to notify the concerned national authorities of the measures it intends to take (Article 28(5) and (6) SSR). This is not only an expression of the principle of loyal cooperation enshrined in Article 4(3) TEU; it also ensures that microprudential supervision by ESMA is linked to the macroprudential supervision by the ESRB. Finally, all measures taken by ESMA must be reviewed, at the latest, every three months, and automatically expire if ESMA does not renew them in accordance with Article 28(10) SSR.

[52] Jonathan Bauerschmidt, 'Artikel 26 VO 236/2012' in Christoph Seibt, Petra Buck-Heeb, and Rafael Harnos (eds), *BeckOK Wertpapierhandelsrecht* (CH Beck 2026), para 1.

[53] Jonathan Bauerschmidt, 'Artikel 28 VO 236/2012' in Seibt, Buck-Heeb, and Harnos (n 52), paras 39 ff.

[54] ibid, paras 7 ff.

[55] Art 24(3) of Commission Delegated Regulation (EU) 918/2012 [2012] OJ L274, p 1.

2 *Short Selling* judgment of 2014

The UK challenged the empowerment of ESMA to intervene on the financial market because it allegedly violated the *Meroni* case law by conferring powers entailing large margins of discretion.

In response, the Court noted that the Short Selling Regulation does not confer any powers on ESMA beyond the regulatory framework established by the ESMA Regulation 1095/2010 itself.[56] Moreover, ESMA's powers are sufficiently framed by the substantive conditions set out in Article 28(2) and (3) SSR.[57] Thus, ESMA must examine a significant number of cumulative factors before taking action. Finally, the procedural requirement to consult the ESRB and National Competent Authority further circumscribes ESMA's margin of discretion.[58] From this, the Court concluded that ESMA's empowerment in Article 28 SSR is precisely delineated and amenable to judicial review in light of the *Meroni* case law, and thus ESMA is not vested with a very large margin of discretion allowing it to set actual economic policy.[59]

The UK also challenged the compliance of ESMA's empowerment with the *Romano* judgment because Article 28 SSR allegedly allowed the adoption of quasi-legislative measures of general application.

In response, the Court recalled that the *Romano* judgment concerned soft law measures.[60] Conversely, for ESMA, the Union legislator deliberately chose to confer powers which may have general application. In fact, in the strictly circumscribed circumstances, emergency measures may affect a range of natural and legal persons who have engaged in short-selling activities. From this it does not follow, however, that the empowerment in Article 28 SSR is at odds with the principle established in the *Romano* judgment. Rather, it follows from Articles 263 and 277 TFEU, which were revised in the Lisbon Treaty to also include references to bodies, offices, and agencies of the Union, that the institutional framework expressly permits such Union entities to adopt acts of general application.[61] This is also supported by the discussions in the European Convention of 2002–2003—later reflected in the Lisbon Treaty—according to

[56] Case C-270/12 *United Kingdom v Parliament and Council (Short Selling)*, ECLI:EU:C:2014:18, para 44.
[57] ibid, paras 46 f.
[58] ibid, para 50.
[59] ibid, paras 53 f.
[60] ibid, para 63, with reference to *Romano* (n 15), para 20.
[61] *UK v Parliament and Council (Short Selling)* (n 56), paras 64 f.

which direct actions against all legal acts of bodies, offices, and agencies of the Union should be allowed before the Court.[62]

Finally, the UK also called into question Article 114 TFEU as legal basis for Article 28 SSR because it did not aim at harmonizing national law, but rather at replacing national decisions with supranational decisions. Advocate General Jääskinen showed some sympathy with this argument. In his opinion, Article 114 TFEU cannot be used to authorize an EU agency to take decisions against market participants when national authorities disagree about the appropriate measure. The result of such an authorization would not be the harmonization of the internal market but the replacement of national decisions by supranational decisions.[63] Similar criticism was previously expressed by scholars.[64]

The Court did not uphold this argument. Rather, it pointed out the discretion of the legislator to choose the most appropriate technique for the approximation of laws. Discretion is particularly important where the approximation requires highly technical and specialist analyses to be made and developments in a specific field to be taken into account. Moreover, echoing the *ENISA* judgment, the legislator may deem it necessary to provide for the establishment of an EU body responsible for contributing to the implementation of a process of harmonization.[65] Finally, the legislator may also empower such a body to issue binding decisions for specific market participants in order to address serious threats to the orderly functioning and integrity of the financial markets or financial stability.[66]

The *Short Selling* judgment is an important confirmation of the *Meroni* case law: decisions with a wide margin of discretion must not be transferred to Union agencies. At the same time, the Court also significantly developed its case law by specifying that clearly defined intervention powers without wide discretion may be delegated to Union agencies. This clarification has been largely welcomed by scholars.[67]

[62] See especially the Final report of the discussion circle on the Court of Justice of 25 March 2003, CONV 636/03, paras 24–26.

[63] Case C-270/12 *United Kingdom v Parliament and Council (Short Selling)*, EU:C:2013:562, Opinion of AG Jääskinen, paras 51 f. He proposed to use the competence of art 352 TFEU.

[64] Jörn Axel Kämmerer, 'Das neue Europäische Finanzaufsichtssystem (ESFS)' (2011) Neue Zeitschrift für Verwaltungsrecht 1281, 1283; Niamh Moloney, 'EU Financial Market Regulation after the Global Financial Crisis' (2010) 47 Common Market Law Review 1317, 1340 f; Christoph Ohler, 'Rechtmäßige Errichtung der Gemeinschaftsagentur ENISA' (2006) Europäische Zeitschrift für Wirtschaftsrecht 372.

[65] *UK v Parliament and Council (Short Selling)* (n 56), paras 102–04, with reference to *ENISA* (n 20), para 44.

[66] *UK v Parliament and Council (Short Selling)* (n 56), para 108.

[67] Carl Fredrik Bergström, 'Shaping the New System for Delegation of Powers to EU Agencies' (2015) 52 Common Market Law Review 219–42, 241; Christian Calliess, 'Artikel 13 EUV' in Christian Calliess and Matthias Ruffert (eds), *EUV/AEUV Kommentar* (6th edn, CH Beck 2022), para 52.

3 ESMA measures during Covid

In the course of the Covid-19 pandemic, ESMA used its intervention powers under Article 28 SSR for the first time. On 16 March 2020, ESMA lowered the reporting threshold so that holders of net short positions in shares traded on regulated markets in the EU were temporarily obliged to report their positions to National Competent Authorities if they reached or exceeded 0.1% of the issued share capital; a measure extended three times.[68] ESMA justified its intervention as a precautionary measure in response to the exceptional Covid-19 pandemic, and to enable authorities to better monitor financial markets. For ESMA, the circumstance constituted a serious threat to market confidence and financial stability. Since ESMA only lowered the reporting threshold, it considered the measure to be proportionate.[69] In conformity with its obligations, ESMA consulted the ESRB and notified National Competent Authorities beforehand.[70]

This example shows that ESMA uses its intervention powers cautiously. In particular, it did not use its powers under Article 28(1)(b) SSR to prohibit or otherwise restrict entering into short sales. Rather, ESMA coordinated measures adopted by National Competent Authorities in accordance with its role under Article 26 SSR.[71] In addition to these measures, ESMA was also active in advising the Commission. Shortly after the ESMA measure lapsed, the Commission acted by way of delegated regulation,[72] and with a favourable ESMA opinion.[73] This shows that ESMA uses intervention powers restrictively and instead advises the Commission, which, as a Union institution, has much broader discretion to adopt the necessary acts to safeguard financial stability of the Union.

V Complex administrative procedures in the Single Resolution Mechanism

The *Meroni* case law is also crucial to understanding the involvement of EU agencies in complex administrative procedures. As part of the second pillar of

[68] ESMA Decision of 16 March 2020, ESMA70-155-9546; extended by Decisions of 11 June 2020, ESMA71-99-1342; 16 September 2020 ESMA70-155-11072 and 16 December 2020, ESMA70-155-11608.

[69] ibid, recitals (26)–(51).

[70] ibid, recitals (52) and (53).

[71] See, for an overview of some of the national measures, ESMA Final Report: Review of certain aspects of the Short Selling Regulation of 22 March 2022, ESMA70-448-10, pp 11 ff.

[72] Commission Delegated Regulation (EU) 2022/27 of 27 September 2021 amending Regulation (EU) No 236/2012 [2022] OJ L6, p 9.

[73] ESMA, Opinion for the adjustment of the threshold for the notification of net short positions in shares set out in Article 5(2) of Regulation (EU) No 236/2012 of 13 May 2021, ESMA70-156-4262.

the Banking Union, the Union legislator adopted, in 2014, a legal framework to resolve ailing banks which are close to insolvency. Whereas insolvency is dealt with by courts retrospectively in order to fulfil the claims of creditors, banking resolution is carried out by the executive branch prospectively, in order to ensure financial stability. The Bank Recovery and Resolution Directive 2014/59/EU[74] (BRRD) harmonized national resolution law and procedures, while the Single Resolution Mechanism Regulation 806/2014[75] (SRMR) established the Single Resolution Board (SRB) as a Union agency which is called upon to resolve a bank in the course of a weekend. Like ESMA, the SRB is established under Article 114 TFEU.[76] Unlike ESMA, the SRB does not act autonomously but, rather, is one (important) actor in the complex decision-making procedure for resolving banks (1). This raises the question of responsibility (2), in order to assess whether this administrative procedure is *Meroni*-compliant (3).

1 Decision-making for resolving a bank

The decision-making for resolving a bank was one of the key elements during legislative deliberations. Whereas the initial proposal foresaw an *ex ante* control of the SRB by the Commission, through the adoption of the resolution decision,[77] the resolution procedure adopted by the Union legislature foresees an *ex post* control of the SRB by the Commission and, where applicable, the Council. Clearly circumscribed powers for the SRB, and control by Union institutions, is necessary in light of the *Meroni* doctrine, since the resolution of a bank is not only a technical task but requires policy choices.

In order to make the decision-making compliant with the *Meroni* doctrine, the resolution procedure under Article 18 of the SRMR has two distinct phases, involving the SRB as a EU agency, as well as the ECB, the Commission, and the Council as Union institutions.

First, in the initial assessment phase under Article 18(1)–(5) SRMR, it has to be assessed whether: (a) the bank is failing or likely to fail, involving the assessment by the ECB; (b) there is no reasonable prospect of alternative

[74] Directive 2014/59/EU establishing a framework for the recovery and resolution of credit institutions and investment firms [2014] OJ L173, p 190.

[75] Regulation (EU) 806/2014 establishing uniform rules and a uniform procedure for the resolution of credit institutions and certain investment firms in the framework of a Single Resolution Mechanism and a Single Resolution Fund [2014] OJ L225, p 1.

[76] See, in more detail, Karl-Philipp Wojcik, 'Bail-in in the Banking Union' (2016) 53 Common Market Law Review 91, 100 ff; Alberto de Gregorio Merino, 'Institutional Report' in Gyula Bándi and others (eds), *FIDE Report on European Banking Union* (Kluwer 2016) 204 ff.

[77] See arts 14, 16(6), and 16(7) of the initial Commission Proposal, COM (2013) 520 final.

private sector measures within a reasonable time frame, based on an assessment by the SRB or, where applicable, by national authorities in close cooperation with the ECB; and (c) resolution action must be in the public interest.

Second, the subsequent adoption and endorsement phase in Article 18(6)–(8) SRMR sets out how the resolution scheme is adopted and enters into force. To this end, the SRB adopts a resolution scheme which, in accordance with Article 18(6) SRMR: (a) places an entity under resolution; (b) determines the application of resolution tools; and (c) determines the use of the Single Resolution Fund. This resolution scheme, however, only enters into force 'if no objection has been expressed by the Council or by the Commission within a period of 24 hours after its transmission by the Board', in accordance with Article 18(7), 5th subparagraph. To this end, the SRB immediately transmits the resolution scheme to the Commission.

Pursuant to Article 18(7), 2nd subparagraph, SRMR, within 24 hours of transmission, the Commission shall either endorse the resolution scheme, or object to it with regard to the discretionary aspects in cases not covered by the 3rd subparagraph. In addition, Article 18(7), 3rd subparagraph, SRMR foresees the involvement of the Council. The Commission may propose to the Council to: (a) object to the resolution scheme on the ground that it does not fulfil the criterion of public interest; or (b) approve or object to a material modification of the amount provided by the Single Resolution Fund in the resolution scheme. Where there are modifications or objections by the Union institutions to the resolution scheme, the SRB has to modify the resolution scheme within eight hours, pursuant to Article 18(7), 7th subparagraph, SRMR.

The rationale for this adoption and endorsement phase and the relevance for the *Meroni* case law is explained in recital (24) SRMR, underlining that each resolution entails discretionary decisions. Moreover, recital (26) SRMR further sets out that the

> procedure relating to the adoption of the resolution scheme, which involves the Commission and the Council, strengthens the necessary operational independence of the Board while respecting the principle of delegation of powers to agencies as interpreted by the Court of Justice . . . Therefore, this Regulation provides that the resolution scheme adopted by the Board enters into force only if, within 24 hours after its adoption by the Board, there are no objections from the Council or the Commission or the resolution scheme is approved by the Commission.

As the Union legislator expressly reserved the decision on the discretionary aspects in the resolution procedure to the institutions of the Union, the SRB has not received autonomous powers but, rather, acts in a complex administrative procedure.

2 Responsibility in complex administrative procedures

The complex administrative procedure established in Article 18 SRMR raises intricate questions on who is responsible for this resulting administrative act. The concept of responsibility has, due to its inflationary use in political, philosophical, and also legal discourses, remained dependent on its respective context.[78] Nevertheless, the word already contains an important point of reference for a more detailed definition: responsibility requires answers to be given.[79] Responsibility thus describes a duty to justify oneself and to give reasons for one's behaviour. Responding before a court is understood as a 'paradigm' for responsibility and gives insights for the roles of those involved in court proceedings, such as applicants or defendants.[80]

A formal structure of responsibility—which can also be used in legal discourse—should distinguish between six elements:[81] responsibility requires (1) a subject capable of acting, which (2) through attribution (3) is held responsible for a certain action or omission and the resulting consequences. However, the attribution necessary when linking the subject and object of responsibility does not result from the responsibility itself but requires a value judgement. Thus, responsibility also requires (4) justification before a forum,

[78] See only Mark Bovens, *The Quest for Responsibility – Accountability and Citizenship in Complex Organisations* (CUP 1998) 22 ff; Horst Dreier, 'Verantwortung im demokratischen Verfassungsstaat' (2000) *ARSP Beiheft* 74, 9–38; Paul Ricoeur, 'Le concept de responsabilité' (1994) Esprit, 28–48; Pierre Rosanvallon, *Le bon gouvernement* (Seuil 2015) 253–78; Herbert LA Hart, *Punishment and Responsibility* (OUP 2008 (1970)) 211–30 and 264 f distinguishes between role-responsibility, causal-responsibility, liability-responsibility, and capacity-responsibility – four different, and by no means exhaustive, meanings of responsibility.

[79] See the Latin '*respondere*'; English 'responsiblility' and 'responsible'; and French '*responsabilité*' and '*responsable*'.

[80] See, in more detail, Jonathan Bauerschmidt, *Die Rechtsperson der Europäischen Union im Wandel* (n 12), 58 ff.

[81] Andreas Voßkuhle, 'Gesetzgeberische Regelungsstrategien der Verantwortungsteilung zwischen öffentlichem und privatem Sektor' in Gunnar F Schuppert (ed), *Verantwortungsteilung als Schlüsselbegriff eines sich verändernden Verhältnisses von öffentlichem und privatem Sektor* (Nomos 1990) 47–90, at 52–57; 'Beteiligung Privater an der Wahrnehmung öffentlicher Aufgaben und staatliche Verantwortung' (2003) 62 Veröffentlichungen der Vereinigung der Deutschen Staatsrechtslehrer (VVDStRL) 266–335, at 270, fn 9.

and can only be acceptable if the subject responsible (5) has room for manoeuvre and (6) there is a standard by which the subject can be judged.

This formal structure of responsibility has different dimensions depending on who is responsible to whom. Especially in organizations with a sophisticated division of labour, many persons are involved at different levels and to varying degrees in making a decision. This 'problem of many hands' makes it extremely difficult to determine who takes responsibility in complex organizations.[82] This is not a particularly novel insight but, rather, a conundrum that haunts, in particular, the executive, as Alexander Hamilton already observed in the *Federalist Papers*. For him:

> Responsibility is of two kinds to censure and to punishment. The first is the more important of the two, especially in an elective office. Man, in public trust, will much oftener act in such a manner as to render him unworthy of being any longer trusted, than in such a manner as to make him obnoxious to legal punishment.

Having distinguished between political and legal responsibility, he turns to the first branch of government to find that:

> the multiplication of the Executive adds to the difficulty of detection in either case. It often becomes impossible, amidst mutual accusations, to determine on whom the blame or the punishment of a pernicious measure, or series of pernicious measures, ought really to fall. It is shifted from one to another with so much dexterity, and under such plausible appearances, that the public opinion is left in suspense about the real author.[83]

When faced with the problem of many hands, the Court of Justice, in 1981, gave a landmark judgment in *IBM v Commission*. Where acts or decisions are adopted by a 'procedure involving several stages, in particular where they are the culmination of an internal procedure', those acts are open to review only 'if it is a measure definitively laying down the position . . . on the conclusion of that procedure, and not a provisional measure intended to pave the way for the final decision'.[84] This often repeated jurisprudence[85] entails that intermediate

[82] See, on this fundamental problem, Dennis F Thompson, 'Moral Responsibility of Public Officials: The Problem of Many Hands' (1980) 74 American Political Science Review 905.
[83] Alexander Hamilton, *The Federalist Papers* (Signet Classics 1787 (2003)), no 70, 426.
[84] Case 60/81 *IBM v Commission*, ECLI:EU:C:1981:264, para 10.
[85] See only Case C-322/09 P *NDSHT v Commission*, ECLI:EU:C:2010:701, para 48 and the case law cited.

measures which only prepare final decisions cannot, in principle, be attacked by themselves.[86] In other words, in complex administrative procedures, the Court solves the problem of many hands by looking at the final act rather than any preparatory act.

3 Compliance with *Meroni* and responsibility for resolution procedure

The compliance with the *Meroni* case law and the responsibility in the resolution procedure have recently been examined by the General Court and the Court of Justice.

In the *Banco Popular* cases, concerning the resolution of this Spanish bank, the General Court recently had to examine the *Meroni*-compliance of the procedure applied. This Court, in particular, assessed the legislative procedure and referred to an opinion of the Council Legal Service on the matter. Subsequent changes in the legislative process, taking into account that opinion, are a clear sign that the Union legislature did not intend to confer broad discretionary powers on the SRB. Although the SRB adopts the resolution scheme, 'legal and political responsibility for determining the European Union's resolution policy' is conferred on Union institutions, which avoids the actual transfer of responsibility, in the meaning of the *Meroni* judgment.[87]

The General Court also assessed the contention that, given the deadline of 24 hours, the Commission only 'rubber-stamps' the resolution scheme and does not assume real responsibility, in circumvention of the *Meroni* judgment. The General Court referred to the general obligation of the SRB to cooperate with the Union institutions under Article 30 SRMR. Moreover, a Commission representative participates in the meetings of the executive sessions and plenary sessions of the SRB as permanent observer, in accordance with Article 43(3) SRMR. Thus, the Commission is involved already at an early stage of the resolution procedure, where it can assess discretionary aspects. From this, the General Court concluded that the Commission's involvement in the resolution scheme 'is not a mere formality'.[88] These findings are welcome clarifications

[86] Case C-463/10 P and C-475/10 P *Deutsche Post and Germany v Commission*, ECLI:EU:C:2011:656, para 50; C-415/15 P *Stichting Woonpunt and Others v Commission*, ECLI:EU:C:2017:216, para 44.

[87] Case T-510/17 *Del Valle Ruiz v Commission and SRB*, ECLI:EU:T:2022:312, para 218; Case T-628/17 *Aeris Invest v Commission and SRB*, ECLI:EU:T:2022:315, para 133.

[88] *Del Valle Ruiz v Commission and SRB* (n 87), paras 231 f.

by the General Court on the overall *Meroni*-compliance of the resolution procedure.

However, an important question remained open: are direct actions pursuant to Article 263 TFEU to be brought against the SRB because it adopted the resolution scheme, or against the Commission because it endorsed this scheme (or even against both)? For the General Court, direct actions could be brought against the SRB's resolution scheme only.[89] Upon appeal, the Court of Justice held that the *Meroni* judgment is also relevant for identifying the author for resolution actions and the act which may be attacked to review its legality.[90] In deviating from the Opinion of Advocate General Ćapeta, who had argued that it was the Union legislator's choice, rather than the *Meroni* doctrine, which was relevant for identifying the author,[91] the Court convincingly interpreted the SRMR in light of that doctrine, and thus used it as the constitutional yardstick to review the legislative choices. In fact, the Court in *Meroni* focused also on the shift of responsibility between institutions and additional bodies established in the framework of the Treaties. And it was precisely because only institutions are empowered to take decisions entailing large political margins of discretion that such powers may not be delegated to independent bodies.[92] In other words, the broad political responsibility may only be borne by institutions which are then also legally responsible for their acts.

This is also supported by the *IBM v Commission* line of reasoning, since, in the complex administrative procedure involving several stages, only the Commission's endorsement definitively lays down the Union's position in the resolution procedure.[93] The same applies in the case that the Commission does not act within the 24 hours foreseen in Article 18(7), 2nd subparagraph, SRMR, as this silence must be regarded as a tacit endorsement of a resolution scheme in whose preparation the Commission was involved.[94] Moreover, a distinction between the discretionary aspects (for which the Commission would be responsible) and the non-discretionary aspects (for which the SRB would be responsible) may be very difficult to operationalize in practice, as discretionary and non-discretionary elements are inextricably linked, which would make it very difficult for any applicant to determine who should be attacked for

[89] Case T-481/17 *Fundación Tatiana*, ECLI:EU:T:2022:311, paras 114–49.
[90] Case C-551/22 P *Commission v SRB*, ECLI:EU:C:2024:520, paras 70–74, 81, 82, and 88, 89.
[91] Case C-551/22 P *Commission v SRB*, ECLI:EU:C:2023:846, Opinion of AG Ćapeta of 9 November 2023, paras 98 ff.
[92] *Meroni* (n 3), pp 151 f.
[93] *Commission v SRB* (n 90), para 92, with reference to *IBM v Commission* (n 84), para 10.
[94] See, on the Commission involvement, *Del Valle Ruiz v Commission and SRB* (n 87), paras 231 f.

which parts.[95] Thus, there are good reasons why the Commission is the main defending institution in the case of a resolution action, in the end, even with the important role of the SRB in the preparatory phase.

Finally, where no resolution action in the framework of the SRMR is pursued and the procedure ends in the course of the assessment phase of Article 18(1)–(5) SRMR, the SRB is the defending body. This was already confirmed by the Court of Justice in the *ABLV* cases. Examining the ECB's 'failing or likely to fail' assessment, the Court held that this is a mere preparatory act. In a complex administrative procedure, action would have to be brought against the SRB if it decides not to take resolution action in the assessment phase.[96] Similarly, the SRB is the defending body in the case where no resolution action is pursued because it makes the clearly delimited and technical assessment that resolution is not in the public interest as defined in Article 18(1)(c) and (5) SRMR, with the effect of the bank being wound up under normal insolvency proceedings.[97] In sum, simply letting events run their course without an intervention by EU public authorities poses less of an issue for the *Meroni* doctrine.

VI Conclusion: the many faces of *Meroni*

The *Meroni* judgment is one of the most important early decisions by the Court of Justice. It is as pivotal for the institutional system set up by the Treaties as the *Costa v ENEL* judgment is for the relation between the Union and its Member States. The *Meroni* judgment is not only the starting point for the Court's jurisprudence on institutional balance, now enshrined in Article 13(2), 1st sentence, TEU; it also forms the crucial background for understanding the powers and procedures established in and under the Treaties in relation to the EU as a whole. Therefore, it comes as no surprise that the *Meroni* judgment and the ensuing case law constituting the *Meroni* doctrine govern the delegation of powers to bodies which are not established in the Treaties.

The *Meroni* doctrine had a profound impact on establishing the Banking Union, which saw a proliferation of new bodies with different kinds of powers. Whether it is the internal delegation in the SSM, the delegation of autonomous

[95] *Commission v SRB* (n 90), para 87.

[96] Joined Cases C-551/19 P and C-552/19 P *ABLV Bank v ECB*, ECLI:EU:C:2021:369, para 66. Confirmed in Case C-202/21 *ABLV Bank v SRB*, ECLI:EU:C:2022:734, para 185 and *Commission v SRB* (n 90), para 92.

[97] See Case C-602/22 P *ABLV Bank v SRB*, ECLI:EU:C:2025:347, Opinion of AG Biondi, paras 44–50.

powers on ESMA, or the creation of complex administrative procedures in the SRM, the *Meroni* case law had an impact, as it led the EU legislator to avoid the delegation of broad discretionary powers, which only the Union institutions established by the Treaties may exercise.

This reveals the many faces of the *Meroni* judgment: it is not only of paramount constitutional importance for the overall institutional set-up of the Union; it also creates important boundaries for lawmakers when delegating autonomous or preparatory powers to EU agencies, and when devising the (sometimes very complex) administrative procedures which may also involve Union institutions. These considerations have important implications for judicial review and are also relevant for identifying the authors of decisions. Thus, the *Meroni* judgment prompts decision-makers, lawyers, and scholars alike to ask intricate questions of legal and political responsibility. And when answering these questions, we will discover that, beyond the complexities, the many faces of *Meroni* have a unifying effect, as they require us to think about the EU as a whole.

10

Reformed European Stability Mechanism Fully Respectful of Union Law

*Andrea Westerhof Löfflerová**

I Introduction

On 27 January 2021, after several years of intensive negotiations, representatives of the EU Member States signed two important international treaties. First, the then 19 euro area Member States[1] signed the Agreement amending the Treaty Establishing the European Stability Mechanism (ESM Amendment).[2] Second, all 27 EU Member States signed the Agreement amending the agreement on the Transfer and Mutualisation of Contributions to the Single Resolution Mechanism (IGA Amendment).[3]

The signature of these two international treaties formalized the political agreement on the ESM reform package that was reached on 30 November 2020 at the Eurogroup, in an inclusive format, ie with the participation of all Member

* The views expressed by the author are strictly personal and do not engage the institution for which she works. This chapter builds on an earlier contribution to EU Law Live.

[1] Estonia, due to a change of government, signed a few days later, on 8 February 2021.

[2] Agreement amending the Treaty Establishing the European Stability Mechanism between the Kingdom of Belgium, the Federal Republic of Germany, the Republic of Estonia, Ireland, the Hellenic Republic, the Kingdom of Spain, the French Republic, the Italian Republic, the Republic of Cyprus, the Republic of Latvia, the Republic of Lithuania, the Grand Duchy of Luxembourg, the Republic of Malta, the Kingdom of the Netherlands, the Republic of Austria, the Portuguese Republic, the Republic of Slovenia, the Slovak Republic and the Republic of Finland, to be found at www.consilium.europa.eu/media/48069/agreement-amending-the-treaty-establishing-the-european-stability-mechanism-27-january-2021_en.pdf, accessed 9 June 2026.

[3] Agreement amending the Agreement on the Transfer and Mutualisation of Contributions to the Single Resolution Fund between the Kingdom of Belgium, the Republic of Bulgaria, the Czech Republic, the Kingdom of Denmark, the Federal Republic of Germany, the Republic of Estonia, Ireland, the Hellenic Republic, the Kingdom of Spain, the French Republic, the Republic of Croatia, the Italian Republic, the Republic of Cyprus, the Republic of Latvia, the Republic of Lithuania, the Grand Duchy of Luxembourg, the Republic of Malta, the Kingdom of the Netherlands, the Republic of Austria, the Republic of Poland, the Portuguese Republic, Romania, the Republic of Slovenia, the Slovak Republic, and the Republic of Finland, to be found at www.consilium.europa.eu/media/48068/agreement-amending-the-intergovernmental-agreement-on-the-transfer-and-mutualisation-of-contributions-to-the-single-resolution-fund-27-january-2021_en.pdf, accessed 9 June 2026.

Andrea Westerhof Löfflerová, *Reformed European Stability Mechanism Fully Respectful of Union Law*
In: *EU Banking Union*. Edited by: Jonathan Bauerschmidt, Raffaele D'Ambrosio, Diane Fromage, Daniela Jaros, and Paul Weismann, Oxford University Press.
DOI: 10.1093/9780198949756.003.0011

States[4]—a reform that was designed to strengthen the crisis-prevention and crisis-resolution capacities of the euro area, and of the Union as a whole.

The signature launched the ratification procedures in the Member States, in accordance with their national constitutional requirements. To date, the ESM Amendment has been ratified by all its signatories[5] with the exception of Italy. Similarly, the IGA Amendment has been ratified by all the signatories participating in the Banking Union, with the exception of Italy. Both the ESM Treaty and the ESM Amendment have also been acceded to by Croatia, which has meanwhile become the twentieth member of the euro area. The accession by Bulgaria, who became the twenty-first member of the euro area, is currently underway.

The lack of Italy's ratification[6] means that neither of the two amendments can yet enter into force. However regrettable the delay, it remains a fact that, once Italy has submitted its instruments of ratification,[7] the reform of the ESM in force will represent a fundamental milestone for further development of the Economic and Monetary Union (EMU), and for the completion of the Banking Union.

The purpose of this chapter is to present the main elements of the reformed ESM Treaty, to pinpoint the main legal challenges that the discussions have brought about, and to show that the ESM, even after the revision of its founding document, will continue to orbit the Union in a manner that is loyal to it, in full respect of the powers of Union institutions and of the primacy and autonomy of the EU legal framework.

II A quick recapitulation on the ESM and the SRM

The ESM was born from the financial crisis that hit Europe in 2008 and the subsequent sovereign debt crisis. It is an international financial institution,

[4] To be found at website of the Eurogroup at www.consilium.europa.eu/en/press/press-releases/2020/11/30/statement-of-the-eurogroup-in-inclusive-format-on-the-esm-reform-and-the-early-introduction-of-the-backstop-to-the-single-resolution-fund, accessed 9 June 2026.

[5] For instance, in Germany, the ratification of both amendments has been subject to a constitutional complaint which has been rejected by the German Constitutional Court—see BVerfG, Judgment of the Second Senate of 9 December 2022 - 2 BvR 1111821. See also Michal Kianička, 'Bundesverfassungsgericht on NGEU and ESM reform: Is the German Constitutional Court (legally) avoiding its EU counterpart?' (*EU Law Live*, 20 January 2023), to be found at Op-Ed: "Bundesverfassungsgericht on NGEU and ESM reform: Is the German Constitutional Court (legally) avoiding its EU counterpart?" by Michal Kianička" - EU Law Live.

[6] See Giampaolo Galli, 'The Reform of the ESM and Why It Is So Controversial in Italy' (2020) 15 Capital Markets Law Journal 262–76.

[7] Although the Italian parliament voted against the ratification on 21 December 2023, the Italian government is not prevented from resubmitting the motion for ratification to the Parliament again in the future.

established in 2012 in Luxembourg. The ESM operates under public international law. Its founding document—the Treaty establishing the European Stability Mechanism[8]—is an intergovernmental treaty concluded among the euro area Member States. The ESM mandate is to mobilize funding and provide financial assistance, under strict conditions, to ESM members who are euro area Member States which are experiencing or are threatened by severe financing problems, if providing such financial assistance is indispensable to safeguard the financial stability of the euro area as a whole, and of its Member States. Its purpose, thus, is to help avoid and overcome financial crises and to maintain long-term financial stability and prosperity by providing, as a lender of last resort, loans and other types of financial assistance to euro area Member States.

The financial crisis also demonstrated the need for better regulation and supervision of the EU financial sector, particularly in the euro area. As a consequence, euro-area countries decided to pursue a deeper integration of their banking systems. The creation of the Banking Union, in 2014, was a powerful response to the financial crisis, with significant progress on an EU Single Rulebook and the establishment of a new European architecture for banking supervision and resolution. The Banking Union is currently based on two fully operational pillars that apply to 21 Member States,[9] namely the Single Supervisory Mechanism (SSM) and the Single Resolution Mechanism (SRM).

As for the latter, the SRM was created in 2014 by the SRM Regulation[10] and became operational in 2016. It established a uniform procedure for the resolution of credit institutions that are subject to the SSM. It is made up of the Single Resolution Board (SRB), an EU regulatory agency with legal personality, seated in Brussels, and the Single Resolution Fund (the Fund). The SRB is the owner of the Fund, and may use it only to the extent necessary to ensure the effective application of the resolution tools, and for the purposes specified in Article 76 of the SRM Regulation. The Fund is financed entirely by (*ex ante* and *ex post*) contributions from the banking sector. Although the Fund as such, the rules for its use, and the rules for the calculation of the bank contributions are established by the SRM Regulation, a Union act, the rules concerning the collection and transfer of those contributions to the Fund are governed

[8] The authentic wording of the ESM Treaty as it currently stands can be found at www.esm.europa.eu/sites/default/files/20150203_-_esm_treaty_-_en.pdf, accessed 9 June 2026.

[9] 21 euro area Member States; see art 4(1) of the SRM Regulation.

[10] Regulation (EU) 806/2014 of the European Parliament and of the Council of 15 July 2014 establishing uniform rules and a uniform procedure for the resolution of credit institutions and certain investment firms in the framework of a Single Resolution Mechanism and a Single Resolution Fund [2014] OJ L225, pp 1–90.

by an instrument of an intergovernmental nature, namely the Agreement on the Transfer and Mutualisation of Contributions to the Single Resolution Fund (IGA).[11] Although signed by all EU Member States, the IGA applies, according to its Article 12, only among the Member States participating in the Banking Union.

III Objectives, instruments, and challenges

As the objective of the reform of the ESM Treaty was, among others, to grant the ESM a new function as a lender vis-à-vis the SRB, such objective required that, in addition to the ESM Amendment, an amendment to the IGA was negotiated in parallel.

1 What are the key innovations brought by the ESM Amendment?

The ESM reform will streamline the access to one of the ESM tools, namely the ESM's precautionary credit line.[12] This tool is available to ESM Members that, although in need of financial assistance, are not yet in such dire straits as to have lost access to financing on the markets. The reform will also bring about an important recalibration of the roles of the ESM and of the Commission in the design, negotiation, and monitoring of future financial assistance programmes, and in crisis preparedness. The reformed ESM Treaty also foresees better tools to promote debt sustainability of the Member States.[13]

Although the ESM is currently permitted to provide financial assistance only to ESM members—ie euro area Member States—the most significant innovation of the ESM reform rests in granting the ESM the mandate to provide financial assistance to the SRB, an EU agency in charge of the resolution of the Union's most important banks.[14] This is a quintessential quality jump.

[11] The IGA can be found at Treaties and Agreements database of the Council of the EU at Search the Treaties and Agreements database - Consilium.

[12] It is worth mentioning that, in December 2017, the Commission submitted a proposal for a Council Regulation on the establishment of the European Monetary Fund which aimed at 'repatriating' the ESM into the EU legal order. The proposal was based on art 352 TFEU, according to which the Council acts by unanimity on a proposal of the Commission and a consent of the European Parliament. It was, however, clear after a single discussion in the Council that no unanimity existed to even start discussing the proposal.

[13] For a more detailed description of the reform, see, for instance, Jasper Aerts and Pedro Bizarro, 'The Reform of the European Stability Mechanism' (2020) 15(2) Capital Markets Law Journal 159–74.

[14] See, in particular, art 3(2) ('The ESM may provide the backstop facility to the SRB for the SRF to support the application of the resolution tools and exercise of resolution powers of the SRB as enshrined in the EU law.') and art 18A of the reformed ESM Treaty.

The ESM will be able to provide a backstop—a safeguard—for the SRB as regards the availability of financial means needed for it to exercise its functions. As already explained, the Fund is financed by contributions from the banking sector. However, the SRM Regulation also envisages, in its Articles 73 and 74, the possibility for the SRB to conclude financial arrangements for raising additional financial means, should this be necessary. Indeed, ensuring effective and sufficient financing of the Fund is of paramount importance to the credibility of the SRM as a whole. And although it has been clear from the inception of the SRM that a safety vault should exist that would increase the Fund's firepower, should its size prove too low, the decision on how and by whom such a backstop should be provided has only been made in the reformed ESM.

The ESM will thus newly be able to provide a common backstop to the SRB in the form of a revolving credit line under which loans may be provided to the SRB. The common backstop is conceived as a last-resort safety net to be used if ever the SRB does not have sufficient means in its Fund, for instance in the event of a systemic crisis or a resolution of a major systemically important bank.[15]

2 Why was the IGA Amendment needed?

At the inception of the SRM, the political agreement[16] envisaged a common backstop being in place by the end of 2023, ie at the end of the eight-year initial period during which the Fund was built up from so-called *ex ante* bank contributions.[17] During that initial period, *ex ante* contributions were not immediately and fully mutualized (ie available for the SRB, to be used for a resolution of any bank in the Banking Union) but were attributed to national compartments that were only progressively mutualized according to a schedule determined in Article 5 of the IGA, and which only ceased to exist at the end of 2023.

Given the traditional interlinkages, in the discussions on the deepening of the EMU, between risk sharing and risk reduction, the fact that sufficient progress had been achieved in reducing risks in the banking sector paved the way for the so-called early introduction of the common backstop. The backstop would become available at the beginning of 2022, ie two years ahead of the

[15] The term '*common* backstop' is used as a shorthand for the backstop facility, to be provided by the ESM—essentially on behalf of the euro area Member States as ESM Members—and a parallel credit line, to be provided to the SRB on equivalent terms by non-euro area Member States participating in the Banking Union, as defined in art 4(1) of the SRM Regulation.

[16] See recital 13 of the IGA and recitals of the IGA Amendment.

[17] Art 70 of the SRM Regulation.

originally conceived schedule. To that end, a targeted amendment had to be negotiated. It only concerned Article 5(1) of the IGA—the famous 'waterfall'—and was intended to bring forward the mutualization of the so-called extraordinary *ex post* contributions[18] from the banking sector.[19]

3 How about the ESM 'secondary law' instruments?

In addition to the two international amending agreements, an entire set of ESM secondary-level rules has been negotiated and politically agreed. The idea was to have the entire package ready, also in view of the national ratification procedures. In practice, these secondary-level rules would be formally adopted by the relevant ESM bodies once the ESM Amendment had entered into force.

These secondary-level rules[20] include a draft resolution of the ESM Board of Governors to grant the backstop facility to the SRB; a draft resolution of the ESM Board of Governors determining the so-called nominal cap, ie the maximum amount of the backstop that the ESM may, at any moment in time, provide to SRB[21] and the procedure for the verification of the condition of permanence of the legal framework, before the common backstop can be granted to the SRB (the Backstop Resolution);[22] a draft guideline of the ESM Board of Directors on the backstop facility to the SRB for the Fund (the Backstop Guideline); and a draft guideline on the precautionary financial assistance. In addition, draft loan agreements between the ESM, as the lender, and the SRB, as the borrower, have been prepared.

4 The key constitutional and institutional challenges

The negotiation process among the Member States acting *inter se* as contracting parties to two international agreements took place in 2019 and 2020 at the Eurogroup and its preparatory bodies, namely the Euro Working Group

[18] ibid, art 71.

[19] Given the envisaged timeline, the IGA Amendment effectively became obsolete at the end of 2023.

[20] These can be found among the documents endorsed by Eurogroup of 4 December 2019, at www.consilium.europa.eu/en/meetings/eurogroup/2019/12/04, accessed 9 June 2026.

[21] This nominal cap is currently envisaged at the level of 68 billion euros, which corresponded to the target level of the Fund, estimated at the relevant time (December 2019). It is worth observing that, since Single Resolution Fund currently amounts to over 81 billion euros, it is possible, and even highly probable, that the nominal cap will be adjusted at the moment of the formal adoption of the resolution by the ESM Board of Governors.

[22] See section V.2, below.

and its Task Force for Coordinated Action.[23] The discussions involved numerous legal challenges and innovations. As both the ESM Treaty and the IGA are intergovernmental agreements outside the EU legal framework, the key legal concern was the need to ensure their (continued) consistency with EU law and, ultimately, to preserve the primacy of EU law and the autonomy of the Union legal order, and of the Union decision-making.

Two of the most interesting constitutional issues brought about concerned: (i) the relationship between the ESM and the Union institutions; and (ii) the relationship between Union law, the ESM rules, and the constitutional requirements of the Member States.

IV Relationship between the ESM and the Union institutions: The Commission remains a central actor

Some of the most important legal discussions on the reformed ESM Treaty centred, without exaggeration, around the correct calibration of the roles of the ESM, on the one hand, and of the Commission, the European Central Bank (ECB), and the SRB, on the other.

It has been asserted or implied that the reform of the ESM had significantly expanded the role of the ESM in the EU economic governance.[24] However, as will be shown below, the ESM has not been endowed with a role in the economic governance of the Union, nor does the amendment to the ESM Treaty lead to an alteration of the institutional architecture of the EU economic governance.

It is true that (some) Member States would have liked to have seen the ESM transformed into a European version of the International Monetary Fund and vested with powers of economic surveillance in respect of the euro area. At the root of those aspirations was the reform of the EMU, which has been undertaken since 2010 through successive instruments known as the Six-Pack and the Two-Pack. That reform has reinforced the role of the Commission in the economic governance of the Union, in the hope that, unlike the Council, which has been perceived as responding too much to political, rather than legal or

[23] For a detailed explanation of the genesis of the reform, see, for instance, Menelaos Markakis, 'The Reform of the European Stability Mechanism: Process, Substance, and the Pandemic' (2020) 47(4) Legal Issues of Economic Integration 359–84.

[24] For instance, in the European Parliament's internal analysis: Cristina Dias and Alice Zoppè, 'The proposed amendments to the Treaty establishing the European Stability Mechanism' (European Parliamentary Research Service, January 2021); or Anna Peychev, 'Reforming the European Stability Mechanism. Too Much but Never Enough' (2021) Wilfried Martens Centre for European Studies.

economic, criteria,[25] the Commission would exercise the task of economic surveillance in a technical, non-political manner. However, the opposite became true: as the task remained political, the Commission, as a technical institution, was politicized.[26] It was this development that led some Member States to require that the ESM—seen as a purely technical body—acts as an alternative enforcer of the rules of economic governance.

However, an attribution of powers in the area of economic governance to the ESM faces major legal obstacles, stemming from the fact that the ESM is an intergovernmental body outside the EU legal framework. The compatibility of the current ESM Treaty with EU law has already been famously verified by the Court of Justice of the EU (CJEU) in *Pringle*.[27] For the CJEU, the ESM Treaty qualified as an instrument ancillary to the achievement of Union's objectives which 'serves to complement the new regulatory framework for strengthened economic governance of the Union, rather than as a mechanism that would encroach upon the competencies of the Union'.[28]

The CJEU has given its blessing to intergovernmental instruments concluded by the Member States *inter se*, provided that they do not interfere with or put in jeopardy the competences of the Union and of its institutions. More specifically, an intergovernmental instrument must respect the principles of autonomy and primacy of the Union legal order,[29] and mechanisms that anchor the intergovernmental action to Union law, such as attribution of certain tasks of management and jurisdiction to EU institutions. Finally, the intergovernmental agreement must not encroach upon the competences of the Union or its institutions. When negotiating, concluding, and implementing an intergovernmental agreement, the Member States have to comply with the principle of sincere cooperation set out in Article 4(3) TEU.[30] To put it briefly, the ESM may not become a new institution of economic governance of the euro area, replacing the Commission and the Council, and its powers may not overlap with the powers of these EU institutions.

While the revised ESM Treaty uncontestably foresees an enhanced role of the ESM, it must be emphasized that, in view of the above fundamental

[25] Let us recall that, in 2004, the Council of the EU failed to apply the excessive deficit procedure rules to France and Germany. See also Case C-27/04 *Commission v Council*, ECLI:EU:C:2004:436.

[26] The Commission immediately adopted a highly politicized Flexibility Communication and, in the summer of 2016, decided not to apply sanctions to Spain and Portugal. See, for instance, Mark Dawson, 'How Can EU Contain Economic Discretion?' in Joana Mendes (ed), *EU Executive Discretion and the Limits of Law* (OUP 2019).

[27] Case C-370/12 *Pringle*, ECLI:EU:C:2012:756.

[28] ibid, para 58.

[29] ibid, in particular paras 68 and 69, 109, and 121. In the ESM Treaty, this is complied with by means of including consistency clauses of the ESM with EU law.

[30] ibid, paras 148 ff.

legal limitations, such role is confined to issues concerning the *ESM's own governance.*

As a result, the ESM may carry out debt-sustainability assessments of the Member States that are, or are to become, *beneficiaries* of the ESM financial assistance; the ESM may *for that purpose* negotiate the memorandum of understanding with such a Member State and sign it; and the ESM may *to this end* monitor compliance of such Member State with the conditionality requirements set out in such memorandum of understanding. However, the ESM never acts alone, and the ESM's actions are always subject to a consistency check by the Commission. The revised ESM Treaty explicitly provides that the ESM exercises its enhanced role '*together*' with the Commission (which, in turn, acts in liaison with the ECB). This is fundamental in order to ensure that the ESM and the Commission always act within *their respective competences.* It is in this manner that the Commission maintains the effective power to vet the conditions associated with any ESM financial assistance programme, provided, of course, that these are consistent with the measures of economic governance adopted under EU law. Indeed, even under the revised ESM Treaty, the Commission is still required to (co-)sign the memorandum of understanding (co-)negotiated with the ESM.

As the ESM may not, and will not, assume functions and tasks conferred on Union institutions under the Treaties, the ESM does not have a role of general economic surveillance vis-à-vis the economic policies of Member States—a role which is reserved to the Commission and the Council. To this end, the revised ESM Treaty contains a raft of provisions that must be read in mutual conjunction, and which provide guarantees that are essential for distinguishing between, on the one hand, the rules applicable under the Stability and Growth Pact and, on the other, the rules for the purpose of granting ESM financial assistance to the ESM members.

This distinction between competences and powers also applies when it comes to the role of the ESM *outside* the ESM programmes. The ESM will be able to examine the macroeconomic and financial situation of the ESM members, including the sustainability of their public debt, and will be able to carry out analysis of the relevant information and data. However, the purpose of such actions is only *internal*; namely, the ESM is endowed with such powers only 'in order to internally prepare and enable it to appropriately and in a timely manner pursue the tasks conferred on it by the ESM Treaty' (Article 3(1) of the revised ESM Treaty). It follows that these are not self-standing powers but powers that must be understood as subsumed into the already existing tasks of the ESM. Moreover, in exercising such analytical functions, the

ESM must again collaborate with the Commission (and, by that token, with the ECB) to ensure full consistency with the Union framework for economic policy coordination. Recital 15a of the revised ESM Treaty makes it clear that the ESM does not serve the purpose of economic policy coordination among ESM members, a role which is reserved by the Treaties for the Union institutions. Consequently, rather than adding brand-new attributions to the ESM, the revised ESM Treaty clarifies what the ESM is permitted to do under the existing legal framework.

Furthermore, Article 12(4) of the revised ESM Treaty contains a *general consistency clause*[31] which makes it clear that it is for the Commission to ensure that all ESM financial-assistance operations are consistent with Union law, and in particular with the measures of economic policy coordination.[32] This important role of the Commission as the guardian of the Treaties was underlined by the CJEU, in the context of financial assistance to Cyprus, in *Chrysostomides*.[33]

It follows that the Commission maintains its role as the guardian of the EU Treaties, in particular the role of ensuring consistency of the ESM's actions with the EU economic policy coordination framework, and the ESM performs its (enhanced) analytical and assessment roles from the perspective of a lender.

V Autonomy of the EU legal framework: A delicate balance between Union law, ESM rules, and constitutional requirements of the Member States

In addition to ensuring that the intergovernmental action by the Member States does not encroach upon the competences of the Union institutions, another difficulty consisted in finding a delicate balance between the constitutional requirements of the Member States, on the one hand, and the limits imposed by Union law, on the other.[34]

[31] In addition to the specific consistency clauses in art 13(3) ESM Treaty, see also ibid, para 121.

[32] See recitals 5b and 16, and arts 3(1), 12(1a) and (4), and 14(2) of the revised ESM Treaty.

[33] Joined Cases C-597/18P, C-598/18P, C-603/18P, and C-604/18P, ECLI:EU:C:2020:1028, para 96.

[34] See also Jean-Paul Keppenne, Tim Rusche, and Laura Estrella Blaya, 'An ESM Backstop Facility to the Single Resolution Board: The Difficult Marriage of an EU Mechanism and an Intergovernmental Institution' in Diane Fromage and Bruno de Witte (eds), 'Recent Evolutions in the Economic and Monetary Union and the European Banking Union: A Reflection' (2019) Maastricht Law Faculty Working Paper Series, 2019/03, 43–45.

These tensions were particularly present in discussions on the conditions for access to, and use of, the common backstop to the SRB, and concerned, in particular: (1) the sharing of information; and (2) the permanence of the legal framework.

1 Information sharing between the ESM and the SRB

As regards the information sharing, the issue concerned the scope, and the conditions under which the SRB, as the borrower, would provide information to the ESM, as the lender, for the purpose of obtaining the backstop facility from the ESM. Two potentially conflicting interests needed to be reconciled.

On the one hand, there was a need for the national parliaments of (some) Member States to have sufficient information at their disposal. Indeed, in some Member States, a prior approval by the national parliament is necessary before the representative of that Member State can take a part in a vote in the relevant ESM decision-making bodies,[35] as the activation of the common backstop is considered as potentially affecting the national budgetary sovereignty, of which national parliaments are the holders.[36]

As a result, some Member States required an enhanced system of information sharing. More specifically, they required that the SRB, when submitting a request to the ESM for a loan under the common backstop facility, would provide the ESM with as much information as possible, so that the national parliaments would feel comfortable, and could consider themselves to be effectively exercising their budgetary control, before giving a 'mandate' to their finance minister, as a member of the Board of Governors, to vote within the ESM.

It is worth recalling, in this respect, that the German Constitutional Court ruled in 2012, in its judgment concerning the ESM Treaty,[37] that, as regards decisions to be taken by the ESM bodies, the respect of national budgetary sovereignty entailed the need to provide the Bundestag with 'effective and comprehensive information' in order for it to be able to develop an informed opinion.[38] This judgment prompted the Member States, as signatories of the ESM Treaty,

[35] The personal composition of the ESM Board of Governors in practice coincides with that of the Eurogroup and consists of ministers of finance of the euro area Member States. According to the revised ESM Treaty, the ESM Board of Governors and the ESM Board of Directors take all decisions relevant to the common backstop, by mutual agreement.

[36] This is, in particular, the case of Germany, Austria, the Netherlands, and Estonia.

[37] BVerfG, Judgment of the Second Senate of 12 September 2012 - 2 BvR 1390/12.

[38] See ibid, paras 153, as well as 152 and 156.

to make an interpretative declaration[39] that explicitly clarified that provisions in the ESM Treaty that concern professional secrecy do not prevent the provision of comprehensive information to the national parliaments, as foreseen by national regulation. It also declared this element to constitute an essential basis for the consent of the Member States, as the contracting parties, to be bound by the ESM Treaty.

On the other hand, information that could be legally shared by the SRB as a Union agency is subject to serious constraints, bearing in mind the principles of primacy of Union law and autonomy of the Union legal order. Given that the common backstop would be granted to the SRB in respect of a resolution of a *specific bank*, sharing of bank-specific information was extremely sensitive, as any untimely divulgation of sensitive information could lead to further deterioration of the bank's situation.

There were essentially three constraints to any information sharing by the SRB in the context of the common backstop.

First, in accordance with Article 88 of the SRM Regulation, the SRB would be allowed to share information with the ESM, provided that this would fall within the exercise of the *SRB functions*, as defined in the SRM Regulation. Since, in the context of the common backstop, the SRB would exercise its borrowing mandate in accordance with Article 74 of the SRM Regulation, any information shared with the ESM (and, subsequently, by the members of the ESM bodies with their respective national parliaments) would have to be confined to information that is relevant for such borrowing mandate of the ESM.

Second, any information shared by the SRB with the ESM would only be shared for the *purpose* of the evaluation, by the ESM—as a lender—of the borrowing transaction, and more specifically of the repayment capacity of the SRB. It thus must be excluded that the provision of information by the SRB to the ESM would lead to the ESM or the national parliaments becoming a 'second chamber of control' of the SRB's actions under the Union bank resolution framework.[40]

Third, any information sharing by the SRB with the ESM must be subject to the respect of *confidentiality requirements of Union law*, namely Article 339 TFEU, in general, and Article 88 SRM Regulation, in particular.

[39] To be found at website of the Council of the EU at www.consilium.europa.eu/uedocs/cms_data/docs/pressdata/en/ecofin/132615.pdf, accessed 9 June 2026.

[40] In line with the CJEU's *Meroni* doctrine, as confirmed by recent case law (see Case C–551/22 P *Commission v SRB*, ECLI:EU:C:2024:520), the policymaking aspects of the SRB decision-making are subject to the Commission's and/or the Council's approval. See recital 24 and art 18(7) of the SRM Regulation.

In order to stay well within the above legal constraints, Article 18a(5) of the revised ESM Treaty specifies that the request for a loan by the SRB must contain all relevant information while respecting confidentiality requirements of EU law. This basic premise is then further spelled out in the Backstop Guideline. Article 1(3) of the Backstop Guideline recalls that the Guideline is to be applied in accordance with the 2012 interpretative declaration, mentioned above. A two-step approach for the provision of information is foreseen in Article 4 of the Backstop Guideline. First, a defined list of items is presumed to allow the ESM to take informed decisions on loans and respective disbursements under the backstop facility.[41] Second, a possibility is foreseen for the ESM managing director to ask for additional relevant explanations, which the SRB would provide unless their disclosure would interfere with the exercise of its functions. Any information is provided subject to its confidential treatment, as spelled out in Article 10 of the Backstop Guideline.[42] Article 4(1c) of the Backstop Guideline also clarifies that the use of any information thus provided shall respect the tasks and powers conferred by Union law on the Union institutions and agencies, including the specific merits of each resolution action, and shall be used for the purpose of ensuring the ESM functions as laid down in Article 18a and Annex IV to the ESM Treaty, most notably for determining the SRB capacity of servicing the loan within the relevant maturity.

2 Permanence of the legal framework

The second issue where possible tensions between the respective ESM and EU legal orders were at the centre stage is the requirement of the permanence of the legal framework for banking resolution. That requirement is formulated in Article 18a(8) and (9) of the revised ESM Treaty. It makes the granting of the backstop facility to the SRB, and its use, contingent upon compliance with that condition, and attaches consequences to situations where that condition is no longer complied with after the backstop facility has been granted to the SRB.

The permanence-of-legal-framework provisions in the ESM Treaty were inspired by the IGA—more particularly by its Article 9(1), according to which the use of the Fund on a mutual basis and the transfer of contributions to the

[41] Art 4(1a) of the Backstop Guideline.

[42] 'The treatment of confidential information exchanged between the ESM and SRB in accordance with Article 4 is subject to professional secrecy obligations in accordance with Article 34 ESMT and EU law and shall be subject to appropriate mechanisms for maintaining confidentiality.'

Fund is contingent upon the permanence of the legal framework on resolution, which consists of specifically identified core provisions of the Union bank resolution regulations, namely the SRM Regulation and the Banking Resolution and Recovery Directive (BRRD).[43] The permanence-of-the-legal-framework condition is complied with where the core resolution rules have not been amended by the EU legislator or, if they ever have been amended, the amendment has resulted in rules that are equivalent to those rules or lead to the same result as those rules.

These core resolution rules consist of procedural rules on the adoption of a resolution scheme as laid down under Article 18 of the SRM Regulation; the decision-making rules of the SRB laid down in Articles 52 and 55 of the SRM Regulation; general principles concerning resolution, as laid down in Article 15 of the SRM Regulation, notably the principles that the shareholders of the institution under resolution bear first losses and that the creditors of the institution under resolution bear losses after the shareholders in accordance with the order of priority of their claims, enshrined in Article 15(1)(a) and (b); and the rules on the resolution tools referred to under Article 22(2) of the SRM Regulation, notably those concerning the application of the bail-in tool laid down under Article 27 of the SRM Regulation and Articles 43 and 44 of the BRRD and the specific thresholds that they establish related to the imposition of losses on shareholders and on creditors and the contribution of the Fund to a particular resolution action.[44]

However, the permanence of the legal framework in the IGA, and in the ESM, are fundamentally different in two aspects.

First, in the IGA, the permanence of the legal framework represented a *rebus sic stantibus* clause, ie a fundamental-change-of-circumstances clause, a customary law principle codified in Article 62 of the Vienna Convention on the Law of Treaties (VCLT), and thus constituted an essential basis for the consent of the Member States, as contracting parties to the IGA, to be bound by that international treaty.[45] As such, it would allow a contracting party to the IGA to suspend, under certain conditions, some of its obligations under that international treaty. In the common-backstop context, on the other hand, the

[43] Directive (EU) 2014/59 establishing a framework for the recovery and resolution of credit institutions and investment firms [2014] OJ L173, pp 190–348.

[44] See also recitals 17 and 18 of the IGA. It is difficult, *in abstracto*, to fathom when exactly the permanence of the legal framework will be considered by a Member State—a contracting party to the IGA—to not to be complied with; in other words, when an amendment to EU banking resolution rules will, figuratively speaking, cross the line in such a fatal way that the contracting party will no longer consider itself bound by the IGA.

[45] See recital 17 of the IGA.

permanence of the legal framework has a very different function; namely, it constitutes a condition for the ESM to be able to grant the backstop facility to the SRB and to approve loans and disbursements under such facility.[46] In the case of non-compliance with the permanence of the legal framework, a comprehensive review is initiated and an explicit decision by the ESM Board of Governors is required for the ESM to be able to (continue to) provide the SRB with the backstop facility. In other words, and importantly, the permanence-of-legal-framework condition in the ESM does not, differently from the IGA, allow an ESM Member to suspend its obligations under the ESM Treaty.[47]

The second difference lies in the scope of the perimeter of the legal framework whose permanence is sought after, as the legal framework targeted in the revised ESM Treaty is broader than that in the IGA. This is because, in May 2019, an important set of amendments (the Banking Package) was adopted, inter alia, to the SRM Regulation and the BRRD, and (some) Member States considered it essential that additional key elements of that Banking Package be relevant for the permanence of the legal framework under the revised ESM Treaty.

This brought about concerns—already discussed in the context of the IGA—about the autonomy of the EU legal framework and its decision-making. More specifically, it has been argued that including the extended permanence of legal framework condition in the revised ESM Treaty would constitute an obstacle for legislative changes to the EU legal framework for bank resolution to be adopted in the Council by the applicable majority of votes,[48] as any euro area Member State outvoted within the Council would be able to threaten to disable the common backstop within the ESM.

It should, however, be observed that the relationship between the common backstop and the EU legal framework is more remote than in the case of the IGA. While the IGA and the SRM Regulation are clearly intertwined, as both the built-up, and the use, of the Fund are made dependent on the entry into force of the IGA,[49] the constitution of the Fund and its use are, as a matter of principle, not dependent on the common backstop.

[46] See article 18a(8) and (9) of the revised ESM Treaty and Annex IV thereto.

[47] A fundamental change of circumstances within the meaning of art 62 of the VCLT could be invoked by a party to an international treaty as a ground for terminating or withdrawing from a treaty, or as a ground for suspending the operation of the treaty.

[48] The legal basis for the adoption of both the SRM Regulation and BRRD, and of their Banking Package amendments, is art 114 TFEU, for the purpose of which the Council acts by a qualified majority of votes.

[49] It is recalled that, in the *Unified Patent Regulation* case, C-146/13, ECLI:EU:C:2015:298, the CJEU dismissed the arguments based on the principle of autonomy of the EU legal framework, in respect of a situation of mutual dependence analogous to that between the SRM Regulation and the IGA.

The enlargement of the scope of the permanence-of-legal-framework condition in the revised ESM Treaty is, thus, legally acceptable. Yet, it was still necessary to devise a procedure that would allow the verification of the compliance with the thus extended permanence-of-legal-framework condition in a manner that would limit the consequences to the ESM realm only and, more specifically, that would avoid—because of its intertwined relationship with the EU legal framework—any spillover effect of the ESM condition on that under the IGA.

It was these considerations that shaped the design of the procedure for the verification of the permanence of the legal framework under the revised ESM and its consequences for the common backstop facility to be granted by the ESM to the SRB and its use. The relevant provisions are defined in the draft Backstop Resolution, as foreseen in Article 37(4) of the reformed ESM Treaty.[50] The procedure is designed in two parallel strands:[51] one for the permanence of legal framework that corresponds in its scope to that in the IGA,[52] and the other for the 'Banking Package-related' permanence of legal framework that goes beyond the scope of the IGA.[53] Under the agreed rules, if an ESM member submits an application for the verification of the compliance with the permanence of the legal framework to the CJEU, under Article 273 TFEU,[54] such ESM Member must specify that the Court's verification is to be made separately in respect of each of the two 'legs' of the permanence-of-legal-framework condition. In the same vein, it is explicitly excluded that a Court judgment in respect of the 'Banking Package-related' permanence affects performance or execution of obligations under the IGA.[55]

Although, at the first sight, the procedural provisions might seem complicated, the contrary is true. They work with clear concepts with predictable results, in order to avoid duplication, inconsistency, or even dysfunctionality, which could occur if ever the same set of criteria was subject to two different types of judicial scrutiny with differently calibrated procedures. As a result, any finding concerning the extended scope of the permanence-of-legal-framework

[50] According to art 37(4), any dispute between the ESM Members concerning the compliance with the condition of the permanence of the legal framework for bank resolution laid down in art 18a may be directly submitted to the Court of Justice of the EU in line with the procedure to be determined by the ESM Board of Directors pursuant to art 18a(1) and (8). The judgment of the Court of Justice shall be binding on the parties of the procedure, and the ESM shall act in conformity with such judgment.

[51] See cls 2(1)(a) and (b) of the draft Backstop Resolution.

[52] As defined in art 18a(9)(a) of the revised ESM Treaty.

[53] As defined in ibid, art 18a(9)(b).

[54] Under art 37(4) of the revised ESM Treaty and art 273 TFEU.

[55] See cl 2(1)(c) of the draft Backstop Resolution.

condition for the ESM purposes may have no unintended consequences on the IGA and, thus, on the use of the Fund by the SRB for the purpose of undertaking a resolution action under Union law.

VI Conclusion: The ESM remains loyal and complementary to the Union legal order

It can be concluded that the ESM is—and under the revised ESM Treaty remains—an instrument that is loyal and complementary to the Union legal order. The ESM pursues Union objectives by safeguarding the stability of the euro area, and it supplements Union policies by assisting in the coordination of economic policies of the Member States. The common backstop to be provided by the ESM is a significant step towards completing the European Banking Union and breaking the vicious circle between banks and sovereigns. The ESM is respectful of the autonomy of the EU legal framework and does not deconstruct the powers of Union institutions. By including a set of consistency clauses, the revised ESM Treaty highlights the ESM's respect for primacy of Union law and features mechanisms that continue to firmly anchor the intergovernmental action to Union law by reserving a key role within the ESM to the European Commission.

Recent developments have shown that the intergovernmental method has not become the new paradigm of the Union integration, as some have feared in the light of the intensely intergovernmental response to the euro crisis.[56] For instance, the legal construction that underlies the Next Generation EU Programme, the Union's flagship innovative recovery plan as a reaction to the Covid-19 crisis, is firmly anchored in the Union legal order, although, very initially, intergovernmental montages were also envisaged.

On the other hand, the ESM story shows that, in those cases where the intergovernmental method is—for a reason—retained, an instrument such as the ESM does not need to be an alien construction to the Union—rather the contrary. If it is properly designed and in accordance with the requirements enunciated by the CJEU in *Pringle*, it fortifies the Union by furthering its objectives, rather than clashing with it.[57] It is uncontested that not only has ESM's functioning not been detrimental to the Union legal order, but it has fundamentally

[56] See, for a well-balanced assessment and overview, eg Bruno de Witte, 'Euro Crisis Responses and the EU Legal Order' (2015) 11(3) European Constitutional Law Review 434–57.

[57] See Alberto de Gregorio Merino, 'Institutional Report' in Gyula Bándi and others (eds), *European Banking Union: Congress Proceedings* vol 1 (The XXVII FIDE Congress in Budapest, 2016) (Wolters Kluwer 2016) 185–86.

strengthened the Union in the area of economic governance and enhanced the role of the Union institutions, in particular the European Commission.

For these reasons, the ESM in its current wording, and as reformed in the future by the ESM Amendment, can be regarded as an instrument that, in spite of its intergovernmental nature, belongs to the Union legal order in a wider sense.

11

The Financing of the Single Resolution Fund through *Ex Ante* Contributions

Innovative Financing and Legal Challenges

Eugénie d'Ursel[*]

I Introduction

The creation of the Banking Union is one of the key developments in the European Union (EU) in recent times, with extensive constitutional, financial, and institutional consequences. The celebration of its 10-year anniversary provides the opportunity to reflect upon it.

This chapter will focus on one of the key objectives of the Banking Union: its financing, aiming at ensuring that, in the future, taxpayers do not pay for failures of the banking sector. More specifically, the emphasis will be on the second pillar of the Banking Union, namely the Single Resolution Mechanism (SRM), and its financing by means of the *ex ante* contributions of the Single Resolution Fund (the 'Fund'). These contributions ensure the financing of the Fund by banks themselves. They have been in the spotlight of legal discussions since their inception, and have been, and still are, subject to a lot of litigation. Interestingly enough, the legal framework related to *ex ante* contributions was not subject to a direct challenge in front of the Court of Justice of the European Union after its adoption. However, several banks have challenged (yearly) the annual decision fixing the amount of their *ex ante* contributions. To date, there have been at least nine cases at the Court of Justice and 152 cases in front of the General Court (both pending and closed ones) on this topic.[1] While most of these cases dealt exclusively with legal questions related to the decisions

[*] The views expressed are strictly personal and do not express the views of the Council of the European Union or the European Council or the European Commission.

[1] As at 25 June 2024. The number of cases did not increase as substantially as before since then, as no additional contributions were raised after 2023.

Eugénie d'Ursel, *The Financing of the Single Resolution Fund through* Ex Ante *Contributions*
In: *EU Banking Union*. Edited by: Jonathan Bauerschmidt, Raffaele D'Ambrosio, Diane Fromage, Daniela Jaros, and Paul Weismann, Oxford University Press.
DOI: 10.1093/9780198949756.003.0012

adopted by the Single Resolution Board (SRB), several dozen included questioning of the validity of several acts establishing the legal framework.[2]

After introducing the legal framework and key concepts (section II), this chapter aims at analysing the interaction between general principles of EU law and a technical area. This will be assessed in a threefold case study focusing on the question of the legal basis and the principles of legal certainty and proportionality (section III).

II The financing of the Fund through *ex ante* contributions

The key acts making up the framework for the calculation rules will be introduced (subsection 1). To get a full picture, it is also important to understand who has to pay such contributions and the applicable procedure (subsection 2).

1 The legal framework applicable to *ex ante* contributions

Two legislative acts are of particular relevance here: the Bank Recovery and Resolution Directive (BRRD)[3] and the Single Resolution Mechanism Regulation (SRMR).[4] The BRRD harmonizes the rules applicable to the recovery and resolution of banks within the whole EU.[5] Under that directive, banking resolution remains national, but subject to enhanced coordination in cross-border cases. On the other hand, the SRMR provides for a centralized approach and establishes uniform rules for the resolution of the covered entities.[6] Contrary to the BRRD, the SRMR applies specifically to entities established in

[2] Litigation concerning SRB decisions gave rise to interesting developments going beyond this contribution: see, eg Concetta Brescia Morra and Federico Della Negra, 'Overview on the Litigation on the '*Ex Ante Contributions*' to the SRF: the Strict Standard of Review Adopted by the Court to Ensure Effective Legal Protection' in Chiara Zilioli and Karl-Philipp Wojcik, *Judicial Review in the European Banking Union* (Edward Elgar 2021) 551–63.

[3] Directive 2014/59/EU of the European Parliament and of the Council of 15 May 2014 establishing a framework for the recovery and resolution of credit institutions and investment firms and amending Council Directive 82/891/EEC, and Directives 2001/24/EC, 2002/47/EC, 2004/25/EC, 2005/56/EC, 2007/36/EC, 2011/35/EU, 2012/30/EU and 2013/36/EU, and Regulations (EU) No 1093/2010 and (EU) No 648/2012 of the European Parliament and of the Council Text with EEA relevance [2014] OJ L173/190.

[4] Regulation (EU) 806/2014 of the European Parliament and of the Council of 15 July 2014 establishing uniform rules and a uniform procedure for the resolution of credit institutions and certain investment firms in the framework of a Single Resolution Mechanism and a Single Resolution Fund and amending Regulation (EU) No 1093/2010 [2014] OJ L225/1.

[5] Art 1 of the BRRD.

[6] Art 1 of the SRMR.

participating Member States—more specifically, those whose currency is the euro, or whose currency is not the euro, but which have established a close co-operation (namely Bulgaria).[7]

The Fund serves the purpose of ensuring the efficient application of the resolution tools and exercise of the resolution powers.[8] It is an autonomous financing mechanism. This autonomous character is related to its innovative financing: the Fund is financed by the banking sector itself by means of financial contributions referred to as *ex ante* (Article 70), raised on an annual basis during the initial period, or extraordinary *ex post* (Article 71) contributions, raised exceptionally when financial means become insufficient. The Fund reached the end of the build-up phase in 2023 with an amount of approximately 77.6 billion[9] euros, through financing exclusively by *ex ante* contributions. Since then, the Fund's target remains reached and no additional contributions were raised. The target level of the Fund will be verified again at the beginning of 2027 and currently amounts to 81 billion euros.[10]

Other acts also have to be taken into account: Council Implementing Regulation 2015/81[11] (the 'Implementing Regulation'), Commission Delegated Regulation 2015/63[12] (the 'Delegated Regulation'), and Commission Delegated Regulation 2017/747.[13] The Implementing Regulation provides uniform conditions of application of the SRMR by specifying the conditions for the implementation of the SRB's obligation to calculate the individual contributions. The Delegated Regulation supplements the BRRD by specifying, inter alia, the methodology for the calculation of the *ex ante* contributions. The

[7] Arts 2 and 4 of the SRMR and art 2 of Council Regulation (EU) 1024/2013 of 15 October 2013 conferring specific tasks on the European Central Bank concerning policies relating to the prudential supervision of credit institutions [2013] OJ L287/63.

[8] Art 67 of the SRMR.

[9] Single Resolution Fund, Single Resolution Fund grows by EUR 11.3 billion to reach EUR 77.6 billion, Press Release, 6 July 2023, https://www.srb.europa.eu/en/content/single-resolution-fund-grows-eu113-billion-reach-eu-776-billion.

[10] Single Resolution Fund, For the third year, the SRB will not impose Single Resolution Fund levies, Press Release, 13 February 2026, For the third year, the SRB will not impose Single Resolution Fund levies | Single Resolution Board.

[11] Council Implementing Regulation (EU) 2015/81 of 19 December 2014 specifying uniform conditions of application of Regulation (EU) No 806/2014 of the European Parliament and of the Council with regard to ex ante contributions to the Single Resolution Fund [2015] OJ L15/1.

[12] Commission Delegated Regulation (EU) 2015/63 of 21 October 2014 supplementing Directive 2014/59/EU of the European Parliament and of the Council with regard to ex ante contributions to resolution financing arrangements [2015] OJ L11/44.

[13] Commission Delegated Regulation (EU) 2017/747 of 15 December 2015 supplementing Regulation (EU) No 806/2014 of the European Parliament and the Council with regard to the criteria relating to the calculation of ex ante contributions, and on the circumstances and conditions under which the payment of extraordinary ex post contributions may be partially or entirely deferred [2017] OJ L113/2.

SRB, while applying this framework, adopts an annual decision fixing the *ex ante* contributions for a given year.

Another relevant act in this area is the Intergovernmental Agreement on the transfer and mutualization of contributions to the Fund, concluded on 21 May 2014 between 26 Member States (with the exception of Sweden). This Intergovernmental Agreement deals with the transfer of contributions raised at national level to national compartments.

2 The calculation of the *ex ante* contributions

The legal framework provides for comprehensive rules for the constitution of the Fund and the calculation of the *ex ante* contributions.

a) The target level
The starting point is the establishment of the target level of the Fund. The annual *ex ante* contributions then have to be calculated with the goal of ensuring that this target level is met.

The available means of the Fund shall reach overall at least 1% of the amount of covered deposits of all institutions authorized in all of the participating Member States by the end of an initial period of eight years.[14] The initial period ended on 31 December 2023. In order to calculate the annual *ex ante* contributions of each institution, the SRB is also in charge of the calculation of the annual target level, in accordance with Article 70(2) of the SRMR. To that end, the SRB fixes the annual target level after consulting the European Central Bank (ECB) or the National Competent Authorities, and in close cooperation with national resolution authorities (NRAs), while taking due account of the phase of the business cycle and the impact that pro-cyclical contributions may have on the financial position of contributing institutions.[15]

This annual target level corresponds to the total amount of *ex ante* contributions that have to be collected in a given year to reach the global target level by

[14] Art 69(1) of the SRMR.
[15] Art 70(2) of the SRMR; and Commission Delegated Regulation (EU) 2017/747 of 17 December 2015 supplementing Regulation (EU) No 806/2014 of the European Parliament and the Council with regard to the criteria relating to the calculation of ex ante contributions, and on the circumstances and conditions under which the payment of extraordinary ex post contributions may be partially or entirely deferred [2017] OJ L113/2 art 3(1).

the end of 2023. The SRB then has to calculate and divide this amount among the contributing institutions in such a way as to ensure that this annual target level is met. For illustration purposes, the annual target level for 2023 was set at 11,702,958,514.31 euros.[16]

b) Calculation method of individual contributions

The key basic rule is the following:

> the individual contribution of each institution shall be raised at least annually and shall be calculated pro-rata to the amount of its liabilities (excluding own funds) less covered deposits, with respect to the aggregate liabilities (excluding own funds) less covered deposits, of all of the institutions authorised in the territories of all of the participating Member States.[17]

Such individual contributions are based on two elements: (i) a flat contribution; and (ii) a risk-adjusted contribution.[18]

The flat contribution is based pro rata on the amount of an institution's liabilities excluding own funds and covered deposits, with respect to the total liabilities, excluding own funds and covered deposits, of all of the institutions authorized in the territories of the participating Member States.[19]

The risk-adjusted contribution is based on the criteria laid down in Article 103(7) of Directive 2014/59/EU and has to take into account the principle of proportionality, without creating distortions between banking sector structures of the Member States.[20] Article 103(7) of the BRRD is the legal basis for the adoption of the Delegated Regulation.[21] The relevant provisions of the Delegated Regulation are Articles 4 to 13, as well as its Annex I.

[16] Single Resolution Board, 2023 SRF levies (ex ante contributions), https://www.srb.europa.eu/en/content/2023-srf-levies-ex-ante-contributions.

[17] Art 70(1) of the SRMR. The consequence of this is that credit institutions financed almost exclusively by deposits will pay low *ex ante* contributions but will have to contribute to national deposit guarantees schemes, as highlighted by Danny Busch and Guido Ferrarini (eds), *European Banking Union* (2nd edn, OUP 2020) point 9.47.

[18] Art 70(2) of the SRMR.

[19] ibid, art 70(2), subpara 2(a).

[20] ibid, subpara 2(b).

[21] ibid, art 70(6) recalls that the Delegated Regulation is relevant here.

3 Who pays *ex ante* contributions and how are they raised and collected?

a) Who pays?

The contributions are raised directly from the banking sector. This was an essential element in the aftermath of the sovereign debt crisis, to ensure that taxpayers no longer have to pay for the failure of banks.

Indeed, the contributions are financed by the entities covered by the SRMR, referred to in its Article 2, namely credit institutions, parent undertakings, and some investment firms and financial institutions, in all cases where established in a participating Member State.[22] This covers a wide variety of institutions of different sizes. In light of the principle of proportionality and the fact that small institutions are deemed not to have a high risk profile, and are often systematically less risky compared with large institutions, the calculation of their annual contribution has been simplified and consists of a lump sum.[23]

b) The procedure for raising and collecting *ex ante* contributions annually

The process of raising and collecting *ex ante* contributions is the result of a collaboration between the SRB and NRAs.[24]

In a nutshell, this requires the adoption of a decision by the SRB.[25] In practice, the SRB specifies the data to be reported in accordance with Article 6 of the Implementing Regulation and requests institutions to report such data to the relevant NRA, which then provides the information to the SRB.[26] This decision is made up of a general part describing the calculation method, and of an annex containing the relevant figures applicable to each contributing institution. As the annex is individual, and contains business secrets, it is sent only to the relevant concerned institution. The decision is then communicated by the SRB to the relevant NRAs, which further notify the institutions authorized in their Member States of such decision on the calculation of the annual contributions due by those institutions.[27] The NRAs collect and transfer the contributions to the Fund in accordance with the Intergovernmental Agreement.

[22] Art 67(4) of the SRMR.
[23] Recitals 15–19 and arts 10 and 11 of the Delegated Regulation, and recital 9 and art 8(5) of the Implementing Regulation.
[24] This section serves contextualizing purposes: for a detailed explanation of the adoption process, please see Busch and Ferrarini (n 17) point 9.48; and Brescia Morra and Della Negra (n 2) 554–55.
[25] Art 55 of the SRMR and arts 8(1) and 9(1) of the SRB Rules of Procedure (Decision of the Plenary Session of the SRB of 29 April 2015 adopting the Rules of Procedure of the SRB and its executive session (SRB/2015/8)). See Case C-414/18 *Iccrea Banca* [2019] ECLI:EU:C:2019:1036, where the Court clarified the respective roles of the SRB and NRA.
[26] Arts 4 and 14 of the Delegated Regulation and art 4 of the Implementing Regulation.
[27] Art 14(4) of the Delegated Regulation.

III *Ex ante* contributions' interaction with general principles of EU law

Ex ante contributions operate within the general EU legal order and, therefore, are the concrete expression of the relevant rules of the Treaties. This section will assess some chosen interactions between *ex ante* contributions and general principles of EU law.

1 Article 114 TFEU as legal basis for the SRMR, and for the financing of the Fund

a) Article 114 TFEU as a legal basis

The legal basis of the SRMR is Article 114 TFEU.[28] The question of the suitable legal basis for the adoption of the SRMR led to vivid debates during its elaboration process.[29] The topic has recently been brought back for discussion at the Court of Justice.[30]

The question of the legal basis for a Union act must rest on objective factors amenable to judicial review.[31] As far as Article 114 TFEU is concerned, it is also settled case law that it can serve as a legal basis only where it is actually and objectively apparent, for the legal act, that its purpose is to improve the conditions for the establishment and functioning of the internal market, and that it serves as a legal basis for the approximation of laws.[32]

Article 114 TFEU is a lengthy provision but its two first paragraphs are the most relevant for this section. While the first paragraph confers a legislative empowerment to adopt the relevant measures, the second one clarifies that

[28] See Manuel Kellerbauer, Marcus Klamert, and Jonathan Tomkin (eds), *The EU Treaties and the Charter of Fundamental Rights: A Commentary* (OUP 2019) ch 'Article 114 TFEU'.

[29] Alberto de Gregorio Merino, 'Institutional Report' in Gyula Bándi and others (eds), *European Banking Union Congress Proceedings* (XXVII FIDE Congress in Budapest) (Wolters Kluwer 2016) 208 ff.

[30] A similar question was raised concerning the BRRD in *Portigon*, where the Court also considered that art 114 is the right legal basis: Case T-360/21 *Portigon AG v SRB* [2024] ECLI:EU:T:2024:332, paras 36 to 80.

[31] See Case C-300/89 *Commission v Council* (Titanium dioxide) [1991]ECLI:EU:C:1991:244, para 10; Case C-84/94 *United Kingdom v Council* [1996] ECLI:EU:C:1996:431, para 25; Joined Cases C-164/97 and C-165/97 *Parliament v Council* [1999] ECLI:EU:C:1999:99, para 12; Case C-269/97 *Commission v Council* [2000] ECLI:EU:C:2000:183, para 43; Case C-336/00 *Huber* [2002] ECLI:EU:C:2002:509, para 30; Case C-338/01 *Commission v Council* [2004] ECLI:EU:C:2004:253, para 54; Case C-110/03 *Belgium v Commission* [2005] ECR I-0000, para 78; and Case C-347/03 *Regione autonoma Friuli-Venezia Giulia* [2005] ECLI:EU:C:2005:285, para 72.

[32] Case C-270/12 *United Kingdom v European Parliament and Council* (Short selling) [2014] ECLI:EU:C:2014:18, para 100.

this empowerment shall not apply to fiscal provisions. Some credit institutions have argued that *ex ante* contributions would actually be taxes and should, therefore, not have been adopted on the basis of Article 114 TFEU but, rather, on the basis of fiscal legal bases. This argument has never been upheld by the Court. On the contrary, the case law of the Court has already clarified that Article 114 TFEU is the appropriate legal basis, in two key judgments: *Dexia*[33] and *Portigon*.[34] The *Dexia* judgment was appealed by Dexia. This appeal was dismissed in its entirety,[35] and the *Dexia* judgment hence became definitive.

b) Article 114(1) TFEU as the legal basis of the SRMR

First of all, the SRMR clearly serves the purpose of improving the functioning of the internal market by putting in place a uniform and efficient single framework for resolution, and to guarantee the coherent and centralized application of resolution rules.[36] This aims at guaranteeing financial stability, which was one of the key focuses of the proposal.[37] This focus on financial stability has been highlighted by the Court in *Landesbank Baden-Württemberg*.[38] Indeed, divergences between national resolution rules in different Member States, and the lack of a unified decision-making process were identified as factors contributing to financial instability[39] that had to be addressed by providing uniform rules to ensure financial stability and avoid fragmentation of the internal market.[40] Ensuring effective resolution decisions for failing banks is essential for the completion of the internal market in financial services, as is explained very clearly in recital 12 of the SRMR. Finally, it appears from recitals 9 and 19 of the SRMR that, as long as the financing of resolution remained national, the single market would remain fragmented. In light of the above, the SRMR clearly aims at improving the conditions for the functioning of the internal market. This was confirmed by the General Court in paragraphs 39 to 40 of *Dexia* and 44 to 45 of *Portigon*.

[33] Case T-405/21 *Dexia Crédit Local v Single Resolution Board* [2024] ECLI:EU:T:2024:33.
[34] *Portigon AG v SRB* (n 30).
[35] Case C-254/24 P *Dexia SA v Single Resolution Board* [2025] ECLI:EU:2025:585.
[36] Art 1 and recitals 8 and 22 of the SRMR.
[37] Commission, 'Proposal for a Regulation of the European parliament and of the council establishing uniform rules and a uniform procedure for the resolution of credit institutions and certain investment firms in the framework of a Single Resolution Mechanism and a Single Bank Resolution Fund and amending Regulation (EU) No 1093/2010 of the European Parliament and of the Council' COM (2013) 0520 final, s 4.3.1, p 14.
[38] Joined Cases C-584/20 P and C-621/20 P *Commission v Landesbank Baden-Württemberg* [2021] ECLI:EU:C:2021:601, para 42.
[39] Recitals 2 to 4 and 12 of the SRMR.
[40] ibid, recital 10.

This conclusion also applies specifically to the financing mechanism provided for in the SRMR, including the *ex ante* contributions. This centralized financing contributes to ensuring a competitive level playing field, as credit institutions are not dependent on the means available at national level, and also contributes to eliminating fragmentation in the internal market. Indeed, the SRM would not achieve its goal without the support of a centralized financing system.[41] This was also confirmed in paragraphs 42 to 48 of *Dexia* and 52 to 53 of *Portigon*. The establishment of the Fund and its financing through *ex ante* contributions are, therefore, necessary to ensure the good functioning of the SRM, and to allow it to achieve its financial stability and internal-market-related goals.

Second of all, the SRMR also clearly serves the purpose of the approximation of laws. While assessing this question, the Court takes into consideration the fact that the EU legislature benefits from a wide margin of discretion as to the choice of the most appropriate harmonization technique for achieving the desired result, especially in technical areas.[42] The Court has already confirmed that *ex ante* contributions correspond to a technical area where the EU legislature benefits from a wide margin of discretion.[43] The Court further held that the measures to be adopted in the area of resolution require a specific professional and technical expertise, and that the SRB was clearly established to guarantee uniform application of the resolution procedure (paragraphs 49 to 51 of *Dexia*). As a consequence, the case law indicated that the provisions of the SRMR on the calculation of *ex ante* contributions are an essential element of resolution rules and contribute to avoiding diverging national practices that could impact competition on the internal market (paragraph 52 of *Dexia*).

It is, therefore, clear that Article 114 TFEU is the correct legal basis for the adoption of the SRMR, including its provisions on the calculation of *ex ante* contributions.

[41] De Gregorio Merino (n 29) Vol 1, 207.

[42] Case C-66/04 *United Kingdom of Great Britain and Northern Ireland v European Parliament and Council of the European Union* [2005] ECLI:EU:C:2005:743, para 45; *UK v Parliament and Council* (Short selling) (n 32), para 102 ff; Case C-547/14 *Philip Morris Brands SARL and Others v Secretary of State for Health* [2016] ECLI:EU:C:2016:325, para 63; Case C-549/15 *E.ON Biofor Sverige AB v Statens energimyndighet* [2017] ECLI:EU:C:2017:490, para 30.

[43] *Commission v Landesbank Baden-Württemberg* (n 38), para 118; Case C-663/20 P *SRB v Hypo Vorarlberg Bank* [2022] ECLI:EU:C:2022:162, para 77; and Case C-664/20 P *SRB v Portigon and Commission* [2022] ECLI:EU:C:2022:161, para 80.

c) *Ex ante* contributions are not fiscal provisions in the sense of Article 114(2) TFEU

Fiscal provisions are excluded from the scope of Article 114(1) TFEU. This exception, provided for in Article 114(2) TFEU, has been scrutinized by the Court in two key judgments.[44] In this context, the Court held that there is nothing in the Treaties to indicate how the concept of 'fiscal provisions' should be construed and, that being said, held that 'it is, however, necessary to point out that, by reason of their general character, those words cover not only all areas of taxation, without drawing any distinction between the types of duties or taxes concerned, but also all aspects of taxation, whether material rules or procedural rules'.[45] According to the Court, this would cover 'not only the rate of tax but also the basis of assessment and the detailed rules for levying the various duties'.[46] This statement does not provide concrete guidance as to what constitutes 'fiscal provisions' in the sense of Article 114(2) TFEU.

More recently, the Court further elaborated its analysis in the *Airbnb Ireland* judgment.[47] In this judgment, the Court assessed the relationship between Chapter 2 of Title VII of the TFEU. dealing with 'tax provisions', and Chapter 3 of Title VII on the 'approximation of laws', which includes Article 114 TFEU. The Court held that 'everything relating to Chapter 3, namely the approximation of laws, does not relate to what falls within Chapter 2'.[48] It arises from this that Article 114(2) TFEU excludes from the scope of Article 114(1) TFEU measures to be adopted on the basis of Chapter 2 of Title VII. Chapter 2 contains four provisions that can be divided into two groups: on the one hand, Articles 110 to 112 TFEU, which are related to internal taxation, and, on the other, Article 113 TFEU, which concerns harmonization of indirect taxation like turnover taxes, excise duties, and value added tax. It is clear that *ex ante* contributions cannot be characterized as internal taxation or as indirect taxes. Hence, the findings of the Court in *Airbnb Ireland* lead to the conclusion that such contributions do not fall within the scope of the exclusion in Article 114(2) TFEU.

The fact that *ex ante* contributions cannot be categorized as fiscal provisions also arises from the broader case law of the Court on taxation. In *Air Transport Association of America*, the Court used the criterion of applying a basis of

[44] *Commission v Council* (n 31); and Case C-533/03 *Commission v Council* [2006] ECLI:EU:C:2006:64.

[45] *Commission v Council* (n 44), para 63; and *Commission v Council* (n 44), para 47.

[46] *Commission v Council* (n 44), para 65.

[47] Case C-83/21 *Airbnb Ireland* [2022] ECLI:EU:C:2022:1018.

[48] ibid, para 25.

assessment and a rate defined in advance to distinguish taxes from other types of levies.[49]

This criterion has been relied on by the Grand Chamber of the Court of Justice to assess the nature of *ex ante* contributions. In *Landesbank Baden-Württemberg*,[50] the Court indeed held that *ex ante* contributions, by their specific nature, actually respond to an insurance-based logic and not to applying a rate to a basis of assessment. The key excerpt can be found in paragraph 113 of the judgment, which contains a direct reference to the Opinion of Advocate General Richard de la Tour, and more specifically to point 143 of this Opinion, which was incorporated into the judgment. This incorporation of point 143 of the Opinion is a key element, as it excluded expressly the qualification of *ex ante* contributions either as fiscal or parafiscal levies.[51] The Court's reasoning in *Landesbank Baden-Württemberg* was expressly repeated in posterior judgments, more specifically in *Hypo Vorarlberg Bank*[52] and *Portigon*.[53] The Court, therefore, indicated that *ex ante* contributions do not qualify as fiscal provisions in the sense of Article 114(2) TFEU.[54]

This reasoning was confirmed in *Dexia* (paragraphs 61 to 82). On top of the elements mentioned above, it is interesting to note that the General Court relied on *Schräder*[55] to show that the fact that a levy is raised from the members of a given sector and is directly devoted to the sole financing of the expenses of such sector is an indication that it is not of a fiscal nature (paragraphs 64 and 65 of *Dexia*). The Court, in *Dexia*, relied on and further elaborated on the findings of *Landesbank Baden-Württemberg* on the insurance-based logic by showing that credit institutions receive benefits from the Fund. The first

[49] Case C-366/10 *Air Transport Association of America and Others v Secretary of State for Energy and Climate Change* [2011] ECLI:EU:C:2011:864, para 143.

[50] *Commission v Landesbank Baden-Württemberg* (n 38), para 113. This is an implicit reference, as the *Air Transport Association of America* judgment is not quoted but applied in substance.

[51] Advocate General Kokott relied specifically on this finding in para 65 of her opinion in the *ABVL* judgment: Case C-202/21 P *ABLV Bank AS v Single Resolution Board* [2022] ECLI:EU:C:2022:327, Opinion of AG Kokott, para 65.

[52] *SRB v Hypo Vorarlberg Bank* (n 43), para 75.

[53] *SRB v Portigon and Commission* (n 43), para 78.

[54] In addition to this confirmation of the nature of *ex ante* contributions, by the Court, it is interesting to mention other interesting arguments raised by scholars to support the conclusion that *ex ante* contributions are not fiscal provisions. See, in this sense, the arguments of Bauerschmidt, based on the case law on Protocol 7, and on a comparison with the national level and a specific assessment of the situation in Germany, in Jonathan Bauerschmidt, 'Financial Stability as the Objective of the Banking Union' (2020) 17(2) European Company and Financial Law Review 174; and Jonathan Bauerschmidt, 'Der Einheitliche Bankenabwicklungsmechanismus' in Jonathan Bauerschmidt and others (eds), *Konstitutionalisierung in Zeiten globaler Krisen* (Nomos 2015) 360–62.

[55] Case 265/87 *Hermann Schräder HS Kraftfutter GmbH & Co KG v Hauptzollamt Gronau* [1989] ECLI:EU:C:1989:303, para 9.

benefit is the fact that contributing institutions could be subject to resolution measures, including the use of the Fund, provided that they fulfil the applicable conditions. This is a benefit not available to non-contributing institutions (paragraph 73 of *Dexia*). The second benefit is the stability of the financial sector which is guaranteed by the Fund (paragraph 74 of *Dexia*). Contributing institutions clearly benefit from the resolution of other institutions. While financial stability is beneficial to all kinds of actors, it should be highlighted that credit institutions are the first beneficiary of financial stability, which allows them to operate on a stable market and ensure the good development of their businesses.

2 Legal certainty

Legal certainty is a general principle of EU law requiring that rules of EU law be clear and precise so that interested parties can ascertain their position in situations and legal relationships governed by EU law.[56]

It is, nevertheless, clear that absolute certainty does not exist in law, and that this principle must be applied while taking into account the relevant general context. Indeed, the Court has already held that where a degree of uncertainty regarding the meaning and the scope of a rule of law is inherent in that rule, the judicial review should be limited to whether the legal measure at stake displays such ambiguity as to make it difficult to resolve with sufficient certainty any doubts as to the scope or meaning of the measure.[57]

When it comes to the *ex ante* contributions, the Court has already held that legal certainty cannot be interpreted as precluding the EU legislature from having recourse, in a norm that it adopts, to an abstract legal notion, nor as requiring that such an abstract norm refer to the various specific hypotheses in which it applies, given that all those hypotheses could not be determined in advance by the legislature.[58]

[56] See: C–482/17 *Czech Republic v European Parliament and Council of the European Union* [2019] ECLI:EU:C:2019:1035, para 148; Case C–14/18 P *Alfamicro v European Commission* [2019] ECLI:EU:C:2019:159, para 75; Case C–76/06 *Britannia Alloys & Chemicals v Commission* [2007] ECLI:EU:C:2007:326, para 79 (and the cited case law); and Case T–829/16 *Mouvement pour une Europe des nations et des libertés v European Parliament* [2018] ECLI:EU:T:2018:840, para 68 (confirmed on appeal by the Order of 25 September 2019 in Case C–60/19 *Mouvement pour une Europe des nations et des libertés v European Parliament* [2019] ECLI:EU:C:2019:783).

[57] *Belgium v Commission* (n 31), para 31; Joined Cases T–147/09 and T–148/09 *Trelleborg Industrie SAS* [2013] ECLI:EU:T:2013:259, para 96; and Case T–240/04 *French Republic v Commission* [2007] ECR II-04035, para 49.

[58] Case T–383/21 *La Banque Postale* [2023] ECLI:EU:T:2023:845, para 190 and the cited case law. This was repeated in Cases T–384/21, T–385/21, T–387/21, T–388/21, and T–397/21.

It is also settled case law that judicial review must, having regard to the discretionary powers conferred on the EU legislator, be limited to examining whether the measure in question is vitiated by a manifest error or misuse of powers, or whether there has been a manifest excess of the limits of the discretion.[59]

In this regard, a wide discretion is recognized by the Court when the legislature is asked to intervene in an area which entails political, economic, and social choices on its part, and in which it is called upon to undertake complex assessments.[60] When it comes to *ex ante* contributions, their annual individual calculation is based on a very elaborated calculation method, and on underlying evolving economic data that cannot be anticipated years in advance, as they have to reflect the socio-economic and political developments that can have an impact on financial stability, and involve confidential data related to each contributing institution.

Before assessing the case law related to *ex ante* contributions in light of the principle of legal certainty, it is interesting to analyse other similar and comparable systems which were assessed by the Court in light of the principle of legal certainty.

The legal framework applicable to *ex ante* contributions is a clear system that is not based on legal uncertainty but on factual uncertainty related to the need to take into account recent and accurate data in a given year. Such a situation is not specific to *ex ante* contributions but is inherent to complex regulatory environments dealing with an evolving market or sector. Other systems partly based on factual uncertainty have already been challenged on the basis of a legal certainty plea, but were upheld by the Court.

The upheld systems include both a system based on the evolution of the global situation in a given sector and a system based on the situation of other operators. These are two features that can also be found in the calculation method of the *ex ante* contributions, which is based on the evolution of covered deposits and, therefore, on the situation of other operators in the banking sector.

A first example illustrating this trend can be found in the *Arcelor* judgment,[61] where a plea of illegality based on legal certainty was rejected in a

[59] Case C-331/88 *Fedesa* [1990] ECLI:EU:C:1990:391, para 8; Case C-405/92 *Etablissements Armand Mondiet SA* [1993] ECLI:EU:C:1993:906, para 32.

[60] *Commission v Landesbank Baden-Württemberg* (n 38), para 117; and Case C-203/12 *Bilerud Karlsborg and Bilerud Skärblacka* [2013] ECLI:EU:C:2013:664, para 35; Case C-210/03 *Swedish Match* [2004] ECLI:EU:C:2004:802, para 48; Case C-233/94 *Germany v European Parliament and Council* [1997] ECLI:EU:C:1997:231, para 56; Case C-84/34 *United Kingdom v Council* [1996] ECLI:EU:C:1996:431, para 58.

[61] Case T-16/04 *Arcelor v Parliament and Council* [2010] ECLI:EU:T:2010:54.

context comparable to the one of *ex ante* contributions. This judgment is about the allowance trading scheme for greenhouse gas emissions and the question of pricing. The applicant argued that there would be a breach of legal certainty because it would be required to buy allowances at prices that would be unpredictable. It is undoubtedly a complex area where prices are determined by the evolution of market forces. The Court considered that the increase in the cost of emissions and, consequently, in the price of allowances, which depends on a series of economic parameters, cannot be regulated in advance by the EU legislature without reducing, or even completely removing, the economic incentives which constitute the very basis of the allowance trading scheme, and thereby adversely affecting the effectiveness of the allowance trading scheme.[62] The Court considered that the establishment of such system, including its economic premises, came within the broad discretion of the EU legislature.[63] Such a system cannot be considered as contrary to the principle of legal certainty, as clearly stated by the Court in paragraph 203 of this judgment. The Court even held that deciding otherwise would be incompatible with the wide margin of discretion of the EU legislature.[64] This system shares similarities with the *ex ante* system, and the conclusions reached by the Court are aligned with those reached in *ex ante* cases.

A second illustration can be found in the *T & L Sugars Ltd and Sidul Açúcares*[65] judgment, where a plea based on legal certainty was rejected in a context similar to the one of *ex ante* contributions. This judgment concerns the regulation of the sugar market. A system was established at EU level providing that the quantity of sugar that could be imported at a reduced rate, as well as the level of such reduction, had to be set while taking into account the current situation and the predictable evolution of the sugar markets.[66] The applicants alleged that the principle of legal certainty had been breached because the system put in place would make customs duties unpredictable, and because the system would also not be fixed through the application of consistent and objective criteria. The Court confirmed the validity of such system and, more specifically, a methodology taking into account the evolution of the situation on the global sugar market. This led to a rejection of the plea related to legal certainty.[67]

[62] ibid, para 201.
[63] ibid, para 202.
[64] ibid, paras 201, 205, and 206.
[65] Case T–103/12 *T & L Sugars Ltd* [2019] ECLI:EU:T:2016:682, paras 145–52.
[66] A summary of the system can be found in ibid, paras 87, 88, 148, and 149.
[67] ibid, para 151.

These cases have to be put in perspective with the developments on the *ex ante* contributions. The Court held that, in light of the EU legislature's the wide margin of discretion, it had validly opted for a calculation method capable of ensuring dynamic adjustment of the financing of the Fund according to developments in the financial sector.[68]

The Court further established that:

> the persons concerned are in a position to verify whether their ex ante contribution to the SRF was fixed arbitrarily, in disregard of the reality of their economic situation or through the use of data relating to the rest of the financial sector which are not plausible. Those persons concerned can therefore understand the reasons for the decision calculating their ex ante contribution to the SRF.[69]

In addition to that, the Court proclaimed that the persons concerned benefitted from sufficient information to understand how their situation was taken into account, and that a concerned person should be provided with the calculation methodology and sufficient information to understand how its situation was accounted for but not with the elements, which are confidential, as they concern other institutions.[70] While assessing the calculation method, the Court described it as 'precise' and considered that the various steps in the calculation process were 'detailed'.[71] More recently, the Court relied specifically on *Landesbank Baden-Württemberg*, in several judgments, to reject a plea of illegality of the SRMR based on legal certainty and an alleged lack of clarity of the calculation method of the *ex ante* contributions.[72] No appeal was lodged against these judgments, which became definitive.

In conclusion, the Court has never upheld a plea of illegality against the SRMR or the BRRD based on legal certainty. On the contrary, the Court unequivocally held that the EU legislature enjoyed a wide margin of discretion, that the choices made on that basis were valid, and that the rules were sufficiently foreseeable, clear, and precise.

[68] *Commission v Landesbank Baden-Württemberg* (n 38), para 118; *SRB v Hypo Vorarlberg Bank* (n 43), para 77; and *SRB v Portigon and Commission* (n 43), para 80.

[69] *Commission v Landesbank Baden Württemberg* (n 38), para 123.

[70] Case C-633/20 *SRB v Hypo Vorarlberg Bank* [2022] ECLI:EU:C:2022:162, paras 79–80 and *SRB v Portigon and Commission* (n 43), paras 82–83.

[71] *Commission v Landesbank Baden-Württemberg* (n 38), paras 108 and 128.

[72] *La Banque Postale* (n 58), para 189 ff. This was repeated in cases T-384/21, T-385/21, T-387/21, T-388/21, and T-397/21.

The assessment of the recent case law on *ex ante* contributions, put in the perspective of the two judgments on the allowance trading scheme and the sugar market, shows a trend in the case law of the Court in its assessment of legal certainty. Hence, a mechanism or methodology fixing a price or contribution on the basis of underlying data related to a specific (evolving) market or the situation of other operators is clearly in line with the principle of legal certainty.

3 Proportionality

The principle of proportionality requires that acts of the EU institutions be appropriate for attaining the legitimate objectives pursued by the legislation at issue, and that they do not exceed the limits of what is necessary in order to achieve those objectives.[73]

When EU institutions have, in a complex and evolving context, to make technical choices and complex assessments, in areas entailing political and economic choices, they must be allowed a broad discretion.[74] In terms of judicial review, the criterion to be applied is not whether the measure adopted was the only or the best possible measure, but only whether such measure is manifestly inappropriate having regard to the objectives pursued, since its legality can only be affected in such scenario.[75] The Court is not allowed to substitute its assessment of technical facts for that of the legislature.[76]

While assessing the proportionality of the *ex ante* framework, one must keep in mind the impact of the sovereign debt crisis and the role played by credit institutions in that crisis. The system put in place serves the main goals of preventing the occurrence of another crisis, and of ensuring financial stability

[73] TFEU art 5(4) and, inter alia, C-358/14 *Poland v European Parliament and Council* [2016] ECLI:EU:C:2016:323, point 78; and Case C-477/1 *Pillbox 38* [2016] ECLI:EU:C:2016:324, point 48. For a summary regarding the principle of proportionality, see Koen Lenaerts, 'Proportionality as a matrix principle promoting the effectiveness of EU law and the legitimacy of EU action in continuity and change – how the challenges of today prepare the ground for tomorrow' (2022) (ECB Legal Conference 2021), 27–42.

[74] See *Czech Republic v Parliament and Council* (n 56), para 77; C-101/12 *Schaible* [2013] ECLI:EU:C:2013:661, para 47; C-620/18 *Hungary v European Parliament* [2020] ECLI:EU:C:2020:1001, para 112.

[75] See *Czech Republic v Parliament and Council* (n 56), para 77; C-58/08 *Vodafone* [2010] ECLI:EU:C:2010:321, para 52; *Schaible* (n 74), para 48; *Hungary v European Parliament* (n 74), para 112.

[76] Case C-128/17 *Poland v European Parliament and Council* [2019] ECLI:EU:C:2019:194, para 95; and Case C-5/16 *Poland v Parliament and Council* [2018] ECLI:EU:C:2018:483, para 150.

while maintaining free movement of capital. These are very important objectives, and the means used to achieve them are clearly appropriate.

Early on, the Court considered specifically that frameworks regulating economically complex situations trigger limited judicial review. One of the earliest manifestations of this can be traced back to a judgment on the deposit guarantee schemes.[77] The situation of *ex ante* contributions is very similar. The legal framework applicable to *ex ante* contributions is the result of a complex assessment in an area which entails political and economic choices where the legislator benefits from a broad discretion. This has been confirmed expressly by the Court in several instances: in the *Landesbank-Baden Würtenberg* judgment,[78] and, subsequently, in the *Hypo Vorarlberg Bank*[79] and *Portigon*[80] judgments.

Indeed, the EU legislature was very careful to ensure that the designed system would fully embrace the principle of proportionality, especially in light of the far-reaching and novel nature of the Fund. This was at the heart of the process from its inception and is reflected at all stages. The key importance of the principle of proportionality in this framework is reflected in the explanatory memoranda of the SRMR[81] and BRRD.[82]

The calculation method of *ex ante* contributions is designed to take into account the proportionality principle, and is nourished by it. Indeed, several mechanisms were put in place to ensure compliance with this principle. The two most striking illustrations of this are: (i) the calculation of the contribution of a given institution pro rata with the amount of its liabilities, combined with an adjustment of such contribution to the risk it effectively presents; and (ii) the establishment of a lump-sum contribution for small institutions.

The proportionality principle resonates through the whole act. Recital 45 of the SRMR sets the general tone and is supplemented by recital 114 dealing specifically with proportionality in the context of the calculation method of *ex*

[77] *Germany v Parliament and Council* (n 60), paras 55–56.

[78] *Commission v Landesbank Baden-Württemberg* (n 38), paras 117–18.

[79] *SRB v Hypo Vorarlberg Bank* (n 43), para 77.

[80] *SRB v Portigon and Commission* (n 43), para 80.

[81] Proposal for a Regulation of the European Parliament and of the Council establishing uniform rules and a uniform procedure for the resolution of credit institutions and certain investment firms in the framework of a Single Resolution Mechanism and a Single Bank Resolution Fund and amending Regulation (EU) No 1093/2010 of the European Parliament and of the Council, (COM/2013/0520 final - 2013/0253 (COD)), Explanatory Memorandum, section ibid, s 3.3.

[82] Commission, 'Proposal for a Directive of the European Parliament and of the Council establishing a framework for the recovery and resolution of credit institutions and investment firms and amending Council Directives 77/91/EEC and 82/891/EC, Directives 2001/24/EC, 2002/47/EC, 2004/25/EC, 2005/56/EC, 2007/36/EC and 2011/35/EC and Regulation (EU) No 1093/2010 COM (2012) 280 final, s 4.3, and SWD (2012) 166 final, s 5.2.

ante contributions. The key importance of the principle of proportionality in the calculation of *ex ante* contributions is even expressly emphasized in Article 70(2)(a), which sets out the principle that the flat contribution is pro rata based on an institution's liabilities, and in Article 70(2)(b), which defines the risk-adjusted contribution, inter alia, by reference to the principle of proportionality. This way of calculating the contribution of each institution on the basis of its actual financial model, situation, and the risk it effectively presents is a straight manifestation of the principle of proportionality.

In addition, the system applicable to small institutions takes into account the different profiles of small institutions, with different corresponding lump sums as set out in Article 10 of the Delegated Regulation. The rationale behind this way of proceeding is elaborated in recital 18 of the Delegated Regulation, which justifies it through the need to avoid disproportionate differences. The principle of proportionality is so central in the design of the system that the Delegated Regulation provides for an adjustment mechanism in Article 10(8). According to this provision, when a small institution has a risk profile disproportionate to its small size, a reasoned decision may be taken by the SRB not to apply the lump-sum contribution to it, but to calculate its contribution according to the general methodology.

The General Court recently had to assess a plea of illegality of the SRMR based on an alleged breach of the principle of proportionality. In this context, it fully dismissed the plea.[83]

In light of the above, it is evident that the principle of proportionality is at the heart of the *ex ante* framework, which fully complies with it.

IV Conclusion

The financing of the SRM was designed to reply to the shortcomings identified in the aftermath of the sovereign debt crisis. The SRM provides far-reaching tools to prevent the occurrence of similar crises in the future. The complexity of the financial sector and the interconnection between its actors, as well as the need to comply with essential principles of EU law, led to the drawing-up of a complex and innovative piece of legal architecture. This architecture, while complex, is nevertheless fully comprehensive and functional. The system put in place is quite unique, and is the manifestation of very ambitious and

[83] *La Banque Postale* (n 58), para 148 ff. This was repeated in Cases T-384/21, T-385/21, T-387/21, T-388/21, and T-397/21.

protective choices made at EU level to protect financial stability, free movement of capital, and taxpayers. This complexity may sometimes dampen the enthusiasm to take interest in this fundamental area. This contribution synthetized the key elements forming the financing system of *ex ante* contributions, in order to make it tangible to a wider public.

Every policy area and the corresponding acts of EU institutions can only be elaborated within the limits set out by the Treaties. The framework applicable to the financing of the SRM is no exception and provides for a very interesting case study to assess the question of this interplay. This contribution focused on the question of the legal basis and compliance with general principles of legal certainty and proportionality. It shows the constant deep attention to ensure compliance with these principles that drove the design and elaboration process of the framework. The analysis of the case law confirmed this way of proceeding. The existence of extensive litigation in this area makes it very interesting, and new developments will need to be followed closely.

12

European System of Financial Supervision and AMLA

Matthias Deissenberger[*]

I Introduction

The three European Supervisory Authorities (ESAs)—the European Banking Authority (EBA), the European Insurance and Occupational Pensions Authority (EIOPA), and the European Securities and Markets Authority (ESMA)—were created in 2011, in response to the global financial crisis. This chapter summarizes, from a historical perspective, the reasons leading to the creation of the ESAs after the financial crisis, detailing their organization and institutional mandate. It takes stock of the evolution of the ESAs a decade after their inception, taking into account relevant case law and the institutional changes introduced by the 2019 ESAs review. It contrasts the current institutional framework of the ESAs, a tried-and-tested example of agencification at Union level, with the framework of the Anti-Money Laundering Authority (Authority for Anti-Money Laundering and Countering the Financing of Terrorism, or 'AMLA'), created in 2024. In this context, the limitations of the ESAs' powers and governance structure, leading, amongst other things, to the genesis of the AMLA—with the aim to remedy weaknesses in the AML framework that lead to the emergence of new obstacles to the proper functioning of the internal market, both due to internal risks and external threats—is assessed. Furthermore, remaining challenges are highlighted that might merit further legislative developments; against the background of expanding supervisory mandates, a particular focus will be on the agencies' role as supervisors.

* The views expressed in this chapter are purely personal and do not necessarily represent those of ESMA or of any of its staff members. All errors or omissions are those of the author. This chapter was completed on 1 December 2024; all websites were live as at that date.

Matthias Deissenberger, *European System of Financial Supervision and AMLA* In: *EU Banking Union*. Edited by: Jonathan Bauerschmidt, Raffaele D'Ambrosio, Diane Fromage, Daniela Jaros, and Paul Weismann, Oxford University Press. © Oxford University Press 2026. DOI: 10.1093/9780198949756.003.0013

II Creation of the ESAs

The Great Financial Crisis of 2008 highlighted how interconnected the financial markets are, and how quickly contagion spreads among financial markets participants. The relevant legislative and regulatory frameworks, as well as the supervisory powers, were not adequate, resulting in major vulnerabilities for the Union's (incomplete) single financial market and the real economy:

> The financial crisis in 2008 exposed important shortcomings in financial supervision, both in particular cases and in relation to the financial system as a whole. Nationally based supervisory models have lagged behind financial globalisation and the integrated and interconnected reality of European financial markets, in which many financial institutions operate across borders. The crisis exposed shortcomings in the areas of cooperation, coordination, consistent application of Union law and trust between national supervisors.[1]

In 2010, as an institutional response, the European System of Financial Supervision (ESFS)—an integrated network of European Union (EU) financial supervisors (see Figure 12.1)—was established to address the vulnerabilities, and to achieve effective macro- and microprudential regulation, as well as supranational supervision of financial activities:[2]

> The Union has reached the limits of what can be done with the present status of the Committees of European Supervisors. The Union cannot remain in a situation where there is no mechanism to ensure that national supervisors arrive at the best possible supervisory decisions for cross-border financial market participants; where there is insufficient cooperation and information exchange between national supervisors; where joint action by national

[1] Recital 1 of the ESAs' Regulations: Regulation (EU) 1093/2010 of the European Parliament and of the Council of 24 November 2010 establishing a European Supervisory Authority (European Banking Authority), amending Decision No 716/2009/EC and repealing Commission Decision 2009/78/EC [2010] OJ L331, p 12; Regulation (EU) 1094/2010 of the European Parliament and of the Council of 24 November 2010 establishing a European Supervisory Authority (European Insurance and Occupational Pensions Authority), amending Decision No 716/2009/EC and repealing Commission Decision 2009/79/EC [2010] OJ L331, p 48; Regulation (EU) 1095/2010 of the European Parliament and of the Council of 24 November 2010 establishing a European Supervisory Authority (European Securities and Markets Authority), amending Decision No 716/2009/EC and repealing Commission Decision 2009/77/EC [2010] OJ L331, p 84.

[2] See also Asen Lefterov, 'How Feasible Is the Proposal for Establishing a New European System of Financial Supervisors?' (2011) 38(1) Legal Issues of Economic Integration 33–64; Emiliano Grossman and Patrick Leblond, 'European Financial Integration: Finally the Great Leap Forward?' (2011) 49(2) Journal of Common Market Studies 413.

> authorities requires complicated arrangements to take account of the patchwork of regulatory and supervisory requirements; where national solutions are most often the only feasible option in responding to problems at the level of the Union; and where different interpretations of the same legal text exist. The European System of Financial Supervision (hereinafter the ESFS') should be designed to overcome those deficiencies and provide a system that is in line with the objective of a stable and single Union financial market for financial services, linking national supervisors within a strong Union network.[3]

Article 2(2) of the European Supervisory Authorities Regulations (ESAs' Regulations)[4] stipulates that the ESFS is composed of the European Systemic Risk Board (ESRB),[5] in charge of macrofinancial supervision; the three European Supervisory Authorities (ESAs) (the European Banking Authority (EBA), the European Securities and Markets Authority (ESMA), and the European Insurance and Occupational Pensions Authority (EIOPA)), in charge of the microprudential supervision of banks, markets, and insurance, respectively; the ESAs Joint Committee (headed by the chairpersons of the ESAs); and the National Competent Authorities (NCAs).

The ESAs are EU agencies[6] and work with NCAs to contribute to the elaboration of a Single Rulebook for the financial sector, and to promote supervisory convergence throughout the Union. The treaty basis for the establishment of the ESAs is Article 114 of the Treaty of the Functioning of the European Union (TFEU).[7]

[3] Recital 8 of the ESAs Regulations, Regulation (EU) 1093/2010 of the European Parliament and of the Council of 24 November 2010 establishing a European Supervisory Authority (European Banking Authority), amending Decision No 716/2009/EC and repealing Commission Decision 2009/78/EC [2010] OJ L331; Regulation (EU) 1094/2010 of the European Parliament and of the Council of 24 November 2010 establishing a European Supervisory Authority (European Insurance and Occupational Pensions Authority), amending Decision No 716/2009/EC and repealing Commission Decision 2009/79/EC [2010] OJ L331, 15.12.2010; Regulation (EU) 1095/2010 of the European Parliament and of the Council of 24 November 2010 establishing a European Supervisory Authority (European Securities and Markets Authority), amending Decision No 716/2009/EC and repealing Commission Decision 2009/77/EC [2010] OJ L331.

[4] See ESA Regulations: Regulation (EU) 1093/2010, p 12; Regulation (EU) 1094/2010, p 48; Regulation (EU) 1095/2010, p 84.

[5] ESRB's founding Regulations: Regulation (EU) 1092/2010 of the European Parliament and of the Council of 24 November 2010 on European Union macro-prudential oversight of the financial system and establishing a European Systemic Risk Board [2010] OJ L331, p 1; Council Regulation (EU) 1096/2010 of 17 November 2010 conferring specific tasks upon the European Central Bank concerning the functioning of the European Systemic Risk Board [2010] OJ L331, p 162.

[6] For further information on EU agencies, see Stefan Griller and Andreas Orator, 'Everything under Control? The "Way Forward" for European Agencies in the Footsteps of the Meroni Doctrine' (2010) 25 European Law Review 3, 7–9; and on the ESAs specifically, Niamh Moloney, *The Age of ESMA: Governing EU Financial Markets* (Hart 2018).

[7] See C–270/12 *United Kingdom v Council and Parliament*, ECLI:EU:C:2014:18.

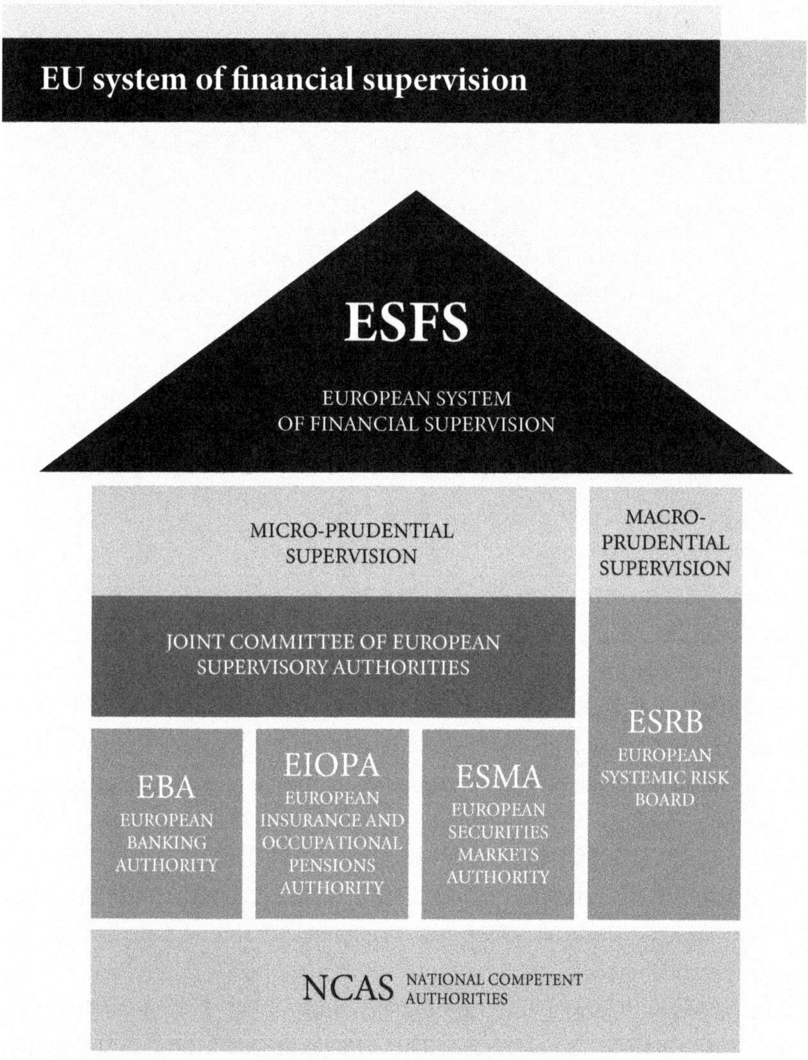

Figure 12.1 Overview of the ESFS

Reproduced with permission from Council of the European Union (2019). EU system of financial supervision, https://www.consilium.europa.eu/en/infographics/financial-supervision-architecture/.

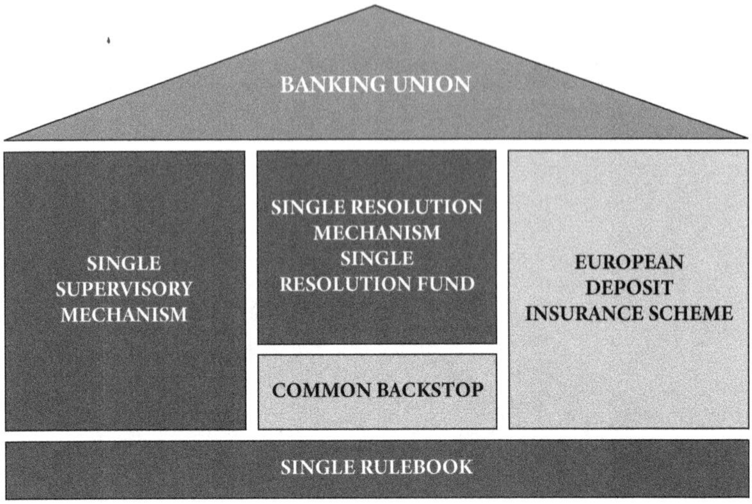

Figure 12.2 Overview of the Banking Union Pillars
Source: European Commission, https://ec.europa.eu/newsroom/fisma/items/703494.

Soon after its establishment, deficits of the ESFS became apparent, leading to the creation of the European Banking Union (EBU) in 2012.[8] The EBU is composed of three pillars (see Figure 12.2): the Single Supervisory Mechanism (SSM), as part of the European Central Bank (ECB) in charge of the prudential supervision of credit institutions; the Single Resolution Mechanism (SRM), a common mechanism for the resolution of credit institutions, headed by the Single Resolution Board (SRB), an EU agency like the ESAs, albeit with a different governance structure and different sources of financing; and the European Deposit Insurance Scheme (EDIS), which has still to be established.[9]

The creation of the ESFS and the EBU has, thus, brought important changes to the institutional system of the EU. These have included the creation of new agencies, as well as structural reform of the ECB.

III Structural features of the ESAs

The three ESAs' Regulations are almost identical.

[8] European Commission, 'Communication on Completing the Banking Union' COM (2017) 592 final.

[9] For general information on the EBU, see Giuseppe Boccuzzi, *The European Banking Union: Supervision and Resolution* (Palgrave Macmillan 2016).

When creating the ESAs, the legislative discussion revolved mainly around the European Banking Authority,

> the text of its regulation being considered applicable ne varietur to the two other authorities. This assimilation was considered essential both in the preparatory stages by Commission and Council and by the integrated national regulators. Although the level of development and the way of functioning of the pre-existing three committees was relatively different, this legislative technique has resulted in focusing on the issues of the banking regulators, traditionally more cautious in accepting more dynamic integrative techniques. As it was already accepted that ESMA would have direct supervisory powers – on the credit agencies – this aspect and its specific needs, e.g. on enforcement and sanctioning were not reflected in the final text.[10]

Consequently, the governance structures of the ESAs, as well as their tasks and powers, are to a large extent alike; still, differences developed in practice. Banking, capital markets, and the insurance sector are interconnected but intrinsically different. Furthermore, the EU legal framework applicable to these sectors varies considerably; capital markets legislation is split over a large number of regulations and directives, while EBU legislation is vastly consolidated in a few legislative acts.

Moreover, subsequent legislation introduced after the founding of the ESAs broadened ESMA's responsibilities and attributed to it the unique role of direct supervisor. Only recently have the other ESAs gained some limited supervisory roles as well.[11]

The ESAs are 'decision-making' agencies; they have the power to take individual decisions that are legally binding on third parties.[12] However, the ESAs cannot develop their own policy choices through rule-making. This is in stark contrast to regulatory authorities in other countries, such as, for example, the

[10] Eddy O Wymeersch, 'Europe's New Financial Regulatory Bodies' (11 April 2011), p 450. Available at SSRN: https://ssrn.com/abstract=1813811 or http://dx.doi.org/10.2139/ssrn.1813811.

[11] See DORA Regulation, Regulation (EU) 2022/2554 of the European Parliament and of the Council of 14 December 2022 on digital operational resilience for the financial sector and amending Regulations (EC) No 1060/2009, (EU) No 648/2012, (EU) No 600/2014, (EU) No 909/2014 and (EU) 2016/1011 (Text with EEA relevance) [2022] OJ L333, pp 1–79; see MiCA Regulation, (EU) 2023/1114 of the European Parliament and of the Council of 31 May 2023 on markets in crypto-assets, and amending Regulations (EU) No 1093/2010 and (EU) No 1095/2010 and Directives 2013/36/EU and (EU) 2019/1937 (Text with EEA relevance) [2023] OJ L150, pp 40–205.

[12] Paul Craig, 'Agencies' in *EU Administrative Law (Collected Courses of the Academy of European Law)* (1st edn, OUP 2006; online edn, Oxford Academic, 22 March 2012),https://doi.org/10.1093/acprof:oso/9780199296811.003.0005, 151–98.

British Financial Conduct Authority (FCA).[13] Decisions of the ESAs can be reviewed. The vast majority can be contested before the Joint Board of Appeal (JBoA) of the ESAs. The few decisions that do not fall under the competence of this internal review mechanism can be appealed directly before the Court of Justice of the European Union (CJEU) pursuant to Article 263 TFEU.[14]

The JBoA is a joint body of the ESAs, operating fully impartially and independently. It is composed of six members and six alternates, who shall be individuals of high repute with a proven record of relevant knowledge of Union law, and of having international professional experience, to a sufficiently high level in the fields of banking, insurance, occupational pensions, securities markets, or other financial services, to provide expert legal advice on the legality, including proportionality, of the respective ESA's exercise of its powers.[15] The JBoA is competent to review the decisions made by the ESAs; decisions of the ESAs on breach of Union law; to address an emergency situation; mediation between NCAs; and any other decision which is taken by the ESAs in accordance with the sectoral legislation within their remit, and which is either addressed directly to the appellant or, if addressed to another person, is of direct and individual concern to the appellant.[16]

The decisions of the JBoA can be contested before the CJEU under Article 263 of the TFEU.[17] It should be noted that, recently, a significant amendment to the Statute of the CJEU, intended to maintain the efficacy of appeal proceedings against decisions of the General Court, in view of the high number of appeals lodged with the Court of Justice, limited the appeals allowed to proceed. The mechanism for the determination by the Court of Justice of whether an appeal is allowed to proceed concerns appeals in cases which have already

[13] See, eg s 137A ff, Financial Services and Markets Act 2000, available at https://www.legislation.gov.uk/ukpga/2000/8/contents.

[14] Jörn Axel Kämmerer, 'Das neue Europäische Finanzaufsichtssystem (ESFS)' (2011) Neue Zeitschrift für Verwaltungsrecht 1281; Niamh Moloney, 'EU Financial Market Regulation after the Global Financial Crisis' (2010) 47 Common Market Law Review 1317; Eilís Ferran and Kern Alexander, 'Can Soft Law Bodies Be Effective? The Special Case of the European Systemic Risk Board' (2010) 35 European Law Review 751; Paul Weissmann, 'The European Financial Market Supervisory Authorities and their Power to Issue Binding Decisions' (2012) 27 Journal of International Banking Law and Regulation 495; Jonathan Bauerschmidt, 'Financial Stability as the Objective of the Banking Union' (2020) European Company and Financial Law Review 155.

[15] See ESAs Regulations: Regulation (EU) 1093/2010, Regulation (EU) 1094/2010, Regulation (EU) 1095/2010, arts 58(2) and 59(1).

[16] For further details, see Merijn Chamon and Diane Fromage, 'Between Added Value and Untapped Potential: The Boards of Appeal in the Field of EU Financial Regulation' in Merijn Chamon, Annalisa Volpato, and Mariolina Eliantonio (eds), *Boards of Appeal of EU Agencies* (OUP 2022); David Ramos-Muñoz and Marco Lamandini, 'Law and Practice of Financial Appeal Bodies (ESAs' Board of Appeal, SRB Appeal Panel): A View from the Inside' (2020) 57(1) Common Market Law Review 119.

[17] See ESAs Regulations: Regulation (EU) 1093/2010, Regulation (EU) 1094/2010, Regulation (EU) 1095/2010, arts 58–61.

been considered twice—initially by an independent board of appeal of a body, office, or agency of the Union, and then by the General Court. This 'filter' allows the Court of Justice to focus on the appeals that raise important legal questions. The JBoA has been added to the list of boards of appeal in Article 58a of the Statute of the Court.[18] The limitation of appeals allowed further increases the significance of the JBoA. The Board of Appeal adopts its own rules of procedure, pursuant to Article 60(6) of the ESAs' Regulations.

Reviewability of the ESAs' decisions was a key element in the CJEU's decision to uphold the legality of the delegation of product intervention powers to ESMA under Regulation (EU) No 236/2012 (Short Selling Regulation).[19] The ability to challenge ESAs' acts is, however, limited: in two judgments related to the EBA, the CJEU has confirmed that Article 263 TFEU excludes the CJEU's review of a recommendation or guidelines in the context of an action for annulment; it follows, however, from Article 19(3)(b) TEU and the first paragraph of Article 267(b) TFEU, that the Court has jurisdiction to give preliminary rulings on the interpretation and validity of acts of the institutions of the Union, without any exception.[20] Thus, ESAs' soft law instruments can only be indirectly challenged via a request for a preliminary ruling, making the national courts the first guarantors of EU law.[21] These rulings are also of relevance for other agencies, such as AMLA, as they apply equally to their soft law instruments.

Even though the ESAs have existed for more than a decade, fewer than 20 decisions have been referred to the JBoA. This is mainly due to the limited number of contestable decisions, as soft law instruments and draft technical standards—as they are mere preparatory acts—cannot be challenged before the JBoA.[22] Therefore, the JBoA only convenes when required by an appeals

[18] Regulation (EU, Euratom) 2024/2019 of the European Parliament and of the Council of 11 April 2024 amending Protocol No 3 on the Statute of the Court of Justice of the European Union [2024] OJ L2024/2019.

[19] Sophie Vuarlot-Dignac and Eugenia Siracusa, 'The European System of Financial Supervision and in Particular the European Securities and Markets Authority' in Federico Fabbrini and Marco Ventoruzzo (eds), *Research Handbook on EU Economic Law* (Edward Elgar 2019) 406.

[20] *Fédération bancaire française (FBF) v Autorité de contrôle prudentiel et de résolution (ACPR)*. Request for a preliminary ruling from the Conseil d'État C–911/19, ECLI:EU:C:2021:599; C–501/18 *Balgarska Narodna Banka*, ECLI:EU:C:2021:249.

[21] For a more detailed analysis, see Merijn Chamon and Nathan de Arriba-Sellier, 'FBF: On the Justiciability of Soft Law and Broadening the Discretion of EU Agencies: ECJ (Grand Chamber) 15 July 2021, Case C-911/19, Fédération Bancaire Française (FBF) v Autorité de Contrôle Prudentiel et de Résolution, ECLI:EU:C:2021:599' (2020) 18(2) European Constitutional Law Review 286–314; Marloes van Rijsbergen, 'On the Enforceability of EU Agencies' Soft Law at the National Level: The Case of the European Securities and Markets Authority' (2014) 10(5) Utrecht Law Review 116.

[22] JBoA Decision 2019 05, Creditreform Rating AG/EBA, para 60: 'In the instant case, however, the appealed act is not a decision under Article 60 of the ESAs Regulation because it is merely a preparatory act without immediate legal effects vis-à-vis the appellant; it is a proposal for a draft implementing

procedure or other circumstances. In this context, it is important to highlight that the ESAs, as well as the JBoA, are expert bodies. Hence, the JBoA is equipped to assess the highly technical decisions taken by the ESAs and has to conduct an in-depth assessment. In this context, the CJEU ruled, in a case concerning the EU Agency for the Cooperation of Energy Regulators (ACER), that:

> The Court considers that the case-law according to which complex technical, scientific and economic assessments are subject to limited review by the EU judicature does not apply to the review carried out by the appellate bodies of the agencies of the European Union. . . . The intensity of the review carried out by the Board of Appeal is thus greater than that of the review carried out by the EU judicature. In so doing, the Court confirmed, in essence, that it would be contrary to the very nature of appellate bodies within agencies for those bodies to conduct the limited review reserved to the Courts of the European Union.[23]

The ESAs are 'quasi-regulatory' agencies;[24] they contribute to the EU's rule-making process mainly by developing draft delegated and implementing acts (ie technical standards), which are then formally adopted by the Commission.[25] Recital 23 of the ESAs Regulations clarifies that technical standards adopted by the ESAs should be subject to amendments only in very restricted and extraordinary circumstances, since the Authority is the actor in close contact with, and knowing best, the daily functioning of financial markets. Amendments should only be considered if the standards were incompatible with Union law, did not respect the principle of proportionality, or ran counter to the fundamental principles of the internal market for financial services as reflected in the acquis of Union financial services legislation.[26] This goes hand in hand

regulation, which will be adopted through endorsement via a final decision of the European Commission according to Article 15 of the ESAs Regulations.'

[23] Case T-735/18 *Aquind v ACER*, ECLI:EU:T:2020:542, para 61.
[24] Craig (n 12) 151–98.
[25] See also Niamh Moloney, 'The European Securities and Markets Authority and Institutional Design for the EU Financial Market – A Tale of Two Competences: Part (1) Rule-Making' (2011) 12(1) European Business Organization Law Review 41; Niamh Moloney, 'The European Securities and Markets Authority and Institutional Design for the EU Financial Market – A Tale of Two Competences: Part (2) Rules in Action' (2011) 12(2) European Business Organization Law Review 177.
[26] See ESAs Regulations: Regulation (EU) 1093/2010, Regulation (EU) 1094/2010, and Regulation (EU) 1095/2010.

with the limitation on the ESAs to only issue (further) soft law instruments in areas not already covered by technical standards.[27]

It is key to remember that, despite the establishment of EU agencies, the NCAs remain important actors; together with the ESAs, they form the micro pillar of the ESFS. They still conduct the majority of day-to-day (EU) supervision and cooperate closely with the ESAs and participate in the creation of the Single Rulebook under the ESAs framework. Furthermore, they play an important role in the governance of the ESAs, as outlined further below.

Lastly, the Joint Committee institutionalizes the cooperation among ESAs on matters of a transversal nature or relevance. Recent legal acts such as DORA[28] show that enhanced cooperation between the ESAs is, more and more, seen by the legislator as a cornerstone to tackle complex transversal challenges such as ICT regulation.

IV ESAs' governance

The governance structure of each ESA comprises a Board of Supervisors, a Management Board, a chairperson, an executive director, and the already described JBoA.[29] Furthermore, in order to facilitate consultation with stakeholders, each ESA is supported by a stakeholder group.

The Board of Supervisors is the principal decision-making organ of the ESAs. The main role of each respective Board of Supervisors is to make all policy decisions of the ESA. It takes policy decisions, such as adopting draft technical standards, guidelines, opinions, and the issues advice to the EU institutions, as well as enforcement decisions. The Board of Supervisors also has the power to approve the budget. It consists of the chairperson, the heads of the NCAs in the EU and the European Economic Area (EEA), and non-voting representatives from the European Commission, the ESRB and the other two ESAs; at the EBA, an ECB representative also participates. The Board is supported by several standing committees and working groups dealing with technical issues. The voting members are the heads of the EU NCAs, and the

27 See ibid, recital 26: 'In areas not covered by regulatory or implementing technical standards, the Authority should have the power to issue guidelines and recommendations on the application of Union law. In order to ensure transparency and to strengthen compliance by national supervisory authorities with those guidelines and recommendations, it should be possible for the Authority to publish the reasons for supervisory authorities' non-compliance with those guidelines and recommendations.'

28 See DORA Regulation (n 11); MiCA Regulation (n 11).

29 See ESAs Regulations: Regulation (EU) 1093/2010, Regulation (EU) 1094/2010, and Regulation (EU) 1095/2010, art 6.

chairperson can vote regarding certain matters; before the 2019 ESAs review, the chairperson had no voting powers at all. At the EBA, for the adoption of all regulatory products, a double qualified majority of euro-area participating and non-participating Member States is required. Given the ever-decreasing number of non-euro countries, this gives them an outsized influence in the voting procedure. The Board of Supervisors must meet at least twice a year. In practice, the Board of Supervisors meets at least every second month. Decisions can also be taken by written procedure, without convening a physical meeting. The members of the Board of Supervisors must act independently and objectively in the sole interest of the Union. It has been debated whether this can be achieved in practice, given the current governance structure.[30]

The main role of the Management Board is the operational management of its respective ESA, ensuring that the ESA carries out its mission and performs the tasks assigned to it in accordance with the respective ESAs Regulation. Key tasks are the development and implementation of a multi-annual work programme, as well as budget and staff resource matters. Composition-wise, the Board is composed of the chairperson and six members selected from the Board of Supervisors by its members. The executive director and a representative from the Commission attend as non-voting participants, except on budget matters, where the Commission has a vote.

The chairperson is responsible for representing the Authority, including at international organizations—preparing the work of the Board of Supervisors and chairing the meetings of both the Board of Supervisors and the Management Board, including setting the agenda. The chairperson has a right to vote in the Management Board, and—as already mentioned above—partially in the Board of Supervisors. The role of the independent chairperson, as well as their selection and removal procedures, ensure the ESAs' accountability. The ESAs are vertically politically accountable to the Council and Parliament.[31] Despite the chairperson of the respective ESA acting in full independence, they can be summoned by the European Parliament. Additionally, the chairperson shall, when requested, report in writing on the activities of the ESA, and shall also do so at least 15 days before making their annual statement before the European Parliament. The chairperson can only be removed by the European Parliament following a decision of the Council, adopted after consulting the Board of Supervisors.[32]

[30] Elizabeth Howell, 'EU Agencification and the Rise of ESMA: Are Its Governance Arrangements Fit for Purpose?' (2019) 78(2) Cambridge Law Journal 324–54.

[31] See ESAs Regulations: Regulation (EU) 1093/2010, Regulation (EU) 1094/2010, and Regulation (EU) 1095/2010, art 3.

[32] ibid, art 48.

Extrajudicial accountability encompasses quasi-judicial forums such as the European Ombudsman, who has issued decisions on several complaints against the ESAs.[33] Under the ESAs' Regulations, the ESAs are subject to considerable obligations, including reporting requirements; these include the transmission of their work programmes[34] and an annual report on their activities.[35]

The independent executive director is responsible for the daily management of the ESA, preparing the work of the Management Board and implementing the work programme. According to the ESAs' Regulations, the executive director may attend the meetings of the Board of Supervisors without the right to vote. In practice, the ESAs' executive directors play a larger role within the Authorities' institutional frameworks. They tend to always attend board meetings. At ESMA—historically, the only ESA with supervisory mandates—the executive director acts as direct overseer of ESMA's direct supervision activities. The executive director decides the cases to be referred to enforcement, and in these circumstances, appoints an independent investigating officer according to the applicable sectoral legislation.[36]

V Review of the founding Regulations of the ESAs and establishment of the AMLA

The founding Regulations of the ESAs provide for a review procedure on a three-year basis. The legislation circumscribes the fields the review shall cover in detail.[37] Amongst others, it is meant to cover the overall architecture of the ESFS, as well as the adequacy of the ESAs' resources, and goes well beyond a simple assessment of the effectiveness and convergence in supervisory practices reached by competent authorities.

The first review took place in 2014,[38] as provided for in the founding Regulations. Being so close to the ESAs' inception, it was of a very general

[33] See, eg Case 2168/2019/KR, 'How the European Banking Authority (EBA) handled the move of its former executive director to become CEO of a financial industry lobby group'. Available at https://www.ombudsman.europa.eu/en/case/en/56050.

[34] See ESAs Regulations: Regulation (EU) 1093/2010, Regulation (EU) 1094/2010, and Regulation (EU) 1095/2010, art 43(4).

[35] See ibid, art 3.

[36] Vuarlot-Dignac and Siracusa (n 19) 406.

[37] See ESAs Regulations: Regulation (EU) 1093/2010, Regulation (EU) 1094/2010, and Regulation (EU) 1095/2010, art 81.

[38] Report from the Commission to the European Parliament and the Council on the operation of the ESAs and the EFSF, COM 2014/509.

nature and did not lead to amendments of the ESAs' Regulations. The report already proposed potential main areas for possible improvement in the medium term. Amongst them are governance-related ones, such as strengthening the position of the chairperson, but also to amend the composition and mandate of the Management Board in order to confer more permanent and executive functions on it, as well as 'improvements to the funding arrangements of the ESAs, including the use of alternative sources of funding, ideally abolishing EU and national contributions'. The report also mentions a conversion of the ESAs' product intervention power in Article 9(5) of the ESAs' Regulations into a self-standing empowerment.[39] It is noteworthy that the main areas of improvement highlighted above—and identified in the report—have not, to date, undergone substantial reform since the inception of the ESAs.

A comprehensive study conducted for the European Parliament's ECON Committee at roughly the same time, on the evolution of the ESFS, reached very similar, albeit not fully identical, conclusions, and furthermore already recognized the different evolutions of the ESAs:[40]

> Less than three years is a short observation period. However, although almost identical Regulations established the ESAs, their scope has evolved very differently. The EBA has had to deal with a severe banking crisis, and its founding legislation has already been modified to take account of the planned Single Supervisory Mechanism (SSM) . . . The scope of the ESMA has been significantly expanded to new areas, including direct EU-wide supervision of credit rating agencies (CRAs); this direct supervisory power is unique among the ESAs.

The second review took place in 2017; it echoed several of the proposals made in the previous report, and was launched within a broader Capital Markets Union scheme.[41] The legislative proposal[42] included, amongst other things,

[39] For a more comprehensive overview, see Kostas Botopoulos, 'The European Supervisory Authorities: Role-models or in Need of Re-modelling?' (2020) 21 ERA Forum 177–98, https://doi.org/10.1007/s12027-020-00609-7.

[40] Mazars, 'Review of the New ESFS: Study for the European Parliament's ECON Committee' (October 2013 (IP/A/ECON/ST/2012-23)), s 2.1.3.

[41] Communication from the Commission to the European Parliament, the Council, the European Central Bank, the European Economic and Social Committee and the Committee of the Regions Reinforcing integrated supervision to strengthen Capital Markets Union and financial integration in a changing environment, COM/2017/0542 final.

[42] Proposal for a Regulation of the European Parliament and of the Council Amending Regulation (EU) No 1093/2010 establishing a European Supervisory Authority (European Banking Authority); Regulation (EU) No 1094/2010 establishing a European Supervisory Authority (European Insurance

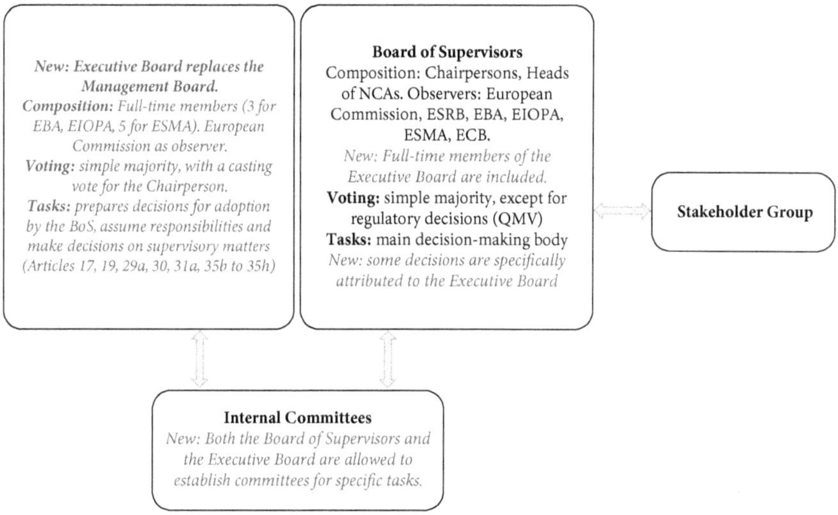

Figure 12.3 The figure depicts changes proposed to the governance of the ESAs by the European Commission during the second ESAs review in 2017
Source: European Commission (2017), https://eur-lex.europa.eu/legal-content/EN/TXT/PDF/?uri=CELEX:52017DC0542.

a new governance structure with a full-time Executive Board; a new funding structure, independent from national supervisors and consisting of contributions by industry and market participants; and more direct supervisory powers for ESMA. Furthermore, new objectives, covering technological innovation and risks, were introduced.

Proposed governance changes are set out in Figure 12.3 below:[43]

Proposed change of the ESAs' funding is set out in Figure 12.4 below:[44]

The communication[45] accompanying the legislative proposal recognizes the inherent differences between the different financial sectors.

and Occupational Pensions Authority); Regulation (EU) No 1095/2010 establishing a European Supervisory Authority (European Securities and Markets Authority); Regulation (EU) No 345/2013 on European venture capital funds; Regulation (EU) No 346/2013 on European social entrepreneurship funds; Regulation (EU) No 600/2014 on markets in financial instruments; Regulation (EU) 2015/760 on European long-term investment funds; Regulation (EU) 2016/1011 on indices used as benchmarks in financial instruments and financial contracts or to measure the performance of investment funds; and Regulation (EU) 2017/1129 on the prospectus to be published when securities are offered to the public or admitted to trading on a regulated market, COM/2017/0536 final.

[43] Communication from the Commission (n 41) 8.
[44] ibid 9.
[45] Communication from the Commission to the European Parliament, the Council, the European Central Bank, the European Economic and Social Committee and the Committee of the Regions

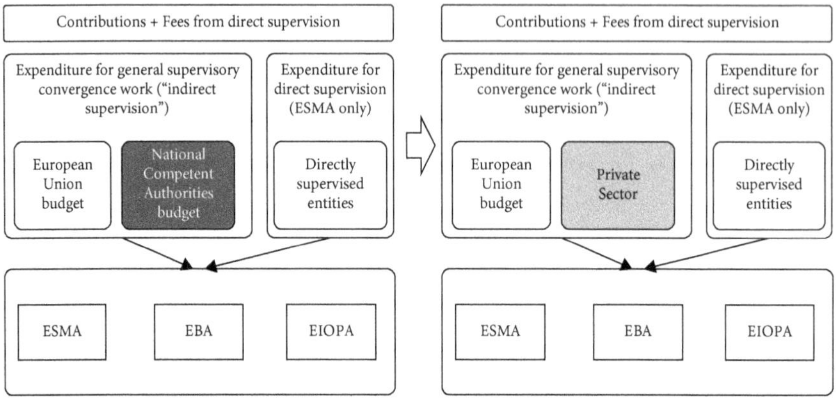

Figure 12.4 The figure depicts changes proposed to the funding of the ESAs by the European Commission during the second ESAs review in 2017

Source: European Commission (2017), https://eur-lex.europa.eu/legal-content/EN/TXT/PDF/?uri=CELEX:52017DC0542.

Consolidation of banking supervision within the SSM is recognized:

> The banking sector already benefits from consistent supervision by the Single Supervisory Mechanism within the Banking Union, in which 19 Member States participate. The geographical scope of Single Supervisory Mechanism supervision will extend, as additional Member States join the Banking Union. However, it is important that the Single Supervisory Mechanism operates within a consistent supervisory framework for the wider EU . . . To this end, the role of the European Banking Authority in promoting supervisory convergence in the EU banking sector should be enhanced.

At the same time, the lack of capital market integration is highlighted:

> With a few exceptions, EU capital markets are supervised at national level . . . As the Capital Markets Union will bring about further financial integration, it is crucial to strengthen the capacity of the European Supervisory Authorities to ensure consistent supervision and uniform enforcement of the single rulebook. This will support well-functioning capital markets by reducing barriers to cross-border investment, simplifying the business

Reinforcing integrated supervision to strengthen Capital Markets Union and financial integration in a changing environment, COM/2017/0542 final.

> environment and reducing compliance costs for firms operating on a cross-border basis resulting from divergent implementation of the rules. From an investor's perspective, consistent supervision and uniform enforcement of the rules contributes to enhancing investor protection and the building confidence in capital markets. Moreover, direct supervision by the European Securities Markets Authority could significantly contribute to ensuring consistent supervision and represents first concrete steps towards a Single European Capital Markets Supervisor.

Political reality proved different; the majority of Member States did not support a further Europeanization of financial supervision.[46] After a series of money-laundering scandals, improving the EU's anti-money-laundering framework became a new priority in 2018.

The Commission was especially concerned that:

> there is no clear articulation between the prudential and anti-money laundering rules for financial institutions. The Commission also has concerns about delayed supervisory reactions and shortcomings with respect to cooperation and information sharing – both at domestic level, between prudential and anti-money laundering authorities, and across borders, between authorities in different Member States or in third countries.[47]

Finally, political agreement was reached in March 2019, and the new legislative framework was endorsed in April and published in the Official Journal just before year's end.[48] The amendment did not live up to the Commission's ambitious legislative proposal. It contained small improvements to the ESA's

[46] See, eg ESA-Review Beitrag aus dem Jahresbericht 2018 der BaFin, available at https://www.bafin.de/DE/PublikationenDaten/Jahresbericht/Jahresbericht2018/Kapitel2/Kapitel2_8/Kapitel2_8_1/kapitel2_8_1_artikel.html;jsessionid = 9EF34983E5146FA807F60A20CB088E4B.internet012?nn = 19655328#U3.

[47] Communication from the Commission to the European Parliament, the European Council, the Council, the European Central Bank, The Economic and Social Committee and the Committee of the Regions—Strengthening the Union framework for prudential and anti-money laundering supervision for financial institutions, COM (2018) 645 final.

[48] Regulation (EU) 2019/2175 of the European Parliament and of the Council of 18 December 2019 amending Regulation (EU) No 1093/2010 establishing a European Supervisory Authority (European Banking Authority), Regulation (EU) No 1094/2010 establishing a European Supervisory Authority (European Insurance and Occupational Pensions Authority), Regulation (EU) No 1095/2010 establishing a European Supervisory Authority (European Securities and Markets Authority), Regulation (EU) No 600/2014 on markets in financial instruments, Regulation (EU) 2016/1011 on indices used as benchmarks in financial instruments and financial contracts or to measure the performance of investment funds, and Regulation (EU) 2015/847 on information accompanying transfers of funds (Text with EEA relevance) [2019] OJ L334, pp 1–145.

governance; however, an independent Executive Board with full-time members that ensure effective, impartial, and EU-oriented decisions with regard to the coordination of supervisory practices was not established besides the Board of Supervisors. Also, the funding structure remained essentially unchanged; industry funding was not introduced. The major changes were the centralization of AML powers, from the other ESAs, at the EBA, and a further extension of ESMA's direct supervisory powers. Technological innovation and sustainability objectives were also introduced.[49]

Despite the AML reforms, major issues continued to be unresolved; the AML framework remained basically a national supervisory framework with a coordinating role for the EBA. Under its new AML mandate, the EBA was mostly empowered with indirect supervision, but had no direct supervisory power, except for its power to impose an individual decision directly on an obliged entity where the relevant NCA failed to comply with the EBA's prior instructions.[50] The inadequacy of decentralized AML supervision by NCAs was identified by the European Commission as inadequate to handle cross-border AML cases involving banks and financial institutions operating in several Member States.[51] Therefore, in 2021, the Commission proposed to confer the competence of AML supervision on an EU agency—AMLA.[52] AMLA's founding regulation was published on 19 June 2024 in the Official Journal,[53] together with the AML Regulation[54] and the 6th AML Directive.[55] AMLA will

[49] For a more comprehensive overview, see Botopoulos (n 39).

[50] As the EBA Framework has been replaced by the new AMLA Regime, it will not be described in detail here. For a more detailed overview, see Gianni Lo Schiavo, 'The Single Supervisory Mechanism (SSM) and the EU Anti-Money Laundering Framework Compared: Governance, Rules, Challenges and Opportunities' (2022) 23 Journal of Banking Regulations 91, https://doi.org/10.1057/s41261-021-00166-0.

[51] Commission, 'Report from the Commission to the European Parliament and the Council on the assessment of recent alleged money laundering cases involving EU credit institutions' COM (2019) 373 final.

[52] Proposal for a Regulation of the European Parliament and of the Council establishing the Authority for Anti-Money Laundering and Countering the Financing of Terrorism and amending Regulations (EU) No 1093/2010, (EU) 1094/2010, (EU) 1095/2010 (COM/2021/421 final) (AMLA Proposal).

[53] Regulation (EU) 2024/1620 of the European Parliament and of the Council of 31 May 2024 establishing the Authority for Anti-Money Laundering and Countering the Financing of Terrorism and amending Regulations (EU) No 1093/2010, (EU) No 1094/2010 and (EU) No 1095/2010 (Text with EEA relevance) [2024] OJ L2024/1620 (AMLAR, hereinafter 'AMLR').

[54] Regulation (EU) 2024/1624 of the European Parliament and of the Council of 31 May 2024 on the prevention of the use of the financial system for the purposes of money laundering or terrorist financing (Text with EEA relevance) [2024] OJ L2024/1624.

[55] Directive (EU) 2024/1640 of the European Parliament and of the Council of 31 May 2024 on the mechanisms to be put in place by Member States for the prevention of the use of the financial system for the purposes of money laundering or terrorist financing, amending Directive (EU) 2019/1937, and amending and repealing Directive (EU) 2015/849 (Text with EEA relevance) [2024] OJ L2024/1640.

assume most of its tasks and powers from 1 July 2025, and direct supervision as of 2028.[56]

The treaty basis for the establishment of AMLA, similarly to the ESAs, is Article 114 TFEU. Hence, AMLA, similarly to the ESAs, is limited in its decision-making by its Treaty basis and the application of the *Meroni*[57] doctrine. The CJEU developed the *Meroni* doctrine in 1958, and further developed it in *Romano*[58] and the ESMA *Short Selling*[59] case.[60] Most recently, the court touched upon the issue in *Fundación Tatiana Pérez*.[61] Accordingly, EU agencies can be recipients of executive discretionary powers if this discretion is limited. The delegation of clearly defined executive powers is permitted, since the acts to be taken by the Authority—ESMA in the specific case; AMLA and the other ESAs by extension—are subject to 'strict judicial review', provided that their exercise can be assessed 'in the light of the objective criteria determined by the delegating authority'.[62] The powers can, however, never involve a margin of political judgement, as this would be contrary to the balance of power between the institutions.[63]

VI Main responsibilities of AMLA

To bring AML/CFT supervision to an efficient and uniform level across the Union, AMLA was, in a nutshell, provided with the following main powers:

- Direct supervision of a certain number of selected obliged entities (SOEs) in the financial sector, including crypto-asset service providers.[64] To enable efficient supervision, AMLA can apply investigative measures, administrative measures, periodic penalty payments, and administrative

[56] AMLA Proposal (n 52), arts 4 and 108; recitals 8 and 86.
[57] C-9/56 *Meroni v High Authority (Meroni I)*, ECLI:EU:C:1958:7; Case 10/56 *Meroni v High Authority (Meroni II)*, ECLI:EU:C:1958:8.
[58] C-98/80 *Giuseppe Romano v Institut national d'assurance maladie-invalidité*, ECLI:EU:C:1981:104.
[59] See *UK v Council and Parliament* (n 7).
[60] See also Miroslava Scholten and Marloes van Rijsbergen, 'The ESMA-Short Selling Case: Erecting a New Delegation Doctrine in the EU upon the Meroni-Romano Remnants' (2014) 41(4) Legal Issues of Economic Integration 389–406.
[61] C-551/22 P *Commission v SRB*, ECLI:EU:C:2024:520.
[62] Silvia Allegrezza, 'The Proposed Anti-Money Laundering Authority, FIU Cooperation, Powers and Exchanges of Information: A Critical Assessment' (2022) 27–28.
[63] See *UK v Council and Parliament* (n 7), para 72.
[64] AMLR, arts 12–13.

pecuniary sanctions.[65] These powers are similar to the supervisory powers the ESAs have under their respective sectoral legislation.[66]

- In addition to the powers set out directly in AMLAR, AMLA can also exercise the powers conferred on to NCAs under relevant Union law—including national law transposing directives—or instruct NCAs to use their powers under national law. This leads to difficult interpretation and application issues, a problem already known from the SSM,[67] as a clear delineation between supervisory powers under Union law, on the one hand, and national supervisory powers under national law, on the other, is not always easily possible. It will be interesting to observe how AMLA, the NCAs, and potentially the CJEU, resolve any issues arising, and whether they are able to develop a consistent methodology.
- Direct supervision of SOEs will take place in the form of Joint Supervisory Teams (JSTs) composed of AMLA and NCA staff and coordinated by a staff member of AMLA ('JST coordinator'), a structure already well known from the SSM's supervision of significant supervised entities.[68] Also in the sphere of the ESAs, similar concepts start to be explored. When conducting DORA oversight activities, in particular, general investigations or inspections, the Lead Overseer shall be assisted by a Joint Examination Team (JET) established for each critical ICT third-party service provider.[69] These JETs are composed of ESA and NCA staff.
- To select SOEs, AMLAR foresees a two-step process. The first step is a risk assessment of obliged entities that operate in several countries; the second step is a selection based on criteria related to their specific risk profile.[70]

[65] For a detailed overview, see Stanislaw Tosza and Olivier Voordeckers, 'An Anti-money laundering Authority for the European Union: A New Center of Gravity in AML Enforcement' (2024) 25 ERA Forum 405–24. https://doi.org/10.1007/s12027-024-00805-9.

[66] See, eg arts 61–73, Regulation (EU) 648/2012 of the European Parliament and of the Council of 4 July 2012 on OTC derivatives, central counterparties and trade repositories Text with EEA relevance [2012] OJ L201, pp 1–59.

[67] Raffaele D'Ambrosio, 'Single Supervision Mechanism: Organs and Procedures' in Mario P Chiti and Vittorio Santoro (eds), *The Palgrave Handbook of European Banking Union Law* (Palgrave Macmillan 2019); Lena Boucon and Daniela Jaros, 'The Application of National Law by the European Central Bank Within the EU Banking Union's Single Supervisory Mechanism: A New Mode of European Integration?' (2018) 10 European Journal of Legal Studies 155, 167.

[68] Regulation (EU) 468/2014 of the European Central Bank of 16 April 2014 establishing the framework for cooperation within the Single Supervisory Mechanism between the European Central Bank and National Competent Authorities and with national designated authorities (SSM Framework Regulation) (ECB/2014/17) [2014] OJ L141, pp 1–50; see also Dominik Schlarb, 'Rethinking Anti-money Laundering Supervision: The Single Supervisory Mechanism - A Model for a European Anti-money Laundering Supervisor?' (2022) 13(1) New Journal of European Criminal Law 69–90.

[69] DORA Regulation (n 11); See MiCA Regulation (n 11), art 40.

[70] AMLR, art 12; for a detailed explanation of the process, see Tosza and Voordeckers (n 65).

- Coordination and oversight of AML/CFT supervisors of the financial sector, the non-financial sector, and Financial Intelligence Units (FIUs). AMLA is responsible for the effective and consistent functioning of the AML/CFT supervisory system. NCAs remain responsible for the direct AML/CFT supervision of non-SOEs. However, they will do so under the oversight of AMLA. NCAs shall provide the AMLA with all information concerning obliged entities that remain directly supervised at national level which is necessary for the fulfilment of AMLA's tasks.

To achieve this goal, AMLA has several powers.
Key powers regarding the supervision of-non-selected obliged entities[71] are:

- Assessments of the state of supervisory convergence.
  A periodic assessment of the activities of NCAs, as well as of their tools and resources. Establishing the extent to which NCAs perform their tasks in accordance with Directive (EU) 2024/1640 and ensuring consistent high-level supervisory standards and practices.
- Coordination and facilitation of the work of the AML/CFT supervisory colleges in the financial sector.
  Conceptually similar to the ESAs, AMLA shall ensure the functioning of supervisory colleges within its powers.
- Requests to act in exceptional circumstances following indications of serious, repeated, or systematic breaches.
  Where the situation of any non-selected obliged entity deteriorates rapidly and significantly—in particular, where such deterioration might negatively impact several Member States or the Union as a whole or undermine the integrity of the Union's financial system—AMLA can take certain actions enumerated in Article 32 AMLAR. As a last recourse, AMLA can request the Commission to grant permission to temporarily transfer the relevant tasks and powers related to direct supervision of the non-selected obliged entity from the financial supervisor concerned, to AMLA. Commission approval is rooted in the institutional set-up applicable to an EU agency.[72]
  Additionally, NCAs can request that supervision is transferred from the national level to AMLA for a non-obliged entity, in certain exceptional circumstances.[73]

[71] AMLR, arts 30–34.
[72] Allegrezza (n 62) 27–28; Miroslava Scholten and Marloes van Rijsbergen, 'The Limits of Agencification in the European Union' (2014) 15(7) German Law Journal 1223–55.
[73] AMLR, art 14.

- Settlement of disagreements between financial supervisors in cross-border situations

  Conceptually similar to the ESAs, AMLA can mediate between NCAs in the case of disagreement.
- Action in cases of systematic failures of supervision.

  Another well-known tool from the ESAs' world, breaches-of-Union-law investigations are also at AMLA's disposal. It shall be noted that AMLA, similarly to the ESAs, has discretion regarding the initiation of investigations, both when it receives requests from entities mentioned in the respective founding Regulations and when it acts on its own initative. This has been clarified by the CJEU for the EBA.[74]

Furthermore, AMLA will be complementing EU AML/CFT rules by developing regulatory[75] and implementing technical standards[76] and issuing guidelines and recommendations,[77] as well as opinions and technical advice[78]—regulatory tools already well known from the ESAs. Hence, AMLA will be assuming EBA's regulatory powers in the area of AML. These regulatory tools include the development and maintenance—in cooperation with the supervisory authorities—of an up-to-date and harmonized AML/CFT supervisory methodology detailing the risk-based approach to supervision of obliged entities in the Union. That methodology shall comprise guidelines, recommendations, opinions, and other measures and instruments as appropriate, including, in particular, regulatory and implementing technical standards.[79] AMLA will also establish a central AML/CFT database, which will rely heavily on the AML/CFT database established in accordance with Article 9a of Regulation (EU) No 1093/2010 (EBA Regulation).[80]

Despite AMLA's role as supervisor of SOEs, the NCAs will still play an important role. NCAs will remain fully responsible for the direct supervision of all non-SOEs. However, in exceptional circumstances, AMLA can take over such direct supervision.[81] Furthermore, as already mentioned, direct supervision of SOEs will take place in the form of JSTs, composed of AMLA and NCA staff. AMLA and the NCAs form the AML 'supervisory system'.[82]

[74] Case C–577/15 P *SV Capital OÜ v European Banking Authority (EBA)*, ECLI:EU:C:2016:947.
[75] AMLR, art 49.
[76] AMLR, art 53.
[77] AMLR, art 54.
[78] AMLR, art 55.
[79] AMLR, art 8.
[80] AMLR, art 11.
[81] AMLR, art 14.
[82] AMLR, art 2(3).

VII AMLA governance

AMLA will be governed by two collegial bodies: the Executive Board and the General Board.[83]

The Executive Board will be composed of the chair and five full-time members, including the vice-chair and a Commission representative (the latter only participating when AMLA decides on matters of internal administration, for example the adoption of budgets, rules of procedure, etc.). The supervisory mandate of AMLA is the main task of the Executive Board. It is responsible for the execution of AMLA's supervisory tasks; it takes all decisions—drafted by JSTs—towards individual obliged entities or, in the case of indirect supervision, towards individual supervisory authorities. The Executive Board will also take decisions regarding the draft budget and all matters relating to the operations and the functioning of AMLA.[84]

The General Board will have two alternative compositions: a supervisory composition, with heads of public authorities responsible for AML supervision, and an FIU composition, with heads of FIUs from all EU Member States; additionally, a chairperson and a non-voting Commission representative participate in the General Board. Where the General Board sits in supervisory composition, it may provide its opinion on any decision concerning SOEs before adopting the final decision by the Executive Board, thus participating in the supervisory function of AMLA.[85]

The chair represents the Authority and chairs the two governing bodies—the General Board and the Executive Board—which includes the responsibility for preparing the work of both boards, including setting the agenda, convening and chairing all the meetings, and tabling items for decision. Furthermore, the chair shall assign specific areas of responsibility to the members of the Executive Board.[86]

The executive director is responsible for the daily management of AMLA, the preparation and implementation of the annual work programme, and the budget establishment and implementation; he or she is accountable to the Executive Board.[87]

[83] For a more detailed overview, see Georgios Pavlidis, 'The Birth of the New Anti-money Laundering Authority: Harnessing the Power of EU-wide Supervision' (2023) 31(2) Journal of Financial Crime 322–30.
[84] AMLR, arts 63–66.
[85] AMLR, arts 57–62.
[86] AMLR, arts 68–69.
[87] AMLR, arts 70–71.

In addition, AMLA has an Administrative Board of Review (ABoR).[88] It is similar in structure and function to the ECB's Administrative Board of Review.[89] This differs substantially from the JBoA of the ESAs, which has much broader powers. The JBoA can confirm or remit a contested decision to an ESA.[90] Hence, despite not having the power to annul contested decisions, the legal effects of the decisions of the JBoA lead to a similar outcome, since the ESAs have to amend their decisions if these are remitted to them.[91] In contrast, the ABoR can only express an opinion which shall be taken into account by the Executive Board. This is very uncommon, since decision-making agencies normally have fully fledged appeals bodies.[92] Additionally, the amendments, already mentioned above,[93] to Article 58a of the Statute of the Court apply to all independent boards of appeal set up after 1 May 2019. As AMLA is *sensu stricto* not a board of appeal, Article 58a does not apply to the AMLA ABoR. Given the contentious nature of AML supervision, this should lead to an increased workload at both Court instances in the future. Consideration could be given to merging the ESA's JBoA, the SRB's Appeals Panel,[94] and AMLA's ABoR into a Joint Board of Appeal, elevating the ABoR to a fully fledged board of appeal in the process. This would centralize appeal proceedings at a truly specialized appeals body, transforming these part-time boards into permanent ones, with a permanent secretariat (instead of the ESAs acting as secretariat on a rotating basis for the JBoA), alleviating the CJEU's caseload and becoming de facto specialized 'courts' of first instance.

[88] AMLR, arts 72–75.

[89] Council Regulation (EU) 1024/2013 of 15 October 2013 conferring specific tasks on the European Central Bank concerning policies relating to the prudential supervision of credit institutions [2013] OJ L287, pp 63–89, art 24; For a more detailed overview, see Eleni Koupepidou, 'Administrative Pre-litigation Review Mechanism in the SSM: The Administrative Board of Review' in Chiara Zilioli and Karl-Philipp Wojcik, *Judicial Review in the European Banking Union* (Edward Elgar 2021).

[90] See ESAs Regulations: Regulation (EU) 1093/2010, Regulation (EU) 1094/2010, and Regulation (EU) 1095/2010, art 60.

[91] Chamon and Fromage (n 16) 25.

[92] Merijn Chamon, Annalisa Volpato, and Mariolina Eliantonio, 'Introduction' in Chamon, Volpato, and Eliantonio (eds) (n 16) 2–3; Chamon and Fromage (n 16) 8–33.

[93] Regulation (EU, Euratom) 2024/2019 of the European Parliament and of the Council of 11 April 2024 amending Protocol No 3 on the Statute of the Court of Justice of the European Union [2024] OJ L2024/2019.

[94] Regulation (EU) 806/2014 of the European Parliament and of the Council of 15 July 2014 establishing uniform rules and a uniform procedure for the resolution of credit institutions and certain investment firms in the framework of a Single Resolution Mechanism and a Single Resolution Fund and amending Regulation (EU) No 1093/2010 [2014] OJ L225, pp 1–90, art 85.

VIII AMLA as a blueprint for the future evolution of the ESAs?

As AMLA is the last iteration in the universe of agencies in the financial services area, the obvious question must be asked: can the AMLA framework serve as the foundation for future reforms of the ESAs?

It is clear that the AMLA framework incorporates some of the suggestions brought forward by the Commission during the 2019 ESAs review. AMLA has a General Board and an Executive Board, and AMLA's supervisory activities—direct and indirect—are industry financed, which contrasts with the ESAs, where only direct supervision is industry financed.

1 Financing of the agencies

AMLA activities will be funded by the EU budget and fees, with strict separation between the costs for fee-funded and not-fee-funded activities. Fees should only cover task-related expenditures. Fees should be levied on selected and non-selected obliged entities. The amount of the fee to be collected from a non-selected obliged entity, in proportion to its income or turnover, shall not exceed 20% of the amount of the fee to be collected from selected obliged entities with the same level of income or turnover.[95]

2 ESAs

The ESAs' financing structure can best be illustrated and compared with AMLA using the example of ESMA, as the only ESA with a broad supervisory mandate besides its regulatory mandate.

The ESAs' Regulations prescribe that the ESAs' budgets consist of a combination of the following: (a) obligatory contributions from NCAs; (b) a subsidy from the Union; (c) any fees paid to the Authority in the cases specified in the relevant instruments of Union law; (d) any voluntary contribution from Member States and observers; and (e) agreed charges for publications, training, and any other services specifically requested by one or more NCAs.[96]

[95] AMLR, arts 76–77.

[96] See ESAs' Regulations: Regulation (EU) 1093/2010, Regulation (EU) 1094/2010, and Regulation (EU) 1095/2010, art 62.

As regards the proportion of funding from the NCAs and the Union, the current funding model of the ESAs for non-supervisory tasks is based on a political agreement reached during the establishment of the ESAs. The agreement is recorded in Recital 68 of the ESAs' Regulations as follows: 'The Authority should be appropriately financed. At least initially, it should be financed 40 % from Union funds and 60 % through contributions from Member States, made in accordance with the weighting of votes set out in Article 3(3) of the Protocol (No 36) on transitional provisions.'

Whereas the distribution of the 60% contribution from Member States in accordance with Protocol No 36[97] is given legal effect in Article 62 of the ESAs' Regulations, the overall 60% level remains a political agreement between the Member States and the Union. Such practice has been applied since the establishment of the ESAs in 2011. While the funding arrangements have not evolved since the ESAs' inception, their mandates have expanded. This can be easily observed by looking at ESMA's expanded mandate. Since its establishment, ESMA has been granted several supervisory mandates on the principle of full cost recovery, so that the cost of ESMA's direct supervision—not indirect supervision—is fully funded by the supervised entities, leading to a current and expected revenue stream from supervised entities (varying considerably in size), including CRAs; from trade repositories under European Market Infrastructure Regulation; from trade repositories under SFTR; from securitization repositories; from third countries' CCPs Tier 1; from third countries' CCPs Tier 2; from Data Reporting Service Providers' approved reporting mechanisms; from Data Reporting Service Providers' approved publication arrangements; from Data Reporting Service Providers' consolidated tape providers; from benchmark administrators; from Critical ICT Third-party Providers; from ESG ratings; and from EU green bonds. Fees will also be collected under DORA. The expanded mandate has led to a considerable increase of regulatory costs, including those of indirect supervision, borne by the NCAs and the Union.

3 Observations and (possible) way forward

There are key differences between AMLA and the ESAs. AMLA is, first and foremost, a supervisor, while at least two of the three ESAs—namely EBA and EIOPA—are, first and foremost, regulators, mainly tasked with

[97] Treaty on the Functioning of the European Union—Protocol (No 36) on transitional provisions, OJ C115, 9.5.2008, pp 322–26.

supervisory convergence via the establishment of a Single Rulebook in a particular area. Hence, of the three ESAs, only ESMA resembles AMLA in the sense of also having broader and continuously expanding supervisory mandates. Therefore, it could be contemplated to apply AMLA's funding framework to ESMA, taking into account the differences between the two agencies. AMLA 'only' supervises AML/CFT, with its supervisory mandate contained in its founding Regulation;[98] ESMA's supervisory mandate is, on the other hand, scattered across a high number of legislative acts and not contained in its founding Regulation[99] (as is the case for the other ESAs), leading to different rules applying across ESMA's supervised entities. Additionally, supervised entities are not homogenous. A possible solution could be to establish a central supervisory mandate in ESMA's founding Regulation, leaving only sectoral rules, where deviation is necessary, in sectoral legislation. The outcome could be a drastic reduction in complexity and an end to the ever-growing duplication of slightly different rules with each new sectoral act broadening ESMA's supervisory mandate.

However, even if a centralization of supervision cannot be achieved, inspiration could be drawn from AMLA's funding framework. Currently, the 60% NCA contribution at the ESAs is calculated in accordance with the contributions from Member States under Protocol No 36. This fails to take into account the high concentration of certain financial activities in specific Member States, essentially leading to Member States without such (or with only marginal such) financial activities cross-subsidizing the development of a Single Rulebook for entities potentially not active at all in their Member States. Possible solutions could be to devise a contribution mechanism taking into account such distortions, ensuring a proportionate contribution not purely linked to the mechanism in Protocol No 36. It must also be highlighted that, under the current mechanism, budget contributions by the NCAs and the voting power of the NCAs in the Board of Supervisors are not aligned. Furthermore, Member States with a small share of supervised entities in the capital markets area have, as a consequence, very small NCAs who have to contribute an outsized amount of their budget to ESMA's budget; consideration could, therefore, be given to moving the contribution obligation from the NCA to the Member State level.

[98] Regulation (EU) 2024/1620 of the European Parliament and of the Council of 31 May 2024 establishing the Authority for Anti-Money Laundering and Countering the Financing of Terrorism and amending Regulations (EU) No 1093/2010, (EU) No 1094/2010 and (EU) No 1095/2010 (Text with EEA relevance) [2024] OJ L2024/1620 (AMLAR).

[99] See ESAs' Regulations: Regulation (EU) 1093/2010, Regulation (EU) 1094/2010, and Regulation (EU) 1095/2010.

AMLA elegantly avoids such issues by solely relying on EU and fee funding, which could be another solution for the ESAs.

In this context, it must be borne in mind that funding is intrinsically linked with governance, and therefore a reduction in NCA contributions would require a refined governance structure.[100] While such a reform did not succeed previously, the carving out of the EBA's AML mandate and transferring it to AMLA (together with the transfer of certain national supervisory mandates from NCAs) with an independent Executive Board shows that there seemed to be political agreement, or at least compromise, that such a governance form is preferential for an agency mainly tasked with supervision. This raises the question whether it can be justified to treat the three ESAs as if they were the same creature, or if it is time to face reality and acknowledge that they are indeed very different, and hence should be treated differently.

It is undisputed that AMLA's governance structure is superior to the current ESAs' structure, as independent decision-making is fostered to a larger extent, via independent board members. Hence, AMLA should serve as inspiration for a possible reform of all ESAs. However, if this is politically not feasible, it should at least serve as inspiration for an overhaul of ESMA's governance structure, given its role as supervisor, especially in light of calls for a future expansion of ESMA's role. The *Draghi report*,[101] the *Letta report*,[102] and the *Noyer report*,[103] all published in 2024, call for an expansion of ESMA's role (see Table 12.1).[104]

Christine Lagarde even boldly calls for turning ESMA into a European Securities and Exchange Commission (SEC).[105] It is worth remembering that the *de Larosière report*[106] laid the foundation for the creation of the ESAs in

[100] Howell (n 30) 346–49.

[101] Mario Draghi, 'The future of European competitiveness—A competitiveness strategy for Europe' (2024). Available at https://commission.europa.eu/topics/strengthening-european-competitiveness/eu-competitiveness-looking-ahead_en#paragraph_47059.

[102] Enrico Letta, 'Much more than a market—Speed, Security, Solidarity Empowering the Single Market to deliver a sustainable future and prosperity for all EU Citizens' (2024). Available at https://www.consilium.europa.eu/media/ny3j24sm/much-more-than-a-market-report-by-enrico-letta.pdf.

[103] Christian Noyer, 'Developing European capital markets to finance the future' (2024). Available at https://www.tresor.economie.gouv.fr/Articles/e3283a8f-69de-46c2-9b8a-4b8836394798/files/6b8593b5-ca31-45a3-b61c-11c95cf0fc4b.

[104] Kai Gereon Spitzer, Giacomo Loi, and Maja Sabol, 'How to achieve CMU, after all? An analysis of the recommendations for Capital Markets Union in the Draghi, Letta and Noyer reports' (Economic Governance and EMU Scrutiny Unit (EGOV) Directorate-General for Internal Policies, updated January 2025). Available at https://www.europarl.europa.eu/RegData/etudes/IDAN/2024/760263/IPOL_IDA(2024)760263_EN.pdf.

[105] Christine Lagarde, President of the ECB, 'A Kantian shift for the capital markets union' (Speech at the European Banking Congress, Frankfurt am Main, 17 November 2023). Available at https://www.ecb.europa.eu/press/key/date/2023/html/ecb.sp231117~88389f194b.en.html.

[106] The de Larosiére Group report, 'The High-Level Group on Financial Supervision in the EU'. Available at https://ec.europa.eu/economy_finance/publications/pages/publication14527_en.pdf.

Table 12.1 Overview of key CMU proposals in Letta, Draghi, and Noyer reports

Proposal	Letta report	Draghi report	Noyer report
Securitization			
Simpler transparency and due diligence requirements	✓	✓	✓
Lower capital requirements	✓	✓	✓
Broader liquidity buffer eligibility (LCR)			✓
Relax prudential framework for insurers			✓
Public securitization platform			✓
Green securitization			
Supervision			
Stronger role for ESMA	✓	✓	✓
'Pathways' towards SSM-style model	✓		
European SEC		✓	
Opt-in into central supervision			✓
Executive board for ESMA			
Add European appointees to Board of Supervisors	✓	✓	
Market Infrastructure			
Consolidation of CCPs and CSDs	✓	✓	
Convergence of securities law as path to foster			✓
Allow TARGET2 Securities to become an EU CSD			✓
Pensions and Savings			
Introduction of common EU savings product	✓		
EU label for national savings product			✓
Incentives for Pillar 2 pension schemes	✓	✓	✓
Harmonization of Business Law			
European Business Code and European Company Statute	✓		
EU-wide legal statute for innovative start-ups			

Source: EGOV own elaboration based on Letta, Draghi, and Noyer reports.

their current form, and only the future will tell whether this new round of reports will create the same spark for reform as the 2009 report, the difference being that, this time, the crisis we face is not a financial crisis but a multifaceted crisis about the EU's, as well as the Member States', (continued) significance in a multipolar world.

Modern risk-based supervision is not cost-free; therefore, any credible agency with a large-scale supervisory mandate needs stable funding. Hence, a further expansion of ESMA's supervisory powers will, at some point, require a revision of its funding structure. However, as the 2019 ESAs' review has shown, a prerequisite for a revision of the funding structure is a more independent governance. Therefore, at some point, one of the two will have to give; either ESMA's supervisory powers will only grow marginally, and the dream of a European SEC will not materialize, or supervision will be expanded, requiring, at some point, a governance reform, ensuring sufficient independence. Here, AMLA seems the logical inspiration; considering that is was politically feasible in the area of AML, why should it not be an adequate approach for other areas of financial supervision? In this context, it also has to be borne in mind that, instead of establishing AMLA, EBA's mandate could have been expanded, which was not pursued; one has to wonder whether EBA's structure played a role in this decision.

13

The Width and Length of Composite Decision-Making in the European Banking Union

Filipe Brito Bastos and Ieva Hūna[*]

I Composite decision-making, the Court, and the Banking Union's tenth anniversary

Ten years after its foundations were laid, it is fair to say that the rise of the European Banking Union (EBU) has been transformative for European Union (EU) administrative law, and vice versa. The Single Supervisory Mechanism (SSM) and the Single Resolution Mechanism (SRM) proved unique in the history of EU administrative law, both for the intensity and for the complexity of administrative integration between national and Union authorities.[1] Both networks use the full arsenal of tools for administrative cooperation known to EU administrative law, from information sharing to teamed-up cooperation and joint decision-making.[2] Consequently, the SSM and SRM have become test cases for the challenges that multilevel administration can raise for basic rule-of-law requirements, such as effective judicial protection and reasoned administrative decisions.[3] In turn, past experiences in EU administrative law, drawn from unrelated policy fields, have provided important insights for Banking

* Filipe Brito Bastos' contribution to this work was supported by the Portuguese Foundation for Science and Technology. The two authors would like to thank Bernardo Pinto and Rafael Guerra, research assistants at NOVA PEARL, for their collaboration.

[1] For an overview of the institutional aspects of the SSM and SRM, see Alexander Türk, 'European Banking Union and Its Relation with European Union Institutions' in Mario Chiti and Vittorio Santoro (eds), *The Palgrave Handbook of European Banking Union Law* (Palgrave Macmillan 2019).

[2] See, eg Filipe Brito Bastos, 'Composite Procedures in the SSM and SRM - an Analytical Overview' in Chiara Zilioli and Karl-Philipp Wojcik (eds), *Judicial Review in the European Banking Union* (Edward Elgar 2021).

[3] See, eg Argyro Karagianni and Miroslava Scholten, 'Accountability Gaps in the Single Supervisory Mechanism (SSM) Framework' (2018) 34(2) Utrecht Journal of International and European Law 185.

Filipe Brito Bastos and Ieva Hūna, *The Width and Length of Composite Decision-Making in the European Banking Union* In: *EU Banking Union*. Edited by: Jonathan Bauerschmidt, Raffaele D'Ambrosio, Diane Fromage, Daniela Jaros, and Paul Weismann, Oxford University Press. © Oxford University Press 2026.
DOI: 10.1093/9780198949756.003.0014

Union academics and practitioners to better understand the legal architecture of its enforcement systems.

When the SSM became operational, few would have believed that some of the most sensitive questions concerning judicial control of ECB supervisory decisions would be settled in a case initiated by Silvio Berlusconi and extensively informed by EU case law concerning administrative procedures for agricultural subsidies, protected designations of origin, access to documents, and even for the regulation of genetically modified organisms.[4]

The kind of administrative procedures in question—composite administrative procedures—exist in many policy areas, from the protection of natural habitats to data protection, but are a particularly important feature of the Banking Union's governance.[5] They can be understood as procedures where national and Union administrations adopt a sequence of measures in terms of *decisional interdependence*—one way to put this is that the Union administration may not exercise its own competences within the administrative procedure before the national administration has exercised its own, or the other way around.[6]

The difficulties in ensuring effective judicial protection in composite administrative decision-making have now been known for over 30 years.[7] The *Berlusconi* ruling provided EU administrative lawyers with further long-awaited answers on the boundaries of the jurisdiction of the Court of Justice of the European Union (CJEU).[8] The judgment clarified the conditions under which the CJEU's jurisdiction extends not just to the review of final Union-level decisions, at the conclusion of a composite administrative procedure, but to the review of preparatory acts that national authorities adopt in the preceding procedural stages.

[4] Case C–219/17 *Berlusconi and Fininvest*, ECLI:EU:C:2018:502, Opinion of AG Campos Sánchez-Bordona.

[5] Vittorio di Bucci, 'Procedural and Judicial Implications of Composite Procedures in the Banking Union' in Zilioli and Wojcik (eds) (n 2) 114, § 8.01.

[6] Filipe Brito Bastos, *Judging Composite Decision-Making: The Transformation of European Administrative Law* (Hart 2024) 57–58, supported by the definition of 'composite administrative procedure' in art I-4 (3) of the ReNEUAL Model Rules in EU Administrative Procedure.

[7] See the judgment in case C–97/91 *Oleificio Borelli*, ECLI:EU:C:1992:491. For an extended analysis, see Filipe Brito Bastos, 'The Borelli Doctrine Revisited: Three Issues of Coherence in a Landmark Ruling for EU Administrative Justice' (2015) 8 Review of European Administrative Law 269; and Mariolina Eliantonio, 'Judicial Review in an Integrated Administration: The Case of "Composite Procedures"' (2014) 7 Review of European Administrative Law 65, 82; Ieva Hūna, 'The CJEU and the Ship of Theseus. Acts of Mixed Authorship in Composite Procedures' (*EU Law Live Weekend Edition*, 15 February 2025), no 218, https://eulawlive.com/weekend-edition/weekend-edition-no218/, accessed 17 May 2026.

[8] Judgment in Case C–219/17 *Berlusconi and Fininvest*, ECLI:EU:C:2018:1023.

This chapter considers an important gap that *Berlusconi* did not address: what exactly constitutes a national preparatory act? Which national measures are conceived to be a part of a composite administrative procedure—and hence reviewable by the CJEU—and which are simply decisions taken at the conclusion of a purely national administrative procedure, which are solely for the national courts to review? The question has, by now, become decisive in how two other rulings drew the jurisdictional boundaries between national courts and the CJEU.

The chapter will be organized as follows: section II situates national preparatory acts in the broader context of the Banking Union's administrative governance, and of the particular role which it ascribes to national authorities. Section III recalls the key findings of the landmark *Berlusconi* ruling and points out the loose end that it left: the scope of the concept of a 'preparatory act'. Section IV examines how the question has been addressed in two subsequent Banking Union judgments. In *Satabank*, the CJEU had to clarify where the national stage of a composite administrative procedure begins—which we refer to as the 'length' of the composite procedure. In *Pilatus*, the CJEU had to clarify how national authorities' preparatory acts are to be distinguished from decisions taken in purely national administrative procedures that develop at the same time as a related, albeit distinct, composite administrative procedure—the 'width' of the composite procedure. Section V concludes the chapter by considering the constitutional dilemmas in finding a test to discern purely preparatory national measures. As with other well-known issues in composite decision-making, difficult choices loom between the uniformity and autonomy of Union law, on the one hand, and effective judicial protection, on the other.

II Decision-making in the Banking Union and the role of national preparatory acts

The SSM and the SRM reflect a familiar pattern in European administrative law. Since the Member States are reluctant to centralize enforcement in the Union administration, and since the risks of completely decentralized enforcement to the uniformity of Union law are well known, the Union legislator strikes a balance of national and Union power. This balance tends to combine centralized and decentralized enforcement by allocating distinct roles to Union and national authorities within a multilevel network with reciprocal duties of administrative cooperation.[9] Such cooperation can take many forms,

[9] See Ellen Mastenbroek and Dorte Martinsen, 'Filling the Gap in the European Administrative Space: The Role of Administrative Networks in EU Implementation and Enforcement' (2018) 25

from the exchange of information to the creation of joint teams composed of national and Union officials. Crucially, one form of cooperation requires national and Union authorities in the Banking Union to do far more than simply assisting one another in better exercising their respective decision-making powers. Indeed, in a composite administrative procedure, both levels exercise decision-making powers *jointly*, acting as a single administration rather than separate EU and national administrations.[10]

The SSM Regulation (SSMR) and the SRM Regulation (SRMR) vest National Competent Authorities (NCAs) and national resolution authorities (NRAs) with quite different tasks.[11] Nonetheless, NCAs as well as NRAs are critical in providing the European Central Bank (ECB) and the Single Resolution Board (SRB) with the operational support and preparatory work that they need to exercise decision-making power at the Union level. However, the CJEU case law has shown that composite administrative procedures have proven particularly challenging from the perspective of judicial control. Typically, the role of NCAs and NRAs is to adopt preparatory acts that pave the way for the ECB and SRB to take the administrative procedures' final decisions.

In the SRM, NRAs are involved in multiple composite procedures. Article 8(1) and (4) of the SRMR require NRAs to provide the SRB with the information 'necessary' for it to draw up and implement resolution plans.[12] However, the most contentious instance of composite decision-making in the SRM has concerned NRAs' contribution in gathering data for the SRB to calculate how much each credit institution must pay into the Single Resolution Fund as *ex ante* contributions.

In the SSM, NCAs are vested 'with an ancillary role that is functionally and operationally embedded in all SSMR procedural modules setting out the

Journal of European Public Policy 422, 424; and Tobias Bach and Eva Ruffing, 'The Transformative Effects of Transnational Administrative Coordination in the European Multi-level System' in Edoardo Ongaro and Sandra van Thiel (eds), *The Palgrave Handbook of Public Administration and Management in Europe* (Palgrave Macmillan 2017) 748–51.

[10] Jan Jans and others, *Europeanisation of Public Law* (2nd edn, Europa Law Publishing 2015) 31.

[11] Council Regulation (EU) 1024/2013 of 15 October 2013 conferring specific tasks on the European Central Bank concerning policies relating to the prudential supervision of credit institutions (SSMR), art 2(8); and Regulation (EU) 806/2014 of the European Parliament and of the Council of 15 July 2014 establishing uniform rules and a uniform procedure for the resolution of credit institutions and certain investment firms in the framework of a Single Resolution Mechanism and a Single Resolution Fund and amending Regulation (EU) No 1093/2010 (SRMR), art 7 (3).

[12] Despite the provisions' wording, the NRAs' obligations in the SRMR's context are part of a composite administrative procedure rather than an example of mere information exchange. See Brito Bastos, 'Composite Procedures in the SSM and SRM' (n 2) § 7.37.

exercise of ECB powers'.[13] In setting up the SSM, the Union legislator opted for the balance of power to be clearly tilted to the benefit of the ECB,[14] and the CJEU has reinforced the ECB's dominance further.[15] NCAs cannot issue or revoke bank licences, nor can they authorize qualifying holdings, and are limited to *proposing* a specific decision on any of these three actions, for the ECB to exercise its 'exclusive decision-making power' in the framework of the so-called common procedures.[16] The ECB can also require NCAs' assistance in the 'preparation and implementation' of any act adopted pursuant to one of the ECB's supervisory powers.[17]

From the very inception of the SSM and SRM, EU administrative law literature noticed how composite decision-making in the two systems sat awkwardly with the Union's dualistic system of judicial review.[18] The CJEU has always held that this system is based on a 'strict separation' between the jurisdictions of national and Union courts, whereby only the former are competent to review national decisions and only the latter are competent to review Union decisions. Composite administrative decision-making, in contrast, results in final decisions that cannot be adopted without the cumulative involvement of national and Union authorities.[19]

As we discuss below, the CJEU addressed the mismatch between dual judicial control and interdependent decision-making in *Berlusconi*, by claiming exclusive jurisdiction to review final Union-level decisions (of the ECB and SRB) *and* to review the legality of national (NCA and NRA) measures to initiate procedures, preparatory acts, or non-binding proposals that precede such

[13] Alessandro Cuomo, 'Unus Pro Omnibus, Omnes Pro Uno: The Single Supervisory Mechanism as a Unitary Multilevel Administration' (2022) 72(3) Rivista Trimestrale di Diritto Pubblico 707, 727.

[14] Filippo Annunziata and Mariateresa Maggiolino, 'The Single Supervisory Mechanism and the European Framework for the Enforcement of Competition Law: A Comparison between Two Models for Economic Governance in the EU' (2023) 24 Journal of Banking Regulation 264, 269–70.

[15] Pierre Schammo, 'Institutional Change in the Banking Union: The Case of the Single Supervisory Mechanism' (2021) Yearbook of European Law 265, 292 ff. See also the judgments in Cases T–122/15 *Landeskreditbank Baden-Württemberg v ECB*, ECLI:EU:T:2017:337 and C–450/17 P *Landeskreditbank Baden-Württemberg v ECB*, ECLI:EU:C:2019:372.

[16] See Judgment in Case T–330/19 *PBN Banka AS v European Central Bank*, ECLI:EU:T:2022:775, para 119.

[17] SSMR (n 11), art 6(3); and Regulation (EU) 468/2014 of the European Central Bank of 16 April 2014 establishing the framework for cooperation within the Single Supervisory Mechanism between the European Central Bank and National Competent Authorities and with national designated authorities (SSM Framework Regulation), arts 90–98.

[18] For the SSM, see Laura Wissink, Ton Duijkersloot, and Rob Widdershoven, 'Shifts in Competences between Member States and the EU in the New Supervisory System for Credit Institutions and Their Consequences for Judicial Protection' (2014) 10(5) Utrecht Law Review 92. For the SRM, see Jolien Timmerman, 'Guess Who? The SRB as the Accountable Actor in Legal Review Procedures' (2019) 1 Review of European Administrative Law 155.

[19] For an overview of how the CJEU has attempted to solve this mismatch, see Brito Bastos, *Judging Composite Decision-Making* (n 6).

decisions.[20] Yet, even after *Berlusconi*, serious doubts have remained as to how to ensure judicial protection in the face of the complexity of the administrative procedures in the SSM and SRM.[21]

III *Berlusconi*—the questions left unsettled

In the landmark judgment in *Berlusconi*, the CJEU laid down the basic rules for the judicial review of composite procedures in the case of EU decisional dominance, ie where the Union administration exercises the decisive powers.[22] However, for the present purposes, the judgment in *Berlusconi* will serve to illustrate not what the CJEU clarified but rather what it left unsettled—namely the understanding of a preparatory act, and thus the scope of a composite procedure at large.

The judgment concerned the Italian business magnate and politician Silvio Berlusconi, who had been denied an authorization for a qualified holding of the Italian bank Banca Mediolanum. A qualified holding is an ownership of more than 10% of the shares of the undertaking. Since this allows the holder to have a significant influence over a credit institution, the acquisition of a qualified holding is subject to an authorization procedure.[23] The NCA first assesses whether the acquisition leading to a qualified holding meets a set of requirements, including that of the acquirer's good repute, and forwards this assessment to the ECB together with a proposal to adopt the final decision authorizing or opposing the acquisition. According to the assessment of the Italian NCA, namely the Bank of Italy, Berlusconi did not meet the good-repute prerequisite of a good reputation, which led it to propose that the ECB refuse to issue the authorization (hereinafter 'the Proposal'). The ECB followed the proposal and adopted a final decision refusing the authorization of the acquisition of the qualified holding (hereinafter 'the ECB decision'). Berlusconi sought

[20] *Berlusconi* (n 8); Judgment in Case C-414/18 *Iccrea Banca*, ECLI:EU:C:2019:1036.

[21] In the SSM, see Filipe Brito Bastos, 'Judicial Review of Composite Administrative Procedures in the Single Supervisory Mechanism: Berlusconi' (2019) 56 Common Market Law Review 1355; Marta Simoncini, 'Challenges of Justice in the European Banking Union: Administrative Integration and Mismatches in Jurisdiction' (2021) 40 Yearbook of European Law 310; and Laura Wissink, *Effective Legal Protection in Banking Supervision* (Europa Law Publishing 2021). In the SRM, see Menelaos Markakis, 'Composite Procedures and Judicial Review in the Single Resolution Mechanism: Iccrea Banca' (2021) 13 Review of European Administrative Law 109.

[22] For a more developed account of the novelty brought by the judgement in *Berlusconi*, see Brito Bastos, *Judging Composite Decision-Making* (n 6) 189 ff; Mariolina Eliantonio, 'Access to Justice in Composite Procedures for the Implementation of EU Law: The Story So Far' (28 February 2023) 16. Available at SSRN: https://ssrn.com/abstract = 4373333.

[23] SSMR (n 11), art 15; and SSM Framework Regulation (n 17), arts 85–87.

the annulment of the ECB decision in the General Court.[24] He also sought the annulment of a number of preceding acts of the Bank of Italy, including the Proposal, in the Italian courts, which subsequently submitted a reference for a preliminary ruling to the CJEU. The CJEU was asked to determine, inter alia, whether the Italian courts or the CJEU had jurisdiction to review the challenged acts of the Bank of Italy.

In its judgment, the CJEU deemed that, in the decision-making procedure at hand, the NCA adopts acts that are preparatory to a final decision of the ECB. The exclusive decision-making power in this procedure is vested in the ECB,[25] and it was not bound by the preparatory acts of the Bank of Italy, including the Proposal.[26] In such situations of EU decisional dominance, Article 263 TFEU, in light of the principle of sincere cooperation, precludes the national court from reviewing the national preparatory acts.[27] The final EU act—in this case, the ECB decision—is the only reviewable act in the procedure, and its review falls under the CJEU's exclusive jurisdiction.[28] The national courts must refrain from reviewing the national preparatory acts, to avoid divergent assessments in one and the same procedure and avoid compromising the exclusive jurisdiction of the CJEU.[29]

Iccrea Banca extended the same line of reasoning from the SSM to the SRM.[30] As in *Berlusconi*, the CJEU claimed exclusive jurisdiction to review the entirety of administrative procedures—in this case, leading to SRB decisions determining the amount of banks' *ex ante* contributions—including acts of operational support, such as collection and sharing of data, that are adopted by NRAs at a preparatory stage.

Notwithstanding the enhancement of judicial protection in composite decision-making, the judgments in *Berlusconi* and *Iccrea Banca* leave open a number of questions which complicate the application of the rules that they pronounced. In *Berlusconi* and *Iccrea Banca*, the CJEU undertook to review not only the EU concluding act of the composite administrative procedure but also, incidentally, the respective decisions of the Bank of Italy, which it saw as national preparatory acts in the composite administrative procedure. What remains uncertain, however, is the scope of the procedure itself. How can one tell

[24] Leading to the judgment in Case T–913/16 *Finanziaria d'investimento Fininvest SpA (Fininvest) and Silvio Berlusconi v European Central Bank*, ECLI:EU:T:2022:279.
[25] *Berlusconi* (n 8), paras 44 and 55.
[26] ibid, para 55.
[27] ibid, para 47.
[28] ibid, para 49.
[29] ibid, paras 50 and 57.
[30] *Iccrea Banca* (n 20). For an extended analysis, see Markakis (n 21).

whether a national measure constitutes a preparatory act within a composite administrative procedure, and can therefore be reviewed only by the CJEU as part of the review of the final EU decision, or whether a national measure has been taken within a related, but purely national, administrative procedure, and can therefore be reviewed only by the national courts?

Having a clear answer to these questions is important both from a conceptual and a practical perspective. Conceptually, determining what acts a composite administrative procedure is composed of means nothing less than defining the phenomenon itself. Practically, the answer is important for two reasons. First, it is crucial to determine the scope of the CJEU's jurisdiction in reviewing composite administrative procedures. Second, whether the rule pronounced in *Berlusconi* applies to a particular unlawful national act might be crucial in deciding on the validity of the final decision taken on the EU level. In the words of Advocate General Campos Sánchez-Bordona, such a national preparatory act might 'contaminate the entire procedure',[31] thereby putting in question the legality of the final EU decision.[32]

IV The length and width of composite administrative procedures

One way to approach the question of preparatory acts in a composite procedure is through a metaphorical length and width of the procedure. The length of a composite procedure concerns the question, how far back in the procedural sequence does the composite procedure stretch? The width of a composite procedure, by contrast, requires determining whether a measure adjacent to the procedural sequence should also be considered as part of it.

1 The length—*Satabank*

The challenge of determining the length of a composite procedure is exemplified by the judgment in *Satabank*, which concerned the procedure for the withdrawal of authorization of a failing credit institution.[33] Important to note, in this judgment, is that the CJEU found this procedure to be a composite

[31] Opinion of AG Campos Sánchez-Bordona in *Berlusconi* (n 4), para 112.
[32] For the situations in which this is permitted, see Brito Bastos, *Judging Composite Decision-Making* (n 6) 201 ff.
[33] Judgment in Case T-72/20 *Satabank v ECB*, ECLI:EU:T:2023:149.

procedure.[34] Indeed, *Satabank* was the first ruling expressly distinguishing a concept of composite administrative procedures. Although the importance of this development cannot be overstated, *Satabank* highlights another important aspect as to the length of a composite procedure.

Satabank was a credit institution under Maltese law, supervised by the Malta Financial Services Authority (MFSA), acting as the NCA under the SSMR. Upon suspicion of money laundering, the Maltese authorities launched an investigation into Satabank, and the MFSA issued a decision requiring Satabank to discontinue its activity, freeze its accounts, and begin returning the funds to the owners as controls were carried out. The MFSA also appointed a so-called competent person to take charge of Satabank's assets and assume control over its business (the NCA decision).

Foreseeing that the ECB would eventually withdraw its authorization as a credit institution, Satabank requested access to the file concerning it, to be able to exercise its rights of defence. The ECB refused, as Satabank was not subject to any supervisory procedure by the ECB and, therefore, the access was not justified (the 'ECB refusal'). The Maltese authorities and not the ECB had ongoing proceedings concerning Satabank. Eventually, the NCA submitted to the ECB a draft decision proposing to withdraw the authorization according to the procedure set out in the SSMR (the 'NCA proposal'). Satabank again requested, from the ECB, access to the file concerning it, which this time the ECB granted. The ECB eventually withdrew its authorization. Satabank challenged the ECB refusal decision, by which it was initially denied access to the file, in the General Court.

The General Court confirmed the conclusion of the ECB that Satabank could not rely on its rights of defence in a supervisory procedure, and thus its right of access to the file, since no supervisory procedure by the ECB was in place at the time of the ECB refusal. The right of access to the file exists only in a direct supervisory procedure, which had not begun at the time of the first request. Eventually, the General Court concluded that access to the file had to be granted, based on general provisions on public access to documents, and thus annulled the ECB refusal decision.

The main interest of the present inquiry, however, is the General Court's conclusion that the newly recognized composite procedure had not begun at the time of the ECB rejection. The General Court had to decide whether the procedure for withdrawal of authorization had already begun at the time when Satabank requested access to the file for the first time—that is, when

[34] ibid, para 70.

the case was still entirely in the hands of the NCA. This meant deciding whether the NCA decision by which it ordered Satabank to discontinue activity had been initiated and was part of the composite administrative procedure.

This raises the broader question of the length of a composite procedure. A composite procedure, at its core, is a sequence of measures taken by authorities on the EU and national levels. The final measure in this sequence is usually not difficult to identify and is most likely the last one which is addressed to the person concerned. The beginning of the composite procedure is a lot more ambiguous. How far back in the sequence of measures does the composite procedure span?

The General Court did not explicitly reflect on the length of a composite procedure. However, the judgment suggests a possible answer to these questions. The General Court decided that the NCA decision did not form part of what it conceived as a composite procedure. It reasoned that, 'it is not apparent from Article 14(5) of the SSMR that the procedure for withdrawal of authorisation before the ECB is initiated as a result of the adoption by a national competent authority of a decision ordering a credit institution to discontinue any activity'.[35] Thus, the NCA decision did not have 'the effect of opening, on that date, the procedure for the withdrawal' of the authorization of Satabank;[36] it was, rather, the MFSA draft decision to withdraw the authorization of Satabank.

This conclusion becomes a lot less apparent when one looks further into how the procedure in *Satabank* had been set up. The withdrawal of authorization of a credit institution can be decided by the ECB on its own initiative or upon a proposal to do so from the respective NCA. In the case of Satabank, the Maltese NCA had proposed to the ECB a draft decision on the withdrawal, arising from the requirements of its national law, and the ECB had then taken 'a decision on the proposed withdrawal taking full account of the justification for withdrawal put forward by the NCA.'[37] However, one may look beyond the set-up of the SSMR. The proposal of the NCA was preceded by a procedure on a national level, which was set in national—namely Maltese—law. The reasoning of the General Court in *Satabank* excluded this national administrative activity from the scope of the composite procedure. Therefore, the answer of the General Court to the question of the span of a composite procedure is

[35] ibid, para 74.
[36] ibid.
[37] SSMR (n 11), art 14(5).

that it stretches only as far back in the procedural sequence as is determined in the governing EU legislation.

However, there are good reasons to doubt whether the General Court in *Satabank* intended to speak about the span of composite administrative procedures in general. Although, in *Satabank*, the General Court first mentioned the concept of a composite procedure when deciding if the NCA decision was already a part of it, the General Court did not appear to speak of composite procedures in general. The argumentation analysed previously was presented after the General Court had found that the previous case law on composite procedures did not provide a resolution to the case, as the *Berlusconi* judgment '[did] not concern the question of which stage of the composite administrative procedure gives rise to the right of access to the file of credit institutions before the ECB'.[38] It was after this conclusion that it turned specifically to Article 14(5) of the SSMR.

This suggests that the CJEU has most likely not yet spoken its last word on the length of a composite procedure. As composite procedures become increasingly prevalent in the EU legal order, it will very likely have to return to this question and establish a clear stance on it. Given the abundance of composite procedures in the EBU and the intensive litigation that it gives rise to, a clarification will likely, again, originate from this area.

2 The width—*Pilatus*

Pilatus offered the CJEU an opportunity to illustrate the width of composite administrative procedures. Pilatus Bank was a Maltese credit institution. The bank's ultimate owner, Ali Sadr, indirectly held 100% of capital and voting rights. In 2018, Sadr was arrested in the United States and charged with illegally funnelling $115 million, originally intended to finance a project in Venezuela, for Iranian citizens and firms and, allegedly, for Pilatus Bank itself.

The arrest had immediate consequences in the bank's activities, with a sudden and large increase in withdrawal requests, worth the equivalent of 40% of deposits. The MFSA immediately took action and adopted a series of directives. Besides imposing a moratorium on withdrawals by shareholders and members of the board of directors, the MFSA determined the removal of Sadr from the role of director, and the suspension of his voting rights and role as legal and judicial representative. An additional directive appointed a

[38] *Satabank* (n 33), para 73.

competent person with the role of exercising the main powers of the bank's governing bodies. Lastly, the MFSA submitted a proposal to the ECB to withdraw Pilatus Bank's authorization to operate as a credit institution. The ECB agreed with the MFSA and decided to revoke said authorization.

Pilatus challenged the ECB decision before the General Court, arguing, in essence, that the ECB had merely implemented the MFSA's allegedly illegal directives.[39] However, the General Court refused to apply the same reasoning as in *Berlusconi*. It held that the directives did not qualify as initiating acts, preparatory acts, or proposals in the administrative procedure leading to the ECB decision. Even though it conceded that the 'directives at issue concern the same situation', the General Court found that they constituted 'other decisions' which were not adopted pursuant to the ECB's competences to withdraw authorizations under Article 4(1)(a) of the SSMR.[40] Put differently, because they were not provided for in the SSMR, and because they constituted self-standing decisions made exclusively under national law, the MFSA directives were beyond the competence or control of the ECB, and were therefore to be reviewed by national courts, and not by the CJEU when reviewing the final ECB decision.[41]

Pilatus appealed to the Court of Justice. The Court ultimately ruled that the actions were inadmissible because of the implications of the MFSA's directives for the lawfulness of Pilatus Bank's legal representation in the General Court.[42] However, the Advocate General had proposed an altogether different view.[43] Because the MFSA's directives affected the ability of Pilatus Bank to exercise the rights of the defence in the administrative procedure, and because the ECB had the obligation to ensure respect for said rights, the directives had to be reviewed, along with the ECB's decision, before the EU courts.[44] The Advocate General further noted that the illegality of the MFSA's directives could also affect the legality of its proposal for the ECB to revoke Pilatus Bank's authorization. If the CJEU has exclusive jurisdiction to review the final ECB decision and its preceding NCA proposal, then such a review should extend to national measures taken to pave the way for the proposal itself, and which may render it illegal.[45] In essence, because the MFSA directives were preparatory acts

[39] Judgment in Case T-27/19 *Pilatus Bank plc v European Central Bank*, ECLI:EU:T:2022:46.
[40] ibid, paras 46–47.
[41] ibid, paras 242–50.
[42] Judgments in Case C-750/21 P *Pilatus Bank plc v European Central Bank*, ECLI:EU:C:2024:124 and Case C-256/22 P *Pilatus Bank plc v European Central Bank*, ECLI:EU:C:2024:125.
[43] Cases C-750/21 P and C-256/22 P *Pilatus Bank plc v European Central Bank*, ECLI:EU:C:2023:431, Opinion of AG Kokott.
[44] ibid, para 68.
[45] ibid, paras 71–72.

leading to the MFSA's proposal to the ECB, they had to be taken as national preparatory acts within the meaning of the *Berlusconi* case law.[46]

Knowing whether, so to say, 'preparatory acts to national preparatory acts' come under the scope of *Berlusconi* review is an important question. Had it examined the merits of the *Pilatus* case, the Court of Justice would have provided some clues. In our view, such clues would have been all the more important because the General Court's stance on the review of the MFSA's directives is difficult to reconcile with past case law on the judicial review of some composite administrative procedures.

Indeed, the MFSA's directives fulfilled the purpose of interim measures. They were adopted in connection with the MFSA's proposal for the ECB to withdraw Pilatus Bank's authorization. The directives aimed to contain the risks to financial stability caused by the reputational damage the bank had suffered following Ali Sadr's arrest and criminal charges, while the full administrative procedure was still pending and until the ECB took the final decision. The directives, in essence, meant to support and ensure the effectiveness of the ECB's decision if it were to decide in favour of withdrawing the licence.

All these characteristics make national precautionary interim measures such as those adopted by the MFSA remarkably similar to another kind of national measures—safeguard measures. In safeguard-clause administrative procedures, national authorities adopt measures that temporarily derogate from EU law requirements (for example, provisional bans of medicines authorized under EU law, due to new public health concerns). The measures are subsequently confirmed, amended, or rejected by a final decision of the European Commission. In such administrative procedures, there is no contradiction between characterizing a national measure as the final decision in a national administrative procedure *and* as a non-binding preparatory act in a composite decision-making process. The national interim measure has, so to say, a double life.[47] It constitutes a final administrative decision within the national administrative system, in the sense that it produces binding legal effects on affected parties without the need for an additional subsequent decision—for the duration of the safeguard-clause procedure, that is. The national safeguard measure, however, is also a non-binding preparatory act in the sense that the Union authority, in resolving the case in a definitive manner, is entirely free to make its own assessment and overturn the national measure.[48] The national

[46] ibid, para 75.
[47] Brito Bastos, *Judging Composite Decision-Making* (n 6) 65.
[48] See Case C-120/14 P *Klein*, ECLI:EU:C:2015:252, paras 64 and 76.

measure is adopted in a single administrative procedure which, as the CJEU puts it, 'takes place partly at national level and partly at European Union level', ie a composite administrative procedure.[49]

The comparison between measures such as those adopted by the MFSA and national safeguard measures is particularly apt. It is true that, unlike national safeguard measures, decisions such as those adopted by the MFSA are not intended to introduce a temporary derogation from EU law. It is also true that national authorities' safeguard measures initiate an administrative procedure, while decisions such as those adopted by the MFSA are adopted after the administrative procedure has been initiated, and in order to support the effectiveness of subsequent steps (such as the final ECB decision to withdraw the authorization). However, they have something fundamental in common. In both instances, the national measure, which already entails binding legal effects in the domestic legal system, determines the legal position of affected parties within the national procedural stage, and can also have an impact within the EU procedural stage, in particular if the Union authority—though not bound to do so—chooses to follow the national authority's stance. In the specific case of the concrete measures that the MFSA took, their binding legal effects had a lasting impact in the administrative procedure. Indeed, under Article 22 of the SSMR, it falls to the ECB to ensure respect for the rights of the defence before taking final supervisory decisions. In the context of the case, the MFSA's measures impeded the applicant from accessing resources and information held in the bank's premises and IT systems. Such access would have facilitated Pilatus Bank's exercise of the right to be heard in the administrative procedure that led to the withdrawal of its authorization by the ECB.

The CJEU's case law provides important guidance on how to ensure judicial review of composite administrative procedures emerging from safeguard clauses.[50] Given that the national measures are final administrative decisions within the national administrative system, they can be judicially challenged, as final decisions, before national courts.[51] However, the national safeguard measures can be reviewed by the CJEU as part of a judicial challenge against a final Union-level decision that confirms them—precisely as if they had been national preparatory acts all along.[52] It is unclear to us why the same line of

[49] See Case T-465/11 *Globula a.s. v European Commission*, ECLI:EU:T:2013:406, para 32.

[50] See Brito Bastos, *Judging Composite Decision-Making* (n 6) 174 and 199–200.

[51] See, eg Joined Cases C-58/10 to C-68/10 *Monsanto SAS v Ministre de l'Agriculture et de la Pêche*, ECLI:EU:C:2011:553, para 79.

[52] See, eg Case T-168/16 *Grizzly Tools GmbH & Co KG v European Commission*, ECLI:EU:T:2018:246.

reasoning could not have applied to the MFSA's directives or any other measures taken by an NCA that entail binding legal effects domestically and contribute, condition, or support the decision-making stage at Union level. The same reasoning could apply whenever the NCA adopts binding measures—such as interim measures, or investigatory orders for private parties to provide certain information—that are instrumental to the preparatory work that they conduct before the ECB takes final decisions. This includes binding national measures taken to support the non-binding preparatory acts that NCAs submit to the ECB under the common procedures—such as proposals for withdrawal, for granting authorizations, or (not) to oppose a qualifying holding—or when the ECB requires NCAs' assistance before taking supervisory decisions over significant credit institutions.

V The definition of 'preparatory act' and the problem of autonomy

The difficulty of determining which measures should be conceived as a preparatory act is not merely an absence of drawing a clear line between where the composite administrative procedure starts and unrelated prior national administrative activity ends. The root of the problem is of a conceptual and, even more so, a constitutional nature.

A preparatory act in EU law is not clearly defined and conceptually developed. As with the area of EU administrative law at large, the concept has been crafted largely by the CJEU, which has primarily been concerned with the resolution of the specific case before it, leaving the conceptual work in the background. Furthermore, there have been very few scholarly contributions on the matter. However, establishing what a 'preparatory act' can mean, in the Banking Union or in general, may become easier once we consider what the *preparation of a decision* can consist of within an administrative procedure.

Administrative procedures are, at their core, predefined sequences of measures leading to administrative decisions.[53] Some measures are meant to establish the points of fact and law that will form the basis for the final decision and, in that sense, are preparatory acts. Of those measures, some will constitute legal acts—ie actions intended to produce legal effects—such as advisory

[53] See Giacinto della Cananea, *Due Process of Law beyond the State: Requirements of Administrative Procedure* (OUP 2016) 22; and Javier Barnes, 'Administrative Procedure' in Peter Cane and others (eds), *The Oxford Handbook of Comparative Administrative Law* (OUP 2020).

bodies' opinions, the designation of the case worker, or notifications requiring a person to provide certain information or inviting a person to submit observations to exercise the right to be heard. Other preparatory measures are merely factual conduct and do not intend to produce legal effects, such as the simple forwarding of information to a specific authority. What all these rather diverse acts have in common is that they are merely instrumental for a specific final decision and lack any autonomous function beyond the administrative procedure leading to it.[54] CJEU case law implies this same idea when it defines the tests for a Union decision to be judicially reviewable. Besides the final decision itself, which manifests the administration's definitive will on a case, decision-making processes may include 'special procedures' or subprocedures that define part of the final decision—these are *binding* preparatory acts. However, some preparatory acts are *non-binding* and constitute purely provisional measures that simply 'pave the way' for the final decision to be made.[55]

Berlusconi offered the CJEU the chance to clarify that, whereas binding national preparatory acts taken in composite administrative procedures must be reviewed by national courts alone, just as if they were final administrative decisions, non-binding national preparatory acts can only be reviewed by the CJEU, as part of the review of final Union decisions.[56] The meaning of 'non-binding national preparatory act' thus circumscribes the scope of the *Berlusconi* case law. In light of the above, if we take 'non-binding national preparatory act' to mean a measure by a national authority that is merely instrumental and paves the way for a final EU-level decision, without obliging the Union administration to decide in accordance with that measure, then one can identify several categories of non-binding national preparatory acts. When taken together, the CJEU's case law at present, the SSMR, and the SRMR suggest that one may distinguish between three such categories.

The first category of national preparatory acts concerns those that are specifically provided for in the Banking Union's legislative framework. For instance, Articles 14 and 15 SSMR clearly refer to NCAs' proposals for ECB final decisions granting or revoking bank licences or authorizing the acquisition of qualifying holdings. The SSM Framework Regulation, when fleshing out the

[54] This notion of preparatory act as instrumental is common to, for instance, Spanish law (García de Enterría and Tomás-Ramón Hernández, *Curso de Derecho Administrativo*, I (16th edn, Civitas 2013) 615–17); Portuguese law (Mário Aroso de Almeida, *Teoria Geral do Direito Administrativo* (7th edn, Almedina 2021)); French law (René Chapus, *Droit Du Contentieux Administratif* (13th edn, Montchrestien 2008) 600–01); and Latvian law (Jautrīte Briede, Edvīns Danovskis, and Anita Kovaļevska, *Administratīvā Procesa Tiesības* (Latvijas Vēstnesis 2003) 129).

[55] Judgment in Case C–60/81 *IBM v Commission*, ECLI:EU:C:1981:264, paras 10–12; and Judgment in Case T–404/08 *Fluorsid and Minmet v Commission*, ECLI:EU:T:2013:321, para 133.

[56] *Berlusconi* (n 8), paras 44–46.

more detailed aspects of common procedures, also alludes to national preparatory acts, such as, for example, the forwarding of information to the ECB as to the deadline within which it must take the final decision in a procedure to grant a bank licence (Article 73(2)). Article 7(4)(b) SRMR provides that NRAs may send requests for the SRB to decide to exercise direct resolution powers in respect of a specific less significant credit institution. In *Iccrea*, the CJEU held that the NRA's role in gathering and forwarding data to the SRB, for it to decide the contributions that banks must pay into the Single Resolution Fund, amounted to the adoption of preparatory acts that came under the scope of the *Berlusconi* case law.[57] In contrast, the two judgments analysed above, *Satabank* and *Pilatus*, implied that the CJEU takes a rather restrictive view of what counts as a national preparatory act. In both judgments, the test was whether the NCAs' measures were foreseen as steps in the SSMR's composite administrative procedures. In *Satabank* the General Court explicitly reasoned that 'it is *not apparent from Article 14(5) of the SSMR* that the procedure for withdrawal of authorisation before the ECB is initiated as a result' of the NCA measure in question.[58] Even more explicitly in *Pilatus Bank*, the General Court reasoned that, 'although the MFSA's directives at issue concern the same situation, they are other decisions which were not adopted pursuant to Article 4(1)(a) of Regulation No 1024/2013'.[59]

However, preparatory acts, in the sense of measures instrumental to build the legal and factual basis of an administrative procedure's final decision, can take countless forms. The national measures alluded to in the SSMR and SRMR are necessarily only a fraction of the preparatory acts that NCAs and NRAs must adopt. To give an example, the SSMR and the SSM Framework Regulation foresee only one national preparatory act in the common procedure leading to the withdrawal of a credit institution's authorization—the NCA's proposal for the ECB to withdraw the authorization (Article 14(5) SSMR and Article 80 SSM Framework Regulation). Neither regulation foresees any of the steps that the NCA may have to take before even concluding that proposing withdrawal is justified—like the decision to designate a rapporteur for the proposal, requests for expert opinions from different services within the NCA, the gathering of evidence that the credit institution fails to comply with regulatory standards, or requests for information from the credit institution, to name just a few. For this reason, many national preparatory acts needed in the national stages of

[57] *Iccrea Banca* (n 20), paras 38–42. See also Judgment in Joined Cases T-351/18 and T-584/18 *Urselhosprom and Versobank*, ECLI:EU:T:2021:669, para 223.
[58] *Satabank* (n 33), para 74. Emphasis added.
[59] *Pilatus Bank* (n 39), para 47.

composite administrative procedures are taken pursuant to national administrative law provisions, whenever the SSMR, the SSM Framework Regulation, and SRMR are silent. Indeed, as with most composite administrative procedures, SSM and SRM composite procedures are legislated as incomplete administrative procedures.[60] They are instituted by Union legislation which only governs some aspects of the decision-making process—predominantly those aspects that specifically concern the interactions between the two levels of administration—and leaves all remaining aspects of the procedural stages taking place at national level for national administrative laws.

Given such heavy reliance on national administrative procedural rules, one could expect that the answer as to what constitutes a national preparatory act in a composite procedure, as opposed to a measure taken within a purely national administrative procedure, should be found in national laws. However, even with regard to preparatory acts provided for only in national legislation, a distinction should be made. The second and third categories of national preparatory acts distinguish between those instances where NCAs and NRAs take preparatory acts by instruction of the ECB or SRB and those instances where NCAs and NRAs take preparatory acts by their own initiative.

The second category of preparatory acts we identify consists of those adopted in the exercise of a competence established under national law, in support of a final Union-level decision, by request of the ECB or SRB. In our view, *any* such act must count as a preparatory act for the purposes of *Berlusconi* and CJEU review of national procedural stages. Given that NCAs and NRAs must comply with ECB and SRB instructions, the measures they take under national law are treated by the ECB and SRB themselves as acts they need to support a final decision. This, we argue, results from Articles 4(1), 6(3), and 9(1) of the SSMR. In the SRM, the Court took the view that NRAs' operational support to the SRB, consisting of collecting data to assist the SRB in calculating *ex ante* contributions of credit institutions into the Single Resolution Fund, 'following the SRB's direction', constituted national preparatory acts in the sense of *Berlusconi*.[61] In the same logic, one should regard as preparatory acts the draft resolution plans for credit institutions that the SRB requires NRAs to draw up.[62]

[60] See Daria de Pretis, 'Procedimenti amministrativi nazionali e procedimenti amministrativi europei' in Giandomenico Falcon (ed), *Il procedimento amministrativo nei diritti europei e nel diritto comunitario* (CEDAM 2008) 68.

[61] Opinion of AG Campos Sánchez-Bordona in Berlusconi (n 4), para 40, supported by the Court in *Iccrea* (n 20), para 47.

[62] SRMR (n 11), art 8.

The third category consists of national measures which, like the second category, are taken under national law provisions but, in contrast, are *not* requested by the ECB or SRB. Instead, the measures in question are adopted at the initiative of the national authorities with the aim of contributing, in a more or less direct manner, to preparing the final Union decision. The particular challenge that this third category of preparatory acts raises is that they have no legal basis in Union legislation, be it directly—as acts that the SSMR and SRMR explicitly govern as steps in a composite administrative procedure, as NCA proposals for ECB decisions—or even indirectly, as national acts that are taken if the ECB and SRB consider them as useful for preparing a final decision. Because they have no legal basis in Union legislation, the acts spontaneously taken by NCAs and NRAs are governed and foreseen exclusively in national law. Hence, in principle, only national law can provide the answer as to whether a given NCA or NRA act qualifies as a preparatory act within an administrative procedure or as something else.

However, if national law determines what counts as a preparatory act in a composite administrative procedure, then national law determines whether the *Berlusconi* case law applies and, accordingly, whether the CJEU's jurisdiction extends to the national procedural stage. This is difficult to reconcile with the principles of the autonomy and uniformity of the EU legal order, and the tenet according to which the application of EU law rules—such as those concerning the CJEU's jurisdiction—cannot be made dependent upon national law. It remains unclear how the lack of a Union law definition of 'national preparatory act' can be squared with the risk that national law conceptions condition the ability of the CJEU to ensure judicial review and offer effective judicial protection under the *Berlusconi* case law.

VI Conclusion: fine-tuning judicial review in and with the Banking Union

Ever since it was established, the Banking Union has birthed some of the most significant recent innovations in EU administrative law. *Berlusconi* is only comparable in historical significance to the *Borelli* judgment of the early 1990s, when the CJEU first ruled that composite decision-making required important adaptations to the normally strict division between judicial review by national and Union courts.

Even with the clarifications in the *Berlusconi* judgment, the CJEU's case law ever since has shown that challenges originating in the Banking Union's composite administrative procedures are far from resolved. *Satabank* and *Pilatus Bank* illustrate well how apparently simple questions can add further complexity to the boundaries of the CJEU's judicial review. We noted that the two judgments suggest the need to circumscribe the notion of 'national preparatory act' from self-standing national administrative measures that are not taken within the national preparatory stage of a composite administrative procedure—be they measures taken in national administrative procedure *prior* to said national procedural stage (the question of 'length' of the procedure, illustrated in *Satabank*) or measures taken *in parallel* to it (the question of 'width', illustrated in *Pilatus*). At present, the CJEU has provided a lot less clarity as to what constitutes a 'national preparatory act', after all, than as to what does not.

Inevitably, mounting litigation will lead the CJEU to shed further light on that question and, consequently, on how judicial review of the Banking Union's composite administrative procedures should be carried out in doing so, continuing the task started in *Borelli* and *Berlusconi* and further refining the delimitation of jurisdictions between the CJEU and national courts. As has been the case for 10 years now, new CJEU rulings will be followed closely by EU administrative lawyers. The Banking Union is bound to remain one of the most important sources of much-needed answers on the constitutional and legal framework of composite procedures, whatever the policy sectors in which they may be found.

14

The Cooperation between European and National Authorities in the Single Resolution Mechanism

Edoardo Rulli[*]

I Introduction

The Banking Union was set up in response to the 2008/09 financial crisis, notably after this crisis had spillovers which exacerbated the risks stemming from the sovereign debt—banks nexus (2011/12). When the sovereign debt of certain Member States was at risk of distress, Union policymakers gathered political support to work towards deeper integration of the banking systems of the euro area, with the possibility for non-euro-area Member States to join the cooperation mechanism.[1] Following the Council's 2012 road map,[2] the Union proposed to set up three 'mechanisms', also known as the pillars of the Banking Union. These are the Single Supervisory Mechanism (SSM), established in 2013,[3] the Single Resolution Mechanism (SRM), established in 2014,[4] and a system for the insurance of deposits, which has not seen the light of day so far.[5]

* Views are personal and do not necessarily reflect those of the staff who work in the author's organization. The author would like to thank Annagiulia de Meis, Diane Fromage, Paola Lucantoni, and Paul Weismann for the useful comments.

1 'Council agrees general approach on Single Resolution Mechanism', 18 December 2012 http://www.consilium.europa.eu/uedocs/cms_data/docs/pressdata/en/ecofin/140190.pdf, accessed 7 May 2026.

2 Herman Van Rompuy, 'Towards a Genuine Economic and Monetary Union' (Brussels, 5 December 2012), https://www.consilium.europa.eu/media/23818/134069.pdf, accessed 7 May 2026.

3 Council Regulation (EU) 1024/2013 of 15 October 2013 conferring specific tasks on the European Central Bank concerning policies relating to the prudential supervision of credit institutions [2013] OJ L287/63.

4 Regulation (EU) 806/2014 of the European Parliament and of the Council of 15 July 2014 establishing uniform rules and a uniform procedure for the resolution of credit institutions and certain investment firms in the framework of a Single Resolution Mechanism and a Single Resolution Fund and amending Regulation (EU) No 1093/2010 [2014] OJ L225/1.

5 Daniel Gros and Dirk Schoenmaker, 'European Deposit Insurance and Resolution in the Banking Union' (2014) 52(3) Journal of Common Market Studies 529.

Edoardo Rulli, *The Cooperation between European and National Authorities in the Single Resolution Mechanism* In: *EU Banking Union*. Edited by: Jonathan Bauerschmidt, Raffaele D'Ambrosio, Diane Fromage, Daniela Jaros, and Paul Weismann, Oxford University Press. © Oxford University Press 2026.
DOI: 10.1093/9780198949756.003.0015

II Banking Union: what is it for?

The Banking Union is one of the most successful, albeit still incomplete, frameworks for the cooperation between the Union level and the national level.[6] It is a *sui generis* form of enhanced cooperation within the Union:[7] a set of Member States agreed to centralize, at the European Union (EU) level, crucial bank supervisory functions.

The Banking Union works based on composite *mechanisms*, which allow a shared decision-making between the Union centralized level[8] and the national dimensions, thus responding to the logic of the shared competence enshrined in the internal market.[9] Today, 21 Member States are part of the Banking Union.[10]

The rationale of the Banking Union goes much further than simply reinforcing the cooperation among certain Member States' supervisory/resolution authorities. It is a tool to pave the way for a deeper integration of the internal market for banking services as a whole, in all 27 Member States. This idea is spelled out in recital 3 of the Single Supervisory Mechanism Regulation (SSMR), where the Banking Union comes in as the ram's head of the internal market for banking. According to this recital, this is something that is, in fact, 'essential in order to foster economic growth in the Union and adequate funding of the real economy'. The idea is mirrored in recital 1 of the SSMR.

This shows the dual nature of the Banking Union: (i) a *mechanism* allowing cooperation; and (ii) a *token* of what a more integrated internal market for banking would look like, once the geographical scope of application of the

[6] Iain Hardie and David Howarth, 'Die Krise but not La Crise? The Financial Crisis and the Transformation of German and French Banking Systems' (2009) 47(5) Journal of Common Market Studies 1017; Dermot Hodson, 'The Eurozone in 2012: "Whatever It Takes" to Preserve the Euro?' (2013) 51(2) Journal of Common Market Studies 183; David Howarth and Lucia Quaglia, 'Banking Union as Holy Grail: Rebuilding the Single Market in Financial Services, Stabilizing Europe's Banks and "Completing" Economic and Monetary Union' (2013) 51(2) Journal of Common Market Studies 103.

[7] At the moment, the Banking Union comprises 21 out of 27 EU Member States.

[8] On the ECB's dual role as a central bank and a prudential supervisor, see Diane Fromage, 'Assessing and (Re-)situating Today's ECB in the EU's Institutional Landscape' in Thomas Beukers, Diane Fromage, and Giorgio Monti (eds), *The New European Central Bank: Taking Stock and Looking Ahead* (OUP 2023). On the role of the ECB-SSM in supervision, see Paul Weismann, 'The Supervisory Board of the ECB: An Agency-Like Body to Stabilise the Banking Sector?' in Johannes Pollak and Peter Smolinski (eds), *The Role of EU Agencies in the Eurozone and Migration Crisis: Impact and Future Challenges* (Palgrave Macmillan 2021) 80.

[9] With reference to the division of competences between the central and the national level, see Raffaele D'Ambrosio, 'Single Supervisory Mechanism: Organs and Procedures' in Mario P Chiti and Vittorio Santoro (eds), *The Palgrave Handbook of European Banking Union Law* (Palgrave Macmillan 2019) 159.

[10] These are all the Member States which form part of the euro area, plus Bulgaria.

Banking Union coincides with that of the EU, ie once the *Banking Union* matches the *internal market*.

III Banking Union and Single Rulebook

The Banking Union is backed by the Single Rulebook, a term that identifies the pieces of legislation harmonizing the European banking laws. The Single Rulebook applies to all banks active in the internal market.

The relationship between the Single Rulebook and the Banking Union is crucial to recognizing the dual nature of the Banking Union as a cooperation mechanism for present times and a blueprint for the future of the internal market. The Banking Union fosters cooperation in banking matters across the EU, but, at the same time, it should not supersede the logic of the internal market. To ensure that this balance is kept, the Banking Union benefits from the existence of a common regulatory basis, the Single Rulebook, and rests on it. Recent case law has confirmed that the Banking Union is 'underpinned by a comprehensive and detailed single rulebook for financial services, valid for the internal market as a whole'.[11]

At the same time, the Banking Union finds its limits in the Single Rulebook, because the reinforced cooperation among the 21 Member States 'must not compromise the unity and integrity of the single market which remains one of the greatest achievements of European integration'.[12]

So, the Single Rulebook is the framework on which the Banking Union is being developed and the perimeter within which it is developing. The legal framework of the Banking Union builds on top of the Single Rulebook but cannot trespass upon it.[13]

The key elements of the Single Rulebook are the Capital Requirements Regulation (CRR) and the Capital Requirements Directive (CRD). In the context of crisis management and resolution, they are complemented by the

[11] Case T–510/17 *Del Valle Ruíz v European Commission and Single Resolution Board* [2022], ECLI:EU:T:2022:312, Judgment of the General Court (Third Chamber, Extended Composition). A more recent Court of Justice case, Case C–551/22 *Commission v Fundación Tatiana Pérez de Guzmán el Bueno et al* [2024], ECLI:EU:C:2024:520, the same interpretative approach on the relationship between the Banking Union project and the internal market project. See para 81, in which the Court notes that the SRM Regulation involves 'a balancing of various objectives and interests, relating to the safeguarding of the financial stability of the European Union and the integrity of the *internal market*, the taking into account of the budgetary sovereignty of the Member States and the protection of the interests of shareholders and creditors'.

[12] Communication from the Commission to the European Parliament and the Council, A Roadmap towards a Banking Union (2012) COM/2012/0510 final.

[13] Recital 11 of the SSMR.

Bank Recovery and Resolution Directive (BRRD) and the Deposit Guarantee Schemes Directive (DGSD). The Single Rulebook is further detailed by regulatory and implementing technical standards developed by the European Banking Authority.

The Banking Union's two pillars are set up against that legal background. Yet, each of the two has its own specific features. First and foremost, despite the common name 'mechanism', they rest on different legal bases. The legal basis of the SSM is Article 127(6) of the TFEU, which allows the EU to empower the European Central Bank (ECB) to exercise specific tasks in the field of prudential supervision of credit institutions,[14] in addition to monetary policy tasks.[15] The legal basis of the SRM is Article 114 of the TFEU, which is, more in general, the TFEU's provision allowing for the approximation of laws to progress towards a more integrated single market.[16]

In relation to bank crisis-management aspects, the framework was set up in 2014. While the BRRD defines the general Union rules and procedures for the resolution of banks, the central resolution mechanism of the Banking Union has its legal basis in the Single Resolution Mechanism Regulation (SRMR), which only applies in the Member States participating in the Banking Union.

The SRMR regulates two main elements of the framework. It sets up the central Union resolution authority—the Single Resolution Board (SRB)—and the Single Resolution Fund (SRF). In addition, it mirrors, and sometimes specifies, how the rules included in the BRRD need to apply in the Banking Union context. While the SSMR has never been amended,[17] the SRMR was revised in 2019.[18] Another important step in the development of the SRM is that, in

[14] The TFEU lists three sets of tasks for the ECB. The first is the monetary tasks in the context of the Eurosystem, laid down in art 127(2) TFEU; the second is the supervisory task conferred upon it by virtue of art 127(6) TFEU; and the third is the financial stability task within the Eurosystem under Article 127(5) TFEU. On this, see Christos V Gortsos, 'Definition and Evolution up to the Creation of the Banking Union', *The European Banking Regulation Handbook, Volume I: Theory of Banking Regulation, International Standards, Evolution and Institutional Aspects of European Banking Law* (Palgrave Macmillan 2023).

[15] For a historical perspective, see Emmanuel Mourlon-Druol, 'Banking Union in Historical Perspective: The Initiative of the European Commission in the 1960s–1970s' (2016) Journal of Common Market Studies 913. Specifically on the SSM, see the critical stance on the allocation of supervisory powers between the ECB and the NCAs within the ECB, in D'Ambrosio (n 9) 163.

[16] In general, see Rosa M Lastra, 'Banking Union and Single Market: Conflict or Companionship?' (2013) 36 Fordham International Law Journal 1190; Tomi Tuominen, 'The European Banking Union: A Shift in the Internal Market Paradigm?' (2017) 54(5) Common Market Law Review 1359. More recently, Gortsos (n 14) 201.

[17] Art 127(6) of the TFEU requires unanimity for the Council, after consulting the European Parliament and the ECB, to confer specific tasks upon the latter concerning policies relating to the prudential supervision of credit institutions.

[18] In the context of the revision of a wider 'Banking Package' comprising amendments to the CRR/CRD and to the BRRD.

November 2020, the Eurogroup agreed on the creation and early introduction of a common backstop to the SRF, in the form of the European Stability Mechanism (ESM).[19]

IV The Banking Union and its 'mechanisms'

The word 'mechanism' has a variety of meanings. In science, the term normally describes the ways in which a phenomenon takes place, often in different phases or because of multiple factors (for example, a reaction *mechanism* in chemistry). In engineering, the term refers to the parts that make up any machine or device, and to the way such parts connect to one another in such a way as to cause certain movements (for example, the transmission *mechanism*, in the case of engines).

In Union law, it is used only in the case of the pillars of the Banking Union (SSM and SRM), and in the case of the ESM. The latter is a purely intergovernmental body—as such, not part of the *aquis communitaire*[20]—which, following its latest reform, is linked to the Banking Union construct, as it can serve as the backstop for the SRF.[21]

The SSM, SRM, and ESM all have the word *mechanism* in their names. Like in chemistry or engineering, this indicates that those bodies have a commonality. They all put together different levels in the decision-making: the centralized European one and the national ones. This composite multilevel cooperation[22] is not without inefficiencies[23] and does not always exclude some of the actors involved from pursuing a national interest.[24]

The SRMR includes among its general principles the need for the SRM to act in the interest of the internal market (Article 6(2) of the SRMR) and, at the

[19] See the Eurogroup, 'Statement of the Eurogroup in inclusive format on the ESM reform and the early introduction of the backstop to the Single Resolution Fund' (30 November 2020). The Agreement Amending the Treaty Establishing the European Stability Mechanism is still pending ratification.

[20] It is, rather, an intergovernmental organization set up by euro-area countries to serve as a backstop (lender of last resort) to overcome financial crises of its members.

[21] The ESM is also mentioned in art 30(6) of the SRMR, which requires the SRB to endeavour to cooperate with the ESM, 'in particular in the extraordinary circumstances referred to in Article 27(9) and where such a facility has granted, or is likely to grant, direct or indirect financial assistance to entities established in a participating Member State'.

[22] Christina Eckes and Raffaele D'Ambrosio, 'Composite Administrative Procedures in the European Union' (2020) 20 ECB Legal Working Paper 4.

[23] Diane Fromage, Mariolina Eliantonio, and Kathryn Wright, 'Soft Law and Multilevel Cooperation as Sources of (New) Constitutional Challenges in EU Economic and Monetary Integration: Introduction to the Special Issue' (2022) 23 Journal of Banking Regulation 1.

[24] Tobias Tröger and Anastasia Kotovskaia, 'National Interests and Supranational Resolution in the European Banking Union' (2023) 34(5) European Business Law Review 781.

same time, the interests of the Member States where a bank operates (Article 6(3) of the SRMR). The first reason for this is that national interests are not necessarily in conflict with the Union interest. More importantly, even when potential conflicts arise, the Banking Union *mechanisms* are there to find an appropriate balance in pursuing their objectives. In the case of the SRM, those are the objectives listed in Article 14(2) of the SRMR, which need to 'be balanced, as appropriate, to the nature and circumstances of each case' (Article 14(3) of the SRMR). The second reason is that the SRM (similarly to the SSM) ensures that decisions across participating Member States of the Banking Union are effectively taken at central Union level, thus avoiding uncoordinated national actions, which were the norm until the Great Financial Crisis.

One can argue that, in the context of the Banking Union, Union law developed a specific meaning for the word *mechanism*. The term now illustrates the way a Union body allows for participative decision-making that can mediate different interests and perspectives to achieve a common objective.

V The Single Resolution Mechanism

Resolution planning is the main business of the SRB. The SRMR requires the SRB to draw up the resolution plans *annually*, which gives rise to a task that is, in the resolution domain, equivalent to the Supervisory Review and Evaluation Process (SREP)[25] of the supervisory world. The SRB draws up resolution plans with the national resolution authorities (NRAs). In practice, this takes place via established teams including SRB staff and NRAs' staff. These teams are named internal resolution teams (IRTs) and are regulated by Article 83, paragraphs 3 and 4 of the SRMR. The adjective internal means 'internal' to the SRM, as opposed to the lighter form of cooperation that SRB needs to set up with non-Banking Union NRAs—that is, the resolution college.[26] The latter is more of a forum to exchange information than a work platform.

A resolution plan is a document that describes the bank, its business, and the way it could be resolved should it be determined to be failing or likely to fail. Each bank has a resolution plan which includes: (i) the description of the preferred resolution strategy for that bank (bail-in, asset separation, sale of business, or bridge bank); and (ii) the necessary amount of own funds

[25] Arts 97–101 of the CRD.
[26] Art 88 of the BRRD.

and eligible liabilities (MREL) that a bank needs to hold at all times to be resolvable.

An integral part of the resolution planning is the resolvability assessment;[27] that is, an assessment of 'the extent to which institutions and groups are resolvable' without the assumption of any external assistance (public support, central bank liquidity, etc.).[28]

When it comes to set the MREL, the Board needs to adopt a separate decision from that endorsing the resolution plan. However, the resolution plan and the MREL determination are closely related, as the resolution strategy set out in the resolution plan can influence MREL level. If the resolution plan envisages that a bank will be resolved using the bail-in tool, then there is a need to have sufficient MREL to ensure that losses can be written down and that balance sheet solvency can be restored by converting liabilities into capital. This obvious economical link is acknowledged in the SRMR, which, in Article 12(4), requires the SRB to make any MREL determination 'in parallel with the development and maintenance of the resolution plans'. Once the MREL decision has been made, it is sent on to the NRA of the Member State in the territory of which the bank is located, and, in line with the division of tasks set out in Article 7(3) of the SRMR, that NRA notifies the decision to the bank and monitors its compliance.

In addition, the SRB has the task to adopt the resolution scheme to address concrete cases of banking crisis.[29] The resolution scheme benefits from the preparatory work developed during the resolution planning phase, but is not bound by it, as both endogenous and idiosyncratic factors playing out in a crisis scenario can change the assumptions on which the resolution plan was based.

In all cases, the SRB needs to cooperate with other stakeholders, primarily the supervisor and the NRAs. On the resolution scheme, the Board needs also to cooperate with the Commission and, potentially, the Council. On this specific point, recent case law has affirmed that it is only through the Commission's endorsement decision that the resolution action adopted by the SRB in the resolution scheme produces binding legal effects.[30]

[27] Art 20 of the SRMR.

[28] If the SRB determines that a bank is not resolvable, it can take action to address the impediment to resolvability, via the NRAs that act at local level. On the SRM's tasks, and on the allocation of those tasks between the SRB and the NRAs, see Michele Cossa, Raffaele D'Ambrosio, and Andrea Vignini, 'The SRM: Allocation of Tasks and Powers between the SRB and the NRAs and Organisational Issues' in Raffaele D'Ambrosio (ed), *Law and Practice of the Banking Union and of Its Governing Institutions (Cases and Materials)* (2020) Quaderni di Ricerca Giuridica no 88, Banca d'Italia, 330.

[29] Art 18(1) of the SRMR uses the verb 'to adopt'.

[30] *Commission v Fundación Tatiana Pérez de Guzmán el Bueno et al* (n 11), paras 81–88.

VI The Single Resolution Board and the development of a 'resolution-administrative practice'

The SRB's role as a central decision-maker evolved over time as it developed implementing policies which became a standard within the European resolution community.

During the first 10 years of its existence, the SRB proved capable of developing a 'resolution-administrative practice' that is effectively supranational. Even though the SRB exercises its powers via the NRA, the role of the SRB as an EU body has been steadily growing because of the tension between two separate sets of rules, both included in the SRMR; in other words, this is the distinction between the SRM as a *mechanism* for cooperation between the EU and the national level and the SRB as the standing central Banking Union *body* in charge of resolution.

The first set of rules is the one which identifies the SRB as the resolution authority of significant banks and relevant cross-border groups. Around that set of rules, the SRB has established its policies, practice, and influence. For example, Article 5 of the SRMR authorizes the SRB to carry out the tasks that the BRRD assigns to the NRA, which suggests that the sole resolution authority for significant banks is the SRB. Other examples are Article 6(1) and (2), which refer to SRB's 'policies', thus implying the SRB's role as the central authority for designing how bank resolution policy should be implemented, and Article 31(1)(a) of the SRMR, which mandates the SRB to issue 'guidelines and general instructions' to NRAs. In all those cases, the SRB details how tasks are to be performed, and resolution decisions are adopted by NRAs.

The second set of rules requires the SRB to channel its decisions and actions through the NRAs in order for them to take effect on the banks. The main example here is Article 29 of the SRMR, which states that NRAs shall take the necessary action to *implement* decisions referred to in the SRMR, which are, of course, decisions of the SRB. Concrete examples of these mechanics are the notification of the MREL determination (the SRB communicates it to the national level; the national level notifies the bank) and the execution of the resolution scheme (the SRB adopts it; the national level implements it and checks its execution).

In finding the balance between these two sets of rules, the SRB developed an administrative practice. Examples are:

1. The SRB developed a policy for determining the MREL requirement applicable to the banks under its remit (SRB MREL policy). The need

for such a policy is not spelled out in the SRMR, which only provides an option, as already said, to issue guidelines and instructions. The SRB MREL policy is now widely accepted in the Banking Union and used as a blueprint for the MREL-setting of banks not falling under the SRB's remit (less-significant banks). In addition, it inspires the action of non-Banking Union resolution authorities that may either use it as a benchmark[31] or indirectly apply it in the context of resolution colleges, in the case of groups where one bank is situated in the Banking Union and another is outside the Banking Union.[32] Finally, the SRB MREL policy is now mentioned in court proceedings, so that it is not unlikely that the European Court of Justice case law may eventually refer to it.[33]

2. The SRB established a Banking Union-specific reporting exercise to collect MREL data from the banks within its remit. In this domain, the SRMR[34] only provides for a rather general rule under which the Board requires that the NRAs 'verify and ensure that entities and groups maintain the requirements for own funds and eligible liabilities'. Based on such legal basis, the SRB built up a resolution reporting mechanism that ensures that the Board, via the national level, gets up-to-date MREL data. To achieve that, the Board developed guidance[35] which is updated on an annual basis, and is in line with the reporting templates developed by the European Banking Authorities (EBA Implementing Technical Standards). Under the SRB's guidance, banks incorporated within the Banking Union need to report MREL data to their NRA. Banks incorporated in the Union, but outside the Banking Union and part of a group with a Banking Union footprint, need to report to the NRA of the Banking Union jurisdiction in which the (ultimate) parent entity is incorporated. This shows how the SRB set up a reporting mechanism which centralizes MREL data. Also, those data are gathered in a quarterly

[31] IMF Country Report No 23/180, Sweden, p 22, para 45: 'The SNDO [Swedish National Debt Office] has a comprehensive MREL policy and has made good progress in ensuring implementation by banks. In particular, the SNDO has taken opportunities when implementing the BRRD 2 to maintain its pre-existing MREL levels for its banks. The overall outcome under the SNDO's MREL policy is that Swedish institutions are subject to somewhat higher (risk-weighted) requirements (both overall and subordination requirement) than institutions within the Banking Union (SRB MREL-policy).'

[32] See, for instance, the Hungarian central bank's principles for setting a minimum requirement for own funds and eligible liabilities (MREL), which constantly refer to the SRB MREL policy. These are available here: mnb-s-principles-for-setting-minimum-requirement-for-own-funds-and-eligible-liabilities-mrel.pdf.

[33] Case T–71/22 *BNP Paribas v SRB*: the bank pleads that the Court 'declare that the contested provisions of the MREL Policy must be disapplied'.

[34] Art 12(5) of the SRMR.

[35] Available here: https://www.srb.europa.eu/system/files/media/document/Guidance_2024_LDR_v1.0.pdf, accessed 8 May 2026.

published document (MREL dashboard)[36] which provides markets with data on the stability of the system as whole.

3. The SRB directly grants the prior permission for the early redemptions of MREL instruments. This task was introduced by the CRR2 in 2019.[37] It is the power for resolution authorities to authorize in advance the liability management exercises of banks: if a bank wants to early call, redeem, buy back, or repurchase one of its own debt instruments counting towards the MREL, it needs to obtain the prior authorization of the resolution authorities.[38] In the absence of an explicit provision of the SRMR[39] attributing to the SRB the competence to authorize significant institutions to perform MREL redemptions, the SRB has built on top of its administrative practice and developed an implementation policy, which is publicly available.[40]
4. Regulation (EU) 2019/877 (SRMR2) introduced a tool for the SRB to enforce the potential failure of banks to comply with the buffer requirements sitting on top of the MREL stack. This is referred to as the Maximum Distributable Amount related to MREL (M-MDA).[41] In practice, the Board may restrict the possibility for a bank to distribute dividends and pay out coupons if such bank fails to comply with its combined buffer requirement when considered on top of the MREL stack.[42] The SRMR rules on the application of M-MDA restrictions grant significant discretion to the SRB, since the matter is highly technical and the SRB needs to ensure MREL compliance and, at the same time, adequate coordination with the supervisor. Yet, the SRB specified, in the context of its MREL policy,[43] how the application of that MREL compliance's

[36] Available here: https://www.srb.europa.eu/en/content/mrel-dashboard-0, accessed 8 May 2026.

[37] Arts 77 and 78a of the CRR.

[38] This power mirrors the one which the CRR has long granted to bank supervisors: arts 77 and 78 of the CRR.

[39] This apparent issue is now also addressed in the SRMR3 proposal, which would clarify in art 12 of the SRMR that, for entities under its direct remit, the Board is responsible for granting the permission to call, redeem, repay, or repurchase eligible liabilities instruments under art 78a of Regulation (EU) No 575/2013.

[40] Available here: https://www.srb.europa.eu/en/content/srb-approach-prior-permissions-regime-1, accessed 8 May 2026. Such guidance also bridged the gap between the entry into application of the CRR2 and the development, by the EBA, of the criteria for the early redemption of MREL, which only entered in force four years later (on 9 May 2023). See Commission Delegated Regulation (EU) 2023/827, amending Delegated Regulation (EU) No 241/2014 and providing further details on certain elements of resolution prior permissions, such as the information to be submitted by institutions, the assessment criteria to be applied by resolution authorities, and the time limits for issuing decisions.

[41] Art 10a of the SRMR.

[42] See art 141a(1) of the CRD.

[43] s 8.1, available here: https://www.srb.europa.eu/system/files/media/document/MREL%20Policy%202024_clean%20version_web.pdf, accessed 8 May 2026.

enforcement tool would play out in practice. This, on the one hand, implies a degree of self-containment from the SRB's side. On the other hand, it shows that the SRB was able to set out the perimeter within which to exercise such broad discretion, which ensures predictability of its decisions and effective *ex post* checks on the SRB's administrative action.

VII The SRB's 'footprint' in Union law beyond resolution

Over time, the SRB's footprint expanded throughout several legislative acts which are relevant beyond the Banking Union:

1) First, since 2019, the SRB has been granted specific tasks under the CRR. The reason is that CRR2 amended the original CRR to include a set of provisions that are also relevant for the bank resolution framework. Notably, reference is made to the implementation of the Total Loss-absorbing Capacity (TLAC) term sheet in Union law.[44] Those standards required the introduction, in the CRR provisions on the TLAC for global systemically important institutions (G-SIIs) (Articles 92a and 92b of the CRR),[45] of conditions for eligible liabilities instruments to count towards the compliance with the CRR TLAC requirements (Article 72b of the CRR), and a prior permission regime requiring banks to seek authorization from the resolution authority before buying back TLAC and MREL instruments (Article 77 and 78a of the CRR). The latter prior permission regimes build on top of the different regime which was already in place for buybacks of own funds instruments (Article 78 of the CRR). Yet, with the CRR2, TLAC and MREL requirements became relevant also for bank supervisors: only if a bank complies with the TLAC and MREL can a supervisor authorize a capital buyback (see Article 78 of the CRR, as amended by CRR2). It is against that background that Article 2 of the CRR vests the SRB with the powers to ensure that banks comply with the resolution-related rules included in the CRR and in the CRD. In addition, the CRR specifically requires the SRB and the SSM to ensure

[44] Financial Stability Board, 'Press release: "FSB issues final Total Loss-Absorbing Capacity standard for global systemically important banks", 9 November 2015.

[45] In practice, TLAC was introduced for G-SIIs only, as part of the MREL requirement. In the financial jargon, is often referred as Pillar 1 MREL, in the sense that it constitutes the statutory part of the MREL that a GSII must meet, whereas the Pillar 2 MREL is set by the resolution authority on a case-by-case basis.

'the regular and reliable exchange of relevant information' (Article 2(4) of the CRR).

2. Second, the SRB now also plays a role in the domain of central counterparties (CCPs). CCPs are businesses which put themselves in between market participants. It is usually said that CCPs are the buyer to every seller, and the seller to every buyer. Essentially, they handle financial transactions until they are settled, manage exposures, and reduce risks (especially contagion risk). In this sense, they act as an insurance cover for their members, which are normally required to provide collateral to the CCP and pay a fee for the service. It may not seem clear what the relation is between the Banking Union central resolution authority and CCPs. However, the relation follows Regulation (EU) 2021/23, which introduced Union-wide applicable rules for the crisis management of CCPs. While it is for Member States to identify the resolution authority of a CCP, the Regulation provides that the SRB is a mandatory member of CCP resolution colleges. Based on that piece of Union law, the SRB has, since 2022, been engaging with CCPs, and participates in CCP resolution colleges (Article 4(2) of Regulation (EU) 2021/23).
3. Third, under Regulation (EU) 2022/2554 on digital operational resilience for the financial sector (DORA), the SRB: (i) receives reports on major ICT-related incidents and significant cyber threats in relation to the banks falling within its remit; and (ii) may establish mechanisms to enable the sharing of effective practices across financial sectors to enhance situational awareness and identify common cyber vulnerabilities and risks across sectors, with the ESAs, ECB, and the European Union Agency for Cybersecurity (ENISA).[46]
4. Fourth, the SRB is one of the entities which has access to the securitization repositories, which gather information on securitizations from originators, sponsors, and securitization special purpose entities. While the main purpose of these repositories is to provide investors with a single and supervised source of the data necessary for performing their due diligence, securitization-related information can be relevant also for resolution authorities.

[46] Regulation (EU) 2019/881 of the European Parliament and of the Council of 17 April 2019 on ENISA (the European Union Agency for Cybersecurity) and on information and communications technology cybersecurity certification and repealing Regulation (EU) No 526/2013 (2019) OJ L151/15.

VIII Single Resolution Mechanism prospects: SRMR3

In April 2023, the European Commission proposed a set of measures commonly known as proposals for the reform of the 'crisis management and deposit insurance framework'. The package includes a proposal for a Regulation amending Regulation (EU) No 806/2014 (SRMR3).

The proposed SRMR3 aims at introducing adjustments to the SRMR in force. These are targeted amendments which concern four areas: (1) the allocation of tasks between the SRB and the NRAs; (2) certain ECB powers around early intervention measures; (3) early warning in the case of a bank failing or being likely to fail; and (4) the division of tasks between the ECB and the national supervisors as regards the failing-or-likely-to-fail assessment.

1 Allocation of tasks between the SRB and the NRAs

In terms of allocation of tasks within the Banking Union, Article 7 of the SRMR currently provides that the SRB has direct responsibility for the banks directly supervised by the ECB (significant institutions); for those banks that, despite being Less Significant Institutions, have a cross-border footprint; and for any other bank for which the SRB or the NRA has decided that the SRB would exercise direct responsibility. In these three cases, the SRB is the resolution authority; in all other cases, the competent resolution authority is the NRA. While this situation clearly follows the reading of the current Article 7 of the SRMR, other provisions of the current SRMR only refer to the SRB and not the national authorities. SRMR3 aims at fixing that, clarifying in Article 7 that 'any references to the Board . . . shall be read as references to the national resolution authorities'. This clarification avoids the risk of confusion between resolution authorities (SRB and NRA).

The SRMR3 aims at clarifying how the SRB should apply certain powers granted by the CRR or by the BRRD to resolution authorities which are not explicitly mentioned in the SRMR. One example is that, for banks falling under the SRB's direct powers, the latter is responsible for granting the permission to call, redeem, repay, or repurchase eligible liabilities instruments under Article 78a of the CRR. In this case, it is the SRB that directly exercises the power, given that such power stems from a Regulation (CRR) which is self-applicable. Another example is the power to suspend some financial obligations following the determination that the institution or entity is failing or likely to fail, pursuant to Article 33a of the BRRD. In that case, the SRMR would clarify that the

SRB should apply the power and instruct the NRA to implement the SRB decision. The difference is justified by the fact that the application of this power needs to be framed in accordance with national law provisions, notably in the area of contract law.

2 Certain ECB powers around early intervention measures

SRMR3 would introduce a set of provisions into the SRMR mirroring those already listed in Articles 27 to 29 of the BRRD, which empower supervisors to take actions on the bank managers. These measures complement those which have long existed in the supervisory framework (Article 104 of the CRD). In a nutshell, these are powers that competent authorities would apply as soon as ongoing supervision reveals that problems faced by a bank may lead to infringements of requirements, or that infringements are likely to occur in the near future.[47]

SRMR3 would not alter the current set-up of the supervisory powers and intervention measures. Rather, it would provide the ECB with a directly applicable legal basis (Articles 13 to 13c of the SRMR3) for the exercise of those powers (ie they would be included in the SRMR, a regulation, which does not need transposition into national laws).[48]

3 Early warning in the case of a bank failing or being likely to fail

SRMR3 would also include a new Article 13c to require the supervisor to notify the SRB early of any material risk that a bank will meet the conditions for being assessed as failing or likely to fail. This would serve as an early warning and to deliver to the resolution authority an overview of the alternative solutions that may prevent the failure of the institution or entity concerned within a reasonable time frame. The memorandum accompanying the Commission's SRMR3 proposal explains that this notification aims at anticipating the start of the pre-resolution dialogue between the SSM and the SRM, obviously in the interests of time. It also adds that this anticipation can be read as an element of

[47] European Banking Authority, 'Report on the application of early intervention measures in the European Union in accordance with articles 27–29 of the BRRD' (2012) EBA/REP/2021/12.

[48] In the past, questions on how the ECB should apply the national law provisions resulting from the BRRD arose in Case T-501/19 *Corneli v ECB* [2022], ECLI:EU:T:2022:402, annulling an ECB decision on an early intervention measure (temporary administration).

alignment to recent case law of the Court of Justice of the EU related to a case taking place in the Banking Union, according to which the ECB's assessment is a preparatory measure designed to allow the SRB to take a decision regarding the resolution of a bank.[49]

4 Division of tasks between the ECB and the national supervisors as regards the failing-or-likely-to-fail assessment

SRMR3 also aims at introducing changes to Article 18 of the SRMR to clarify the allocation of tasks between the ECB and the NCAs when it comes to assessing whether a bank is failing or likely to fail. The change is justified in the case of cross-border groups, which are supervised at national level, but for which the SRB is the competent resolution authority.

IX Conclusions

The SRM reflects one of the key operational features of the Banking Union—that is, its functioning based on 'mechanisms'. These mechanisms allow for a decision-making which brings the Union level and the national ones together. A *mechanism* such as the SRM should be able to compose the different interests at stake, and to lead to a (Banking) Union-wide decision which puts together those different interests. Even though certain authors deem this feature to limit the ability of the SRB to act as a fully fledged supranational authority that pursues a supranational interest,[50] it is in fact Union law that mandates the SRB to mediate among different interests and identify the (Banking) Union-wide interest to be pursued (Article 6 of the SRMR). Considering that, this work concludes that, in the context of the Banking Union, the term *mechanism* illustrates the way an EU body allows for a participative decision-making able to mediate different interests and perspectives to achieve a common objective.

The SRB carries out the function of composing interests in all the forms of cooperation taking place in the context of the SRM (resolution planning, MREL-setting, and resolution schemes). During the first 10 years of its existence (2015–24), the SRB delivered on its tasks. Even if it cannot be concluded

[49] T-281/18 *ABLV Bank v ECB*, order [2019], paras 34 to 36; C-551/19 P and C-552/19 P *ABLV Bank v ECB* [2021], paras 62 to 71.

[50] Tröger and Kotovskaia (n 24) 781.

that the SRB was always able to identify and pursue a public interest that is purely supranational,[51] it can be argued that it proved capable of building up its leadership from among the resolution authorities. In doing so, it leveraged the supranational setting of its decision-making and developed a 'resolution-administrative practice' that is indeed supranational.

This supranational character is not put into question by the fact that the SRB exercises certain powers via the NRA (nor by the fact that resolution schemes need to be endorsed by the Commission). These are, rather, inherent features of the way the SRM is built up, ie around two distinct sets of rules, both included in the SRMR, under which the SRM is both a *mechanism* for cooperation between the EU, the national level, and the SRB, and the standing central Banking Union *body* in charge of resolution.

[51] A question for another paper could be, does such a supranational interest exist?

15

The Complementary Nature of the State Aid in the Banking Union

Audronė Steiblytė

I Introduction

During the 2007–08 financial crisis, the process of bailing out banks with taxpayers' money contributed to the transformation of the banking crisis into the European sovereign debt crisis. During that crisis, a number of Member States had to seek outside assistance in order to be able to repay or refinance their governments' debts, to bail out banks subject to national supervision. At the legislative level, the Union responded to the crisis by creating the so-called Single Rulebook[1] for the EU financial sector, which applies in all Member States and ensures a level playing field across the internal market by means of requiring all credit institutions in the Union to comply with it. The Single Rulebook comprises a set of Union legal acts establishing capital requirements applicable to credit institutions, foreseeing the creation of deposit guarantee schemes (DGSs), and setting out rules necessary to ensure the orderly resolution of failing-or-likely-to-fail (FOLTF) banks.

The euro-area debt crisis, however, demonstrated that euro-area Member States needed a closer integration of their banking systems. Moreover, in the wake of the crisis, several Member States introduced national mechanisms meant to deal in a rapid and effective manner with credit institutions in distress. Those mechanisms created a risk of fragmenting the internal market. As a consequence, the creation of the Banking Union was anticipated in 2012[2] as

[1] The term 'Single Rulebook' was first used by the European Council in its conclusions of 19 June 2009 that confirmed the establishment of the European System of Financial Supervisors, comprising three new European Supervisory Authorities (the European Banking Authority (EBA), in the field of banking, by Regulation (EU) 1093/2010 of the European Parliament and of the Council of 24 November 2010 establishing a European Supervisory Authority [2010] OJ L331, p 12).

[2] In December 2012, the president of the European Council, in cooperation with the presidents of the Commission, the European Central Bank, and the Eurogroup, drew up a road map leading to the

Audronė Steiblytė, *The Complementary Nature of the State Aid in the Banking Union* In: *EU Banking Union*. Edited by: Jonathan Bauerschmidt, Raffaele D'Ambrosio, Diane Fromage, Daniela Jaros, and Paul Weismann, Oxford University Press. © Oxford University Press 2026. DOI: 10.1093/9780198949756.003.0016

a means to improve the integration, resilience, and supervision of the banking sector in the euro area. The Banking Union[3] is currently founded on two pillars[4]—the Single Supervisory Mechanism (SSM)[5] and the Single Resolution Mechanism (SRM).[6] The regulation establishing the SRM complements the Directive for the recovery and resolution of credit institutions and investment firms (Banking Recovery and Resolution Directive, or BRRD),[7] which sets out rules concerning resolution of FOLTF banks for the entire single market.

This chapter will analyse some selected aspects of the applicable resolution and State aid frameworks with the aim of understanding to what extent they are interdependent and what role State aid, as well as the rules for the assessment of its compatibility with the internal market, still plays in the Banking Union, especially having in mind that the resolution framework aimed at diminishing reliance on public support. After presenting the key relevant features of the resolution framework for this analysis, the chapter will specifically look into Fund aid, and assistance from national DGSs.

II Certain relevant features of the resolution framework

One of the key aims of the BRRD and the Single Resolution Mechanism Regulation (hereinafter also referred to as the 'resolution framework')[8] is to reduce or even cut the dependence of banks on sovereigns, and, as a

achievement of the genuine economic and monetary union that required a closer integrated financial framework in the form of the Banking Union.

[3] Non-euro-area Member States may choose to join the Banking Union by becoming a 'participating Member State', as defined in art 2(1) of Regulation (EU) No 806/2014 establishing uniform rules and a uniform procedure for the resolution of credit institutions and certain investment firms in the framework of a Single Resolution Mechanism and a Single Resolution Fund (SRMR), [2014] OJ L225, p 1.

[4] In 2015, the Commission adopted a proposal concerning the third anticipated pillar, the European Deposit Insurance Scheme (EDIS), which should have provided insurance for all retail depositors in the Banking Union.

[5] Council Regulation (EU) 1024/2013 of 15 October 2013 conferring specific tasks on the European Central Bank concerning policies relating to the prudential supervision of credit institutions [2013] OJ L287, p 63.

[6] Regulation (EU) 806/2014 of the European Parliament and of the Council of 15 July 2014 establishing uniform rules and a uniform procedure for the resolution of credit institutions and certain investment firms in the framework of a Single Resolution Mechanism and a Single Resolution Fund and amending Regulation (EU) No 1093/2010 [2014] OJ L225, p 1.

[7] Directive 2014/59/EU of the European Parliament and of the Council of 15 May 2014 establishing a framework for the recovery and resolution of credit institutions and investment firms and amending Council Directive 82/891/EEC, and Directives 2001/24/EC, 2002/47/EC, 2004/25/EC, 2005/56/EC, 2007/36/EC, 2011/35/EU, 2012/30/EU and 2013/36/EU, and Regulations (EU) No 1093/2010 and (EU) No 648/2012, of the European Parliament and of the Council [2014] OJ L173, p 190.

[8] Also known as forming part of the Crisis Management and Deposit Insurance (CMDI) framework, which also includes the Deposit Guarantee Schemes Directive.

consequence, on public support. As explained in recital 73 SRMR, '[a]n effective resolution regime should minimise the costs of the resolution of a failing institution borne by the taxpayers'. In other words, the resolution of the FOLTF bank must, inter alia, be the means of reducing reliance on public funding. The resolution should primarily be financed by the resolution funds[9] which are annually capitalized by banks themselves. The overarching aim to minimize the reliance on extraordinary public financial support[10] is also directly reflected in the resolution objectives, compliance with which is assessed when determining whether the resolution of a FOLTF bank is in the public interest.[11] The objective 'to protect public funds by minimising reliance on extraordinary public financial support' stands on an equal footing with the other resolution objectives fixed by the Union legislator: to ensure the continuity of critical functions of the FOLTF bank; to avoid a significant adverse effect on the financial system, in particular by preventing contagion, including to market infrastructures, and by maintaining market discipline; to protect depositors and investors, covered respectively by the Deposit Guarantee Schemes Directive[12] and the Investor Guarantee Schemes Directive;[13] and to protect funds and assets of the bank's clients.

Until now, in the Banking Union, the assessment of public interest, which involves a certain margin of discretion, has been applied restrictively by the Single Resolution Board (SRB),[14] and has led to the resolution of only three FOLTF banks.[15]

The resolution framework limits the recourse to the State aid[16] that comes from taxpayers, primarily by making the resources of the resolution funds available to FOLTF banks. Nevertheless, the role of the State aid legal framework in the Banking Union remains significant, and the types of scenarios in

[9] The national resolution funds created in accordance with the BRRD and the Single Resolution Fund established under the SRMR.

[10] Art 2(28) BRRD contains the following definition: '"Extraordinary public financial support" means State aid within the meaning of Article 107(1) TFEU, or any other public financial support at supra-national level, which, if provided for at national level, would constitute State aid, that is provided in order to preserve or restore the viability, liquidity or solvency of an institution or entity.'

[11] FOLTF banks are only resolved by preserving their vital functions if that is in the public interest. As set out in Article 18(5) SRMR, the bank resolution is in the public interest only if three cumulative conditions are met: (i) the resolution is necessary for the achievement of one or more of the resolution objectives; (ii) the resolution is proportionate to those relevant objectives; and (iii) the winding up of the credit institution under normal insolvency proceedings would not meet those resolution objectives to the same extent.

[12] Directive 2014/49/EU on deposit guarantee schemes, OJ L173, p 149.

[13] Directive 97/9/EC on investor-compensation schemes, OJ L84, p 22.

[14] And subsequently endorsed by the Commission.

[15] Banco Popular Español, SA and two entities of the Sberbank Europe AG group.

[16] The Commission establishes whether the measure constitutes State aid, following its Notice on the notion of State aid as referred to in art 107(1) TFEU ([2016] OJ C262, p 1).

which that framework applies are varied. Even though not directly analysed in this chapter, the support from the national resolution funds managed by the national resolution authorities outside the Banking Union is considered to be state resources, as the resources come under the control of public authorities and, therefore, the support has to be notified to the Commission as State aid, in accordance with Article 108(3) TFEU. For an advantage to be 'aid' within the meaning of Article 107(1) TFEU, it must, inter alia, be granted directly or indirectly through state resources and be imputable to the state.[17] Where public authorities like the national resolution authority are involved in the adoption of that measure, there is no doubt that the measure is imputable to the state.[18] The question of whether state resources are being used arises when the financing originates from private parties, such as banks which pay *ex ante* contributions to the resolution fund. In such a case, for those contributions to constitute state resources, they must constantly remain under public control and, therefore, be available to the public authorities.[19] The resources of the national resolution funds become state resources because the national resolution authorities have a full power of disposal over the national resolution funds, as they determine whether the resources of these funds will be used for the specific resolution of a FOLTF bank and, if so, to what extent.

While ensuring that, in principle, the FOLTF banks in resolution will not have access to public money, the resolution framework, however, envisages that public funding may still be used for precautionary or preventive measures, as well as for FOLTF banks whose resolution is not in the public interest, and which therefore must make an orderly exit from the market in accordance with normal insolvency proceedings. In other words, in the Banking Union, the resolution framework allows the use of State aid in various scenarios, such as precautionary and preventive recapitalization, resolution supported from the national resolution funds, public support for the resolution of banks falling under the SRB competence,[20] and aid for banks whose resolution is not in public interest, which are subject to normal insolvency proceedings.

The necessity of State aid to a struggling bank (where 'extraordinary public financial support is required') automatically places it into the FOLTF

[17] Judgments of 15 May 2019 in Case C-706/17 *Achema*, ECLI:EU:C:2019:407, para 47, and of 19 December 2019 in Case C-385/18 *Arriva Italia*, ECLI:EU:C:2019:1121, para 33.

[18] *Arriva Italia* (n 17), paras 34 and 65.

[19] Judgment of 13 September 2017 in Case C-329/15 *ENEA*, ECLI:EU:C:2017:671, paras 25 and 31 and *Achema* (n 17), paras 53, 66, and 67.

[20] In accordance with art 7(2) SRMR, the competence of the SRB encompasses the banking entities and groups directly supervised by the ECB, and other cross-border banking groups which have entities established in more than one participating Member State.

category,[21] leading to the resolution or liquidation of such a bank. The credit institution must be declared to be failing or likely to fail by its supervisor, unless the bank's situation falls into well-defined exceptions related to the necessity to remedy a serious disturbance in the economy of a Member State and preserve financial stability. The measure of support must then be destined for a solvent bank and be of a precautionary and temporary nature, and is not to be used to offset losses that the entity has incurred or is likely to incur in the near future.[22] This type of precautionary State aid still has to be assessed for its compatibility with the internal market, including the proportionality aspect. If the Commission finds this aid incompatible, the bank will very probably not be able to avoid the FOLTF status. Furthermore, the SRMR[23] permits only three specific forms of precautionary measures which would not trigger FOLTF: (i) a state guarantee to back liquidity facilities provided by central banks in accordance with the central banks' conditions; (ii) a state guarantee of newly issued liabilities; and (iii) an injection of own funds or purchase of capital instruments at prices and on terms that do not confer an advantage upon the bank. The latter scenario can validly apply only where a number of other cumulative circumstances, such as the bank continuing to comply with all the requirements necessary for it to continue possessing its banking authorization, are satisfied.

It has been argued in the literature[24] that, with Article 32(4) BRRD and Article 18(4) SRMR being identical, it would be difficult to justify extraordinary public financial support to solvent but non-systemic banks because that support would not be necessary 'to preserve financial stability', which is one of the two already mentioned cumulative conditions—remedy a serious disturbance and preserve financial stability. The national authorities, rather than the SRB, would then have to declare such banks FOLTF and assess whether their resolution would be in public interest.

The resolution framework (SRMR and BRRD) does not regulate the exit of the FOLTF bank whose resolution is not in the public interest and, therefore, does not set out any conditions for the possible State aid measures necessary to help the exit of such a bank. The decision to wind up the FOLTF bank is taken by the relevant national authorities alone, without the SRB's involvement. Member States, however, have different 'normal insolvency proceedings' and their initiation might be subject to diverging requirements and conditions. The

[21] ibid, art 18(4)(d).
[22] ibid, art 18(4).
[23] ibid, art 18(4)(d).
[24] Phedon Nicolaides, 'State Aid after the Banking Union: Serious Disturbance and Public Interest' (2022) 23 Journal of Banking Regulation 79.

Union law, nevertheless, requires that an entity must be wound up in an orderly manner in accordance with the applicable national law and taking due regard to the resolution objectives with respect to which the resolution authority assessed the public interest necessity. As a consequence, a FOLTF entity for which there is no reasonable prospect of private or public sector measures, and the resolution of which is not in public interest, may not remain active on the market.[25] The State aid for banks subject to normal insolvency proceedings is assessed by the Commission under Article 107 TFEU.

III Some particularities of State aid assessment of precautionary and liquidation support

The intended precautionary support, as well as liquidation support, for a FOLTF bank[26] is assessed by the Commission as, respectively, liquidity, restructurization, or liquidation aid, under the 2013 Banking Communication,[27] which provides detailed guidance on the criteria for the compatibility of State aid with the internal market pursuant to Article 107(3)(b) TFEU for the financial sector.

In general, State aid can take different forms and be granted, inter alia, as subsidies or financial instruments, such as guarantees or loans. The resolution framework, however, limits the choice of the form of State aid for precautionary measures.

While the State aid rules, due to their earlier adoption and amendments, are almost silent on the existence of the resolution framework, the Commission assesses the requirements of the resolution framework in each of its State aid decisions on banks, as provisions that are indissolubly linked[28] to the object of State aid. This is, in particular, evident in the case of precautionary recapitalization of a bank, for which the resolution framework sets out its own requirements, incompatibility with which would have an effect on the compatibility or incompatibility of the aid viewed as a whole.

[25] Audronė Steiblytė, 'Public Interest for Resolution Action in the Light of the *ABLV* Cases' in Chiara Zilioli and Karl-Philip Wojcik (eds), *Judicial Review in the European Banking Union* (Edward Elgar 2021) 564–70.

[26] Support from the national resolution funds for the resolution of a FOLTF bank outside the Banking Union is State aid, and is therefore assessed by the Commission in accordance with the 2013 Banking Communication (Communication from the Commission on the application, from 1 August 2013, of State aid rules to support measures in favour of banks in the context of the financial crisis [2013] OJ C216, p 1).

[27] ibid.

[28] Judgment of 22 March 1977, Case 74/76 *Iannelli and Volpi*, ECLI:EU:C:1977:51, para 14.

The State aid framework for banks and the resolution framework regulate certain aspects of support for banks in a different manner. One such prominent aspect is the requirement that holders of financial instruments of the FOLTF bank contribute to the loss absorption with their own resources. For the purpose of the State aid assessment, burden-sharing requirements[29] envisage that, where the absorption of losses by equity is insufficient, hybrid capital holders and subordinated debt holders must also contribute to the absorption before support for the bank can be granted.[30] The resolution framework addresses the matter by introducing a bail-in tool which requires a contribution of a minimum of 8% of total liabilities of the FOLTF bank, including own funds, to the loss absorption before the resolution fund can be accessed. Some authors see the bail-in as the 'focal point' of the entire resolution framework.[31] Differently from the State aid rules, the bail-in tool also provides for a contribution from senior bondholders or depositors, meaning that, depending on the specific situation of the FOLTF bank, the burden-sharing requirement might be less burdensome than the bail-in requirement. It follows that, in certain scenarios, senior bondholders and depositors might escape burden sharing where the FOLTF bank is liquidated under normal insolvency proceedings because the bank's resolution is not in public interest, while the same senior bondholders and depositors would have been subject to bail-in if the bank had been resolved.[32] It can also be noted that, in situations which are regulated by the State aid rules alone, such as precautionary recapitalizations, the Member State can decide to notify its State aid measure intended for a bank even if the measure does not comply with all the relevant aspects described in the 2013 Banking Communication, including the application of burden sharing to subordinated creditors. The Member State government will then have to justify the inapplicability of the 2013 Banking Communication to the measure in question due to exceptional circumstances, while the Commission will verify the correctness of the Member State's assumptions.[33]

[29] See points 15 to 19 of the 2013 Banking Communication (n 26). The burden sharing envisaged by the 2013 Banking Communication was examined by the Court of Justice in Case C-526/14 *Kotnik and others*, ECLI:EU:C:2016:570.

[30] Point 41 of the 2013 Banking Communication (n 26).

[31] Karel Lannoo, 'Bank State Aid under BRRD and SRM' (2014) 41 European State Aid Quarterly 630–35.

[32] Art 15(1)(g) SRMR establishes a no-creditor-worse-off (NCWO) principle which is meant to ensure that the shareholders and creditors affected by resolution will not be worse off than in the case where the bank had entered into normal insolvency proceedings.

[33] Stefano Lucchini and others, 'State Aid and the Banking System in the Financial Crisis: From Bail-out to Bail-in' (2017) 8(2) Journal of European Competition Law & Practice 88.

As the assessment of the State aid primarily focuses on the task to mitigate competition distortions, the State aid rules for banks follow a different structure from that of the logic and terminology built into the resolution framework. More specifically, the liquidation aid where a bank exits the market is considered to be less distortive than the restructuring aid where a bank remains on the market. That asymmetry is, in particular, evident where the FOLTF bank is resolved using the aid from the Single Resolution Fund (Fund aid). The compatibility criteria of restructuring aid are applied for the use of the Fund aid with the bail-in tool, where the bank is supposed to remain on the market. But where the resolution of a FOLTF bank requires the use of the sale-of-business and bridge-bank tools, the Commission relies on the criteria for liquidation aid even if, in the resolution logic, the bank is resolved (as in the public interest) and not liquidated following normal insolvency proceedings. It follows that an effort in interpretation has to be made in order to ensure that the State aid rules for banks and the resolution framework are applied in a coherent manner.

By introducing the above-mentioned parameters for the precautionary recapitalization, which would not lead to the FOLTF status of the bank and, therefore, to its possible resolution, the resolution framework limited the formal access door to State aid. The intention of that legislative construction quite probably was to channel the banks with more severe underlying issues through the assessment of public interest under Article 18(1)(c) SRMR. Those banks could then possibly obtain financing from the Single Resolution Fund (SRF), subject to the resolution procedure, and if that financing was required for their successful resolution.

IV Fund aid

One could possibly anticipate that in the Banking Union, the support from the SRF, owned by the SRB,[34] which is a Union agency, and alimented by private resources of the banks themselves, would not be subject to the State aid type of assessment. That possibility, however, was not legally realistic because the distortive effects of Fund aid are equal to those of State aid assistance granted from national resolution. The SRMR, therefore, creates a requirement for the support from the SRF to be assessed under Article 107 TFEU too,[35] because it 'is essential for the good functioning of the internal market that the same

[34] Art 67(3) SRMR.
[35] ibid, art 19(3).

rules apply to all resolution actions, regardless of whether they are taken by the resolution authorities under Directive 2014/59/EU or within the framework of the SRM'.[36] If the resolution of the FOLTF bank requires the use of the SRF, the SRB must notify the Commission of the proposed use of the SRF, as the Member State would notify the intended State aid measure. The notification by the SRB must include all the information necessary for the Commission to make the assessment of whether the Fund aid is compatible with the internal market. That responsibility might weigh heavily on the SRB, especially the first time it proposes to use the Fund aid, because of the possible lack of administrative experience and knowledge in the matter.

So far, the SRB has not had any direct experience as to what information the Commission might require when carrying out the assessment of the intended Fund aid. The stakes could be particularly high, as it is possible that the Commission would take a negative decision regarding the compatibility of the proposed Fund aid with the internal market, if it did not receive elements which would allow the Commission to declare that aid compatible. A different approach towards the lack of information would not be justified, as the SRB should be afforded equal treatment to that given to a comparably situated Member State. The reference to 'all of the information necessary to enable the Commission to make its assessments'[37] is rather general and might be subject to interpretation, as from the outset it is not fully clear what documents should be submitted as a part of the notification. Submitting the draft resolution scheme as part of the notification could ensure that the assessment of the Fund aid is carried out in full awareness of the upcoming resolution action; however, in practice, that might not always be possible because, for example, the drafting of the scheme might not yet have been completed.

When carrying out the preliminary investigation of the notified Fund aid, the Commission 'shall apply to the use of the Fund the criteria established for the application of State aid rules as enshrined in Article 107 TFEU'.[38] The State aid rules provided for in Article 107(3) TFEU, therefore, do not apply by analogy but instead apply directly to the Fund aid as envisaged by SRMR provisions. On that premise, for instance, as there is no presumption of compatibility of State aid with the internal market, that same principle would also apply to the Fund aid. More specifically, the assessment of the Fund aid will be carried out by the Commission under the 2013 Banking Communication[39] in

[36] ibid, recital 29.
[37] ibid, art 19(3) SRMR.
[38] ibid, 2nd subpara.
[39] In total, six communications could currently be applied when assessing State aid for the banks in difficulty: the 2009 Recapitalisation Communication (Communication from the Commission—The

the same way that State aid for banks was assessed before the entry into force of the resolution framework. As the 2013 Banking Communication helps to ensure legal certainty in relation to the large margin of discretion that the Commission possesses in interpreting the compatibility provisions in Article 107(3) TFEU, it is definitely a useful tool for the SRB to anticipate the parameters of the Commission's assessment.

In a manner equal to the classical State aid, a conclusion on the compatibility of Fund aid could only be reached if the proposed Fund aid measure does not violate the intrinsically linked provisions, in particular those of the resolution framework. The Commission cannot deem a State aid measure compatible with the internal market if the measure, by reason of some modalities or the method of its financing, breaches intrinsically linked provisions of Union law, which include general principles of Union law.[40] That assessment of compliance with intrinsically linked provisions gains additional significance because, in accordance with Article 19(1) SRMR,[41] the Fund aid decision is adopted before the adoption of the resolution scheme and, therefore, the assessment will possibly partly pre-empt the assessment of certain elements of the scheme.

While there is no hierarchy or subordination between the resolution framework and the State aid rules for banks in difficulty, and both of them aim at contributing to the overarching objective of financial stability, the main

recapitalisation of financial institutions in the current financial crisis: limitation of aid to the minimum necessary and safeguards against undue distortions of competition [2009] OJ C10, p 2); the 2009 Impaired Assets Communication (Communication from the Commission on the treatment of impaired assets in the Community banking sector, [2009] OJ C72, p 1); the 2009 Restructuring Communication (Commission communication on the return to viability and the assessment of restructuring measures in the financial sector in the current crisis under the State aid rules [2009] OJ C195, p 9); the 2010 Prolongation Communication (Communication from the Commission on the application, from 1 January 2011, of State aid rules to support measures in favour of banks in the context of the financial crisis [2010] OJ C329, p 7); the 2011 Prolongation Communication (Communication from the Commission on the application, from 1 January 2012, of State aid rules to support measures in favour of banks in the context of the financial crisis [2011] OJ C356, p 7); and the 2013 Banking Communication (n 26).

[40] Among many, see *Iannelli and Volpi* (n 28), para 14: 'Those aspects of aid which contravene specific provisions of the Treaty . . . may be so indissolubly linked to the object of the aid that it is impossible to evaluate them separately so that their effect on compatibility or incompatibility of the aid viewed as a whole must therefore of necessity be determined in the light of the procedure prescribed in Article 93'. See also: Case C-225/91 *Matra*, ECLI:EU:C:1993:239; Case C-594/18 P *Hinkley Point C*, ECLI:EU:C:2020:742; or Case C-284/21 P *Braesch*, ECLI:EU:C:2023:58, judgment of 31 January 2021, para 96; judgment of 15 April 2008 in Case C-390/06 *Nuova Agricast*, ECLI:EU:C:2008:224, para 50.

[41] Art 19(1) SRMR sets out that, '[w]here resolution action involves the granting of State aid pursuant to Article 107(1) TFEU or of Fund aid in accordance with paragraph 3 of this Article, the adoption of the resolution scheme under Article 18(6) of this Regulation shall not take place until such time as the Commission has adopted a positive or conditional decision concerning the compatibility of the use of such aid with the internal market.'

conceptual decision on 'what happens to the FOLTF bank' and how to ensure financial stability is predominantly taken in accordance with the resolution framework. The scenarios of precautionary support and liquidation in which State aid still plays a prominent role, as Fund aid is not available, are, to a certain extent, of secondary importance for the smooth functioning of financial markets in comparison with the possible effects of a FOLTF bank when the successful achievement of the resolution objectives[42] is at stake.

The State aid policy of the Union nevertheless has its own autonomous function—to protect the internal market from undue distortions and contribute to the creation of a competitive level playing field. The Commission, therefore, retains its *ex ante* control power directly over the support for banks under Article 108 TFEU, as well as by means of Article 19 SRMR. Aid granted in contravention of Article 108(3) TFEU that requires a prior notification constitutes 'unlawful aid'.[43] Therefore, not only the Member States for the classical State aid, but also the SRB for the Fund aid, are obliged to notify the intended aid to the Commission and cannot grant it before the Commission's approval. During the resolution process, the Commission's negative assessment under Article 107 TFEU might prevent the entire intended resolution action of the FOLTF bank if the Commission finds the Fund aid incompatible with the internal market. In such a scenario, if time allows, the SRB might still try to remedy the flaws and re-notify the Fund aid or try to resolve the bank using an alternative strategy that does not involve the use of the Fund.

When the Fund aid is used for a FOLFT bank, the SRB cannot adopt a resolution scheme for the FOLTF bank until the Commission has adopted a positive or conditional decision concerning the compatibility of such aid with the internal market. The resolution procedure has several very tight deadlines, counted in hours,[44] and the Commission has to adopt not only the already mentioned Fund aid-related decision but also the decision regarding the resolution scheme. The latter decision might be of three types: endorsing the resolution scheme adopted by the Board,[45] proposing to the Council to object to the resolution scheme because it does not fulfil the criterion of public interest,[46] or objecting to the scheme itself with regard to the other remaining discretionary aspects of the scheme. For the purposes of each of the two decisions in the

[42] ibid, art 14.
[43] Art 1(f) of the Procedural Regulation (EU) 2015/1589 laying down detailed rules for the application of Article 108 TFEU, [2015] OJ L248, p 9. Lawfulness (or 'legality') of an aid measure is thus a different concept from 'compatibility'.
[44] Art 18(7) SRMR.
[45] ibid, 2nd subpara.
[46] ibid, 3rd subpara.

resolution procedure, the Commission uses distinct legal bases and carries out relevant distinct assessments. Following that logic, the Fund aid decision and the decision endorsing the resolution scheme would also be subject to distinct judicial review procedures.

The procedure for adopting a resolution scheme for a FOLTF bank, where Fund aid is necessary, demonstrates that the assessment in accordance with Article 107 TFEU continues to play an important role. That assessment would be carried out by following the 2013 Banking Communication, which therefore, in principle, retains the same significance and role in resolution procedures in the entire internal market—outside as well as inside the Banking Union. Other authors also observe that the Commission continues to play a central role in determining whether the Fund aid is compatible with the internal market, and that this role is not affected by the technical competences granted to the SRB by the SRMR.[47]

Within the Banking Union, financial support to the failing bank might sometimes come from several sources—not only the SRF, but also the DGS or a protection scheme established under national law to which banks contribute voluntarily.[48] In some of these set-ups the Commission might even need to adopt a Fund aid decision and the State aid decision, both being necessary for the subsequent adoption and enforcement of the resolution scheme. The State aid measures would, in such a scenario, be notified to the Commission not by the Board, but by the relevant Member State. It is quite probable that, procedurally, the Commission would adopt a decision on the State aid and a separate decision on the Fund aid, given that each of those two decisions would require a different legal basis (Article 107 TFEU and Article 19 SRMR) and have different addressees (the Member State and the SRB). It should be mentioned that the Fund aid is not State aid within the meaning of Article 107(1) TFEU, and the Commission has no power to examine Fund aid under Article 108 TFEU, which, inter alia, envisages a formal investigation procedure.[49] In accordance with Article 108(2) TFEU, the Commission is obliged to open a

[47] Maria Rosaria Miserendino, 'State Aid for the Banking Sector: What Has Changed After the New BRRD and SRM Regulation?' (2018) 17(2) European State Aid Law Quarterly 204.

[48] The aim of such a protection scheme created by banks is often to ensure the liquidity and solvency of its members, including by supporting the possible resolution of a failing-or-likely-to-fail member by providing liquidity or capital support through loans or guarantees, with funds coming from the own resources of the scheme members.

[49] The 3rd subpara of art 19(3) SRMR directly envisages a special comparable in-depth investigation procedure if the Commission has serious doubts as to the compatibility of the proposed use of the Fund with the internal market, or where the SRB has failed to provide the necessary information for the assessment of the Fund aid pursuant to a request of the Commission.

formal investigation if it has serious doubts[50] about the compatibility of the State aid with the internal market. According to settled case law,[51] the concept of serious difficulties coincides with that of doubts and is objective in nature. Such doubts must give rise to the initiation of a formal investigation procedure in which the interested parties referred to in Article 1(h) of Regulation (EU) 2015/1589 may participate. However, in order to ensure that the Fund aid is subject to an equivalent regime, the third subparagraph of Article 19(3) SRMR introduces a rule explicitly providing that, where the Commission has serious doubts as to the compatibility of the proposed use of the Fund with the internal market, or where the Board has failed to provide the necessary information pursuant to a request of the Commission, the Commission is obliged to open an in-depth investigation.

In the same vein, the competence assigned to the Commission under Article 19 SRMR is limited to the compatibility assessment of Fund aid, and the Commission has no power to examine State aid under Article 19 SRMR. In other words, conceptually and formally, the Commission assesses the State aid and the Fund aid under separate legal bases—respectively under Article 107 TFEU and Article 19 SRMR—even though the Union legislator decided in Article 19 SRMR that the Fund aid has to be assessed in accordance with the same rules as the State aid. However, assessment under the same compatibility criteria does not conceptually transform the Fund aid into State aid. The Fund aid cannot constitute State aid, as it is not imputable to the state or granted from the state's resources.

V Assistance from DGS

Apart from the Fund aid, another less probable but still apparent source of funding[52] for a FOLTF bank is a national deposit scheme. The intervention by the DGS is a State aid measure where all the cumulative[53] conditions set

[50] Art 4(4) of Regulation (EU) 2015/1589 laying down detailed rules for the application of Article 108 of the Treaty on the Functioning of the European Union ([2015] OJ L248, p 9) provides that, '[w]here the Commission, after a preliminary examination, finds that doubts are raised as to the compatibility with the internal market of a notified measure, it shall decide to initiate proceedings pursuant to Article 108(2) TFEU.'

[51] See, inter alia, judgment of 6 October 2021 in Case T-167/19 *Tempus Energy Germany GmbH and T Energy Sweden AB v Commission*, ECLI:EU:T:2021:645, para 49.

[52] Art 79 SRMR regulates the use of deposit guarantee schemes in the context of resolution.

[53] For a measure to be qualified as State aid within the meaning of art 107(1) TFEU, the following cumulative criteria must be met: (i) it must be granted by the State and through State resources; (ii) it must confer an advantage upon an undertaking; (iii) it must be selective, ie favour certain undertakings or the production of certain goods; and (iv) it must distort or threaten to distort competition and it must affect trade between Member States.

out in Article 107(1) TFEU are fulfilled. When exercising State aid control, the Commission must first determine whether a measure constitutes State aid. For that purpose, the Commission relies on its notice summarizing its case practice and the jurisprudence of the European courts regarding the notion of State aid.[54]

Where the financial support is provided by a DGS governed by private law and that DGS is neither an organization of the state nor a public undertaking, that measure taken by a DGS would not, following the *Tercas* judgment, qualify as State aid, if the measure is not imputable to the state.[55] The correct qualification of a specific intervention by the DGS has a particular importance if it is granted as precautionary support, because of a far-reaching consequence of whether that intervention will trigger the FOLTF declaration.

The outcome of the assessment of the measure taken by a DGS would, in principle, depend on the features of the specific scheme and the particular measure. The measure is not imputable to the state only where the Member State does not have any discretion left regarding the use of the funds or granting of advantages.[56] Where Union law, however, makes the contribution from a DGS mandatory without any doubt, and the conditions of that mandatory DGS intervention are clearly set out in Union law, the imputability to the state would normally be absent. It looks like the wording of Article 79(1) SRMR read together with Article 109 BRRD could allow to maintain that the DGS intervention is mandatory—'the deposit guarantee scheme to which the institution is affiliated shall be liable'—and that the conditions for determining the relevant amounts of intervention are sufficiently well defined. The outcome might, however, differ where not the SRB but the national resolution authorities handle resolution in accordance with Article 109 BRRD alone, which indicates that 'Member States shall ensure that, where the resolution authorities take resolution action, and provided that that action ensures that depositors continue to have access to their deposits, the deposit guarantee scheme to which the institution is affiliated is liable for specific amounts'. As some DGSs are private and others public, there is currently quite some uncertainty as to which DGSs could support preventive measures without triggering a FOLTF declaration of the bank.

[54] Commission Notice on the notion of State aid as referred to in Article 107(1) of the Treaty on the Functioning of the European Union, C/2016/2946 ([2016] OJ C262, p 1).

[55] Judgment of 2 March 2021 in Case C-425/19 P *Commission v Italy et al (Tercas)*, ECLI:EU:C:2021:154.

[56] Judgment of 5 April 2006 in Case T-351/02 *Deutsche Bahn AG v Commission*, ECLI:EU:C:2006:104.

In April 2023, the Commission adopted a package of proposals to reform the CMDI framework[57] that, inter alia, aim at facilitating the use of DGS funds for the purpose of implementing the resolution tools. The alternative use of DGS funds, if compared with the primary functions of paying out covered deposits, is also expected to be subject to a harmonized least-cost test. The package is currently being negotiated by the co-legislators. The coherence aspect between the State aid rules and the resolution framework could also be addressed from the State aid side, especially as regards the burden-sharing requirements and conditions to access funding to support tools within and outside resolution.

VI Conclusion

In the Banking Union, the Commission, in charge of the State aid control, could find itself rather closely knitted together with the bank supervisory and resolution authorities—albeit, of course, that all those actors are in charge of their own parallel assessments—every time State aid or Fund aid must be provided to a bank.

While the resolution framework aimed at significantly reducing access to public money for bank resolution, the public funding may still be rather widely used for precautionary measures, as well as for FOLTF banks whose resolution is not in public interest, in the latter case for their orderly exit from the market. The applicable resolution and State aid frameworks are tightly intertwined and interdependent, even if they have certain mutual incoherences. The State aid rules still play an important complementary role in assessing support for banks in the Banking Union.

[57] For the general description, see the Commission's Communication on the review of the CMDI framework contributing to completing the Banking Union, COM (2023) 225 final.

16

Cooperation between National Authorities and the Banking Union regarding Macroprudential Policy

Lawmakers' Intentions and Reality after 10 Years of the EU Macroprudential Framework

Ursula Hauser-Rethaller[*]

I Relevance of macroprudential policy

Macroprudential policy and the Banking Union (BU) are both consequences of the Great Financial Crisis of 2008–09. Both were established in order to avoid another financial crisis and sustain financial stability. While the Basel Committee on Banking Supervision (BCBS) had already published its macroprudential framework[1] in December 2010, the implementation[2] into the European legal framework[3] was finished in 2013, and the macroprudential framework only became legally binding on 1 January 2016 (with transitional provisions until 2018). Since then, its relevance has increased continuously, as, on the one hand, relevant/competent authorities are increasingly setting and modifying macroprudential policy measures, and, on the other, the Covid-19 pandemic and its strong effects on business cycles and inflation have raised

* This text expresses the personal opinion of the author and not that of the Austrian Financial Market Authority.

[1] Basel Committee on Banking Supervision, 'Basel III: A global regulatory framework for more resilient banks and banking systems, December 2010' (Bank for International Settlements 2011).

[2] In addition to implementing the rules laid down by the BCBS, the EU framework added a few elements, most importantly the systemic risk buffer.

[3] Directive 2013/36/EU of the European Parliament and of the Council of 26 June 2013 on access to the activity of credit institutions and the prudential supervision of credit institutions and investment firms, amending Directive 2002/87/EC and repealing Directives 2006/48/EC and 2006/49/EC [2013] OJ L176/338 (Capital Requirements Directive (CRD IV)).

Ursula Hauser-Rethaller, *Cooperation between National Authorities and the Banking Union regarding Macroprudential Policy* In: *EU Banking Union*. Edited by: Jonathan Bauerschmidt, Raffaele D'Ambrosio, Diane Fromage, Daniela Jaros, and Paul Weismann, Oxford University Press. © Oxford University Press 2026.
DOI: 10.1093/9780198949756.003.0017

concerns about maintaining financial stability and adequacy of measures, not only in the supervisory community but also in broader policy discussions.

The increased importance of financial stability in the European Union (EU) led to the establishment of the European Systemic Risk Board (ESRB)[4] in 2010, which was designed with the purpose of establishing 'a Union level body charged with overseeing risk in the financial system as a whole'.[5] The ESRB is responsible for the coordination of macroprudential policies in the EU and the European Economic Area (EEA), and for the issuance of recommendations and warnings in the context of risks to financial market stability at the European level. With the same regulation, an overarching body for ensuring the supervision of the Union's financial system, the European System of Financial Supervision (ESFS), which encompasses all players with regard to microprudential supervision as well as macroprudential supervision for all financial sectors, was created too.[6] While the ESRB now fulfils a leading role in standard-setting, analysing, coordinating,[7] and shaping macroprudential policy in the EU, the ESFS as a body, in contrast to its members, remained of limited relevance. The ESRB also has a central role in ensuring that reciprocation of macroprudential measures in other Member States works smoothly.

1 What is macroprudential policy? What is its purpose?

The ultimate goal of macroprudential policy is to ensure financial market stability.[8] This is achieved by: (a) measures to strengthen the resilience of the financial system; and (b) measures to reduce the systemic risks and, consequently, to smooth the financial cycle. Microprudential supervision, which has a much longer history, in contrast, focuses on the soundness of each

[4] Regulation (EU) 1092/2010 of the European Parliament and of the Council of 24 November 2010 on European Union macro-prudential oversight of the financial system and establishing a European Systemic Risk Board [2010] OJ L331/1 amended by Regulation (EU) 2019/2176 of the European Parliament and the Council of 18 December 2019 amending Regulation (EU) No 1092/2010 on European Union macro-prudential oversight of the financial system and establishing a European Systemic Risk Board (Text with EEA relevance) [2019] OJ L334/146.

[5] ibid, recital 4.

[6] ibid, art 1(2).

[7] The CRD V (Directive 2019/878/EU of the European Parliament and of the Council of 20 May 2019 amending Directive 2013/36/EU as regards exempted entities, financial holding companies, mixed financial holding companies, remuneration, supervisory measures and powers and capital conservation measures (Text with EEA relevance) [2019] OJ L150/253) has established a central coordinative role for the ESRB. All macroprudential measures must be notified by NDAs to the ESRB, which in turn forwards the notifications to all other NDAs and publishes all macroprudential measures applicable in any Member State on its website.

[8] This is laid down in art 3 of Regulation (EU) 1092/2010.

single institution and its ability to fulfil its obligations vis-à-vis its creditors, counterparties, and the supervisor. While microprudential supervision and macroprudential supervision share the same ultimate goal—financial market stability—the fundamental difference[9] is in the perspective: while the former focuses on individual institutions, the latter focuses on the system as a whole (financial and not only banking) and its interdependencies.[10] Macroprudential supervision is about the identification and mitigation of systemic risks, which can materialize in contagion effects, as, for example, in the case of bank failures or bursting house-price bubbles, or when market liquidity is under stress. Consequently, the focus of analysis, the analytical tools, and the policy instruments differ. Notwithstanding the differences, coordination and cooperation between the two fields of banking supervision lead to superior outcomes.

Empirical research shows that the financial system develops over time in cycles, with boom phases followed by downturns and bust phases. Financial cycles do not run in parallel with business cycles, as financial cycles span over more years and are more costly when a bust phase is followed by a recession.[11] Therefore, risks to financial stability need to be addressed separately from the business cycle. Monetary policy, which is the main task of the European Central Bank (ECB) in the Economic and Monetary Union (EMU), aims at a different goal—to achieve price stability. Monetary policy instruments often yield detrimental effects on financial market stability. Price stability and financial market stability do not go hand in hand, and may even be conflicting goals, and thus require different sets of instruments. Therefore, macroprudential policy and macroprudential supervision need distinctive measures and institutional settings of their own to fulfil their purpose.

The toolbox for macroprudential policy comprises:

(1) Capital-based measures like buffers, ie an additional amount of capital, determined as a fraction of a bank's risk-exposure amount,[12] and add-ons to risk weights used for the calculation of risk-exposure amounts.

[9] For a more detailed distinction, see IMF, 'Macroprudential Policy', https://www.imf.org/en/publications/sprolls/macroprudential-policy, accessed 17 May 2026.

[10] The differences between macroprudential and microprudential supervision and the necessity that each approach takes into account the other one are explained in paras 145–51 of 'The high level group on financial supervision in the EU', chaired by Jacques de Larosière, Report (2009), https://ec.europa.eu/economy_finance/publications/pages/publication14527_en.pdf, accessed 17 May 2026.

[11] Claudio Borio, 'The Financial Cycle and Macroeconomics: What Have We Learnt?' (2014) 45 Journal of Banking & Finance 182.

[12] As defined in art 92(3) of Regulation (EU) 575/2013 of the European Parliament and of the Council of 26 June 2013 on prudential requirements for credit institutions and investment firms and amending Regulation (EU) No 648/2012 [2013] OJ L176/1.

(2) Borrower-based measures (BBMs) that require lending for specific purposes to meet minimum/maximum ratios, for example for loan-to-value, debt-to-income, or debt service-to-income.
(3) Measures addressing liquidity.
(4) Other measures, for example addressing large exposures.

This chapter focuses on the tools mentioned under points 1 and 2, as the others are currently of limited relevance for setting macroprudential policy measures within the existing framework in the BU.[13] While the current common macroprudential framework defines a strong role for the national competent/designated authorities, the role of the ECB seems a subordinated one. The following sections take a closer look at the challenges and conflicts resulting from these arrangements and the cooperation necessary between the national authorities and the ECB. They take a closer look at how the current framework strikes the balance between the necessary subsidiarity and country-specific differentiation of macroprudential measures and the goal to ensure a level playing field via consequent harmonization.

II The legal framework for macroprudential policy in the EU

The macroprudential policy framework in the EU is based on several sources:

(1) The Capital Requirement Directive (CRD IV)[14] and its amendments CRD V[15] and CRD VI,[16] implemented by national law.
(2) Directly applicable EU regulations, such as the Capital Requirements Regulation (CRR)[17] and its amendments.[18]

[13] For a detailed description, see Vitor Constâncio (ed), 'Macroprudential policy at the ECB: Institutional framework, strategy, analytical tools and policies', ECB Occasional Paper Series No 227 (2019).

[14] CRD IV (n 3).

[15] CRD V (n 7).

[16] Directive (EU) 2024/1619 of the European Parliament and of the Council of 31 May 2024 amending Directive 2013/36/EU as regards supervisory powers, sanctions, third-country branches, and environmental, social and governance risks [2024] OJ L2024/1619.

[17] Regulation (EU) 575/2013 of the European Parliament and of the Council of 26 June 2013 on prudential requirements for credit institutions and investment firms and amending Regulation (EU) No 648/2012 [2013] OJ L176/1 (CRR). Relevant changes were introduced by CRR III, Regulation (EU) 2024/1623 of the European Parliament and of the Council of 31 May 2024 amending Regulation (EU) No 575/2013 as regards requirements for credit risk, credit valuation adjustment risk, operational risk, market risk and the output floor OJ L1623.

[18] The amendment relevant for macroprudential policy is CRR II, Regulation (EU) 2019/876 of the European Parliament and of the Council of 20 May 2019 amending Regulation (EU) No 575/2013 as regards the leverage ratio, the net stable funding ratio, requirements for own funds and eligible liabilities,

(3) National legislation.
(4) EU soft law, for example recommendations by the European Systemic Risk Board (ESRB) or guidelines and opinions issued by the European Banking Authority (EBA).
(5) National soft law (recommendations and warnings of national financial stability boards).

The same list, in general, also applies to microprudential supervision. As already mentioned, microprudential supervision has been in place much longer than macroprudential supervision, which is also reflected by the fact that the main sources of the macroprudential framework, mentioned under points 1 and 2—the CRD and the CRR—mainly focus on microprudential supervision, which is executed by the competent authorities (CAs), as defined in Article 4 CRD IV.[19] The role of the ECB as competent authority is defined in the Single Supervisory Mechanism Regulation (SSMR).[20] Compared with the microprudential framework, the macroprudential framework accounts only for a small part of the regulatory framework of the CRD and CRR.

In addition to these sources, publications from the BCBS are also of relevance for the interpretation and application of the EU macroprudential policy framework.

1 Common EU and BU legal framework

a) CRD IV–VI

The backbone of the macroprudential framework applicable in the BU is the CRD, ie CRD IV[21] amended by CRD V and CRD VI,[22] which sets out the buffer regime comprising:

(1) the countercyclical capital buffer (CCyB);

counterparty credit risk, market risk, exposures to central counterparties, exposures to collective investment undertakings, large exposures, reporting and disclosure requirements, and Regulation (EU) No 648/2012 [2019] OJ L150/1.

19 CRD IV (n 3).
20 Council Regulation (EU) No 1024/2013 of 15 October 2013 conferring specific tasks on the European Central Bank concerning policies relating to the prudential supervision of credit institutions [2013] OJ L287/63 (SSMR).
21 CRD IV (n 3).
22 Further references to the 'CRD' refer to CRD IV–VI. The minor changes to the macroprudential framework laid down in CRD VI apply from 11 January 2026.

(2) the buffer for identified global systemically important institutions (G-SIIB);
(3) the buffer for other systemically important institutions (O-SIIB),
(4) the systemic risk buffer (SyRB); and
(5) the capital conservation buffer, which has, contrary to the other buffers, a fixed value of 2.5% that requires no further policy action.[23]

The CRD determines the risks to be addressed by the buffers, as well as procedural questions like who sets the measure and who needs to be informed or to consent. The CRD, furthermore, defines disclosure requirements and reciprocation measures, and, finally, capital conservation measures, which determine the consequences for institutions that breach the combined buffer. However, neither an analytical framework nor a common set of indicators for measuring the risks to be addressed are defined in the CRD or the CRR. This is left to soft law issued by the EBA and the ESRB.[24] The CRR[25] and the CRD leave it to the Member States to entrust either the National Competent Authority (NCA) for microprudential supervision or another 'designated authority' with setting macroprudential policy measures. In any case, this authority is not the ECB. This leads to the situation that, in some countries, setting macroprudential policy measures is located at the same authorities as microprudential supervision for Less Significant Institutions, while in a few countries this is left to another authority. For the remainder of this text, this authority is, in any case, referred to as the 'national designated authority' (NDA). It is important to distinguish further between the 'national designated authority' and the 'macroprudential authority' that the ESRB has defined for its purposes.[26] Apart from the different legal bases, the distinction of powers and purpose is a subtle one: the macroprudential authority is the body that takes the decision on macroprudential policy measures, whereas the NDA is responsible for setting the legal act necessary to implement the decision.[27] While, for 13 Member States of the ESRB, the macroprudential authority is different from the NDA,

[23] Art 458 CRR gives the National Competent Authority or the national designated authority the option to increase the capital conservation buffer in extreme circumstances. This option has, so far, never been used.

[24] The responsibility of the ESRB to issue principles for the design of macroprudential policy measures is clarified in recital 86 of the CRD IV, and by Regulation (EU) No 1092/2010.

[25] For example, art 124(8), CRR.

[26] This refers to the macroprudential authority established in accordance with Recommendation of the European Systemic Risk Board of 22 December 2011 on the macro-prudential mandate of national authorities (Recommendation ESRB/2011/3) [2012] OJ C41/1.

[27] This distinction is explained in Donato Salomone, *National Authorities for Macroprudential Supervision Within the European Union* (2024) Quaderni di Ricerca Giuridica della Consulenza Legale (102), Banca d'Italia.

for the remaining Member States of the ESRB it is the same authority—in most cases, the central bank.[28]

b) CRR

The CRR defines some additional macroprudential policy options available to the national authorities:

(1) The NDA can increase the risk weights for exposures secured by real-estate property located in the Member State's territory, for which risk-weighted exposure amounts are calculated using the Standardised Approach for credit risk (SA).[29] For exposures for which risk-weighted exposure amounts are calculated according to the IRB[30] approach, the loss given default (LGD) input floor values for retail exposures secured by real-estate property located in the Member State's territory can be increased, too.[31] Standards for the assessment of the appropriateness of risk weights and LGD input floor values in this context are specified by an EU delegated regulation.[32]

(2) In a case where risks to financial market stability with 'the potential to have serious negative consequences to the financial system and the real economy in a specific Member State'[33] are identified 'that cannot be addressed by means of other macroprudential tools set out in this Regulation and in Directive 2013/36/EU as effectively as by implementing stricter national measures',[34] NDAs can adopt measures with respect to own funds requirements or liquidity requirements, risk weights for exposures secured by real-estate property, large exposure requirements, the level of the capital conservation buffer, disclosure requirements, or intra-financial sector exposures. To ensure that such a measure is implemented only when no other measure can address the identified risks, the CRR demands a cooperative process that requires

[28] For a complete list, see www.esrb.191125_list_national_macroprudential_authorities, accessed 8 September 2025.
[29] Art 124(9) CRR.
[30] IRB stands for 'internal ratings-based'.
[31] Art 164(6) CRR.
[32] Commission delegated regulation (EU) 2023/206 of 5 October 2022 supplementing Regulation (EU) No 575/2013 of the European Parliament and of the Council with regard to regulatory technical standards specifying the types of factors to be considered for the assessment of the appropriateness of risk weights for exposures secured by immovable property and the conditions to be taken into account for the assessment of the appropriateness of minimum loss given default values for exposures secured by immovable property [2023] OJ L29/1.
[33] Art 458 CRR.
[34] ibid.

the NDA to notify the European Commission and the ESRB, which in turn informs the Council, the EBA, and the European Parliament. On the basis of information provided by the NDA (as required by the CRR), the EBA and the ESRB provide an opinion to the Commission, the Council, and the NDA. In a case where the opinions provide robust evidence that the negative impact of the proposed measure on the internal market outweighs the positive effects on financial stability, the Commission can propose the Council to adopt an implementing act in order to reject the draft national measures. In that case, the Council decides by qualified majority whether to adopt the proposed implementing act to reject the draft national measures. Otherwise, the NDA may implement the measure as notified. In addition to this lengthy process, Member States of the BU need to follow the process required by Article 5 SSMR.

c) European instruments of soft law

EBA guidelines and ESRB recommendations are legally non-binding instruments and are subject to a comply-or-explain mechanism. This means that the addressee either declares compliance with the stated rules or explains why compliance is not possible or not justified. The EBA and the ESRB monitor Member States' compliance with their soft law acts.[35]

The EBA guidelines on defining sectoral systemic risk buffers[36] specify, in the context of the application of the sectoral systemic risk buffer, the criteria for the identification of a 'sector'. Two further EBA guidelines specify the indicators to be used to identify global systemically important institutions,[37] and the methodology for identification of other systemically important institutions.[38] However, the mentioned guidelines do not specify rules for determination of the buffer sizes. For the Banking Union, the ECB[39] has thus published

[35] For an introduction into, and discussion of, European soft law instruments, see Diane Fromage and others, 'Soft Law and Multilevel Cooperation as Sources of (New) Constitutional Challenges' in 'EU Economic and Monetary Integration: Introduction to the Special Issue (2022) 23(1) Journal of Banking Regulation 1.

[36] EBA, 'Final guidelines on the appropriate subsets of sectoral exposures to which competent or designated authorities may apply a systemic risk buffer in accordance with Article 133(5)(f) of Directive 2013/36/EU', EBA/GL/2020/13.

[37] EBA, 'Revised guidelines on the further specification of the indicators of global systemic importance and their disclosure', EBA/GL/2016/01.

[38] EBA, 'Guidelines On the criteria to determine the conditions of application of Article 131(3) of Directive 2013/36/EU (CRD) in relation to the assessment of other systemically important institutions (O-SIIs)', EBA/GL/2014/10.

[39] ECB, 'Governing Council statement on macroprudential policies – the ECB's framework for assessing capital buffers of other systemically important institutions' (2024) https://www.ecb.europa.eu/press/govcstatement/pdf/ecb.govcstatement202412~b1f786e5f1.en.pdf, accessed 15 September

minimum values for O-SII buffer rates depending on the score as determined according to the methodology determined by EBA/GL/2014/10. This floor methodology is used by the ECB as the reference for assessing O-SII buffers notified by NDAs. It is worth noting that, in the context of macroprudential supervision, the ECB is not an addressee of the relevant EBA guidelines, contrary to microprudential supervision, where the ECB has the status of a competent authority.[40] However, it is hard to imagine that the ECB would issue any soft law instrument, in the context of the exercise of Article 5 SSMR, contradicting EBA soft law, as in the ECB's internal decision process the NDAs that have declared compliance with the EBA guideline would find it difficult to agree to such an act.

ESRB recommendations[41] may address risks in specific Member States or in the EU in total, or may give guidance on specific aspects of macroprudential policies. The most relevant recommendations not addressed to a specific country concern reciprocation of macroprudential measures in other Member States[42] and guidance for setting the CCyB.[43]

2 National transpositions and national rules

The parts of the framework determined by directives (CRD IV–VI) require transposition into national banking laws. This allows the national legislature to add rules with regard to two dimensions: (a) procedural requirements on the decision process until the NDA sets the measure, whether it requires any recommendations, non-objections, or even consent by national bodies; and (b) which legal instrument (law, regulation) is chosen.

A large proportion of countries in the BU have established a financial market stability board, which is the macroprudential authority 'entrusted with the conduct of macro-prudential policy' following Recommendation B of the

2025. Further details on the methodology are provided in Maciej Grodzicki and others, 'Enhancing the ECB's O-SII framework' in ECB Macroprudential Bulletin (2025) 30 https://www.ecb.europa.eu/press/financial-stability-publications/macroprudential-bulletin/html/ecb.mpbu202508_01.en.html, accessed 15 September 2025.

40 Art 4(1) no 40 CRR.

41 For a complete list of all ESRB recommendations so far, see https://www.esrb.europa.eu/mppa, accessed 15 September 2025.

42 ESRB, 'Recommendation of the European Systemic Risk Board of 15 December 2015 on the assessment of cross-border effects of and voluntary reciprocity for macroprudential policy measures' (ESRB/2015/2) [2016] OJ C97/9 and amendments.

43 ESRB, 'Recommendation of the European Systemic Risk Board of 18 June 2014 on guidance for setting countercyclical buffer rates' (ESRB/2014/1) [2014] OJ C293/01.

ESRB recommendation 2011/3.[44] Some of them have—in analogy to the ESRB competencies—the power to issue warnings and recommendations to the NDA. The remaining countries of the BU have entrusted their central banks with the conduct of macroprudential policy. In this case, the central bank is also the NDA, as specified by the CRD and the CRR. The compositions and concrete institutional settings of the financial market stability boards in the different Member States are diverse and, in terms of governance, two different outcomes are possible: in some frameworks the NDA or the institution that governs the NDA has the decisive vote in the financial market stability board; in other frameworks this is not the case. This means, for the latter case, that the financial market stability board is not only a consultative panel for the NDA, but that it can take decisions that are not in line with the NDA's assessment.

The EU framework does not provide a legal basis for NDAs to establish BBMs, ie macroprudential measures that define concrete credit standards as, for example, a maximum tolerable ratio of the borrowers' debt to their income, but it encourages national legislatures to do so.[45] The legal basis for such measures is, therefore, determined exclusively in the national legislations. This has an important implication for the cooperation between NDAs and the ECB, as Article 5 SSMR is only applicable when NDAs set macroprudential policies based on EU law, and is thus not applicable to BBMs. The ESRB can recommend BBMs,[46] and monitors their application and effectiveness, but has to accept the boundaries of the diverse legal frameworks for BBMs in Member States.

3 The interaction framework

a) At EU level: The role of the ESRB

At the EU level, the ESRB is the body responsible for macroprudential oversight.[47] Its duties encompass monitoring and assessing systemic risk and analysing all relevant information,[48] issuing warnings and recommendations

[44] ESRB, 'Recommendation of the European Systemic Risk Board of 22 December 2011 on the macro-prudential mandate of national authorities' (ESRB/2011/3) [2012] OJ C41/01.

[45] See recital 22 of the CRD V.

[46] For example, Recommendation of the European Systemic Risk Board of 2 December 2021 on medium-term vulnerabilities in the residential real estate sector in Austria, ESRB/2021/11 [2022] OJ C122/02.

[47] See recital 6 of Regulation (EU) 1092/2010 of the European Parliament and of the Council of 24 November 2010 on European Union macro-prudential oversight of the financial system and establishing a European Systemic Risk Board [2010] OJ L331/1.

[48] See ibid, recital 10.

and following up[49] on these, and coordination and communication of macroprudential policies pursued by Member States.[50] The responsibility of the ESRB encompasses all financial sectors as well as guarantee schemes. In a case where the ESRB identifies serious risks, the Council must be informed. The ESRB is well connected with all other relevant institutions in this context, due to a broad membership and other arrangements, and it also gets scientific support. However, it has no legal powers to enforce compliance with its recommendations or trigger desired action after its warnings. When pursuing its tasks, the ESRB needs to rely on the power of clear and transparent analysis and scientific evidence and the factual power of transparency. Recommendations can be made public,[51] which also helps ensure compliance, whereas compliance reports are usually not published.

The ESRB fulfils an important role by ensuring transparency and knowledge sharing. It provides easily accessible information on all macroprudential measures in place in the EEA, all (published) recommendations, and a large number of studies, handbooks, and papers on macroprudential policies, giving NDAs guidance on good practices, and on which methodologies to use for analysis and design of measures. Further, the ESRB publishes regular and occasional reports assessing risks to financial stability as well as suggestions for further development of the framework.

b) At BU level

Contrary to microprudential supervision, where full competence for the supervision of significant institutions has been transferred to the ECB,[52] with NCAs contributing to, but not deciding on, microprudential measures, setting macroprudential measures has been a joint endeavour of the NDAs and the ECB since the creation of the BU. Article 5(1) SSMR specifies that NDAs must notify the ECB of all macroprudential measures intended to be taken, including all changes to existing macroprudential measures, 10 working days before the NDA decides on the measure. Article 104 of the SSM Framework Regulation[53] additionally requires NDAs to inform the ECB as early as possible

[49] See ibid, recital 11.

[50] A detailed description of the full set of macroprudential measures available in the EU and the duties of the ESRB can be found in the ESRB's flagship report: ESRB, 'Flagship Report on Macro-prudential Policy in the Banking Sector' (2014), https://www.esrb.europa.eu/pub/pdf/other/140303_flagship_report.pdf, accessed 17 May 2026.

[51] See art 3, para 2(c) of Regulation (EU) 1092/2010. For publications, see www.esrb.europa.eu/mppa/recommendations, accessed 15 September 2025.

[52] As defined in art 4 SSMR.

[53] Regulation (EU) 468/2014 of the European Central Bank of 16 April 2014 establishing the framework for cooperation within the Single Supervisory Mechanism between the European Central Bank

if they intend to apply a macroprudential tool. The information should contain as much information as possible on the systemic risks and the intended tools, including the intended application date. In the case where the ECB assesses the measure as insufficient to address the identified risks to financial stability, the ECB has the power to impose a stricter measure (top-up power) via an ECB decision that is directly applicable in the Member State concerned. When exercising the top-up power, the ECB acts as the designated authority.[54] However, Article 5(4) SSMR explicitly requires close cooperation and a formal communication process between the NDA concerned and the ECB before the ECB can exercise its power and issue such a decision. Articles 104 and 105 of the SSM Framework Regulation, as well as Article 13h of the Rules of Procedure of the ECB,[55] determine the precise decision and approbation process with the ECB in that context, which requires that the ECB notifies the NDA of its intention to exercise its top-up power and gives the NDA the opportunity to object within five working days, and the ECB has to 'duly consider those reasons prior to proceeding with the decision as appropriate'.[56] Article 5(5) SSMR, moreover, requires the ECB to 'take into account the specific situation of the financial system, economic situation and the economic cycle in individual Member States or parts thereof'. Interestingly, the ECB needs, in its decision, reference to the national implementation of the relevant article of the CRD, ie Articles 130–140, as a legal basis for the content of the decision.[57] However, any procedural rules—for example, consent of a national body—contained in the national implementations of these articles are irrelevant for the ECB, as it derives its powers from Article 5 SSMR.[58]

What are the intentions of the EU legislature that we can infer from Article 5 SSM Regulation and the CRD IV–V?

(1) Recital 24 of the SSMR implies that setting macroprudential measures is, in the first place, the responsibility of the NDAs, with the ECB in a coordinating role: 'In order to ensure full coordination, where national

and National Competent Authorities and with national designated authorities (SSM Framework Regulation) [2014] OJ L141/1.

[54] Art 9(1) SSMR.

[55] Decision of the European Central Bank of 19 February 2004 adopting the Rules of Procedure of the European Central Bank, OJ L80/33 amended by Decision ECB/2004/2 of the European Central Bank of 22 January 2014, L95/56.

[56] Art 5(4), last sentence of SSMR.

[57] Art 102 of SSM Framework Regulation.

[58] Further aspects of the application of national law by the ECB are discussed in the contribution of Daniela Jaros to this book.

competent authorities or national designated authorities impose such measures, the ECB should be duly notified. Moreover, where necessary the ECB should be able to apply higher requirements and more stringent measures, subject to close coordination with national authorities.' This role in macroprudential supervision as coordinator and watchdog is in contrast to the ECB's responsibilities and powers as microprudential authority, as determined in Article 4 SSMR. The conclusion from this marked difference in institutional settings could be that macroprudential policy within the BU should address the national level, or in some cases even regional levels,[59] but not the level of the BU. This implies that the national financial markets and economies are the units of analysis preceding any measures, and that national specificities and institutional settings need to be taken into account. Consequently, the discretionary leeway that the CRD and CRR give to the NDA when identifying risks to financial stability and determining the measure and its size remains, in the first place, with the NDA.

(2) The NDA is the institution that needs to start the formal process of setting a macroprudential measure by filing a notification at the ECB.[60] In the case where the NDA does not notify (as it does not set) a buffer, Article 102 SSM Framework Regulation clarifies: 'If an NDA does not set a buffer rate, this does not prevent the ECB from setting a buffer requirement in accordance with this regulation and Article 5(2) of the SSM Regulation.' It remains unclear whether 'buffer rate' in that sentence should be read literally or whether it should encompass also measures pursuant to Articles 124(9), 164(6), or 458 CRR. The literal reading leads to an interpretation of Article 5(2) SSMR regarding Articles 124(9), 164(6), or 458 CRR that concludes that the ECB cannot top-up if the NDA does not intend to take a measure and therefore the ECB is not notified pursuant to Art 5(1) of the SSM Regulation. Consequently, it can be inferred that the primary targets of the legislature, for the top-up power, are the CCyB, the systemic risk buffer, and the O-SII/G-SII buffers.

[59] See the options to set a sectoral systemic risk buffer defined in art 133(5) CRD V, as detailed further by EBA, 'Final guidelines on the appropriate subsets of sectoral exposures to which competent or designated authorities may apply a systemic risk buffer in accordance with Article 133(5)(f) of Directive 2013/36/EU', EBA/GL/2020/13.

[60] Recital 24 of the SSM Regulation demands that, 'where national competent authorities or national designated authorities impose such measures, the ECB should be duly notified'.

(3) The EU legislature has introduced the top-up power of the ECB to prevent NDAs from being hesitant to take measures, or from taking them too late or too leniently (inaction bias). This means that, if an NDA underestimates the risks to financial stability and takes insufficient measures, the ECB[61] should identify insufficient measures and communicate this to the NDA, with the preferential outcome being the NDA adjusting its measures accordingly. Otherwise, the ECB may issue a decision setting an appropriate level of the measure under discussion.

(4) A uniform macroprudential measure for the whole BU is not a desired outcome;[62] thus, the ECB has no such power. The top-up power requires the ECB to analyse the risks to financial stability in each Member State of the BU and come up with its own assessment of the optimal macroprudential measures to be taken, as otherwise the ECB would not be in the position to justify any top-up.[63] The risk that risks to financial stability remain unidentified is, thus, reduced by the top-up power. A comprehensive assessment requires an exchange of information, data, assessment methodologies, and views between the NDA and the ECB already during the analysis process. This can lead to situations where the NDA's and the ECB's results from their respective assessments converge to congruent conclusions, as all relevant information has been shared.

(5) Macroprudential policy measures should be taken at the time when and to the extent that it is necessary to tame risks to financial stability, and released[64] when risks have decreased to a sufficient extent.[65] To reach this goal, the EU legislature has foreseen two mechanisms. First, to prevent excessive macroprudential measures with detrimental effects to the real economy, there are rules on public disclosure of the nature of and reasoning for the measure, together with a high level of transparency

[61] In this context, it is interesting to mention art 5(3) SSMR, which gives any Member State of the BU the right to propose to the ECB that it uses its top-up power.

[62] Using the powers of art 458(2)(d)(vi) CRR to impose an add-on to the capital conservation buffer could be an example that, under some circumstances, might make sense.

[63] See art 5(5) SSMR, which requires the ECB to take account of the specific situation and the business cycle in the Member State concerned.

[64] O-SII buffers cannot be fully released as long as any systemically relevant banks are domiciled in a country. Other systemic risks of the structure of a banking system may remain constant for many years, too.

[65] Recital 80 CRD IV states, for the CCyB, the aim to build up capital when system-wide risks build up and release capital during stressed periods. Recital 85 CRD IV explains the purpose of the systemic risk buffer to 'prevent and mitigate long-term non-cyclical systemic or macroprudential risks not covered by Regulation (EU) No 575/2013, where there is a risk of disruption in the financial system with the potential to have serious negative consequences for the financial system and the real economy in a specific Member State'.

towards the ESRB,[66] the ECB, other NDAs, and the EBA. For buffer levels above 3%, the European Commission must be involved, and for measures pursuant to Article 458 CRR, even the Council and the European Parliament must be involved. Second, to prevent inaction, the ESRB can issue recommendations, and the ECB may use its top-up power.

c) Interaction between the ESRB and the ECB

Although the ESRB is chaired by the president of the ECB and gets analytical, administrative, and logistical support from the ECB and has no legal personality of its own,[67] this does not imply that the ESRB acts on behalf of the ECB or executes ECB policies. The ESRB is independent from the ECB in its decisions and strategies pursued. By fulfilling its mandate, to ensure an 'effective macro-prudential oversight of the Union financial system',[68] the ECB, within its macroprudential competencies, is also subject to the ESRB's surveillance. Thus, cooperation within the BU on macroprudential policies is embedded into the even larger cooperative network within the ESRB, and must take the cooperation requirements for interactions with the European Commission, the Council, and the European Parliament into account.[69] The CRD IV states the intention that the ESRB should 'ensure consistent macroprudential oversight across the Union'.[70]

As far as the exercise of powers is concerned, the crucial difference between the ECB and the ESRB is that the latter can exercise 'soft powers'[71] by publishing recommendations or warnings. In particular, the ESRB may issue warnings or recommendations to address significant systemic risks to financial stability in the EU. The ESRB then monitors the follow-up actions undertaken by the addressees of its warnings or recommendations and analyses if, and to what extent, the systemic risk has been mitigated. In addition, specific Union legislation requires that the ESRB be consulted, and mandates it to issue opinions regarding certain issues of financial stability or macroprudential policy.[72]

[66] The notification templates are available on the ESRB's webpage: https://www.esrb.europa.eu/national_policy/html/index.en.html, accessed 8 September 2025.

[67] Council Regulation (EU) 1096/2010 of 17 November 2010 conferring specific tasks upon the European Central Bank concerning the functioning of the European Systemic Risk Board [2010] OJ L331/162.

[68] See recital 33 of Regulation (EU) 1092/2010.

[69] As required, eg by arts 131 and 133 CRD V.

[70] See recital 86, CRD IV.

[71] The ESRB also uses the term 'soft power' when describing its policy. See https://www.esrb.europa.eu/mppa/html/index.en.html, accessed 15 September 2025.

[72] For example, ESRB opinions are required pursuant to art 458(4), second sentence, CRR or art 133(11) CRD V.

The ECB, in contrast, is endowed by Article 5 SSMR to exercise its powers by means of legal acts.

4 Cooperation within the BU: ECB, competent authorities, and NDAs/national central banks

When it comes to cooperation, distinguishing between setting and releasing/adapting the macroprudential policy measure, on the one hand, and supervision and enforcement of the measure in place, on the other, is important.

a) Cooperation on policy-setting

Every 12 or 6 months, each of the central banks of the BU publishes a report on the financial stability for their jurisdiction, as does the ECB for the euro area. The Financial Stability Review (FSR) of the ECB[73] semi-annually provides a comprehensive overview of potential risks to financial stability in the euro area and outlines its current stance on macroprudential policies. It comprises recurrent analysis of risks to the economic environment and financial markets, as well as risks to the banking and non-banking sectors, complemented by an in-depth analysis of current issues in focus. While it focuses on a holistic view of the euro area, differences in developments of the Member States are also reported. The report concludes with a chapter on macroprudential policy issues where recent policy measures and policy initiatives which go beyond the macroprudential toolkit but influence financial market stability are described and analysed. The FSR takes a general stance regarding macroprudential policy measures, but no recommendations are made to individual countries. The FSR is the main publication of the ECB[74] to communicate to the public, financial markets, and the financial industry the ECB's assessment of financial stability and its macroprudential policy stance. It is important to note, however, that the FSR is not only a product of the ECB but the result of cooperation within the BU, ie between the ECB, the NDAs, and the national central banks. This can be claimed for two reasons. The report needs endorsement by the Governing Council of the ECB (GovC),[75] where the representatives of the

[73] ECB, 'Financial Stability Review', https://www.ecb.europa.eu/press/financial-stability-publications/fsr/html/index.en.html, accessed 15 September 2025.

[74] More specific analysis is published via the macroeconomic bulletin and occasional papers. Occasionally, the Governing Council may also publish statements regarding macroprudential issues, eg the 'Governing Council statement on macroprudential policies' as of 28 June 2024.

[75] Art 23.2 of the Rules of Procedure of the ECB.

central banks can address concerns. More importantly, the FSR is 'prepared with involvement'[76] of the Financial Stability Committee (FSC), which is composed, among others, of one representative of each central bank and of each NDA, if the NDA is a separate entity, of the Member States of the BU.[77] While this does not imply that Member States' views are always shared by the ECB, the involvement of the FSC implies a communication/discussion process between the ECB and Member States on how they assess the current situation and, consequently, the risks in the financial markets. Optimally, this results in a shared view on economic reality and risks to be addressed in the BU, and thus serves as a basis for the subsequent discussion process on macroprudential policies.

Recommendation B(3) of the ESRB recommendation of the macroprudential mandate of national authorities[78] calls for a leading role of the national central bank in the macroprudential policy-setting. For the Member States of the BU, this is ensured either by the central bank also being the NDA, or by a relevant role of the central bank in the national financial market stability board. The national central banks provide, in their financial stability reports, their views on the potential risks to financial stability, and vulnerabilities, of their financial systems, which in turn is the starting point for their considerations of macroprudential policy actions. In any case, the NDAs (which are, in the majority of countries of the BU, the central banks) are required to: (i) analyse cyclical risks on a quarterly basis; (ii) assess which institutions qualify as O-SIIs or G-SIIs and determine their scores on an annual basis; (iii) assess the adequacy of risk weights and LGD input floor values for exposures fully secured by immovable property; and (iv) where a systemic risk buffer exists, reassess this SyRB every two years. Most proposals for changes in national macroprudential policies emanate from these types of regular analysis, although the input stemming from the sharing of methodologies, views, and good practices among NDAs/central banks and the ECB via the discussions in the FSC, the ESRB, and their dedicated substructures should not be underestimated.

Since the SSMR entered into force, the ECB has not issued one single decision pursuant to Article 5(2) SSMR. So, from a purely legal perspective, the SSM has not used its top-up power so far. However, we should refrain from concluding that the top-up power does not work as intended. As the ECB does not publish[79] any agendas or protocols from its meetings or correspondences

[76] See ECB, 'Financial Stability Review, May 2024' 3.
[77] Art 9.4 of the Rules of Procedure of the ECB.
[78] Recommendation of the European Systemic Risk Board of 22 December 2011 on the macroprudential mandate of national authorities (ESRB/2011/3) [2012] OJ C41/01.
[79] Art 23.1 of the Rules of Procedure of the ECB.

with the NDAs or central banks of its Member States, the communication and decision processes that have led to this outcome can hardly be analysed. On a few occasions, the ECB has published a Governing Council statement on macroprudential policies, addressing the NDAs and communicating the ECB's general policy stance on the current situation. With the most recent one,[80] the ECB—with reference to the still-elevated current risks—encourages all NDAs in the BU to maintain the current resilience of the banking system and to keep existing BBMs.

b) Cooperation on enforcement of the measure

As soon as a macroprudential measure is in force, it should be clear which authority is responsible for monitoring compliance with the measure and taking supervisory actions in the case of non-compliance. For all macroprudential measures set on the basis of Union law,[81] the ECB is, pursuant to Article 4 of the SSMR, responsible for ensuring the compliance of significant institutions, and the NCAs are responsible for that of Less Significant Institutions. This makes perfect sense, as the monitoring of capital ratios and the assessment and enforcement of the capital conservation plan that leads the way to replenishing a buffer after non-fulfilment of a buffer requirement are so much intertwined with day-to-day microprudential supervision that anyone but the NCA would, at best, be inefficient in performing that task. For macroprudential policy measures based on national laws,[82] the ECB has no responsibility for monitoring or enforcement.

c) Does the framework function as intended and fulfil its purpose?

A reality check shows that the intentions[83] to: (a) leave the responsibility for setting macroprudential policies in the BU with the Member States; and (b) therefore regard the Member States as the primary unit of analysis; with (c) the ECB as a provider of a 'second opinion', and as a coordinator, are currently being realized. Macroprudential policies are set at the national level by measures taken by the NDA, and both national central banks and the ECB regularly analyse risks to financial stability and how these risks can be

[80] ECB, Governing Council statement on macroprudential policies, 7 July 2025, https://www.ecb.europa.eu/press/govcstatement/pdf/ecb.govcstatement202507~143971cee9.en.pdf, accessed 17 May 2026.

[81] See section II.1 above.

[82] See section II.2 above.

[83] See section II.3 above.

mitigated. When it comes to addressing the inaction bias, however, the answer is less straightforward.

Since the outbreak of the Covid-19 pandemic, the economies of the BU have been exposed to a series of shocks. Although these shocks, and the subsequent increase in inflation and economic slowdown in Europe, have had a massive impact on the financial system, this has not resulted in a financial crisis in any country of the BU so far. This is, first, due to the resilience of the banking sector, resulting, among other things,[84] from macroprudential measures that have been taken in the BU over the last decade. The capital available at banks to cushion losses has increased substantially due to the CCyB, O-SII buffers, G-SII buffers, and SyRB that have been set. Risks identified in some residential real-estate markets have been addressed by BBMs and/or by buffers or increased risk weights for exposures secured by mortgages. Second, macroprudential measures in the BU, together with microprudential measures, have also had some impact on the build-up of risks. Most countries released existing CCyBs at the beginning of the pandemic to keep credit supply stable, and increased CCyB rates when cyclical risks rose in the late phase of, and after, the pandemic. To tame risks from the residential real-estate markets, BBMs were introduced—and have led to decent credit standards preventing over-indebtedness of households from mortgage loans—together with measures pursuant to Article 458 CRR and, more recently, sectoral systemic risk buffers. Consequently, in the present author's view, the framework has performed well since its introduction. However, as risks to financial markets of the BU are still elevated, and in view of the numerous geopolitical risks that can easily transform into shocks, we might identify shortcomings in the framework that require adaptation in the future. Keeping and even increasing resilience will remain a priority of macroprudential policy.[85]

d) Pros and cons of cooperation in the BU

On the positive side, we can conclude that different perspectives lead to superior outcomes: as the ECB applies its standardized analyses to each member of the BU, developments of systemic risk in each Member State can be traced and compared with each other. NDAs, for their part, focus on the analysis of systemic risks in their respective financial markets, considering, besides standardized reporting and economic data, also local information that is not

[84] The liquidity rules introduced via the CRR have also contributed substantially to resilience, as we have learned from the banking turmoil in the US and Switzerland in March 2023 ('Spring Crisis').

[85] See, eg ECB, 'Financial Stability Report, May 2024' 5.

available to the ECB, which may lead to divergent conclusions about the nature or severity of risks to financial stability. Thus, national assessments are subject to regular challenge by the ECB.

The downside of the current framework is that, in a case of diverging views, the cooperative framework does not rule out inaction bias, although the opposite is intended. As there is no uniform standard for the analysis of risks to financial stability, discussions on the severity of risk(s) to be addressed, and consequently on the adequate measure(s), are in some cases not straightforward to decide, specifically when measures are already in place and their sufficiency to address the identified risks is under discussion. This is possible because the criteria for the assessment of the intensity of the risks to financial stability, which are the precondition for any policy measures, and for the determination of buffer sizes, are defined in EU law only vaguely. This is most pronounced for the SyRB, for which no clear common understanding exists, as to which structural risks should be covered, but also prevalent for the determination of the sizes of the O-SII buffers and, also for the measurement and identification of cyclical risks for the purpose of setting a CCyB. Thus, NDAs have some relevant discretion in their assessment of risks to financial stability, and in determining adequate (sufficient, non-distorting) macroprudential measures. Although the discretion is reduced by in-depth analysis, sophisticated modelling, and stress testing, or even collection of additional data, it has not been eliminated so far. This feature of the macroprudential policy framework is of high relevance for the cooperation between NDAs and the ECB. As macroprudential measures need to be well justified and transparent, and may be subject to public discussion once announced, ambiguity in the necessity and/or design of the measure to be taken creates a strong incentive for inaction where a valid counterargument is already on the table. However, the top-up power of the ECB is still appropriate to prevent inaction due to reasons other than divergence of assessments, ie in the case where the NDA refrains from setting the measure although there are no objective arguments to disagree with the ECB's assessment.

The cooperative process within the BU may also have detrimental effects on the optimal timing of measures. There is an intrinsic risk that measures may be taken too late due to the extended justification and procedural needs required by EU legislation when measures are taken. While it is clear that, in order to reach the intended goals of transparency vis-à-vis the numerous involved institutions (ESRB, ECB, NDAs, EBA, European Commission, Council, depending on the type of policy measure) that aim at avoiding market distortions, any measure must be well analysed and substantiated before the documentation for the required notifications can be sent. This, together with the decision-taking in the involved institutions, takes time, which bears the risk that the measure is taken later than is optimal. This drawback stems mainly from the cooperative framework laid down in the CRD and CRR and adhered to by the members of the BU.

With regard to the question to be answered by this chapter, it should be considered that, due to the described embeddedness of the macroprudential policies of the BU in the ESRB, cooperation within the BU takes place within the framework of the ESRB, which influences cooperation and, thus, outcomes within the BU. Does this duplicate work or render the competencies of the BU superfluous? No. Within the EMU, which by its nature deprives national central banks of the instrument of an own monetary policy tailored to the economic cycles of the individual countries, macroprudential policy at the national level can work as a counterbalance. Thus, macroprudential policy can play a supporting role for the ECB's monetary policy, as the risks to the financial system that can emerge unintendedly from an accommodative monetary policy can be reduced by tightening macroprudential policy measures. Hence, it is useful that macroprudential policies within the EMU are more closely coordinated than in the EU.

III Conclusion

After 10 years of the BU, the intentions of the EU legislature seem, in several dimensions, to have been met by reality. Macroprudential policies are set at the national level by NDAs, in a joint and cooperative effort with the ECB and national central banks, with a strong role for the ECB in watching buffer sizes. However, inaction bias has not been fully eliminated as, due to the cooperative design and the high level of transparency required when setting macroprudential measures, disagreement between NDAs and the ECB stemming from differences in the assessment of economic reality may yield less stringent macroprudential measures or measures set later in the financial cycle.

To reduce the remaining inaction bias, the BU would gain from a full harmonization of data used and more harmonized indicators and methodologies applied for analysis of risks to financial stability, to reach further convergence on a common understanding about the risk levels in each Member

State, and thus on adequate policy measures. Although the data issue is continuously addressed by the ESRB,[86] the BU is far from a fully harmonized reporting framework for macroprudential purposes, which is already in place for microprudential supervision.

In view of the challenges ahead for macroprudential policy—for example, the design of macroprudential measures to address climate risks via a (sectoral) SyRB—a fully harmonized reporting framework for macroprudential purposes seems crucial. While the discussion on whether climate risks in the banking sector need to be addressed via macroprudential measures is still ongoing,[87] CRD VI clarifies that the SyRB may be used to address climate risks. As climate risks concern all Member States of the BU to some extent, although in different dimensions, the similarities and interlinkages seem so obvious that a common methodology based on harmonized data is the evident way forward. The ongoing discussion on a 'positive neutral' CCyB rate[88] also points in that direction.[89] If the European legislature decides[90] that a positive CCyB may also be set in phases of the financial cycle with non-elevated cyclical risks, the BU should reach a more precise common understanding of how to identify phases of the financial cycle with non-elevated cyclical risks and how to transform this assessment into buffer sizes.

[86] European Systemic Risk Board, 'Recommendation of the Systemic Risk Board of 21 March 2019 amending Recommendation ESRB/2016/14 on closing real estate data gaps' (ESRB/2019/3), OJ 2019/C271/01 and related publications, as well as 'Recommendation of the Systemic Risk Board of 1 December 2022 on vulnerabilities in the commercial real estate sector in the European Economic Area' (ESRB/2022/9), OJ 2023/C39/01.

[87] ESRB and ECB Project Team on Climate Risk, 'Towards macroprudential frameworks for managing climate risk: December 2023' (ECB/ESRB, 2023), https://www.esrb.europa.eu/pub/pdf/reports/esrb.report202312~d7881028b8.en.pdf?bc89d982ac0f87466507bbe82686f64a, accessed 17 May 2026.

[88] For an introduction on the notion of a positive neutral CCyB rate, see BIS, 'Newsletter on positive cycle-neutral countercyclical capital buffer rates' (5 October 2022) https://www.bis.org/publ/bcbs_nl30.htm, accessed 17 May 2026.

[89] The current state of discussion is summarized in Luis Herrera, Mara Pirovano, and Valerio Scalone, 'The Importance of Being Positive: Costs and Benefits of a Positive Neutral Rate for the Countercyclical Capital Buffer' (2024) ECB Macroprudential Bulletin 24.

[90] The legislative review mandated by art 513 of the CRR on the Union's macroprudential framework is still pending.

17

Close Cooperation to the Test

The Participation of Non-euro-area Member States in the Banking Union

Agnese Pizzolla[*]

I Introduction

The identification of the geographical scope of the Single Supervisory Mechanism (SSM) has been at the forefront of the discussion on how to design the new European system of banking supervision since the very inception of the Banking Union. Reflecting on the causes and consequences of the global financial crisis, the proponents of the Banking Union saw the Europeanization of banking supervision as essential to foster effective application of the Single Rulebook, risk control, and crisis-prevention measures throughout the European Union (EU). A single European supervisor was the looked-for response to 'ensure that the supervision of banks *in all EU Member States* is equally effective in reducing the probability of bank failures and preventing the need for intervention by joint deposit guarantees or resolution funds'.[1]

Having considered this premise, it might have been surprising that, when the draft of Regulation (EU) 1024/2013 (SSMR)[2] was submitted to the Council, just a few months after the presentation of the Banking Union project,[3] the institutional set-up of the to-be-established SSM already presented a substantial deviation from the EU-wide model pitched by the early road maps. Participation was envisaged as compulsory and automatic only for euro-area Member States, while non-euro-area ones were to be granted the possibility

* The views expressed here are those of the author, and do not necessarily reflect those of the ECB.

1 Herman van Rompuy, 'Towards a genuine Economic and Monetary Union' (Brussels, 26 June 2012) 4 (emphasis added).

2 Regulation 1024/2013 conferring specific tasks on the European Central Bank concerning policies relating to the prudential supervision of credit institutions [2013] OJ L287/63–89 (SSMR).

3 Commission, 'Proposal for a Council Regulation conferring specific tasks on the European Central Bank concerning policies relating to the prudential supervision of credit institutions' COM (2012) 511.

Agnese Pizzolla, *Close Cooperation to the Test* In: *EU Banking Union*. Edited by: Jonathan Bauerschmidt, Raffaele D'Ambrosio, Diane Fromage, Daniela Jaros, and Paul Weismann, Oxford University Press. © Oxford University Press 2026. DOI: 10.1093/9780198949756.003.0018

to voluntarily 'opt in' through the establishment of a 'close cooperation' between the European Central Bank (ECB) and their own National Competent Authority (NCA). While the soundness and economic growth of the internal market of the Union as a whole remained a main concern for the EU legislator,[4] the SSMR was de facto establishing a mechanism for banking supervision which, at least in its initial phase, was meant to overlap with the euro area.[5] It was indeed only in 2020, with Bulgaria[6] and Croatia[7] becoming the first two non-euro-area Member States to join the Banking Union, that the SSM underwent its first enlargement, with the opt-in mechanism provided for in the SSMR eventually being put to the test.

Today, both Bulgaria and Croatia participate in the SSM as euro-area Member States, having adopted the euro as their currency on 1 January 2026 and 1 January 2023, respectively.[8] With the conclusion of their participation under close cooperation, there could not be a better time to take stock of their experience, drawing some lessons from that first test.[9]

II Close cooperation: Main features and early considerations

The legal basis chosen for the SSMR—namely Article 127(6) of the Treaty on the Functioning of the European Union[10]—did not, in itself, bind the EU

[4] See, with reference, SSMR, recitals 1 to 10.

[5] Participation in the SSM has been considered as the gateway to the overall participation in the Banking Union. Regulation (EU) 806/2014 indeed defines participating Member States in the Single Resolution Mechanism (SRM) as those Member States which are 'participating Member States according to [the SSMR]'. No separate accession process is envisaged for the SRM.

[6] Decision (EU) 2020/1015 of the European Central Bank of 24 June 2020 on the establishment of close cooperation between the European Central Bank and Българска народна банка (Bulgarian National Bank) (ECB/2020/30) [2020] OJ L224I, p 1.

[7] Decision (EU) 2020/1016 of the European Central Bank of 24 June 2020 on the establishment of close cooperation between the European Central Bank and Hrvatska Narodna Banka (ECB/2020/31) [2020] OJ L224I, p 4.

[8] At the time of writing, there are no other non-euro-area Member States participating in the SSM under the arrangement of close cooperation, nor are there pending procedures for the establishment of close cooperation with any of them.

[9] This chapter focuses on the institutional and legal dimension of close cooperation. For an economic governance-oriented analysis of the Bulgarian and Croatian banking system performance after the establishment of close cooperation, see Zsolt Darvas and Catarina Martins, 'Close cooperation for bank supervision: The cases of Bulgaria and Croatia', In-depth analysis requested by the ECON committee (March 2022).

[10] Treaty on the functioning of European Union (OJ C326, 26.10.2012, p 47) (hereinafter 'TFEU'), art 127(6): 'The Council, acting by means of regulations in accordance with a special legislative procedure, may unanimously, and after consulting the European Parliament and the European Central Bank, confer specific tasks upon the European Central Bank concerning policies relating to the prudential supervision of credit institutions and other financial institutions with the exception of insurance undertakings.'

legislator to restrict the geographical scope of the SSM to the euro area.[11] Nonetheless, the design of the SSM was undoubtedly affected by the choice of the ECB as European supervisor.[12] Following the decision not to amend the Treaties, the establishment of a EU-wide Banking Union was soon dismissed, in the face of two major legal obstacles:[13] first, the fixed composition of the ECB Governing Council—limited to representatives of euro-area central banks[14]—entailed that the non-euro-area Member States could not be granted a seat in the ultimate ECB decision-making body; and second, the limits to the exercise of binding legal powers by the ECB outside the euro area[15] would have imposed significant constraints on the actual exercise of prudential supervision vis-à-vis credit institutions established in those Member States.[16]

To overcome such constraints, the EU legislator introduced close cooperation in the SSM institutional set-up as a unique inter-institutional arrangement between the ECB and the NCAs of non-euro-area Member States,[17] aiming at enabling their participation 'on equal footing' with euro-area ones.[18] Close cooperation was designed as specifically pursuing two corrective

[11] It should be recalled that the SSMR is not the first instance in which art 127(6) TFEU has been used to confer tasks on the ECB. The often forgotten precedent of Council Regulation (EU) 1096/2010 of 17 November 2010 conferring specific tasks upon the European Central Bank concerning the functioning of the European Systemic Risk Board ([2010] OJ L331, p 162) proves, in case there was such a need, that it is possible to use this provision as a legal basis for legal acts which display their effects in all Member States, not just the euro area.

[12] See, with reference, Alberto de Gregorio Merino, 'Institutional Report' in Gyla Bándi and others (eds), *FIDE Report on European Banking Union, Budapest 2016* (Wolters Kluwer 2016) 168–74, addressing the questions of why the ECB was chosen as supervisory institution and whether art 127(6) TFEU was a suitable legal basis, bearing in mind the powers granted to the ECB.

[13] SSMR, recital 11 hints at such constraints when, in opening up the participation in the Banking Union to non-euro-area Member States, it clarifies that such participation should take place 'to the extent that this is institutionally possible'.

[14] TFEU, art 283(1).

[15] ibid, art 139(2).

[16] See, with reference, de Gregorio Merino, 'Institutional Report' (n 12) 173–75, where the author describes well the tension between the wider scope of application of art 127(6) TFEU and the more limited scope of the jurisdiction of the ECB in adopting legal acts in the field of supervision under a joint reading of arts 25.2, 34.1, and 42 of the ECB Statute.

[17] It is not uncommon, especially in early writings, to find close cooperation being referred to as a 'contractual mechanism' (Eddy Wymeersch, 'The Single Supervisory Mechanism or "SSM", Part One of the Banking Union' (2014) ECGI Working Paper Series in Law no 240, 62) or an 'agreement' (Concetta Brescia Morra, 'From the Single Supervisory Mechanism to the Banking Union: The role of the ECB and the EBA' (2014) LUISS Guido Carli/School of European Political Economy, Working Paper no 02, 5; and Rene Smits and others, 'Mocomila Report (2014): European Banking Union' (2014) Working Paper Series no 9 (European Center of Economic and Financial Law, 2014) 10). Such a position seems now to have been largely abandoned in favour of an institutional EU-law-centric point of view.

[18] Under the Commission proposal, non-euro-area Member States with close cooperation would not have been full participants in the SSM. Unsurprisingly, such a proposal did not find political favour, especially in those Member States which could have been most affected, and it was strongly criticized at the October 2012 Council meeting, the conclusions of which called for an 'equitable treatment and representation of both euro area and non-euro area Member States participating in the SSM'. See European Council conclusions on completing EMU (18 October 2012). As a result of negotiation, art 2(1) SSMR now defines Participating Member States as follows: 'a Member State whose currency is the euro or a

aims: on the one hand, to preserve the role of the ECB as European supervisor, ensuring that it could fully exercise its tasks also outside the euro area, and, on the other hand, to ensure proper safeguards for the position of non-euro-area Member States in the context of the ECB decision-making.

In its final adopted wording, Article 7 SSMR—which constitutes the cornerstone of the close-cooperation regulatory framework—provides that:

> the ECB [carries] out the tasks in the areas referred to in articles 4(1), 4(2) and 5 in relation to credit institutions established in a Member State whose currency is not the euro, where close cooperation has been established between the ECB and the national competent authority of such Member State. To that end, the ECB may address instructions to the national competent authority or to the national designated authority of the participating Member State whose currency is not the euro.

In particular, in relation to the exercise of binding legal powers, Article 7(4) SSMR further specifies that, '[w]here the ECB considers that a measure relating to [supervisory tasks] should be adopted by the national competent authority of a concerned Member State in relation to a credit institution, financial holding company or mixed-financial holding company, it shall address instructions to that authority, specifying a relevant timeframe.'

In order to ensure the effectiveness of this system, the procedure for the establishment of close cooperation foresees, on the side of the requesting Member State, the adoption of relevant national law to ensure that its NCA will be obliged to adopt any measure in relation to credit institutions as requested by the ECB:[19] EU and national measures—ie ECB instructions and NCA implementing acts—both become necessary for the exercise of supervisory powers in non-euro-area SSM-participating Member States.

In order to address the lack of representation of non-euro-area NCAs in the ECB Governing Council, the SSMR further provides for two 'reasoned disagreement' procedures, giving to NCAs in close cooperation a second opportunity to voice their dissenting views during the decision-making process, after having expressed their vote in the Supervisory Board. By activating these procedures, NCAs in close cooperation can indeed formally express disagreement

Member State whose currency is not the euro which has established a close cooperation in accordance with article 7'.

[19] SSMR, art 7(2)(a) and (c).

with a draft decision of the Supervisory Board[20] or with an objection of the Governing Council to a draft decision of the Supervisory Board.[21]

Additional specifications as to the establishment, functioning, and potential suspension and termination of close cooperation were later introduced through the adoption of ECB legal acts, namely Part IX of Regulation (EU) 468/2014 of the European Central Bank (ECB/2014/17) (SSM Framework Regulation) and Decision ECB/2014/5[22] (DCC), creating a comprehensive framework ready to be activated at the first 'opt-in' request.

Given its peculiar features, close cooperation surely sparked the curiosity and the interest of institutional observers in non-euro-area Member States,[23] but it was also met with a certain degree of scepticism. Soon, questions arose on whether the benefits of participating in the SSM would outweigh the loss of autonomy by NCAs, and whether the potentially convoluted administrative procedures provided for in the relevant legal framework would function smoothly or would, rather, obstruct the everyday work of supervisory authorities. While commentators pondered the pros and cons of joining the Banking Union through close cooperation,[24] non-euro-area Member States ultimately leaned towards a 'wait-and-see' approach, deferring concrete discussions on opting in until a later, unspecified time when the system would have been tested. Unsurprisingly, no one was eager to be the first to venture into

[20] ibid, art 7(8). It is recalled that, pursuant to art 26(6) SSMR, decisions of the Supervisory Board are taken by a simple majority of its members.

[21] ibid, art 7(7).

[22] In setting the procedure for the establishment of close cooperation, the ECB requested Member States to ensure that legal acts adopted by the ECB pursuant to the SSMR would be binding and enforceable in their territory, thus reinforcing the role of NCA intermediation in all aspects related to the exercise of legislative powers by the ECB. See, with reference, art 3(2)(a) of Decision of the European Central Bank of 31 January 2014 on the close cooperation with the National Competent Authorities of participating Member States whose currency is not the euro (ECB/2014/5) ('Decision on close cooperation' or 'DCC').

[23] Most notably, the governments of both Denmark and Sweden commissioned independent in-depth studies aimed at assessing pros and cons of joining the Banking Union via the establishment of close cooperation between their respective NCAs and the ECB. See, with reference, Danish Working Group, 'Report on Possible Danish Participation in the Banking Union: lessons learnt since 2015' (2019); Swedish Government Inquiries, 'Sweden and the Banking Union' SOU 2019:52 (2019). For Denmark, see also Danmarks Nationalbank (DNB), 'Danish participation in the Banking Union, Monetary Review, 4th quarter' (2014).

[24] See, eg Zsolt Darvas and Guntram B Wolff, 'Should non-euro area countries join the single supervisory mechanism?' (2013) 6 Bruegel Policy Contribution; Kornél Kisgergely and Anikó Szombati, 'Banking union through Hungarian eyes – the MNB's assessment of a possible close cooperation' (2014) MNB Occasional Papers 115; Laurian Lungu and Ella V Kállai, 'When should Romania join the European banking union, sooner or later?' (2015) Strategy and Policy Studies (SPOS); Katalin Méró and Dora Piroska, 'Banking Union and Banking Nationalism — Explaining Opt-out Choices of Hungary, Poland and the Czech Republic' (2016) 35(3) Policy and Society 215–26. See also Pia Hüttl and Dirk Schoenmaker, 'Should the 'Outs' Join the European Banking Union?' (2015) 5 European Economy 89–112, providing an interesting analysis of the cross-border rationale for joining the Banking Union.

such unknown territory. It was only years later that the desire of Bulgaria and Croatia to adopt the euro as their currency eventually compelled them to take a leap and to pursue the establishment of close cooperation as a preparatory step to their participation in the euro area.

III Close cooperation and the adoption of the euro: A link through the ERM-II precommitments

The establishment of close cooperation between the ECB and the NCA of a non-euro-area Member State has been designed having in mind an 'opt-in' system whose activation is left at the sole discretion of the Member States concerned. Neither the SSMR nor subsequent legal instruments enacted by the ECB indicate the existence of a direct connection between close cooperation and the adoption of the euro. From a legal standpoint, the establishment of close cooperation and the adoption of the euro remain independent processes, subject to different rules, conditions, and procedures.[25]

Despite that, early commentators already reflected on the opportunity for Member States interested in adopting the euro as their currency to join the Banking Union through the establishment of close cooperation as an intermediate preparatory step.[26] Emphasis was put on the potential favourable implications for the credit ratings of the participating Member States, arguing that early participation in the SSM could have helped enhance their creditworthiness in a post-crisis environment, thereby smoothing the path for a subsequent transition into the Economic and Monetary Union (EMU).[27] This would have, in turn, reflected on the broader economic expectations about the credibility and resilience of their banking systems, stemming from a closer alignment with the Banking Union's regulatory framework, which was considered to be particularly relevant for non-euro-area Member States in order to signal a commitment to rigorous supervisory standards. From the early stages, it was commonly believed that the two processes would turn out to be somehow connected.

[25] Of this view, see also Alberto de Gregorio Merino, 'The Banking Union in EU Law: an EU Institutional Law Perspective' in Gianni Lo Schiavo (ed), *The European Banking Union and the Role of Law* (Edward Elgar 2019) 29, 38, according to which '[c]lose cooperation is a very special construct which does not mark the accession of a Member State to any acquis of the Union with all consequences in terms of supremacy and direct application.'

[26] Hüttl and Schoenmaker (n 24).

[27] Wymeersch (n 17) 61. See also SSMR, recitals 9 and 10, linking the Banking Union project to the development of a deeper economic and monetary union.

The path of Bulgaria and Croatia towards the adoption of the euro proved this prediction to be, to a large extent, correct.[28] For both Member States, the interest in establishing close cooperation between the ECB and their respective NCAs, and thus to join the Banking Union, came into focus in the context of broader discussions on the adoption of the euro as their currency. Expectations of early commentators were, however, arguably surpassed when both countries indicated their intention to join the Banking Union as a precommitment in the process to join the Exchange Rate Mechanism (ERM-II),[29] thus formalizing a link between two processes which would otherwise have continued, at best, to run on parallel tracks.[30]

In the statement of 24 July 2018, the Eurogroup president Mario Centeno commended the accession of Bulgaria to the ERM-II as particularly significant from an integration perspective, since it marked the first time that a Member State's national currency would have joined the ERM-II since the start of the Banking Union.[31] The rationale for linking the two processes was made explicit in that very same statement: since euro-area Member States are automatically and compulsorily participating in the Banking Union, participating in ERM-II with a view to later adopting the euro involved preparing for joining the Banking Union as well, establishing close cooperation at the same time as joining the ERM-II was considered 'very helpful' to this aim. The statement further expressed the expectation that a similar process would be followed in the future for other Member States wishing to join ERM-II, in line with the principle of equal treatment.[32] This was indeed the case when Croatia applied one year later, in July 2019.

[28] See, in this respect, Maria Nieto and Dalvinder Singh, 'Incentive compatible relationship between the ERM-II and close cooperation in the Banking Union: the cases of Bulgaria and Croatia' (2021) Banco d'España Occasional Paper no 2117, where, as the title of the work suggests, the authors take the case of Bulgaria and Croatia to explain the alignment between ERM-II and close cooperation in terms of an 'incentive compatible relationship'.

[29] Ettore Dorrucci and others, 'The European exchange rate mechanism (ERM-II) as a preparatory phase on the path towards euro adoption – the cases of Bulgaria and Croatia' (2020) 8 ECB Economic Bulletin.

[30] It should be recalled that the participation in ERM-II is not necessarily linked to the adoption of the euro as a currency, as it also serves the purpose of contributing to the smooth functioning of the single European market by fostering exchange-rate stability. Most notably, Denmark is party to the ERM-II despite being a Member State with a formal derogation from the obligation to adopt the euro under Protocol 22. Nonetheless, as one of the convergence criteria for entry to the euro area, a Member State must participate in the mechanism without severe tensions and without devaluing its central rate against the euro, on its own initiative, for at least two years before it can qualify to adopt the euro.

[31] Mario Centeno, 'Common understanding of the commitments taken by Bulgaria as participating member' in 'Ad-hoc Meeting of 12 July to Discuss the Prospects of Bulgaria Participating in the ERM-II Mechanism' (Brussels, 24 July 2018).

[32] Against the overall cautious wording of the Eurogroup president's statement, reference to the 'principle of equal treatment' could be read as a political commitment rather than an intention to legally bind the Member States concerned to a specific course of action. Nonetheless, the use of such a term rather than a more generic wording, as well as the circumstance that a precise reference to the 'principle of

The formalization of a link between the establishment of close cooperation and the participation in the ERM-II significantly affected the understanding of the role that such arrangement plays in fostering the integration of non-euro-area Member States. The experience of Bulgaria and Croatia suggests that, both from the side of non-euro-area Member States and from the side of European institutions, establishing close cooperation was, at least to a certain extent, less about the intrinsic benefits of joining the Banking Union and more about its role as a preparatory stepping stone toward euro-area membership. Notably, both Member States sought to finalize the process for the establishment of close cooperation under the understanding that they would have been able to join the Banking Union and the ERM-II simultaneously. This aim was explicitly articulated by both Bulgaria and Croatia in their respective letters on ERM-II participation[33] and subsequently endorsed by the ERM-II parties.[34] The emphasis on synchronizing these processes was especially pronounced in Bulgaria's case, where the formal request for close cooperation under Article 7(2)(a) SSMR was submitted on 18 July 2018, ie only after the publication of the ERM-II precommitments (29 June 2018) and their subsequent endorsement by the ERM-II parties (12 July 2018). Croatia's approach differed in timing, as the request for the establishment of close cooperation was submitted on 27 May 2019, ie ahead of the formalization of the precommitments for the ERM-II (4 July 2019) and their subsequent endorsement by the ERM-II parties (8 July 2019). While the timing of this submission suggests that Croatia opted for a more proactive strategy, it still aligns with the broader goal of ensuring that close cooperation and ERM-II accession would proceed in tandem: temporal proximity suggests that negotiations for the latter were surely already ongoing when the request to establish close cooperation was submitted.[35] Full synchronization was eventually achieved for both Member States, with the establishment of close cooperation and the

equal treatment' appears twice in a relatively short statement, suggests that this statement bears weight as a commitment (able to raise legitimate expectations) that comparable situations will not be treated differently and that different situations will not be treated in the same way, unless such treatment is objectively justified.

[33] Joint letter of the minister of finance and the governor of the Bulgarian National Bank concerning the intentions of the country to apply for participation in the ERM-II mechanism, 29 June 2018; Joint letter of the minister of finance and the governor of the Croatian National Bank, 4 July 2019.
[34] Statement on Bulgaria's path towards ERM-II participation, 12 July 2018; Statement on Croatia's path towards ERM-II participation, 8 July 2019.
[35] On the reasoning behind Croatia's intention to join the Banking Union, see Marta Božina Beroš, Ivana Parać, and Ivana Bajakić, 'The "inbetweeners" in the Banking Union: insights from the experience of ECB-CNB close cooperation' (2025) *Pravni vjesnik* 41.1 (2025) 45–66.

participation in ERM-II being announced simultaneously, for both of them, on 10 July 2020.[36]

Without prejudice to the potential benefits deriving from the participation in the Banking Union in itself, linking close cooperation to the ERM-II, and thus ultimately to the adoption of the euro, is an approach which, if confirmed in the future, carries the potential of altering the very nature of close cooperation as a purely voluntary opt-in arrangement. While it certainly remains possible for non-euro-area Member States to join only the Banking Union without simultaneously initiating the process for the adoption of the euro, the reverse scenario now appears far less likely. Striving for equal treatment, all non-euro-area Member States will indeed be expected to join the Banking Union via close cooperation, as a preparatory step for accession to the ERM-II. In turn, this may close the possibility for those Member States to join only the ERM-II and postpone their participation in the Banking Union until the moment it becomes compulsory for them, as euro-area Member States. At least for the Member States aiming at adopting the euro as their currency, close cooperation may no longer be a totally voluntary 'opt-in' mechanism, but may rather become a de facto compulsory transitional phase; a waiting chamber for 'full' membership—more of a means to an end than an independent objective.

Losing the voluntary element of close cooperation would be relevant not just in itself. It would, rather, be prone to having much wider repercussions on the effectiveness of those protective mechanisms which the SSMR introduced to safeguard the position of Member States with an NCA in close cooperation. The voluntary 'opt-in' design of close cooperation indeed entailed the possibility for Member States with an NCA in close cooperation to 'opt out' from participation in the Banking Union, either because of the unsuccessful outcome of a reasoned disagreement procedure[37] or at their own discretion after three years from the establishment of close cooperation.[38] While this would surely remain true on paper, terminating close cooperation would also inevitably risk undermining the possibility for that Member State to adopt the euro as their currency, making it extremely unlikely for this to happen. Similarly, the lack of feasibility of terminating close cooperation may result in a weakening in the usefulness of the reasoned disagreement procedures as a protective

[36] To be precise, the ECB decisions on the establishment of close cooperation were adopted by the ECB Governing Council on 24 June 2020, in order for Bulgaria and Croatia to present all the precommitments as having been fulfilled when formally requesting accession to the ERM-II. However, the adoption of these decisions was initially not announced to the public, to meet the synchronization expectations, and in order not to disrupt the confidentiality of the ERM-II accession process.

[37] SSMR, art 7(7) and (8).

[38] ibid, art 7(6).

mechanism within the ECB decision-making. These procedures would surely still represent an important tool in the overall SSM institutional structure, as they allow Member States with an NCA in close cooperation to reiterate their views and request a determination by the Governing Council or Supervisory Board to be reassessed and reconsidered; however, without the leverage of an opt-out 'nuclear option',[39] the Member States concerned would be left with the tight choice of accepting the outcome of the procedure or terminating close cooperation, with unknown, but potentially fatal, consequences as to their euro-area accession process.[40]

IV Close cooperation, national legislation, and the integration of legal frameworks

1 National law as integral feature of close cooperation

Mindful of the limits to the ECB's powers outside the euro area, the EU legislator designed close cooperation heavily relying on an intertwined relationship between Union law and the national law of the Member State concerned, in order to enable the exercise of the ECB's supervisory tasks. While the SSMR, the SSM Framework Regulation, and the DCC established a comprehensive legal framework regulating the set-up of close cooperation, resorting to the national law of the Member State with an NCA in close cooperation was, in turn, deemed necessary to ensure that the ECB could effectively exercise its powers vis-à-vis supervised entities established in non-euro-area SSM-participating Member States.

Article 7 SSMR provides that, in order to establish close cooperation, a Member State shall undertake to ensure that its NCA (or national designated authority (NDA) for the exercise of macroprudential tasks) will abide by any guidelines or requests issued by the ECB,[41] and to provide all information on

[39] Niamh Moloney, 'Close cooperation: the SSM institutional framework and lessons from the ESAs' in 'Building Bridges: Central Banking Law in an Interconnected World' (ECB Legal Conference 2019) 301–02, https://www.ecb.europa.eu/press/legconf/pdf/ecb.ecblegalconferenceproceedings201912~9325c45957.en.pdf, accessed 9 June 2026, stressing that these mitigants are in any case of a 'last resort' nature.

[40] Nieto and Singh (n 28) 19 went even further, arguing that 'the commitment to join the Monetary Union minimises the authority risk for the ECB, as safeguards become insignificant and termination is a non-issue'.

[41] SSMR, art 7(2)(b), first indent.

the credit institutions established in that Member State that the ECB may require for the purpose of carrying out a comprehensive assessment of those credit institutions,[42] as well as that the Member State shall adopt relevant national legislation to ensure that its NCA will be obliged to adopt any measure in relation to credit institutions requested by the ECB.[43] Such requirements are reiterated and further specified under Article 3(2)(a) DCC, according to which the request to enter into close cooperation shall be accompanied, among other things, by an undertaking that the requesting Member State will adopt the relevant national legislation to ensure that legal acts adopted by the ECB pursuant to the SSMR are binding and enforceable in the requesting Member State, and that its NCA and NDA are obliged to adopt any measure requested by the ECB in relation to the supervised entities. It is ultimately the national law of the Member State concerned that creates the necessary bridge between the exercise of supervisory powers by the ECB and the imposition of requirements on credit institutions, guaranteeing the functioning of the close cooperation arrangement.

Given the key role of national legislation, the framework regulating the establishment of close cooperation ensures that the legal acts adopted by Member States to comply with the requirements under Article 7 SSMR are subject to in-depth scrutiny by the ECB. Not only is the ECB called on to adopt an opinion on such legislation,[44] but it is also to conduct a broader assessment which takes into account its practical implementation.[45] Through such a holistic approach, the ECB can thus verify, before the establishment of close cooperation, that the national legislation adopted by the requesting Member State will allow the smooth functioning of the arrangement, and that its practical implementation will not constitute an obstacle to the exercise of its supervisory powers to their fullest extent.

[42] ibid, art 7(2)(b), second indent.

[43] ibid, art 7(2)(c).

[44] DCC, art 3(2)(b). It should be noted that, irrespective of the explicit provision to this effect in the decision on close cooperation, Member States would in any case have been obliged to consult the ECB, in light of the competence of the ECB to deliver opinions on the national law of Member States, specifically based on arts 127(4) and 282(5) TFEU and the third and sixth indents of art 2(1) of Council Decision 98/415/EC1, as the draft laws relate to the institutional set-up of central banks, as well as rules applicable to financial institutions in so far as they materially influence the stability of financial institutions and markets and the ECB's tasks concerning the prudential supervision of credit institutions pursuant to art 127(6) TFEU.

[45] DCC, art 4(3).

2 Same requirements, multiple solutions: How Bulgaria and Croatia fulfilled the requirements for the establishment of close cooperation

While the outcome of the broader legal assessment conducted by the ECB under Article 4(4) DCC remains confidential,[46] analysis of the ECB opinions[47] and of the legislation adopted at various stages by both Bulgaria and Croatia provides interesting elements of comparison, shedding a light on the way in which close cooperation is affected by, and in turn affects, the national law of the requesting Member States.

For the purpose of fulfilling the requirements under Article 7(2) SSMR, both Bulgaria and Croatia amended, in a comparable manner, the national legislation governing the exercise of banking supervision within their respective jurisdictions, namely the Bulgarian Law on Credit Institutions (hereinafter 'BLCI')[48] and the Croatian Credit Institution Act (hereinafter 'CCIA').[49] In both instances, the relevant legal framework was amended in order to impose an obligation on the respective NCA—the Bulgarian National Bank (BNB) and the Croatian National Bank (HNB)—to adopt any measure in relation to credit institutions as requested by the ECB, and to abide by ECB guidelines and requests. The amendments to both the BLCI and the CCIA distinguished

[46] Under art 4(4) DCC, the ECB preliminary assessment of the request to establish close cooperation is communicated by the ECB to the requesting Member State and is subject to confidentiality. While, in line with the practice of the ECB, the results of the comprehensive assessment were published by the ECB (on 26 July 2019 for Bulgaria, and on 5 June 2020 for Croatia), this was not the case for the outcome of legal assessment and the overall preliminary assessment, whose content therefore remains unknown to the public.

[47] Opinion of the European Central Bank of 9 November 2018 on national legislation to be adopted for the purpose of establishing close cooperation between the European Central Bank and Българска народна банка (Bulgarian National Bank) (CON/2018/49) (hereinafter 'Opinion CON/2018/49'); Opinion of the European Central Bank of 30 January 2020 on the sanctioning powers of BNB within close cooperation and the official exchange rate of the Bulgarian lev (CON/2020/5) (hereinafter 'Opinion CON/2020/5'); Opinion of the European Central Bank of 22 December 2020 on the interaction between the European Central Bank and the Bulgarian National Bank within the framework of close cooperation in the Single Supervisory Mechanism (CON/2020/36) (hereinafter 'Opinion CON/2020/36'); Opinion of the European Central Bank of 8 July 2019 on national legislation to be adopted for the purpose of establishing close cooperation between the European Central Bank and Hrvatska narodna banka (CON/2019/25) (hereinafter 'Opinion CON/2019/25'); Opinion of the European Central Bank of 25 March 2020 on close cooperation between the European Central Bank and Hrvatska narodna banka (HNB) within the Single Supervisory Mechanism, and on the macroprudential mandate and tools of HNB (CON/2020/10) (hereinafter 'Opinion CON/2020/10').

[48] Закон за кредитните институции [Law on Credit Institutions], published in *Darjaven Vestnik* No 59, 21 July 2006, as amended in issue 106 of 2018, which introduced ch 11a BLCI on close cooperation (now repealed).

[49] Zakon o kreditnim institucijama [Credit Institutions Act], published in OG 159/2013, amended by Zakon o dopunama Zakona o kreditnim institucijama [Act on Amendments to the Credit Institutions Act], published in OG 70/2019, which introduced arts 11a to 11e CCIA on close cooperation (now repealed).

between the powers of the ECB with respect to significant and less significant credit institutions, as well as powers with respect to the adoption of macroprudential measures.

Setting aside minor differences in the wording, the provisions adopted to this effect by Bulgaria and Croatia mirrored the text of Article 7(2)(b) and (c) SSMR, as well as Article 3(2) DCC, introducing into their respective legal frameworks the few new articles necessary to meet the pre-requirement for the establishment of close cooperation. In both instances, the ECB described these provisions as 'addressing in a cohesive manner several aspects related to the establishment and operation of close cooperation with the ECB', and considered them to be sufficient to meet the requirements set forth under Article 7(2) SSMR, under the understanding that these self-contained amendments, read in conjunction with the rest of the respective acts, would enable the exercise of prudential supervision over credit institutions established in those Member States.[50]

Despite the seemingly straightforward approach adopted by both Member States, interesting elements arise from the analysis of these provisions, in particular with reference to the specific way in which national law was used to ensure a sound exercise of supervisory powers by the ECB.

A first interesting example can be found in the way in which both Bulgaria and Croatia complied with Article 7(2)(b) SSMR, according to which Member States requesting the establishment of close cooperation must undertake to provide all information requested by the ECB in relation to credit institutions established in their jurisdiction, for the purpose of conducting a comprehensive assessment of those entities.

As, under the EU legal framework, credit institutions could not be the direct addressees of the ECB's requests for information, it was inevitable for the SSMR to impose such an obligation on the requesting Member States themselves. National law was, however, used to 'circumvent' this limitation. Both in the case of Bulgaria and Croatia, the obligation upon Member States to provide the ECB with information was met by amending the relevant national legal framework so that both the BLCI and the CCIA, in turn, imposed such an obligation directly upon credit institutions.[51] This approach prompted the ECB to specify, in its opinions, that this solution should not be read as affecting the position of the ECB in relation to credit institutions or as conferring powers on

[50] Opinion CON/2018/49, para 3.1.1; Opinion CON/2019/25, para 3.1.1.
[51] Transitional and final provisions of the BLCI, art 13a (now repealed); CCIA, art 11b(2) (now repealed).

the ECB beyond those provided for under the SSMR, emphasizing that, even after the establishment of close cooperation, the relevant NCA would remain the authority responsible for adopting decisions addressed to credit institutions. Nonetheless, in practice this allowed the ECB to liaise directly with the credit institutions in order to obtain all necessary information to conduct the comprehensive assessment, without the intermediation of the Member States or their respective NCAs.

While the two Member States adopted the same solution in order to comply with Article 7(2)(b) SSMR, significantly different approaches were pursued with regard to the broader obligation under Article 3(2) DCC to ensure that legal acts adopted by the ECB pursuant to the SSMR would be binding and enforceable within their jurisdiction.

The approach followed by Croatia aimed at streamlining the process as much as possible. A provision was added to the CCIA simply prescribing that legal acts adopted by the ECB pursuant to the SSMR would be binding and enforceable in the Republic of Croatia.[52] In doing so, Croatia avoided the need to engage in a national legislative process any time the ECB adopted a new legal act, eliminating the risk of divergences between the applicable regulatory frameworks. It also avoided burdening the HNB with the additional responsibility of monitoring and implementing such legal acts, through the adoption of primary or secondary administrative acts, in order for them to also become binding and enforceable vis-à-vis credit institutions established in Croatia.[53] Such a pragmatic solution did not encompass, however, the implementation of instructions aimed at the exercise of supervisory powers via-à-vis credit institutions, for which the CCIA still required the adoption of an implementing act by the HNB, in line with article 7(4) SSMR.

The approach followed by Bulgaria differed significantly. Possibly because of constitutional law constraints, Bulgaria did not rely on an open cross reference to fulfil such an obligation but, rather, entrusted upon the BNB the responsibility to take all the necessary measures to implement the ECB's legal acts adopted pursuant to the SSMR, including by issuing the necessary administrative acts.[54] Bulgaria thus opted for a case-by-case approach, relying on the BNB for ensuring not only the implementation of the instructions aimed at the exercise of supervisory powers via-à-vis credit institutions but also the

[52] CCIA, art 11a(2) (now repealed).

[53] Opinion CON/2019/25, para 3.3.1. Despite being a more straightforward approach, the introduction of this provision required further amendments as regards the definition of 'legal acts adopted by the ECB' provided for in the draft law. See, with reference, Opinion CON/2019/25, para 3.3.2.

[54] BLCI, art 121b(2) (now repealed).

enforceability of the entire SSM legal framework, including other legal acts adopted by the ECB under the SSMR.

Given the more prominent role envisaged for the BNB, the legislative amendments prepared by Bulgaria to comply with the requirements for the establishment of close cooperation included, from the very beginning of the process, a review of the Law on the Bulgarian National Bank (Law on BNB).[55] The need to adjust the national legal framework in view of close cooperation was thus addressed also from a governance and institutional perspective, with a review of the Law on BNB which complemented the amendments to the BLCI. In particular, the Law on BNB was amended to clarify that, with the establishment of close cooperation, the powers of the BNB Governing Council with regard to prudential supervision,[56] as well as the powers of the deputy governor in charge of banking supervision,[57] would be exercised under the framework set forth under Article 7 SSMR. To this effect, it was further provided that the rules on the independence of the BNB, the governor, and the members of the BNB Governing Council, according to which they shall not seek or take any instructions from Union institutions, would not apply to the ECB with respect to the exercise of supervisory tasks under the close cooperation arrangement.[58] Croatia deemed such amendments not to be necessary for the purpose of fulfilling the pre-requirements for the establishment of close cooperation.

Despite these divergencies, the ECB deemed both the Bulgarian and Croatian amendments to ensure that legal acts adopted by the ECB pursuant to the SSMR would be binding and enforceable, and to ensure that their NCAs would be obliged to adopt any measure requested by the ECB in relation to the supervised entities in accordance with Article 7(4) SSMR,[59] endorsing different but equally acceptable ways to comply with the requirements to establish close cooperation.

3 Towards a deeper integration of legal frameworks

For both Bulgaria and Croatia, the fulfilment of the preconditions for the establishment of close cooperation only marked the initial step in a broader and

[55] Published in *Darjaven Vestnik* No 46, 10 June 1997, as amended (now repealed).
[56] Law on BNB, art 16 (now repealed).
[57] ibid, art 20(3) (now repealed).
[58] ibid, art 44(2) (now repealed).
[59] Opinion CON/2018/49; Opinion CON/2019/25. In both instances, it was stressed that the opinions remained without prejudice to the broader legal assessment to be conducted by the ECB in accordance with art 4 DCC.

more complex process of review of their respective legal frameworks, aimed at ensuring an effective operationalization of close cooperation with the ECB.[60]

Prior to the establishment of close cooperation, Croatia undertook a meticulous, in-depth review of its national legislation to ensure full alignment with the SSMR and to facilitate seamless collaboration between the HNB and the ECB.[61] Most notably, it pursued a detailed analysis of the CCIA, identifying all supervisory procedures that would require an interaction between the ECB and the HNB, and amended all relevant provisions in order to make explicit the role played by the ECB in the overall exercise of supervisory powers and facilitate the joint decision-making procedures.[62] The review of the CCIA against the provisions of the SSMR additionally led the Croatian legislation to attribute new supervisory powers to the HNB, in order to make sure that the NCA itself had at its disposal powers at least equivalent to those of the ECB, so that no obstacle could arise when adopting national administrative acts addressed to credit institutions upon the ECB's instruction.[63]

These changes were further complemented by the amendment of the Law on the Croatian National Bank (Law on HNB).[64] While adopted at a later stage, and thus not strictly for the purpose of fulfilling the preconditions for the establishment of close cooperation, from a substantive point of view the review of the Law on HNB closely resembled the approach adopted by Bulgaria when reviewing the Law on BNB. In particular, these amendments subjected the exercise of supervisory powers by the HNB Governing Council to the framework set forth by the SSMR,[65] as well as laying down the competences that the HNB's governor exercises within the framework of close cooperation, including the regulation of detailed conditions for, and methods of, exercising prudential supervision.[66]

[60] It is important to note that, between 2019 and 2020, both Member States introduced a significant number of legislative changes to update their respective legal frameworks in light of their participation in the SRM and the ERM-II. However, for the purposes of this analysis, the focus will be exclusively on the legislative acts specifically aimed at establishing and ensuring the effective functioning of close cooperation with the ECB.

[61] Opinion CON/2020/10.

[62] See, with reference, ibid, s 3.

[63] Zakon o dopunama Zakona o kreditnim institucijama [Act on Amendments to the Credit Institutions Act], published in OG 146/2020. Among such changes, what stands out in particular is the attribution to the HNB of the power to impose administrative sanctions to credit institutions and responsible persons of credit institutions' management boards, which was previously subject to judicial proceedings. On this new system for the imposition of administrative sanctions, see Beroš, Parać, and Bajakić (n 35) 55–56.

[64] Zakon o Hrvatskoj narodnoj banci [Act on the Croatian National Bank], published in OG 75/2008, amended by Zakona o izmjenama i dopunama Zakona o Hrvatskoj narodnoj banci [Act on Amendments to the Act on the Croatian National Bank] published in OG 47/2020.

[65] Act on Amendments to the Act on the Croatian National Bank, arts 9 and 28, amending art 42(3) and art 104 of the Law on HNB.

[66] Act on Amendments to the Act on the Croatian National Bank, art 10, amending art 43 of the Law on HNB.

By comparison, Bulgaria adopted a more incremental approach, introducing narrow and tailored amendments into its legal framework after the establishment of close cooperation. These amendments were focused mainly on the alignment of specific procedures and on the introduction of procedural safeguards, like the exercise of right to be heard, the setting of deadlines, and the adjustment of the procedure for the imposition of sanctions. With these exceptions aside, it was left to the legislation already adopted for the purpose of fulling the criteria under Article 7 SSMR to bring together the EU and the national legal framework.

Different approaches necessarily entailed different strength and weaknesses. On the one hand, Croatia's thorough and proactive legislative reforms ensured that its legal framework was fully prepared for the demands of close cooperation from the outset. However, by mirroring, in national law, procedures which were already at least in part regulated under Union law, it also exposed the system to a higher risk of inconsistencies, potentially putting at stake legal certainty rather than enhancing it. On the other hand, Bulgaria's approach arguably exposed it to higher initial risks, as relevant procedures had to be adjusted when close cooperation was already operational. At the same time, however, this resulted in a more adaptive strategy, allowing Bulgaria to make targeted adjustments to its legal framework in response to specific issues as they arose from a first-hand knowledge of the functioning of close cooperation.

In both cases, the establishment of close cooperation undoubtedly represented a significant opportunity for these Member States to align their respective regulatory frameworks, going beyond the mere fulfilment of the essential prerequisites set forth under Article 7 SSMR. Together with the more informal alignment of supervisory practices, this additional legislative effort surely represented a key moment in the path towards the integration of both countries into the Banking Union, setting a precedent to be followed for other non-euro-area Member States which may join the SSM in the future.

V The lessons not learned: What is next?

Despite Bulgaria and Croatia having participated in the SSM under the close cooperation arrangement for some years, very little is known about how such participation worked in practice. After the establishment of close cooperation, supervision of Bulgarian and Croatian credit institutions swiftly transitioned into a 'business as usual' mode, and the amount of information being made available with respect to the actual exercise of supervisory tasks by the ECB soon aligned to that of the rest of the SSM-participating Member States.

Notwithstanding this, a few lessons can surely be learnt from the experience of these Member States. Today, we know more about how close cooperation served a key role in their path towards the adoption of the euro, and how close cooperation proved to be an effective tool to foster integration of non-euro-area Member States, leading to a significant alignment of regulatory frameworks and supervisory practices. Both Bulgaria and Croatia seamlessly transitioned from close cooperation to participation in the SSM as euro-area Member States, confirming the key role played by such an arrangement in paving their way towards the adoption of the euro. Overall, the results of this 'first test' have been, in this sense, undoubtedly positive.

At the same time, one cannot avoid noticing that many of the questions posed by early commentators remain unanswered today. The safeguards in the decision-making process, in particular the 'reasoned disagreement' procedures, have never been tested, and nor have the procedures for the suspension and termination of close cooperation. Neither ECB instructions nor any of the national administrative acts implementing them have been challenged before Union or national courts,[67] leaving unexplored the potential vulnerabilities within the legal architecture that governs the interaction between EU and national legal acts.

Considering this from a positive angle, the circumstance that these procedures have never been activated can be seen as an indicator of the full integration of Bulgaria and Croatia into the SSM. It suggests that, despite the peculiarities of the close cooperation arrangement, the transition of these Member States from a national to a European system of prudential supervision has, overall, been smooth, and that the administrative procedures necessary for the adoption of measures addressed to credit institutions, feared as potentially too convoluted by early commentators and interested Member States alike, eventually worked without major hiccups. On the other hand, this may also simply reflect that, in the relatively short time close cooperation was in place, neither the participation of Bulgaria nor of Croatia in the SSM happened to bring about significant challenges in its practical implementation.

While successful, this test seems to have involved relatively straightforward scenarios and not to have given rise to conflictual situations which could have, in turn, led to a full exploration of the complexities that might arise in more demanding circumstances. Despite the experience of Bulgaria and Croatia, close

[67] See, on this topic, Agnese Pizzolla, 'Close Cooperation and Aspects of Judicial Review' in Chiara Zilioli and Karl-Philipp Wojcik (eds), *Judicial Review in the European Banking Union* (Edward Elgar 2021) 236–50.

cooperation has not yet undergone a rigorous examination under 'stressed' conditions, with important questions waiting to be answered. Significant gaps remain in our understanding of its resilience and efficacy in the face of potential conflicts, which could emerge either between different institutional actors involved in the supervisory framework or between supervisory authorities and the supervised entities themselves. Such scenarios might include disagreements over regulatory interpretations, enforcement actions, or crisis-management protocols, which could test the robustness and flexibility of the close cooperation model.

The current lack of information on how close cooperation would function in adverse conditions also leaves open the questions posed by early commentators about the long-term sustainability of this arrangement, especially when disassociated from the adoption of the euro, as could be the case for Member States that do not intend to adopt the euro—like Denmark or Sweden—or for those which are not yet close to meeting the convergence criteria. Surely, close cooperation has proved to be a key tool for easing the transition of Member States into 'full' membership, in particular by anticipating, and thus smoothing, the need for preparatory work related to banking supervision at the time of adoption of the euro as a currency. However, without evidence as to the resilience of close cooperation in hypothetical conflictual situations, its potential as a viable and reliable framework remains, to a certain extent, uncertain. Close cooperation, as it stands, might ultimately be used only as a temporary arrangement for non-euro-area Member States in the perspective of joining the euro area, rather than as a long-term solution to deepen their integration within the Union.

A better understanding of both the strengths and the limits of this arrangement will be critical for designing a robust framework that accommodates close cooperation both as a transitional and a permanent arrangement for Member States in an evolving economic landscape. But this may be a question for the Banking Union's twentieth anniversary.

18

Divergent Paths in Banking Union Oversight

A Comparative Analysis of SRB and ECB Internal Review Bodies

*Jakub Kerlin**

I Introduction and the current stage of research

This chapter argues that, while both the Single Resolution Board's Appeal Panel (SRB AP) and the European Central Bank's Administrative Board of Review (ECB ABoR) share similar legal frameworks, their differing scopes of control and decision-making procedures reflect deeper institutional imbalances that warrant further legal scrutiny. The focus on the Single Resolution Board (SRB) and European Central Bank (ECB) internal review bodies is critical because these two institutions represent the cornerstone of financial regulation within the European Union (EU). Their quasi-judicial mechanisms serve as gatekeepers to the Court of Justice of the European Union (CJEU), making them uniquely positioned to influence decisions related to financial stability of the Union.

The topic of internal administrative review bodies within EU law is both legally significant and extensively researched. An overview of the literature reveals that, while these review bodies may be perceived as a niche area, they are well studied by scholars, with high-quality legal and policy analysis.

Most scholarly works examine the main features and functions of internal review bodies in a comparative manner, analysing their establishment, composition, competences, and procedural frameworks.[1]

* The views and opinions expressed in this chapter are the personal views and opinions of the author, and they do not necessarily reflect the position of the organization that the author works for.

[1] Merijn Chamon and Diane Fromage, *Between Added Value and Untapped Potential: Boards of Appeal of EU Financial Agencies* (OUP 2022).

Jakub Kerlin, *Divergent Paths in Banking Union Oversight* In: *EU Banking Union*. Edited by: Jonathan Bauerschmidt, Raffaele D'Ambrosio, Diane Fromage, Daniela Jaros, and Paul Weismann, Oxford University Press. © Oxford University Press 2026. DOI: 10.1093/9780198949756.003.0019

Some scholars discuss the delegation of powers and their limits,[2] as well as institutional balance.[3] Different perspectives are also provided, such as that of the European Parliament, where Lukácsi[4] argues that boards of appeal of EU agencies occupy a unique space due to their dual nature—a blend of quasi-judicial review and substantive policy assessment. Unlike traditional EU judicial bodies, these internal boards of appeal may go beyond technical and economic assessments to review decisions based on various considerations. This flexibility allows them to potentially annul (remit) or even replace agency decisions, thereby exercising significant control over executive actions.

One of the key questions explored is the standard of review applied by these internal bodies. Lamandini and Ramos Muñoz[5] conclude that the standard of review for internal bodies in EU financial law should align closely with the more exacting standards recently applied by Union courts. According to them, this shift from a 'hands-off' approach by the judiciary to a more intensive 'hands-on' scrutiny ensures substantive legality and detailed factual accuracy without stepping into *de novo* evaluations. In this context, others focus on the role of procedural guarantees or fundamental rights in quasi-judicial reviews.[6]

Targeted studies focus on specific bodies, such as the SRB AP,[7] the European Chemical Agency Board of Appeal,[8] the European Aviation Safety Agency Board of Appeal,[9] and the European Railways Agency Board of Appeal.[10] Additionally, some works explore the links between internal boards of review and the European Court of Justice (ECJ), examining past[11] statute changes

[2] Merijn Chamon, 'EU Agencies Between Meroni and Romano or the Devil and the Deep Blue Sea' (2011) 48 Common Market Law Review 1055.

[3] Marc Jaeger, 'The General Court's Power to Alter EUIPO Decisions: A Matter of Institutional Balance' (2016) Acta Universitatis Szegediensis: acta juridica et politica 257.

[4] Tamás Lukácsi, 'EU Agencies' Boards of Appeal and the Future of the EU System of Judicial Protection: A Perspective from the European Parliament' in Proceedings of the Final Conference of the Jean Monnet Module on EU Specialized Judicial Protection 'Quo vadis, Boards of Appeal?', 8–9 February, University of Ferrara, Special Issue 2 (2024).

[5] Marco Lamandini and David Ramos Muñoz, 'Aquind and the Standard of Review of the ESAs Joint Board of Appeal and of the SRB Appeal Panel' in Proceedings of the Final Conference of the Jean Monnet Module (n 4).

[6] Giulia Agrati, 'Procedural Guarantees in Litigation Before the Boards of Appeal' in Proceedings of the Final Conference of the Jean Monnet Module (n 4).

[7] Yves Herinckx, *Judicial Protection in the Single Resolution Mechanism* (Intersentia 2017).

[8] Marcus Navin-Jones, 'A Legal Review of EU Boards of Appeal in Particular the European Chemicals Agency Board of Appeal' (2015) 21 European Public Law 143.

[9] Marta Simoncini and Mafalda Verissimo, *The EASA Board of Appeal in Search of Identity: An Effective Filter between Administration and Courts?* (OUP 2022).

[10] Marcel Verslype, 'The Scrutiny Performed by the ERA Board of Appeal: Some General and Operational Remarks, Waiting for a Settled Practice' in Proceedings of the Final Conference of the Jean Monnet Module (n 4).

[11] Jacopo Alberti, 'A New Era for EU Agencies' Boards of Appeal? A Preliminary Assessment of the Recent Reform of CJEU's Statute and its Implication on EU Administrative Adjudication' in Martina Conticelli, Maurizia De Bellis, and Giacinto Della Cananea (eds), *EU Executive Governance: Agencies and Procedures* (G. Giappichelli Editore 2019) 204–32.

and the most recent[12] ones, with some of these works being critical of these changes.[13] Most of these works propose future legislative improvements *(de lege ferenda).*

Taking all of the above into account, a valid question remains: is there scope for any new research in this area? This chapter argues affirmatively and focuses specifically on the Banking Union dimension.

The creation of the European Banking Union has resulted in the delegation of certain powers to entities operating within the Single Resolution Mechanism (as is the case of the SRB) and the Single Supervisory Mechanism (as is the case of the ECB). Decisions entrusted to these entities, which operate within a relatively new and judicially untested legal framework and often possess a broad range of technical powers, are based on complex economic assessments or require the processing of large amounts of information and data. Consequently, the legislator intended to introduce an internal administrative review system for them. In this context, it is important to note a subtle but significant fact: the initial proposals from the European Commission for both the Single Supervisory Mechanism Regulation (SSM Regulation)[14] and the Single Resolution Mechanism Regulation (SRM Regulation)[15] did not include provisions for appeal bodies at all. These appeal bodies were introduced later in the legislative process, following consultations with the European Parliament and negotiations within the Council.[16] However, there is limited official legislative explanation available in the public domain to clarify the reasoning

[12] Paolo Stancanelli and Alejandro Menendez Fernández, 'Role and Perspective of the Boards of Appeals of EU Agencies in Light of the Reform of the Statute of the Court of Justice' in Proceedings of the Final Conference of the Jean Monnet Module (n 4).

[13] Henning Berger, 'ECJ reform reduces judicial protection against substantial decisions of the SRB and the ESAs to one instance' (*White & Case*, 13 June 2024) <https://www.whitecase.com/insight-alert/ecj-reform-reduces-judicial-protection-against-substantial-decisions-srb-and-esas one#:~:text = The%20ECJ%20reform%20reduces%20judicial> accessed 6 October 2024.

[14] Council Regulation (EU) 1024/2013 of 15 October 2013 conferring specific tasks on the European Central Bank concerning policies relating to the prudential supervision of credit institutions [2013] OJ L287/63.

[15] Regulation (EU) 806/2014 of the European Parliament and of the Council of 15 July 2014 establishing uniform rules and a uniform procedure for the resolution of credit institutions and certain investment firms in the framework of a Single Resolution Mechanism and a Single Resolution Fund and amending Regulation (EU) No 1093/2010, [2014] OJ L225, p 1.

[16] For the Council's general approach to the SRM, see Council of the European Union, 'Proposal for a Regulation of the European Parliament and of the Council establishing uniform rules and a uniform procedure for the resolution of credit institutions and certain investment firms in the framework of a Single Resolution Mechanism and a Single Bank Resolution Fund and amending Regulation (EU) No 1093/2010 of the European Parliament and of the Council' (Report from the Presidency to COREPER II and Council, Interinstitutional File: 2013/0253(COD), 16 December 2013, 17743/13), available at <https://data.consilium.europa.eu/doc/document/ST-17743-2013-INIT/en/pdf>, and accompanying document Council of the European Union, 'Proposal for a

behind the rationale for their inclusion and the lack of such a proposal by the Commission, although the appeal body concept was already widely known in EU law at the time of presenting these legislative texts.

What warrants additional legal study is a comparison of the legislator's approach to the powers of internal review boards within the same branch of EU law—the Banking Union. Specifically, a study comparing the SRB and ECB, which both service the same credit institutions, from two perspectives—supervisory and resolution—could be insightful. This chapter aims to analyse the status quo and compare the bodies operating within the European Banking Union, and to identify spheres that may not yet be fully visible at first sight. The comparative analysis undertaken in this chapter is based mainly on legal textual analysis, a review of procedural data from the ECB and SRB, and current literature. The criteria for comparison include legal frameworks, procedural timelines, and the outcomes of decisions.

This chapter begins by examining the establishment and mandates of the internal review bodies, followed by an analysis of their governance and composition. It then delves into the scope of review and selected procedural aspects. The chapter then discusses the form of order, notification, transparency, and the broader comparative dimension, highlighting key differences and similarities. Finally, attention has been given to the judicial activities of both bodies, including the implications of recent ECJ reforms. In this context, this chapter maps the practical functioning and transparency disparities of both bodies and then contextualizes these findings against the recent entry into force of appeal-filtering mechanism that altered the balance of judicial review by restricting appellate access to CJEU for SRB litigants.

Regulation of the European Parliament and of the Council establishing uniform rules and a uniform procedure for the resolution of credit institutions and certain investment firms in the framework of a Single Resolution Mechanism and a Single Bank Resolution Fund and amending Regulation (EU) No 1093/2010 of the European Parliament and of the Council - Presidency compromise' (17 December 2013) Interinstitutional File 2013/0253(COD), 17742/13, available at <https://data.consilium.europa.eu/doc/document/ST-17742-2013-INIT/en/pdf>, and in particular art 37c of the proposal. For the SSM part, see eg European Parliament, 'Report on the Proposal for a Council Regulation Conferring Specific Tasks on the European Central Bank Concerning Policies Relating to the Prudential Supervision of Credit Institutions' (2012) COM(2012)0511, C7-0314/2012, 2012/0242(CNS), available at <https://www.europarl.europa.eu/doceo/document/A-7-2012-0392_EN.html>, as well as Council of the European Union, 'Proposal for a Council Regulation Conferring Specific Tasks on the European Central Bank Concerning Policies Relating to the Prudential Supervision of Credit Institutions: Final Compromise Text' (Interinstitutional File: 2012/0242 (CNS), 7776/13, Brussels, 25 March 2013), available at <https://language-tools.ec.europa.eu/eDraftingLabServices/Default>, and in particular art 17c.

II The subject of a study—two internal review bodies

This chapter takes into account the framework of institutional design theory, which posits that the effectiveness of quasi-judicial bodies is, to some extent, contingent upon their legal independence, procedural transparency, and enforcement power.[17]

The SRM is operated by the SRB. The SRM's Appeal Panel is established by Article 85 of the SRM Regulation and is indirectly linked to recital 120 of the same regulation, which outlines the rationale behind the review of decisions made within the SRM system. In contrast, the SSM is operated by the ECB. The SSM's Board of Review is established by Article 24 of the SSM Regulation and is directly contextualized in recital 64 of that regulation. A closer examination of the internal review systems' logic is warranted, to better understand their structure and functions.

The literature reveals a general consensus on the rationale behind establishing internal review bodies, which are predominantly found in EU agencies but are also present in the ECB, as my research shows. As noted by Herinckx,[18] these bodies provide individuals affected by decisions with 'a first layer of legal review' before they potentially appeal their case to the EU Courts. This initial review process is designed to be simpler, faster, and more cost-effective for appellants, compared with formal legal proceedings at the CJEU. The advantages often cited include minimal procedural formalities, rapid review timelines, and no requirement for representation by an external qualified legal counsel.

Furthermore, these appeal bodies are in principle composed of members not solely from legal backgrounds, enabling them to address complex matters (for example, economic matters) more effectively, and have a deep understanding of the issues at hand. This multidisciplinary approach is believed to enhance the quality and relevance of the review process, making it a valuable component of the EU's administrative framework.

The SSM was established first, and it is evident that the SRM provisions drew significant inspiration from the ECB's internal review system. Both bodies share a similar conceptual framework, yet distinct differences are also apparent in their implementation, which are worth examining. The comparison framework of this chapter focuses on three main axes: legal basis and structure, scope of review, and procedural mechanisms.

[17] Alec Stone Sweet, 'Judicialization and Governance' (1999) 32 Comparative Political Studies 147.
[18] Yves Herinckx (n 7).

III Establishment and mandate

Both the SSM and SRM Regulations mandate the establishment of review bodies—the Administrative Board of Review for the ECB and the Appeal Panel for the SRB. These bodies are tasked with overseeing decisions made within their respective regulatory frameworks. However, there is a notable disparity in their mandates.

The ECB ABoR is specifically designed to 'carry out an internal administrative review of the decisions' made by the ECB, assessing both 'procedural adherence and substantive compliance' with the SSM Regulation.[19] In contrast, the SRB AP is tasked solely with 'deciding on appeals',[20] lacking a clearly defined scope or standard of review, as it is not directly outlined in the SRM Regulation. Unlike the comprehensive mandate of the ECB ABoR, the SRB AP's role is less explicitly delineated.

The establishing provisions of both the SSM and the SRM Regulations, in paragraph 1 of each, underscore that neither appeal body can initiate reviews autonomously; rather, they must be triggered by an individual actor requesting a review. This procedural requirement ensures that the review bodies operate in response to specific appeals rather than on their own initiative.

Overall, while the ECB ABoR operates under a structured framework with more detailed review criteria, the SRB AP functions within a less defined scope, relying on appeals initiated by interested parties to engage in its oversight role.

IV Governance and composition

The subsequent provisions of the SSM and SRM Regulations' articles concerning appeal bodies focus on the composition of the appeal bodies within the SSM and SRM frameworks. Each body comprises five primary members and two alternates, appointed for a five-year term by their respective institutions, with the possibility of extension.[21] Despite institutional appointment, members shall operate independently in the public interest and are not bound by instructions. The selection process is open, requiring a public call for expressions of interest, published in the Official Journal of the European Union.

[19] Art 24(1) SSM Regulation.
[20] Art 85(1) SRM Regulation.
[21] Art 24(2) SSM Regulation and Art 85(2) SRM Regulation.

Members of both bodies must publicly declare commitments and interests that could compromise their independence.

Additionally, the regulations outline resources to support the powers of both the Appeal Panel and the Administrative Board of Review under each framework. While the exact nature of these resources is unspecified, they likely include materials or staff necessary for the bodies' functioning. This raises ambiguity, as the independence of appeal bodies' members contrasts with typical staff subordination to an appointing authority, potentially creating a dual reporting structure not explicitly addressed in the regulations.[22] The absence of internal organizational provisions in the regulations—such as a registry, secretariat functions, or remuneration rules—necessitates that these bodies must self-organize to the greatest extent possible. This includes establishing fundamental operational rules, such as adopting their own operating rules (for ABoR) or rules of procedure (for AP), which is actually specified in the regulation.[23] This likely requires providing these bodies with some supportive measures from the primary organization. Decisions on appeals require a majority vote from at least three of the five members, but it appears that other organizational measures may be taken solely by the chair of the appeal body.

The selection criteria for both bodies are nearly identical, requiring individuals of distinguished reputation from Member States with proven expertise in banking or financial services. The SSM emphasizes supervisory experience, while the SRM mandates expertise in resolution matters.

Exclusion criteria clearly prohibit current staff of the institution establishing the review body (ECB for SSM, SRB for SRM) and members of the respective SSM or SRM systems from participating in these bodies. The criteria also exclude personnel from other national or Union institutions involved in tasks defined by ECB or SRB regulations.

An intriguing aspect arises regarding the exclusion of ECB staff from becoming members of the SRM Appeal Panel due to the ECB's role in SRM tasks. Conversely, while the SSM Regulation does not assign tasks to the SRB, SRB staff may serve on the ECB's Administrative Board of Review. However, although not formally prohibited, the selection of SRB staff for such a role appears unlikely.

[22] Merijn Chamon and Diane Fromage, *Between Added Value and Untapped Potential* (n 1); Herinckx (n 7).

[23] Art 24(10) SSM Regulation and art 85(10) SRM Regulation.

A significant difference between the Appeal Panel and the Administrative Board of Review lies in the required expertise. The Appeal Panel (as a whole) must possess 'expertise to provide expert legal advice on the legality of the Board's exercise of its powers', while the Administrative Board of Review has to possess 'expertise to assess the exercise of the powers of the ECB under the SSM Regulation'. This distinction underscores the unique roles and responsibilities of each body within their regulatory frameworks, highlighting their distinct approaches to internal review and oversight.

V The scope of review

In the case of the SSM, the scope of review encompasses an open catalogue of all possible ECB decisions under the SSM Regulation. The primary requirement is that the decision must directly and individually concern the appellant (either a natural or a legal person). This includes, but is not limited to, decisions related to authorizing credit institutions, withdrawing authorizations, assessing notifications of the acquisition and disposal of qualifying holdings in credit institutions, and carrying out supervisory reviews, as outlined in Article 4 of the SSM Regulation. A legislative safeguard, designed to prevent an endless loop of administrative reviews, ensures that, once a decision has been appealed and reissued, further appeals to the ABoR are inadmissible, as explicitly stated in Article 24(5). This represents a sound legislative technique that ensures procedural economy and finality of the internal review.

The SRB Appeal Panel's provisions are structured both similarly, to some extent, yet differently. The criterion of direct and individual concern is equally applicable. However, the types of decisions that can be appealed are explicitly defined in the SRM. The SRB Appeal Panel has exclusive competence to examine the Board's decisions in specific matters only: (i) addressing or removing substantive impediments to resolution (Article 10(10) SRM Regulation); (ii) applying simplified obligations or waiving the drafting of resolution plans (Article 11 SRM Regulation); (iii) determining the minimum requirement for own funds and eligible liabilities (MREL) (Article 12(1) SRM Regulation); (iv) imposing fines (Articles 38–41 SRM Regulation); (v) raising contributions for administrative expenditures (Article 65(3) SRM Regulation); (vi) raising extraordinary *ex post* contributions (Article 71 SRM Regulation);

and (vii) granting or denying access to documents under the public access framework (Article 90(3) SRM Regulation).

The literature is divided on the selection of these specific decisions for internal review in the SRB, as the reasoning behind this categorization is not explicitly stated by the legislator. Herinckx,[24] for example, questions the rationale for legislator choices, noting the absence of a clear explanation or a logical pattern that can be established. One possible, albeit tenuous, theory is that decisions with significant legal gravity (bringing a distinct change to the legal position) or financial impact are intended to be directed immediately to the CJEU rather than through internal review. It could be speculated, for instance, that the exclusion of '(non)-resolution decisions' by the SRB or Commission[25] from the scope of Appeal Panel review was deliberate, as such significant decisions may impact the very existence of the bank. On the other hand, the SSM has decisions of severe gravity (for example, withdrawal of authorization) going through the ECB ABoR process. It is also noteworthy that competent authorities or resolution authorities can be the addressees of decisions, allowing them to bring actions as well (as happened, for example, to the SRB, an act of which was challenged by the national resolution authority).[26]

It is worth noting that, during discussions on expanding the SRB's powers to include the European Deposit Insurance Scheme (EDIS), the Council also proposed broadening the scope of the Appeal Panel's authority.[27] This expansion would have included, for example, the power to disqualify entities from the guarantee system, determination of the amount of funding, and determination of *ex ante* and *ex post* contributions to EDIS. However, divergent views among Member States were reported on this proposal, which may support the above-described speculations on a political nature of the compromise in the legislative process of what to include in the scope of the review of the Appeal Panel, rather than a pattern for choices made that can be clearly established.

[24] Yves Herinckx (n 7).

[25] For further details on the determination of the ultimate author of the resolution decision— whether it is the SRB or the Commission—in accordance with art 18 of the SRB Regulation, see Case C-551/22 P *European Commission v Fundación Tatiana Pérez de Guzmán el Bueno* [2024] ECLI:EU:C:2024:520.

[26] One notable example is Case 1/2023, where a national resolution authority appealed against the SRB's decision on setting the minimum requirement for own funds and eligible liabilities (MREL). The appeal was based on the argument that the SRB's decision did not adequately consider the specific circumstances of the financial institution involved.

[27] Council, 'Proposal for a Regulation of the European Parliament and of the Council amending Regulation (EU) 806/2014 in order to establish a European Deposit Insurance Scheme (First reading)' (Brussels, 14 June 2016) 10036/16, LIMITE, EF 175, ECOFIN 573, CODEC 856, Interinstitutional File: 2015/0270 (COD).

VI Selected procedural aspects

In the context of the SSM, the time frame for lodging an appeal is one month, while for the SRM it extends to six weeks. These deadlines commence from the date the decision is notified to or becomes known by the concerned person.

Under the SSM, a 'request for review' must be submitted in writing to the ECB. Conversely, in the SRM, the procedural submission is termed an 'appeal' and is lodged directly with the Appeal Panel rather than the SRB. Both submissions require a statement of grounds. The SRB Appeal Panel must decide on the appeal within one month from its lodging. Unlike other EU procedures, such as those for access to documents, there is no default condition attached to non-compliance by the reviewing body with this requirement for a timely decision on the case brought.

The Appeal Panel is also required to invite parties to submit observations within specified time limits, and allows for oral representations, a process seemingly constrained within the one-month time frame. It remains unclear whether this one-month period is intended to encompass the timeframe allocated for the SRB, which is acting as the respondent, to submit its formal response to the appeal before the Appeal Panel issues its final decision.

In contrast, the ECB ABoR under the SSM operates differently. It first assesses the admissibility of the review, a procedural step without a specific time frame. Subsequently, it issues an opinion on the request for review. The ABoR must decide within a period appropriate to the urgency of the matter and no later than two months from receiving the request.

In the SRM mechanism, the focus is not on the admissibility issues seen in the SSM, but on a clearer procedural path related to the merits. This clarity in the SRM Regulation eliminates the need for an additional administrative step to determine admissibility. One may argue why there is such a difference between the systems. The hypothesis might be that Appeal Panel serves as an appellate entity somewhat disconnected from the SRB, possessing a distinctly more powerful set of tools. In contrast, the ABoR's review is merely a procedural step in the ECB's decision-making process, despite its official independence. Therefore, the admissibility criteria are less distinct.

VII Form of order—effect of the review

For the SSM, the effects of the review process are rather straightforward. Upon analysing the 'request for review', the ECB ABoR issues an opinion.

Subsequently, the ABoR forwards the case to the Supervisory Board of the ECB for preparation of a new draft decision. The Supervisory Board considers the ABoR's opinion and promptly submits a new draft decision to the ECB Governing Council. This new draft decision can either: (i) annul the initial decision; (ii) replace it with an identical decision; or (iii) replace it with an amended decision. A special non-objection procedure is in place, where the new draft decision is deemed adopted unless the Governing Council objects within 10 working days.

In contrast, the SRB operates differently. The Appeal Panel assesses the admissibility, although this step is less explicitly distinct than in the SSM framework. The SRB AP verifies the merits of the appeal and holds broader powers than the ABoR. It may either: (i) confirm the Board's decision; or (ii) remit the case back to the SRB. The latter option is particularly impactful, as the Board must comply with the AP's decision and adopt an amended decision accordingly. This raises several significant issues, such as whether the SRB can bring the AP's decision to the ECJ—a scenario that seems unlikely due to potential lack of interest, and unity (indivisibility) of the agency in external relations. The SRB's lack of influence over the AP presents a structural challenge. Unlike the ABoR, whose decisions are integrated into the ECB's decision-making process, the AP operates independently. The SRB provides only secretarial support to the AP, whereas ECB services actively support the ABoR. One may argue that this detachment results in a weaker position for the SRB when compared with banks challenging decisions before the AP. This structural disjunction indicates a potential imbalance within the system which could have significant implications for the coherence and efficacy of the regulatory framework. Moreover, if the applicant and the SRB disagree with the new decision following the AP's decision, confusion may arise in properly implementing the AP's decision practically within the SRB. This situation may necessitate especially revisiting the functioning of the 'revolving door' principle, the existence of which potentially results in the revised decision (after first review) returning to the AP for further consideration on (in fact) the same subject.

Importantly, neither the submission of a 'request for review' nor an appeal to the AP suspends the effects of the contested decision. However, the ECB Governing Council (based on a proposal by the ABoR) or the AP itself may suspend the application of the decision if deemed necessary. A notable difference is that, while the AP decides on suspension autonomously, the decision for suspension by the ABoR rests with the Governing Council, which aligns with the natural logic of the ECB's internal review system, where the final decision rests not with the appeal body but with the executive decision-making body—in this case, the Governing Council.

VIII Notification and transparency

The decision of the SRB AP must be reasoned and communicated to all parties involved,[28] which is a simpler process compared with that of the ECB ABoR. As previously highlighted, the ECB ABoR opinion, the new draft decision prepared by the Supervisory Board, and the final decision of the Governing Council (three acts in total) must all be reasoned and communicated to the parties concerned,[29] presumably jointly. An intriguing procedural issue may arise in this context: the Governing Council might opt to decide through a non-objection procedure (Article 24(7) SSM Regulation). This method typically does not produce an explicit, separate act, which raises questions about meeting the standard of adequate and sufficient reasoning required by the regulation. This is particularly problematic if the ABoR opinion is not followed, as the reasons for deviating from and not adhering to the ABoR opinion may remain unknown to the bank.

IX Judicial activities of both bodies: A quick overview

While the primary focus of this chapter is not on the judicial activities of ABoR and the SRB AP, it is nonetheless essential to provide a brief analysis of their practical functioning. Both bodies were designed to serve as internal review mechanisms, yet their practical uses and outcomes have diverged significantly.

The ECB issues over 2,000 supervisory decisions annually,[30] indicating the considerable potential scope for ABoR interventions and opinions. Although banks have invoked the ABoR's review powers, specific data regarding the exact number of cases remains unavailable. Reports[31] suggest that ABoR has reviewed 'numerous' ECB decisions, spanning a wide array of issues. These

[28] Art 85(9) SRM Regulation.

[29] Art 24(9) SSM Regulation.

[30] European Central Bank, 'Assessing the Resilience of the European Banking Sector: Lessons from Recent Stress Tests' (*ECB Banking Supervision Newsletter*, 17 May 2023) <https://www.bankingsupervision.europa.eu/press/publications/newsletter/2023/html/ssm.nl230517_4.en.html> accessed 6 October 2024.

[31] European Central Bank, 'Administrative Board of Review: Review of 2022 Activities' (December 2022) <https://www.bankingsupervision.europa.eu/ecb/pub/pdf/ssm.aborreview202212~ce9fb4e503.en.pdf> accessed 6 October 2024.

issues include the classification of credit institutions within the SSM, the scope of consolidated supervision, breaches of prudential rules (such as large exposure limits), corporate governance matters, and the power to adopt supervisory measures based on national law. Additionally, ABoR has reviewed decisions on supervisory compliance, the withdrawal of banking licences, administrative sanctions, acquisitions of qualifying holdings, and the use of internal models for regulatory capital calculations. However, the absence of detailed statistics and the lack of publicly available opinions have limited the transparency of ABoR's contributions to the broader legal framework. Notably, it is known that eight cases reviewed by ABoR have subsequently been brought before the ECJ, underscoring the significant legal gravity of these decisions. Despite this, ABoR's decisions remain largely inaccessible, thereby preventing broader analysis by scholars, practitioners, or other stakeholders. This lack of public disclosure limits the ability to evaluate how ABoR jurisprudence influences ECB decision-making processes.

In contrast, the SRB, through its Appeal Panel, operates within a more complex landscape, as not all SRB decisions are subject to review by the Appeal Panel. Although comprehensive statistics are scarce, it is estimated that the number of decisions potentially falling under Article 85 of the SRM Regulation could easily surpass 100 a year. This is largely due to the annual determination of the minimum requirement for own funds and eligible liabilities (MREL), as well as issues related to access to documents and administrative contributions (collected for the functioning of the agency), which must be addressed by the SRB.

The SRB AP is notably more transparent in its operations, offering access to its case registry and providing annual summaries of its judicial activities. As of 2023, the registry listed 106 records, though not all represent separate cases; some were also clearly inadmissible and dealt with by short orders. From the available data, it is clear that the AP dealt with a broad array of appeals between 2016 and 2023, primarily centred on MREL determinations and access to documents particularly those triggered by the Banco Popular resolution.

Oral hearings are a common feature of SRB AP proceedings: for instance, the SRB AP held six hearings in 2023. Moreover, the AP has remitted several decisions back to the SRB for further review. In terms of procedural developments, it can be observed that the AP has continuously refined its operations. A major procedural advancement came in 2023, when the AP adopted revised rules of procedure to improve its efficiency and streamline its processes, based on prior experience.

While neither the ABoR nor the SRB AP handle an overwhelming volume of cases, both bodies play an important role in shaping regulatory and supervisory practices within their respective frameworks. The SRB AP, in particular, has demonstrated a more transparent approach, with some visible remittals to the SRB and tangible effects on SRB decisions, which must have been amended in the aftermath of the AP control. The occasional escalation of cases to the General Court from both bodies further underscores their significance.[32] Despite these contributions, the limited public accessibility of ABoR's decisions points to the need for greater transparency and empirical analysis to fully assess the impact of these internal review mechanisms on the broader European financial regulatory landscape.

X Comparative dimension—analysis

The above analysis, and scholars mentioned in the introduction, suggest that the procedural establishment of both internal review bodies was desirable within the Banking Union. Although the Banking Union encompasses the complementary systems of the SSM and SRM, credit institutions subject to these systems face different scopes of legal review by these bodies, which may lead to some confusion.

1 Similarities

The SSM and SRM review bodies exhibit several similarities. The legal provisions establishing these bodies share common origins and structures. Neither body can act *ex officio*; their reviews are triggered only by a specific request from a party. Their composition is almost identical, with each comprising five members and two alternates. Decisions are made by a majority of at least three members. Both bodies are required to act independently and in the public interest, with members making public declarations of commitments and interests, indicating any direct or indirect interests that might prejudice their

[32] For the ECB see, eg Case T-122/15 *L-Bank v ECB* [2017] ECLI:EU:T:2017:337; Case T-712/15 *Akréa v ECB* [2017] EU:T:2017:900; Case T-133/16 *Crédit Agricole v ECB* [2018] ECLI:EU:T:2018:219; Case T-247/16 *Trasta Komercbanka v ECB* [2017] ECLI:EU:T:2017:623; Case T-321/17 *Niemelä and Others v ECB* [2019] EU:T:2019:373; Case T-150/18 *BNP Paribas v ECB* [2020] ECLI:EU:T:2020:1; Case T-584/18 *Versobank v ECB* [2020] ECLI:EU:T:2020:214. For the SRB, see, eg Case T-540/22 *France v SRB* [2024] ECLI:EU:T:2024:461.

independence. The status of members in both bodies is also similar: they must be independent, act in the public interest, and not be bound by any instructions. All members must be individuals of high repute from Member States; it is worth acknowledging that the members are not limited to participating Member States. They shall possess a proven track record of relevant high-level knowledge and experience in banking or financial services. However, unlike the governing bodies of these institutions, gender and geographical diversity are not criteria for the selection of the members of the internal review bodies. Additionally, the lack of a requirement of a legal background among members might hinder the smooth functioning of the review bodies. While economic or banking knowledge is beneficial in understanding the essence of the cases, the procedures of the internal review bodies are ultimately legalistic and centred on the law and legal principles, not economic or policy deliberations. Also, decisions must be drafted in legal language, a skill that experts from other disciplines may not necessarily possess. This aspect warrants reconsideration. However, the similarities between the bodies end here.

2 Differences

Despite their similarities, the differences between the SSM and SRM review bodies are significant. While both bodies share a common heritage, they differ in age and nature. The SSM is the older entity, having been created as an experiment within a well-established EU institution recognized by the Treaties. In contrast, the SRM was established later, as an agency based on Article 114 of the Treaty on the Functioning of the EU.

The distinct legal origins and foundations of the ECB and SRB are mirrored in the legislative approaches taken to define their respective internal review bodies. In establishing the internal review body for the SRM, the legislator refined the provisions and operational framework of the Appeal Panel, drawing inspiration from the SSM, while also implementing certain amendments. This iterative process somewhat emulates the established framework of the SSM, with the SSM serving as a precedent for the SRM. However, the legislator introduced modifications to the rules governing the SRB AP and opted for a different set of tools, including the remittal of cases to the SRB—an approach not observed in the SSM review process.

One notable difference is the context provided by the regulations. The ECB's ABoR is well defined in the recitals, whereas the SRB's AP is not mentioned in its respective recitals. The purposes of these bodies also differ: the ECB's ABoR is a pure internal review body, while the SRB's AP is tasked with 'deciding on appeals', aligning it more closely with the judicial system.

The standard of review further distinguishes these bodies. The SRB's standard of review is not defined, whereas the ECB's ABoR conducts purely internal administrative review of ECB decisions. Exclusion criteria for membership also vary: ECB staff cannot participate in the SRB Appeal Panel, but SRB staff can, theoretically, participate in the ECB's ABoR.

The scope of decisions subject to review differs as well. The ECB's ABoR has an open catalogue of decisions to be reviewed if they are of direct and individual concern. Conversely, the SRB's AP has a closed catalogue, excluding highly litigious matters like decisions not to take resolution action or decisions on the calculation of *ex ante* contributions, which go directly to the General Court.

In terms of power, the ECB's ABoR has limited authority and cannot alter the ECB's final decision in a specific case. In contrast, the SRB's AP has the final word, and the SRB must comply with its decisions. The divergence in the remittal powers of the SRB and ECB review bodies raises questions about the consistency of legal oversight within the Banking Union. This difference in authority also impacts on transparency. The SRB operates within a transparent framework, building case law accessible to public, whereas the ECB's ABoR does not provide access to its opinions to the wider public.

Procedural differences include the time frame for bringing an appeal (one month for the ABoR and six weeks for the AP) and the time allowed to decide (unspecified for the ECB, but one month for the SRB). Additionally, procedural submissions differ: requests to the ECB are addressed to the ECB directly, while appeals to the SRB are addressed straight to the AP, as its internal body. In addition, it would be of considerable interest to compare the average duration of procedures, provided that relevant data is available. According to research conducted within the AP case register, it typically takes slightly more than one year to adjudicate a case on its merits. In contrast, the ABOR does not publish data on the duration of its procedures.

These distinctions highlight the unique roles and operational nuances of the SSM and SRM review bodies within the Banking Union. In conclusion, there may be a sound rationale behind the differences between the SSM and SRM review bodies, but it is not apparent on first sight. Their purpose should be revisited, focusing on expediency and the informal functioning needed to quickly review technical decisions in the SRM and SSM. Meanwhile, the differences can cause confusion for appellants—credit institutions operating within a single European Banking Union—about the different review systems and the effects of their actions. While the purpose of these bodies is worth supporting, procedural simplification and unification of rules within the Banking Union is desirable.

XI Further disparity—ECJ perspective

In December 2022, the CJEU proposed an amendment to its Statute, which it submitted to the EU co-legislators. One key proposal was to amend Article 58a, which concerns the filtering mechanism for appeals against General Court judgments that have already been reviewed by independent boards of appeal within certain EU agencies. The amendment to the Statute suggested extending this provision to include other EU bodies, including the SRB, but obviously not including the ECB, in the case of which ABoR issues only an opinion, which makes it outside the scope of the ECJ review. It appears that the specific proposal in question did not undergo extensive debate, likely due to its lack of controversy among the public. Nevertheless, a brief discussion from the perspective of that chapter is warranted, particularly noting that the amendment has now entered into force.[33]

Firstly, it is important to note that the CJEU comprises two instances: the General Court (the lower-tier EU court) and the Court of Justice (the upper-tier EU court). Normally, judgments of the General Court can be appealed before the Court of Justice.

In 2019, to reduce the workload of the Court of Justice, a filtering mechanism was established for appeals against General Court judgments reviewed by independent boards of appeal within certain EU bodies and agencies. Article 58a of the Statute was introduced, stipulating that the Court of Justice would only proceed with such appeals if they raised significant issues concerning the unity, consistency, or development of Union law.

Initially, Article 58a applied only to certain EU agencies and did not include the SRB AP. The current amendment aims to include the SRB and other EU bodies within its scope, enhancing consistency across EU institutions.

Now, when the SRB was included within Article 58a, appealing General Court judgments related to SRB decisions became more difficult, an issue that was recently spotted by the industry.[34] The CJEU will only proceed with

[33] Regulation (EU, Euratom) 2024/2019 of the European Parliament and of the Council of 11 April 2024 amending Protocol No 3 on the Statute of the Court of Justice of the European Union PE/85/2023/REV/2, [2024] OJ L2024/2019.

[34] Henning Berger (n 13).

appeals if they demonstrate significance concerning Union law's unity, consistency, or development. The appellant must provide a separate request outlining these reasons and all necessary information for the Court to rule on the request. Since 2019, the CJEU has reviewed a number of cases to determine whether appeals should proceed. Appeals from individual applicants have regularly been rejected, while requests from EU agencies have more frequently been allowed.

The amendment could create disparities between the internal review mechanisms of the SSM and SRM. If the SRB or credit institution needs to appeal a General Court judgment, it must demonstrate both legal error and significance concerning Union law, which could be challenging. A stricter application of Article 58a criteria may limit access to the Court of Justice in such cases. However, the amendment might benefit the SRB and increase the role of the AP by curtailing prolonged and costly litigation in cases where both the SRB AP and the General Court have dismissed an appeal on the same grounds. The filtering mechanism was introduced to address such situations, where many appeals were dismissed by the Court of Justice as manifestly unfounded or inadmissible. However, given the novel legal framework, and the pleas of illegality often brought by the applicants, the Court of Justice may be more inclined to allow appeals lodged in the SRB cases to proceed.

One could claim that this statute amendment could imbalance access to the Court of Justice within the European Banking Union. For the ECB, no filtering mechanism applies, ensuring that judicial review always includes a second instance at the Court of Justice. In contrast, the SRB would face the filtering mechanism, potentially limiting access to the second instance. Conversely, the reform raises significant questions regarding the necessity to restructure the AP both legislatively and operationally. This restructuring aims to enhance its independence and resourcefulness, particularly if the legislator and judicial system accord greater weight to its reviews.

XII Conclusion

The comparative analysis of the SRB Appeal Panel and the ECB Administrative Board of Review highlights both similarities and differences in their operational frameworks within the European Banking Union. Both bodies serve as internal review mechanisms, but their distinct legal bases, scopes, and procedural characteristics reflect different institutional objectives and legislative intents.

The establishment of internal review bodies in the Banking Union seems to have been beneficial. Both the SSM and SRM review bodies share similarities in their structure, origins, and independence requirements; however, their different legal review scopes may confuse interested parties, ie credit institutions.

Despite their similarities related to selection criteria of members or composition, the SSM and SRM review bodies differ significantly in age, nature, and legislative approach. The ECB's Administrative Board of Review (ABoR) and the SRB's Appeal Panel (AP) serve different purposes and have distinct contexts in their regulations. The SRB's AP has the final word on decisions, while the ECB's ABoR has limited authority and cannot remit decisions, but opines on them only. Procedural differences, such as in time frames for appeals and the scope of decisions, further highlight the distinct roles of these bodies.

The amendment to Article 58a of the ECJ Statute raises the difficulty of appealing SRB decisions to the ECJ, enhances the role of the SRB AP, and creates disparities in access to the Court of Justice for credit institutions appealing from the SRM side of the regulatory framework. Although the amendment could streamline litigation for the SRM part of the European Banking Union, it may also create an imbalance in judicial review access within it.

Future reforms should consider harmonizing the scope and powers of internal review bodies across EU institutions, in particular for financial institutions, ensuring a consistent legal approach that upholds procedural fairness, institutional accountability, and coherence of applicable rules. Further research could focus on how these reforms might be implemented within the broader context of the EU financial regulatory agenda and development of the Banking Union. Enhanced transparency is also recommended, mandating public accessibility of decisions and opinions rendered by both the SRB AP and the ECB ABoR, for greater accountability and scholarly evaluation. Clarifying legislative intent for the inclusion and exclusion of decisions appealable to internal bodies is necessary to mitigate current ambiguities. Simplifying procedural timelines and requirements can ensure expedited and effective review processes, especially for urgent matters. Lastly, a flexible approach to the filtering mechanism applied to SRB decisions by the ECJ might be essential to maintain balanced access to judicial oversight by the Court of Justice across the European Banking Union.

In conclusion, the intricacies of the SRB AP and the ECB ABoR reflect broader themes of institutional design within the EU's financial regulatory architecture. By acknowledging their respective strengths and addressing identified gaps, future reforms can enhance the operational coherence and effectiveness of these crucial oversight mechanisms, fortifying the principle of legal certainty and reinforcing the robustness of the internal review process within the Banking Union. The granular differences in the operational design, mandate, and procedural constraints of both bodies yield an asymmetric landscape of internal review within the Banking Union. To provide a comprehensive structural overview, Table 18.1 maps the core divergent parameters of the ECB ABoR and the SRB AP side by side.

Table 18.1 Comparative Analysis of the ECB Administrative Board of Review and the SRB Appeal Panel Frameworks

Name of the review body	ECB's Administrative Board of Review	SRB's Appeal Panel
Year of establishment	2013	2016
Context from the recital of the basic regulation	Recital 64: The ECB should provide natural and legal persons with the possibility to request a review of decisions taken under the powers conferred on it by this Regulation and addressed to them, or which are of direct and individual concern to them. The scope of the review should pertain to the procedural and substantive conformity with this regulation of such decisions while respecting the margin of discretion left to the ECB to decide on the opportunity to take those decisions. For that purpose, and for reasons of procedural economy, the ECB should establish an administrative board of review to carry out such internal review. To compose the board, the Governing Council of the ECB should appoint individuals of a high repute. In making its decision, the Governing Council should, to the extent possible, ensure an appropriate geographical and gender balance across the Member States. The procedure laid down for the review should provide for the Supervisory Board to reconsider its former draft decision as appropriate.	n/a
Legal basis for establishment and functioning	Article 24, SSM Regulation	Article 85, SRM Regulation

Table 18.1 Continued

Name of the review body	ECB's Administrative Board of Review	SRB's Appeal Panel
Purpose of establishment	for the purposes of carrying out an internal administrative review of the decisions taken by the ECB	for the purposes of deciding on appeals
Scope/standard of review	The scope of the internal administrative review shall pertain to the procedural and substantive conformity with this Regulation of such decisions.	Not defined
Effects of the review	- shall express an opinion and remit the case to the Supervisory Board for preparation of a new draft decision	- confirm the decision taken by the Board; or - remit the case to the latter
Implementation	- The Supervisory Board shall take into account the ABoR's opinion and shall promptly submit a new draft decision to the Governing Council. - The new draft decision shall abrogate the initial decision, replace it with a decision of identical content, or replace it with an amended decision. - The new draft decision shall be deemed adopted unless the Governing Council objects within a maximum period of 10 working days.	The Board shall be bound by the decision of Appeal Panel and it shall adopt an amended decision regarding the case concerned.
Possibility of *ex officio* control	at the request of the party	
Composition	5 individuals	
Alternates	2 individuals	
Selection criteria from selection	Individuals: - of high repute; - from Member States; - having a proven record of relevant knowledge and professional experience, including supervisory experience, to a sufficiently high level in the fields of banking or other financial services.	Individuals: - of high repute; - from the Member States; - with a proven record of relevant knowledge and professional experience, including resolution experience, to a sufficiently high level in the fields of banking or other financial services.

(continued)

Table 18.1 Continued

Name of the review body	ECB's Administrative Board of Review	SRB's Appeal Panel
Exclusions	excluding current staff of the ECB, as well as current staff of competent authorities or other national or Union institutions, bodies, offices, and agencies who are involved in the carrying out of the tasks conferred on the ECB by the SSM Regulation	excluding current staff of the Board, as well as current staff of resolution authorities or other national or Union institutions, bodies, offices, and agencies who are involved in performing the tasks conferred on the Board by the SRM Regulation
Status of Members	- independent - acting in the public interest - not bound by any instructions	
Are ECB staff excluded from being a member of the body	Yes	
Are SRB staff excluded from being a member of the body	No	Yes
Modalities of decision-making	on the basis of a majority of at least three of its five members	
Independence assurances	- shall act independently and in the public interest - shall make a public declaration of commitments and a public declaration of interests indicating any direct or indirect interest which might be considered prejudicial to their independence, or the absence of any such interest	
Scope of review	open catalogue all SSM-based decisions	closed catalogue only specific SRM-based decisions
Time to bring an appeal	1 month	6 weeks
Time from when the deadline to bring an appeal runs	The date of notification of the decision to the person concerned, or, in the absence of a notification, the day on which the decision came to the knowledge of the person concerned.	
Name of the document	request for review	appeal

Table 18.1 Continued

Name of the review body	ECB's Administrative Board of Review	SRB's Appeal Panel
Procedural requirement	in writing; at the ECB	in writing; directly to Appeal Panel
Act of the body	decision on admissibility opinion	decision
Time to take decision	For admissibility—not specified. For opinion—appropriate to the urgency of the matter and no later than two months from the receipt.	one month
'Revolving doors' review	No	Yes

19

The Accountability of the Single Supervisory Mechanism and the Single Resolution Mechanism to the European Parliament

*Menelaos Markakis**

I Introduction

The European Banking Union, which is now celebrating its tenth anniversary, is often heralded as a major achievement of European integration.[1] Created in 2014 in response to the financial crisis that had engulfed Europe at the time, it is regarded as 'a crucial step in achieving the EU's economic and monetary union'.[2] In simple terms, the Banking Union aims to 'strengthen banks' safety and soundness to ensure that they can withstand future financial crises', to 'resolve non-viable banks without resorting to using taxpayers' money and with minimal impact on the real economy', and to 'reduce market fragmentation by harmonised banking rules and supervision'.[3] It currently has two

* The author is very grateful to the editors of this volume for their helpful comments. The usual disclaimer applies.

[1] See generally, just in terms of books, Gianni Lo Schiavo (ed), *The European Banking Union and the Role of Law* (Edward Elgar 2019); Danny Busch and Guido Ferrarini (eds), *The European Banking Union* (2nd edn, OUP 2020); Christoph Ohler, 'Banking Supervision' (ch 37) and Christos Gortsos, 'Banking Resolution: The EU Framework Governing the Resolution of Credit Institutions' (ch 38) both in Fabian Amtenbrink and Christoph Herrmann (eds), assisted by René Repasi, *The EU Law of Economic and Monetary Union* (OUP 2020); Christos Gortsos, *European Central Banking Law: The Role of the European Central Bank and National Central Banks under European Law* (Palgrave Macmillan 2021); Thomas Beukers, Diane Fromage, and Giorgio Monti (eds), *The New European Central Bank: Taking Stock and Looking Ahead* (OUP 2022); Klaus Tuori, *The European Central Bank and the European Macroeconomic Constitution: From Ensuring Stability to Fighting Crises* (CUP 2022) ch 9; Gianni Lo Schiavo, *EU Banking Law and Regulation* (OUP 2024).

[2] See Council of the European Union, 'Banking Union', <https://www.consilium.europa.eu/en/policies/banking-union/>, accessed 11 September 2025.

[3] ibid.

Menelaos Markakis, *The Accountability of the Single Supervisory Mechanism and the Single Resolution Mechanism to the European Parliament* In: *EU Banking Union*. Edited by: Jonathan Bauerschmidt, Raffaele D'Ambrosio, Diane Fromage, Daniela Jaros, and Paul Weismann, Oxford University Press. © Oxford University Press 2026. DOI: 10.1093/9780198949756.003.0020

fully operational pillars: the Single Supervisory Mechanism (SSM) and the Single Resolution Mechanism (SRM). As explained in more detail elsewhere in this edited volume, the European Central Bank (ECB) has acquired a role in banking supervision within the SSM, where it directly supervises big (or 'significant') banks in the 21 EU Member States participating in the Banking Union and ensures a consistent approach in the supervision of small and medium-sized (or 'less significant') banks by National Competent Authorities.[4] For banks and financial institutions established in those Member States and subject to the supervision of the ECB and the national authorities within the framework of the SSM, a centralized power of resolution has been established in the context of the SRM and entrusted to the Single Resolution Board ('SRB' or 'the Board') and national resolution authorities.[5] The activities of the SRB are backed by the Single Resolution Fund (SRF), which is also governed by a separate international agreement.[6] The SRF is funded by bank contributions and 'can be used to ensure the efficient application of resolution tools for resolving failing banks, after other options, such as the bail-in tool, have been exhausted'.[7]

This chapter does not intend to examine the effectiveness of the arrangements for the supervision and resolution of banks in the European Banking Union. Instead, it aims to evaluate the accountability arrangements in the SSM and the SRM. It focuses on one particular aspect of the accountability arrangements in the Banking Union, namely the accountability of the SSM and the SRM to the European Parliament.[8] Notably, it looks at public hearings at the European Parliament in the 2019–24 legislative term, thus complementing the existing literature which chiefly focuses on public hearings regarding the SSM in the 2014–19 legislative period.[9] In line with the overall multidimensional

[4] Council Regulation (EU) 1024/2013 of 15 October 2013 conferring specific tasks on the European Central Bank concerning policies relating to the prudential supervision of credit institutions [2013] OJ L287/63 (hereinafter 'SSM Regulation').

[5] Regulation (EU) 806/2014 of the European Parliament and of the Council of 15 July 2014 establishing uniform rules and a uniform procedure for the resolution of credit institutions and certain investment firms in the framework of a Single Resolution Mechanism and a Single Resolution Fund and amending Regulation (EU) No 1093/2010 [2014] OJ L225/1, as currently in force (hereinafter 'SRM Regulation').

[6] Intergovernmental Agreement on the transfer and mutualisation of contributions to the Single Resolution Fund, <https://www.consilium.europa.eu/media/48068/agreement-amending-the-intergovernmental-agreement-on-the-transfer-and-mutualisation-of-contributions-to-the-single-resolution-fund-27-january-2021_en.pdf>, accessed 17 February 2025.

[7] See Single Resolution Board, 'Single Resolution Fund', <https://www.srb.europa.eu/en/single-resolution-fund>, accessed 17 February 2025.

[8] On other aspects of the SSM's and the SRM's accountability, see the chapters by Jakub Kerlin and Carlos Soler Ruiz in this edited volume.

[9] Fabian Amtenbrink and Menelaos Markakis, 'Towards a Meaningful Prudential Supervision Dialogue in the Euro Area? A Study of the Interaction between the European Parliament and the European Central Bank in the Single Supervisory Mechanism' (2019) 44 European Law Review 3

focus of this edited volume, which transverses the pillars of the Banking Union, this chapter will examine the accountability of *both* the ECB and the SRB to the European Parliament for the activities of the SSM and the SRM, respectively.[10]

The chapter is structured as follows. The discussion begins with the accountability arrangements in the SSM and the SRM. The focus then shifts to the public hearings with the Chair of the ECB's Supervisory Board and the Chair of the SRB at the European Parliament. The chapter will examine both the evidence from those public hearings and the manner in which they are organized, including the provision of expertise. The final section concludes with an overall assessment of those public hearings, as well as some suggestions for the way forward, from a normative standpoint.

examines 13 public hearings that took place on 19 June 2018, 26 March 2018, 9 November 2017, 19 June 2017, 23 March 2017, 9 November 2016, 13 June 2016, 22 March 2016, 19 October 2015, 25 June 2015, 31 March 2015, 3 November 2014, and 18 March 2014. Adina Akbik, *The European Parliament as an Accountability Forum: Overseeing the Economic and Monetary Union* (CUP 2022) ch 4 focuses on 283 letters with questions, and 13 public hearings that took place at the Committee on Economic and Monetary Affairs (ECON Committee) between October 2013 (ie since the adoption of the SSM Regulation) and April 2018. See also Adina Maricut-Akbik, 'Contesting the European Central Bank in Banking Supervision: Accountability in Practice at the European Parliament' (2020) 58 Journal of Common Market Studies 1199. The analysis published most recently by Diane Fromage, 'Democratic Accountability in the Banking Union: Is There Really a Gap?' in Mark Dawson (ed), *Substantive Accountability in Europe's New Economic Governance* (CUP 2023) ch 5 covers the period between November 2014 (namely the start of the functioning of the SSM) and April 2022. Ferdinand Dreher and others, 'The ECB's Accountability to the European Parliament 2019-2024: Commitment in Times of Change' ECB Economic Bulletin Issue 7/2024 <https://www.ecb.europa.eu/press/economic-bulletin/articles/2024/html/ecb.ebart202407_01~7014b80a90.en.html>, accessed 17 February 2025, 75–92 focuses on public hearings and written questions asked by Members of the European Parliament to the Chair of the Supervisory Board, during the ninth parliamentary term. Andrea Resti, '10 Years of Parliamentary Scrutiny over the Single Supervisory Mechanism: Are Current Transparency and Accountability Mechanisms Adequate for the Next Legislative Term?' (August 2024) <https://www.europarl.europa.eu/thinktank/en/document/IPOL_STU(2024)755728>, accessed 17 February 2025, builds on the work by Akbik, cited above, and reviews how the different interaction channels between the SSM and the European Parliament have been utilized since 2014, as well as how their usage has evolved over time.

[10] The accountability of the Commission and Council for the exercise of their tasks in the SRM falls outside the scope of this contribution. See, however, Fromage, 'Democratic Accountability in the Banking Union' (n 9). Kai Gereon Spitzer and Marcel Magnus, 'Parliamentary Scrutiny of the SRB: Discretion in Applying the Resolution Objectives and Mechanisms for Accountability to Parliament' (June 2024) <https://www.europarl.europa.eu/thinktank/en/document/IPOL_BRI(2024)755734>, accessed 17 February 2025, 5 observe that: 'Since the legislator has vested the Commission with overriding – but . . . limited – possibility to endorse and reject resolution schemes, an interest in also holding the Commission to account for its role may arise. The legislation does not entail a specific mechanism to this end. The public structured dialogues with the competent Commissioner theoretically provide an opportunity to hold the Commission to account for how it exercises control over the SRB. One may note in this context that the Parliament has recently introduced the possibility in its rules to activate a new format for "special scrutiny hearings", to enable Parliament "to question one or more Commissioners, or any other relevant person, on an issue of major political importance"... The Council's role in the resolution process is yet more limited than the Commission's, but may eventually be decisive. Possibly, the fact that the Council has to provide reasons for its decisions may constitute an entry point for discussions between the institutions and the new "special scrutiny hearings" might again provide a possible format in the future.'

II The accountability arrangements in the SSM and the SRM

The literature on accountability in the Banking Union is appropriately large.[11] This section focuses on one particular aspect of the accountability arrangements in the Banking Union, namely the accountability of the SSM and the SRM to the European Parliament. What follows will examine the SSM's and the SRM's accountability, in turn.

[11] See, among many others, Christopher Gandrud and Mark Hallerberg, 'Does Banking Union Worsen the EU's Democratic Deficit? The Need for Greater Supervisory Data Transparency' (2015) 53 Journal of Common Market Studies 769; Gijsbert ter Kuile, Laura Wissink, and Willem Bovenschen, 'Tailor-Made Accountability within the Single Supervisory Mechanism' (2015) 52 Common Market Law Review 155; Jean-Victor Louis, 'Democracy and the European Central Bank. Some Comments on Independence and Accountability' in Gregorio Garzón Clariana (ed), *Democracy in the New Economic Governance of the European Union* (Marcial Pons 2015) 109–50; Charikleia Vlachou, 'Ensuring the Democratic Accountability of the Single Resolution Board: Which Role for the European Parliament and National Parliaments?' (2017) Revue Internationale des Services Financiers 8; Diane Fromage and Renato Ibrido, 'The "Banking Dialogue" as a Model to Improve Parliamentary Involvement in the Monetary Dialogue?' (2018) 40 Journal of European Integration 295; Amtenbrink and Markakis, 'Towards a Meaningful Prudential Supervision Dialogue in the Euro Area?' (n 9); Marta Božina Beroš, 'The ECB's Accountability within the SSM Framework: Mind the (Transparency) Gap' (2019) 26 Maastricht Journal of European and Comparative Law 122; Diane Fromage and others, 'ECB Independence and Accountability Today: Towards a (Necessary) Redefinition?' (2019) 26 Maastricht Journal of European and Comparative Law 3; Diane Fromage, 'Guaranteeing the ECB's Democratic Accountability in the Post-Banking Union Era: An Ever More Difficult Task?' (2019) Maastricht Journal of European and Comparative Law 48; Diane Fromage and Renato Ibrido, 'Accountability and Democratic Oversight in the European Banking Union' in Lo Schiavo (ed), *The European Banking Union and the Role of Law* (n 1) ch 4; Phedon Nicolaides, 'Accountability of the ECB's Supervisory Activities (SSM): Evolving and Responsive' (2019) 26 Maastricht Journal of European and Comparative Law 136; Marta Božina Beroš and Marin Beroš, 'The Single Resolution Board: What About Accountability?' in Johannes Pollak and Peter Slominski (eds), *The Role of EU Agencies in the Eurozone and Migration Crisis: Impact and Future Challenges* (Springer 2021) 127–48; Édouard Fernandez-Bollo, 'Democratic Accountability within the Framework of the SSM and the SRM as a Complement to Judicial Review' in Chiara Zilioli and Karl-Philipp Wojcik (eds), *Judicial Review in the European Banking Union* (Edward Elgar 2021) ch 2; Menelaos Markakis, *Accountability in the Economic and Monetary Union: Foundations, Policy, and Governance* (OUP 2020) ch 5; Marco Lamandini and David Ramos Muñoz, 'SSM and SRB Accountability at European Level: What Room for Improvements?' (April 2020), https://www.europarl.europa.eu/RegData/etudes/STUD/2020/645711/IPOL_STU(2020)645711_EN.pdf, accessed 17 February 2025; René Smits, 'SSM and the SRB Accountability at European Level: Room for Improvements?' (April 2020), https://www.europarl.europa.eu/RegData/etudes/STUD/2020/645726/IPOL_STU(2020)645726_EN.pdf, accessed 17 February 2025; Jonathan Zeitlin and Filipe Brito Bastos, 'SSM and the SRB Accountability at European Level: Room for Improvements?' (May 2020), https://www.europarl.europa.eu/RegData/etudes/IDAN/2020/645747/IPOL_IDA(2020)645747_EN.pdf, accessed 17 February 2025; Marco Lamandini and David Ramos Muñoz, 'Banking Union's Accountability System in Practice: A Health Check-up to Europe's Financial Heart' (2022) 28 European Law Journal 187; Fromage, 'Democratic Accountability in the Banking Union' (n 9); Dreher, Hernborg, Mochhoury, Mulder, and Schölermann, 'The ECB's Accountability to the European Parliament 2019-2024' (n 9); Rosa Lastra and Sara Dietz, 'Accountability of the European Banking Union: Accountability in Banking Supervision and Banking Resolution under Review' (September 2024), https://www.europarl.europa.eu/RegData/etudes/IDAN/2024/760238/IPOL_IDA(2024)760238_EN.pdf, accessed 17 February 2025; Resti, '10 Years of Parliamentary Scrutiny over the Single Supervisory Mechanism' (n 9).

1 The accountability of the Supervisory Board of the ECB to the European Parliament

It is hard to overstate the importance of accountability and transparency in the context of the SSM. It is rightly noted in the preamble to the SSM Regulation that:

> The conferral of supervisory tasks implies a significant responsibility for the ECB to safeguard financial stability in the Union, and to use its supervisory powers in the most effective and proportionate way. Any shift of supervisory powers from the Member State to the Union level should be balanced by appropriate transparency and accountability requirements. The ECB should therefore be accountable for the exercise of those tasks towards the European Parliament and the Council as democratically legitimised institutions representing the citizens of the Union and the Member States. That should include regular reporting, and responding to questions by the European Parliament in accordance with its Rules of Procedure, and by the euro Group in accordance with its procedures. Any reporting obligations should be subject to the relevant professional secrecy requirements.[12]

The key accountability provisions in the SSM Regulation are Articles 20 and 21. The former provision concerns (political) accountability at the EU level, whereas the latter provision refers to the role of national parliaments in the SSM. The accountability provisions in the SSM Regulation should be read together with the Interinstitutional Agreement between the European Parliament and the ECB on the practical modalities of the exercise of democratic accountability and oversight over the exercise of the tasks conferred on the ECB within the framework of the SSM ('IIA' or the 'Interinstitutional Agreement'),[13] as well as the Memorandum of Understanding between the Council of the EU and the ECB on the cooperation on procedures related to the SSM.[14] As will also be seen below:

[12] SSM Regulation, preamble recital 55. See also preamble recital 56 on the role of national parliaments.
[13] See <https://eur-lex.europa.eu/legal-content/EN/TXT/?uri=celex%3A32013Q1130%2801%29>, accessed 17 February 2025.
[14] See <https://eur-lex.europa.eu/legal-content/IT/TXT/?uri=CELLAR%3A021e8fcb-96ac-11ea-aac4-01aa75ed71a1>, accessed 17 February 2025.

> The IIA complements the SSM Regulation by granting additional information and consultation rights to the European Parliament concerning the records of the proceedings of the Supervisory Board, the principles and kinds of indicators or information used in developing acts and policy recommendations, informal exchanges of views on draft acts, and so on.[15]

Overall, it is argued that '[t]he SSM Regulation, read together with the IIA between the European Parliament and the ECB and the MoU with the Council, introduces a relatively detailed framework on the provision of information to and institutional contacts with the EU institutions.'[16]

It is provided in the SSM Regulation that the ECB shall be accountable to the European Parliament and to the Council for the implementation of the SSM Regulation.[17] More specifically, the ECB shall submit on an annual basis to the European Parliament, the Council, the Commission, and the Eurogroup a report on the execution of the tasks conferred on it by the SSM Regulation.[18] The Chair of the Supervisory Board shall present that report in public to the European Parliament, and to the Eurogroup in the presence of representatives from any non-euro-area Member States that are participating in the Banking Union.[19] The Interinstitutional Agreement lays down in detail the contents of that report and also provides that it shall be made available in draft form to the European Parliament, on a confidential basis, four working days in advance of the hearing. It further requires that the final report be published on the SSM website.[20] Moreover, the Chair of the Supervisory Board may, at the request of the Eurogroup, be heard on the execution of its supervisory tasks.[21] At the request of the European Parliament, (s)he shall participate in a hearing on the execution of these supervisory tasks, before the competent committees of the European Parliament.[22] In this connection, the Interinstitutional Agreement distinguishes between ordinary public hearings, ad hoc exchanges of views, and special confidential meetings with the Chair of the Supervisory Board, all of which 'can cover all aspects of the activity and functioning of the SSM covered by [the SSM Regulation]'.[23] The ECB shall also reply orally or in writing

[15] Fabian Amtenbrink and Menelaos Markakis, 'The Legitimacy and Accountability of the European Central Bank at the Age of Twenty' in Beukers, Fromage, and Monti (eds), *The New European Central Bank* (n 1) 282.
[16] ibid 281.
[17] SSM Regulation, art 20(1).
[18] ibid, art 20(2).
[19] ibid, art 20(3).
[20] IIA, s I.1.
[21] SSM Regulation, art 20(4).
[22] ibid, art 20(5).
[23] IIA, s I.2.

to questions put to it by the European Parliament or the Eurogroup.[24] Upon request, the Chair of the Supervisory Board shall hold confidential oral discussions behind closed doors with the Chair and Vice-Chairs of the competent committee of the European Parliament concerning the Supervisory Board's supervisory tasks, where such discussions are required for the exercise of the European Parliament's powers under the Treaty on the Functioning of the European Union (TFEU).[25] Furthermore, the ECB shall cooperate sincerely with any investigations by the European Parliament, subject to the TFEU.[26]

An important element of *ex ante* accountability is injected with regard to the appointment of the Chair and Vice-Chair of the Supervisory Board. After hearing the Supervisory Board, the ECB submits a proposal for the appointment of the Chair and the Vice-Chair to the European Parliament for approval. Following the approval of this proposal by the European Parliament, the Council shall adopt an implementing decision to appoint them. The Chair shall be chosen on the basis of an open selection procedure, on which the European Parliament and the Council shall be kept duly informed. The Vice-Chair is chosen from among the members of the ECB's Executive Board.[27] Considerably more detail on this selection procedure is provided in the Interinstitutional Agreement.[28]

The European Parliament's approval is also required for the removal of the Chair and the Vice-Chair of the Supervisory Board from office. More specifically, although there is no provision for performance-based dismissal, if the Chair of the Supervisory Board no longer fulfils the conditions required for the performance of her/his duties or has been guilty of serious misconduct, the Council may, following a proposal by the ECB which has been approved by the European Parliament, adopt an implementing decision to remove her/him from office.[29] The same procedure is followed for removing the Vice-Chair of the Supervisory Board from office, following her/his compulsory retirement as a member of the Executive Board.[30] The European Parliament or the Council may, in a certain sense, take the initiative here, as they may inform the ECB that they consider the conditions for the removal of the Chair or the Vice-Chair from office to have been fulfilled, to which the ECB shall respond.[31]

[24] SSM Regulation, art 20(6).
[25] ibid, art 20(8).
[26] ibid, art 20(9).
[27] ibid, art 26(3).
[28] IIA, s II.
[29] SSM Regulation, first subpara of art 26(4).
[30] ibid, second subpara of art 26(4).
[31] ibid, third subpara of art 26(4).

It should be noted that '[t]he role of the European Parliament in the appointment and dismissal of the Chair and Vice-Chair of the Supervisory Board is considerably greater than its role in the appointment of the members of the ECB's Executive Board.'[32] It will be recalled that the President, the Vice-President, and the four other members of the Executive Board are appointed by the European Council, acting by a qualified majority, on a recommendation from the Council, after it has *consulted* the European Parliament and the Governing Council of the ECB.[33] It will be further recalled that, if a member of the Executive Board no longer fulfils the conditions required for the performance of her/his duties, or if (s)he has been guilty of serious misconduct, the Court of Justice may, on application by the Governing Council or the Executive Board of the ECB, compulsorily retire her/him.[34] No involvement of the European Parliament is foreseen by EU primary law in this context. Seen in this light, the Parliament plays a far more important role in the appointment and dismissal of the Chair and Vice-Chair of the ECB's Supervisory Board than it does in the area of monetary policy. However, the procedure to be followed for the appointment or the removal from office of Executive Board members is not only relevant for monetary policy; it is also important for the governance of the SSM, as Executive Board members are also members of the ECB's Governing Council,[35] which formally adopts or objects to the draft decisions prepared by the Supervisory Board (non-objection procedure).[36] 'This perforce limits the extent to which the European Parliament and Council could influence the composition of the SSM's decision-making bodies.'[37] In this connection, it is rather unsurprising that the European Parliament has asked that its role in the appointment of ECB Executive Board members be enhanced by requiring that it consents to the recommendations of the Council.[38] This would improve *ex ante* accountability for both monetary policy and banking supervision.

Nor is the European Parliament granted other—potent—instruments of accountability which would allow it to assign consequences to its judgment

[32] Amtenbrink and Markakis, 'The Legitimacy and Accountability of the European Central Bank at the Age of Twenty' (n 15) 283.
[33] See the second subpara of art 283(2) TFEU.
[34] Protocol (No 4) on the statute of the European System of Central Banks and of the European Central Bank, art 11.4.
[35] Art 283(1) TFEU.
[36] SSM Regulation, art 26(8).
[37] Amtenbrink and Markakis, 'The Legitimacy and Accountability of the European Central Bank at the Age of Twenty' (n 15) 284.
[38] See European Parliament resolution of 12 December 2013 on constitutional problems of a multitier governance in the European Union (2012/2078(INI)) <https://www.europarl.europa.eu/doceo/document/TA-7-2013-0598_EN.html>, accessed 17 February 2025, para 66.

of the performance of the ECB in the SSM.[39] The reader may be excused for thinking that, since the SSM Regulation constitutes *secondary* Union law, it could in theory be amended by the European Parliament acting together with the other EU institutions, in order to impose additional obligations on the ECB and/or to amend the accountability framework applicable to its activities. However, the SSM Regulation was adopted on the basis of Article 127(6) TFEU, which provides for a *special* legislative procedure with the Council at its helm, acting unanimously, after merely *consulting* the European Parliament and the ECB. It has been observed elsewhere that, 'by providing the European Parliament merely with the right to be consulted in the legislative procedure, Article 127(6) TFEU is a relic from the dark ages of European parliamentarianism, when the consultation procedure was the main *modus operandi* in supranational law-making'.[40] 'Referring in this context to the independent position of the ECB is somewhat misplaced, as the role accorded to the Council under art.127(6) TFEU means that another Union political institution can amend the SSM Regulation.'[41] It should, however, be observed that it would, in principle, be possible under the *current* Treaty framework for the European Council to decide to switch from a special to an ordinary legislative procedure, in the absence of opposition by national parliaments.[42] This would render the European Parliament a veritable co-legislator with the Council in this context and equip it with a potent instrument of accountability. Any amendments to the legal framework of the Banking Union that could ensue thereafter would, naturally, have to take into account any relevant Treaty constraints as well as other international standards.[43]

Last but definitely not least, the European Parliament also produces an annual report on the Banking Union, which 'allows Members to formulate concrete demands to the . . . institutions and bodies involved in the Banking Union'.[44] The report is adopted by the European Parliament by means of a resolution. These reports 'mostly consist of high-level recommendations' and 'usually address a wide range of issues'.[45] The ECB Banking Supervision replies

[39] Budgetary accountability is covered elsewhere: see Markakis, *Accountability in the Economic and Monetary Union* (n 11) 167–69, and the chapter by Carlos Soler Ruiz in this volume.

[40] Amtenbrink and Markakis, 'The Legitimacy and Accountability of the European Central Bank at the Age of Twenty' (n 15) 283.

[41] Amtenbrink and Markakis, 'Towards a Meaningful Prudential Supervision Dialogue in the Euro Area?' (n 9) 22.

[42] See the second, as well as the third and fourth, subparas of art 48(7) TEU. See further Markakis, *Accountability in the Economic and Monetary Union* (n 11) 327.

[43] Louis, 'Democracy and the European Central Bank' (n 11) 137–38.

[44] Spitzer and Magnus, 'Parliamentary Scrutiny of the SRB' (n 10) 3.

[45] Resti, '10 Years of Parliamentary Scrutiny over the Single Supervisory Mechanism' (n 9) 22.

to the comments and suggestions provided by the European Parliament. Naturally, the feedback by the ECB focuses selectively on a number of issues raised in the European Parliament's resolution.[46] Unfortunately, this is not a two-way street in the case of the SRM, as 'the SRB has so far not publicly responded to these reports'.[47]

2 The accountability of the Single Resolution Board to the European Parliament

The discussion thus far has focused on the accountability of the ECB to the European Parliament for its banking supervisory activities. It now turns to consider the accountability of the SRB to the European Parliament.

It is provided in the preamble to the SRM Regulation that:

> In order to ensure transparency and democratic control, as well as to safeguard the rights of the Union institutions, the Board should be accountable to the European Parliament and to the Council for any decisions taken on the basis of this Regulation. For reasons of transparency and democratic control, national parliaments should have certain rights to obtain information about the activities of, and to engage in a dialogue with, the Board.[48]

The key accountability provisions in the SRM Regulation are Articles 45 and 46. The former provision refers to the accountability of the Board to the European Parliament, the Council, and the Commission, whereas the latter provision concerns the role of national parliaments of the participating Member States.[49] The relevant arrangements are complemented by the Agreement concluded between the European Parliament and the SRB on the practical modalities of the exercise of democratic accountability and oversight over the exercise of the tasks conferred on the SRB within the framework of the

[46] See, eg European Parliament, 'REPORT on Banking Union - Annual Report 2023' (2023/2078(INI)), https://www.europarl.europa.eu/doceo/document/A-9-2023-0431_EN.html, accessed 17 February 2025; European Central Bank, 'Feedback on the Input Provided by the European Parliament as Part of Its Resolution on Banking Union 2023', https://www.bankingsupervision.europa.eu/press/other-publications/publications/feedbackar/html/ssm.feedbackar202403.en.html, accessed 17 February 2025.

[47] Spitzer and Magnus, 'Parliamentary Scrutiny of the SRB' (n 10) 3.

[48] SRM Regulation, preamble recital 42. See also ibid, preamble recital 43 on the role of national parliaments.

[49] As noted above, budgetary accountability is examined elsewhere: see Markakis, *Accountability in the Economic and Monetary Union* (n 11) 167–69, and the chapter by Carlos Soler Ruiz in this volume.

SRM.[50] This Agreement contains similar provisions to the Interinstitutional Agreement examined above. Relevant differences with regard to accountability at EU level will be highlighted below, where appropriate.

More specifically, it is provided in the SRM Regulation that the Board shall be accountable to the European Parliament, the Council, and the Commission, for the implementation of the SRM Regulation.[51] The Board shall submit an annual report to the European Parliament, the national parliaments of participating Member States, the Council, the Commission, and the European Court of Auditors, on the performance of the tasks conferred on it by the SRM Regulation. Subject to requirements of professional secrecy, the report shall be published on the Board's website.[52] The Chair shall present that report in public to the European Parliament, and to the Council.[53] The Agreement between the European Parliament and the SRB lays down in detail the contents of that report and also provides that it shall be made available in draft form to the European Parliament on a confidential basis seven working days in advance of the public hearing and of its official publication.[54] At the request of the European Parliament, the Chair shall participate—at least annually—in a hearing by the competent committee of the European Parliament on the performance of the resolution tasks by the Board.[55] The Agreement between the European Parliament and the SRB increases the frequency of such hearings to twice a year and also refers to ad hoc exchanges of views with the Parliament's competent committee on issues within the Board's responsibility.[56] The Chair may also be heard by the Council, at the Council's request, on the performance of the resolution tasks by the Board.[57] The Board shall reply orally or in writing to questions addressed to it by the European Parliament or by the Council.[58] Upon request, the Chair shall hold confidential oral discussions behind closed doors with the Chair and Vice-Chairs of the competent committee of the European Parliament, where such discussions are required for the exercise of

[50] See <https://eur-lex.europa.eu/legal-content/EN/TXT/?uri=CELEX%3A32015Q1224%2801%29>, accessed 17 February 2025.
[51] SRM Regulation, art 45(1).
[52] ibid, art 45(2).
[53] ibid, art 45(3).
[54] Agreement between the European Parliament and the SRB, s I.1.
[55] SRM Regulation, art 45(4).
[56] Agreement between the European Parliament and the SRB, s I.2.
[57] SRM Regulation, art 45(5). For the practice of joint hearings with the Chair of the Supervisory Board and the Chair of the SRB at the Eurogroup, see Fromage, 'Democratic Accountability in the Banking Union' (n 9) 123–24, who also argues that 'it probably would have been best to entrust the Council with the task of controlling both the ECB-SSM and the SRB in the first place, also to guarantee higher transparency and thus higher accountability standards' (ibid 124).
[58] SRM Regulation, art 45(6).

the European Parliament's powers under the TFEU.[59] During any investigations by the European Parliament, the Board shall cooperate with it, subject to the TFEU and regulations referred to in Article 226 thereof.[60]

The procedure for the appointment of the Chair, Vice-Chair, and four further full-time members of the Board differs from the one explained above with regard to the Chair and Vice-Chair of the Supervisory Board, but again injects an element of *ex ante* accountability into the process, in that the European Parliament's approval is required for their appointment. More specifically, the Chair, the Vice-Chair, and the other four full-time members shall be chosen on the basis of an open selection procedure. The European Parliament and the Council shall be kept duly informed at every stage of that procedure in a timely manner. After hearing the Board, the Commission shall provide to the European Parliament a shortlist of candidates for these positions and inform the Council of the shortlist. The Commission shall submit a proposal for the appointment of the Chair, the Vice-Chair, and the four further full-time members to the European Parliament for approval. Following the approval of that proposal, the Council shall adopt an implementing decision to appoint them.[61] Considerably more detailed arrangements regarding those selection procedures are laid down in the Agreement between the European Parliament and the SRB.[62]

The European Parliament's approval is also required for the removal of the Chair, Vice-Chair, or another full-time member from office. More specifically, if one of those officials no longer fulfils the conditions required for the performance of her/his duties or has been guilty of serious misconduct, the Council may, on a proposal from the Commission which has been approved by the European Parliament, adopt an implementing decision to remove her/him from office. For those purposes, the European Parliament or the Council may inform the Commission that it considers the conditions for her/his removal from office to have been fulfilled, to which the Commission shall respond.[63] Performance-based dismissal is, again, not possible.

Last but definitely not least, the SRM Regulation was adopted on the basis of Article 114 TFEU, which, in stark contrast to the legal basis used for the adoption of the SSM Regulation, provides for the use of the *ordinary* legislative procedure. Consequently, it is, in principle, possible for the European Parliament

[59] ibid, art 45(7).
[60] ibid, art 45(8).
[61] ibid, art 56(4) and (6).
[62] Agreement between the European Parliament and the SRB, s II.
[63] SRM Regulation, art 56(9).

and Council, following a proposal by the Commission and after consulting the Economic and Social Committee, to amend the SRM Regulation so as to impose additional obligations or requirements on the SRB and/or to change its accountability framework. The potence of this accountability instrument is tempered by the fact that any changes to the relevant legal rules would have to take cognizance of EU Treaty constraints and the relevant case law of the CJEU (notably, the *Meroni* doctrine),[64] the need to maintain consistency with the Bank Recovery and Resolution Directive[65] and other relevant Union law, and other international agreements or standards, including the Agreement on the transfer and mutualisation of contributions to the SRF.[66]

III Parliamentary hearings

1 Internal organization and expertise provided

This section focuses on public hearings at the Committee on Economic and Monetary Affairs (ECON) of the European Parliament, with the Chairpersons of the Supervisory Board and of the SRB. As noted above, '[t]he hearings took place two or three times per year and lasted for about 1 hour, consisting of a short introductory presentation by the chairperson and question time.'[67] It is noted in the relevant literature that:

> It has been customary for the representatives of the invited EU institution to provide a brief introduction, followed by a question and answer session with the Members of the competent committee. During this session, Members are typically allocated five-minute slots to ask questions and engage in discussion with the invitee. The insights gained from these scrutiny hearings are

[64] Case 9-56 *Meroni & Co., Industrie Metallurgiche, SpA v High Authority of the European Coal and Steel Community* ECLI:EU:C:1958:7; see also Case C–270/12 (Grand Chamber) *United Kingdom of Great Britain and Northern Ireland v European Parliament and Council of the European Union* ECLI:EU:C:2014:18.

[65] Directive 2014/59/EU of the European Parliament and of the Council of 15 May 2014 establishing a framework for the recovery and resolution of credit institutions and investment firms and amending Council Directive 82/891/EEC, and Directives 2001/24/EC, 2002/47/EC, 2004/25/EC, 2005/56/EC, 2007/36/EC, 2011/35/EU, 2012/30/EU and 2013/36/EU, and Regulations (EU) No 1093/2010 and (EU) No 648/2012, of the European Parliament and of the Council [2014] OJ L173/190, as currently in force.

[66] See also Markakis, *Accountability in the Economic and Monetary Union* (n 11) 164.

[67] Economic Governance and EMU Scrutiny Unit, 'The Institutional Role of the European Parliament in the Economic and Monetary Union' (June 2024), <https://www.europarl.europa.eu/RegData/etudes/IDAN/2024/760227/IPOL_IDA(2024)760227_EN.pdf>, accessed 17 February 2025, 16.

> channelled into the [European Parliament]'s annual reports, such as the report on the European Semester, the report on the ECB, and the report on the Banking Union. Furthermore, the plenary of the House typically holds discussions on these topics once a year.[68]

In terms of the expertise provided to the ECON Committee, the Economic Governance and EMU Scrutiny Unit (commonly referred to as EGOV), which is part of the Directorate-General for Internal Policies of the Union (DG IPOL), is supporting the committee's scrutiny activities also in the area of the Banking Union, through briefings and preparatory meetings in advance of each of those public dialogues and hearings, relying on both internal and external expertise.[69] EGOV's role is crucial in supporting the European Parliament and its relevant committees and bodies in their scrutiny-related work in EMU and the Banking Union, as well as—one may even go as far as saying—in facilitating academic research and external accountability by experts in this area.[70] More specifically, EGOV prepares a briefing in advance of each hearing, 'reflecting on recent developments that Members may wish to raise with the chairperson'.[71] Moreover, '[e]xternal briefings and expertise are commissioned to external experts, upon request by the competent committee, to complement the internal expertise and provide normative assessments and/or policy recommendations' on supervision and resolution topics.[72] The thematic papers commissioned from external experts 'provide a more normative assessment of the issues at stake'.[73] 'In order to support the scrutiny activities in the area of Banking Union, a dedicated panel of experts was first established

[68] Kajus Hagelstam, Samuel De Lemos, and Giacomo Loi, 'Enhanced Political Ownership and Transparency of the EU Economic Governance Framework' (21 December 2023), <https://www.europarl.europa.eu/RegData/etudes/IDAN/2023/741517/IPOL_IDA(2023)741517_EN.pdf>, accessed 17 February 2025, 3.

[69] Economic Governance and EMU Scrutiny Unit, 'The Institutional Role of the European Parliament in the Economic and Monetary Union' (n 67) 4.

[70] By way of example, EGOV have prepared an overview of all public hearings in the 2019–24 legislative term, including links to the transcripts and video recordings, its briefing for each hearing, and an overview of all papers written by external experts: Marcel Magnus and Kai Spitzer, 'Single Supervisory Mechanism: Accountability Arrangements (9th Parliamentary Term)' (April 2024), <https://www.europarl.europa.eu/thinktank/en/document/IPOL_BRI(2020)659623>, accessed 17 February 2025; Marcel Magnus and Kai Spitzer, 'Single Resolution Board: Accountability Arrangements (9th Parliamentary Term)' (April 2024), https://www.europarl.europa.eu/thinktank/en/document/IPOL_BRI(2020)659621, accessed 17 February 2025.

[71] Economic Governance and EMU Scrutiny Unit, 'The Institutional Role of the European Parliament in the Economic and Monetary Union' (n 67) 15.

[72] Economic Governance and EMU Scrutiny Unit, 'EGOV 2023 Annual Activity Report' (April 2024), <https://www.europarl.europa.eu/RegData/etudes/IDAN/2024/755740/IPOL_IDA(2024)755740_EN.pdf>, accessed 17 February 2025, 4.

[73] Hagelstam, De Lemos, and Loi, 'Enhanced Political Ownership and Transparency of the EU Economic Governance Framework' (n 68) 4.

in January 2016 and has been used ever since, in advance of hearings with the SSM and SRB.'[74] There are also thematic papers prepared by EGOV itself, on top of its regular briefings for the hearings, which aim to monitor, on a regular or ad hoc basis, developments in the Banking Union.[75]

Furthermore, there is a Banking Union Working Group, which was set up in October 2014 and is currently composed of 22 ECON Members, including the ECON Chair.[76] It is responsible for monitoring the implementation of, and dealing with, any related matters concerning the SSM and the SRM, scrutinizing the exercise of the tasks of the ECB as bank supervisor and of the SRB, and holding meetings with representatives of the SSM and the SRM, as well as with relevant stakeholders.[77] EGOV also prepares briefings for the Banking Union Working Group.[78]

2 Hearings on the SSM

The hearings in the 2019–24 parliamentary term cover the very first hearing with Claudia Buch as the new Chair of the ECB's Supervisory Board, as well as 14 hearings with Andrea Enria, the former Chair of the Supervisory Board.[79] As was noted by Claudia Buch in her opening statement on 21 March 2024:

> Accountability to the European institutions and to the European Parliament is really essential for us. We are doing more now also to even more to reach out to all stakeholders, to explain what risks we see, how we address them, and I think we have achieved a lot together, and I'm really looking forward

[74] Economic Governance and EMU Scrutiny Unit, 'EGOV 2023 Annual Activity Report' (n 72) 4.

[75] Economic Governance and EMU Scrutiny Unit, 'The Institutional Role of the European Parliament in the Economic and Monetary Union' (n 67) 16; Economic Governance and EMU Scrutiny Unit, 'EGOV 2023 Annual Activity Report' (n 72) 3–4.

[76] See 'Banking Union Working Group (BUWG)' (July 2024), <https://www.europarl.europa.eu/cmsdata/286605/BUWG%20composition%202024%2007%2001.pdf>, accessed 17 February 2025.

[77] See European Parliament, 'Banking Union Working Group', https://www.europarl.europa.eu/committees/en/banking-union-working-group/product-details/20160630CPU09281, accessed 17 February 2025. See also Amtenbrink and Markakis, 'Towards a Meaningful Prudential Supervision Dialogue in the Euro Area?' (n 9) 16–17. Dreher, Hernborg, Mochhoury, Mulder, and Schölermann, 'The ECB's Accountability to the European Parliament 2019-2024' (n 9) 89 report that the Chair of the Supervisory Board participated in 12 closed-door meetings with members of the Banking Union Working Group during the 9th parliamentary term.

[78] Economic Governance and EMU Scrutiny Unit, 'EGOV 2023 Annual Activity Report' (n 72) 4.

[79] The current author watched, on the European Parliament's Multimedia Centre, the video recordings from 15 public hearings that took place on 21 March 2024, 7 November 2023, 28 June 2023, 21 March 2023 (two separate hearings, one together with the Chair of the European Banking Authority), 1 December 2022, 30 June 2022, 31 March 2022, 14 October 2021, 1 July 2021, 23 March 2021, 27 October 2020, 5 May 2020, 12 December 2019, and 4 September 2019.

> to working with the European Parliament over the next term to complete the Banking Union and also to support your work to further strengthen the regulatory framework.

The meetings are structured as follows. There is an introductory statement by the Chair of the Supervisory Board for around 10 minutes, followed by a Q&A session. There is a first round of questions (one per political group), during which one and a half to two minutes is allocated for the initial question and three minutes are given for the answer. There is also the possibility—within the same slot—of a follow-up question of a half a minute, with one minute given for the answer. Thereafter, there is a second round of questions in a more traditional format—one minute is allocated for the question and two minutes for the answer. If time allows, there can be questions on a catch-the-eye basis towards the end of the session.[80] However, it should be noted that, in some cases, there has been a very short—or even no—second round of questions.[81] Compared with what the current author has observed in the past for ECB banking supervision or monetary dialogues, there are fewer questions asked by Members of the European Parliament (MEPs).[82]

Overall, MEPs are asking a variety of well-informed questions, for example regarding the implementation of the Basel framework and the banking package, the completion of the Banking Union, the crisis management and deposit insurance (CMDI) reform, non-performing loans, the profitability of banks, and non-banks. In hearings earlier in the parliamentary term, there was also a focus on the establishment of an anti-money laundering authority, or on the impact of the Covid-19 crisis and Brexit on banks. It is readily apparent that, in a non-crisis context, there are fewer questions by MEPs on the situations of specific banks,[83] or that these, mercifully, concern non-EU banks that fall outside the remit of the SSM, whether this is Silicon Valley Bank or Swiss banks.[84] There are, of course, also questions on issues that do not fall within

[80] See the introduction by Irene Tinagli at the meeting of 28 June 2023.

[81] See, eg the meetings of 28 June and 7 November 2023.

[82] cf Amtenbrink and Markakis, 'Towards a Meaningful Prudential Supervision Dialogue in the Euro Area?' (n 9) 18. The format of the monetary dialogues has also changed: see the introduction by Irene Tinagli at the monetary dialogue with the President of the ECB on 20 June 2022. I am grateful to Diane Fromage and Alessandro Giovannini for this observation.

[83] cf Fabian Amtenbrink and Menelaos Markakis, 'Towards a Meaningful Prudential Supervision Dialogue in the Euro Area?' (n 9) 18. See, however, the meeting of 31 March 2022 with regard to the liquidity crisis at Sberbank, as well as RCB Bank, which transformed into a non-bank institution; or, eg the question asked by Fulvio Martusciello (European People's Party (PPE)) at the hearing of 12 December 2019 regarding Banca Popolare di Bari—a 'less significant' institution based in Italy.

[84] See also the exchange of views of 21 March 2023 with the Chair of the European Banking Authority and the Chair of the ECB's Supervisory Board on the failure of Silicon Valley Bank and the implications for financial stability in Europe.

the remit of ECB banking supervision, such as on the ECB's bond-buying programmes.[85] MEPs from Member States that are not (yet) participating in the Banking Union are also active in asking questions. As was noted above, a briefing is prepared by EGOV for each public hearing with the Chair of the Supervisory Board. However, it should be noted that the questions posed by MEPs do not strictly focus on the issues addressed in those briefings.[86] Furthermore, so far as their questions are concerned, the MEPs do not seem to take issue with the accountability and transparency arrangements in the SSM, nor with their practical implementation.[87]

3 Hearings on the SRM

The hearings in the 2019–24 legislative term included four hearings with the current Chair of the SRB, Dominique Laboureix, as well as 10 hearings with Elke König, the former—and very first—Chair of the SRB.[88] These hearings follow a very similar format to the one explained above for the public hearings with the Chair of the Supervisory Board. As noted by the Chair of the ECON Committee at the hearing of 18 July 2023:

> So, today's meeting will be organised as follows: Mr Laboureix will have the floor for an introductory statement of a maximum five minutes, and afterwards we will turn to the Q&A session with the first round of questions. One slot per political group and longer slots for speakers in the first round of Q&As with follow-up questions allowed. So, one minute for the initial question and three minutes for the answer with the follow-up, which would be half a minute and one minute maximum for the answer and then a second round of questions where we apply the d'Hondt system—so one minute for

[85] See, eg the question asked by Michiel Hoogeveen (ECR) at the meeting of 28 June 2023 or the question by Eugen Jurzyca (ECR) at the meeting of 27 October 2020. An exceptionally high number of questions that fall outside the remit of the SSM were asked by MEPs at the hearing on 5 May 2020, as it took place only an hour and a half after the *PSPP* judgment was delivered by the Bundesverfassungsgericht: BVerfG, Judgment of the Second Senate of 5 May 2020–2 BvR 859/15, paras 1–237, https://www.bverfg.de/e/rs20200505_2bvr085915en, accessed 12 September 2025.

[86] This is not a new phenomenon: see Amtenbrink and Markakis, 'Towards a Meaningful Prudential Supervision Dialogue in the Euro Area?' (n 9) 21.

[87] Save for two questions asked by Sven Giegold (Verts/Greens/European Free Alliance (ALE)) at the hearings of 12 December 2019 and 4 September 2019, concerning the statistics on fit-and-proper assessments and the disclosure of Pillar 2 requirements, respectively.

[88] The current author watched, on the European Parliament's Multimedia Centre, the video recordings from 14 public hearings that took place on 21 March 2024, 4 December 2023, 18 July 2023, 1 March 2023, 30 November 2022, 13 July 2022, 14 March 2022, 1 December 2021, 1 July 2021, 23 March 2021, 27 October 2020, 5 May 2020, 3 December 2019, and 22 July 2019.

> the question and two minutes for the answer. And then, if time allows, we may have slots allocated on a catch-the-eye basis.

It should be noted that there can be slight variations of this format, depending on the public hearing concerned. A notable difference is that the former Chair of the SRB used to be given 10 minutes (instead of five) for her introductory statement.[89] It should be noted from the outset that, overall, there are noticeably few(er) questions asked by MEPs at those hearings.[90] The current Chair of the SRB gives characteristically long-winded answers, whereas that was not the case with his predecessor. Furthermore, it is readily apparent that there is no strict distinction or separation between those hearings where the annual report of the SRB is presented and the other hearings, in terms of the format followed or the ensuing discussion.[91] This coheres with the current author's observations from the other SSM/SRM hearings.

Similarly to what was observed above, MEPs are asking well-informed questions. Although extremely rare, there are even some (explicit) references to the papers written by external experts.[92] In terms of the questions asked, there is some overlap with the topics discussed in the public hearings with the Chair of the Supervisory Board, for example with regard to the CMDI reform and its implications, or the European Deposit Insurance Scheme, which is directly pertinent to the completion of the Banking Union. There are also questions on other SRM-related topics, such as the use of resolution tools, the minimum requirement for own funds and eligible liabilities (MREL),[93] resolution funding, and gender balance for managerial positions at the SRB. Earlier in the parliamentary term, there were also questions on the economic impact on banks of Russia's aggression against Ukraine, the resolution of Sberbank,[94] and—to a more limited extent—on the impact of Brexit.[95] Interestingly for the subject matter of this chapter, there have also been questions about transparency

[89] See the introduction by Irene Tinagli at the meetings of 30 November 2022 and 13 July 2022.

[90] At the hearing of 30 November 2022, René Repasi (Socialists and Democrats, S&D) remarked, with some degree of surprise, that he 'thought having the second S&D slot would mean [waiting for] another half an hour'.

[91] As mentioned, eg by the Chair of the SRB at the meeting of 13 July 2022: 'I will not dwell into the report in great detail, although I'm happy to answer any questions because I firmly believe you are more interested in what's going on today than reflecting on the past. I want to use the time this morning to provide a short update on a number of topics we've been working on.'

[92] At the meeting of 1 December 2021, Margarita Marques (S&D) referred to the paper by Marco Bodellini and Willem Pieter de Groen, and then went on to refer to the paper by Christos Gortsos, as well as to a European Court of Auditors report that had been published a few days before the hearing.

[93] Including on the Daisy Chains proposal regarding 'internal MREL' in banking groups—see, eg the meeting of 1 December 2021.

[94] See the meeting of 14 March 2022.

[95] See, eg the meetings of 3 December 2019 and 22 July 2019.

regarding the work of the SRB and the institutions within its remit.[96] Even more so, certain improvements in terms of transparency have originated from requests by MEPs during those hearings.[97]

IV Conclusions

There will be no attempt to summarize the preceding arguments in their entirety. Instead, this concluding section will highlight certain features that are of particular importance. First of all, to state what is perhaps obvious to the reader at this juncture, the existing mechanisms of accountability are not only written on a piece of paper or legislation but are also employed in practice: 'hearings and exchanges of views are organised, questions are posed, and reports are produced'.[98] Overall, the SSM and SRM Regulations, together with the Interinstitutional Agreement between the European Parliament and the ECB and the Agreement between the European Parliament and the SRB, introduce a relatively detailed framework on the provision of information to, and the institutional contacts with, the European Parliament.[99] As far as the parliamentary hearings are concerned, this is, in the current author's view, a relatively well-functioning dialogue, within the confines of the framework provided by the respective arrangements. Arguably, the personality of the respective Chairs plays a role in the smooth operation of the accountability arrangements. The way in which these meetings are scheduled is also very interesting. On various occasions, a hearing with the Chair of the ECB's Supervisory Board took place either before or after an exchange of views with the Chair of the SRB, or after a hearing with the Chair of the European Systemic Risk Board.[100] This may allow for better synergies between the respective accountability mechanisms,

[96] See, eg the question by Danuta Maria Hübner (PPE) at the hearing of 1 March 2023, as well as the Chair's answer. At the meeting of 23 March 2021, Eero Heinäluoma (S&D) asked about the publication of MREL decisions. The SRB Chair responded that they published aggregate MREL build-up numbers on their website. Subsequent hearings also focused on the publication of the resolvability heat-map.

[97] As noted, eg by the Chair of the SRB at the meeting of 13 July 2022: 'And here I would just refer to the MREL dashboard that, not least because of the requests of this House, we now publish quarterly on our website. Sometimes it's good to have someone to push.' See, in this connection, the interaction between Sven Giegold (Verts/ALE) and the Chair of the SRB at the meeting of 27 October 2020.

[98] Fromage, 'Democratic Accountability in the Banking Union' (n 9) 125.

[99] See also Amtenbrink and Markakis, 'The Legitimacy and Accountability of the European Central Bank at the Age of Twenty' (n 15) 281.

[100] An interesting parallel may be noted here, since 'the Chair of the Supervisory Board and the Chair of the SRB commonly appear together before the Eurogroup': Fromage, 'Democratic Accountability in the Banking Union' (n 9) 123.

and it is often the case that MEPs refer in their questions to the hearing that preceded the meeting on that day.

As we have seen, the hearings do not sharply focus on whether the SSM and the SRM are achieving their objectives or not, but rather focus more on the provision of information or requests for policy views.[101] What is more, as readily admitted in a recent study published as part of the ECB *Economic Bulletin*, '[a]mong other considerations, the diversity of supervisory tools, the absence of a single quantifiable supervisory objective, and banking data confidentiality create distinct scrutiny challenges.'[102] The same considerations could be said to apply, *mutatis mutandis*, to banking resolution.[103] Clearly, confidentiality in banking supervision and resolution—for example, the respective Chairs never address the situations of individual banks at the public hearings—is 'a further hindrance in MEPs' quest for accountability'.[104] In this connection, it is argued in the relevant literature that 'an appropriate opening of professional secrecy provisions could improve the accountability vis-à-vis the European Parliament'.[105]

In the present author's view, there is always scope for improvement of both the formal accountability arrangements and their practical implementation. As so often suggested in the relevant literature, it starts with making better use of the existing accountability arrangements, thereby 'asking more informed questions, making more demands for policy changes where necessary, and ensuring better synergies between the mechanisms that exist in parallel',[106] including interparliamentary cooperation and meetings, where appropriate.[107] It also entails—for the SSM and the SRM—being more responsive, where appropriate, to demands for scrutiny, or simply feedback, by the European Parliament. Changes to the relevant accountability and transparency arrangements, where needed, are possible by means of amending the SSM and the SRM Regulations, and/or by adapting the relevant agreements with

[101] See also ibid 126. Akbik, *The European Parliament as an Accountability Forum* (n 9) 85 observes that '[r]equests for policy views cannot be considered a form of oversight because they do not concern the past activity of the ECB in terms of decisions or conduct.'

[102] Dreher, Hernborg, Mochhoury, Mulder, and Schölermann, 'The ECB's Accountability to the European Parliament 2019-2024' (n 9) 89.

[103] See also Markakis, *Accountability in the Economic and Monetary Union* (n 11) ch 5.

[104] Fromage, 'Democratic Accountability in the Banking Union' (n 9) 126. See also the reform proposals by Smits, 'SSM and the SRB Accountability at European Level' (n 11) 13 ff.

[105] Smits, 'SSM and the SRB Accountability at European Level' (n 11) 28; see also René Smits and Nikolai Badenhoop, 'Towards a Single Standard of Professional Secrecy for Supervisory Authorities – A Reform Proposal' (2019) 44 European Law Review 295.

[106] Fromage, 'Democratic Accountability in the Banking Union' (n 9) 131.

[107] See also ibid; Economic Governance and EMU Scrutiny Unit, 'The Institutional Role of the European Parliament in the Economic and Monetary Union' (n 67) 4.

the European Parliament, viz. the Interinstitutional Agreement between the European Parliament and the ECB, and the Agreement between the European Parliament and the SRB. The present author agrees that 'the thoroughness of scrutiny could and should be enhanced in order to ensure that decision[s] and practices by supervisory authorities and authorities acting within banking resolution are truly challenged'.[108] Obviously, this also implicates the other accountability mechanisms examined elsewhere in this volume.[109] 'The experience from the past ten years shows that effective accountability can only be achieved via the interplay of various mechanisms of which parliamentary scrutiny is only one – albeit essential – pillar.'[110] Much like the European Banking Union, which is imperfect or incomplete, ensuring the robustness of the accountability and transparency arrangements in the Banking Union also remains a work in progress.

[108] Lastra and Dietz, 'Accountability of the European Banking Union' (n 11) 16.
[109] See the chapters by Jakub Kerlin and Carlos Soler Ruiz.
[110] Lastra and Dietz, 'Accountability of the European Banking Union' (n 11) 26.

20

The Role of the European Court of Auditors in the Administrative Accountability of the Banking Union

Carlos Soler Ruiz[*]

I Public sector auditing as a way to enhance accountability: The audit mandate and powers of the European Court of Auditors

Governments and other public sector entities are accountable for their management and performance, and for the use of resources.[1] Public sector auditing provides legislative and oversight bodies—those charged with governance and the general public—with information and assessments about the performance of government policies, programmes, or operations.[2] Public sector audits contribute to good governance by, among other things, enhancing accountability and transparency, and can be categorized into financial, compliance, and performance audits.[3] The United Nations has recognized 'the important role of supreme audit institutions in promoting the efficiency, accountability, effectiveness and transparency of public administration'.[4]

* Disclaimer: the text expresses the personal opinion of the author and not that of the European Court of Auditors, the European Commission, or any other institution, body, office, agency, or supreme audit institution of the EU.

[1] ISSAI 100/17 – International Organisation of Supreme Audit Institutions, *Fundamental Principles of Public-sector Auditing* (INTOSAI 2019) 10 https://www.issai.org/wp-content/uploads/2019/08/ISSAI-100-Fundamental-Principles-of-Public-Sector-Auditing-1.pdf accessed 31 August 2024.

[2] ISSAI 100/18 – International Organisation of Supreme Audit Institutions, *Fundamental Principles of Public-sector Auditing* (INTOSAI 2019) 10 https://www.issai.org/wp-content/uploads/2019/08/ISSAI-100-Fundamental-Principles-of-Public-Sector-Auditing-1.pdf accessed 31 August 2024.

[3] ISSAI 100/20–22 – International Organisation of Supreme Audit Institutions, *Fundamental Principles of Public-sector Auditing* (INTOSAI 2019) 10–11 https://www.issai.org/wp-content/uploads/2019/08/ISSAI-100-Fundamental-Principles-of-Public-Sector-Auditing-1.pdf accessed 31 August 2024.

[4] United Nations, 'Resolution adopted by the General Assembly on 22 December 2011' A/RES/66/209 (15 March 2012) https://documents.un.org/doc/undoc/gen/n11/471/36/pdf/n1147136.pdf accessed 31 August 2024.

Carlos Soler Ruiz, *The Role of the European Court of Auditors in the Administrative Accountability of the Banking Union* In: *EU Banking Union*. Edited by: Jonathan Bauerschmidt, Raffaele D'Ambrosio, Diane Fromage, Daniela Jaros, and Paul Weismann, Oxford University Press.
DOI: 10.1093/9780198949756.003.0021

The European Court of Auditors (ECA) is the supreme audit institution (SAI) of the EU. Its audit powers, competences, and responsibilities are laid down in primary law: pursuant to Article 13(2) of the TEU, the ECA must, like any other institution, 'act within the limits of the powers conferred on it in the Treaties, and in conformity with the procedures, conditions and objectives set out in them', and, in accordance with Article 285 of the TFEU, 'the Court of Auditors shall carry out the Union's audit'.

Article 287(1) of the TFEU defines the scope of the examination that the ECA is obliged to perform. This scope consists of the accounts of all revenue and expenditure of the EU, or of any body, office, or agency set up by the EU. In its second subparagraph, the same provision continues to define the scope of the examination: the ECA has two sort of audits to perform in order to provide the European Parliament (EP) and the Council with a statement of assurance:

(a) A traditional *financial audit* to verify the *reliability of the accounts* of the EU or any body, office, or agencies set up by the EU. The audit objective in this case is to ascertain that these accounts provide the true and fair view of the auditee's financial position as at the end of the year audited, the results of its operations, its cash flows, and the changes in net assets for the year then ended.[5]
(b) A *compliance audit* to verify the *legality and regularity of the underlying transactions*. It does so by examining, according to Article 287(2) of the TFEU, whether all revenue has been received and all expenditure incurred in a lawful and regular manner, and reporting on any cases of irregularity.

The ECA performs its audits in accordance with international auditing standards, in particular the International Organization of Supreme Audit Institutions (INTOSAI) professional standards and other pronouncements. Pursuant to Article 287(1) TFEU and Article 70(6) of the EU Financial Regulation,[6] the ECA draws up an *annual report* on the EU budget and *specific annual reports*[7] on each body, office, or agency after the close of each financial

[5] See, eg para 3.38.5 of European Court of Auditors, *Annual Report on EU Agencies for the Financial Year 2022* (Publications Office of the European Union 2023) 312.

[6] Regulation (EU, Euratom) 2024/2509 of the European Parliament and of the Council of 23 September 2024 on the financial rules applicable to the general budget of the Union (recast) [2018] OJ L2024/2509 (hereinafter 'EU Financial Regulation').

[7] The specific annual reports are consolidated in ch 3 of the European Court of Auditors, *Annual Report on the EU Agencies from the Financial Year 2017* onwards, and in ch 3 of the European Court of Auditors, *Annual Report on the Joint Undertakings from the Financial Year 2018* onwards.

year and presents them to the EP and the Council. These reports provide the basis for the yearly discharge exercise for the EU budget.

Apart from these financial and compliance audits, the ECA carries out *performance audits*. Indeed, Article 287(2) of the TFEU also requires the ECA to 'examine whether the financial management has been sound', reporting 'in particular on any cases of irregularity'.

The observations arising from these performance audits are usually published in the form of *special reports*. Therefore, apart from the annual reports, the ECA, pursuant to Article 287(4) of the TFEU, 'may also, at any time, submit observations, particularly in the form of special reports, on specific questions'. This does not prevent the annual reports from containing 'an assessment of the soundness of financial management', as provided for by Article 258(2) of the EU Financial Regulation.

Pursuant to Article 287(4) of the TFEU, the ECA can deliver *opinions* during the legislative process, either in the cases provided by the law or at the request of any of the other institutions of the EU, outside the cases of mandatory consultation.

Finally, the ECA can also deliver *reviews*[8] to describe and analyse areas of EU policy or management issues using publicly available information. Reviews are different from audit reports because they do not intend to address evaluative questions and do not provide assurance or make new recommendations.[9]

II Audit mandate of the ECA on the Banking Union

The negative consequences of any future financial crisis would have on the public finances and, ultimately, for the real economy, make a case for a strong audit remit on the Banking Union (BU) as a crucial element of its accountability. This section examines how this audit remit has been granted to the ECA in both primary and secondary law, and how this applies to the BU and its two operational pillars. It also shows how the ECA has contributed to the discharge of the administrative accountability of the BU during its first 10 years of existence through the main sorts of audits and products: the financial and

[8] For example, European Court of Auditors, *Review No 5/2020: How the EU Took Account of Lessons Learned from the 2008-2012 Financial and Sovereign Debt Crises* (Publications Office of the European Union 2020).

[9] See European Court of Auditors, 'AWARE ECA Methodology and Guidance' https://methodology.eca.europa.eu/aware/review/Pages/Aims-of-reviews.aspx accessed 31 August 2024.

compliance audits and the performance audits, and its special reports, annual reports, reviews, and opinions.

A full administrative accountability of the main players of the BU at EU level is possible only if the legal framework provides the SAI of the EU—the ECA—with a clear remit and vests it with unlimited powers to audit: (i) the reliability of their accounts (*financial audit*); (ii) the legality and regularity of their underlying transactions (*compliance audit*); and (iii) whether their policies, programmes, or operations have been implemented in accordance with the sound financial management principles of economy, efficiency, and effectiveness (*performance audit*).[10]

The objectives of the BU and its pillars are reproduced below for the purpose of identifying potential gaps in the administrative accountability of the BU. Indeed, if the legal framework does not allow the ECA to verify, for example, how one of the two operational pillars of the BU delivers its intended objectives, there is a gap in the administrative accountability of that pillar and in the BU in general.

The BU has three pillars: the Single Supervisory Mechanism (SSM), the Single Resolution Mechanism (SRM), and the not-yet-established European Deposit and Insurance Scheme (EDIS). The SSM was set up in 2013.[11] It is aimed at protecting the safety and soundness of credit institutions so as to help ensure the stability of the EU financial system as a whole.[12] The SRM was established in 2015. As the General Court (GC) has emphasized, pursuant to preamble recitals 12, 58, and 61 of the Single Resolution Mechanism Regulation (hereinafter 'SRM Regulation'),[13] the stability of the financial markets is one of the objectives pursued by the SRM.[14] The Commission submitted a proposal

[10] See the fifth element of the ECA model of six elements for a strong accountability and audit chain shown in European Court of Auditors, *Landscape Review: Gaps, Overlaps and Challenges: A Landscape Review of EU Accountability and Public Audit Arrangements* (Publications Office of the European Union 2014) 6.

[11] Council Regulation (EU) 1024/2013 of 15 October 2013 conferring specific tasks on the European Central Bank concerning policies relating to the prudential supervision of credit institutions [2013] OJ L287/63 (hereinafter 'SSM Regulation').

[12] See Joined Cases C-152/18 P and C-153/18 P *Crédit mutuel Arkéa v ECB*, ECLI:EU:C:2019:810, paras 55–56.

[13] Regulation (EU) 806/2014 of the European Parliament and of the Council of 15 July 2014 establishing uniform rules and a uniform procedure for the resolution of credit institutions and certain investment firms in the framework of a Single Resolution Mechanism and a Single Resolution Fund and amending Regulation (EU) No 1093/2010 [2014] OJ L225/1 (hereinafter 'SRM Regulation').

[14] See Case T-570/17 *Algebris (UK) and Anchorage Capital Group v Commission*, ECLI:EU:T:2022:314, para 341; and Case T-510/17 *Del Valle Ruiz and Others v Commission and SRB*, ECLI:EU:T:2022:312, para 135.

for the creation of an EDIS in November 2015.[15] This proposal has not yet been adopted by the EU legislature.

1 Audit mandate on the SSM

The SSM consists of the European Central Bank (ECB) and the National Competent Authorities (NCAs) of 21 Member States participating in the euro area. As regards the ECB, the broad audit powers granted to the ECA by Article 287 of the TFEU are limited to the 'examination of the operational efficiency of the management of the ECB', by Article 27(2) of the Protocol (No 4) on the Statute of the European System of Central Banks (ESCB) and of the ECB (hereinafter 'the Statute'). Article 27(1) of the Statute provides that the ECB's accounts are audited by 'an independent external auditor recommended by the Governing Council and approved by the Council' and not by the ECA. The concept of 'operational efficiency of the management' of the ECB is not defined either in the Statute or in secondary legislation.

Before the creation of the SSM,[16] the ECA delivered annual reports on the operational efficiency of the management of the ECB. These annual reports were limited in scope to different management topics but did not provide for an interpretation of what 'operational efficiency of the management' of the ECB means.[17] Efficiency normally shows the relationship between the inputs consumed and outputs delivered by the entity, in such a way that doing more (outputs) with less (inputs) represents an increase in the efficiency of that entity. The operational efficiency ratio of an entity is obtained by dividing its operating expenses (input) by its revenue (output).

However, this does not mean that the ECA examination should be limited to the inputs and outputs of the ECB or to its operating expenses and revenue. Furthermore, the principle of efficiency, pursuant to ISSAI 300/11, 'means getting the most from the available resources. It is concerned with the relationship between resources employed and outputs delivered in terms of quantity,

[15] Commission, 'Proposal for a Regulation of the European Parliament and of the Council amending Regulation (EU) 806/2014 in order to establish a European Deposit Insurance Scheme' COM (2015) 586 final (24 November 2015) https://eur-lex.europa.eu/legal-content/EN/TXT/?uri = CELEX:52015PC0586 accessed 31 August 2024.

[16] From the financial year 1998 until the financial year 2010, both inclusive, plus one additional report: European Court of Auditors, 'Report on the audit of the management by the European Central Bank of its carbon footprint together with the replies of the European Central Bank' [2014] OJ C 158/01.

[17] It is worth mentioning that the word 'operational' does not exist in the French and German versions of the Treaty.

quality and timing'.[18] In the same vein, Article 33(1)(b) of the EU Financial Regulation lays down that the principle of efficiency 'concerns the best relationship between the resources employed, the activities undertaken and the achievement of objectives'.

Article 20 of the SSM Regulation, devoted to accountability and reporting, extends, in its paragraph 7, this examination of the operational efficiency of the management of the ECB, carried out by the ECA following Article 27(2) of the Statute, to 'the supervisory tasks conferred on the ECB by this Regulation'. As stated in preamble recital 55 of the SSM Regulation, 'any shift of supervisory powers from the Member State to the Union level should be balanced by appropriate transparency and accountability requirements'.[19]

The Communication from the ECA to the EP clarifies the interpretation of efficiency and states that the 'ECA considers that the interpretation of efficiency in banking supervision is not necessarily the same as in monetary policy' and that, 'in the area of supervisory activities, the assessment of efficiency implies an assessment of whether the supervising institutions are performing their duties in a manner that minimizes the risk of financial instability and potential cost for budgetary resources'.[20]

2 Audits on the SSM

This subsection examines the four special reports produced by the ECA on the SSM. The first one focused mainly on the governance and accountability arrangements of the SSM, while the second was on the crisis management for banks. It shows the practical limitations in the access to evidence experienced by the ECA auditors during the audits that concluded with these two special reports, and how they have been addressed with the signature of a Memorandum of Understanding (MoU) between the ECA and the ECB.

[18] ISSAI 300/11 – International Organisation of Supreme Audit Institutions, *Performance Audit Principles* (INTOSAI 2019) 9 https://www.issai.org/wp-content/uploads/2019/08/ISSAI-300 accessed 31 August 2024.

[19] Quoted in the Memorandum of Understanding between the ECA and the ECB regarding audits on the ECB's supervisory tasks, https://www.eca.europa.eu/lists/ecadocuments/mou_eca-ecb/mou_eca-ecb.pdf, accessed 31 August 2024 (hereinafter 'MoU between the ECA and the ECB'), preamble recital (c).

[20] European Court of Auditors, 'Communication to the European Parliament concerning the European Parliament's request to be kept informed regarding the problem of access to information in relation to the European Central Bank, as laid down in paragraph 29 of the 2016 discharge procedure (2017/2188(DEC))' (European Court of Auditors 2018) 6 https://www.eca.europa.eu/other%20publications/pl19_ecb/pl19_ecb_en.pdf accessed 31 August 2024.

As a result of this MoU, the two special reports produced after the signature of the MoU—one on the fight against money laundering and another on the supervision of the banks' credit risk—showed no scope limitation, as happened with the first ones. However, as explained before, there are legal hurdles preventing the ECA from examining, in the field of the SSM, sound financial management principles other than the operational efficiency of the management of the ECB, in respect of the supervisory tasks conferred on the ECB by SSM Regulation.

The ECA has produced four special reports on the SSM. The first special report was published in 2016.[21] It focused on governance and accountability arrangements of the SSM, organization and resources allocation of the Joint Supervisory Teams, and on-site supervision. The report was published with a limitation in its scope in the areas of governance, off-site supervision, and on-site inspections.[22] It showed, in its Annex II, the areas that were not satisfactorily audited because of the refusal of the ECB to provide the requested evidence. Annex III reported examples of the consequences of the missing evidence on the audit assessment of the ECA.

Although Article 20(7) of the SSM Regulation extends the ECA examination on the operational efficiency of the management of the ECB to 'the supervisory tasks conferred on the ECB by this Regulation', the report noted limitations of access to the information required by the ECA to assess the operational efficiency of:

(a) the management of the ECB's comprehensive assessments, ie asset quality reviews and stress testing;
(b) Joint Supervisory Teams; and
(c) the planning and implementation of supervisory activities, the decision-making process, and the actual work done in the context of on-site inspections.[23]

In the ECA president's letter of 7 February 2013 to the president of the EU Parliament, in relation to the new SSM functions of the ECB, the ECA already indicated that 'its examination of the "operational efficiency of the management of the ECB" will encompass the audit of sound financial management, as it applies to other bodies within its remit'.[24]

[21] European Court of Auditors, *Special Report No 29/2016: Single Supervisory Mechanism—Good Start but Further Improvements Needed* (Publications Office of the European Union 2016).
[22] See ibid 9, para V.
[23] See ibid 20.
[24] European Court of Auditors, *Landscape Review* (n 10) 39.

However, in the present author's opinion, the ECA's examination of the operational efficiency, in this report, was limited de facto by the information provided by the ECB, and focused largely on organizational and human resources matters, in line with the annual reports issued before the setting-up of the SSM, but in the new areas of off-site supervision and on-site inspection. Only the part of the report devoted to the governance and accountability arrangements focused more on other sound financial aspects, such as the effectiveness of bank supervision. Nonetheless, the report highlights the lack of a formal performance framework to provide assurance about the achievement of SSM objectives.[25]

To overcome this weakness in the accountability arrangements, the ECA recommended the ECB to 'fully cooperate with the Court in order to enable it to exercise its mandate and thereby enhance accountability'.[26] The ECB disagreed, in its reply to the report, with the ECA's statements that 'the ECB provided very little of the information requested'[27] and that 'that the audit has confirmed an audit gap which has emerged since the establishment of the SSM'.[28]

The ECA published a second report on the SSM in 2018.[29] The audit examined one supervisory task—the crisis management. The report submitted observations related to the ECB's organizational set-up and resources allocation for the assessment of recovery plans and the supervision of banks, external cooperation and coordination concerning crisis management, assessment of banks' recovery plans, and crisis identification and crisis response.

Once again, the report mentioned limitations in the access to important evidence, preventing the ECA [from confirming] 'the operational efficiency of crisis management at the ECB in practice',[30] although it was able 'to draw overall conclusions about the design of the ECB's processes'.[31]

Annex I reports on the scope limitations[32] regarding the sampling of recovery plans, which made the ECA unable 'to express an opinion on the

[25] European Court of Auditors, *Special Report No 29/2016* (n 21) 46–47.
[26] ibid 81.
[27] ibid 123.
[28] ibid 128.
[29] European Court of Auditors, *Special Report No 2/2018: The Operational Efficiency of the ECB's Crisis Management for Banks* (Publications Office of the European Union 2018).
[30] ibid 11.
[31] ibid.
[32] A limitation on the scope of the audit is the auditor's inability to obtain sufficient appropriate audit evidence. See ISA 705 (revised)/11–14 – International Auditing and Assurance Standards Board, *International Standard on Auditing 705 (Revised) Modifications to the Opinion in the Independent Auditor's Report* (IFAC 2015) 3–4 https://www.iaasb.org/publications/international-standard-auditing-isa-705-revised-modifications-opinion-independent-auditor-s-report-3 accessed 1 September 2024.

operational efficiency in practice of the assessment of recovery plans',[33] and on the sampling of crisis banks, which prevented the ECA from expressing an opinion on the operational efficiency of crisis management activities in practice.[34] Finally, paragraph 112 of the special report refers to the provision of redacted documents concerning early intervention processes. In line with the previous report, the ECB disagreed, in its reply, with 'the ECA's statement that it cannot draw conclusions regarding the operational efficiency of the management of this process owing to the lack of evidence provided by the ECB'.[35]

Apart from this limitation in the access to evidence, the ECA, in the present author's view, drew conclusions on the 'operational efficiency' of the audited areas but not on the effectiveness of the ECB's supervision of bank crisis.

The ECA recommended that the ECB grant the former 'access to all documents or information requested in order to carry out its task, in the interests of accountability'.[36] On 9 October 2019, the ECA and the ECB signed an MoU regarding audits on the ECB's supervisory tasks, with the purpose 'to ensure that the supervisory powers transferred from Member States to ECB Banking Supervision are balanced by appropriate transparency and accountability requirements'.[37]

In the MoU, both parties acknowledge that the operational efficiency of the management, referred to in Article 27(2) of the Statute and Article 20(7) of the SSM Regulation, is not defined in EU Law, but admit that Article 33 of the EU Financial Regulation may be used as a source of interpretation 'in the examination of the ECB's supervisory activities by the ECA in line with its mandate'.[38]

The first audit performed by the ECA after the entry into force of the MoU was on the EU's efforts to fight money laundering.[39] This audit evaluated, among other things, the ECB's integration of money laundering and terrorism financing (ML/TF) risks into prudential supervision. The audit examined whether the ECB had efficiently integrated ML/TF risks into its prudential supervision of banks and efficiently shared information with national supervisors.[40] Although the audit examined aspects of efficiency and effectiveness,[41]

[33] European Court of Auditors, *Special Report No 2/2018* (n 29) Annex I, 53.
[34] ibid, Annex I, 53.
[35] ibid, ECB's replies, 2.
[36] ibid 51.
[37] European Central Bank, 'ECB and ECA agree Memorandum of Understanding' (ECB, 29 August 2019) 3–4 https://www.bankingsupervision.europa.eu/press/pr/date/2019/html/ssm.pr190828~549dd2c932.en.html accessed 1 September 2024.
[38] MoU between the ECA and the ECB (n 19), preamble recital (e).
[39] European Court of Auditors, *Special Report No 13/2021: EU Efforts to Fight Money Laundering in the Banking Sector Are Fragmented and Implementation is Insufficient* (Publications Office of the European Union 2021).
[40] ibid 15.
[41] ibid.

the examination of the ECB's prudential supervision and sharing of information appeared to have been made solely from the efficiency point of view. The ECA has not reported any scope limitation on this audit.

The ECA also published, in 2021, a special report on sustainable finance.[42] However, the audit did not cover the ECB's actions to promote sustainable finance,[43] although it referred to some important actions, such as the ECB's economy-wide climate stress test,[44] and to the ECB's policy to support the use of EU taxonomy-aligned bonds.[45]

Another audit carried out upon the entry into force of the MoU was focused on the EU supervision of banks' credit risk.[46] The ECA confirmed that, during this audit, it 'obtained full access to the documents we requested and full co-operation from ECB staff throughout the process'.[47] The special report issued on this audit contained, in its Annex, a follow-up on the ECA's recommendations of its Special Report No 29/2016, which had been postponed beyond the regular period of three years, due to the pandemic.[48]

The audit examined the operational efficiency of 'the ECB's approach to supervision of credit risk in banks; and in addressing legacy non-performing loans' by assessing the relationship between resources employed, ie inputs and outputs.[49] The audit did not examine other sound financial management aspects of the ECB's supervision of credit risk to conclude whether: (i) it had delivered its intended objectives (effectiveness); or (ii) the resources used by the ECB had been made available in due time, in appropriate quantity and quality, and at the best price (economy).[50]

Obviously, the ECA is free to examine only the operational efficiency, but the examination of the principles of effectiveness and economy is limited by the legal framework, which not only prevents the examination of the ECB's

[42] European Court of Auditors, *Special Report No 22/2021: Sustainable Finance: More Consistent EU Action Needed to Redirect Finance towards Sustainable Investment* (Publications Office of the European Union 2021).
[43] ibid 14.
[44] ibid 6.
[45] ibid 21.
[46] European Court of Auditors, *Special Report No 12/2023: EU Supervision of Banks' Credit Risk – The ECB Stepped Up Its efforts but More Is Needed to Increase Assurance That Credit Risk is Properly Managed and Covered* (Publications Office of the European Union 2023).
[47] ibid 14.
[48] European Court of Auditors, *Report on the Performance of the EU Budget – Status at the End of 2019* (Publications Office of the European Union 2020) 235. The follow-up of the recommendations of Special Report No 2/2018 can be found in European Court of Auditors, *Report on the Performance of the EU Budget – Status at the End of 2021* (Publications Office of the European Union 2022) Annex 3.2, 124.
[49] European Court of Auditors, *Special Report No 12/2023* (n 46) 15.
[50] EU Financial Regulation, art 33.

accounts but also the examination of either the effectiveness or the economy of the ECB's supervisory policy within the SSM.

3 Audit mandate on the SRM

Although the ECA has no legal mandate to audit the accounts of the ECB, the SRM Regulation, in its Article 63, grants the ECA the mandate to audit the SRB accounts, in line with the generic mandate to audit 'any other body, office, or agency set up by the EU' contained in the primary legislation.[51] This is the *financial and compliance audit*, which concludes with a *statement of assurance* as to the reliability of the SRB accounts and the legality and regularity of the underlying transactions. This audit should be published by 15 November of year n+1: the ECA transmits its annual EU agencies report to the budgetary authority, including the statement of assurance of each agency, within chapter 3 of the report. The final accounts of the SRB are published in the *Official Journal of the EU*.[52]

On the other hand, paragraph 4 of Article (4) of the SRM Regulation entrusts the ECA to prepare annually, by 1 December of the year n+1, a *report on any contingent liabilities* 'arising as a result of the performance by the Board, the Council and the Commission of their tasks under this Regulation'. This report examines whether the accounting treatment, in the accounts of the SRB, the Council, and the Commission, of their financial exposure because of pending litigation due to their performance under the SRM Regulation is appropriate.

This accounting treatment of the contingent liabilities is based on the probability of an outflow of resources due to an unfavourable outcome of the pending legal cases before the EU and national courts. If the probability of an outflow of economic resources due to an unfavourable outcome of this pending litigation is assessed as possible,[53] a contingent liability must be disclosed in the notes to the financial statements, to enable users to understand its nature, timing, and amount; if the probability is assessed as probable,[54] a provision must be recognized in the accounts.[55]

[51] TFEU, art 287(1).

[52] SRM Regulation, art 63; European Court of Auditors, *Annual Report on EU Agencies for 2022* (n 5) 24.

[53] Probability assessed as between 10% and 50%, in the case of the SRB and Council, and between 20% and 50%, in the case of the Commission.

[54] More than 50%.

[55] See, eg European Court of Auditors, *Report (Pursuant to Article 92(4) Regulation (EU) No 806/2014) on Any Contingent Liabilities Arising as a Result of the Performance by the Single Resolution Board, the Council or the Commission of Their Tasks under This Regulation for the 2020 Financial Year* (Publications Office of the European Union 2021) 9–10.

This pending litigation involving the SRB, the Commission, and the Council can be triggered mainly by their resolution or non-resolution decisions, the no-creditor-worse-off principle, or the administrative contributions of the banking industry to the SRB's operating expenses or their *ex ante* contributions to the SRF.

Both the ECA, in its annual reports, and the SRB, in its final accounts, from the financial years 2015–22, have highlighted that 'it is difficult to predict the outcome of these legal proceedings at this stage due to the complex, specific and unprecedented legal system of the legal framework for resolution'.[56] These difficulties arise from the absence of a consolidated case law on this new legal framework for resolution.

Apart from the above reports, the ECA can deliver special reports because of *performance audits* carried out on its own initiative, pursuant to Article 287(4) of the TFEU, or at the request of the EP and of the Council, as provided for in Article 92(5) of the SRM Regulation. Article 45(2) of the same regulation obliges the SRB to submit to the ECA, among other stakeholders, an annual report on the performance of its tasks conferred by the SRM Regulation. These audits can examine whether the SRM is delivering on its intended objectives (effectiveness) or whether its design and implementation comply with other sound financial management principles, such as efficiency or economy.

Finally, paragraphs 1 to 3 of Article 92 of the SRM Regulation oblige the ECA to produce a *special report* that examines whether:

(a) sufficient regard was had to the economy, efficiency, and effectiveness with which the Fund has been used, in particular the need to minimize the use of the Fund;
(b) the assessment of Fund aid was efficient and rigorous.

This is a regulatory audit which focuses on sound financial management aspects of the use of the SRF, and of the assessment of its aid. The audited period differs from other regulatory audits as it comprises not the natural or calendar year but a period with the same length of 12 months but running, pursuant to paragraph 1 of the above Article, from 1 April of year n to 31 March of year n+1.

The reporting deadline expires on 30 September of year n+1. This means that, if the Fund is used on 31 March of year n+1, the ECA has only six months to carry out a complex audit and to produce the special report. On the

[56] ibid 18.

contrary, if the Fund is used on 1 April of year n, it has nearly 18 months, until 30 September of the year n+1, to finalize the audit and the special report.

It is a regulatory audit because its scope and timing are determined by the SRM Regulation, and its time schedule differs from the standard period of 13 months set up in Article 259(1) of the EU Financial Regulation to draw up and adopt a special report.

The resolution scheme will determine, as prescribed by Article 23 of the SRM Regulation, 'the specific amounts and purposes for which the Fund shall be used' and the same provision states that, 'in the course of the resolution process, the Board may amend and update the resolution scheme as appropriate in light of the circumstances of the case'. For practical reasons of compliance with the short deadlines provided for in Article 92(3), of the SRM, this audit should start as soon as the resolution scheme or its amendment enters into force.

The purposes of the use of the Fund are enumerated in paragraph 1(a) to (g) of Article 76 of the SRM Regulation. One of them is to compensate shareholders if a valuation carried out pursuant to Article 20 (16) of the SRM Regulation (valuation 3) determines that they would have been better off had the bank been wound up under normal insolvency proceedings.[57] In this case, the resolution scheme should be amended accordingly, even in the case that this valuation 3 has been produced as a result of the annulment by the CJEU of a previous SRB decision based on a valuation 3 issued within the same resolution process.

The interpretation of the audit objectives defined by Article 92(2) of the SRM Regulation could make use of the definition of 'sound financial management', which encompasses the principles of *economy, efficiency, and effectiveness*, laid down by Article 33(1) of the EU Financial Regulation.[58] Concerning the *efficient and rigorous* assessment of the Fund aid, the audit could analyse whether the Commission has complied with Article 19 of the SRM Regulation and, as required by this Article, with its own Banking Communication.[59]

Article 66 of the SRM Regulation enables the ECA to audit—either based on documents or on the spot—beneficiaries, contractors, and subcontractors who have received funds from the Board. Even though the word 'fund' is used here in a wider sense than the SRF, it is clear the ECA has audit powers over

[57] SRM Regulation, preamble recital 62, and art 76(1)(e).

[58] The definition of the sound financial management principles in the ECA AWARE methodology stems from art 33 of the EU Financial Regulation. See European Court of Auditors, 'AWARE ECA Methodology and Guidance' https://methodology.eca.europa.eu/aware/PA accessed 1 September 2024.

[59] Commission, 'Communication from the Commission on the application, from 1 August 2013, of State aid rules to support measures in favour of banks in the context of the financial crisis ('Banking Communication') Text with EEA relevance' [2013] OJ C 216/1.

the bank under resolution, its subsidiaries, an asset management vehicle, or a bridge institution, as potential recipients of the SRF, in accordance with Article 76(1) of the SRM Regulation.

Finally, pursuant to Article 92(8) of the SRM Regulation, the ECA 'shall have the power to obtain from the Board, the Council and the Commission any information relevant for performing the tasks conferred on it by this Article', and 'within such a timeframe as may be specified by the Court of Auditors'. This does not mean that the ECA is obliged to justify before the SRB, the Council, and the Commission its 'need to know' or how relevant the information requested is for the audits described in this Article.

On the contrary, in the present author's view, this provision needs to be interpreted systematically together with Article 287(3) of the TFEU and Article 257 of the EU Financial Regulation. Pursuant to that provision of the Treaty, the supply of information is not subject to the prior consent or approval of either its holder or a third party, for example the originator of the document, since 'any bodies, offices or agencies managing revenue or expenditure on behalf of the Union' shall forward to the Court of Auditors, at its request, *any document or information* necessary to carry out its task'.[60]

4 Audits on the SRM

The SRB became operational as an independent EU agency on 1 January 2015. The ECA has issued unqualified (clean) opinions on the reliability of the accounts[61] and on the legality and regularity of the underlying transactions of the SRB from the financial year 2015 to date. However, the ECA has included in its specific annual reports,[62] from the financial year 2016 onwards, 'emphasis of matter'[63] and 'other matter'[64] paragraphs to highlight the following weaknesses in the legal framework:

[60] Such a provision of primary law cannot be called into question by any provision of secondary law, as recognized by the CJ in Case C–539/09 *Commission v Germany*, ECLI:EU:C:2011:733, para 82. Emphasis added.

[61] An opinion reporting that there is a reasonable assurance that the accounts are free from material misstatement.

[62] The specific annual reports are consolidated in ch 3 of the European Court of Auditors, *Annual Report on the EU Agencies from the Financial Year*, from 2017 onwards.

[63] An 'emphasis of matter' paragraph does not call into question the auditor's opinion expressed in the statement of assurance but draws the reader's attention to matters that are fundamental to understanding the accounts. See European Court of Auditors, 'AWARE ECA Methodology and Guidance' https://methodology.eca.europa.eu/aware/GAP/Pages/CA-FA/Reporting/Emphasis-of-matter-and-other-matter.aspx accessed 1 September 2024.

[64] An 'other matter' paragraph is used by the auditor to communicate matters, other than those that are presented or disclosed in the annual accounts, that are relevant to readers' understanding of the

(a) 'the SRM Regulation does not provide for a comprehensive and consistent control framework to ensure the reliability of the information' provided by the credit institutions to the SRB for the calculation of the Fund contributions;[65] and
(b) the SRB 'cannot release details on the risk-assessed contribution calculations per credit institution as they are interlinked and include confidential information about other credit institutions. This affects the transparency of these calculations'.[66]

In the specific annual report of the financial year 2017, the ECA started to use an 'emphasis of matter' paragraph to draw the reader's attention to the fact that pending litigation concerning the SRM Regulation was not subject to the audit concluding in this statement of assurance. From the financial years 2018 to 2022, this paragraph referred also to the fact that the possible impact of the pending litigation[67] on the SRB's financial statements was subject to a separate audit on contingent liabilities pursuant to Article 92(4) of the SRM Regulation.

audit, the auditor's responsibilities, or the auditor's report. See ISA 706 (revised)/10 – International Auditing and Assurance Standards Board, *Handbook of International Quality Control, Auditing, Review, Other Assurance, and Related Services Pronouncement* (IFAC 2021) 838 https://www.ifac.org/_flysystem/azure-private/publications/files/IAASB-2020-Handbook-Volume-1.pdf#INTERNATIONAL%20STANDARD%20ON%20AUDITING%20706%20(REVISED) accessed 1 September 2024.

[65] European Court of Auditors, *Report on the Annual Accounts of the Single Resolution Board for the Financial Year 2016, together with the Board's Reply* [2017] OJ C 417/258; and European Court of Auditors, *Annual Report on EU Agencies for the Financial Year 2017* [2018] C 434/200. In European Court of Auditors, *Annual Report on EU Agencies for the Financial Year 2018* [2019] C 417/182; European Court of Auditors, *Annual Report on EU Agencies for the Financial Year 2019* (Publication Office of the European Union 2020) 27; European Court of Auditors, *Annual Report on EU Agencies for the Financial Year 2020* (Publication Office of the European Union 2021) 36; European Court of Auditors, *Annual Report on EU Agencies for the Financial Year 2021* (Publication Office of the European Union 2022) 38; European Court of Auditors, *Annual Report on EU Agencies for 2022* (n 5) 33; European Court of Auditors, *Annual Report on EU Agencies for the Financial Year 2023* (Publication Office of the European Union 2024) 327; and European Court of Auditors, *Annual Report on EU Agencies for the Financial Year 2024* (Publication Office of the European Union 2025) 276, these matters are shown, with similar formulations, within an 'other matter' paragraph.

[66] European Court of Auditors, *Report on the Annual Accounts of the SRB for 2016* (n 65); *Annual Report on EU Agencies 2017* (n 65); *Annual Report on EU Agencies for 2018* (n 65); and *Annual Report on EU Agencies for 2019* (n 65) 27. In European Court of Auditors, *Annual report on EU Agencies for 2020* (n 65) 36, this quotation slightly varies by replacing 'per credit institution' with 'for each credit institution'. For European Court of Auditors, *Annual Report on EU Agencies for the 2021* (n 65) 38, and *Annual Report on EU Agencies for 2022* (n 5) 33, 'credit institution' was replaced by 'bank' and the last sentence was slightly nuanced with '[t]his may affect the transparency of these calculations'. European Court of Auditors, *Annual Report on EU Agencies for 2023* (n 65) 327, and *Annual Report on EU Agencies for the Financial Year 2024* (n 65) does not contain the last sentence.

[67] Including administrative appeals.

For the financial years 2023 and 2024, the ECA used an 'other matter' paragraph to indicate that this audit on contingent liabilities had been reported as an appendix to the specific annual reports on the SRB.[68]

The formulation of the 'other matter' paragraph slightly changed in the reports for the financial years 2021 and 2022, to reflect the judgment of the Court of Justice (CJ) of 15 July 2021 in *Commission v Landesbank Baden-Württemberg and SRB*.[69] In the reports for the financial years 2023 and 2024, the ECA also noted improvements in the transparency of the contribution calculation process.[70]

The ECA has issued, based on Article 94(2) of the SRM Regulation, a separate report on the contingent liabilities of the SRB, the Commission, and the Council arising from the performance of their tasks under that regulation, from 2015 until 2022. For the financial years 2023 and 2024, these reporting obligations were met in the appendix of the specific annual reports on the SRB.[71] These specific annual reports have never challenged the disclosures and accounting treatment shown by the SRB, the Commission, and the Council in their financial statements of the pending litigation.

The judgments (and orders) of the GC and the CJ issued so far on the resolution-related cases of *Banco Popular Español (BPE) SA*, *Sberbank dd*, and *Sberbank banka dd* have not contradicted the assessments made by the SRB, the Commission, and the Council that no contingent liability should be disclosed thereof because the probability of an outflow of resources is remote.[72]

[68] European Court of Auditors, *Annual Report on EU Agencies for 2023* (n 65) 326.

[69] Joined Cases C-584/20 P and C-621/20 P *Commission v Landesbank Baden-Württemberg and SRB* ECLI:EU:C:2021:601: 'The SRB cannot release details of the risk assessed contribution calculation for each credit institution, as they are interlinked and include confidential information about other credit institutions. Although this may affect the transparency of these calculations, the Court of Justice considered that the SRB's obligation to state reasons for its ex-ante contribution decisions must be balanced against the principle of the protection of business secrets. It ruled.'

[70] European Court of Auditors, *Annual Report on EU Agencies for 2023* (n 65) 327 and *Annual Report on EU Agencies for the Financial Year 2024* (n 65) 280.

[71] ibid 326.

[72] See Case T-599/18 *Aeris Invest v CRU*, ECLI:EU:T:2019:740; Case T-2/19 *Algebris (UK) and Anchorage Capital Group v CRU*, ECLI:EU:T:2019:741; Case T-512/19 *Del Valle Ruiz and Others v SRB*, ECLI:EU:T:2022:331; Case C-874/19 P *Aeris Invest v SRB*, ECLI:EU:C:2021:1040; Case C-934/19 P *Algebris (UK) and Anchorage Capital Group v SRB*, ECLI:EU:C:2021:1042 (the three BPE valuation 2 cases); Case T-557/17 *Liaño Reig v CRU*, ECLI:EU:T:2019:771; Case C-947/19 P *Liaño Reig v SRB*, ECLI:EU:C:2021:172; Case T-481/17 *Fundación Tatiana Pérez de Guzmán el Bueno and SFL v SRB*, ECLI:EU:T:2022:311; *Del Valle Ruiz* (n 14); Case T-523/17 *Eleveté Invest Group and Others v Commission and SRB*, ECLI:EU:T:2022:313; *Algebris (UK)* (n 14); Case T-628/17 *Aeris Invest v Commission and SRB*, ECLI:EU:T:2022:315; Case C-539/22 P *Del Valle Ruíz and Others v Commission and SRB*; Case C-551/22 P *Commission v SRB*, ECLI:EU:C:2024:520 (the six BPE annulment and damages pilot cases); Case T-257/20 *González Calvet v SRB*, ECLI:EU:T:2020:541; Case C-27/21 P *González Calvet v SRB*, ECLI:EU:C:2021:789; Joined Cases T-302/20, T-303/20, and T-307/20 *Del Valle Ruíz and Others v SRB* ECLI:EU:T:2023:735; Case T-330/20 *ACMO and Others v SRB*, ECLI:EU:T:2023:733; Case 340/20 *Galván Fernández-Guillén v CRU*, ECLI:EU:T:2023:732;

The same applies to the litigation against the SRB concerning its non-resolution decisions of *ABLV Bank AS*, *PNB Banka AS*, and *Sberbank Europe AG*.[73]

The ECA published, in 2017, its first special report on the SRM.[74] This performance audit examined whether the SRB is equipped to carry out bank resolutions effectively and analysed the quality of the SRB's resolution planning for individual banks; whether the SRB was adequately set up to comply with its statutory framework for resolution planning and whether the SRB had adequate human resources to carry out its tasks; and whether the cooperation framework is adequate.[75]

The report noted some challenges in obtaining the requested evidence. It stated that the evidence provided by the SRB enabled the ECA 'to draw the conclusions in this report with confidence', but that 'not all documentation requested was provided'.[76] The list of missing evidence is shown in Annex II of the special report. Therefore, in this case the report does not show a scope limitation but some gaps in the information provided, and in the assessments made by the ECA.

In particular, the report highlights that the absence of certain policy documents meant that the ECA:

> did not fully assess whether the SRB's policies are entirely in line with the Single Rulebook, and access principally to anonymised data in relation to resolution plans meant that we did not assess their completeness and internal

Case T-304/20 *Molina Fernández v SRB*, ECLI:EU:T:2023:734 (the seven BPE valuation 3 cases); Case T-525/22 *Sberbank v Commission and SRB*, ECLI:EU:T:2023:633; Case T-526/22 *Sberbank of Russia v Commission and SRB*, ECLI:EU:T:2023:628; Case T-524/22 *MeSoFa v Council and Others*, ECLI:EU:T:2023:558; Case T-523/22 *MeSoFa v Council and Others*, ECLI:EU:T:2023:559; Case C-693/23 P(I) *Sberbank of Russia v MeSoFa and Others*, ECLI:EU:C:2024:271; Case C-690/23 P(I) *Sberbank of Russia v MeSoFa and Others* ECLI:EU:C:2024:272; and Case C-676/23 P(I) *Sberbank of Russia v MeSoFa and SRB*, ECLI:EU:C:2024:273; Case C-709/23 P *MeSoFA v Commission and SRB*, ECLI:EU:C:2024:630 and in Case C-708/23 P *MeSoFA v Commission and SRB*, ECLI:EU:C:2024:631; Case C-791/23 *Sberbank v Commission and SRB*, P ECLI:EU:C:354; and Case C-792/23 P *Sberbank v Commission and SRB*, ECLI:EU:C:355 (Sberbank dd and Sberbank banka dd annulment cases).

[73] See Case T-280/18 *ABLV Bank v SRB*, ECLI:EU:T:2022:429; Case T-282/18 *Bernis and Others v CRU*, ECLI:EU:T:2020:209, rectified by Order of the GC of 16 July 2020, ECLI:EU:T:2020:359 and Case C-364/20 P *Bernis and Others v SRB*, ECLI:EU:C:2022:115 (annulment of ABLV Bank AS non-resolution decision); Case T-732/19 *PNB Banka and Others v SRB*, ECLI:EU:T:2023:721 (annulment of PNB Banka AS non-resolution decision); Case T-527/22 *Sberbank of Russia v SRB*, EUCLI:EU:T:2023: 629; Case T-450/22 *MeSoFa v SRB*, ECLI:EU:T:2025:608; Case C-676/23 P(I) *Sberbank of Russia v MeSoFa and SRB*, ECLI:EU:C:2024:273; and Case C-793/23 P *Sberbank of Russia v SRB*, ECLI:EU:C:356 (annulment of Sberbank Europe AG non-resolution decision).

[74] European Court of Auditors, *Special Report No 23/2017: Single Resolution Board: Work on a Challenging Banking Union Task Started, but Still a Long Way to Go* (Publications Office of the European Union 2017).

[75] ibid 13.

[76] ibid 6.

consistency. Nonetheless, we were able to form some well evidenced conclusions on resolution plans, as will be evident from this report.[77]

Furthermore, according to the report, the SRB removed all bank-specific data and data originating with the ECB from the selected chapters of the resolution plans examined within the sample. This approach allowed the audit team to look in some detail at critical aspects of the plans and to draw important conclusions but did not allow the auditors to fully understand their completeness and internal consistency, requiring them to seek additional information, which was provided for three banks.[78]

In 2021, the ECA published its second special report on the SRM.[79] The report focused on the SRB's oversight of resolution plans for Less Significant Institutions (LSIs) and contained a follow-up of the previous audit. The audit examined whether the policy framework and organizational set-up were appropriate, and the quality and timing of the resolution plans adopted for banks.[80]

The report refers to problems in accessing the audit evidence: 'the SRB staff redacted documents by blacklining all information and data that would allow us to identify the bank to which the resolution plan in the sample related'.[81] This prevented the auditors from reconciling MREL calculations, assessing the criticality of bank functions, or examining the consistency of the SRB's assessments of the criticality of bank functions across the resolution plans.[82]

In addition, the report notes the absence of the provision of any document originating from the ECB and held by the SRB: (i) bank recovery plans; and (ii) the ECB's feedback on the SRB's draft resolution plans.[83] The ECA auditors were offered the possibility to access the documents in a physical data room at the SRB's premises, but the Covid-19 pandemic confinement measures prevented them from reviewing the documents at the SRB's facilities.[84]

As explained before, in the present author's view, provisions of both primary[85] and secondary law[86] grant the ECA access to all the information and

[77] ibid 14–15.
[78] ibid 13.
[79] European Court of Auditors, *Special Report No 1/2021: Resolution Planning in the Single Resolution Mechanism* (Publications Office of the European Union 2021).
[80] ibid 4.
[81] ibid 15.
[82] ibid.
[83] ibid.
[84] ibid.
[85] TFEU, art 287(3).
[86] EU Financial Regulation, art 257; SRM Regulation, art 92(8).

IT systems it considers necessary for the performance of its duties. Pursuant to them, all the other EU institutions and agencies shall afford the ECA such information and access. Article 287(3) of the TFEU does not make this access conditional on the prior consent of the originator of the requested document. The above provision of primary law cannot be called into question by any provision of secondary law.[87]

The ECA has never audited the use of the SRF pursuant to Article 92(1) to (3) of the SRM because the resolution schemes of BPE, Sberbank dd, and Sberbank banka dd did not provide for the use of the SRF and no amendment has yet been made to them enabling the SRB to use it.

The ECA has examined the new crisis-management framework for banks failing or likely to fail, which consists of the Bank Recovery and Resolution Directive (BRRD)[88] and the SRM Regulation. It published a review, in 2020,[89] which contains interesting findings putting into question the effectiveness of the framework to achieve its objectives to ensure that failing banks are wound up at minimal cost to the taxpayer.[90]

Indeed, the review highlights, among other weaknesses, the heterogeneous application by the EU resolution authorities of the public interest test[91] and the use by Member States of: (i) public funds to bail out and support national insolvency proceedings; (ii) precautionary recapitalizations and recapitalizations to support banks that do not meet their capital requirements; and (iii) public guarantees to support the sale of NPLs. The latter two support measures are not considered to be State aid because they are based on market terms.[92] The heterogeneous application of the public interest test has also been found by the ECA's audit on State aid for banks.[93]

The SRM Regulation authorizes the SRB to contract, for the SRF, 'borrowings or other forms of support from institutions, financial institutions or other third parties in the event that the *ex-ante* and *ex-post* contributions from the

[87] *Commission v Germany* (n 60), para 82.

[88] Directive 2014/59/EU of the European Parliament and of the Council of 15 May 2014 establishing a framework for the recovery and resolution of credit institutions and investment firms and amending Council Directive 82/891/EEC, and Directives 2001/24/EC, 2002/47/EC, 2004/25/EC, 2005/56/EC, 2007/36/EC, 2011/35/EU, 2012/30/EU, and 2013/36/EU, and Regulations (EU) No 1093/2010 and (EU) No 648/2012, of the European Parliament and of the Council (hereafter BRR Directive) [2014] OJ L173/190.

[89] European Court of Auditors, *Review No 5/2020* (n 8).

[90] BRR Directive (n 85), preamble recital 1.

[91] European Court of Auditors, *Review No 5/2020* (n 8) 35.

[92] ibid 36.

[93] See European Court of Auditors, *Special Report No 21/2020: Control of State Aid to Financial Institutions in the EU: In Need of a Fitness Check* (Publications Office of the European Union 2020) 49.

bank industry are not immediately accessible or do not cover the expenses incurred by the use of the Fund in relation to resolution actions'.[94]

To cater for this contingency, the Member States to the ESM signed, on 27 January and 8 February 2021, the Agreement amending the ESM Treaty. The amendment includes a backstop to the SRF, which would provide a credit line up to a nominal cap of 68 billion euros.[95] The reformed Treaty will come into force when ratified by the parliaments of all ESM members. The Italian parliament refused to ratify the amending agreement to the ESM Treaty.[96] As such, the ESM backstop to the SRF is not formally established and cannot be used yet.

III Flaws and limitations of the current accountability framework

This section analyses the main flaws and limitations of the system enshrined by the current legal framework with a view to identifying the main gaps in the administrative accountability deriving from this framework for each pillar of the BU. As mentioned at the beginning of this chapter, public sector audits contribute to good governance by, among other things, enhancing accountability and transparency, and can be categorized into financial, compliance, and performance audits.

In the same vein, the ECA has defined, in a landscape review, a model of six elements for a strong accountability and audit chain; one of these elements is 'a strong mandate for independent external audit to verify accounts, compliance and performance'.[97]

As the ECA is the independent external auditor of the EU, it could be argued that a comprehensive administrative accountability of the main players of the BU at EU level should be possible, including where the legal framework provides the ECA with a clear remit and express powers to carry out financial, compliance, and performance audits with respect to those entities which play an important part in achieving EU objectives.

[94] SRM Regulation, preamble recital 102, and art 73(1).

[95] European Stability Mechanism, 'ESM Treaty Reform Explainer' (2024) https://www.esm.europa.eu/about-esm/esm-treaty-reform-explainer? accessed 1 September 2024.

[96] European Stability Mechanism, 'Statement by ESM Managing Director Pierre Gramegna on the decision of the Italian Parliament not to ratify the revised ESM Treaty' (21 December 2023) https://www.esm.europa.eu/press-releases/statement-esm-managing-director-pierre-gramegna-decision-italian-parliament-not accessed 1 September 2024.

[97] European Court of Auditors, *Landscape Review* (n 10) 6.

If the legal framework does not allow the ECA to verify, for example, how one of the two operational pillars of the BU delivers its intended objectives, there is a gap in the administrative accountability of that pillar, and in the BU in general.

1 Flaws and limitations in respect of the SSM

This subsection analyses potential flaws and limitations in the audit arrangements set up by the current legislative framework governing the SSM, which may result in an eventual gap in its administrative accountability, and the efforts made to address them.

The limitations on the ECA's audit mandate on the accounts of the ECB are, purportedly, a consequence of the independence of the ECB,[98] enshrined in Article 130 of the TFEU in respect of other 'institutions, bodies, offices or agencies, from any government of a Member State or from any other body', and the ban on any of them influencing 'the members of the decision-making bodies of the ECB or of the national central banks in the performance of their tasks'.

The accounts of the ECB are not audited by the ECA but by 'an independent external auditor recommended by the Governing Council and approved by the Council', in accordance with Article 27(2) of the Statute. Nor are they consolidated in the annual accounts of the EU and, therefore, they are excluded from the ordinary discharge procedure before the EU budgetary authorities.[99]

As mentioned before, Article 20(7) of the SRM Regulation limits the audit powers of the ECA in respect of the SSM to an examination of the 'operational efficiency of the management of the ECB'. However, the Contact Committee identified an audit gap on the SSM because:

> those SAIs of euro area countries that previously had a mandate to audit the supervision of all banks are now – since the introduction of the SSM – no longer able to perform this role for the 'significant' banks. The loss of mandate encountered by these national SAIs is not compensated by the current audit mandate of the ECA vis-à-vis the ECB.[100]

[98] Contact Committee of the Supreme Audit Institutions of the European Union, *Preparation for Resolution of Medium-sized and Small Banks in the Euro Area* (Contact Committee 2020) 50 https://www.eca.europa.eu/sites/CC/Lists/CCDocuments/Task_Force_EBU_2020/Task_Force_EBU_2020_EN.pdf accessed 1 September 2024.

[99] Commission, *Consolidated Annual Accounts of the European Union – Financial Year 2021* (Publications Office of the European Union 2022) 139.

[100] Contact Committee of the Supreme Audit Institutions of the European Union, 'EU Contact Committee statement (CC 1/2018) on deficiencies in the accountability and audit arrangements of the

In order to close the audit gaps identified, the Contact Committee requested 'national governments and parliaments, as well as the Parliament, the Council and the Commission of the European Union to strengthen the relevant accountability and audit arrangements' to align the ECA's mandate on the SSM with its mandate concerning the institutions of the EU.[101]

Yves Mersch, Member of the Executive Board of the ECB, in his keynote address of 30 March 2017, declared that the ECB enjoys a different sort of independence as a supervisor than as a monetary authority, calling for 'a differentiated application of the concept of the audit of the operational efficiency of the management of the ECB'.[102] Other SAIs have full audit rights on supervisory authorities.[103]

The MoU has not made it possible for the ECA's examination of the 'operational efficiency of the management of the ECB' to encompass the audit of sound financial management, as applies to other bodies within its remit,[104] or the request of the Contact Committee to align the ECA's mandate on the SSM with its mandate concerning the other institutions of the EU.[105]

It could be argued that the references made by the MoU to Article 33 of the EU Financial Regulation as a source of interpretation of the meaning of the 'operational efficiency of the management of the ECB' could be used to extend the ECA mandate to the principles of both economy and effectiveness, as this Article offers a wider definition of efficiency than the INTOSAI standards.

Indeed, Article 33(1)(b) of the EU Financial Regulation lays down that the principle of efficiency concerns the *best relationship* between the resources employed (which implies an economic use of resources), the activities undertaken, and the achievement of objectives (which means that the activities performed have been effective).

supervisory mechanism for banks in the euro area' (13 November 2018) 1 https://www.eca.europa.eu/sites/cc/Lists/CCDocuments/CC_STATEMENT_2018/CC-STATEMENT-SSM-DEFICIENCIES-EN.pdf accessed 1 September 2024.

[101] ibid.

[102] European Central Bank, 'Central bank independence revisited: Keynote address by Yves Mersch, Member of the Executive Board of the ECB, at the "Symposium on Building the Financial System of the 21st Century: An Agenda for Europe and the United States", Frankfurt am Main, 30 March 2017' https://www.ecb.europa.eu/press/key/date/2017/html/sp170330.en.html accessed 1 September 2024.

[103] For a comparative analysis with other non-EU SAIs, see European Court of Auditors, *Special Report No 29/2016* (n 21) 46, Annex V. See also Task Force on European Banking Union to the Contact Committee of Supreme Audit Institutions of the European Union and the European Court of Auditors, *Report on Prudential Supervision of Medium-sized and Small ('Less Significant') Institutions in the European Union after the Introduction of the Single Supervisory Mechanism*, app 1 (Contact Committee 2017) 13,https://www.eca.europa.eu/sites/cc/Lists/CCDocuments/Task_Force_EBU/Task_Force_EBU.pdf, accessed 1 September 2024.

[104] See European Court of Auditors, *Landscape Review* (n 10) 39.

[105] Contact Committee, *EU Contact Committee Statement (CC 1/2018)* (n 100) 1.

However, in the present author's view, the ECA did not move beyond the narrow boundaries of the examination of the operational efficiency of the management of the ECB, pursuant to the relevant provisions of the Statute and of the SSM Regulation,[106] in the two audits carried out after the entry into force of the MoU. In the last of these audits, the ECA followed an interpretation of efficiency more in line with the INTOSAI standards,[107] as stated in paragraph 20 of Special Report No 12/2023: 'we assessed the relationship between resources employed (i.e. staff, tools and processes) and outputs'.

In this sense, I fully support the Contact Committee's call for a new definition of the ECA's audit mandate over the ECB's function of prudential supervision, to reflect that Article 27(2) of the Statute is only meant to protect the independence of monetary policy.[108]

2 Flaws and limitations in respect of the SRM

This section seeks to identify potential flaws and limitations in the audit arrangements laid down by the current legislative framework concerning the SRM, which may result in an eventual gap in its administrative accountability. To this end, it is necessary to examine both the legislative process and the incipient case law in the field, to get a better understanding of the provisions of Article 90 of the SRM Regulation and their practical limitations.

The impact assessment preceding the BRRD showed, as a preferred option over the creation of an EU resolution authority, resolution colleges between resolution authorities, a cooperation arrangement with the assistance of the EBA.[109] Eventually, the SRB was created as a specific EU agency, departing from the model of all other agencies, 'to ensure a swift and effective decision-making process in resolution'.[110]

There is no limitation on the audit powers conferred on the ECA by the TFEU, the EU Financial Regulation, and the SRM Regulation in respect of the

[106] The Statute, art 27(2), and SSM Regulation, art 20(7).

[107] ISSAI 300/11 (n 18) 9.

[108] Contact Committee, *Preparation for Resolution of Medium-sized and Small Banks in the Euro Area* (n 98) 50.

[109] Commission, 'Commission Staff Working Document. Impact assessment accompanying the document Proposal for a Directive of the European Parliament and of the Council establishing a framework for the recovery and resolution of credit institutions and investment firms and amending Council Directives 77/91/EEC and 82/891/EC, Directives 2001/24/EC, 2002/47/EC, 2004/25/EC, 2005/56/EC, 2007/36/EC and 2011/35/EC and Regulation (EU) No 1093/2010' COM (2012) 280 final https://eur-lex.europa.eu/legal-content/EN/TXT/PDF/?uri=CELEX:52012SC0166 accessed 31 August 2024.

[110] SRM Regulation, preamble recital 31.

SRB. The ECA can audit the accounts of the SRB and can perform compliance and performance audits on the SRB, as on any other EU agency. It has no limits on its access to the information, documents, and IT systems it considers necessary for the performance of its duties, without having regard to the originator or holder of this information.[111]

As such, the ECA has shown no scope limitation in any of its audits on the SRB since the latter started its operations. Certainly, the ECA's reports have indicated some difficulties in the practical implementation of the sharing of information, mainly on documents originating with the ECB, but these challenges related only to the place of the examination of these documents, a secured room on the SRB premises,[112] and to the redaction and anonymization of bank-related information.[113]

However, the type of report on the use of the SRF provided for by Article 90(1) to (3) of the SRM Regulation, in its current drafting, raises more questions than answers and could face serious challenges concerning its timely implementation, with 'a worst-case scenario' of six months for the planning, execution of the audit, and reporting. This is an unrealistic deadline, bearing in mind the full range of topics to be audited pursuant to Article 90(2) of the SRM Regulation:

(a) an examination of the use of the SRF from the point of view of the sound financial management principles of economy, efficiency, and effectiveness; and
(b) an evaluation of the Commission's assessment of the Fund aid from the point of view of efficiency and rigour.

This report on the use of the SRF was not initially foreseen in the Commission's proposal[114] of 10 July 2013, but was introduced by the EP in an amendment[115] of 6 February 2014. The provisions under this amendment would allow the ECA to perform its assessment of the sound financial management of the use of

[111] TFEU, art 287(3); EU Financial Regulation, art 257(1); SRM Regulation, arts 66(2) and 92(8).
[112] See European Court of Auditors, *Special Report No 1/2021* (n 79) 15.
[113] European Court of Auditors, *Special Report No 23/2017* (n 74) 13–15; and ibid.
[114] Commission, 'Proposal for a Regulation of the European Union and of the Council establishing uniform rules and a uniform procedure for the resolution of credit institutions and certain investment firms in the framework of a Single Resolution Mechanism and a Single Bank Resolution Fund and amending Regulation (EU) No 1093/2010 of the European Parliament and of the Council' COM (2013) 520 final https://eur-lex.europa.eu/LexUriServ/LexUriServ.do?uri = COM:2013:0520:FIN:EN:PDF accessed 31 August 2024.
[115] European Parliament, 'Resolution of credit institutions and certain investment firms in the framework of a Single Resolution Mechanism and a Single Bank Resolution Fund' P7_TA(2014)0095 https://www.europarl.europa.eu/doceo/document/TA-7-2014-0095_EN.pdf accessed 1 September 2024.

the SRF, and to report on it, with a longer deadline of 11 months, but it would be performed together with the statement of assurance of the annual accounts of the SRB and with an examination of the contingent liabilities of the SRB, the Commission, or otherwise arising as a result of the performance of their duties under the SRM Regulation.

The current drafting of Article 92(1) to (3) of the SRM Regulation was introduced by an amendment of the EP of 15 April 2014, with a wider scope and a shorter deadline.[116] From the accountability point of view, it is indeed very important that the ECA prepares a report on the use of the SRF and sends it to the Commission and to the budgetary authorities, because the funds raised by the banking industries of the Member States participating in the BU must be used not only in accordance with the provisions of the SRM Regulation[117] but also in accordance with the sound financial management principles and the principle of fair competition in the internal market that Article 107(3)(b) of the TFEU aims to protect.[118]

However, it is not clear how deep the scope of the ECA's examination should be under paragraph 2 of Article 92 of the SRM Regulation. The ECA, as the independent external auditor of the EU, can autonomously decide on the scope of its examination. However, 'use of the Fund' is an undefined legal concept, as is the 'efficient and rigorous' assessment of the Fund aid.

In addition, the reference to the 'effectiveness with which the Fund has been used, in particular the need to minimise the use of the Fund' seems to suggest that a minimum amount of the SRF should be used (principle of economy) to achieve the resolution objectives (principle of effectiveness).[119] This interpretation is in line with the last subparagraph of Article 14(2) of the SRM Regulation, which lays down that, '[w]hen pursuing the objectives referred to in the first subparagraph, the Board, the Council, the Commission and, where relevant, the national resolution authorities, shall seek to minimise the cost of resolution and avoid destruction of value unless necessary to achieve the resolution objectives.' The assessment of whether the use of the SRF has been minimized would also require an examination of the valuations carried out

116 European Parliament, 'Position of the European Parliament adopted at first reading on 15 April 2014 with a view to the adoption of Regulation (EU) No . . . /2014 of the European Parliament and of the Council establishing uniform rules and a uniform procedure for the resolution of credit institutions and certain investment firms in the framework of a Single Resolution Mechanism and a Single Resolution Fund and amending Regulation (EU) No 1093/2010 of the European Parliament and of the Council' EP-PE_TC1-COD(2013)0253 https://www.europarl.europa.eu/doceo/document/TC1-COD-2013-0253_EN.pdf accessed 1 September 2024.

117 SRM Regulation, arts 19, 50(1), and 76–79.

118 As developed by the Banking Communication (n 59).

119 SRM Regulation, 1st subpara of art 14(2).

pursuant to Article 20 of the SRM Regulation. In particular, valuation 3, which assesses whether shareholders and creditors would have been better off under normal insolvency proceedings, may have an impact on the amount of the SRF to be used.[120] In this sense, the CJ has ruled that 'the application in the present case of the [NCWO principle], according to which no creditor may be treated worse, guarantees the applicants fair compensation in accordance with the requirements of Article 17(1) of the Charter'.[121]

For this examination, should the ECA reperform these valuations or should its examination be limited to verifying whether:

(a) the valuations are fair, prudent, and realistic;[122]
(b) the evidence relied upon is factually accurate, reliable, consistent, complete, and robust;[123] and
(c) the factual assessments used are plausible?[124]

In any case, the CJ has declared that the SRB has 'a broad discretion, in particular as to the assessment of highly complex scientific and technical facts', and that 'the EU judicature cannot substitute its assessment of scientific and technical facts for that of the authorities of the European Union'.[125] The CJ has also ruled that, 'given the time constraints and the information available, some uncertainties and approximations are inherent in any provisional valuation', and that the reservations expressed by the external valuer 'cannot mean that valuation 2 was not "fair, prudent and realistic" within the meaning of Article 20(1) of Regulation No 806/2014'.[126]

Therefore, given the time constraints, it is, in the present author's view, not realistic that the auditors perform an examination of the valuations that goes beyond the boundaries of judicial review, as defined by the case law for the EU judicature. In addition, eventual divergent valuations—one from the SRB and a reperformed valuation carried out by the ECA—would risk triggering litigation against the SRB valuation.

The provisions do not clarify what an 'efficient and rigorous' assessment of the Fund aid is. The Commission's assessment is bound by Article 107(3)(b) of the TFEU, Article 19 of the SRM Regulation, and its own Banking

[120] ibid, art 76(1)(e).
[121] See *Algebris (UK)* (n 14), para 428; and *Del Valle Ruiz* (n 14), para 522.
[122] SRM Regulation, art 20(1).
[123] See *Algebris (UK)* (n 14), para 108; and *Del Valle Ruiz* (n 14), para 110.
[124] See *Algebris (UK)* (n 14), para 109; and *Del Valle Ruiz* (n 14), para 111.
[125] See *Algebris (UK)* (n 14), para 105; and *Del Valle Ruiz* (n 14), para 107.
[126] See *Algebris (UK)* (n 14), para 242; and *Del Valle Ruiz* (n 14), para 302.

Communication,[127] with the guidance offered by its case practice and the EU courts' case law.[128] As explained before, 'efficiency' means, in line with the INTOSAI standards, 'getting the most from the available resources. It is concerned with the relationship between resources employed and outputs delivered in terms of quantity, quality and timing'.[129]

In this case, it could be interpreted to be a thorough and robust assessment of the Fund aid that has minimized the use of resources. However, the parameters under which such rigour, thoroughness, and robustness should be judged are not defined in the above provisions.

Finally, Article 92(1) to (3) of the SRM Regulation does not clarify whether this audit should be one-off per each resolution scheme (or its amendment) deciding that the SRF should be used, or a recurrent one every year to audit, for example, on the basis of documents,[130] the bank under resolution, its subsidiaries, an asset management vehicle, or a bridge institution, as potential recipients of the SRF, in accordance with Article 76(1).

Concerning the ESM backstop, the ECA has, in the past, pointed out certain gaps in the ESM accountability arrangements,[131] namely the lack of audit mandate in respect of the ESM.[132] In its Special Report No 5/2023, the ECA recommends the Commission, by 2025, to engage with the EU legislature authorities, and with the ESM, with a view to reaching a common position on how to integrate the ESM into the 'EU legal framework'.[133]

IV Conclusions and recommendations

This section shows the conclusions of this chapter on the accountability gaps of each of the two operational pillars of the BU and makes concrete proposals to fill these accountability gaps and to improve the BU landscape.

There is a clear limitation in the audit mandate of the ECA in respect of the ECB in the regulatory framework.[134] The accounts of the ECB are not audited

[127] Banking Communication (n 59).
[128] See European Court of Auditors, *Special Report No 21/2020* (n 93) 45.
[129] ISSAI 300/11 (n 18) 9.
[130] SRM Regulation, art 66(2).
[131] European Court of Auditors, *Landscape Review* (n 10) 60.
[132] European Court of Auditors, *Briefing Paper: Future of EU Finances: Reforming How the EU Budget Operates* (Publications Office of the European Union 2018) 20.
[133] European Court of Auditors, *Special Report No 5/2023: The EU's Financial Landscape – A Patchwork Construction Requiring Further Simplification and Accountability* (Publications Office of the European Union 2023) 44.
[134] The Statute, art 27(2); SSM Regulation, art 20(7).

by the ECA or consolidated within the annual accounts of the EU, and are not part of the discharge procedure before the EU budgetary authorities.

The ECA cannot carry out either a compliance or a performance audit on the ECB on the same terms as on any other EU institution, body, office, or agency, as provided for by Article 287(2) to (4) of the TFEU, because it can only audit 'the operational efficiency of the management of the ECB', including in respect of 'the supervisory tasks conferred on the ECB by this Regulation'.[135] However, in comparative law, we can see examples where the SAIs have no limits on auditing the accounts of and carrying out performance and compliance audits on both supervisory and non-supervisory activities of the NCAs.[136]

The Contact Committee has highlighted that:

> Prior to the implementation of the SSM, the German and Dutch Supreme Audit Institution, for example, had the right to audit the entire process of supervising SIs and LSIs. We now face a situation where the ECA's mandate, as it is currently exercised in practice, falls short of the mandates several national Supreme Audit Institutions, including those of Germany and the Netherlands, had prior to the introduction of the SSM.[137]

I share the recommendations of the Contact Committee calling on the national and EU executive and legislative authorities to strengthen the relevant accountability and audit arrangements to align the ECA's mandate on the SSM with its mandate concerning the institutions of the EU.[138]

Furthermore, to align EU legislation with comparative law, I would support an amendment of both the Statute and secondary legislation to extend the ECA's mandate on performance audits in respect of the ECB, with the sole exception of its monetary policy, which is subject to a strong independent mandate of the ECB and the ESCB.

This alignment with comparative law would entail a further amendment of the Statute. Under this amendment, the reliability of the accounts of the ECB could continue to be audited by the external independent auditor, but under the responsibility of the ECA,[139] which could audit the legality and regularity of the underlying transactions and produce a specific annual report including

[135] SSM Regulation, art 20(7).

[136] For a comparative analysis with other non-EU SAIs, see European Court of Auditors, *Special Report No 29/2016* (n 21) 46, Annex V. See also Task Force on European Banking Union (n 103) app 1.

[137] Contact Committee, *Preparation for Resolution of Medium-sized and Small Banks in the Euro Area* (n 98) 50.

[138] Contact Committee, *EU Contact Committee Statement (CC 1/2018)* (n 100) 1.

[139] This is a similar arrangement to that laid down in the EU Financial Regulation, arts 70(6) and (7).

both the reliability of the accounts of the ECB and the legality and regularity of its underlying budgetary operations.

However, if the legal framework is not changed in the meanwhile, the MoU between the ECA and the ECB provides for the possibility to 'review the functioning and effectiveness of the cooperation and information exchange under this MoU every three years, or earlier if deemed necessary by both parties'.[140]

This review could focus on a wider interpretation of the meaning of 'operational efficiency of the management of the ECB', which could also include aspects of effectiveness and economy, as provided for by Article 33 of the EU Financial Regulation,[141] which recital (e) of the MoU considers 'a source of interpretation in the examination of the ECB's supervisory activities by the ECA in line with its mandate'.

The ECA cannot assess the fulfilment of the objective of the SSM 'that the Union's policy relating to the prudential supervision of credit institutions is implemented in a coherent and effective manner' if it lacks a mandate to audit the effectiveness of the SSM.[142] Therefore, a review of the MoU could aim to support a wider interpretation of the 'operational efficiency', including other sound financial management principles, to further close the audit gap.

Concerning the SRB, there is no gap in the administrative accountability because there are no limitations in the ECA's audit mandate thereon. However, the audit on the use of the Fund, as laid down in paragraphs (1) to (3) of Article 92 of the SRM Regulation, should be changed at the earliest opportunity by the EU legislature, because it does not provide for a satisfactory audit examination thereof. The amended provision should only request the ECA to produce a special report pursuant to Article 287(4) of the TFEU to examine whether the use of the Fund, and the Fund aid assessment, have been carried out in accordance with the principles of sound financial management and fair competition within the internal market.

This special report should be produced within the standard period of 13 months set up by Article 259(1) of the EU Financial Regulation to draw up and adopt a special report. The ECA should independently decide whether to start this audit immediately upon the approval (or amendment) of the resolution scheme, or to wait for the full execution of the use of the Fund in order

[140] MoU between the ECA and the ECB (n 19), para 11.

[141] Art 33(1)(b) of the EU Financial Regulation lays down that the principle of efficiency concerns the *best relationship* between the resources employed (which implies an economic use of resources), the activities undertaken, and the achievement of objectives (which means that the activities performed have been effective).

[142] SSM Regulation, preamble recital 12.

to carry out a more comprehensive examination of all the aspects of this execution, including the recipients of the SRF, or to split this audit into an initial one upon resolution and a follow-up audit after its execution.

Finally, there is an accountability gap in respect of the ESM backstop. To overcome this, I fully share the ECA's recommendations that the Commission engages with the EU legislature, and with the ESM, with a view to reaching a common position on how to integrate the ESM into the 'EU legal framework'.[143]

If the gaps identified above were remedied by following the above recommendations, it would allow the ECA to play its full potential in ensuring the administrative accountability in the Banking Union.

[143] European Court of Auditors, *Special Report No 5/2023* (n 133) 44.

21

Cooperation and Information Exchange In- and Outside the Banking Union

The Use of Memoranda of Understanding

*Jonathan Bauerschmidt, Diane Fromage, and Vanessa Aichstill**

I Introduction

In response to various crises, the framework in place within the EU for prudential regulation and supervision has gradually transformed into the Banking Union, where roles and responsibilities often intersect. This evolution necessitates cooperation for the implementation of this legal regime to function smoothly in practice, and eventually to ensure financial stability at both the EU and global levels. Consequently, a duty to cooperate emerges, rooted in the principle of sincere cooperation enshrined in Article 4(3) TEU.[1] In this evolving landscape of the Banking Union, memoranda of understanding (MoUs) have emerged as critical instruments for fostering effective cooperation and information exchange. MoUs are particularly relevant for non-Banking Union Member States and third countries, which encounter distinct treatment and challenges in aligning their financial regulatory practices, unlike Banking Union Member States, which are directly supervised by the European Central Bank (ECB) and have the Single Resolution Board (SRB) as their resolution authority. Prior to the establishment of MoUs between key institutions, such as the ECB and the SRB, as well as National Competent Authorities (NCAs), cooperation was difficult, undermining the efficiency and coherence of the EU's financial oversight.[2] A fundamental objective of the Banking Union was, thus,

* We warmly thank Daniel Segoin for his insightful comments.

[1] Ann-Katrin Kaufhold, 'Art 3 SSMR' in Jens-Heinrich Binder and others (eds), *European Banking Union: Brussels Commentary* (1st edn, Bloomsbury Publishing 2022) 1.

[2] This issue was discussed as part of the summer school on Financial Agencies and AMLA held in Salzburg from 1–7 July 2024.

Jonathan Bauerschmidt, Diane Fromage, and Vanessa Aichstill, *Cooperation and Information Exchange In- and Outside the Banking Union* In: *EU Banking Union*. Edited by: Jonathan Bauerschmidt, Raffaele D'Ambrosio, Diane Fromage, Daniela Jaros, and Paul Weismann, Oxford University Press.
 DOI: 10.1093/9780198949756.003.0022

the creation of specialized bodies and agencies aimed at enabling seamless cooperation between European and national authorities. MoUs now serve as crucial agreements that establish 'the rules of the game', and embody the principle of loyal cooperation, ensuring that all parties—even outside the EU—are aligned in their efforts to cooperate and exchange information. Their significance is further underscored in the context of the Anti-Money Laundering Authority (AMLA) and the broader AML regime, where future MoUs will be crucial for collaboration,[3] particularly given that the AMLA does not currently permit third-country participation in its governance structures, unlike the European Banking Authority (EBA), for example. Similar challenges are faced by the bodies of the ECB and the SRB, which merely allow Banking Union Member States in close cooperation to be involved in some but not all decision-making bodies. Third countries, in particular, have no legal possibility to participate and must rely solely on MoUs. This discrepancy raises important questions about the legal nature of MoUs, their enforceability, and the mechanisms available for holding parties accountable, particularly through indirect judicial review. As the EU continues to navigate these complex legal and regulatory landscapes, understanding the role and implications of MoUs is essential for ensuring robust and transparent cross-border financial governance.

Against this background, this chapter examines the legal foundations of MoUs and explores those which are most relevant for the Banking Union. Based on a short typology (section II), the following considers the horizontal MoUs by and between the ECB and the SRB (section III), vertical MoUs with Member States in- and outside the Banking Union (section IV), and external MoUs with third countries and international organizations (section V). This allows a look to be taken at some overarching legal issues for MoUs (section VI), before addressing, in conclusion, the question of whether the Banking Union is in need of cooperation instruments that are harder than mere (non-binding) soft law instruments (section VII).

II A short typology of MoUs

Historically, MoUs have evolved from informal arrangements to politically influential tools in international law. They lack legally binding character unless

[3] See art 95 of the AMLA Regulation 2024/1620, [2024] OJ L2024/1620, on cooperation with third countries and international organizations.

explicitly intended.[4] MoUs offer flexibility and speed in agreements, often avoiding parliamentary approval (and involvement, leaving the signatories free(r) in the drafting of the MoUs). On a global scale, MoUs complement formal regulations, facilitating global cooperation and information exchange, both of which are crucial in banking supervision and crisis management. Arguably, soft law instruments in general have shaped international financial law. These instruments can be categorized into three genres:[5] best practices; regulatory reports and observations; as well as information-sharing and enforcement cooperation. More precisely, the last category deals with international financial agreements, which often take the form of MoUs. Early MoUs on cross-border cooperation[6] addressed crisis management during the Great Financial Crisis. Flaws in these agreements led to an enhanced framework, focusing on efficient exchange of information during crises.[7] Despite the establishment of the Banking Union, with the daily cooperation and information exchange taken over by the Joint Supervisory Teams and Internal Resolution Teams it has introduced, MoUs remain vital for cross-border cooperation, especially with non-participating states. The ECB has been actively negotiating and concluding MoUs since 2016,[8] shaping their legal nature and content.

MoUs establish terms of less formal cooperation on bilateral or multilateral bases, concentrating on regulatory and enforcement assistance, information sharing, evidence gathering, and confidentiality rules.[9] These quasi-contractual arrangements for cooperation work in extensive and complicated institutional landscapes of financial governance with a myriad of actors at national, international, and supranational levels in different dimensions. The dimensions covered span various segments of financial markets, encompassing different roles within them as well as both microprudential and macroprudential spheres. Not mentioned in Article 288 TFEU, MoUs are

[4] Jan Klabbers, 'Governance by Academics: the Invention of Memoranda of Understanding' (2020) 80(1) Zeitschrift für ausländisches öffentliches Recht und Völkerrecht 35, 36 ff.

[5] Chris Brummer, 'Why Soft Law Dominates International Finance – And Not Trade' (2011) 13(3) Journal of International Economic Law 623, 628.

[6] ECB, 'Memorandum of Understanding on high-level principles of co-operation between the banking supervisors and central banks of the European Union in crisis management situations' (10 March 2003), available at http://www.ecb.int/press/pr/date/2003/html/pr030310_3.en.html, accessed 1 August 2024; ECB, 'Memorandum of Understanding on co-operation between the Banking Supervisors, Central Banks and Finance Ministries of the European Union in Financial Crisis situations' (18 May 2005), available at http://www.ecb.int/press/pr/date/2005/html/pr050518_1.en.html, accessed 1 August 2024.

[7] Zdenek Kudrna, 'Cross-Border Resolution of Failed Banks in the European Union after the Crisis: Business as Usual' (2012) 50(2) Journal of Common Market Studies 283, 287.

[8] Kaufhold (n 1) 20.

[9] Dariusz Adamski, 'Memoranda of Understanding in the Governance of European Financial Institutions' (2020) 1 European Law Review 100, 101.

atypical acts in EU law and sit outside the typical sources and categories of public international law.[10] The legal nature of such atypical acts is determined by 'objective criteria, such as the content of that act, taking into account, as appropriate, the context in which it was adopted and the powers of the institution which adopted the act'.[11] Nevertheless, in the hierarchy of norms, MoUs must comply with primary and secondary EU law and have been classified as tertiary sources of law.[12] MoUs are mostly foreseen in secondary law and designated as

MoU, or by using closely associated names such as common understandings, memoranda of cooperation, joint agreements, joint declarations or statements, framework agreements, *modi vivendi*, common arrangements, codes of conduct, and terms of reference.[13] Even though not expressly foreseen in secondary law, the power to conclude MoUs can still be inferred from general clauses for cooperation in primary or secondary law.[14] For example, the ECB, as well as the European Supervisory Authorities, 'may . . . enter into administrative arrangements with supervisory authorities, international organisations and the administrations of third countries', but 'those arrangements shall not create legal obligations'.[15]

In terms of substance, many MoUs can be found in the area of financial services related to financial governance. These financial-governance MoUs cover areas and modes of administrative cooperation between authorities working on the oversight of financial institutions, including regulatory and enforcement assistance, information sharing, evidence gathering, and confidentiality rules. They are signed by EU authorities in charge of financial sector regulation and supervision, with stakeholders within and outside the EU.[16] Some MoUs are bank-specific and cover exchange of information, possible on-site inspections, and internal model approval. Others are issue-specific, concern many

[10] Art 296(3) TFEU implicitly acknowledges the existence of a separate category of Union acts: P-J Loewenthal, 'Article 296 TFEU' in Manuel Kellerbauer and others (eds), *The EU Treaties and the Charter of Fundamental Rights: A Commentary* (OUP 2024). See also Final report of Working Group IX on Simplification of 29 November 2002, CONV 424/02, p 6; Case C–409/13 *Council v Commission*, ECLI:EU:C:2014:2470, Opinion of AG Jääskinen in Judgment of 14 April 2015, para 114; and Case 22/70 *Commission v Council (AETR)*, ECLI:EU:C:1971:32, Judgment of 31 March 1971, para 42.

[11] Case C–16/16 P *Belgium v Commission*, ECLI:EU:C:2018:79, Judgment of 20 February 2018, para 32.

[12] Linda Senden and Ton A. van den Brink, 'Checks and Balances of Soft EU Rule-Making' (Parliament Study, 2012) https://www.europarl.europa.eu/RegData/etudes/etudes/join/2012/462433/IPOL-JURI_ET(2012)462433_EN.pdf accessed 2 January 2024.

[13] Pointed out by Alberto de Gregorio Merino, 'Memoranda of understanding: a critical taxonomy' (ECB Legal Conference 2019) 253.

[14] Examples may be found in Adamski (n 9) 18.

[15] Art 8 SSMR; art 33(1) of the ESAs Regulations 1093–1095/2010, [2010] OJ L331.

[16] Adamski (n 9) 101.

supervised entities, and cover exchange of information on global systemically important financial institutions.[17] In contrast to MoUs on external relations,[18] financial-governance MoUs establish goals and modes of administrative co-operation and do not focus on political commitments. Moreover, those MoUs can be conceived as 'rules of practice . . . by which . . . [the] institution imposes a limit on the exercise of its discretion'.[19] Therefore, those MoUs may bind the institutions, agencies, and authorities which conclude them, if the parties so wish and express. Even if the MoUs are intended to be non-binding, the participants frequently adhere to the arrangements for cooperation in order to evade reputational repercussions, although the nature of such agreements presents both theoretical and practical challenges.[20]

To further differentiate between various categories, EU law literature has distinguished between MoUs in the realm of economic policy and financial assistance (strict conditionality MoUs), MoUs concluded within the EU, and MoUs in external relations.[21] This shows the great variety of MoUs in the EU and is a useful basis to further refine these categories for the purpose of the present study focusing on MoUs in the Banking Union. Thus, the following will distinguish between three categories of MoUs:

- horizontal MoUs between Union institutions, bodies, offices, and agencies to regulate their cooperation;
- vertical MoUs between such EU entities and competent authorities of Member States; and
- external MoUs with third countries or international organizations.

The first category takes inspiration from the inter-institutional agreements enshrined in Article 295 TFEU, which allows the European Parliament (EP), the Council, and the Commission to conclude such agreements, which may be of a binding nature. Seen as an expression of the horizontal duty of sincere co-operation enshrined in Article 13(2) TEU, inter-institutional agreements allow Union institutions to further set out the modalities of their cooperation. While horizontal MoUs share many of the features of inter-institutional agreements,

[17] European Central Bank, 'SSM Supervisory Manual', available at https://www.bankingsupervision.europa.eu/ecb/pub/pdf/ssm.supervisorymanual201803.en.pdf accessed 31 December 2023.
[18] Case C-660/13 *Council v Commission (Swiss MoU)*, ECLI:EU:C:2016:616, Judgment of 28 July 2016, para 33.
[19] C-619/13 P *Mamoli Robinetteria v Commission*, Judgment of 26 January 2017, ECLI:EU:C:2017:50, para 51.
[20] Adamski (n 9) 102.
[21] de Gregorio Merino (n 13) 253 ff.

they have a broader personal scope and can be concluded not only by institutions of the EU but also by its bodies, offices, and agencies. The ECB, as an institution, and the SRB, as an agency, can conclude horizontal MoUs yielding legal effects that are comparable, if not identical, to those of agreements concluded under Article 295 TFEU. Important examples are the Interinstitutional Agreement between the EP and the ECB on exercising democratic accountability for the Single Supervisory Mechanism (SSM),[22] and the Agreement on organizing confidential discussions between the chair of the supervisory board and the EP's ECON Committee. Similar agreements exist between the EP and the SRB.[23]

The second category concerns the vertical relation between Union institutions, bodies, offices, and agencies, on the one hand, and the competent authorities of Member States, on the other. They can be conceived as an expression of the vertical principle of sincere cooperation enshrined in Article 4(3) TEU, and seek to ensure the implementation of Union law in accordance with Article 291(1) TFEU. Both the ECB and the SRB have concluded such MoUs with competent authorities of both Member States participating in the Banking Union and those Member States which are not participating.

The third category concerns the broad area of international relations with third countries and international organizations. In particular, for financial services, many external MoUs have been concluded by the ECB and the SRB with supervisory and resolution authorities. This includes, for example, MoUs concluded by the ECB with the Bank of England as well as with financial supervisors in the UK (Financial Conduct Authority), Switzerland (FINMA), and Liechtenstein (FMA). Also, the SRB has concluded cooperation agreements with the Bank of England and the Swiss FINMA.

III Horizontal MoUs by and between the ECB and the SRB

Agreements between the various EU institutions, bodies, offices, and agencies are frequently used tools to arrange cooperation and information exchange. These may take the form of inter-institutional agreements foreseen in Article 295 TFEU. They also encompass other arrangements for horizontal cooperation between entities at EU level. Like inter-institutional agreements pursuant to Article 295, second sentence, TFEU, horizontal MoUs may or may not be of

[22] [2013] OJ L320, p 1.
[23] [2015] OJ L339, p 58.

a legally binding nature. In accordance with the case law for inter-institutional agreements,[24] the legal nature depends on whether the participants in MoUs intend to enter into a binding commitment towards each other.

Important examples of horizontal MoUs are the agreements concluded by the ECB and the SRB with the EP on accountability and oversight for their functions within the Banking Union.[25] Indeed, these proved necessary to operationalize the provisions on accountability contained in the SSM and the SRM Regulations, which go into further detail about.[26] Furthermore, the SRB agreed on an MoU with the Commission covering cooperation and information exchange as mandated in Article 30(1) and (2) of the Single Resolution Mechanism Regulation (SRMR). MoUs between the ECB and the SRB are particularly important, as those entities are primarily tasked to implement the first two pillars of the Banking Union, and as, for instance, information which the ECB possesses should be provided to the SRB instead of the SRB requesting it again from the credit institution.[27]

This illustrates a strong example of necessary cooperation, as supervision and resolution are crucial and interdependent elements in establishing the internal market for financial services. To align with the SSM, the SRM applies to Member States participating in the SSM. Thus, the SRM's scope is linked to that of the SSM, and the ECB's decisions on the classification and authorization of credit institutions influence which entities fall under the SRB's direct responsibility.[28] The SRB and the ECB collaborate closely during resolution planning, early intervention, and resolution phases. Whereas the SRB handles resolution planning, including resolvability assessments and determining minimum requirement for own funds and eligible liabilities (MREL) levels, the ECB manages the request and assessment of recovery plans. In early intervention, the ECB leads in addressing financial deterioration before the SRB needs to resolve the institution using resolution tools, unless standard insolvency proceedings

[24] See only C-25/94 *Commission v Council (FAO)*, ECLI:EU:C:1996:114, Judgment of 19 March 1996, para 49.

[25] [2013] OJ L320, p 1; and [2015] OJ L339, p 58.

[26] See further on this, Diane Fromage and Renato Ibrido, 'Accountability and Democratic Oversight in the European Banking Union' in Gianni Lo Schiavo (ed), *The European Banking Union and the Role of Law* (Edward Elgar 2019) 66–86; Rosa Lastra and Sara Dietz, 'Accountability of the European Banking Union' (European Parliament, Economic Governance and EMU Scrutiny Unit (EGOV), September 2024).

[27] Art 34(1) SRM Regulation, [2014] OJ L225.

[28] Memorandum of Understanding (MoU) between the SRB and the ECB covering, inter alia, information exchange and cooperation of 22 December 2015, [4], available at https://www.srb.europa.eu/system/files/media/document/mou_with_the_single_resolution_board_on_cooperation_and_information_exchange_2018_.pdf, accessed 1 August 2024. For an example, see Case T-397/21 *BNP Paribas v SRB*, ECLI:EU:T:2023:829. In this case, the SRB became competent following the ECB having taken over supervision.

are a viable option.[29] Overall, the SRB is obliged to consult the ECB pursuant to Articles 8(1) and (2) SRMR.

In order to facilitate their cooperation, in accordance with the principle of sincere cooperation under Article 13(2), second sentence, TEU, and as prescribed in secondary law, the ECB and SRB have established three MoUs. These MoUs are based on Article 30(7) SRMR, which allows the SRB to conclude MoUs with the ECB to outline the general terms of their cooperation under Article 30(2) and (4) SRMR in the performance of their respective tasks under EU law. Moreover, Article 34(5) SRMR allows them to conclude MoUs for the exchange of information in the context of investigatory powers. These MoUs must be reviewed on a regular basis and are published subject to the requirements of professional secrecy according to Article 30(7) SRMR. Furthermore, the information exchange under these MoUs is considered to comply with the requirements of professional secrecy pursuant to Article 34(5) SRMR.

The overall objective of these MoUs is to ensure that the ECB and the SRB collaborate effectively to prevent an unnecessary increase in the reporting burden on institutions and duplication in data collection.[30] Accordingly, the SRB may request banks to provide all necessary information for its tasks only after fully utilizing information already available to the ECB or NCAs, as already noted above. For instance, the SRB should have continuous access to any information required for its functions, particularly regarding capital, liquidity, assets, and liabilities. The issue that arises, though, is how the SRB could be aware that the ECB possesses such information, and whether the ECB may share it.

Three aspects of these MoUs merit particular attention. Firstly, the legal nature of these MoUs is explicitly set out in paragraph 4 of each, where the participants state that they do not intend to create any directly or indirectly enforceable rights. Rather, the participants endeavour to fulfil their responsibilities under the MoUs on a best-efforts basis. Moreover, the MoUs neither modify nor supersede any EU or national laws, nor do they affect any provisions under other multilateral or bilateral agreements currently in force and applicable to the participants. To settle potential disagreements, paragraph 16 of each MoU foresees dispute resolution in an amicable and equitable manner, which can be escalated within the respective hierarchies. However, no involvement of courts or external arbiters is foreseen. While the lack of a real and timely effective escalation mechanism could pose challenges in times of crisis,

[29] MoU between the SRB and the ECB (n 28) [5].
[30] ibid [8].

it could still be expected that pragmatic solutions would be found, especially where the stakes are high. Moreover, the lack of judicial oversight underlines again that these MoUs are not intended to be legally binding.

Secondly, regarding data protection,[31] paragraph 14 of each MoU emphasizes that they do not modify or supersede the applicable EU data protection framework. In particular, the MoU on confidential information exchange underlines that the data protection Regulation 2018/1725 for Union institutions, bodies, offices, and agencies applies also as regards transmission to third countries and international organizations.

Thirdly, the MoUs distinguish between the level of cooperation with participating Member States, non-participating Member States, and third countries. This reflects the complexities within and outside the Banking Union and requires the ECB and the SRB to inform each other about their exchanges with the various authorities.

In sum, the MoUs between the ECB and the SRB have been concluded within the clearly defined legal framework of the SRMR. They address a range of practical modalities for exchange of both non-classified and classified information without creating legal obligations or being enforceable before a court. Thus, these MoUs clearly flesh out the requirement of loyal cooperation horizontally between the ECB and the SRB while bearing in mind the complexities of the Banking Union.

IV Vertical MoUs with Member States in- and outside the Banking Union

Whereas the MoUs concluded by and between the ECB and the SRB pertain to their horizontal relationship within the EU, there is a range of MoUs concluded with NCAs pertaining to the vertical relationship between the EU and its Member States. For the Banking Union, there is an additional complexity since not all Member States participate, which leads to different MoUs concluded by the ECB and the SRB with Member States inside and outside the Banking Union. This distinction between participating and non-participating Member States is not only relevant for the correct legal basis to be used, as will be shown, but has also led to different types of MoUs concluded by the ECB and the SRB.

[31] Christos Hadjiemmanuil, 'Art 30 SRMR' in Binder and others (n 1) 23.

For Member States participating in the Banking Union, the ECB is empowered to enter into MoUs with their NCAs. Foreseen in Article 3(1) SSMR and further spelled out in its recital 33, those MoUs set out, in general terms, how the ECB and NCAs will cooperate with one another when carrying out their supervisory tasks under EU law. Conversely, to enable cooperation with non-participating Member States, the ECB is also empowered to conclude MoUs with their NCAs in relation to banks that fall within the scope of the SSM, in accordance with Article 3(6), first subparagraph, SSMR. In addition, the ECB is also tasked to conclude MoUs with the NCAs of non-participating Member States which are home to at least one global systemically important institution.

An examination of the MoUs published on the ECB's website[32] reveals a coherent content for participating Member States, covering general clauses for cooperation and exchange of information as well as investigations and on-site inspections. For non-participating Member States, a multilateral MoU was signed with the six NCAs from the Czech Republic, Denmark, Hungary, Poland, Romania, and Sweden only in 2023.[33] Like the MoUs with participating Member States, this MoU covers general clauses on cooperation and information exchange as well as investigations and inspections. Interestingly, this MoU also contains a clause on staff exchanges and training to promote cooperation and to foster a common supervisory culture, a key element to guarantee financial stability. This relates to Article 31 SSMR on staff and staff exchange, which nullifies the need to include it in MoUs with Banking Union Member States. The ECB also concluded a specific MoU on prudential supervision of significant branches, in 2016,[34] whose participants were broadened in 2017.[35] Rather than setting out a general framework for cooperation, this MoU addresses the supervision of several large banking groups located in the Nordic and Baltic countries, such as Denmark, Estonia, Finland, Iceland, Latvia, Lithuania, Norway, and Sweden. Since these banking groups are considered to be significant under Article 51 of the Capital Requirements Directive 2013/36/EU, the participants engage to take a reciprocal approach in supervision

[32] Retrieved from https://www.bankingsupervision.europa.eu/legalframework, accessed 1 August 2024.

[33] Memorandum of Understanding (MoU) between the ECB and the competent authorities of non-participating Member States for the performance of their supervisory tasks of 25 January 2023.

[34] Memorandum of Understanding (MoU) between Finansinspektionen (Sweden), Finanstilsynet (Norway), Finanstilsynet (Denmark), and Finanssivalvonta (Finland) and the ECB of 2 December 2016.

[35] Access to ibid by Estonia (Finantsinspektsioon; Eesti Pank), Iceland (Icelandic Financial Supervisory Authority), Latvia (Financial and Capital Market Commission), and Lithuania (Bank of Lithuania).

and to take decisions jointly when it comes to identifying which branches are to be designated as significant. To this end, the MoU contains some general clauses on cooperation and exchange of information as well as on assistance for on-site inspections. Interestingly, the MoU also states explicitly that it does not apply to payment systems, consumer protection, and anti-money laundering and terrorist financing, thus emphasizing the limited competences of the ECB as reflected in recital 28 SSMR. The MoU on significant branches is most notable for the fact that it involves participants not only from Member States outside the Banking Union, such as Sweden and Denmark, but also from within the Banking Union, such as Finland and the Baltic countries, and even third countries, such as Norway and Iceland. This reflects the interconnectedness of banks, such as Nordea or Danske Bank, which have, for a long time already, operated across jurisdictions in these countries. It also means that the legal basis for the ECB to enter into this MoU is threefold: Article 3(1) SSMR for participating Member States, Article 3(6) SSMR for non-participating Member States, and Article 8 SSMR for third countries. On a more general note, the ECB can conclude an agreement with the NCAs on the supervision of third-country groups and third-country branches under its remit, on the basis of Articles 47 and 48 of the Capital Requirements Directive (CRD).[36]

While the MoUs concluded by the ECB relate to supervisory matters, the SRB can also conclude MoUs with the competent authorities of Member States in resolution matters. To this end, Articles 30(7) and 34(5) SRMR serve as legal basis to set out the general terms of cooperation and the exchange of information. However, rather than entering into these MoUs, the SRB adopted, in 2018, a decision based on Article 31(1) SRMR establishing the framework for cooperation with NRAs.[37] Comprising 45 articles, this extensive framework covers a broad range of topics setting out general provisions for the operation of the SRM, direct SRB responsibility, entities and groups under direct NRA responsibility, resolution colleges within the SRM, access to information, investigations and on-site inspections, cooperation regarding the Single Resolution Fund (SRF), and transitional and final provisions. In contrast to MoUs, which must be agreed to by all participants, the framework for cooperation was adopted by the SRB alone. While this makes the framework formally

[36] Memorandum of Understanding (MoU) between the ECB and competent authorities for the performance of their supervisory tasks in relation to the supervision of Third-Country Groups and Third-Country Branches, available at https://www.bankingsupervision.europa.eu/legalframework/mous, accessed 1 August 2024.

[37] Decision of the Single Resolution Board of 17 December 2018 establishing the framework for the practical arrangements for the cooperation within the Single Resolution Mechanism between the Single Resolution Board and National Resolution Authorities (SRB/PS/2018/15).

a unilateral act, it was adopted by the SRB in its plenary session pursuant to Article 50(1)(q) SRMR, which involves all NRAs. And due to the framework's comprehensive scope, there does not seem to be a necessity to conclude bilateral MoUs between the SRB and the NRAs. This decision is all the more important as the division of competences between the SRB and NRAs was originally not totally clear, and the decision contributed to solving this problem.[38]

Whereas the collective MoU with all non-participating Member States focuses on supervisory cooperation, the ECB and SRB have, more recently, jointly concluded MoUs with each non-participating Member State, to cover resolution cooperation. The nearly identical content of these was negotiated based on Article 32(2) SRMR, under which the SRB, ECB, and the resolution and competent authorities of non-participating Member States are required to conclude MoUs to coordinate, in general terms, their tasks under the BRRD. This aligns with the cooperation principles enshrined in Article 87 BRRD. Prior to those individual MoUs, the SRB had concluded only one MoU, with the Swedish competent authority,[39] due to the presence of a G-SIB,[40] covering internal and external communication, principles of cooperation, and rules for exchange of information. Like the MoU between the ECB and the SRB, this MoU with the Swedish NRA contains a clause on its non-binding legal nature, as well as on dispute settlement by mutual agreement rather than courts or arbiters, as can be seen from the SRB's website.[41]

Looked at together, the vertical MoUs concluded by the ECB and the SRB with national authorities of Member States show a wide variety: the most comprehensive ones are the MoUs concluded by the ECB with NCAs of participating Member States, or the SRB's decision establishing the framework for cooperation with NRAs. The recent conclusion of MoUs with all non-participating Member States, for supervisory and resolution cooperation, shows that MoUs are a means to solve practical issues of cooperation rather than an end in themselves. They address practical issues for cooperation, where and to the extent that such issues arise. And where they have not been concluded, the ECB and the SRB can rely on the (vertical) principle of loyal cooperation enshrined in Article 4(3) TEU to ensure that the national authorities

[38] European Court of Auditors, 'Special Report: Resolution planning in the Single Resolution Mechanism' (2021) 38–39 https://www.eca.europa.eu/en/publications/SR21_01 accessed 12 September 2024.

[39] Available at https://www.srb.europa.eu/system/files/media/document, accessed 1 August 2024.

[40] SRB Annual Report of 2016, 30, available at https://www.srb.europa.eu/system/files/media/document/srb_2017.2496_annual_report_2016, accessed 1 August 2024.

[41] Retrieved from https://www.srb.europa.eu/en/content/cooperation, accessed 1 August 2024.

facilitate the achievement of the Union's tasks and refrain from any measure which could jeopardize the attainment of the Union's objectives.[42]

V External MoUs with third countries and international organizations

By far the largest number of MoUs concluded in the area of financial services pertain to external relations. In particular, the ECB and the SRB have concluded numerous external MoUs to flesh out the cooperation with their counterparts. In contrast to horizontal and vertical MoUs, which operate within the existing (binding) legal framework set by the Banking Union and the EU rules in the financial domain, these MoUs are not backed by any legally binding instrument. This difference also explains their larger number, as they are the one and only instrument for cooperation with third-country authorities and international organizations (whereas in the EU, and especially in the Banking Union, further instruments exist).

While Articles 138 and 219 TFEU contain specific provisions on the external dimension of the Economic and Monetary Union,[43] no similar Treaty rules exist for the Banking Union, as it is a creation under secondary law. Thus, in accordance with the principle of conferral, the power to enter into external MoUs must come from other sources of primary and secondary law. As regards the conferral of powers in the realm of international supervision,[44] the SSMR, based on Article 127(6) TFEU, in its Article 8 SSMR, allows the ECB to develop contacts and enter into administrative arrangements with supervisory authorities and the administrations of third countries. At the same time, this provision requires that those arrangements shall not create legal obligations in respect of the Union and its Member States, because the ECB is not empowered to take such decisions in the field of supervision.

Indeed, pursuant to Articles 216 to 219 TFEU, international agreements need to follow specific procedures involving a mandate from the Council and the involvement of the EP. Thus, international agreements cannot be entered into by

[42] See only Marcus Klamert, *Principle of Loyalty in EU Law* (OUP 2014) 275 ff on the amplification of primary and secondary law obligations by way of sincere cooperation.

[43] See further on this, Shawn Donnelly and Ramses Wessel, 'The International Dimension of EMU: The Interplay Between the Global Financial Stability Architecture and the European Union'; Marise Cremona and Leino-Sandberg Päivi, 'External Relations of the EU and Euro Area in the Field of EMU'; Marise Cremona and Leino-Sandberg Päivi 'International Agreements of The EU in The Field of EMU', all in Fabian Amtenbrink and Christoph Herrmann (eds), *The EU Law of Economic and Monetary Union* (OUP 2020).

[44] Christoph Ohler, 'Art 8 SSMR' in Binder and others (n 1) 10 ff.

the ECB alone. This also emanates from the Court's jurisprudence in *France v Commission*,[45] a case involving an agreement between the Commission and the US Department of Justice regarding the application of competition laws, and to promote cooperation between the administrations. The Court held that, since only the Community (now the EU) had legal personality, it alone had the capacity to bind itself by concluding agreements with third countries and international organizations.[46] Moreover, since the term 'agreement' in what is now Article 218 TFEU must be interpreted broadly, legally binding commitments can only be entered into by following the relevant procedures under the Treaties.[47] Therefore, only arrangements which are legally non-binding fall outside the scope of Article 218 TFEU and can be entered into by a Union institution with third countries or international organizations.[48]

Based on Article 8 SSMR, the ECB has concluded a total of 22 external MoUs[49] on supervisory matters, which are published on its website (see Table 21.1).[50] Following the same structure and content, these MoUs aim to facilitate cooperation and the exchange of supervisory information between the competent authorities. To this end, these MoUs contain provisions on confidentiality and personal data as well as on cooperation for ongoing supervision, on-site visits, etc. Crucially, these MoUs explicitly state their non-binding nature and that any disputes would be settled by amicable consultations rather than court proceedings. A particular example is the MoU concluded in 2019 with the Bank of England and the UK's Financial Conduct Authority.[51] It not only comprises the usual rules on cooperation and information exchange but also contains, in its Article 10, the intent to invite FCA and PRA to join the work of the college of supervisors in respect of supervised cross-border entities. This must be read in the context of Brexit, where, pursuant to Article 7 of the Withdrawal Agreement, the UK lost all rights of participation in the decision-making procedures of the Union institutions.[52] Thus, it comes as no

[45] C-327/91 *France v Commission*, ECLI:EU:C:1994:305, Judgment of 9 August 1994.
[46] ibid, para 24.
[47] ibid, paras 27 ff.
[48] Case C-233/02 *France v Commission*, ECLI:EU:C:2004:173, Judgment of 23 March 2004, paras 42–45.
[49] Including the one on the Nordic–Baltic region, in which participants include, inter alia, Denmark and Sweden, retrieved from https://www.bankingsupervision.europa.eu/framework/international-cooperation/understanding/html/ssm.mou_2016_fi~cf8d9a74ee.en.pdf?034ba77c6c64989231c179aab8e7c4c7, accessed 1 August 2024.
[50] Retrieved from https://www.bankingsupervision.europa.eu/legalframework in chronological order, accessed 1 August 2024.
[51] Available at https://www.bankingsupervision.europa.eu/legalframework/mous, accessed 1 August 2024.
[52] Agreement on the withdrawal of the United Kingdom of Great Britain and Northern Ireland from the European Union and the European Atomic Energy Community [2019] OJ C384I, p 1.

surprise that the clause on a possible invitation to join the work of the college of supervisors is formulated so vaguely, and is in any case subject to the applicable legal framework which protects the decision-making autonomy of the ECB.

As regards resolution, the SRB may conclude non-binding cooperation agreements with third countries, based on Article 32(4) SRMR and in accordance with the framework established by the EBA under Article 97(2) BRRD. On this basis, the SRB has concluded 18 external MoUs, which are accessible on its website (see Table 21.1).[53] These MoUs are similar in structure and content, covering cooperation and exchange of information as regards resolution

Table 21.1 Overview of MoUs concluded between the ECB/SRB and third states

Country	NCA/NRA	With ECB[54]	With SRB[55]
Albania	Bank of Albania	✓	✓
Abu Dhabi	Abu Dhabi Global Market Financial Services Regulatory Authority	✓	
Argentina	Central Bank of the Argentine Republic		✓
Australia	Australian Prudential Regulation Authority	✓	✓
Brazil	Central Bank of Brazil	✓	✓
Bosnia and Herzegovina	Banking Agency of Republika Srpska	✓	✓
	Banking Agency of the Federation of Bosnia and Herzegovina	✓	✓
Canada	Office of the Superintendent of Financial Institutions Canada	✓	
	Canada Deposit Insurance Corporation		✓
Guernsey	Guernsey Financial Services Commission	✓	
Japan	Bank of Japan		✓
	Japan's Financial Services Agency	✓	✓
Kosovo	Central Bank of the Republic of Kosovo	✓	
Malaysia	Perbadanan Insurans Deposit Malaysia		✓
Mexico	National Banking and Securities Commission of Mexico	✓	
	Mexico's Institute for the Protection of Bank Savings		✓

(*continued*)

[53] Retrieved from https://www.srb.europa.eu/en/content/cooperation in chronological order, accessed 1 August 2024.

[54] Available at https://www.bankingsupervision.europa.eu/legalframework, accessed 1 August 2024.

[55] Available at https://www.srb.europa.eu/en/content/cooperation, accessed 1 August 2024.

Table 21.1 Continued

Country	NCA/NRA	With ECB[54]	With SRB[55]
Moldova	National Bank of Moldova	✓	
Montenegro	Central Bank of Montenegro	✓	✓
New Zealand	Reserve Bank of New Zealand		✓
North Macedonia	National Bank of the Republic of North Macedonia	✓	
Serbia	National Bank of Serbia	✓	✓
South Korea	South Korean's Deposit Insurance Corporation		✓
Switzerland	Swiss Financial Market Supervisory Authority		✓
Türkiye	Banking Regulation and Supervision Agency	✓	
UK	Financial Conduct Authority	✓	
	Bank of England	✓	✓
Uruguay	Central Bank of Uruguay	✓	
US	United States Securities and Exchange Commission	✓	
	Board of Governors of the Federal Reserve System, the Office of the Comptroller of the Currency, the Federal Deposit Insurance Corporation	✓	
	New York State Department of Financial Services	✓	
	Federal Deposit Insurance Corporation		✓

planning and implementation in cross-border situations. In order to emphasize their non-binding nature, each of these MoUs states explicitly that it does not constitute an agreement under international law and does not create any legal obligations.

In summary, the ECB and SRB negotiate almost the same content with all third states regardless of their economic ties and interconnectedness. As expected, major players in the banking sector, and developing countries, are the main contracting partners. The EEA states and Switzerland have MoUs with the ECB and/or SRB but have not disclosed them online for further examination.[56]

[56] For example, see the international agreements of Switzerland https://www.finma.ch/en/~/media/finma/dokumente/dokumentencenter/myfinma/5finma/vereinbarungen-mit-auslaendischen-aufsichtsbehoerden.

VI Overarching legal issues for MoUs

The various horizontal, vertical, and external MoUs examined above raise a number of overarching legal issues.

The first and most intricate issue is their legal nature. The legal bases to conclude the MoUs usually exclude any legally binding effect, and most of the MoUs contain express provisions to this end. That external MoUs must remain legally non-binding even emanates from the jurisprudence of the Court, because otherwise they would have to be concluded in accordance with the procedure for international agreements under Articles 216 to 219 TFEU.[57] There are only few exceptions to the rule that MoUs are legally non-binding: the horizontal MoUs entered into by the ECB and the SRB with the EP are akin to inter-institutional agreements under Article 295 TFEU where the parties have the choice to make such agreements legally binding. In this vein, the two agreements with the EP have not only been published in the Official Journal's L series containing legal texts but they also use prescriptive language ('shall') which shows that the parties intend to be legally bound, in contrast to the other MoUs, which communicate mainly in a language to describe their intention ('will') or possible decisions/acts ('may'). In the case of any doubt regarding the legal nature of MoUs, it can be expected that the Court would apply a non-formalistic approach and look beyond the mere title, to whether such an atypical act is intended to have legal effects.[58] This will allow the Court to exercise its prerogatives under Article 19 TEU, and ensure that, in the interpretation and application of the Treaties, the law is observed.

Second, for an MoU to be considered an act of a Union institution, body, office, or agency, it suffices that only one such entity is a participant. This was already clarified by the Court in *Florescu*, where it had to assess an MoU on financial assistance concluded between the EU, represented by the Commission, and Romania. Before the *Florescu* judgment, the prevailing opinion was that litigants needed to find alternative EU acts to challenge the terms of financial assistance either directly under Article 263 TFEU or indirectly under Article 267 TFEU before Union courts.[59] However, the Court gave the clear and unequivocal response that any act—even atypical acts such as MoUs—concluded by a Union institution,

[57] See judgments in *France v Commission* (n 45) and *France v Commission* (n 48).

[58] See the classical jurisprudence since the judgment of 31 March 1971 in *AETR* (n 10), para 42.

[59] Menelaos Markakis and Paul Dermine, 'Bailouts, the Legal Status of Memoranda of Understanding, and the Scope of Application of the EU Charter: Florescu' (2018) 55(2) Common Market Law Review 643–71.

body, office, or agency may be subject to the interpretation by the Court.[60] This was also confirmed in *Mallis*, where the involvement of the Commission and the ECB in the financial assistance granted to Cyprus under the European Stability Mechanism (ESM) Treaty was at issue.[61]

Third, MoUs must be consistent with EU law. In *Ledra Advertising*, on the non-contractual liability on the Union pursuant to Article 340 TFEU, the Court held that the Commission, acting within the framework of the ESM Treaty, should refrain from signing an MoU whose consistency with EU law it doubts.[62] In addition, the ESM could face judicial scrutiny through preliminary references, including economic governance or fundamental rights, as Euro area States must remain consistent with EU law according to the ESM Treaty.[63] This case law is applicable to MoUs more broadly and ensures that, in the exercise of public power, EU institutions, bodies, offices, and agencies do not escape their obligations under EU law, including the respect of fundamental rights as set out in the EU Charter of Fundamental Rights. Nevertheless, a case-by-case assessment of each MoU will be necessary in order to ascertain whether public power is being exercised and, if so, with effect on whom—other public authorities or also (rarely) individuals, including economic operators? When making this assessment it is also relevant whether the MoU is legally binding or not.

Fourth, even where MoUs are legally non-binding and may contain only political engagements, they must adhere to the Treaties, including especially the principles of conferral, institutional balance, and sincere cooperation. In this vein, the Court of Justice ruled, in *Council v Commission* on the Swiss MoU, about the contribution by Switzerland towards reducing economic and social disparities, and for cooperation in the area of migration in the EU, that a legally non-binding instrument (whatever its name) that contains policy choices in external relations requires prior approval by the Council pursuant to Article 16(1) TEU.[64] Therefore, neither the Commission nor any other Union institution or EU body can use non-binding MoUs to circumvent the mandatory procedures and the division of competences as set out in the Treaties.[65] Moreover,

[60] Case C-258/14 *Florescu and Others*, ECLI:EU:C:2016:995, Judgment of 13 June 2017, paras 30–36.

[61] Case C-105/15 P *Mallis and Malli v Commission and ECB*, ECLI:EU:C:2016:702, Judgment of 20 September 2016, paras 51 ff.

[62] Case C-8/15 P *Ledra Advertising v Commission and ECB*, ECLI:EU:C:2016:701, Judgment of 20 September 2016, para 59.

[63] de Gregorio Merino (n 13).

[64] *Swiss MoU* (n 18), paras 39 ff.

[65] Thomas Verellen, 'On Conferral, Institutional Balance and Non-Binding International Agreements: the Swiss MoU Case' (2016) 2016 1(3) European Papers—A Journal on Law and Integration 1225.

MoUs that contain choices of external policymaking need prior approval by the Council.

Fifth, most MoUs can thus be classified as soft law, which, although legally not binding, can have some political or other practical effects. This classification also provides valuable guidance as regards judicial review by the Court of Justice. As for the annulment procedure under Article 263 TFEU, Advocate General Bobek argued in *Belgium v Commission* that soft law could be reviewed if it establishes formalized, definitive, precise, and practically enforceable rules of behaviour.[66] However, the CJEU disagreed, repeating the classical formulation from the *AETR* judgment that 'any provision adopted by the institutions, whatever their form, which are intended to have binding legal effects are regarded as challengeable acts for the purpose of Article 263 TFEU'.[67] From this it also follows that measures that are not intended to have binding legal effects are excluded from direct actions. The Court's scope of review is somewhat broader under indirect actions where a national court makes a preliminary reference pursuant to Article 267 TFEU. This allows the Court the possibility to give a preliminary ruling on the validity and interpretation of all acts of the institutions of the EU without exception;[68] even if the acts are 'not intended to produce binding effects and are not capable of creating rights that individuals can rely on before a national court they are not without any legal effect'.[69] Therefore, even non-binding MoUs could, in theory, be the subject of a preliminary reference as long as they have some legal effect and the national courts are bound to take them into consideration in order to decide disputes submitted to them. However, this is unlikely to happen in practice, as individuals are unlikely to be affected by MoUs, resulting in few disputes being brought before national courts and subsequently referred to the CJEU.

Sixth, many MoUs set out rules on professional secrecy. This is not surprising since, pursuant to Article 339 TFEU and many acts of secondary law, Union institutions, bodies, offices, and agencies are bound to observe the obligation

[66] Case C-16/16 P *Belgium v Commission*, ECLI:EU:C:2017:959, Opinion of 12 December 2017, paras 109 ff.

[67] Case C-16/16 P *Belgium v Commission*, ECLI:EU:C:2018:79, Judgment of 20 February 2018, para 31.

[68] Case C-137/08, *VB Pénzügyi Lízing*, ECLI:EU:C:2010:659, Judgment of 9 November 2010, para 38.

[69] Case C-207/01 *Altair Chimica*, ECLI:EU:C:2003:451, Judgment of 11 September 2003, para 41; Case C-501/18 *BT v Balgarska Narodna Banka*, ECLI:EU:C:2021:249, Judgment of 25 March 2021, paras 80: For example, in *BT v Balgarska Narodna Banka*, para 101, the Court declared a recommendation by the EBA invalid, in so far as it equated the decision of the Bulgarian National Bank to place a bank under special supervision and to suspend its obligations to a finding of unavailability of deposits.

of professional secrecy. Moreover, the EBA conducts two equivalence assessments: regulatory and supervisory frameworks, and confidentiality.[70] The goal of equivalence is to facilitate cross-border financial activity by ensuring that third countries adopt EU-level prudential standards. Pursuant to Articles 53 to 62 CRD, equivalent third countries can exchange information on this basis without the necessity for an MoU. In particular, for banking supervision Article 53 CRD, and for banking resolution Article 84 BRRD, set out that professional secrecy applies to information received by persons working for the competent authority and auditors or experts in the course of their duties.[71] Moreover, this provision allows disclosure of information in summary or aggregate form to prevent the identification of individual banks. The *Baumeister* case[72] provides a potential benchmark for assessing the confidentiality of information in intra-EU supervisory cooperation; however, it does not offer specific criteria for designating certain subject matter as confidential.[73] The complexity of defining confidentiality persists within the EU and becomes even more challenging when negotiating with non-EU authorities. Financial-governance MoUs do not define what confidential information is. Rather, they presuppose that the participating entities have such information and want to exchange it in a way where they can be assured that their counterpart will continue to protect professional secrecy. While this assurance can easily be given within the Union—since institutions, bodies, offices, and agencies, as well as Member States' authorities, are bound by Article 339 TFEU on professional secrecy of EU officials, and relevant acts of secondary law—with third countries and international organizations, external MoUs play an important role to give such assurance.

VII Conclusion: Is the Banking Union in need of a harder-than-soft-law instrument for inter-institutional cooperation?

Looking, in conclusion, at the various MoUs examined here, their status is in line with the principles of the Basel Committee.[74] They are statements of

[70] Available at https://www.eba.europa.eu/regulation-and-policy/third-country-equivalence-and-international-cooperation, accessed 1 August 2024.

[71] Roberto Ugena, 'Confidentiality clauses in MoUs: the implications of the absence of a definition for confidential information' (ECB Legal Conference 2019, 2 and 3 September 2019, Frankfurt), available at https://www.ecb.europa.eu/press/legconf/pdf/ecb.ecblegalconferenceproceedings201912~9325c45957.en.pdf, accessed 1 August 2024.

[72] Case C–15/16 *Baumeister*, ECLI:EU:C:2018:464, Judgment of 19 June 2026.

[73] ibid.

[74] Basel Committee on Banking Supervision, 'Good practice principles on supervisory colleges' (26 June 2014), available at https://www.bis.org/publ/bcbs287.htm, accessed 1 August 2024.

cooperation but not necessarily legally binding. Instead, they act as a promise of intent, represent a shared understanding of a process by which information flows can be enabled and cross-border supervisory cooperation can be facilitated, and can be specifically tailored to detail, for example, actions to be taken in crises or with respect to supervision arrangements for specific firms. The MoUs should meet criteria of materiality, equivalence, and reliability to ensure that certain standards are upheld, to protect confidential information, and to efficiently use supervisory resources. Supervisory and resolution colleges are another important platform often included in MoUs. The colleges within the Banking Union were replaced by the SSM and SRM, but such colleges are common for non-participating Member States and third states outside the Banking Union.[75]

Ultimately, the question of whether the EU requires a harder-than-soft-law instrument remains complex and nuanced. The answer depends on the legal nature of each MoU and its type—horizontal, vertical, or external—necessitating a case-by-case analysis. On one hand, these instruments are fit for their purpose and effectively capture the reality of cooperation and information exchange, addressing issues of mutual assistance—a success story with global reach. They also provide the necessary flexibility and, indeed, independence to the bodies that conclude them, without being dependent on the legislator or their executive power. On the other hand, the rights to effective judicial protection and to a fair trial, as enshrined in Article 47 of the Charter, must not be overlooked. To prevent another banking turmoil and to protect the rights of all parties involved, both elements must be carefully balanced.

[75] Duncon Alford, 'The Operation of Supervisory Colleges in EU Banking Supervision: A Case Study of Soft Law Becoming Hard Law' (2021) 54(1) The International Lawyer 83, 83 ff; Agnieszka Smoleńska, 'Multilevel Cooperation in the EU Resolution of Cross-border Bank Groups: Lessons from the Non-euro Area Member States Joining the Single Resolution Mechanism (SRM)' (2022) 23 Journal of Banking Regulation 42.

22

Inside the Internal Market, Outside the Banking Union

EEA/EFTA States

Mads Andenas and Carsten Zatschler

I Introduction

By virtue of the European Economic Area (EEA) Agreement, the EEA/EFTA (European Free Trade Association) states, Norway, Iceland, and Liechtenstein,[1] are part of the EU's internal market. The four freedoms are applicable to the financial services sector, as is the bulk of EU secondary legislation.[2] The EEA/EFTA states are thus, formally through the EFTA Surveillance Authority (the 'EFTA SA'),[3] within the ambit of the EBA (European Banking Authority), ESMA (European Securities and Markets Authority), and European Insurance and Occupational Pensions Authority (EIOPA) Regulations.[4] This chapter will

[1] The EEA of 1992 included the EFTA countries—Austria, Finland, Iceland, Liechtenstein, Norway, Sweden, and Switzerland. Switzerland rejected the EEA Agreement in a referendum, and Austria, Finland, and Sweden joined the EU side of the EEA Agreement in 1994. Norway rejected EU membership in a referendum and remained in the EEA, together with Iceland and Liechtenstein.

[2] The impact of banking and financial market regulation goes beyond administrative law and, in particular, the protection of customers/investors reaches far into private and commercial law: see Mads Andenas, 'Commercial Law, Investor Protection, EU and Domestic Law' in Maren Heidemann (ed), *The Future of the Commercial Contract in Scholarship and Law Reform* (Springer 2018) 437–71; Mads Andenas and Federico Della Negra, 'Between Contract Law and Financial Regulation: Towards the Europeanisation of General Contract Law' (2017) 28(4) European Business Law Review 499. The resistance to giving full effect to such legal consequences raises further questions about the compliance in the EEA/EFTA states.

[3] The EFTA Surveillance Authority is customarily referred to as 'ESA' within the EEA/EFTA states. Given the topic of the present book and the potential for confusion with the acronym for the European Supervisory Authorities, the EFTA Surveillance Authority will here be abbreviated as 'EFTA SA'.

[4] Regulation (EU) No 1093/2010 of the European Parliament and of the Council of 24 November 2010 establishing a European Supervisory Authority (European Banking Authority), amending Decision No 716/2009/EC and repealing Commission Decision 2009/78/EC of 24 November 2010 ([2010] OJ L331, p 84), EBA Regulation; Regulation (EU) No 1094/2010 of the European Parliament and of the Council establishing a European Supervisory Authority (European Insurance and Occupational Pensions Authority), amending Decision No 716/2009/EC and repealing Commission Decision 2009/79/EC ([2010] OJ L331, p 48), EIOPA Regulation; Regulation (EU) No 1095/2010 of

Mads Andenas and Carsten Zatschler, *Inside the Internal Market, Outside the Banking Union*
In: *EU Banking Union*. Edited by: Jonathan Bauerschmidt, Raffaele D'Ambrosio, Diane Fromage, Daniela Jaros, and Paul Weismann, Oxford University Press. © Oxford University Press 2026.
DOI: 10.1093/9780198949756.003.0023

describe the extent to which the functioning of the internal market is impacted by the EEA/EFTA states' transposition process reflecting the peculiar legal and political position of these states, and the way in which the EU regulatory structure has been implemented.

In the wake of the financial crisis, the EU established a new and more comprehensive system for regulation and cooperation on the supervision of banks and other financial institutions as discussed in several of the other chapters of this book. More regulation and supervision moved up from the state to the EU level. New financial market regulatory agencies (EBA, ESMA, and EIOPA) were established, incrementally taking over from the Member State regulators, which remained as members of European regulatory systems. That posed new challenges for the EEA/EFTA states. They are part of the European internal market through the EEA Agreement and the EU's financial supervision system, and homogeneity require that the EU reforms were implemented also in the EEA/EFTA states. The EEA/EFTA states are not part of the European Banking Union, which goes further than the EEA with the internal market and its rules. The components of the internal market, such as the internal financial market and the internal banking market, are constituent elements of the EEA and apply equally in the EU and the EEA/EFTA states.

What are the consequences of the EEA/EFTA states staying outside the European Banking Union? It puts the EEA/EFTA states in the same category as EU Member States outside the Banking Union. In the EU, all the euro states are part of Banking Union; non-euro EU Member States may choose to join the Banking Union.[5] The first component, or central pillar, of the Banking Union is the Single Supervisory Mechanism (SSM). The SSM gives the European Central Bank (ECB) certain supervisory powers over the EU financial system. Under the SSM, the ECB is the central prudential supervisor of financial institutions. The ECB also directly supervises the 114 significant banks[6] of the participating countries. These banks hold almost 82% of banking assets in these countries.

the European Parliament and of the Council of 24 November 2010 establishing a European Supervisory Authority (European Securities and Markets Authority), amending Decision No 716/2009/EC and repealing Commission Decision 2009/77/EC ([2010] OJ L331), ESMA Regulation.

[5] The EFTA/EEA states are not part of the Monetary Union, and only EU Member States are members of the European Central Bank and can adopt the euro as their currency.

[6] The criteria for determining whether banks are considered significant—and therefore under the ECB's direct supervision—are set out in the SSM Regulation, Council Regulation (EU) 1024/2013, [2013] OJ L287, pp 63–89, and the SSM Framework Regulation (Regulation (EU) 468/2014 of the European Central Bank, [2014] OJ L141, pp 1–50.

The internal market rules, and post-crisis reforms of these, should apply fully to the EEA/EFTA states in the same way in which these apply to the non-euro EU Member States outside the SSM. That includes the regulatory structure, which needs be mirrored in the EEA/EFTA states, as will be discussed below. It cannot exclude the rules or the regulatory structure of the Banking Union, which continue the move from the national to the EU level beyond the internal market rules and institutions.

In the SSM—going beyond the internal market rules, and not applying to the EEA/EFTA states—the ECB directly supervises the largest banks, while national supervisors continue to monitor the remaining banks.

The other component of the Banking Union going beyond the internal market and remaining outside the EEA, so that it does not yet apply to the EEA/EFTA states, is the Single Resolution Mechanism (SRM), which is the central institution for bank resolution in the EU and one of the main components of the Banking Union.

The handling of bank crises and resolution at the EU level will be strengthened by the proposed European Deposit Insurance Scheme (EDIS), which has not yet been adopted by the EEA Joint Committee.[7] There are no convincing reasons for excluding the SRM or EDIS from the EEA.

As non-euro countries may join the SSM, there should be no barriers against finding an institutional solution to mirror the SSM in the EEA/EFTA states.

The proposed Savings and Investments Union (SIU), following the Letta[8] and Draghi[9] Reports, and the SIU strategy adopted on 19 March 2025,[10] will remedy barriers to financial market regulation within the EU single market, and include moving further domestic regulatory powers up to the EU level.[11]

[7] The EDIS proposal builds on the system of national deposit guarantee schemes (DGSs) regulated by Directive 2014/49/EU. Under this directive, all deposits up to 100,000 euros are protected through national DGSs all over the EU. This directive has not been adopted by the Joint EEA Committee or transposed into national law in the EFTA/EEA states—see more about this below. See also Gaia Chiarini and Diane Fromage, in this volume.

[8] Enrico Letta, *Much more than a Market—Speed, Security, Solidarity: Empowering the Single Market to Deliver a Sustainable Future and Prosperity for all Europeans* (Report to the European Council, April 2024) https://www.consilium.europa.eu/media/ny3j24sm/much-more-than-a-market-report-by-enrico-letta.pdf accessed 29 April 2025.

[9] Mario Draghi, *The Future of European Competitiveness—A Competitiveness Strategy for Europe* (Report to the European Commission, 9 September 2024) https://commission.europa.eu/topics/eu-competitiveness/draghi-report_en accessed 29 April 2025.

[10] Commission, 'Communication from the Commission to the European Parliament, the European Council, the Council, the European Central Bank, the European Economic and Social Committee and the Committee of the Regions—Savings and Investments Union: A Strategy to Foster Citizens' Wealth and Economic Competitiveness in the EU' COM (2025) 124 final.

[11] See, more on the reasons for moving competences from the Member State to the EU, Mads Andenas, *Financial Markets in Europe: Towards a Single Regulator* (Kluwer Law International 2003).

The EEA/EFTA states have aimed at taking part in this, but the institutional measures required are still being worked out.

As will be seen, the full implementation of the internal market in the financial sector, in many instances, continues to be hampered, leading to an uneven playing field where market access by EU financial undertakings is limited and consumers and businesses in the EEA/EFTA states are often put at a disadvantage. Rigid adherence to formalistic notions of sovereignty[12] delays the pace at which secondary legislation is incorporated, first, into the EEA Agreement, and then into national law.[13] Moreover, Iceland and Norway show much resistance to the full application of internal market law,[14] to some extent in the face of strong national stakeholder groups; and the competent supervisory authority, the EFTA SA, is ill-equipped to detect, let alone pursue, all relevant breaches.

Given the seemingly relatively insignificant size of the financial markets of the countries concerned, as well as the comparatively solid capitalization and governance of the undertakings active on those markets, it appears that the EU institutions and Member States have generally been willing to turn a blind eye to the deficiencies. Undertakings and consumers affected have largely been left to their own resorts.

This chapter will start by briefly outlining the (political) reasons for not joining the EU and the Banking Union, before describing the framework within which the four freedoms and EU secondary legislation become applicable in EEA/EFTA states, including the participation of the EEA/EFTA states in the European Supervisory Authorities (ESAs). A concluding section will deal with some of the contentious cases, as well as the ongoing challenges.

[12] But when obligations are undertaken in the EEA Agreement, sovereignty is not a legal argument of interpretation of the EEA obligations entered into: see Mads Andenas, 'Sovereignty' in Carl Baudenbacher (ed), *The Fundamental Principles of EEA Law* (Springer 2017); and Mads Andenas, Tarjei Bekkedal, and Luca Pantaleo, *The Reach of Free Movement* (Springer 2017).

[13] There is, for instance, strong resistance to making use of the Commission's impact assessments, and the EEA/EFTA countries would commence their own impact assessments after the formal adoption of the EU legislative measure, usually without achieving anything but excessive and pointless delay (if delay is not the very point).

[14] The internal market continues as a system and is more than a collection of free-movement rules: see Stephen Weatherill, *The Internal Market as a Legal Concept* (OUP 2016); and Koen Lenaerts and Piet van Nuffel, *EU Constitutional Law* (OUP 2021) in pt II, 'Competences of the European Union, 7: The Internal Market'. In the banking and financial services sector, the position of the EEA/EFTA countries should be comparable to that of the EU Member States that remain outside the EU Banking Union, as explained in the main text above.

II Reasons for not joining the EU and the Banking Union

The notion of sovereignty is deeply entrenched and far-reaching in both Norway and Iceland—more so than in many other countries—and they have not joined the EU as Member States. This may be partially historically explainable by long periods of foreign (Danish/Swedish) control and relatively recently gained independence, as well as the political influence of the agriculture and fisheries communities, and the view on the economic importance of natural resources, such as oil and gas and other energy sources such as hydropower.

Article 115 of the Norwegian Constitution allows the Norwegian parliament to consent to the transfer of sovereign powers to international organizations by an onerous three-quarters majority vote, but predicates this on Norway being a full member of the organization in question.[15] This is also known as the 'membership principle'. This article was invoked for the first time when Norway became a member of the EEA, and for a second time during the arrangements for Norway to participate in the EU ESAs.[16]

Any transfer of tangible powers to an international organization—even one which Norway, Iceland, and Liechtenstein are members of—is loaded, from a political and public opinion point of view. Formally joining a package of EU legislation like the Banking Union—even if that were possible for a non-EU Member State—could be seen to require a significant transfer of sovereignty to EU institutions, particularly to the ECB. Public opinion in the EEA/EFTA states is generally sceptical of further EU integration.[17]

Moreover, as non-eurozone members, the EEA/EFTA states would have limited voting rights and influence within the relevant decision-making bodies. They are hesitant to cede control over their banking sectors without having a commensurate say in how they are regulated and supervised. Finally, and as already mentioned above in the introduction, from a practical point of view, the EEA/EFTA states have relatively stable and well-capitalized banking systems. Norway claimed, without any empirical support, to be concerned that participation in the Banking Union could expose them to risks from weaker banking systems in other EU Member States. At the same time, Norway had

[15] The article was adopted in 1962 to facilitate Norwegian EU membership, which otherwise might have required a separate constitutional amendment.

[16] Tarjei Bekkedal, 'Third State Participation in EU Agencies: Exploring the EEA Precedent' (2019) 56(2) Common Market Law Review 381.

[17] This may turn. The newly elected (2024) government in Iceland has announced that it will hold a referendum on full EU membership by 2027.

objected to the maximum of 100,000 euros for deposit guarantees,[18] invoking the systemic vulnerability of the Norwegian banking system without any convincing support.[19]

However, public opinion in the EEA/EFTA states did not show any interest in these issues, which, after the 2008 financial crisis, attracted little or no controversy anyway. Nevertheless, civil servants in the Ministry of Finance with responsibility for financial market regulation brought the Ministry of Justice into the process by requesting a legal opinion on the constitutionality of the transfer of power to the EU ESAs.[20] The Ministry of Justice practice has been to defer to the practice of the parliament, so that parliament's view and practice would be decisive. Parliament had, in many fields, accepted gradual transfers of power to EU institutions under Article 26(2) of the Constitution, requiring a simple majority in parliament.[21] The prevailing view, and that of the Ministry of Justice, was that this practice determined the interpretation of the Constitution. The Ministry of Finance requesting this legal opinion before parliament had expressed its view opened up the prospect of the Ministry of Justice arresting the gradual transfer of powers to EU bodies. This was initiated by civil servants at the sub-departmental level without the senior civil servant at the top of the Ministry of Finance (or the ministers) being informed fully of the legal context and possible ramifications.

By way of consequence, a compromise had to be found on how to accommodate the concerns of the two Nordic states[22] in the EFTA about sovereignty with the need to have a functioning rule-making and supervision mechanism covering the whole EEA. The Ministry of Justice issued, in 2012 and 2014, two further opinions on the constitutionality of the institutional arrangements of proposed compromises.

Liechtenstein was concerned by the ways in which the delay in implementing the post-2008 reforms excluded internal market access, but had no effective ways of speeding up the adoption by the EEA Joint Committee and subsequent incorporation into the EEA Agreement.

[18] Directive 2014/49/EU of the European Parliament and of the Council of 16 April 2014 on deposit guarantee schemes (recast) [2014] OJ L173, pp 149–78, which was published as a text 'with EEA relevance' (which it obviously has). See the discussion below with references.

[19] Torje Sunde, Jon Lunde, and Ida Sørebø, *EØS-lovgivningen: Fra EU-rett til EØS-rett og norsk rett* (Universitetsforlaget 2024) 83 and fn 223.

[20] Legislation Department, Ministry of Justice JDLOV-2010- 10039 EO TSU: see the introduction of this document.

[21] And not requiring approval under art 115, which requires a three-quarters majority.

[22] This held up the process for adopting EU legislation in the EEA Committee and met with increasingly strong opposition from Liechtenstein, as this delay put the Liechtenstein financial sector at a competitive disadvantage by gradually restricting market access to the EU by certain Liechtenstein financial institutions (it also had similar deleterious effects on the Icelandic and Norwegian financial sectors).

The compromise, as we shall see later on, was rather meaningless. This episode, and the resulting institutional arrangements, show the challenges posed by fragmentation and agency problems even when it comes to such important financial market regulatory issues.

III 'Two-pillar' framework for applying internal market rules in EEA/EFTA states

The EEA Agreement creates a unique framework for non-EU Member States to participate in the EU internal market.

The EEA Agreement enunciates, in its Article 1(1), the objective of creating a homogeneous European Economic Area.[23] It then enumerates the fundamental freedoms, including the freedom of establishment, the free movement of services, and the free movement of capital, and 'the setting up of a system ensuring that competition is not distorted and that the rules thereon are equally respected'.[24]

The EEA Agreement sets up an institutional framework for ensuring that the EFTA/EEA side constitutes a part of the internal market which is homogeneous with the EU internal market and continues to be homogenous with the EU as the internal market develops.

The Preamble and Article 1 of the EEA Agreement state that the aim of the agreement is to promote a continuous and balanced strengthening of trade and economic relations between the contracting parties, with equal conditions of competition and the respect of the same rules. Article 1(2) expressly states that 'the association shall entail' the fundamental freedoms, and lists, in letters (a)–(c), the free movement of goods, persons, services, and capital.

The EEA Agreement aims to extend the European single market, including the four freedoms, to the EFTA states (Iceland, Liechtenstein, and Norway). The EEA Agreement does this by incorporating relevant EU law into the EEA Agreement and establishing mechanisms to ensure the uniform interpretation and application of those rules throughout the EEA. One effect of this is that individuals and economic operators in the EFTA states enjoy the same rights and freedoms as those in the EU Member States: for example, the freedom to move and reside in any EEA state, the freedom to establish a business in any EEA

[23] Also in EEA Agreement, [1994] OJ L1, arts 1(1), 58, 102, and 105. See Opinion 1/91, ECLI:EU:C:1991:490, para 14 ff; and Opinion 1/91, ECLI:EU:C:1992:189.

[24] Baudenbacher (n 12) provides particularly helpful analysis and explanation on EEA law.

state, and the freedom to provide and receive services across borders within the EEA.

Central to this agreement is the so-called two-pillar structure, a mechanism designed to balance the EEA/EFTA states' access to the internal market with their desire to maintain greater constitutional autonomy than would be possible as members of the EU. Internal market rules promulgated in the first pillar, the EU, are automatically adopted for the second pillar, the EEA/EFTA countries. This system demands rapid and limited adaptation when incorporating EU legislation, also in areas where the EU has granted significant powers to the Commission or to EU agencies. The integration of the EU financial supervisory framework, including its ESAs, presented a challenge. Rather contorted solutions attempted to reconcile the EEA two-pillar structure with the need for efficient and integrated financial supervision, and their efficiency may be questioned.

1 The Two-pillar structure: Aiming at full implementation of the internal market rules

At its core, the EEA Agreement's two-pillar structure is built upon the principle of 'homogeneity without transfer of legislative powers'.[25] This means that the EEA/EFTA states participate in the internal market by incorporating relevant EU legislation into their national laws, ensuring a level playing field without formally surrendering sovereignty to EU institutions. The first of the two 'pillars' in this system is the EU pillar: this comprises the EU institutions, primarily the European Commission, the European Parliament, the Council,

[25] Also, for a helpful explanation of the EEA two-pillar structure, see Baudenbacher (n 12). The Norwegian government lawyers' extolling of sovereignty principles dominates the 1,200 pages of Finn Arnesen and others, *Agreement on the European Economic Area: A Commentary* (Bloomsbury 2018). The authors try to develop the arguments, unsuccessfully used by Norwegian government lawyers in the EFTA Court and also in the CJEU, to the effect that the EEA Agreement is a public international law agreement, in order to read down Norway's internal market obligations. Their problem is that not only has this argument consistently been rejected by the EFTA Court and the CJEU, but the CJEU Grand Chamber has emphatically done so in Case C–897/19 PPU *IN, Ruska Federacija intervening*, ECLI:EU:C:2020:262: see the explicit rejection of the Norwegian government argument in the Opinion by the AG: Evgeni Tanchev, Christophe Alfred Pierre Hillion, and Halvard Haukeland Frederiksen, 'The "Special Relationship" between the EU and the EEA EFTA States and the Free Movement of Persons in an Extended Area of Freedom, Security and Justice - Case C-897/19 PPU, Ruska Federacija v. I.N., judgment of the CJEU (Grand Chamber) of 2 April 2020' (2021) 58(3) Common Market Law Review 851. Neither does it stand up under public international law, as discussed in n 11 above, with the reference to Andenas, 'Sovereignty' (n 12). Undeterred, the Norwegian government lawyers use this argument in domestic Norwegian courts, where they have more success, even after the clear rejections in the CJEU and the EFTA Court.

and the Court of Justice of the European Union (CJEU). Second is the EFTA pillar: this consists of institutions mirroring those in the EU, specifically the EFTA Surveillance Authority (EFTA SA) and the EFTA Court.

In addition to these pillars, joint bodies facilitate cooperation and decision-making; most importantly, the EEA Joint Committee, composed of representatives from both pillars, is responsible for incorporating new EEA-relevant EU acts into the EEA Agreement.

This two-pillar system brings up the question of whether legislation or decisions made in the EU pillar have direct effect in the EEA/EFTA states in the same manner as in the EU.

In a formal sense, it may seem that new EU legal acts only become binding in the EEA/EFTA states after being deemed relevant for EU–EFTA cooperation by the EEA Joint Committee and subsequently incorporated into the EEA Agreement. National authorities in the EEA/EFTA states must then incorporate these acts into their national legal systems. This process, which is applicable to all EU internal market legislation, is essential for understanding the operation of taking over EU law also in the financial sector, which will be outlined briefly here.

On closer analysis, the direct effect goes further. Regulations adopted in the EEA Joint Committee are directly effective.[26] Direct effect of directives is controversial also in the EEA/EFTA states, but indirect direct effect goes a long way in resolving the gaps left by the CJEU's doctrines on horizontal direct effect of directives.[27] Indirect direct effect, as a principle of the EU and EEA law, has an important function in the EEA/EFTA states. Individuals and enterprises must be able to claim direct effect of directives against the state after their adoption in the EEA Joint Committee. Indirect direct effect arguments, based on the EEA Agreement, will also apply before the adoption in the EEA Joint Committee. The promulgation of EU secondary legislation may make the fundamental freedom in the EEA Agreement sufficiently clear and precise, if not for full direct effect, to give strong reasons for indirect direct effect at least.

[26] See Tarjei Bekkedal, 'Understanding the Nature of the EEA Agreement: On the Direct Applicability of Regulations' (2020) 57 Common Market Law Review 773.

[27] The EFTA Court and national courts in the EEA/EFTA states apply the indirect direct effect doctrines of the CJEU in the interpretation and application of domestic legislation: see, for instance, Rt 2000 s 1811 *Finanger I*, in which the Norwegian Supreme Court states that its own rules of presumption of compliance with international law obligations go at least as far as CJEU case law on indirect direct effect, to comply with EU Law, mentioning, inter alia, Case C–106/89 *Marleasing* [1990] ECR I-4135.

2 Incorporation of EU acts into EEA law

New EU legislation regarding the internal market is incorporated into the EEA Agreement by decisions of the EEA Joint Committee, which formally makes the legal act a part of the EEA Agreement by adding a mention of the legal act to one of its annexes, stipulating adaptations as appropriate. This requires an ongoing process of scrutiny and adaptation to ensure that the final EEA rules function effectively in the context of the two-pillar structure.[28]

Formally, the EEA Agreement, in its Article 3, provides that the contracting parties shall take all appropriate measures, whether general or particular, to ensure the fulfilment of the obligations arising out of the Agreement. The EEA Agreement, in Article 1, clarifies that these obligations cover the internal market rules.

For the EU, this means incorporating relevant EU legislation into the EEA Agreement by decisions of the EEA Joint Committee. The EEA Joint Committee is established under Article 92 of the EEA Agreement. It meets around eight times per year and takes approximately 250 decisions, incorporating 400 to 600 new EU acts yearly into the EEA Agreement.[29]

The process begins when the European Commission draws up new legislation in a field governed by the EEA Agreement. The Commission informs the other contracting parties in the EEA Joint Committee as soon as possible. At this point, the EEA/EFTA states assess the new legislation to determine its relevance to the EEA and whether it needs to be adapted. This is done by experts[30] in the EFTA states. The EFTA states then discuss the legislation and their proposed amendments in the Standing Committee. The Standing Committee is tasked with coordinating the incorporation process, facilitating consultation between the EEA/EFTA states, and arriving at a common position. The Standing Committee normally meets to finalize its position the day before the EEA Joint Committee. If all parties agree, the EEA Joint Committee can then adopt a decision incorporating the EU act into the EEA Agreement.

Once an act has been incorporated into the EEA Agreement, Article 7 thereof imposes an obligation to make it part of the national legal order. Article 7 of the EEA Agreement is one of its most important provisions, as it sets out

[28] For a detailed description, see 'Legal Notes by the EFTA Secretariat on the EEA Agreement' (*EFTA Bulletin*, June 2019) https://www.efta.int/media-resources/publications/legal-notes-efta-secretariat-eea-agreement.

[29] See the annual reports on the activities of the EEA Joint Committee, https://www.efta.int/eea-relations-eu/eea-institutions-two-pillar-structure/eea-joint-committee.

[30] Officials in the relevant ministries or regulatory bodies.

how acts are to be implemented into the domestic law of the contracting parties. It provides that acts referred to or contained in the annexes to the EEA Agreement or in decisions of the EEA Joint Committee shall be binding upon the contracting parties and shall be made part of their internal legal order, in the same way as under Article 288 of the Treaty on the Functioning of the European Union (TFEU).

An act corresponding to an EU regulation shall, 'as such', be made part of the internal legal order of the contracting parties.

An act corresponding to an EU directive shall leave to the authorities of the contracting parties the choice of form and method of implementation.

The first of the paragraphs above means that regulations are to be made applicable in the EEA/EFTA states without any textual modifications, in the same wording and form in which they are applicable in the EU. The second paragraph means that directives, on the other hand, while binding as to the result to be achieved, leave to the national authorities the choice of form and methods.[31] Directives are really not to be modified by transposing acts. And there is no more room for modifying EU law by implementing measures in the EEA/EFTA states than in the EU.

Article 3 of the EEA Agreement complements Article 7 by imposing an obligation on the contracting parties to ensure that the obligations arising from the EEA Agreement are fulfilled. This means that the contracting parties must take all appropriate measures, whether general or particular, to ensure that they comply with the provisions of the Agreement. This obligation applies to all aspects of the EEA Agreement, including the incorporation of EU acts into EEA law, and will notably involve the abrogation of any acts which may lead to conflict with provisions of EEA law.

The current backlog in the EEA Joint Committee is a challenge to the future of the EEA.[32] One increasing problem has been the time that is required by the national impact assessments before the EEA/EFTA states take a position on the EEA relevance of an EU measure. The EU impact assessments have already examined whether there is a need for EU action and analysed the possible impacts of available solutions. These will have been carried out during the preparation phase, before the European Commission finalized a proposal for a new law. In the EEA/EFTA states, the dispute is over the extent to which

[31] As under art 288 TFEU.

[32] See the Walaas Report, 'Cross-sectoral EU initiatives: The way ahead for the EEA – Report to the Standing Committee of the EFTA States by the Task Force on Files with Distinctive Horizontal Dimensions' (2024); and the Eldring Commission, 'NOU 2024: 7 Norge og EØS: Utvikling og erfaringer', 11 April 2024.

the national impact assessment may duplicate that of the Commission. If the EU measure does not have any interested domestic administrative or political body to sponsor the national impact assessment, it can take an inordinately long time. The duty of loyalty and good faith under Article 3 of the EEA Agreement requires that the EU impact assessments are not unnecessarily duplicated, and also that any specific EEA/EFTA impacts are assessed in parallel to or direct sequence with the Commission impact assessment. This will require the domestic rules on impact assessments for new rules to be applied in accordance with the requirements of EEA law or amended to clarify that such duplication and delay is not allowed.

3 Adaptation of EU acts

Most EU acts can be incorporated into the EEA Agreement without recurring discussions on the need for special adaptations. However, in some cases, adaptations are necessary to ensure that the act functions effectively in the context of the EEA Agreement. These adaptations can be technical or substantive, or exemptions.[33]

a) Technical adaptations

Technical adaptations are required to make the act fit within the framework of the EEA Agreement.

They do not alter the substance of the act. Some common examples include adding the EEA/EFTA states to lists of EU countries. This is necessary to ensure that the EFTA states are included in the scope of the legislation. It includes replacing references to EU primary law with references to the corresponding provisions in the EEA Agreement: a reference to Article 107 TFEU might, for example, be replaced with a reference to Article 61 of the EEA Agreement.

It further includes updating transitional arrangements. This is necessary to ensure that market participants in the EFTA states benefit from transitional arrangements in the same way as EU operators.

The final example is clarifying the role of EEA/EFTA institutions. An adaptation text might, for example, clarify that the EFTA SA is responsible for implementing a particular provision in the EEA/EFTA states.

[33] Legal Notes by the EFTA Secretariat (n 28), Adaptation Texts, para 2.

b) Substantive adaptations

Substantive adaptations may entail a deviation from, or an amendment to, the rules laid down in the EU act. Substantive adaptations can be politically controversial, as they may require the EEA/EFTA states to accept rules that are different from those applicable in the EU. It can be particularly difficult for the EU side to accept exceptions to finely balanced outcomes of the EU legislative process. In effect reopening decisions that have been highly controversial in the EU process may be politically impossible. It will rarely be merited, as the EU will have taken account of the arguments of the EEA/EFTA states.

Examples of situations where substantive adaptations have been made include the delegation of tasks to EU agencies. As the EEA Agreement does not regulate the creation of separate regulatory bodies or agencies in the EFTA pillar to mirror those of the EU, the contracting parties usually need to find solutions to reflect modalities for EFTA participation within the existing EU bodies. The incorporation, by the EEA Joint Committee, of the regulations establishing the three ESAs is a case in point.[34] As will be seen, substantive adaptations were included to ensure that the EFTA SA could exercise similar powers to those enjoyed by the ESAs in the EU. Ultimately, however, the EFTA SA has been left with merely formal powers which do not mirror those of the ESAs in the EU. The system requires that the EFTA domestic regulatory bodies or agencies loyally and tightly follow and abide by what is decided by the EU agencies.

Centralized market authorization schemes are another example, worth mentioning in this chapter, focusing on Banking Union and ESAs in particular, of situations where substantive adaptations may be required. When an EU act establishes a centralized market authorization scheme, substantive adaptation may be necessary to ensure that authorizations granted by the EU institutions are also recognized in the EEA/EFTA states.[35]

c) Exemptions

In some cases, the EEA/EFTA states may also be exempted from applying certain provisions of an EU act. Exemptions are typically granted where there are

[34] Joint Committee Decision No 199/2016 [2017] OJ L46, p 4 (EBA Regulation); Joint Committee Decision No 200/2016 [2017] OJ L46, p 13 (EIOPA Regulation); Joint Committee Decision No 2011/2016 [2017] OJ L46, p 22 (ESMA Regulation).

[35] An example from another field is that the EEA Joint Committee adopted a substantive adaptation to Regulation (EC) No 258/97 concerning novel food and novel food ingredients, to ensure that the EFTA states could grant market authorizations in parallel with the European Commission: see Legal Notes by the EFTA Secretariat (n 28), para 112.

specific reasons why an act should not apply in an EEA/EFTA state, such as geographical factors or constitutional constraints.[36]

4 Challenges for incorporating EU law into EEA law

The incorporation of EU acts into EEA law is a complex and time-consuming process. It requires close cooperation between the EU institutions and the EEA/EFTA states.

A key challenge includes the need to ensure homogeneity, as required by the EEA Treaty.[37] One of the main goals of the EEA Agreement is to create a homogeneous EEA based on common rules and equal conditions of competition (see Article 1(1) thereof). This requires ensuring that EU acts are implemented, interpreted, and applied uniformly throughout the EEA.

Another key challenge is respecting the two-pillar structure, whereby each pillar is responsible for implementing and enforcing EEA rules within its own territory. Article 1 of the EEA Agreement, with the provisions about homogeneity and the main elements of the internal market, requires a straightforward implementation on the EEA/EFTA side. Increasingly, the EEA/EFTA states have developed a sovereignty doctrine which is not based on the EEA Agreement. One line of argument is that the incorporation of EU acts into EEA law must be done in a way that respects this structure and does not undermine the sovereignty of the EEA/EFTA states. But state sovereignty is limited by the treaty obligations, as these are expressed in Article 1 of the EEA Agreement, about a homogenous European Economic Area. There is no room for sovereignty as a principle of interpretation to read down the obligations under the EEA Agreement, as is increasingly argued before the EFTA Court and the EEA/EFTA-state national courts.[38]

Yet another key challenge is managing the volume of EU legislation. The EU produces a large volume of legislation each year. This can make it challenging for the EEA/EFTA states to keep up with the incorporation process,

[36] Where EU legislation allows Member States to derogate from certain provisions of an act, there is no need for an adaptation text in order for the same possibility to apply to the EEA/EFTA states. This follows from para 7 of Protocol 1 EEA. Several rather spurious 'constitutional constraints' have been claimed by the EEA/EFTA states, and the EU side has shown great patience.

[37] See, in particular, art 1 EEA.

[38] Andenas, 'Sovereignty' (n 12); Mads Andenas, 'General Principles at the European Level' in Giacinto della Cananea and Jean-Bernard Auby (eds), *General Principles and Sector-Specific Rules in European Administrative Laws* (OUP 2024); Andenas, Bekkedal, and Pantaleo (n 12).

particularly where adaptation of the EU act is required. There are two main points to make here.

First, that for the EEA/EFTA states, the incorporation is the only way in which they can regulate their markets. They are small countries with limited regulatory capacity. In practice, they can only implement international standards through EU legislation. They have problems in keeping up with EU legislation, and no prospect whatsoever of managing the regulatory challenge on their own at a domestic level.

Second, that the EEA/EFTA states simply do not have the administrative capacity to undertake drawn-out economic, administrative, sustainability, and environmental assessments duplicating the Commission assessments. These assessments often only start in the EFTA/EEA states after the adoption of the EU measure. They delay the adoption at all levels in the EFTA/EEA states. The EEA/EFTA countries need to build on the impact assessments of the Commission or other EU body and only address adaption issues specific to the country in question. In real terms, the legitimate specific adaptation issues are few and limited.

5 Challenges for the application and interpretation of EEA law

The EEA Agreement includes mechanisms to ensure the uniform interpretation and application of EEA law across both pillars. In practice, this only concerns the EEA/EFTA pillar; in order to meet the requirements of effectiveness and loyalty, incorporation and transposition must be timely and carried out almost sequentially, with as limited delay as is possible.

The EEA Agreement's two-pillar structure and the principle of 'homogeneity without transfer of legislative powers' relies on the parallel incorporation and transposition by the EEA Committee and the EEA/EFTA states, as set out above. The obvious vulnerability of the EEA/EFTA pillar requires that the EFTA SA play an even stronger and more independent role, also in preparing for implementation at an early stage. Domestic courts must consistently apply the direct-effect doctrines of the CJEU and the EFTA Court. The EFTA SA's strict compliance with, and enforcement of, EBA and other EU guidelines and recommendations is of paramount importance.[39] Indirect direct effect, as a

[39] The legal consequences of recommendations and guidelines are a classic problem of EU Law: see, eg Mads Andenas, 'The Interplay of the Commission and the Court of Justice in Giving Effect to the Right to Provide Financial Services' in Paul Craig and others, *Lawmaking in the European Union* (Kluwer Law International 1998); and Mads Andenas, 'Harmonising and Regulating Financial Markets' in Mads Andenas and Camilla Baasch Andersen (eds), *Theory and Practice of Harmonisation*

principle of the EU and EEA law, has an important function in the EEA/EFTA states.

The EFTA SA monitors compliance with EEA rules in the EFTA states, at one level mirroring the European Commission's role in the EU; and in accordance with the adaptation texts adopted when incorporating EU acts, establishing agencies into the EEA Agreement, the EFTA SA also replicates the functions of EU agencies within the EFTA pillar. This is a matter of replicating the regulatory activities of the EU agencies, but the EFTA SA can only replicate in the sense of repeating and transmitting, and does so in a technical manner without adding any real impact on the rules or other regulatory activities. The EFTA SA is the intermediary between the EU agencies and the domestic regulators in the EFTA states.

The EFTA Court adjudicates disputes related to the EEA Agreement in the EFTA states, similarly to the CJEU's role in the EU.

The many provisions for cooperation and consultation between the EU and EFTA institutions facilitate harmonization.

IV Incorporation of the EBA Regulation, the ESMA Regulation, the EIOPA Regulation, and the Single Rulebooks into the EEA Agreement

In accordance with the procedures just described, the EBA Regulation, as well as all the acts forming part of the Single Rulebook, have to be incorporated, first, into the EEA Agreement, and then into the national legal orders of each of the EEA/EFTA states.[40] The same applies to the ESMA Regulation and the EIOPA Regulation and these regulators' respective rule books.

1 Single Rulebook

The incorporation of the European System of Financial Supervision (ESFS) into the EEA Agreement poses distinct challenges, depending on the different levels of EU rules within the ESFS framework:

(Edward Elgar 2010). EBA, ESMA, EIOPA and other EU guidelines and recommendations provide a comprehensive legal framework which must be given effect to, and by doing so, the EFTA SAs may contribute to remedying the systemic vulnerabilities of the EFTA pillar of the EEA.

[40] See n 4.

- Level 1 texts, consisting of legislation properly speaking (framework directives and regulations), are incorporated relatively smoothly. The EEA Joint Committee decides on incorporation into an annex of the EEA Agreement, after which the EFTA states implement them through national legislation.
- Level 2 texts, consisting of regulatory technical standards (RTS) and implementing technical standards (ITS), are also incorporated into the annexes to the EEA Agreement through Joint Committee decisions. This process ensures that both the EU and EFTA sides participate in the decision to incorporate these detailed technical rules, respecting the two-pillar structure.
- Level 3 texts, comprising guidelines and recommendations issued by the ESAs, present a more significant challenge. Unlike level 1 and level 2 texts, level 3 guidance does not undergo a formal incorporation process through the EEA Joint Committee. There are no corresponding decisions or annexes specifically dedicated to these guidelines. While considered 'soft law', these guidelines are becoming increasingly influential due to the 'comply-or-explain' approach under Article 16 of the ESA Regulations. National Competent Authorities (NCAs) in the EFTA states are required to publicly declare compliance with ESA guidelines or provide reasons for non-compliance.

This transfer of quasi-legislative power to EU bodies without a formal agreement within the EEA framework is a necessary corollary to the participation in the internal market.[41] The absence of EFTA-pillar involvement in the implementation of level 3 guidance can only be remedied by informal participation in ways in which the system allows. The current practice in EFTA states clarifies the true nature of level 3 guidance, as competent authorities in EFTA states typically publish ESA guidelines directly from the ESAs' websites. They often issue letters to relevant financial institutions urging them to consider these guidelines. This practice, reflecting a pragmatic approach to ensuring a harmonized internal market, clarifies that this is not 'soft law' but binding in the same way in the two pillars of the EU and the EEA/EFTA.

[41] Andri Fannar Bergporsson, 'Adapting the European System of Financial Supervision (ESFS) to the EEA Two-Pillar Structure - A Workable Solution' (2019) 16 European Company and Financial Law Review 557, s 4.2.

2 The decision-making powers of the EU financial regulators (EBA, ESMA, and EIOPA)

The EBA's decision-making powers caused inordinate, seemingly constitutional, problems, particularly in Norway. Similar problems arose with the ESMA Regulation and the EIOPA Regulation. But the EBA, ESMA, and EIOPA Regulations[42] were incorporated into the EEA Agreement by Decision of the EEA Joint Committee No 199/2016 on 30 September 2016.[43] The decision entered into force on 1 October 2016. The incorporation of this regulation, and similar regulations that established the other ESAs, was subject to substantive adaptations allegedly to maintain the two-pillar structure of the EEA Agreement in the way this was regarded from the Norwegian side, and, to a lesser extent, from the Icelandic side, as already pointed out above.

One of the key challenges was that the EBA, ESMA, and EIOPA enjoy extensive decision-making powers which may include the ability to take binding decisions applicable to institutions and individuals within the EFTA states.[44] The Norwegian view was that this created a conflict with the two-pillar structure of the EEA Agreement, which did not envision giving direct powers to the European Commission or EU bodies. It would, in the case where powers to take binding decisions moved up from the national level, require the creation of separate EEA regulatory bodies that would mirror those of the EU. The rather contorted solution that was chosen involved giving the EFTA SA the competence to adopt decisions in the EFTA pillar, based on drafts prepared by the relevant EU supervisory authority. For example, if the EBA were to make a binding decision, it would send a draft of that decision to the EFTA SA, which would then translate that decision into a binding decision applicable within the EFTA states.[45] Whether this process effectively promotes the EFTA states' notions of sovereignty is highly uncertain. But the institutional solution allows them to participate in the harmonized regulatory framework of the European internal market while maintaining claims to formal sovereignty. The EEA

[42] Regulation (EU) 1093/2010 of the European Parliament and of the Council of 24 November 2010 establishing a European Supervisory Authority (European Banking Authority).

[43] EEA Joint Committee Decision No 199/2016 of 30 September 2016 amending Annex IX (Financial services) to the EEA Agreement, https://eur-lex.europa.eu/legal-content/EN/TXT/HTML/?uri = CELEX:22017D0276.

[44] ESMA took over the authorization, regulation, and supervision of rating agencies: see about Decision 199/2016.

[45] See Decision of the EEA Joint Committee No 199/2016 (n 43); See also the Norwegian government legislative proposal to the parliament, Proposisjon til Stortinget (Prop S 100) (2015–2016).

Committee decision of 30 September 2016 included 31 legal acts, going back to the 2010 EBA Regulation.[46]

The EU had taken the view that none of the financial market directives or regulations could be adopted in the EEA Committee before the regulations on the financial market authorities had been adopted. That caused a considerable backlog, with important consequences. The 2016 EEA Committee decision brought the process back on track.

The adaptations to EBA Regulation, as set out in Decision 199/2016, can be summarized as follows: competent authorities of the EFTA states, along with the EFTA SA, have the same rights and obligations as the competent authorities of EU Member States in the work of the EBA. They are entitled to participate in all of the EBA's activities, including the work of its Board of Supervisors and all preparatory bodies, but do not have voting rights.

Decisions taken by the EBA that affect the EFTA states are to be implemented by the EFTA SA. These decisions are based on drafts prepared by the EBA, and the EFTA SAs can also, on its own initiative, request the EBA to prepare drafts if it believes that measures are needed.

The EFTA SA is to exercise the powers of the EBA as they apply to the EFTA states. For example, if the EBA has the power to issue guidelines on a particular topic, the EFTA SA will be responsible for issuing those guidelines as they apply to the EFTA states.

In practice, EFTA state regulators will apply EBA guidelines in advance of the EFTA SA having issued those guidelines, so that they become formally binding in the sense outlined above. That would apply also to other decisions and less formal guidance. The internal market law would be the same, and there would have to be very good reasons for not following the EBA guidelines.

V The EFTA SA: The key player in replicating EU decisions

The EFTA SA plays a critical role in the two-pillar structure, particularly in replicating the decisions of the ESAs (EBA, ESMA, and EIOPA). While the EFTA SA is formally independent, it is functionally dependent on the EU ESAs for its decision-making in financial supervision.

[46] See n 4.

The process of replicating ESA decisions generally follows the four steps described below.[47]

The first step is the drafting by EU ESAs: when an EU ESA makes a decision, for instance, regarding the application of specific regulations, the ESA prepares a draft decision and sends it to the EFTA SA.

The second step is tweaking by the EFTA SA: the EFTA SA adapts the draft decision to ensure its compatibility with the EEA Agreement and the institutional framework of the EFTA pillar. This involves, where necessary, replacing references to EU bodies with their EFTA counterparts (for example, replacing the EBA with the EFTA SA) and ensuring alignment with the EEA Agreement's provisions.

The third and final step is the issuance of the binding decision by the EFTA SA. The EFTA SA formally issues the adapted decision, making it binding on the competent authorities and market operators in the EEA/EFTA states.

The EFTA SA is, under the guise of 'transparency', and with the ostensible aim of obtaining 'technical expertise', required to inform the competent authorities of EFTA states of any decisions about to be adopted by it, providing a reasonable time limit for any response.[48] As the decisions in question are already based on the expertise of the relevant ESA, and there are no real reasons for suspecting a need to inject further 'technical expertise' into the process, it appears that the real aim of this provision is to provide the EFTA states with an early-warning mechanism before a decision is adopted. There are no formalized communication channels between the EU ESAs and the EFTA SA on the work within the ESAs while recommendations are being drafted. There is little the EU ESAs can do to keep the EFTA SA in check.

This procedure applies to a wide range of decisions by the EU ESAs, including binding decisions invoking specific articles of the ESA regulations. For example, Common Article 16 allows ESAs to issue recommendations and, if necessary, binding decisions to national supervisors to address breaches or risks of breaches of Union law.[49] It also includes decisions related to the direct regulation and governance of national markets. This includes authorizing credit rating agencies and overseeing transaction registers. A final example is intervention powers in exceptional circumstances. For example, the Short Selling Regulation[50] empowers ESMA to require information disclosure or

[47] See Protocol 8 to the Surveillance and Court Agreement on the functions and powers of the EFTA Surveillance Authority in the field of financial supervision, as well as the Multilateral Memorandum of Understanding concluded on 26 March 2018 between the EFTA SA and the ESAs.

[48] Art 4 of Protocol 8 to the Surveillance and Court Agreement.

[49] See Common Article 16 of the EBA, ESMA, and EIOPA Regulations (n 4) for full reference.

[50] Regulation (EU) No 236/2012 [2012] OJ L86/1.

impose temporary restrictions on short-selling activities, to address threats to financial stability.

VI Replicating the EU authorities' tasks in banking supervision

To replicate the tasks of the EBA and EIOPA, and in the EFTA pillar, the EEA Agreement utilizes a combination of mechanisms.

First, direct incorporation of EBA regulations:[51] regulations, which are directly applicable in the EU, are typically incorporated into the EEA Agreement through decisions of the EEA Joint Committee. These regulations become legally binding in the EEA/EFTA states following their incorporation and subsequent implementation in national law.

Second, EFTA SA replicating EBA guidelines and recommendations: while EBA guidelines and recommendations are not legally binding in the EU in a strict sense, they aim to foster supervisory convergence and best practices. In the EFTA pillar, the EFTA SA usually issues corresponding guidelines and recommendations based on those issued by the EBA. These EFTA SA guidelines and recommendations are tailored to the specific context of the EEA/EFTA states, ensuring consistency with the EEA Agreement and the EFTA pillar's institutional framework. EBA interpretations and other statements will be important sources outside the framework described here. They will, in practice, determine the interpretation and application of the EU sources that are to be applied in the EEA/EFTA states—see above about the EEA Agreement, Article 1.

Third, EFTA SA participation in EBA activities: the EEA Agreement provides for the participation of EFTA SA representatives in various EBA activities, such as committees, working groups, and task forces. This participation allows the EFTA SA to stay informed about EBA initiatives, contribute to the development of EU banking supervisory policy, and advocate for the interests of the EEA/EFTA states.

Finally, information exchange and cooperation: regular information exchange and cooperation between the EBA and the EFTA SA, as well as between the NCAs of the EEA/EFTA states and their EU counterparts, are crucial for ensuring consistent implementation and application of banking supervisory

[51] The EBA itself, strictly speaking, does not issue regulations in the way that the European Commission or the Council of the EU do. Rather, the EBA is tasked with developing draft regulatory technical standards (RTS) and implementing technical standards (ITS) which are then adopted by the Commission.

rules across the EEA. This cooperation takes various forms, including bilateral meetings, participation in joint supervisory colleges, and the sharing of supervisory data.

Here are four examples of the EFTA SA's role in replicating EBA tasks. First, the Capital Requirements Directive (CRD) and Capital Requirements Regulation (CRR): these are key pieces of legislation establishing prudential requirements for banks in the EU. The EFTA SA plays a role in ensuring that these requirements are implemented and enforced consistently in the EEA/EFTA states, working closely with the EBA and national supervisors.

Second, the SSM: while the SSM only applies to eurozone Member States, its establishment has had implications for the EEA/EFTA states. The EFTA SA works to ensure that the EEA/EFTA states' banking supervisory frameworks are compatible with the SSM and that cooperation with the ECB is effective.

The third example is anti-money laundering (AML) and combating the financing of terrorism (CFT). The EBA plays a significant role in developing and implementing AML/CFT regulations in the EU. The EFTA SA replicates these efforts in the EEA/EFTA states, working with the EBA and national authorities to ensure compliance with international standards and the EU's AML/CFT framework.

The fourth and final example is the EU resolution framework. The EU resolution framework aims to ensure the orderly resolution of failing banks, minimizing the impact on financial stability and taxpayers. The EFTA SA works to ensure that the EEA/EFTA states' resolution frameworks are compatible with the EU's framework and that cooperation with the Single Resolution Board (SRB) is effective.

VII Challenges and concerns: Balancing supranationality with constitutional autonomy

While the two-pillar solution aims to preserve the EEA/EFTA states' constitutional autonomy, a functioning internal market for financial services requires a level playing field, which is hampered, in particular, by: (1) the lag in the making EU law and rules applicable in EEA/EFTA states; (2) structural problems caused by the reluctance of EEA/EFTA states to equip the EFTA SA with the powers and resources required to fully fulfil its role under the EEA Agreement; and (3) an often recalcitrant and opportunistic approach to the EEA Agreement on the part of EEA/EFTA states, attempting to cherry-pick the rules to apply and to mask non-compliance.

Ultimately, these concerns arise independently of the choice of the EEA/EFTA states to remain outside the Banking Union: they are caused by the approach taken towards the EEA Agreement as a whole, and give rise to a lack of homogeneity in other parts of the internal market as well. The reason they stand out in the financial field is the rapid pace at which integration has been proceeding in an economic sector that is already, by its nature, fast-moving and agile, causing additional problems for regulators to keep pace, all the more so where they are under-resourced and lacking political backing.

1 Delayed incorporation of secondary legislation

There is an almost constant severe backlog in the implementation of legal acts on the EEA/EFTA side. This backlog can create challenges for businesses operating in the EEA, as they may face uncertainty regarding the applicable rules and potential delays in the implementation of new regulations.

The delayed incorporation of EU secondary legislation into the EEA Agreement has been a recurring problem, particularly in the area of financial services. This has created legal uncertainty for financial institutions operating in the EEA/EFTA states and has hampered the smooth functioning of the internal market.

There are several reasons for these delays. The EEA/EFTA states have allocated only limited resources to reviewing and implementing EU legislation, and the process of negotiation and consensus-building within the EEA Joint Committee can be slow and cumbersome. In addition, the EEA/EFTA states sometimes resist incorporating EU legislation that they perceive as being against their national interests.

A particularly illustrative example of the delayed incorporation of secondary legislation—albeit from outside the financial field—is the Third Energy Package, a set of EU directives and regulations aimed at liberalizing the EU's energy markets. The EEA/EFTA states were slow to incorporate the Third Energy Package into the EEA Agreement, in part due to concerns about the impact on national energy policies. The Norwegian political disagreement on the Third Energy Package led to the breakdown of the coalition government in 2025, and the incorporation has still not been resolved. This delay has created uncertainty for energy companies operating in the EEA/EFTA states and hindered the development of a single European energy market. It also has serious knock-on consequences for financial markets.

Another example of resistance is the Icelandic government's approach of not responding to or challenging decisions of the EFTA SA on Iceland's lack of implementation of the regulation of financial services.[52]

In the financial sector, the delay in adoption by the EEA Committee only continues. As mentioned above, there was a six-year delay in adopting the EBA, ESMA, and EIOPA Regulations. EEA Committee Decision of 30 September 2016 catching up with this backlog included 31 legal acts, going back to the 2010 EBA Regulation.[53]

The EEA/EFTA states have still not yet transposed the 2014 Deposit Guarantee Directive.[54] The then minister of finance, in 2011, stated that Norway would consider 'vetoing' the adoption of the directive in the EEA Joint Committee.[55] Norway has maintained a coverage of 200,000 euros, double the harmonized coverage level set by the EU directive.[56] The systemic vulnerability of the Norwegian banking system was invoked and is unconvincing. Norwegian banks have a higher capitalization than in most EU Member States. Notably, the Norwegian central bank has argued against the current high ceiling, as it causes distortions in the market, and has not shown any concern for systemic consequences of implementing the lower ceiling of the directive.[57]

[52] See, eg Case E-21/24 *EFTA Surveillance Authority v Iceland*, judgment of 2 April 2025—failure to implement Commission Delegated Regulation (EU) 2023/314 on risk management procedures for the exchange of collateral; Case E-20/24 *EFTA Surveillance Authority v Iceland*—failure to incorporate Regulation (EU) 2022/750 on benchmarks in OTC derivative contracts; Case E-16/24 *EFTA Surveillance Authority v Iceland*—failure to implement Regulation (EU) 2021/1688 on prudential requirements for investment firms; Case E-12/24 *EFTA Surveillance Authority v Iceland*—failure to incorporate Directive (EU) 2019/2034 on the supervision of investment firms; Case E-10/24 *EFTA Surveillance Authority v Iceland*—failure to implement Regulation (EU) 2021/23 on a framework for the recovery and resolution of central counterparties; Case E-7/22 *EFTA Surveillance Authority v Iceland*, judgment of 17 November 2022—failure to implement the regulatory framework for markets in financial instruments under Directive 2014/65/EU (MiFID II) and Regulation (EU) No 600/2014 (MiFIR).

[53] See n 4.

[54] Directive 2014/49/EU of the European Parliament and of the Council of 16 April 2014 on deposit guarantee schemes (recast), which was published as a text with EEA relevance (which it in our view obviously has).

[55] Aftenposten, 11 November 2010, https://www.aftenposten.no/verden/i/Gaw49/eu-stanser-norsk-bankgaranti.

[56] Art 6(1) of Directive 2014/49. A transitional provision in art 19(4) permitting coverage levels of up to 300,000 euros expired on 31 December 2018.

[57] Sunde, Lunde, and Sørebø (n 19) 83 and fn 223 set out the Norwegian sources: Prop 159 L (2016–2018) p 126 and Innst L (2017–2018), in which the parliamentary committee 'underlines the importance of maintaining the Norwegian maximum of 2 mill NKR beyond 2018 and asks the government to continue the negotiations with the EU about this. In Norway we save largely by taking up banking deposits, and a good deposit guarantee is more important for us than others.' See also the treatment on pp 154 and 298.

While the EFTA SA is meticulous in its monitoring of incorporation delays and publishes detailed, well-illustrated 'scoreboards',[58] it is important to bear in mind that the assessment of delays in EEA/EFTA states and compliance with internal market legislation does not take account of the delay in a decision being made by the EEA Committee, only the transposition after the adoption in the EEA Committee, ie after the states have, in principle, agreed to make these texts part of their legal orders. This explains the (false) impression of, in some respects, high compliance in the EEA/EFTA states.

2 Limited role of the EFTA SA

A key concern is the proper functioning of the two-pillar system in transposing EU rules and decisions. This is predicated on the EFTA SA's limited independence in a number of regards, both via-à-vis the EU and the EEA/EFTA states themselves.

Most tangibly, the EFTA SA's reliance on draft decisions from the EU ESAs promotes its efficiency and the proprer functioning of the internal market by effectively limits its independence. While the EFTA SA theoretically has the power to reject a draft decision from an EU ESA, it is highly unlikely to do so, given the EEA Agreement's core objective of maintaining homogeneity (see the EEA Agreement, Articles 1(1), 58, 102, and 105) and the EFTA SA's limited resources. This raises concerns about whether the EFTA SA can act as an independent supervisory authority or merely functions as a 'rubber stamp' for EU decisions.

It is true that, as the EFTA states are also involved in the ESAs (albeit without voting rights), they may raise issues and meet some understanding from the EU side. But this may unavoidably be limited under the current system. Frankly, the impact of the EEA/EFTA states, even as full Member States, would have been limited, and the EEA cannot create any disproportionately increased influence for these three countries. The EU side cannot open up for renegotiation and new outcomes on issues that have been through the long internal market political and legislative process, or for 'adaptations', 'reservations', or 'vetoes' that restrict internal market instruments on the EEA/EFTA side of the EEA.

[58] See, eg the 56th Internal Market Scoreboard, published by the EFTA SA in July 2025: https://www.eftasurv.int/cms/sites/default/files/documents/gopro/Internal%20Market%20Scoreboard%20No%2056.pdf.

The most serious cause for concern in this respect is the resource disparity. A significant difference in resources between the EU ESAs and the EFTA SA exacerbates the power dynamic. The EU ESAs are large, specialized institutions with hundreds of staff dedicated to financial supervision. The EFTA SA, in contrast, has a significantly smaller staff, with only two case handlers responsible for financial services in all three EEA/EFTA states, supported by a relatively small legal department. This resource imbalance raises questions about the EFTA SA's capacity to effectively scrutinize and adapt the complex draft decisions it receives from the EU ESAs, limiting its ability to safeguard the interests of stakeholders on the EEA/EFTA side. While a requirement has been imposed on the EFTA SA to seek 'technical expertise' from the competent authorities of the EFTA states,[59] this provision, in effect, functions merely as an early-warning mechanism to the EFTA states rather than leading to any substantive input from their competent authorities. A realistic view may be that the institutional solution was never intended to provide anything but a 'rubber stamp' procedure.

This may be surprising, seeing the fact that the limited influence of EFTA states in decision-making is a constant cause for debate and concerns about the democratic legitimacy of the system, and whether the EEA/EFTA states are truly equal partners in the internal market's financial supervision is frequently raised. But it is an inevitable and intrinsic consequence of the EEA model that is exacerbated if the EFTA SA is held back by resource constraints imposed by the EEA/EFTA states.

The EEA model may not be helped by the fact that it includes some bypassing of the EFTA SA. This occurs, for example, when specific sectoral legislation has not been fully adapted to the EEA's two-pillar structure, not providing a role for the EFTA SA in the adaptation texts. One obvious example is ESMA's ban on binary options, adopted under Article 40 MiFIR[60] in 2018 and repeatedly renewed,[61] where ESMA acted directly without involving the EFTA SA, raising concerns about the consistency and predictability of the two-pillar system.

[59] Art 4 of Protocol 8 to the Surveillance and Court Agreement between the EFTA States, see n 47.

[60] Regulation (EU) No 600/2014 of the European Parliament and of the Council of 15 May 2014 on markets in financial instruments and amending Regulation (EU) No 648/2012 [2014] OJ L173/84. ¶

[61] Decisions (EU) 2018/795[2018] OJ L136/31; ESMA Decision (EU) 2018/1466 [2018] OJ L245/17; ESMA Decision (EU) 2018/2064 [2018] OJ L329/27; ESMA Decision (EU) 2019/509 [2019] OJ L85/19.

3 Resistance to the full application of internal market law

Iceland and Norway have shown some resistance to the full application of internal market law in the face of strong national stakeholder groups. This resistance has manifested itself in a number of ways, including the adoption or preservation of national rules that are more restrictive; going further in pursuing regulatory aims such as capital adequacy or deposit guarantees than EU law; and the challenge to EFTA SA decisions before the EFTA Court. What is often attempted to be justified as higher regulatory standards may, however, not be suitable and proportionate, and may be serving protectionist purposes.

One egregious recent example of this resistance is the Norwegian government's practice of restricting ownership of undertakings in strategic sectors, including the financial sector.[62]

For about a decade after acceding to the EEA, Norwegian legislation provided that no party could own more than 10% of the share capital of a financial institution.[63] This provision was ostensibly aimed at avoiding financial institutions being run as personal banks where one or a few persons owned the institutions. It was considered that such an ownership arrangement could result in a relationship between the institution and its owners where the shareholders received preferential treatment, which could have negative consequences for the financial system both directly, through increased losses, and indirectly, through loss of confidence in financial institutions. In 2001, the EFTA SA initiated infringement proceedings and issued a Reasoned Opinion concluding (predictably) that the rule was incompatible with Article 40 of the EEA Agreement on the free movement of capital.[64]

The reaction of the Norwegian authorities was, however, not to simply abrogate the 10% rule, but to replace it with a discretion-based rule evaluating whether owners of qualifying holdings were suited to owning such holdings, which, as was evident from the preparatory works, pursued unchanged objectives. By way of consequence, an administrative practice arose whereby individuals or undertakings could not own more than '20% to 25%' of the shares in financial institutions, except where the financial institution engaged only in a niche activity.

[62] Already in the EFTA Court judgment in Case E-2/06, Norwegian conditions for a concession for acquisition of hydropower resources were struck down as violating the free movement of capital and right of establishment through indirect discrimination.

[63] s 2-2 of the Norwegian Law on Financial Activity and Financial Institutions (Lov om finansieringsvirksomhet og finansinstitusjoner) of 10 June 1988 No 40.

[64] Reasoned Opinion 319/01/COL of 30 October 2001. https://www.eftasurv.int/cms/sites/default/files/documents/gopro/3573-109382.pdf.

This administrative practice remained substantially unchallenged for some 15 years. The EFTA SA started making some enquires in 2015, which, however, did not lead to formal infringement proceedings until after the EFTA Court had been seized of the matter by way of a request for an advisory opinion from the Oslo City Court in what has become a seminal case: Case E–8/16 *Netfonds*. In its judgment, the EFTA Court had no difficulty holding that the Norwegian legislation requiring dispersed ownership was in breach of the right of establishment within the EEA. The Court noted that less restrictive measures could be equally effective in attaining the legitimate objective pursued by Norway. The clear finding in the Advisory Opinion even led the Oslo District Court to rule in favour of Netfonds in 2018, awarding NOK 55 million in damages against the Norwegian state. However, the Court of Appeal later overturned this decision, in 2021.[65] It held that the case lacked a cross-border element and, therefore, did not fall within the scope of EEA law. It also found, in the alternative, that the ministry's practice constituted a lawful restriction on the freedom of establishment. This reasoning diverged from the EFTA Court's advisory opinion in Case E–8/16, which had found the ownership restrictions incompatible with EEA law.

Notwithstanding a situation which disclosed a perfectly clear breach of EEA law, delaying tactics on the part of Norway, involving numerous piecemeal amendments of the rules and forbearance on the part of the EFTA SA, meant that it took until 2024 for the EFTA Court to be seized of the matter again,[66] in Case E–24/24 *EFTA SA v Norway*.

These infringement proceedings finally concluded on 30 September 2025, with the EFTA Court in essence confirming its judgment in E–8/16 *Netfonds*, now against an even clearer legal background, given the developments in secondary legislation. The EFTA Court found that Norway's continued administrative practice—requiring prior approval for acquisitions above 25% and applying additional criteria not foreseen in harmonized EU law—is incompatible with the exhaustive assessment regime under CRD IV and Solvency II.[67] The judgment represents the culmination of ESA's long-standing efforts to bring Norway into compliance. That it took over two decades and a second

[65] Borgarting Court of Appeal, judgment of 17 December 2021, LB-2018-141762, *Netfonds Bank AS and Netfonds Livsforsikring AS v The Norwegian State*, available at https://lovdata.no/dokument/LBSIV/avgjorelse/lb-2018-141762.

[66] See EFTA SA Decision 134/23/COL of 27 September 2023; and see EFTA SA, 'ESA refers Norway to the EFTA Court for restricting freedom of establishment for banks and other financial undertakings' (*EFTA SA*, 27 September 2023) https://www.eftasurv.int/newsroom/updates/esa-refers-norway-efta-court-restricting-freedom-establishment-banks-and-other accessed 29 April 2025.

[67] Directive 2009/138/EC, OJ L335/1.

infringement procedure to address such a clear breach is disconcerting. It underscores the fragility of enforcement in the EFTA pillar and the systemic delays that undermine the homogeneity of the internal market.

It has to be hoped that Norway will comply with the judgment not only in form, but also in substance. It is notable that the government has not yet acknowledged the decision or—as would normally be the practice—confirmed that it will comply. The silence is notable, given the clarity of the judgment and its confirmation of long-standing legal principles already established in E–8/16 *Netfonds*. It may reflect either internal deliberations or a reluctance to publicly acknowledge the implications of the ruling, especially in light of the previous resistance to aligning national practice with EEA obligations. Given the fact that Norwegian law and practice regarding ownership of financial institutions has been in breach of EEA law in one way or another for some 30 years, it cannot be excluded that, in effect, the licences of all banks and insurance undertakings are vitiated in some way. That aside, it appears clear that there has been a chilling effect for merger and acquisition activity, and the whole corporate structure and capital acquisition in the Norwegian financial sector will have been impeded, hindering growth while artificially sheltering national champions.

Another illustration of the grounds for concern regarding the level of compliance comes from the competition law enforcement, which, given the highly concentrated nature of the financial sector in the EEA/EFTA states, should be a particular priority.[68] In principle, the EFTA SA enjoys the same powers and has the same duties regarding the enforcement of competition law as the European Commission has within the EU. In practice the modest size of the EFTA SA, and the consequent lack of in-depth expertise and resources, often prevent both a timely and thorough investigation and a sufficiently vigorous follow-up.

By way of consequence, deterrence is weakened, and even where the authority becomes aware of breaches of the competition rules, it will often be able to act only after damage to the market has been done. A good example is the handling of a complaint concerning restrictions in the e-payment services market.

In October 2015, the EFTA SA received a complaint from Trustly Group AB, a Swedish provider of electronic payment services, regarding a coordinated

[68] This is illustrated by the analysis of banking market and ownership concentration in E-16/23 *EFTA Surveillance Authority v The Kingdom of Norway.*

blocking of its ability to provide e-payment services in Norway by several members of the Norwegian banking sector.

The complaint specifically focused on Trustly's inability to access Norway's payment infrastructure through BankID, due to agreements, decisions, or concerted practices by the Norwegian banks. Trustly invoked violations of the competition provisions of the EEA agreement concerning concerted practices and abuse of dominance.[69]

One year later, in October 2016, the EFTA SA initiated proceedings and an in-depth investigation into a potential concerted practice aimed at excluding a new market entrant, against the principal industry association and the largest incumbent banks.[70] A further two years later, the matter was effectively settled, as a consequence of Trustly—which had, in the meantime, been acquired by another investor—withdrawing its complaint in exchange for some undisclosed concessions. The EFTA SA closed its case in April 2019, citing 'reasons of prioritisation', without any finding of impropriety having been made or any penalties being imposed.[71]

A final feature is the lack of dispute resolution mechanisms. The EEA Agreement lacks comprehensive dispute resolution mechanisms for disagreements between the EU and EFTA pillars on the interpretation or application of EEA law. This can lead to prolonged disputes and legal uncertainty, particularly in areas where the division of competences between the two pillars is not clear.

VIII Conclusion

The EEA/EFTA states are integrated into the EU's internal market but remain outside the Banking Union. This situation presents both opportunities and challenges. The EEA/EFTA states benefit from access to the EU's single market in financial services but must comply with EU rules and regulations, with limited influence over their development. The delayed incorporation of secondary legislation, resistance to the full application of internal market law, and ongoing challenges, such as the regulation of e-payments, and *Netfonds*, demonstrate the complexities of being 'inside the internal market, outside the Banking Union'. As the EU continues to deepen integration in the financial

[69] Arts 53 and 54 of the EEA Agreement, equivalent to arts 101 and 102 TFEU.
[70] EFTA SA Decision 195/16/COL of 25 October 2016 in Case No 77452.
[71] EFTA SA Decision 22/19/COL of 2 April 2019, available here: https://www.eftasurv.int/cms/sites/default/files/documents/gopro/4866-Decision%20to%20close.pdf.

services sector, the EEA/EFTA states will need to carefully navigate their relationships with the EU to ensure that they can continue to reap the benefits of internal market membership while also safeguarding their national interests.

There are signs that the European Commission has become less willing to continue to tolerate the lax and tardy enforcement of EEA law in EEA/EFTA states to today's extent, with significant problems arising for competition and the integrity of the financial markets.[72] There are also signs of a stronger will from the EEA/EFTA states to take part in the stepping up of the internal market, as proposed in the 2024 reports by Letta[73] and Draghi,[74] prompting the EU to deepen integration in the financial services sector, most recently with the SIU strategy (2025). The Walaas Report on *Cross-sectoral EU initiatives: The way ahead for the EEA*[75] and the Norwegian Eldring Commission[76] (both of 2024) emphasized the need for improving the EEA/EFTA-pillar compliance and overcoming the backlogs. They reflect views in government also in Iceland and Liechtenstein. So there may be the political will to step up to the plate, cut the backlog in the EEA Joint Committee, improve implementation, and embrace new institutional solutions for moving regulation from the domestic to the European level.

Overall, the EEA/EFTA states' experience within the internal market for financial services, while remaining outside the Banking Union, provides valuable insights into the dynamics of differentiated integration in the EU. Their particular position highlights the challenges of balancing national sovereignty with the requirements of a highly integrated single market, and offers lessons for other countries considering closer ties with the EU in the area of financial services.

[72] The pressure has been mounting, in particular, on the implementation of the EU's Third Energy Package, which in turn contributed to the break-up of the Norwegian coalition government in 2025, as referred to above.

[73] Letta (n 8).

[74] Draghi (n 9).

[75] See the Walaas Report (n 32).

[76] Eldring Commission (n 32).

23
Switzerland and the Banking Union

Carlo Lombardini[*]

I Introduction

The relationship between Switzerland and the European Union (EU) has always been a sensitive subject in Switzerland, a fiercely independent country. Switzerland views direct democracy as a privilege of paramount importance which could be jeopardized by too-close political and legal ties with the EU. At the moment of writing this contribution, intense discussions are being held as to the future relationship with the EU and the countries composing the Union, further to the conclusion of sectorial bilateral agreements which have no impact on the banking and financial sectors.[1]

This chapter will give some explanations regarding banking supervision in Switzerland (section II), and thereafter look at the rules applicable to the relationship between the EU and Switzerland in matters of banking supervision (section III). As a conclusion (section IV), we will make some general remarks regarding Switzerland as a leading offshore banking centre.

II Banking supervision

1 General presentation

The banking sector is supervised by the Swiss Financial Market Supervisory Authority (FINMA). FINMA was created by a special law (FINMASA),[2]

* The author thanks his assistant, Mr Nicola Pantaleo, for its contribution in reviewing the final version of this chapter.

[1] https://www.europa.eda.admin.ch/en, accessed 31 August 2025.

[2] Loi sur l'Autorité fédérale de surveillance des marchés financiers/Federal Act on the Swiss Financial Market Supervisory Authority, Classified Compilation of Federal Legislation (Recueil Systématique du droit fédéral, RS) 956.1. See Rolf Watter and Rashid Bahar (eds), *Basler Kommentar Finanzmarktaufsichtgesezt/Finanzmarktinfrastrukturgesetz* (Helbing Lichtenhahn 2019).

Carlo Lombardini, *Switzerland and the Banking Union* In: *EU Banking Union*. Edited by: Jonathan Bauerschmidt, Raffaele D'Ambrosio, Diane Fromage, Daniela Jaros, and Paul Weismann, Oxford University Press. © Oxford University Press 2026. DOI: 10.1093/9780198949756.003.0024

completed in 2019 by an ordinance adopted[3] by the Swiss government (the Federal Council).

FINMA is an integrated financial market supervisory authority in charge of the supervision of the activities regulated by the so-called financial market laws. These are: (1) the Banking Act;[4] (2) the Federal Law on Financial Institutions;[5] (3) the Federal Act on Collective Investment Schemes;[6] (4) the Federal Act on the Supervision of Insurance Companies;[7] (5) the Federal Act on Combating Money Laundering and Terrorist Financing;[8] (6) the Federal Act on Financial Market Infrastructures and Market Behaviour in Securities and Derivatives Trading;[9] (8) the Federal Act on the Issuance of Bonds of Guarantee;[10] (9) the Federal Act on Financial Services;[11] and (10) the Federal Act on Insurance Contracts.[12] This chapter will deal only with FINMA's position in banking regulation and supervision.

FINMA's tasks are: (1) to authorize and supervise regulated institutions; (2) to identify institutions which should be subject to regulation but are not authorized and put them into liquidation; (3) to sanction institutions and inviduals which do not respect the rules; (4) to declare the bankruptcy or resolution of supervised institutions.

Whereas FINMA is a microprudential regulator, the Swiss National Bank (SNB) is a macroprudential regulator.[13] It identifies systemic banks; it can also propose to the Swiss government that the government adopts countercyclical

[3] Ordonnance relative à la loi sur la surveillance des marchés financiers/Ordinance to the Financial Market Supervision Act, RS 956.11.

[4] Loi fédérale sur les banques et les caisses d'épargne, RS 952.0. See Rolf Watter and others (eds), *Basler Kommentar Bankengesetz* (Helbing Lichtenhahn 2013); Thibaud Giddey, *Histoire de la régulation des banques en Suisse (1914–1972)* (Droz 2019).

[5] Loi fédérale sur les établissements financiers, RS 954.1. See Rashid Bahar and Rolf Watter (eds), *Basler Kommentar Finanzdienstleistungsgesetz/Finanzinstitutsgesetz* (Helbing Lichtenhahn 2023); Rolf Sethe and others (eds), *Kommentar zum Finanzinstitutsgesetz FINIG* (Schulthess 2021).

[6] Loi fédérale sur les placements collectifs de capitaux, RS 951.31. See René Bösch and others (eds), *Basler Kommentar Kollektivanlagengesetz* (Helbing Lichtenhahn 2016).

[7] Loi fédérale sur la surveillance des entreprises d'assurances, RS 961.01.

[8] Loi fédérale concernant la lutte contre le blanchiment d'argent et le financement du terrorisme, RS 955.0. See Ursula Cassani and others (eds), *Commentaire romand Loi sur le blanchiment d'argent* (Helbing Lichtenhahn 2022).

[9] Loi fédérale sur les infrastructures des marchés financiers et le comportement sur le marché en matière de négociation de valeurs mobilières et de dérivés, RS 958.01. See Rolf Sethe and others (eds), *Kommentar zum Finanzmarktinfrastrukturgesetz FinfraG* (Schulthess 2017).

[10] Loi sur l'émission de lettres de gage, RS 211.423.4.

[11] Loi sur les services financiers, RS 950.1 See Alexandre Richa and Philipp Fischer (eds), *Commentaire romand Loi sur les services financiers* (Helbing Lichtenhahn 2022); Bahar and Watter (eds), *Basler Kommentar Finanzdienstleistungsgesetz/Finanzinstitutsgesetz* (n 5); Rolf Sethe and others (eds), *Kommentar zum Finanzdienstleistungsgesetz FIDLEG* (Schulthess 2021).

[12] Loi sur le contrat d'asssurances, RS 221.229.1.

[13] See https://www.snb.ch/en/the-snb/mandates-goals/financial-stability accessed 9 October 2024.

rules regarding equity to be held by banks.[14] More generally, the SNB's mandate is to conduct monetary policy in such a way that prices remain stable and take into account the situation of the Swiss economy. It must also contribute to the stability of the financial system. Interesting statistics on the activities of banks in Switzerland are available on the website of the SNB.[15]

In order to facilitate the flow of information between the various authorities having an interest in the proper functioning of the financial markets, two memoranda of understanding (MoUs) have been concluded: (1) one between FINMA and the SNB;[16] and (2) another between FINMA, the SNB, and the Federal Finance Department.[17]

FINMA represents Switzerland's interests in numerous international bodies.[18] It can cooperate with international or supranational organizations (such as the Basel Committee on Banking Supervision, the International Monetary Fund, the Financial Stability Board, or the Financial Action Task Force) by supplying them with data and figures that may be needed for their missions (article 42b FINMASA). At the international level, the State Secretariat for International Finance (SIF) represents the interests of Switzerland.[19] FINMA cannot take legal commitments on behalf of Switzerland, and it must involve the Federal Departement of Finance in matters which are deemed to be of substantial importance. This concept is vague and there is no public indication as to how it is applied practically.

2 Banking regulations

Federal banking regulations are a consequence of the 1929 crisis. In 1934, the parliament adopted the Banking Act (BA).[20] Before 1934, banking regulation was a matter of cantonal law. From 1934 onwards, it has become a matter exclusively of federal law, with the BA containing the organizational requirements

[14] See, for instance, Federal Council, 'Federal Council requires banks to hold additional capital for residential mortgages' (26 January 2022), https://www.admin.ch/gov/en/start/documentation/media-releases/media-releases-federal-council.msg-id-86922.html accessed 9 October 2024.
[15] Banque nationale suisse, 'Banks in Switzerland' www.snb.ch/fr/the-snb/mandates-goals/statistics/statistics-pub/publication-history/statpub_bankench accessed 9 October 2024.
[16] See https://www.finma.ch/fr/~/media/finma/dokumente/dokumentencenter/myfinma/5finma, accessed 10 October 2024.
[17] See https://www.finma.ch/fr/~/media/finma, accessed 10 October 2024.
[18] See https://www.finma.ch/en/finma/international-activities, accessed 10 October 2024.
[19] See https://www.sif.admin.ch/en, accessed 11 October 2024.
[20] See n 4.

to be satisfied by banks and designating the supervisory authority (the Federal Banking Commission, at the time).

Banking activity is connected to the liability side of the balance sheet and, according to the law (article 1a BA), does not require that loans be granted by a bank, although practically and economically, deposits received by banks are used for that purpose.

Private banking, which contributed to the reputation of Switzerland as a leading financial centre, is not a banking activity but is defined as a financial service covered by the Federal Act on Financial Services.[21] Banks can provide this service without further authorization. So-called securities firms, also supervised by FINMA, but which are financial institutions pursuant to the Federal Law on Financial Institutions,[22] can also provide private banking services: for that purpose, they receive deposits from clients and use these deposits to buy and sell securities and financial instruments on behalf of the clients. They do not, however, grant loans, except Lombard loans.

In 2012, rules were introduced in the BA regarding systemic banks (article 7).[23] These banks are designated as such by the SNB, but they are supervised by FINMA. UBS, the Raiffeisen Group, Zürcher Kantonalbank, and PostFinance[24] are systemic banks.[25] Only UBS is a global systemically important bank, having been designated as such by the Financial Stability Board.

3 FINMA's organization

FINMA is a public-law institution with its own legal personality; it is operationally, institutionally, and financially independent (article 4, para 1, and article 21 FINMASA).

The Federal Council must approve FINMA's strategic objectives (article 9, para 1, lit a, FINMASA), appoint the members of its Board of Directors (article 9, para 3, FINMASA), and approve the appointment of the CEO; the Federal Assembly (the parliament) exercises supreme supervision (article 21, para 4,

[21] See n 11.

[22] See n 5.

[23] David Wyss, 'Too big to fail-Regulierung – Stand in der Schweiz' (2022) 1 Gesellschaft und Kapitalmarktrecht 26 ff.

[24] PostFinance is a 100% owned subsidiary of La Poste Suisse, an entity fully owned by the Swiss Confederation; it is prevented by law from granting credits.

[25] https://www.finma.ch/fr/mise-en-oeuvre/recovery-et-resolution/too-big-to-fail-et-stabilité-du-système/banques-d'importance-systémique/#:~:text = UBS%2C%20le%20groupe%20Raiffeisen%2C%20la,de%20stabilisation%20et%20d'urgence accessed 11 October 2024.

FINMASA). Neither the Federal Council nor the Federal Assembly can influence FINMA's operational activities or decisions.

FINMA's governing bodies are the Board of Directors, the Executive Board, and the Auditors (article 8 FINMASA).

The Board of Directors is responsible for setting FINMA's strategic objectives, adopting ordinances or guidelines, and also deciding on specific matters deemed to be of major importance (article 9 FINMASA).

The fact that the Board of Directors takes individual decisions in specific cases—including on matters relating to the supervision of individual entities, if these matters are deemed to be of substantial importance—means that the Board does not have to deal only with theoretical issues.[26] FINMA defines matters of substantial importance in article 2*bis* of its Organizational Regulations.[27] The approach of FINMA as regards the definition of issues of substantial importance is not binding on the courts.[28]

The Executive Board is responsible for FINMA's operational management, and for taking decisions which are not deemed to be of substantial importance, which means the vast majority of the decisions (article 10 FINMASA).

The decisions rendered by FINMA, be it by the Board of Directors or the Executive Board, are subject to appeals, first to the Federal Administrative Court and thereafter to the Swiss Supreme Court.

4 FINMA as a regulator

FINMA can adopt ordinances and circulars. FINMA may only adopt an ordinance on the basis of an express legal provision (article 7, para 1, lit a, FINMASA). An ordinance must deal with technical issues of secondary importance (article 5, para 1, FINMA Ordinance). Ordinances cannot derogate to legal rules. Some FINMA ordinances are quite important, for instance the Insolvency Ordinance,[29] the Ordinance on Money Laundering,[30] and the Ordinance on Financial Markets

[26] David Wyss, 'Finanzmarktaufsicht zwischen Macht und Ohnmacht Schweizerische' (2022) 6 Revue suisse de droit des affaires et du marché financier 623 ff.

[27] Règlement d'organisation de l'Autorité fédérale de surveillance des marchés financiers du 18 décembre 2008/Organizational Regulations of the Swiss Financial Market Supervisory Authority of 18 December 2008.

[28] Swiss Federal Supreme Court, case 2C_387/2018, 18 December 2018.

[29] Ordonnance de la FINMA sur la procédure d'insolvabilité des établissements des marchés financiers/FINMA Ordinance on Insolvency of financial institutions, RS 952.05.

[30] Ordonnance de la FINMA sur le blanchiment d'argent/FINMA Money Laundering Ordinance, RS 955.033.0.

Audits.[31]

Guidelines (or circulars) enable FINMA to explain how it uses its discretionary powers to interpret financial market legislation. This allows it to establish a known and predictable practice. No specific legal basis is, therefore, required for FINMA to issue a guideline (article 7, para 1, lit b, FINMASA). Guidelines are not binding, but some guidelines contain rules that are quite important, such as Guideline 2017/1 Corporate Governance Banks or Guideline 2010/1 Remuneration Systems.[32]

5 FINMA as a supervisor

FINMA uses specially qualified auditors not only: (1) to review the accounts of banks (accounting audit); but also (2) to assess whether banks fulfil the legal and regulatory requirements they are subject to (prudential audit).[33] Only specially qualified auditors can be used for these activities.[34] The auditors are subject to the Federal Audit Oversight Authority.[35]

The prudential auditor is appointed by the board of directors of a bank, but reports also to FINMA. Year after year, the auditor must agree with FINMA (and not with the bank) how its audit will be carried out and which risks of the bank will be subject to more scrutiny. FINMA can also appoint an auditor to carry out all or part of the audit of a bank, instead of relying on the auditor appointed by the bank. FINMA is more directly involved in the supervision of systemic banks. Allowing auditors to assess the prudential situation of a bank on behalf of the regulator is a Swiss specificity.

FINMA visits banks for on-site supervisory reviews, usually dedicated to specific themes;[36] this allows FINMA to compare institutions with similar business models.

Banks are divided by FINMA into various categories:

[31] Ordonnance sur les audits des marches financiers/Ordinance on Financial Market Audits, RS 956.161.

[32] No rules on remuneration are contained in the BA; the only exception is that, if a bank is helped financially by the authorities, then the Federal Council can order measures (art 10a, BA).

[33] See FINMA, 'FINMA's extended reach', https://www.finma.ch/en/finma/auditing/, accessed 9 October 2024.

[34] Ordonnance sur la surveillance de la revision/Ordinance of the Federal Audit Oversight Authority on the Oversight of Audit Firms, RS 221.302.

[35] See www.rab-asr.ch/#/?lang = en, accessed 10 October 2024.

[36] See https://www.finma.ch/en/supervision/cross-sector-issues/on-site-supervisory-reviews/, accessed 11 October 2024.

- Category 1: extremely large, important, and complex market participants—very high risk. These are the systemic banks.
- Category 2: very important, complex market participants—high risk.
- Category 3: large and complex market participants—significant risk.
- Category 4: medium-sized market participants—medium risk.
- Category 5: small market participants—low risk.

Banks in categories 1 to 3 receive an assessment letter from FINMA at the end of each year. In this letter, FINMA reviews the situation of the bank and stresses both the positive and negative developments. It explains where it expects changes or efforts to be made. FINMA indicates, in the letter, the intensity of the supervision it will exert on the institution.[37]

A special regime has been introduced for so-called small banks. The regime exempts banks in categories 4 and 5 that are particularly liquid and well capitalized from certain supervisory requirements.[38]

6 Bankruptcy and resolution

FINMA is the sole authority which can decide whether a bank has to be subject to bankruptcy procedures or to resolution. Switzerland is a country too small to have different authorities for supervision and for resolution. The BA contains the requirements that have to be met for a bank to be subject to: (1) protective measures; (2) reorganization (resolution); or (3) bankruptcy (article 25, para 1, BA). Important rules on these matters are contained in the Ordinance to the BA[39] and the Ordinance on Bank Insolvency.[40]

FINMA has the authority to decide whether the point of non-viability (the PONV), as defined by Swiss law, has been reached. Detailed rules regarding the resolution of systemic banks were approved in 2012 and have been reviewed on a regular basis. For the resolution of banking groups, FINMA favours a single-point-of-entry strategy with bail-in at the group holding company level.

[37] A bank can be subject to standard supervision, increased supervision, intensive supervision, or intensive and permanent supervision.

[38] Alain Girard, Dusan Ivanovic, and Martin Sennrich, 'Das Kleinbankenregime – Proportionalität in der Aufsicht, «Swiss Made»' (2022) 4 Gesellschaft und Kapitalmarktrecht 447 ff; https://www.finma.ch/fr/surveillance/banques-et-maisons-de-titres/kat-4-und-5-kleinbankenregime/, accessed 10 October 2024.

[39] Ordonnance sur les banques et les caisses d'épargne, RS 952.02.

[40] Ordonnance de la FINMA sur l'insolvabilité bancaire, RS 952.05.

However, when Credit Suisse collapsed in March 2023, none of the rules that had been studied, approved, and reviewed were applied.[41] The Federal Council, and not FINMA, stepped in, issuing an urgent decree to prevent the application of most principles of Swiss contract, corporate, and merger laws, in order to allow the urgent purchase of Credit Suisse by UBS. AT1 bondholders lost everything, while shareholders could still sell their shares to UBS and recover some value. The whole process was severely criticized in Switzerland and abroad, including by the Single Resolution Board (SRB);[42] litigation is pending in order to assess the legality of what happened.

Finally, the specificities of the Swiss deposit protection scheme should be mentioned. Deposit protection is based on rules contained in the BA but enacted by self-regulation of the banking sector via a private-law association.[43] Deposits are covered up to CHF 100,000 per depositor, but the maximum guaranteed amount, to be provided to the deposit guarantee scheme by the various banks, is limited to a percentage of all of the insured deposits in the Swiss banks (article 37h BA, roughly CHF 7.9 billion). The amount is to be divided between banks according to their share of the total of insured deposits in Switzerland.[44] This means that, if a major institution collapsed, not all of its deposits would be covered. This limitation exists to avoid the failure of a bank endangering the other institutions because of the contributions they must pay towards the failed bank's guaranteed deposits.

7 The future of FINMA

The demise of Credit Suisse has been a traumatic event and has led to doubts as to whether FINMA had the appropriate staff, approach, and tools to properly supervise significant banks. A new CEO of FINMA was appointed in April

[41] See https://www.fsb.org/2023/10/fsb-review-of-2023-bank-failures-assesses-implications-for-the-operation-of-the-international-resolution-framework/, accessed 11 October 2024; Bericht der Expertengruppe «Bankenstabilität» 2023, 'Reformbedarf nach dem Untergang der Credit Suisse'; Alvarez & Marsal, 'International Comparison of Key Jurisdictions, Institutional Setup for the Supervision and Resolution of Banks, Expert Opinion', 11 December 2023.

[42] 'Credit Suisse's Collapse Reveals Some Ugly Truths About Switzerland for Investors' (*Bloomberg*, 20 March 2023) https://www.bloomberg.com/news/articles/2023-03-20/credit-suisse-collapse-reveals-some-ugly-truths-about-switzerland-for-investors accessed 11 October 2024. See also 'Dominique Laboureix, chair of the EU's Single Resolution Board, had a clear message for investors in an exclusive interview with CNBC. "In [a banking] resolution here, in the European context, we would follow the hierarchy, and we wanted to tell it very clearly to the investors, to avoid to be misunderstood: we have no choice but to respect this hierarchy," Laboureix said Wednesday.' https://www.srb.europa.eu/en/content/eu-regulators-distance-themselves-credit-suisse-bond-writedowns/, accessed 25 October 2024.

[43] See https://www.esisuisse.ch/de, accessed 11 October 2024.

[44] The share of UBS is CHF 1.8bn (UBS Annual Report 2023, 178).

2024: Mr Stefan Walter, a former director general of the European Central Bank (ECB).

Mr Walter gave a long interview in June 2024 to the *Neue Zurcher Zeitung*.[45] He favours early intervention and more on-site reviews. FINMA would like instruments such as a senior managers' regime,[46] the power to impose fines,[47] and more stringent rules regarding corporate governance. This will require modifications to the Swiss legal framework and more resources to be allocated to FINMA.

A report has been published by a commission set up by the Swiss parliament in order to better understand what led to the collapse of Credit Suisse.[48] The Swiss government submitted various ideas regarding possible modifications of banking regulations, which will lead, in 2026, to legislative proposals.[49]

III The relationship with the Banking Union

1 General remarks

There are significant differences between banking regulation and supervision in Switzerland and in the Banking Union. Most of these have been exposed above. They can be summarized, at a very high level, as follows:

- Supervision is exercised by an administrative authority (FINMA), and the SNB has a very limited role in banking supervision.
- FINMA's tasks are not limited to banking supervision.
- FINMA relies on prudential auditors to fulfil its role.
- FINMA is not only involved in supervision of banks, but also in their resolution.
- FINMA cannot impose fines.
- FINMA does not have early intervention powers.

[45] https://www.nzz.ch/finanzen/der-neue-finma-chef-will-bei-der-ubs-haerter-durchgreifen-wir-haben-den-spielraum-noch-nicht-ausgereizt-sagt-stefan-walter-ld.1833319, accessed 10 October 2024.

[46] PA, 'Individual Accountability Regimes: A Comparative Report, Prepared for the State Secretariat for International Finance', September 2023.

[47] FINMA can order the disgorgement of profits generated by the breach of regulations (art 35 FINMASA) but cannot impose fines. If FINMA were to be given the power to fine institutions or individuals, the whole enforcement procedure, which is quite flexible, would need to be reorganized to be in conformity with the European Convention on Human Rights.

[48] 'La gestion par les autorités fédérales dans le contexte de la crise de Credit Suisse, Rapport de la Commission d'enquête parlementaire du 17 décembre 2024' https://www.parlament.ch/fr/ratsbetrieb/suche-curia-vista/geschaeft?AffairId = 20240098 accessed 28 August 2025.

[49] https://www.news.admin.ch/fr/newnsb/ty6FlsBuspE-AXC9ClLJt accessed 28 August 2025.

- It is difficult for FINMA to pre-emptively restrict banks' business activities, require capital conservation measures, address governance failures, and rectify deficiencies in risk management.[50]
- As a rule, FINMA's decisions are not immediately enforceable.
- Swiss rules are principles-based and not detail-based, and self-regulation still plays a role in Switzerland.

The legal relationship between Switzerland, as a banking centre, and the Banking Union is very limited. There are no treaties or agreements containing rules dealing with this relationship, and Swiss law does not contain any specific rules. The Swiss–EU regulatory dialogue, while existing theoretically, does not seem to bring many concrete developments.[51]

The subsections below will expose the general rules of Swiss law applicable to market access in Switzerland by foreign banks (subsection 2), to access to the EU market by Swiss banks (subsection 3), and to the relationship of FINMA with foreign regulators (subsection 4), which would include the ECB and other EU countries' regulators.

2 Access to the Swiss market by foreign banks

The BA does not contain any rule preventing access to the Swiss market by banks outside of Switzerland, as long as they do not have a regular place of business in Switzerland. If they have a regular place of business, they must set up a branch and be authorized by FINMA. Limited cross-border restrictions exist in financial services legislation.[52]

Foreign banks can set up subsidiaries or branches (article 3*bis*, BA). FINMA favours subsidiaries, since it has a complete supervision of their activities. If a Swiss bank is controlled by foreign interests, it cannot use a business name that may lead the public to believe that it is Swiss-owned (article 3*bis*, para 1, lit b, BA).[53]

[50] https://www.imf.org/en/News/Articles/2025/06/30/07012025-mcs-switzerland-imf-concluding-statement-2025-art-iv-consultation-mission, accessed 31 August 2025.

[51] https://finance.ec.europa.eu/document/download/e4b48301-81b9-414d-87ff-ba3b75b23c3f_en?filename = 240704-eu-switzerland-financial-regulatory-dialogue-joint-statement_en.pdf, accessed 25 October 2024.

[52] Art 26 Federal Act on Financial Services. These restrictions do not apply if client advisers of prudentially supervised foreign financial service providers provide services exclusively to professional or institutional clients.

[53] Thus, Banca della Svizzera Italiana had to become BSI. Subsidiaries controlled by foreign groups usually put 'SUISSE' in their trade name to show that they are Swiss companies.

Usually, private banking activities of foreign groups in Switzerland are carried out via subsidiaries, and commercial banking activities via branches. This is understandable because: (1) to grant a loan, a branch can use the full equity of the company, and hence not be limited to the smaller equity available to a subsidiary; and (2) in the case of branches, no restrictions exist regarding exchange of information with the rest of the legal entity—restrictions exist for subsidiaries. It should be noted, however, that recently a major French banking group decided that its activities in Switzerland, including private banking, should be carried out by Swiss branches of the French company and not by a Swiss subsidiary.[54]

Subsidiaries can transmit information to their parent companies only to the extent permitted by article 4*quinquies* BA,[55] ie where the information is needed by the parent company to be able to exercise proper consolidated supervision of the subsidiary. It is admitted that article 4*quinquies* BA allows, in some cases, transmission of information regarding clients, which would otherwise be covered by banking secrecy and could not be shared. This is the case, for instance: (1) if the parent company needs to be aware of credit risk in the subsidiary which could be relevant at the group level; or (2) for anti-money laundering (AML) purposes. It is a basic principle of Swiss AML rules that the parent company of a group has to be in charge of the proper implementation of AML rules throughout the group, without the possibility of a regulatory arbitrage.[56] Article 4*quinquies* thus allows the transmission of information regarding higher-risk clients, including Politically Exposed Persons, or: (a) clients that were refused by the Swiss entity; (b) holders of accounts closed by the Swiss entity because of reputational or legal risks; (c) clients that have been targeted by an investigation; or (d) clients that have been reported to a Financial Intelligence Unit. However, article 4*quinquies* does not contain a blanket authorization to transmit, to the parent company, information related to all clients. In the case of doubt, article 4*quinquies* BA provides that a bank can ask for FINMA's authorization to either transmit the information or refuse

[54] 'BNP Paribas Suisse devient une succursale de Paris'(*Le Temps*, 16 May 2025) www.letemps.ch.

[55] '1 Banks are authorized to provide their parent companies, which are themselves supervised by a banking or financial market supervisory authority, with non-public information and documents required for consolidated supervision, subject to the following conditions: a. such information is used exclusively for internal control purposes or for the direct supervision of banks or other financial intermediaries subject to authorization; b. the parent company and the authority responsible for consolidated supervision are bound by professional or official secrecy; c. such information may only be passed on to third parties with the prior authorization of the bank or a general authorization contained in an international treaty.'

[56] See art 6, FINMA Ordinance on Money-Laundering.

the transmittal. No cases are publicly known where such authorizations have been requested.

An agreement should be entered into between the Swiss subsidiary and the parent company regarding the scope of the information transmitted and how it will be accessed and used at the parent-company level. The fact that information can be transmitted by the Swiss entity for specific purposes does not mean that this information is generally accessible at the parent-company level by any person expressing an interest. The regulators of the parent company can, of course, have access to this information. The Swiss subsidiary must not be informed of a specific request of the foreign regulator to obtain the information.

Since article 4*quinquies* BA only allows transmittal of information to the parent company, Swiss subsidiaries of foreign groups usually provide, in their general terms and conditions, a waiver of banking confidentiality obligations also towards other members of the same group.

Banks have to be careful in drafting the waiver, since violation of banking secrecy is a criminal offence, even if perpetrated by negligence, and the bank employees involved in the breach are liable personally.[57] Thus, the waiver has to be precise and clearly expressed; it should be individually submitted to the client for acceptance. Doubts exist as to the validity of such general waivers.[58]

3 Access to the EU market by Swiss banks

Historically, EU residents booking their accounts in Switzerland have been important clients of Swiss banks. It is, however, difficult to provide services to these clients from Switzerland because of the rules contained in MiFID II[59] and CRD VI. Swiss banks thus run the risk of breaching either national or EU rules on cross-border services,[60] with possible

[57] Art 47, BA.

[58] Lukas Fahrländer, 'Der nachträgliche Einschub von Datenschutz- und Bankgeheimnisklauseln in AGB' (2024) Aktuelle Juristische Praxis 1163 ff.

[59] Thierry Ammanm, *Der europäische Marktzugang für Schweizer Banken* (Dike Verlag 2020); Marije Louisse and Mirik van Rijn, 'The Third Country Regime for Investment Firms' (2024) 25 European Business Organization Law Review 183 ff; Rolf Sethe, 'MiFID II - Eine Herausforderung für den Finanzplatz Schweiz' (2014) 19 Schweizerische Juristen-Zeitung 477 ff; Rolf Sethe, 'Das Drittstaatenregime von MiFIR und MiFID II' (2014) 6 Schweizerische Zeitschrift für Wirtschafts- und Finanzmarktrecht 615 ff. MiFID II, Directive 2014/65/EU of the European Parliament and of the Council of 15 May 2014 on markets in financial instruments and amending Directive 2002/92/EC and Directive 2011/61/EU. CRD VI, Directive (EU) 2024/1619 of the European Parliament and of the Council of 31 May 2024 amending Directive 2013/36/EU as regards supervisory powers, sanctions, third-country branches, and environmental, social and governance risks.

[60] Susan Emmenegger and Andrea Bigler, 'Fortress Europe: Die Äquivalenzverfahren der EU im Bereich der Finanzdienstleistungen' (2019) 2 Revue suisse de droit des affaires et du marché financier

regulatory,[61] civil,[62] and criminal law risks.[63] They therefore usually access the EU markets via subsidiaries in the EU.[64] It is not clear how profitable this business is; many banks have exited the market.

4 Relationship with foreign regulators

a) General remarks

FINMA cooperates with foreign regulators regarding: (1) provision of banking services in Switzerland by foreign banks; (2) provision of banking services outside Switzerland by Swiss banks; (3) activities of branches or subsidiaries of foreign banks in Switzerland; and (4) activities of branches or subsidiaries of Swiss banks in foreign countries.[65] Proper consolidated supervision of foreign entities controlled by Swiss banks is a subject of interest to FINMA, which has issued a guideline on this matter.[66]

The exchange of information and documents between FINMA and a foreign regulator is admissible if the foreign regulator is subject to confidentiality duties and the information is relevant for the purposes of supervision (article 42, paras 1 and 2, FINMASA). Cooperation is not limited to regulators in charge of consolidated supervision. Information and documents received from FINMA can be further transmitted by the foreign regulator to other authorities, courts, or bodies, but exclusively to implement financial market laws (article 42, para 2, FINMASA). With the prior consent of the Federal Office of Justice—part of the Swiss Ministry of Justice—FINMA can authorize the information transmitted to be forwarded to criminal authorities (article 42, para 5, FINMASA). Information cannot be transmitted to civil law courts or

155 ff. The situation will be different between Switzerland and the UK, further to a treaty that has been negotiated, https://www.sif.admin.ch/en/united-kingdom, accessed 9 October 2024.

61 FINMA requires Swiss banks to be sure they are not violating any foreign cross-border rules, and would sanction a bank which does not properly manage this risk.

62 Foreign courts: (1) could have jurisdiction over a Swiss bank if it targets local clients in the jurisdiction; and (2) could ignore choice-of-courts provisions in favour of Swiss courts. They could also ignore choice-of-law provisions in favour of Swiss law, if contrary to imperative rules of the *lex fori*.

63 See the well-known criminal law case brought against UBS by French authorities, which not only involved laundering of the proceeds of tax fraud but also violation of cross-border rules (*démarchage*, Cour de Cassation, 15 November 2023, n° 22-81.258).

64 The EU subsidiary of UBS (UBS Europe SE), headquartered in Germany, is subject to the direct supervision of the ECB. See also EBA, 'EBA Report—Analysis on the Market Share of Subsidiaries of Third Country Banking Groups in the EU' (EBA/REP/2025/09), April 2025.

65 Carlo Lombardini, 'Entraide administrative internationale dans le secteur financier' in Etienne Poltier, Anne-Christine Favre, and Vincent Martenet (eds), *L'entraide administrative Évolution ou révolution?* (Schulthess 2019) 163 ff.

66 Circulaire 2025/4, Surveillance consolidée des groupes financiers selon la LB et la LEFin.

to tax authorities. Further information and documents can be exchanged for the purposes of liquidation or resolution of regulated entities (article 42, para 3, FINMASA).

FINMA has entered into various MoUs with foreign banking regulators,[67] for the purposes of both standard supervision and crisis management. The documents are not legally binding. FINMA also participates in supervisory colleges with foreign supervisors. FINMA does not disclose information on these matters. With the EU, MoUs have been entered into with the regulators of various countries, and with the ECB. An MoU has also been signed with the SRB.[68] No further details are available as to the contents of these documents or the practice followed by FINMA in exchanging information and documents with foreign regulators.[69]

A recent and important problem regarding cooperation between regulators is connected to the fact that some operationally important functions for banks (IT environment, for instance) are outsourced to entities that are neither authorized nor supervised because they are not active in the financial sector, although the failures of these entities could have substantial consequences for banks. It is, therefore, important that regulators are able to obtain the information they need and exchange it with other regulators.[70] The Federal Council has subjected a bill to the Parliament to cover such cases.[71]

b) Standard cooperation

Cooperation with foreign regulators is usually informal, without the supervised entities being aware of it happening, or of the nature and the extent of the information and documents exchanged.

Communication between regulators usually starts when a bank is active in a foreign market by providing services to clients in this market, or by setting up a branch or subsidiary there. Once a bank has been authorized in Switzerland as a branch or a subsidiary, extensive information can be exchanged by FINMA regarding all relevant subjects, such as: (1) the organization of a supervised entity; (2) the management of its risks; (3) its internal controls; (4) capital and

[67] https://www.finma.ch/en/finma/international-activities/supervisory-cooperation/agreements/ accessed 22 October 2024.

[68] https://www.srb.europa.eu/en/content/srb-and-finma-sign-cooperation-arrangement accessed 22 October 2024.

[69] An MoU between ESMA, the SNB, and FINMA has been published: https://www.esma.europa.eu/sites/default/files/library/mou_esma_finma_snb.pdf accessed 22 October 2024.

[70] Article 23*bis* BA, which obliges entities to which a bank has outsourced important functions to FINMA of major events impacting on them, and gives FINMA the right to inspect them.

[71] Conseil fédéral, Message concernant la modification de la loi sur la surveillance des marchés financiers (FF 2025) 2863 ff.

liquidity; (5) operational issues; (6) audit results; and (7) possible breaches of rules, and enforcement procedures. The information exchanged can also cover information on board members or members of management, in order to ascertain whether they are properly fulfilling their duties. Finally, regulators can also be interested in transactions they identify between banks in different countries that may need clarifications.

Client-related information, ie information containing the names of clients or data which could be used to identify clients, cannot be exchanged informally between regulators. If client-related information is transmitted to a foreign regulator, the principles of article 42a FINMASA must be respected. This provision covers the transmittal of this information both: (1) for the standard purposes of banking supervision; and (2) for cases where the foreign authority (administrative, not criminal) are investigating cases of market abuse, insider trading, non-disclosure of positions on the markets, or other breaches of financial market rules.

In such cases, Swiss law provides for a complicated process whereby the client: (1) is made aware of the request; (2) is entitled to give their opinion; and (3) can appeal any decision granting the request to transmit their identity. This position of Swiss law is not in conformity with international practice. Hence, the law has recently been modified to give FINMA the possibility to restrict, 'in exceptional cases' (article 42a, para 4, FINMASA), the rights granted to clients. The concept is vague and difficult to understand. This is still viewed as unsatisfactory, and the Federal Council is planning to abrogate any possible intervention by clients in the process.[72]

c) On-site visits

With the authorization of FINMA, foreign regulators can come to Switzerland and inspect the branches or subsidiaries of banks which are subject to their supervision, or which are active in their jurisdiction (article 43, para 2, FINMASA). On-site examination allows the foreign regulator to review whether a supervised entity: (1) is appropriately organized; (2) records, limits, and monitors, in an appropriate manner, the risks inherent in its business operations; (3) is managed by persons who guarantee proper business conduct; (4) fulfils the own funds and risk-diversification regulations on a consolidated basis; and (5) properly complies with its reporting duties vis-à-vis the supervisory authorities (article 43, para 3, FINMASA). The general wording used in the provision allows a substantial amount of information to be obtained.

[72] ibid 29.

Some restrictions exist in respect of the right of foreign regulators to directly access private banking clients' files (article 43, para 3*bis* and 3*ter*, FINMASA).[73] FINMA collects this information and forwards it to the requesting authority pursuant to the rules of article 42a FINMASA described above. FINMA can authorize the foreign regulator to inspect a limited number of individual client files. Files must be selected at random, according to criteria set in advance. These restrictions are a heritage of the times when banking secrecy was viewed as of paramount importance to Switzerland. The Federal Council is also planning to abrogate this provision.[74]

d) Direct communication with foreign regulators

Article 42c FINMASA allows direct communications between Swiss-based entities and foreign regulators or entities involved in the supervision of such entities, and the transmittal of information by the Swiss entities to such authorities. This provision of FINMASA has been effective since 2016, and was necessary because Swiss criminal law[75] restricts direct interaction between physical and legal persons in Switzerland and foreign authorities (judicial, administrative, or prosecution authorities). Furthermore, since auditors were more directly involved than FINMA in banking supervision, foreign regulators wanted to be able to be made aware promptly of events happening in Swiss-based subsidiaries or branches.

FINMA needs to be made aware before the foreign regulator of any major event impacting on the Swiss entity (article 42c, para 3, and art 29, para 2, FINMASA). It can also restrict any transmittal of information or documents to a foreign regulator (article 42c, para 5, FINMASA). These provisions were introduced: (1) to make sure that FINMA could take measures to protect clients of the Swiss entities, for instance in cases of major losses in those entities; and (2) to prevent foreign regulators from exerting pressure on Swiss entities to obtain documents and information that could not otherwise be obtained. This last point was very important when the United States wanted to be made aware of the identity of US taxpayers having undeclared accounts with Swiss

[73] *'Opérations de gestion de fortune, de négoce de valeurs mobilières ou de placement pour le compte de clients'.*

[74] Département fédéral des finances (n 71) 40.

[75] Art 271, para 1, Swiss Criminal Code, RS 311.0: 'Any person who carries out activities on behalf of a foreign state on Swiss territory without lawful authority, where such activities are the responsibility of a public authority or public official, any person who carries out such activities for a foreign party or organisation, any person who facilitates such activities, shall be liable to a custodial sentence not exceeding three years or to a monetary penalty, or in serious cases to a custodial sentence of not less than one year.'

banks; the US Department of Justice targeted banks and their employees to exert significant pressure on Switzerland for that purpose.[76]

FINMA issued a guideline on direct cooperation.[77] The Federal Council has prepared a draft law to modify Swiss rules, and to allow for further extensive exchange of information.[78]

IV Final remarks

For a long time, the Swiss banking centre was isolated from other financial centres and prospered thanks to this isolation. This was the period when: (1) Swiss banking secrecy was a shelter against inquiries regarding the tax situations of clients; and (2) Switzerland was viewed as a neutral country. Switzerland thus became a leading (if not *the* leading) offshore banking centre.[79]

The situation changed as a result of the crisis of 2008. Several Swiss banks (and/or their employees) were targeted for helping foreign taxpayers to avoid paying taxes on their assets deposited in Switzerland, and on the income generated by such assets. Prosecutions in foreign countries were triggered by data thefts (the most well known being the 'Falciani case' and the so-called 'Swissleak case'). Closing the inheritance of a past suddenly fraught with previously unidentified dangers was an expensive exercise for Swiss banks.[80] Switzerland now participates in the automatic exchange of information in tax matters and grants very extensive cooperation in tax matters to foreign authorities.

In view of the recent events on the international stage, Switzerland is no longer viewed as really being neutral.[81] Compliance requirements are very stringent and banks who want to serve clients in exotic markets out of

[76] The US set up a program which allowed Swiss banks to avoid prosecution for helping US taxpayers to evade taxation, provided that they cooperated fully with the US Department of Justice and paid a substantial fine: Tax Division, US Department of Justice, 'Swiss Bank Program' (24 September 2024) https://www.justice.gov/tax/swiss-bank-program accessed 9 October 2024.

[77] Circular 2017/6 direct cooperation.

[78] Message concernant la modification (n 71) 4.1.3.

[79] Although widely viewed suspiciously, 'offshore' means only that the clients depositing their assets in Switzerland are based outside the country.

[80] See the US program referred to in n 76. In 2008, UBS ran a very real risk of being prosecuted in the US while it was already in a weak position because of the losses suffered due to the sub-prime crisis: Commissions de gestion des Chambres fédérales, *Les autorités sous la pression de la crise financière et de la transmission de données clients d'UBS aux Etats-Unis, Rapport des Commissions de gestion des Chambres fédérales du 30 mai 2010* (Feuille Fédérale 2011) 2903 ff.

[81] Laura Kayali and Jacopo Barigazzi, 'Putin, cash and guns prompt "explosive" rethink of Swiss neutrality' (*Politico*, 30 August 2024) https://www.politico.eu/article/switzerland-military-neutrality-defense-arms-sales-war-in-ukraine-vladimir-putin/ accessed 11 October 2024.

Switzerland must really investigate and ascertain the source of wealth and funds of the clients they accept, which may be difficult, depending on the jurisdictions involved. Furthermore, banks active in Switzerland in private banking must face high costs in CHF and income generated in currencies like the US dollar or the euro, which lose value against the CHF.

All of these circumstances have an impact on the position of Switzerland as a leading offshore financial centre,[82] and some foreign banking groups may decide that they want to streamline or sell their operations in the country. Under these circumstances, it would certainly be helpful if Swiss banks could have access directly out of Switzerland to the EU market. It is difficult, however, to imagine that this will happen in the near future.

Any further access to the EU market may require substantial modifications of Swiss rules, including rules regarding the organization of banks[83] and banking supervision by FINMA.[84] This would be necessary in order to be able to achieve a recognition of the equivalence between Swiss rules and the EU rules. However, one can wonder whether the EU is using the vague concept of equivalence[85] simply as a decoy, without having any intention of allowing Swiss financial institutions to access the internal market.

[82] 'Despite continued growth in its asset management sector, Switzerland is set to lose ground compared with competitors in the coming years, an annual report predicts. The "Global Wealth Report 2022", published on Thursday by the Boston Consulting Group (BCG), predicts that Switzerland will be pushed out of the world's top three global centres by the UK by 2026.': https://www.swissinfo.ch/eng/business/swiss-financial-centre-faces-growing-global-pressure/47663550 accessed 11 October 2024; see also https://www2.deloitte.com/ch/en/pages/financial-services/articles/international-wealth-management.html?id = ch:2sm:null:4dcom_share:5awa:6dcom:financial_services accessed 24 October 2024.

[83] For instance, the BA, contrary to the CRD, contains hardly any regulation regarding remuneration and no regulation regarding whistle-blowing.

[84] Simon Schären, *Europakompatibles Finanzmarktrecht* (Dike Verlag 2024).

[85] See https://finance.ec.europa.eu/document/download/013005aa-8040-4b1e-b518-bc76b5bb9ba7_en?filename = overview-table- accessed 31 August 2025; https://www.sif.admin.ch/en/equivalence-procedures-eu accessed 31 August 2025.Aline Darbellay, 'Third-Country Regime and Equivalence: The Swiss Perspective' (2024) European Business Organization Law Review 75 ff. https://doi.org/10.1007/s40804-023-00307-0.

Conclusion

Where Does the Banking Union Stand and is it Fit for the Future?

Jonathan Bauerschmidt, Raffaele D'Ambrosio, Diane Fromage, Daniela Jaros, and Paul Weismann

I Introduction

The preceding chapters have sought to identify how the Banking Union, launched in 2012, has developed and where it stands today. In doing so, they examined several aspects related to six dimensions (the horizontal, the substantive, the institutional, the cooperative, the review, and the external dimensions), thereby covering not only the three pillars of the Banking Union, but also considering it from various, differentiated yet complementary, perspectives. In the following, we draw the main conclusions stemming from these analyses.

II Horizontal dimension

It has been shown that thc Banking Union emerged in a context (economic and legal) which is quite peculiar, as it is characterized by the European Union (EU) finding itself in a constant state of crisis, which the EU has increasingly been required to contribute to solving. Yet this had to happen *à Traités constants*—that is, without Treaty change (*Alberto de Gregorio Merino*). This therefore demanded, among other things, that existing legal bases be used in an original manner, and that Member States conclude *inter se* agreements—such as the European Stability Mechanism (ESM) Treaty—outside the EU legal framework. At the same time, innovations were introduced by EU institutions themselves—for example, the Next Generation Programme or the establishment of the Health Emergency Preparedness and Response (HERA)—thereby

Jonathan Bauerschmidt, Raffaele D'Ambrosio, Diane Fromage, Daniela Jaros, and Paul Weismann, *Conclusion* In: *EU Banking Union*. Edited by: Jonathan Bauerschmidt, Raffaele D'Ambrosio, Diane Fromage, Daniela Jaros, and Paul Weismann, Oxford University Press.
DOI: 10.1093/9780198949756.003.0025

pointing to the tension that exists between the 'agencification phenomenon'[1] and the creation of specialized units within the Commission, which could threaten its internal balance.

Another distinctive feature of integration in the banking domain (and in the financial domain in general) is the very important resort to—and, therefore, the role of—soft law. The European Banking Authority (EBA) adopts numerous guidelines, which 'serve as de facto implementing acts because they suggest specific rules to be followed or steps to be taken by the financial institutions' (*Mariolina Eliantonio and Pavliná Hubková*). Also, the guidelines follow a so-called 'comply-or-explain' mechanism, hence making it difficult for authorities not to comply. Beyond that, as shown by these authors as well, they can be 'hardened' at the national level, depending on how they are enforced by the national authorities. They may, nevertheless, bring benefits, as they can serve to clarify or define further formal legally binding provisions. The (necessary) control over these guidelines is to take place in the framework of preliminary references by national courts, since the Court of Justice has denied its capacity to check them in procedures for annulment. This may, however, lead to insufficient review possibilities, which is all the more regrettable as the mechanisms for political and administrative accountability are (too) limited as well.

Another important issue in the context of the (relatively) new Banking Union is the question of how to protect fundamental rights: since banks and their shareholders and creditors are directly affected by (EU) decisions in this area,[1] fundamental rights play a very important role. Rights such as the right to property or procedural fundamental rights may be affected; therefore, it must be borne in mind that, '[i]n matters of bank resolution more generally, the CJEU engages in a limited form of judicial review' (*Paul Weismann*). At the same time, the Banking Union has brought about new grounds for interference with fundamental rights such as the right to property and procedural rights. Therefore, 'the novel tools of EU law and administration introduced by the Banking Union also raise new questions with regard to fundamental rights' (*Weismann*).

Beyond new fundamental rights questions, the Banking Union has also demanded that (new) relationships between (new) EU bodies be established. However, the divide of 'regulatory' and 'supervisory' functions among EU

[1] This is only the second (or the third) area of full integration within the EU. Stefan Grundmann and Hans-Wolfgang Micklitz, 'The European Banking Union and Constitution: The Overall Challenge' in Stefan Grundmann and Hans-Wolfgang Micklitz (eds), *The European Banking Union and Constitution—Beacon for Advanced Integration or Death-Knell for Democracy?* (Hart Publishing 2019).

bodies, notably between the European Central Bank (ECB) and the EBA, may lead to counterproductive rigidities in the area of supervision. In fact, the issue appears to be far-reaching, as the 'current legal framework, though functional, suffers from overlapping competences, legal uncertainty, and high compliance costs' (*Concetta Brescia Morra* and *Federico Pistelli*). Hence, reforms are necessary, notably to enhance flexibility and clarify responsibilities while ensuring democratic accountability.

Thus, collaborative efforts are essential to the functioning of the Banking Union. Yet, its peculiar architecture has raised novel issues, and still demands improvements.

III Substantive dimension

The same applies to the Banking Union in its substantive dimension. The functioning of the Banking Union has, indeed, led to the introduction of unprecedented innovations, including the application of national law by an EU institution—the ECB. However, this has raised important new questions regarding, among other things, the scope of the ECB's power and the relevance of national case law. The ECB is placed in a difficult position: this tension due to its mandate 'to create a level playing field while respecting the diversity of the national legal frameworks it is bound to apply is reflected in [its] tendency to stick to the wording of the directives as far as possible' (*Daniela Jaros*).

Another remaining open question concerns the future of deposit guarantee schemes (DGSs) and their potential future Europeanization. The Banking Union was conceived as a three-pillar structure comprising the Europeanization of banking supervision and resolution, and a European Deposit Insurance Scheme (EDIS). The third pillar is, however, still missing amid the absence of political support by (some of) the Member States. This notwithstanding, a reform of the current Deposit Guarantee Schemes Directive (DGSD) is ongoing. This 'makes further tentative steps to fill the empty space due to the absence of EDIS. Recognizing an increasingly interconnected banking system, the reform of the DGSD further develops provisions for cross-border institutions and third-country branches' (*Diane Fromage* and *Gaia Chiarini*), even if some weaknesses remain.

To avoid bank failures, and hence the resort to DGSs, detailed rules exist that allow the ECB, and supervisors in general, to conduct effective supervision. One such rule is the Supervisory Review and Evaluation Process (SREP), which has been amended on several occasions and, indeed, strengthened since the establishment of the Single Supervisory Mechanism (SSM) in 2014, just like regulatory changes in EU prudential regulation and evolutions in prudential supervision regarding common methodologies and processes that have been witnessed. In this context, the 'main concern in regulation and supervision has been to cater for new and emerging risks in the SREP so that the safety and soundness of banks is preserved' (*Christy Ann Petit*).

A further prong in the EU's efforts to avoid bank failure is to strengthen banks' resilience in terms of capital endowment. Against this background, 'the Union has established a very comprehensive and detailed framework setting broadly three strands of requirements on credit institutions—capital requirements (both risk-based and non-risk-based), loss absorption requirements (both risk-based and non risk-based), and capital buffers', which is 'remarkable' because of the speediness with which the framework was established, and because it is very complex (*David M Brinkman* and *Asen Lefterov*). A move towards simplification while preserving effectiveness would be welcome.

IV Institutional dimension

As regards the institutional dimension, we witness issues that are recurring in the European integration process, including the question of the limitation of the competences that may (or may not) be delegated to EU agencies (*Meroni* doctrine). In fact, this has influenced the delegation of powers to the European Securities and Markets Authority (ESMA) and the decision-making in the Single Resolution Mechanism (SRM), as exemplified yet again in 2024 by the *Fundación Tatiana Pérez* decision of the Court of Justice.[2] In fact, the *Meroni* judgment has 'many faces': 'it is not only of paramount constitutional importance for the overall institutional set-up of the Union; it also creates important boundaries for lawmakers when delegating autonomous or preparatory powers on EU agencies, and when devising the (sometimes very complex) administrative procedures which may also involve Union institutions'. This notwithstanding, 'the many faces of *Meroni* [may be viewed as] hav[ing] a unifying effect, as they require us to think about the European Union as a whole' (*Jonathan Bauerschmidt*).

Another important institutional development is the creation of the Single Resolution Fund (SRF). The financing of the SRF in general, and notably *ex*

[2] See Case C-551/22 P *Commission v Fundación Tatiana Pérez de Guzmán el Bueno, Stiftung für Forschung und Lehre (SFL), Single Resolution Board (SRB)*, ECLI:EU:C:2024:520.

ante contributions, is a key question which has been subject to very intense litigation procedures to date, and deserves to be examined from the perspective of legal basis, and of the principles of legal certainty and proportionality. In all, '[t]he complexity of the financial sector and the interconnection between its actors, as well as the need to comply with essential principles of EU law, led to the drawing-up of a complex and innovative piece of legal architecture [,which,] while complex, is nevertheless fully comprehensive and functional' (*Eugénie d'Ursel*).

Institutional innovations also had to be devised in the process leading to the reform of the ESM. Indeed, the (international) ESM is to serve as a backstop to the SRF, a step that would be crucial to increasing financial stability within the euro area and within the EU, since it would increase resolution capacities. Despite the fact that the ESM (and the agreement for the transfer of funds to the SRM) are intergovernmental agreements developed outside the EU legal order, they remain 'loyal and complementary to the Union legal order' (*Andrea Westerhof Löfflerová*). Specific safeguards were introduced, in the form of consistency clauses, to ensure that primacy is respected, and the European Commission is bound to play a key role in 'anchor[ing] the intergovernmental action to Union law'. In fact, the ESM can even be viewed as 'fortif[ying] the Union by furthering its objectives, rather than clashing with it' (*Westerhof Löfflerová*). This reform of the ESM Treaty is of critical importance because funding is essential to the effective resolution of European banks.

Institutional innovation in this domain of European integration is still very much a defining feature of ongoing developments. The European Supervisory Agencies (ESAs), established in 2010, presented unique features, but the EU's latest agency, the Anti-Money Laundering Agency (AMLA), is institutionally more advanced and bears its own unique peculiarities. In fact, some aspects of the regime of the takeover power and the administrative review, AMLA could serve as a source of inspiration for the reform of the ESAs, and especially the ESMA, for instance in terms of the centralization of the mandate in a single foundation regulation, and in terms of its funding, as well as of the centralization of regulatory and supervisory functions. 'AMLA's governance structure is superior to the current ESAs' structure, as independent decision-making is fostered to a larger extent, via independent board members' (*Matthias Deissenberger*); hence, this could be reproduced too.

V Cooperative dimension

In terms of the Banking Union's cooperative dimension, our authors explored the specificities of collaboration between the relevant actors at the EU level and across the EU and the Member State level.

The so-called composite decision-making procedures involving authorities from both the EU and the Member State level epitomize cooperation within the EU. The shape of these procedures varies significantly. The SSM and SRM not only encompass EU bodies, but also the relevant national authorities of the participating Member States. Thus, it does not come as a surprise that they also provide for a number of composite decision-making procedures. By now, they have resulted in a number of court rulings.

In the context of the Banking Union, the concept of a 'national preparatory act'—preparatory for a decision of the ECB or the Single Resolution Board (SRB)—plays a significant role. Whereas this concept is not defined anywhere in EU (or national) law, the further development of this notion by the Court of Justice of the European Union (CJEU) in the context of the Banking Union, notably in the cases *Berlusconi*, *Satabank*, and *Pilatus*, also leaves something to be desired. In fact, 'the CJEU has provided a lot less clarity as to what constitutes a "national preparatory act"... than as to what does not' (*Brito Bastos* and *Ieva Hūna*).

With regard to cooperation between EU and Member State authorities, the concept of a 'mechanism'—a key feature of the Banking Union—was considered, with a strong focus on the SRM, but also dwelling on the interrelation between the two mechanisms in place. This concept entails a specific, most intense form of cooperation between the EU and national authorities, which allows for a 'synthesis of the different interests at stake' to achieve a common objective (*Edoardo Rulli*). This mode is requested by the law. It has not put supranationality at risk, though. In the past decade, the SRB has built up its leadership and has developed a truly supranational 'resolution-administrative practice'. At the same time, this body has left its 'footprint' (*Rulli*) in legislation which is relevant beyond the Banking Union, thereby exemplifying that cooperation not only takes place within the Banking Union but also has a cooperative outreach.

On the contrary, the Banking Union is also confronted with influences from outside, also requiring a cooperative approach. The parallel application of the bank resolution regime and the specific State aid framework the Commission has tailored for banks may serve as an illustration of this. The former was intended to bring a paradigm change in the troublesome interrelationship between ailing banks and taxpayers' money. In spite of some 'mutual incoherences', the two regimes are 'tightly intertwined and interdependent' (*Audronė Steiblytė*). On this basis, State aid may still be used for precautionary measures, as well as for easing the orderly exit from the market of failing-or-likely-to fail (FOLTF) banks, which—for lack of public interest—do not fall within the scope of the resolution regime. In addition to that, DGS assistance is conceivable. In terms of the legal assessment, a crucial question here is whether the DGS at issue is public or private.

In macroprudential policy over the past decade, 'differences in the assessment of economic reality' (*Ursula Hauser-Rethaller*) between the ECB and national designated authorities when assessing risks to financial stability have rendered cooperation difficult. This is mostly due to a lack of harmonization of the data used, and of the indicators and methodologies applied for its analysis. While this shortcoming has been identified and continuously addressed by the European Systemic Risk Board (ESRB), the progress of harmonization still leaves much to be desired. Also, there is an 'intrinsic risk that measures may be taken too late due to the extended justification and discussion needs required by EU legislation' (*Hauser-Rethaller*). One of the most pressing discussions in macroprudential policy at the moment relates to the involvement of climate-related risks in the data analysis.

One specific form of acting together, in the context of the Banking Union, even has cooperation in its name: 'close cooperation', the voluntary attachment to the Banking Union of Member States outside the euro area. With one historical case—Croatia, which by joining the euro area in 2023 became a regular member of the Banking Union—and one current case (Bulgaria), experience shows that close cooperation 'proved to be an effective tool to foster integration of non-euro-area Member States, leading to a significant alignment of regulatory frameworks and supervisory practices' (*Agnese Pizzolla*). At the same time, a number of tools EU law provides in the given context have remained unused or unchallenged. This bears the risk that shortcomings in the design of close cooperation remain undetected and, thus, leave the actors involved unprepared for more conflictual situations than experienced hitherto.

VI Review dimension

The review dimension is reflected in different regimes contained in or with regard to the Banking Union. One of these regimes is the internal review provided both for decisions taken by the SRB and the ECB. A comparative analysis of the SRB Appeal Panel (AP) and the ECB Administrative Board of Review (ABoR) revealed that they 'share similarities in their structure, origins, and independence requirements; however, their different legal review scopes may confuse interested parties' (*Jakub Kerlin*). The most apparent difference—that the AP may decide on the matter, whereas the ABoR only opines—also has ramifications for the parties' access to the Court of Justice, due to the reform of Article 58a of the CJEU Statute. The discussion on internal review bodies reaches out beyond the SRB and the ECB, and also affects the European Financial Market Supervisory Authorities, AMLA, and even EU agencies outside the field of banking law. Against this background, a harmonization of the scope and powers of internal review bodies across the relevant EU actors would be a desirable aim for future reforms.

The SRB and the ECB are not only *legally* accountable to their respective appeal bodies; they are also held to account *politically* by the European Parliament. The relevant legal provisions are laid down not only in the Single Supervisory Mechanism Regulation (SSMR) and the Single Resolution Mechanism Regulation (SRMR) but also in (inter-institutional) agreements concluded between the European Parliament and, respectively, the SRB and the ECB. Apart from reporting duties, hearings of the chairs of the Supervisory Board of the ECB and of the SRB are at the core of the accountability mechanism. According to the author (*Menelaos Markakis*), in practice these hearings have resulted in a 'relatively well-functioning dialogue'. Nevertheless, there is ample room for improvement. By way of example, the absence of single quantifiable policy objectives and confidentiality duties as regards individual banks impedes the effectiveness of the accountability mechanism. A reform of the relevant legal framework could engender more informed questions/feedback from MEPs, as well as a higher degree of responsiveness of the SRM and the Supervisory Board of the ECB. In conclusion, 'ensuring the robustness of the accountability and transparency arrangements in the Banking Union also remains a work in progress' (*Markakis*).

Another EU institution reviewing the Banking Union is the European Court of Auditors (ECA). The limitations of the ECA's mandate with regard to the ECB as a monetary policy actor play out also in respect of its role under the SSM. Pursuant to Article 27(2) of the E(S)CB Statute, the ECA may examine the ECB only with regard to the 'operational efficiency of [its] management'—a term which is not defined more closely by Union law. This 'accountability gap' (*Carlos Soler Ruiz*) is illustrated by the fact that the ECA's auditing powers with regard to banking supervision are more limited than the auditing powers of national auditing bodies used to be before the ECB became the leading actor in banking supervision, ie prior to the introduction of the SSM.

VII External dimension

Looking at the external dimension of the Banking Union—that is, its relationships with countries which are not part of the Banking Union (and their authorities)—an important tool to lay down the conditions of these relationships are memoranda of understanding (MoUs). At the same time, MoUs have also been concluded by actors within the Banking Union. Taking a look at administrative practice, the authors (*Jonathan Bauerschmidt*, *Diane Fromage*, and *Vanessa Aichstill*) distinguish horizontal, vertical, and external MoUs. More often than not, the parties do not intend an agreement to be on legally binding terms. The main purpose is, rather, to establish 'a shared understanding of a process' (*Bauerschmidt*, *Fromage*, and *Aichstill*). By way of example, this may include detailed guidance for coordinated action in a crisis situation, or with regard to a specific institution, but also institutional arrangements like the creation of supervisory and resolution colleges.

The remaining chapters on the external dimension take a country-specific perspective, reflecting upon the relationship of the Banking Union with the EFTA/EEA countries, and the EFTA country Switzerland. The EFTA/EEA countries are inside the internal market (including the regulation of financial services) but outside the Banking Union—an experience which 'provides valuable insights into the dynamics of differentiated integration in the EU' (*Mads Andenas* and *Carsten Zatschler*). The procedural shortcomings in transforming EU secondary law, as incorporated in the EEA Agreement, into the national law of the EFTA/EEA countries are well known, and so is the lax enforcement of EEA law by the chronically understaffed EFTA Supervisory Authority. These drawbacks can also be observed in the context of financial market-related rules. In addition to these process-related difficulties, in the past the application of specific rules or decisions in the EFTA/EEA states has been impeded by politically motivated opposition.

The financial market of Switzerland, as an 'EFTA-only' country, has for a long time profited from its detachment from other financial centres, and has become a major hub for offshore banking, not least due to the famous Swiss banking secrecy and to Switzerland's neutrality. This has changed in the wake of the Great Financial Crisis, when irregular activities of Swiss banks and the related financial risks were increasingly targeted. Today, Switzerland participates in the automatic exchange of information in tax matters and strongly cooperates with tax authorities of foreign countries. Given this change of circumstances, 'it would certainly be helpful if Swiss banks could have access directly out of Switzerland to the EU market' (*Carlo Lombardini*).

It is apparent that the various contributions to this book allow us to 'take measure' of the fascinating project called Banking Union. Its horizontal dimension, first of all, turned our attention to the constitutional basis of all EU action, ie the Treaties and the various legal bases enshrined therein. Together with the further issues addressed as part of this dimension—soft law, fundamental rights, and the relationship between existing and newly established EU bodies—this section is horizontal in at least two ways: on the one hand, it relates to the various pillars of the Banking Union; on the other, it relates to issues which are relevant also in other EU policy fields, and thus addresses core concerns of EU integration as a whole.

Its substantive dimension allowed us to dive into some of the most interesting material law questions related to the Banking Union: the application of national law by EU bodies; the politically most contested third pillar, EDIS, in regard of which no progress has been made over the past years, which again has given rise to evasive movements relating to national DGSs; and the structured SREP and provisions on the capital-related resilience of credit institutions. Thus, the substantive dimension of the Banking Union encompasses questions of legal interpretation (of national provisions), the (non-)creation of rules for political reasons (EDIS/DGS), the material side of a procedural approach (SREP), and the material basis for the resilience of banks (capital endowment).

From an institutional perspective, *Meroni* was discussed as the core doctrine for the empowerment of secondary-law-based bodies such as the SRB; the legal and political difficulties relating to the ESM backstop were explained; the legal framework of the financing of the SRF was addressed; and the European System of Financial Supervision (ESFS) and AMLA, as further EU regimes in the field of financial market law, were presented. These chapters illustrate that the Banking Union is not in a state of 'splendid isolation', but that it is integrated into many of the ongoing more general discussions of EU law. It was in relation to ESFS, and eventually the Banking Union itself, that the *Meroni* doctrine was revitalized and 'updated', both by the legislator and the Court of Justice. AMLA is the most recent contribution to this development. The interaction between public international law and EU law, on the one hand, and the economic policy of the Member States and the EU's internal market policy, on the other, is epitomized by the ESM backstop. Eventually, the financing of the SRF has come to display the intricacies of multilevel governance, requiring contributions from the private sector to be collected by the Member States, which are then transferred to and administered at the EU level.

The contributions on the cooperative dimension of the Banking Union gave us insights in terms of the cooperation between national and EU bodies in the SRM; the relationship between the law on the supervision, recovery, and resolution of banks, on the one hand, and State aid law, on the other; cooperation in the field of macroprudential supervision; and 'close cooperation' as an option for non-euro-area Member States to participate in the Banking Union.

Cooperation is not only enshrined in the new concept of a 'mechanism', which is key to the set-up of the Banking Union across the levels of the EU and its Member States; it also relates to the coordination of different policy fields with partly overlapping scopes and partly contradictory objectives (banking law/State aid law). In terms of supervision, it not only takes place at the microprudential level, which most of the literature on the Banking Union relates to (as do most of the chapters contained in this book), but also at the macroprudential level. The 'close cooperation' essentially refers to the cooperation between a non-euro-area Member State and an institutional set-up created by the EU primarily for the euro-area Member States. Thereby, it bridges a divide in what is called the 'two-speed Europe'.

The review dimension reflects different ways of holding to account the EU bodies active in the Banking Union. Since the review of the Court of Justice is omnipresent in the contributions to all the dimensions of the Banking Union addressed in this book, we deemed that a chapter specifically dedicated to the role of the Court of Justice was not required. However, the review dimension was explored by addressing the roles of the SRB AP and the ECB ABoR, the European Parliament, and the ECA. This way, the relevant chapters grappled with instances of legal, political, and economic accountability mechanisms applicable to the Banking Union. Due to the placement of the independent ECB at the centre of the SSM, accountability in all its expressions is considerably weaker in relation to the SSM than in relation to the SRM.

As part of the external dimension, our authors addressed the memoranda of understanding which have been concluded with Member States outside the Banking Union, third countries, and their respective authorities, as well as the legal set-up in the EFTA/EEA states, and the EFTA-only country Switzerland. External actors are not part of the Banking Union. Nevertheless, they relate to the EU's internal market (including the financial market) in one way or another. These chapters not only depict how Banking Union actors engage with external actors; they also show the different degrees of specific third countries' integration into the EU's internal market.

By following this multidimensional approach and covering a horizontal, a substantive, an institutional, a cooperative, a review, and an external dimension, this book has made an original contribution for understanding the particulars of the Banking Union, and for assessing its resilience against future challenges. In addition to that, it sought to put these six dimensions into the overall context of EU law, hence offering a holistic view on the development of Banking Union to date.

We hope that readers have enjoyed these chapters as much as we enjoyed editing them.

Index

For the benefit of digital users, indexed terms that span two pages (e.g., 52–53) may, on occasion, appear on only one of those pages.

Tables and figures are indicated by an italic *t* and *f* following the page number.